Dover Memorial Library
Gardner-Webb University
P.O. Box 836
Boiling Springs, N.C. 28017

1046719l

78.21

2010
The Supreme Court Review

2010
The

"Judges as persons, or courts as institutions, are entitled to
no greater immunity from criticism than other persons
or institutions . . . [J]udges must be kept mindful of their limitations and
of their ultimate public responsibility by a vigorous
stream of criticism expressed with candor however blunt."
—*Felix Frankfurter*

". . . while it is proper that people should find fault when
their judges fail, it is only reasonable that they should recognize the
difficulties. . . . Let them be severely brought to book,
when they go wrong, but by those who will take the trouble
to understand them."
—*Learned Hand*

THE LAW SCHOOL
THE UNIVERSITY OF CHICAGO

Supreme Court Review

EDITED BY
DENNIS J. HUTCHINSON
DAVID A. STRAUSS
AND GEOFFREY R. STONE

THE UNIVERSITY OF CHICAGO PRESS
CHICAGO AND LONDON

KF
4546
.S9
2010

KF4546 .S9
The Supreme Court review.
2010

Copying Beyond Fair Use: The code on the first page of an article in this book indicates the copyright owner's consent that copies of the article may be made beyond those permitted by Sections 107 or 108 of the U.S. Copyright Law provided that copies are made only for personal or internal use, or for the personal or internal use of specific clients and provided that the copier pay the stated per-copy fee through the Copyright Clearance Center, Inc., 222 Rosewood Drive, Danvers, Massachusetts 01923. To request permission for other kinds of copying, such as copying for general distribution, for advertising or promotional purposes, for creating new collective works, or for resale, kindly write to the publisher. If no code appears on the first page of an article, permission to reprint may be obtained only from the author.

INTERNATIONAL STANDARD BOOK NUMBER: 978-0-226-36326-4

LIBRARY OF CONGRESS CATALOG CARD NUMBER: 60-14353

THE UNIVERSITY OF CHICAGO PRESS, CHICAGO 60637

THE UNIVERSITY OF CHICAGO PRESS, LTD., LONDON

© 2011 BY THE UNIVERSITY OF CHICAGO, ALL RIGHTS RESERVED, PUBLISHED 2011

PRINTED IN THE UNITED STATES OF AMERICA

The paper used in this publication meets the minimum requirements of American National Standard for Information Sciences–Permanence of Paper for Printed Library Materials, ANSI Z39.48-1984. ∞

TO PHILIP B. KURLAND

In memoriam

il miglior fabbro

CONTENTS

PREFACE

In 1959, Philip B. Kurland approached Edward Levi, then Dean of the University of Chicago Law School, with the request that the Law School provide a subvention for the publication of an annual journal devoted to "sustained, disinterested, and competent criticism of the professional qualities of the [Supreme] Court's opinions." Levi agreed with the need but refused financing, on the ground that the journal should be of sufficient quality to support itself. Beginning in 1960, and for the next seventeen years, Phil single-handedly read every submitted manuscript, selected and edited those for publication, and made the *Supreme Court Review* a journal of sharp analysis but no cause. As he explained in a 1964 letter to Justice Felix Frankfurter, for whom he clerked and who was sometimes erroneously suspected of being the impetus for the publication, "The combination of the *Supreme Court Review* and my *Harvard* [*Law Review*] Foreword will prove rather embarrassing. *The Supreme Court Review* is made up of some articles that compliment the very actions that I condemn in my own article. That's the price of editing a review that has no party line but leaves its authors to express the views that they may have."

Although Phil continued as sole editor through the 1976 volume, he was joined first by Gerhard Casper, and then Dennis J. Hutchinson before stepping down in 1988. David Strauss became an editor two years later, and Geoffrey Stone two years after that. When Phil was first asked by one of his deans to describe the *Review* in a sentence for a Law School publication, he called it "an annual devoted to constructive criticism of the work of the Supreme Court." In later years, perhaps acknowledging his own tart writings and other growing criticism, he revised the annual statement to describe the *Review* as devoted to "consideration of the work of the Court."

Nonetheless, the objective of the publication on the occasion of its fiftieth appearance remains as declared in its first preface: to convey and examine, for professional and "intelligent layman" alike, the "depth, the variety, and the difficulty of the problems confronting the Court and the limited tools available to it for their resolution."

DENNIS J. HUTCHINSON
DAVID A. STRAUSS
GEOFFREY R. STONE

KENNETH L. KARST

THROUGH STREETS BROAD AND NARROW: SIX "CENTRIST" JUSTICES ON THE PATHS TO INCLUSION

Let me bow to Philip Kurland right away. In the printed version of his 1969 Cooley Lectures, the first chapter is entitled "The Tyranny of Labels." He begins by decrying any discussion of the Supreme Court "in terms of comic-strip character," specifically criticizing "catchwords" such as "liberals" and "conservatives."[1] To his list, I want to add "centrists." In this comment, that word carries quotation marks; it is, indeed, a quotation of various observers of the Court, and nothing more. If any reference seems to recognize greater importance in the label, I apologize. In the meanwhile, let us bury the term "swing Justice," which is misleading and offensive.

In the last six decades the Supreme Court has been conspicuous

Kenneth L. Karst is David G. Price and Dallas P. Price Professor of Law Emeritus at UCLA School of Law.

AUTHOR'S NOTE: I offer these remarks in memory of Philip Kurland, founding father of *The Supreme Court Review* in 1960 and its editor for the *Review*'s first quarter century. His views and mine about the Court and the Constitution differed considerably, but anyone whose work appeared in these pages would profit by his editing, which always sought to aid the author in expressing his or her position. The word for him is Integrity. Phil's own writings might include a caustic remark here and there, but he had a better than average feel for the humorous. It is a pity that he cannot see this milestone edition of the *Review* he brought to life. If the title reminds you to learn more about Molly Malone—person or legend or both—consult Sean J. Murphy, Irish Historical Mysteries, at http://home-page.eirecom.het/-seanjmurphy/irhismys/molly.htm.

[1] Philip B. Kurland, *Politics, the Constitution and the Warren Court* 1 (Chicago, 1970).

© 2011 by The University of Chicago. All rights reserved.
978-0-226-36326-4/2011/2010-0001$10.00

in promoting the nation's movement toward inclusion.[2] The Court
has made its most notable contributions to the American civic culture in recognizing the Constitution's guarantees of status equality
for groups that had long been subordinated.[3] But status—not always,
but usually—is a zero-sum game. If millions of Americans have been
gratified by a body of law that has affirmed their equal citizenship,
other millions have seen the same decisions as threats to their own
identities. The disgruntled were quickly perceived as a political
constituency. From President Nixon's "southern strategy"[4] to President Reagan's "social issues agenda"[5] and beyond, the Supreme
Court has been a prime target for political leaders who announce
their intention to stem the tide of cultural revolution. The common
theme, not always stated expressly, is that the Court has "gone too
far" in its decisions on racial desegregation, the status of women
(including access to abortion), and—more recently—the rights of
gay and lesbian Americans. This form of identity politics has had
some influence on constitutional law, but thus far that influence has
been limited, seen mainly in decisions about race-conscious responses to past discrimination.[6] The most visible successes of the
politics of cultural division are not seen directly in the Court's
decisions, but in the attraction of voters to practitioners of backlash
politics.[7] Of course, the candidates thus elected can carry considerable weight in determining who becomes a judge.

---

[2] The idea of inclusion is complex, from any perspective. See Martha Minow, *Making
All the Difference: Inclusion, Exclusion, and American Law* (Cornell, 1990); Judith Shklar,
American Citizenship: The Quest for Inclusion (Harvard, 1991); Lani Guinier, *Admissions
Rituals as Political Acts: Guardians at the Gates of Our Democratic Ideals*, 117 Harv L Rev
114 (2003).

[3] As Dean Minow (cited in note 2) shows, the notion of inclusion can have myriad
meanings. I use the term here in one simple sense: the validation of a social group's
constitutional claim to equal citizenship.

[4] See Alexander P. Lamis, *The Two-Party South* 28–30 (Oxford, 1984).

[5] See Nathan Glazer, *The Social Agenda*, in John Lynn Palmer, ed, *Perspectives on the
Reagan Years* at 5 (Urban Institute, 1986).

[6] Critics from quite a different point of view have chided the post-Warren Court for
selling out the promise of *Brown*, and—cruelest cut—to do so in the name of *Brown* itself.
See notes 55–69 below, and accompanying text. For an overview, see Derrick Bell, *Race,
Racism, and American Law* (Aspen, 6th ed 2008). For an up-to-date example, see Cheryl
Harris and Kimberley West-Falcoun, *Reading Ricci: White(ning) Discrimination, Race-ing
Fairness*, 58 UCLA L Rev 73 (2010).

[7] See Richard H. Pildes, *Why the Center Does Not Hold: Hyperpolarized Democracy in
America*, 99 Cal L Rev (forthcoming 2011), emphasizing the polarizing role of the Voting
Rights Act of 1965. The southern strategy lives.
On "the politics of disgust" as a source of laws denying liberties to gay men and lesbians,

The constituency for cultural counterrevolution[8] has found its main locus in the Republican Party, whose nominees have called for the appointment of judges who would turn the tide. Yet, of the twelve Supreme Court Justices appointed by Republican presidents from 1969 to 2008, only six have largely satisfied the counterrevolutionaries.[9] In this comment I focus on the other six, who have disappointed that constituency: Justices Harry A. Blackmun, Lewis F. Powell, Jr., John Paul Stevens, Sandra Day O'Connor, Anthony M. Kennedy, and David H. Souter. All these have been called "centrists" by commentators, but they have had the label attached to them at different stages in their service on the Court, have taken a variety of doctrinal paths, and have voted differently in a number of the relevant cases. As readers of this *Review* know, Justices Blackmun, Stevens, and Souter did not stay in the zone that some observers called the "center"; for most of their years on the Court, these three were more often labeled as "liberals."[10]

When we ask what justifies discussing these six Justices together, one answer can be found in their shared concern for rights to inclusion, to group status equality. Shared concern, of course, does not imply unanimity; these Justices' interactions, including their differences from each other, are part of the story. Typically, their opinions on our topics purport to make only narrow additions to constitutional doctrine—if, indeed, they admit adding anything at all. But in looking at any cultural form, surely most careful observers will measure the dimensions of a body in motion by noticing its apparent gravitational effects on other bodies' movements in cul-

---

see Martha C. Nussbaum, *From Disgust to Humanity: Sexual Orientation and Constitutional Law* 1–30 and passim (Oxford, 2010).

[8] I commented on this mobilization of the backlash some twenty years ago. Kenneth L. Karst, *Religion, Sex, and Politics: Cultural Counterrevolution in Constitutional Perspective*, 24 UC Davis L Rev 677 (1991), elaborated in Kenneth L. Karst, *Law's Promise, Law's Expression: Visions of Power in the Politics of Race, Gender, and Religion* (Yale, 1993). For a more nuanced analysis of the relations between political movements and constitutional development, see William N. Eskridge, Jr., *Channeling: Identity-Based Social Movements and Public Law*, 150 U Pa L Rev 419 (2001).

[9] These six include four members of the current Court. In a longer-term perspective, the six include all three Chief Justices who have succeeded Earl Warren. Yet, Chief Justice Rehnquist, toward the end, supported rights of equality for women and for nonmarital children—in ways that assure those rights' durability.

[10] Or, if you will, "conservatives." That is the label for Justices Stevens and Souter contributed by Noah Feldman, *Imagining a Liberal Court*, NY Times (magazine), June 27, 2010 (on line). Professor Feldman does acknowledge that, without those two Justices' votes, "the liberal legacy [from *Brown* to *Roe*] would have been reversed." Oh, well. (Phil: Are you listening?)

tural spacetime. In that perspective, some of the opinions discussed here are broad, indeed.

Examining the theme of inclusion in the work of our six Justices, we first consider its place in accommodating contending interests, and then turn to its use in achieving various forms of social utility. The doctrinal subjects at the outset are two: racial diversification in colleges and schools, and women's rights. The women's cases go on, beyond questions of utility, to shape the ideal of women's inclusion into an entitlement to treatment as equal citizens—a frame of mind that has come to infuse our third substantive topic, the validation of gay rights.[11]

I. ON DIVERSITY ADMISSIONS: INCLUSION AS POLITICAL ACCOMMODATION AND AS SOCIAL UTILITY

From the beginning, inclusion was seen as the central purpose of affirmative action in its various forms. Of all opinions of the modern Supreme Court, perhaps the one most frequently called "centrist" is Justice Powell's 1978 opinion in *Regents of the University of California v Bakke*.[12] When the Court first came to grips with the sharply divisive question of affirmative action, Powell's opinion looked in two directions. First, he concluded that the UC Davis medical school had violated both the Equal Protection Clause and Title VI of the 1964 Civil Rights Act by using a racial quota in its admission of applicants.[13] Then, Justice Powell went on to reject

---

[11] Analogous cultural disputes center on the religion clauses of the First Amendment. In opinions on the Establishment Clause, Justices O'Connor and Kennedy differed over the proper articulation for the right, but in *Lee v Weisman*, 505 US 577 (1992), Justice Kennedy brought the clause back to life in an opinion strongly supporting rights of inclusion—using language that might well have been written by Justice O'Connor herself. See Kenneth L. Karst, *Justice O'Connor and the Substance of Equal Citizenship*, 2003 Supreme Court Review 357, 380–84. And in *Church of the Lukumi Babalu Aye, Inc. v Hialeah*, 508 US 520 (1993), Justice Kennedy rescued the Free Exercise Clause from the rubble left by *Employment Div., Dep't of Human Resources v Smith*, 494 US 872 (1990). *Smith* had occasioned a strong dissent from Justice O'Connor, and richly deserved the trimming Justice Kennedy gave it. See generally Kenneth L. Karst, *The Stories in Lukumi: Of Sacrifice and Rebirth*, in Richard W. Garnett and Andrew Koppelman, eds, *First Amendment Stories* (Foundation, forthcoming 2011). In the cultural dispute over government funding for religious schools, the rhetoric of inclusion is deployed on both sides. For discussion of the 2009 Term's decision in the Hastings law school case, see the article by Pamela Karlan in this volume.

[12] 438 US 365 (1978). My thanks to Dennis Hutchinson for his contributions to my thinking about Powell.

[13] Justice Stevens, for himself, Chief Justice Burger, and Justices Stewart and Rehnquist, did not reach the constitutional issue, but concluded that the program violated Title VI. This statutory ground thus became the opinion of the Court, invalidating the UC Davis

the view of California's supreme court that any consideration of race in the school's admissions would be unconstitutional. He concluded that it would be permissible for a public university to adopt an explicit policy aimed at creating a student body with diverse backgrounds.[14] This sort of admissions policy, he said, would base an individual's admission on a whole-person evaluation, in which race might be one factor along with many other individual characteristics or attainments. Such a system should not be treated as racial discrimination. Ever since, the *Bakke* opinion has served as the classic reference to the split-the-difference posture a "centrist" is expected to take.

Justice Powell drew on a wealth of political experience. He had served as head of the Richmond school board that managed to tiptoe around the calls for "massive resistance" to desegregation—quietly opposing the segregationists' proposals for action, but not accomplishing actual integration. Later, he had been president of the American Bar Association. More than a few observers have assumed that his embrace of diversity admissions in *Bakke* was purely political, a way to give some satisfaction to both sides of the passion-filled debate over affirmative action. There is considerable support for this view. Powell wanted to be seen as a careful moderate, worthy to be respected by opinion makers of the present and historians of the future. This desire may account for his inclination to straddle a cultural divide.[15] Surely, though, there is another side to Powell,

---

racial quota. In the 1980s Justice Stevens had come to approve the part of Justice Powell's opinion in *Bakke* that validated diversity admissions. See the text accompanying notes 30–31 and 41–53 to this article; Diane Marie Amann, *John Paul Stevens and Equally Impartial Government*, 43 UC Davis L Rev 885, 908 (2010).

[14] In this conclusion Justice Powell was joined by Justices Brennan, White, Blackmun, and Marshall. The "Brennan four" would have upheld the Davis quota against both the constitutional and statutory challenges. They argued that racial segregation's principal vice had been its use as a badge of inferiority—something that could not be said of the medical school's efforts at integration. On Brennan's role in persuading Powell to make explicit the Court's approval of "diversity" admissions, see Seth Stern and Stephen Wermiel, *Justice Brennan* 445–49 (Houghton Mifflin, 2010).

[15] Dennis J. Hutchinson, *Remembering Lewis F. Powell*, 2 Green Bag 2d 163 (1999); Mark Tushnet, *Justice Lewis F. Powell and the Jurisprudence of Centrism*, 93 Mich L Rev 1854 (1995).

Typically, a contested issue of law offers the judge a choice among resolutions—various combinations of results and doctrinal explanations—that can be characterized as ranged on a political continuum (call them A through E). Any likely answer (say, D) will "split the difference" somewhere. So, if you say you are looking for examples of difference splitting among the Justices (of any era), you will find them. In such an exercise, seeking and finding tend to merge. For example, J. Harvie Wilkinson III, *The Rehnquist Court at Twilight: The Lures and Perils of Split-the-Difference Jurisprudence*, 58 Stan L Rev 1969 (2006).

even the Powell who cast the deciding votes in *Bakke*.

Some observers of the decision have offered explanations that highlight substantive concerns. In the 2003 edition of this *Review* John Jeffries portrayed the Powell opinion as an effort to avoid choosing between two substantive holdings that the Justice found unsatisfactory: (i) that any affirmative action was itself racial discrimination and thus unconstitutional, or (ii) that a race-based admission program was valid as a remedy for past discrimination. The first alternative looked draconian; the second might allow racial quotas to go on indefinitely. The *Bakke* resolution would permit "a short-term departure" from color blindness.[16] More recently it has been suggested that Justice Powell was making another substantive point when he remarked that Americans were "a nation of minorities," diverse as to religion, ethnicity, urban or rural origins, etc.[17] In this sense, Powell said, even white Protestants could be called a minority.[18]

Political maneuvering, then, is part of the Powell story, but it is not the whole story, not even in *Bakke*. Further support for a substantive ingredient in Powell's view of *Bakke* can be found in his majority opinion a year earlier in *Arlington Heights v Metropolitan Housing Corp*.[19] This was the occasion for fleshing out the Court's earlier decision in *Washington v Davis*,[20] which limited constitutional claims of racial discrimination to cases in which governmental actors' discriminatory purposes have been demonstrated. In *Arlington Heights* Justice Powell reiterated that a racially disparate effect of governmental action was not, by itself, the equivalent of a discriminatory purpose. But he also said—for the Court—that a discriminatory intent might be inferred from circumstantial evidence, and

---

[16] John C. Jeffries, Jr., *Bakke Revisited*, 2003 Supreme Court Review 1, 7. Professor Jeffries is Powell's biographer, and in that biography he had called the *Bakke* opinion "pure sophistry." John C. Jeffries, Jr., *Justice Lewis F. Powell, Jr.* 484 (Scribner's, 1994). Sophistry, yes—but, as I see it, not *pure* sophistry.

[17] This is the perspective of legal historian Anders Walker in his article, *Diversity's Strange Career: Recovering the Racial Pluralism of Lewis F. Powell*, 50 Santa Clara L Rev 647, 674–76 (2010).

[18] 428 US at 296, 316, 323. In 1978 Powell's remark might annoy the descendants of Irish or Italian or Latin American Catholics, or of Eastern European Jews, but I doubt that he was ignoring those groups' histories of subjection to discrimination. Rather, he was saying that the tables of minority status can be turned with the passage of time. If he were here today, he might mention that not a single one of today's Justices is a Protestant.

[19] 429 US 252 (1977).

[20] 426 US 229 (1976).

he added a catalogue of ways in which complaining parties might find just that sort of evidence in the facts of their cases. One might describe this position as a "centrist" ploy to split the difference, holding out hope to the losers—hope that, someday, their claims of discrimination might succeed, even though government officials have not explicitly avowed a discriminatory purpose. Still, an alternative interpretation, not wholly oriented to the political, is also possible: in shaping this body of doctrine, Powell was looking for a way to do justice in particularized ways that would make good on the Fourteenth Amendment's promise of fair treatment for individuals. He would not be the only Justice labeled as a "centrist" to find substance in a preference for the particular. Such an inclination may produce opinions that purport to follow narrow paths.[21]

Justice Stevens had joined the Court's opinion in *Washington v Davis*, but he added a concurrence of his own, observing that the best proof of a discriminatory purpose often will be "what actually happened" as a result of the governmental action in question.[22] Later in the same year, Stevens famously remarked, "There is only one Equal Protection Clause."[23] His point, of course, was that a gross characterization of a law as discrimination on the basis of sex[24]— thus dropping it into a category requiring important justification— obscures the real issue in the case before the Court. That issue is whether *this* governmental regulation, applied in *this* case, is one that an impartial government would adopt, considering the utility it provides (or fails to provide) to the public, as measured against the harm that the regulation causes to interests in liberty or equality of those who bear its burdens.[25] Justice Stevens's concern for the particular realities of the case at hand bears a strong resemblance to Justice Powell's focus in *Arlington Heights*.

In *Bakke*, while discussing the constitutionality of diversity ad-

---

[21] The modern classic reference here is Cass R. Sunstein, *One Case at a Time: Judicial Minimalism and the Supreme Court* (Harvard, 1999).

[22] 426 US at 253.

[23] *Craig v Boren*, 429 US 190, 211 (1976).

[24] Or, in later cases, on the basis of race.

[25] See Amann, *John Paul Stevens*, 43 UC Davis L Rev, passim (cited in note 13); Andrew Siegel, *Equal Protection Unmodified: Justice John Paul Stevens and the Case for Unmediated Constitutional Interpretation*, 74 Fordham L Rev 2339 (2006). For the suggestion of a broad doctrinal development along similar lines, specifically mentioning the roles of Justices O'Connor and Kennedy, see Louis D. Bilionis, *The New Scrutiny*, 51 Emory L J 481 (2002).

missions, Justice Powell quoted from a statement by Harvard College in its brief amicus curiae. In Harvard's view, a classroom including all sorts of students—representing a variety of experiences,
material concerns, and career goals—would have important educational utility. The Harvard estimate was, and is, entirely justified.[26]
All six of our so-called "centrist" Justices have come to embrace
this conclusion—some soon, some not so soon. Among the later
arrivals, the bodies in motion[27] included the Justices themselves.

Justice Blackmun was one of the four who voted in *Bakke* to
uphold the medical school's racial admissions quota.[28] From that
point forward, he supported affirmative action plans across a wide
variety of cases. In this region of doctrine, Justices labeled as "centrists" have taken different doctrinal paths, and have demonstrated
a capacity to refine their own positions. A notable example is Justice
Stevens, who began with his opinion in *Bakke* holding that the
medical school's race-based admissions quota violated Title VI. Two
years later he filed a shockingly virulent dissent when the Court
upheld an act of Congress that provided grants to local public works,
presumptively reserving 10 percent of the funds for purchases from
specified racial and ethnic groups.[29] But, beginning in 1986, he
consistently supported forward-looking affirmative action, including its deployment as a corrective to harms worked by past racial
discrimination. In *Wygant v Jackson Board of Education*,[30] a Michigan
school board was faced with reduced funding and had to lay off a
number of teachers. Because the board had been dilatory in hiring
minority teachers, most teachers of long standing were white. The
board decided to retain some minority teachers, laying off some
white teachers who had served longer. Justice Stevens called the

---

[26] In the eighteen years of *Bakke*'s reign in California, my own classes in constitutional
law were regularly enriched by exchanges of views among students who brought not just
racial diversity but a wide variety of diverse experiences and interests to our discussions.
I use the word "interests" in two senses: the questions they found interesting, and the
material interests they had known or could expect. In both senses, race mattered.

[27] See the text following note 10.

[28] Indeed, he added his own opinion to that effect. 438 US at 402. In a predecision
memorandum to himself, he had written, "race is used to enhance the fairness of the
system." Linda Greenhouse, *Becoming Justice Blackmun* 139–31 (Times Books, 2005).

[29] *Fullilove v Klutznick*, 448 US 448, 532, 535 n 5 (1980). Even those of us who disapprove
of Justice Stevens's horrific language must concede that this quota did look like a race-
oriented political deal that lacked a fig leaf.

[30] 476 US 267 (1986).

program "inclusionary," not "exclusionary," in purpose.[31] The role modeling of the minority teachers, he said, would be of great utility in educating a student population heavily composed of minority students. That's not enough, said Justice Powell for a plurality, and his position prevailed.

So: Are we to conclude that an integrated student body serves an important educational function, but an integrated teaching staff does not? Not exactly. What seems to have bothered Justice Powell and others of like mind in *Wygant* was that the layoffs imposed heavy burdens on specifically identified teachers.[32] This is a theme that echoes today: Don't impose an employment discrimination remedy that takes away seemingly "vested" interests of identified individual whites.[33] Justice O'Connor provided the fifth vote to invalidate the compensatory layoff program in *Wygant*, but she added an opinion of her own, generally agreeing with Justice Stevens that inclusion was an important goal for government.[34] Thus began a series of cases in which Justice O'Connor wrote separately, sounding generalized themes of inclusion even as she was voting to hold particular affirmative action programs invalid.[35]

The phrase "no, but . . ." has limited appeal as constitutional doctrine, unless the "but" be given some elaboration. On the one

---

[31] Id at 313, 316. See the discussion in Amann, 43 UC Davis L Rev at 905–07 (cited in note 13).

[32] 476 US at 282–84. Concurring in the judgment, Justice Byron R. White strongly emphasized the difference between race-based hiring goals and layoffs. At one point in the conference's consideration of this case, he said the state could not take "an innocent man's job away. You can't call that a remedy." Dennis J. Hutchinson, *The Man Who Once Was Whizzer White* 424 (Free Press, 1998). White had voted in *Bakke* to uphold the medical school's admissions program, and he had been a strong civil rights advocate in the administration of John F. Kennedy. He might have anticipated a possible backlash here: would the Court's approval of the Jackson program dampen whites' enthusiasm for civil rights remedies?

[33] See *Ricci v DeStefano*, 129 S Ct 2658 (2009), holding unconstitutional a similar remedy in a Title VII case. In that case some white firefighters, whose promised promotions were threatened, dramatized their individual concerns by showing up in uniform to hear the oral argument in the Supreme Court. For guidance through the case, see Richard Primus, *The Future of Disparate Impact*, 108 Mich L Rev 1341 (2010). And see the critique in Harris and West-Falcoun, *Reading Ricci* (cited in note 6). "The Rehnquist Court saw the question of social justice through the use of affirmative action, and its effects on whites." Mark Tushnet, *A Court Divided* 226 (Norton, 2d ed 2006).

[34] Her opinion angered a lawyer in the Reagan Justice Department, who wrote that it weakened the decision's force as a rejection of affirmative action. Jan Crawford Greenburg, *Supreme Conflict: The Inside Story of the Struggle for Control of the Supreme Court* 44 (Penguin, 2007).

[35] See *Richmond v J. A. Croson Co.*, 488 US 469 (1989); *Adarand Constructors, Inc. v Peña*, 515 US 280 (1995).

occasion when Justice William J. Brennan, Jr. convinced a (short-lived) majority to uphold an affirmative action law, Justice O'Connor's dissent did provide a glimpse of her substantive concerns. A broad preference for a racial group, she said, violated the Equal Protection Clause's "simple command that the government must treat citizens as individuals, not as simply components of a racial, religious, sexual or national class."[36] As Vik Amar has pointed out, this look-at-the-whole-person demand echoes the "diversity" portion of Justice Powell's opinion in *Bakke*.[37] And, near the end of her tenure on the Court, Justice O'Connor finally found an affirmative action program she could uphold. In *Grutter v Bollinger*[38] she wrote for the Court, validating a diversity admissions program at the University of Michigan's nationally renowned law school.

To understand Justice O'Connor's opinion, we need to make clear what it was not. Some Michigan faculty members and administrators might have believed—as I do—that the Court should have recognized decades ago that the Constitution prohibits racial classifications that stigmatize, not classifications aimed at the integration of long-excluded minorities.[39] The central guarantee of the Fourteenth Amendment, after all, is equal citizenship. Justice Stevens was right when he distinguished inclusion from exclusion, integration from segregation. In the companion case of *Gratz v Bollinger*,[40] Justice Ruth Bader Ginsburg's dissent noted the lasting effects of a racial caste system that still impeded consideration of a great many talented applicants to highly selective universities such as Michigan.[41] This line of argument—sufficient for me, and maybe for you—would have been a recipe for defeat in the Supreme Court.

To save diversity-oriented affirmative action for the University

---

[36] *Metro Broadcasting, Inc. v FCC*, 497 US 547, 602 (1990) (O'Connor, J, dissenting).

[37] Vikram David Amar, *Of Hobgoblins and Justice O'Connor's Jurisprudence of Equality*, 32 McGeorge L Rev 823, 826–28 (2001).

[38] 539 US 306 (2003).

[39] A huge literature (some of it mine) has made this point with sufficient frequency to make most arguments along this line superfluous. For a first-rate treatment of the theme, with plenty of fresh content, see Elizabeth S. Anderson, *Integration, Affirmative Action, and Strict Scrutiny*, 77 NYU L Rev 1195 (2002).

[40] 539 US 244 (2003). In *Gratz*, Justice O'Connor voted with a different 5–4 majority, holding unconstitutional the same university's system of undergraduate admissions. The university readily solved its problem by redefining the undergraduate admissions system in a way designed to leave *Grutter* intact.

[41] 539 US at 298. Justices Stevens and Souter joined Justice Ginsburg's dissent; Justices O'Connor and Kennedy joined the *Gratz* majority.

of Michigan and for universities generally, UM's advocates esti-
mated that they needed to offer arguments that would be persuasive
to Justice O'Connor, or Justice Kennedy, or both. For more than
a decade, both of them had joined majorities holding that affirmative
action could not be validated as an effort to compensate broadly
for societal discrimination, or even to repair the deformations of a
public institution wrought by its own racial discrimination—unless
the particulars of that discrimination had been formally recognized
in a finding by a court or a legislative body.[42] Those two would not
be expected to abandon that position. UM needed a fifth vote, and
undoubtedly its only chances lay with them.

One out of two was enough, and Justice O'Connor wrote for a
bare majority in *Grutter*, upholding the law school's admissions
program.[43] Her opinion first validated diversity admissions on the
basis Justice Powell had used in *Bakke*: the educational value of a
diverse student body. Surely that argument is at its maximum
strength in the discussion format used in most law school classes,
a format well known to all the Justices. What attracted attention
to Justice O'Connor's opinion, however, was her embrace of other
grounds, drawing on other aspects of the ideal of inclusion. This
feature of the Court's opinion has broad national importance.[44]

As the oral argument in *Grutter* had shown, three briefs amici
curiae had caught the Justices' special notice: one filed by General
Motors Corp., another filed on behalf of sixty-five huge business

---

[42] In *Grutter*, an intervenor group of minority students had argued that the UM law
school's current admissions criteria (prominently featuring undergraduate grades and
LSAT scores) were racially discriminatory. Their argument is discussed by Tomiko Brown-
Nagin, *Elites, Social Movements, and the Law: The Case of Affirmative Action*, 105 Colum L
Rev 1436 (2005). On grades-and-LSAT-score admissions systems as a benefit to children
from privileged families, see Susan Sturm and Lani Guinier, *The Future of Affirmative
Action: Reclaiming the Innovative Ideal*, 84 Cal L Rev 953 (1996). For a more recent local
"take," see Kathryn Ladewski, *Note: Preserving a Racial Hierarchy: A Legal Analysis of the
Disparate Racial Impact of Legacy Preferences in University Admissions*, 103 Mich L Rev 577
(2010).

In modern memory there has been no explicit racial discrimination by the University
of Michigan. Even so, the university would not want to get bogged down in dealing with
the intervenors' arguments.

[43] Justices Stevens and Souter joined Justice O'Connor, but Justice Kennedy dissented.

[44] For a crisp (and yet thorough) analysis of the *Grutter* opinion, see Joel K. Goldstein,
Beyond Bakke: Grutter-Gratz and the Promise of Brown, 48 SLU L J 829 (2004).

Dean Caminker reminds us that the challenges to UM's affirmative action programs
were based, not only on the Equal Protection Clause, but also on Title VI of the Civil
Rights Act of 1964. Title VI applies to both public and private recipients of federal
funding—and thus to virtually all American universities. Evan Caminker, *A Glimpse Behind
and Beyond Grutter*, 48 SLU L J 889, 892 (2004).

corporations, and a third filed on behalf of a group of retired high military and naval officers. These briefs made similar points. The amici officers said that, given the large proportion of enlisted men and women who are members of racial and ethnic minorities, it would harm the effectiveness of the services if nearly all the officers were identified as "white." The service academies themselves were engaged in active programs of diversity admissions, aimed at integrating the officer corps. Furthermore, the services regularly draw officers from ROTC programs in public and private universities.[45] The amici companies reminded the Court that many of their employees—and a great many of their prospective customers in the United States and overseas—were members of racial and ethnic groups called "nonwhite." These businesses typically draw their leaders from the ranks of graduates of universities, including law schools. It would harm the companies (and the national economy) if they were deprived of minority graduates, and thus compelled to operate under leadership almost entirely composed of whites.

To the diversity argument and the arguments of the amici, Justice O'Connor added a third, and broader, concern: the importance of law schools as "the training ground for a large number of the Nation's leaders." This was a matter of legitimacy; the public needed assurance "that the path to leadership is visibly open."[46] Her opinion took account of all these forward-looking utilitarian factors as justifications for diversity admissions.[47] In sum, the arguments combined to justify the law school's diversity admissions "so that all members of a heterogeneous society may participate in the educational institutions that provide the training and education necessary to succeed in America."[48] In the language I have used here, the utility of an integrated leadership class is a strong national interest, broadly shared by all Americans.[49]

---

[45] The armed services' most famous ROTC graduate in our time is General Colin Powell.

[46] 539 US at 332.

[47] See Kenneth L. Karst, *The Revival of Forward-Looking Affirmative Action*, 104 Colum L Rev 60 (2004).

[48] 539 US at 332–33. In the words of a seasoned veteran of the war against racial caste, "affirmative action in higher education has contributed substantially to creating a black middle class and leadership class." Jack Greenberg, *Diversity, the University, and the World Outside*, 103 Colum L Rev 1610, 1611 (2003). See also Guinier, 117 Harv L Rev at 125–36 and passim (cited in note 2).

[49] The *Grutter* and *Gratz* opinions are, to put it softly, not easy to reconcile. For a severe critique of both Justice O'Connor's *Grutter* opinion and Chief Justice Rehnquist's

The interests of the military and business amici are not the interests of individual minority applicants to the university—nor, indeed, the interests of any identified individuals. As William Nelson has reminded us, a critical view, expressed by observers ranging from Professor Derrick Bell to Justice Clarence Thomas, begins with recognition that, in one important sense, these are interests of whites in "using" Americans of minority race or ethnicity—using them, that is, to fight their wars or sell their goods.[50] But the university cannot be charged with cynicism here. As a litigant, UM needed arguments that would persuade a majority of this Court to uphold affirmative action. The concerns of the military and the business interests were broad in their reach, and they were legitimate. The services' and companies' objectives offered significant utility to the whole society, and they undoubtedly had broad appeal for the public—especially the portion of the public that might vote.[51] And Justice O'Connor's third stated purpose for the affirmative action before the Court—the integration of the nation's leadership class—is, indeed, a value shared by the middle class of racial and ethnic minority groups.[52] In the event, she wrote for a 5–4 majority

Gratz opinion, see Ian Ayres and Sydney Foster, *Don't Tell, Don't Ask: Narrow Tailoring After Grutter and Gratz*, 85 Tex L Rev 517 (2007). Unfortunately, these authors conclude by asking judges to perform a task that no Supreme Court Justice—not one, not ever, at any stage of the Court's history—would assign to them. The authors propose that "courts should require [a university to] quantify the overall and marginal costs and benefits of granting racial preferences," and then "determine if the university is using the smallest possible preference to achieve the benefits of the diversity interest." Id at 583. So: If you think a diverse classroom will improve a law school's educational offering, what is the minimum number of diversity candidates the school will need, considering the large number of course offerings, and estimates of enrollment in each of them—that is, estimates of "diversity" and "other" enrollees? Or, if you agree with Justice O'Connor that diversity admissions in highly respected law schools will serve the vital national interest in producing a racially integrated class of national leaders, what might be the smallest possible number of diversity admissions at the UM law school to provide that school's share in the integration? You may bring your notes to this examination.

[50] See William E. Nelson, *Brown v Board of Education and the Jurisprudence of Legal Realism*, 48 SLU L J 795, 833–38 (2004). Indeed, *Grutter* does illustrate Professor Bell's interest-convergence pattern. See Derrick Bell, *Diversity's Distraction*, 103 Colum L Rev 1622, 1624 (2003), looking back to Derrick A. Bell, Jr., *Brown v Board of Education and the Interest-Convergence Dilemma*, 93 Harv L Rev 518 (1980).

[51] UM's leaders had recognized the political attractiveness of the arguments of the military officers and big companies—including attractiveness to Justice O'Connor—but UM, in its own briefing, could only hint at these arguments. In any event, the "amici strategy" to bring the arguments squarely before the Court had its origin in Ann Arbor. See Caminker, 48 SLU L J at 894–96 (cited in note 44). More generally on the military brief, see Jeffrey Toobin, *The Nine: Inside the Secret World of the Supreme Court* 246–64 (Anchor, 2008); Tushnet, *A Court Divided* at 232–34 (cited in note 33).

[52] Little of this value directly benefits persons of low socioeconomic class, for whom the promise of inclusion remains a chimera—and who do not vote. Bertrall L. Ross II,

that opted for affirmative action's historic goal: inclusion. "*Grutter* reconnects equality discourse to concerns about freedom and participation."[53]

Although Justice Kennedy dissented in *Grutter*, he agreed that diversity admissions satisfied the need for a "compelling" governmental interest; his vote was the sixth for that broad position.[54] Now, with the retirement of Justices O'Connor and Souter, Justice Kennedy is the last of our set of six so-called "centrists" to remain on the Court. His definition of an acceptable race-conscious program is partly illuminated by his separate opinion in *Parents Involved in Community Schools v Seattle School District No. 1*.[55] In that case Justice Kennedy agreed with the conclusion of a plurality of four Justices that the Louisville and Seattle school boards' districting systems were unconstitutional. The systems were designed to maintain a substantial degree of racial integration, and they explicitly assigned students using racial percentages. That method required the classification of individual students in racial categories. Chief Justice John G. Roberts, Jr., for the plurality, followed the line of formal racial neutrality that had been central in President Reagan's social issues agenda.[56] He went on to instruct his colleagues in a

Minimum Responsiveness and the Political Exclusion of the Poor, 72 L & Contemp Probs 197 (2009). See generally *Symposium, Race and Socioeconomic Class: Examining an Increasingly Complex Tapestry*, 72 L & Contemp Probs 1 (Trina Jones, ed, Fall 2009). Most recent discussions of this subject recognize their debt to William E. Forbath, *Caste, Class, and Equal Citizenship*, 98 Mich L Rev 1 (1999).

[53] Rachel F. Moran, *Of Doubt and Diversity: The Future of Affirmative Action*, 67 Ohio St L J 201, 237 (2006). Discourse is, indeed, important. But affirmative action cannot make up for the public's neglect of education in minority communities. That neglect is the most important factor contributing to the racial disparities that make affirmative action necessary. See Bryan K. Fair, *Taking Educational Caste Seriously: Why Grutter Will Help Very Little*, 78 Tulane L Rev 1843 (2004). On *Grutter* as a potential stimulus for universities' imagination about race-conscious behavior, see Guinier, 117 Harv L Rev at 198–231 (cited in note 2).

[54] Justice Kennedy dissented in *Grutter* because he thought the law school's actual practice did not really add up to a diversity program; the numbers seemed to him to be too close to a quota. So far as I know, Justice Kennedy's law-teaching experience has not included the administrative responsibilities that would aid in appreciating that a school cannot maintain a "critical mass" of diversity admittees without paying "some attention to numbers." The latter is the phrase used by Harvard College in the brief quoted by Justice Powell in *Bakke*. On the influence of the need for a "critical mass" on diversity admissions, see Kenneth L. Karst, *Justice O'Connor*, 2003 Supreme Court Review at 395–401 (cited in note 11).

[55] 551 US 701, 782 (2007) (Kennedy, J, concurring in the judgment). For a ten-page gem on the *Parents Involved* decision, see Kenneth M. Casebeer, *Memory Lost: Brown v. Board and the Constitutional Economy of Liberty and Race*, 537 U Miami L Rev 537 (2009).

[56] On earlier versions of formal racial neutrality, see Kenneth L. Karst, *Private Discrimination and Public Responsibility: Patterson in Context*, 1989 Supreme Court Review 1, 24–28, 35–46.

tone reminiscent of Felix Frankfurter's willingness to edify the Justices of the 1940s: "The way to stop discrimination on the basis of race is to stop discriminating on the basis of race."[57] In proposing this sweepingly broad rejection of affirmative action, the Chief Justice spoke for the Court's four hardliners on the subject of race, invoking *Brown*—of all cases!—to invalidate school boards' voluntary desegregation. As John Wooden might say, goodness, gracious.[58]

If there is such a thing as secular sacrilege, the plurality has committed that sin here in quoting the 1954 words of counsel for the plaintiffs in *Brown*, omitting the purpose at hand. The Chief Justice quoted Robert L. Carter, who said in the *Brown* oral argument that the Equal Protection Clause forbids the state "to use race as a factor in affording educational opportunities among the citizens." The Chief Justice thus conceals from his readers the main function of school segregation in 1954: to declare the inferiority of black people and to reinforce their systematic subordination to whites. Commenting in 2007 on the Chief Justice's strategic deployment of his words, Judge Carter (now a celebrated Senior Judge of the federal district court) said, "It's to stand that argument [against subordination] on its head to use race the way they [the *Parents Involved* plurality] use it." Other leading lawyers for the *Brown* plaintiffs were equally vehement. Columbia law professor Jack Greenberg called the Chief Justice's invocation of their 1954 argument "preposterous," adding: "The plaintiffs in *Brown* were concerned with the marginalization and subjugation of black people. . . . [T]hat's how race was being used." William T. Coleman, who later became President Ford's Secretary of Transportation, called the Chief Justice's interpretation of the *Brown* counsel "100% wrong."[59] If you think these distinguished lawyers' talk was acerbic,

---

[57] 551 US at 748.

[58] To readers who are not fans: John Wooden died recently, just before his 100th birthday. He was the greatest coach in the history of college basketball, and he arrived in Westwood while I was a UCLA undergraduate. When I am tempted—for example, by this plurality opinion—to indulge in language that is bitter and contemptuous, I look to the mild-spoken Coach for guidance.

[59] All these quotations are from Adam Liptak, *News Analysis: The Same Words, but Differing Views*, NY Times, June 29, 2007, A24. After writing this paragraph I came upon the same criticism—in similar words, and quoting from the Liptak article—by Pamela Karlan, *What Can Brown® Do for You? Principles and the Struggle over the Equal Protection Clause*, 38 Duke L J 1049, 1064–67 (2009). As I often say to her work, Amen.

just imagine what Thurgood Marshall would have said. But don't print it.

Justice Kennedy resisted the Chief Justice's lecture. He pointed out that the reality of race relations in the schools has never been color-blind, nor will it be in the foreseeable future. He made clear that he would uphold a districting system that recognized the educational utility of racially integrated schools, using race-conscious policies to guide the location of schools, the drawing of attendance zones, or the recruitment of teachers.[60] In short, although he rejected school board action that broadly required racial labeling for individual students, he invited board members who favored racial integration to deploy their powers to promote diversity without that sort of labeling.[61] Surely the methods that he envisioned would need to be narrowly adapted to the particular conditions in the district. Louisville's school board responded to this decision with a carefully crafted plan for school assignments, a plan conscious of the values of diversity but not identifying any individual students by race. It remains to be seen whether their new plan will survive an attack on the basis of *Parents Involved*, but a recent evaluation persuasively predicts a positive result for the board.[62]

Heather Gerken suggests that Justice Kennedy's opinion, along with one in an earlier voting rights case,[63] represents his recognition that official consideration of race can have special utility in a particular setting—a particular "domain," in her locution.[64] In *Parents*

---

[60] Ironically, some of these methods evoke memories of the instruments used by segregationist school boards seeking to avoid the reach of *Brown*. As Justice Stevens pointed out in his *Parents Involved* dissent, indirection would not have been necessary in the days when a majority of the Court focused on actual integration, as opposed to a formal racial neutrality that reinforces racial separation in schools. "It is my firm conviction that no Member of the Court that I joined in 1975 would have agreed with today's decision." 551 US at 803. I was teaching the subject in those days, and I share his conviction—with a little uncertainty about Justice Rehnquist. For an estimate that would, indeed, include the Rehnquist vote, see Amann, 43 UC Davis L Rev at 912–13 n 165 (cited in note 13).

[61] 551 US at 788–89. As Bill Eskridge put it, Justice Kennedy, viewing race as "a sensitive criterion," saw Seattle's plan as "a crude racial sorting," less effective in achieving diverse classrooms than the measures he suggested. William N. Eskridge, Jr., *A Pluralist Theory of the Equal Protection Clause*, 11 U Pa J Const L 1239, 1267 (2009). See also Andrew Siegel, *Stevens and the Seattle Schools Case: A Case Study on the Role of Righteous Anger in Constitutional Discourse*, 43 UC Davis L Rev 927, 929 (2010).

[62] Daniel Kiel, *Accepting Justice Kennedy's Dare: The Future of Integration in a Post-PICS World*, 78 Fordham L Rev 2873 (2010).

[63] *League of United Latin American Citizens v Perry*, 148 US 399 (2006).

[64] Heather K. Gerken, *Comment: Justice Kennedy and the Domains of Equal Protection*, 121 Harv L Rev 104 (2007).

Involved the domain is public education, and the school is a place where students should be learning about race in our society. A racially integrated school provides opportunities for that education every day.[65] In this opinion, as Rachel Moran suggests, Justice Kennedy may, indeed, "split the difference" between those who are comfortable with racial separation and those who are not—or, as she more generously puts it, between those who would forbid any official classification based on race, and those who would uphold race-based efforts to achieve integration.[66] As she makes clear, however, Justice Kennedy recognizes the "expressive and associational aspects of the common school."[67] He is careful to identify particular areas in which public school officials can legitimately consider race when they pursue integration as an instrument of inclusion.

For Justice Kennedy, at this writing, the outer constitutional boundaries of race-conscious remedies are yet to be defined.[68] But we do know one thing: He does not have a constitutional objection to the *purpose* of diversifying public schools or universities. To put that more directly, Justice Kennedy plainly accepts, as a broad master principle, that the Constitution allows some governmental efforts to promote racially integrated public education. This is no trifling matter.[69] During Justice Kennedy's tenure, the way remains

---

[65] Judge Alex Kozinski, who is no bleeding heart, made a valuable point when the Ninth Circuit considered the Seattle case: "Schoolmates often become friends, rivals and romantic partners; learning to deal with individuals of different races in these various capacities cannot help but foster the live-and-let-live spirit that is the essence of the American experience." *Parents Involved in Cmty Sch. v Seattle School Dist. No. 1*, 426 F3d 1192, 1195 (en banc) (9th Cir 2005) (concurring in result).

It must be recognized, however, that the Kozinski scenario is beyond hope for the great majority of students, who live in one-race school *districts* that are—by the Court's own decision—immune from judicial orders for interdistrict transfers. *Milliken v Bradley*, 418 US 717 (1974). For illumination of this sad reality by an expert, see James F. Ryan, *Comment: The Supreme Court and Voluntary Integration*, 121 Harv L Rev 131, 144–46 (2007). The one-race districts are not accidental. They result, in great measure, from governmental action taken with race in mind. Nancy A. Denton, *The Permanence of Segregation: Links Between Residential Segregation and School Segregation*, 80 Minn L Rev 795 (1996).

[66] Rachel F. Moran, *Rethinking Race, Equality, and Liberty: The Unfulfilled Purpose of Parents Involved*, 69 Ohio St L J 1321, 1328 (2008). Dean Moran goes on to develop a sophisticated defense of the power (and also the duty) of government to support the right of individuals to make their own choices about racial identity. Her article, along with Guinier, 117 Harv L Rev (cited in note 2), are "must reads" for anyone interested in the longer-term issues raised by *Grutter* and *Gratz*.

[67] Moran, 69 Ohio St L J at 1366 (cited in note 66).

[68] Richard Primus, 108 Mich L Rev (cited in note 33), has analyzed the possible constitutional implications of the interpretation of Title VII in Justice Kennedy's opinion for the Court in *Ricci v DeStefano* (cited in note 33).

[69] Justice Kennedy thus "undermines as a general principle the notion that government

open for public education officials to advance the broad values of inclusion in ways narrowly adapted to the situations they confront.

II. On Women's Rights: Inclusion as Utility, and Then as Entitlement

Starting a generation ago, the Supreme Court's decisions on women's constitutional rights to equal citizenship demonstrated a concern about the relation of inclusion to social utility—but at the turning point there was a catch. Here, the Court began by recognizing the *lack* of utility in a set of exclusionary (and timeworn) assumptions about sex roles that had come to be seen as obsolete in the late twentieth century. Examples included the assumption that women were weak and otherwise unqualified for "men's work"—that is, work outside school teaching, nursing, or caring for children or the elderly—roles traditionally seen as motherly. After World War II had demonstrated women's utility in all sorts of roles, most Americans, directly presented with the issue, would recognize the weakness of such assumptions. The problem was that a great many Americans (not only men, but mostly men) were not giving the matter any thought at all.

The 1970s were the decade in which the women's movement surged ahead. By 1976 the Supreme Court had held, in *Craig v Boren*,[70] that sex discrimination—in that case, a wholesale limit imposed by government on women and not men—violates the Equal Protection Clause unless it contributes in a substantial way to achievement of an important public interest.[71] Within five years, however, Justice William H. Rehnquist—a *Craig* dissenter—had twice led majorities of the Court to narrow the application of *Craig*'s demanding requirements, substituting more permissive language that permitted sex discrimination whenever women and men were

---

cannot act to remedy societal discrimination." Derek W. Black, *Turning Stones of Hope into Boulders of Resistance: The First and Last Task of Social Justice Curriculum, Scholarship, and Practice*, 86 NC L Rev 673, 717 (2008).

[70] 429 US 190 (1976).

[71] Justice Brennan wrote the Court's opinion. In the early 1970s he had sought (with vigor but no success) to persuade the Court to equate sex discrimination with racial discrimination, which could be sustained only on a showing of the most compelling need. Yet Brennan explicitly refused to hire women as law clerks until the 1974 Term. On this sad story, concluding with Justice Ginsburg's generous forgiveness, see Stern and Wermeil, *Justice Brennan* at 385–408 (cited in note 14).

"not similarly situated."[72] To the reader, I suggest the following parlor game, after the wine is consumed: In each round, one side proposes an area of activity in which women and men *are* similarly situated, and the other side gets one point by responding with some way in which the sexes *are not* similarly situated as to that same activity. The respondents will win most of the rounds—all of them, if each side includes a lawyer.

Immediately after this decision, Justice O'Connor joined the Court. Late in her first Term she wrote for a 5–4 majority holding unconstitutional a state university nursing school's refusal to admit a man as a student.[73] Her opinion revitalized the *Craig* standard. Repeatedly referring to women's rights decisions, she made clear that the Court was defining the Constitution's response to a public agency's discrimination against women or men. Indeed, her own experience of sex discrimination[74] is discernible on the opinion's face. In describing the school's exclusion of male applicants, she quoted the late nineteenth-century charter of Mississippi University for Women (MUW), announcing that it would instruct "the girls of the state" in various forms of secretarial work, nursing, and even needlework, "to fit them for the practical affairs of life."[75]

The dissenters in *MUW* were the four Justices appointed by President Nixon, including two from our set of six, Justices Blackmun[76] and Powell. Those two suggested that an all-female school might expand Mississippi women's college choices, but Justice O'Connor pointed out that there had been no shortage of opportunities for women to be trained in nursing. Ever since, the *MUW* decision has served as a founding (at least re-founding) precedent

---

[72] *Michael M. v Superior Court*, 450 US 464, 471 (1981) (5–4); *Rostker v Goldberg*, 453 US 57, 79 (1981) (6–3). For a contemporary criticism that left these opinions in shreds, see Wendy Webster Williams, *The Equality Crisis: Some Reflections on Culture, Courts, and Feminism*, 7 Women's Rights L Rep 175 (1982).

[73] *Mississippi University for Women v Hogan*, 458 US 718 (1982). On interactions among the Justices in this case, see Joan Biskupic, *Sandra Day O'Connor* 129–46 (Harper Collins, 2005). Instead of writing for the Court, Justice Brennan assigned the opinion to Justice O'Connor. Good for him.

[74] For a paragraph on Justice O'Connor's experience after her law school graduation, see id at 28.

[75] 458 US at 720 n 1. Fairness requires the report that Hunter Gholson, MUW's lawyer, began his oral argument by saying, "we are not here to perpetuate a nineteenth-century finishing school to teach young women needlecraft and kindergarten keeping." Biskupic, *Sandra Day O'Connor* at 130 (cited in note 73).

[76] Linda Greenhouse reports that Justice Blackmun was troubled by the case, but dissented anyway. Greenhouse, *Becoming Justice Blackmun* at 221 (cited in note 28).

forbidding law's exclusion of women from the world of work, and more generally their exclusion from the public life of the national community. By 1982 the economic and social utility of women's inclusion would seem obvious to a great majority of Americans, but—beyond any dispute about utility—it is plain today that women are entitled to these forms of inclusion as a simple matter of constitutional principle.

The Court reaffirmed this broad entitlement in *United States v Virginia*,[77] recognizing (7–1)[78] the right of women to be considered for admission to the Virginia Military Institute, a state university. Since its founding, VMI had been limited by state law to male students. Demonstrating the anachronism of this limit, Justice Ginsburg wrote for a majority that included all five of our six so-called "centrist" Justices who remained on the Court.[79] Now women's entitlement to inclusion was virtually its own justification. Quoting from *MUW*, the Court concluded that the exclusion of women from any public program would be invalid unless there were "an exceedingly persuasive justification" for it. Remarkably, Chief Justice Rehnquist concurred in the result, although he would not join the other six in prescribing such a demanding standard of review.[80] The standard as articulated by Justices O'Connor and Ginsburg has not been disavowed, although the Court did limit its application in one minor instance involving a fact situation that seems likely to arise only sporadically.[81] The main point in all these cases, as Ann Scales had put it a decade before the VMI case, "is not freedom to be treated without regard to sex; the issue is freedom from systematic subordination because of sex."[82] That broad substantive entitlement

---

[77] 518 US 515 (1996).

[78] Justice Thomas had recused himself; his son was attending VMI.

[79] That is, Justices Blackmun, Stevens, O'Connor, Kennedy, and Souter.

[80] 518 US at 558–59, adopting the *Craig* standard. A significant part of his opinion was a reply to Justice Scalia's outraged dissent. The Chief Justice later caused another surprise with his opinion for a 6–3 majority in *Nevada Dep't of Human Resources v Hibbs*, 538 US 721 (2003), holding that Congress had the power, under § 5 of the Fourteenth Amendment, to abrogate a state's immunity from judicial enforcement of the Family and Medical Leave Act, an Act of Congress designed in major part to protect women's rights. Justices O'Connor and Souter joined this opinion, Justice Stevens concurred in the judgment, and Justice Kennedy wrote the main dissenting opinion.

[81] *Nguyen v INS*, 533 US 53 (2001) (5–4). Justice Kennedy wrote for a majority that included Justice Stevens; Justice O'Connor wrote for the dissenters, who included Justice Souter.

[82] Ann C. Scales, *The Emergence of Feminist Jurisprudence: An Essay*, 95 Yale L J 1373, 1395 (1986).

to equal citizenship is now settled, under either the Rehnquist or the O'Connor/Ginsburg locution.[83]

The most important illustration of the Scales axiom—and arguably the most important women's claim in modern times—is the right of a woman to make her own decision whether to have an abortion. Justice Blackmun saw his opinion for the Court in *Roe v Wade*[84] as his defining moment, and others have seen it in the same light.[85] Although his language in *Roe* emphasized the importance of supporting a doctor's medical judgment, in later years he explicitly invoked the women's-equality justification for the right of abortion choice.[86] In the decade following *Roe*, Justice Stevens showed some reluctance to invalidate laws limiting women's rights to abortion choice, but by the early 1980s he and Justice Powell had become Justice Blackmun's allies in defending those rights.[87] And after another decade passed, Justice Stevens was working to persuade Justice O'Connor to join them.[88]

Justice Souter, too—after a bit of vamping[89]—became a consistent supporter of women's abortion rights. Indeed, he seems to have been the prime mover in assembling the threesome (Justices O'Connor, Kennedy, and Souter) whose joint opinion preserved a major portion of those rights[90] in *Planned Parenthood of Southeastern*

---

[83] On the role of the women's movement in this evolution, see Reva B. Siegel, *Constitutional Culture, Social Movement Conflict and Constitutional Change: The Case of the De Facto ERA*, 94 Cal L Rev 1323 (2006).

Even after women have attained equal rights in contexts of explicit governmental action, important inequalities remain in women's lives. See, e.g., Martha Albertson Fineman, *The Autonomy Myth: A Theory of Dependency* (New Press, 2004); Angela P. Harris, *Theorizing Class, Gender, and the Law: Three Approaches*, 72 L & Contemp Probs 57 (Fall 2009).

[84] 410 US 113 (1973). On the influence of Justice Brennan on the Court's handling of the abortion issue, beginning with *Eisenstadt v Baird*, 415 US 438 (1972), see Stern and Wermeil, *Justice Brennan* at 369–75 (cited in note 14).

[85] The authoritative exposition is Greenhouse, *Becoming Justice Blackmun* at 74–101 and passim (cited in note 28).

[86] For example, *Thornburgh v American College of Obstetricians and Gynecologists*, 476 US 747, 772 (1986).

[87] For example, *Akron v Akron Center for Reproductive Health, Inc.*, 462 US 416 (1983) (Powell, J, for the Court, joined by Stevens, J).

[88] Linda Greenhouse, *Justice John Paul Stevens as Abortion-Rights Strategist*, 43 UC Davis L Rev 749 (2010).

[89] In *Rust v Sullivan*, 500 US 173 (1991), and in *Bray v Alexandria Women's Health Club*, 506 US 263 (1993).

[90] A major portion, but not all. One price of the agreement to preserve the core of *Roe* seems to have been the validation of the state law requiring a woman who seeks an abortion to review literature about pregnancy and the fetus, and to wait for twenty-four hours before the procedure. These requirements seriously burden abortion choice, and are in-

Pennsylvania v Casey.[91] The majority in that hugely significant decision was composed of the five remaining Justices in our set of six, who had been appointed by Presidents Nixon, Ford, Reagan, and Bush I. In *Casey,* Justice Stevens also played an important role in persuading—and helping—the authors of the joint opinion to shape their opinion so that its most significant features would be the heart of the opinion of the Court.[92]

The drafting of the joint opinion was divided among the three Justices, and the authors separately emphasized that a woman's control over her own pregnancy is essential to her right to full inclusion as a man's equal.[93] Justice O'Connor, explaining the invalidation of Pennsylvania's law requiring a married woman to inform her husband before she has an abortion, said that the law "embodies a view of marriage consonant with the common-law status of married women but is repugnant to our present understanding of marriage and of the nature of rights secured by the Constitution."[94] Justice Kennedy wrote, "The destiny of the woman must be shaped to a large extent on her conception of her spiritual imperatives and her place in society."[95] Justice Souter summed up the main social importance of *Casey* in a paragraph that spoke broadly of women as a group and emphasized their right to inclusion. For two decades since *Roe v Wade,* he wrote,

> People have organized intimate relationships and made choices that define their views of themselves and their places in society, in reliance on

tended to do so. See Sylvia A. Law, *Abortion Compromise—Inevitable and Impossible,* 1992 U Ill L Rev 921, 940–41; Seana Valentine Shiffrin, *Inducing Moral Deliberation: On the Occasional Virtues of Fog,* 123 Harv L Rev 1214, 1234–36 (2010).

[91] 505 US 833 (1992). The opposing movement here had culminated in an initial vote in the conference on *Casey* to take action that would virtually overrule *Roe* without saying so. On that vote and the Chief Justice's draft majority opinion, see Greenburg, *Supreme Conflict* at 152–53 (cited in note 34); Toobin, *The Nine* at 47–70 (cited in note 51). On the crucial work of Justices O'Connor, Kennedy, and Souter to shape that decision, and Justice Scalia's strong reaction, see Greenburg, *Supreme Conflict* at 155–60; Tushnet, *A Court Divided* at 209–13 (cited in note 33).

[92] See Greenhouse, 43 UC Davis L Rev at 776–81 (cited in note 88).

[93] For a fuller discussion, see Karst, 2003 Supreme Court Review at 421–26 (cited in note 11). Justice Kennedy's subsequent detachment from the others in *Stenberg v Carhart,* 530 US 914, 956 (2000), and *Gonzalez v Carhart,* 550 US 124 (2007), marks a doctrinal difference, but almost no diminution of women's actual power of abortion choice. For the reasons why, see Kenneth L. Karst, *The Liberties of Equal Citizens: Groups and the Due Process Clause,* 55 UCLA L Rev 99, 130–31 (2007). On the second *Carhart*'s reinforcement of *Casey*'s concern for women's dignity interest, see Reva B. Siegel, *Dignity and the Politics of Protection: Abortion Restrictions Under Casey and Carhart,* 117 Yale L J 1694 (2008).

[94] 505 US at 894.

[95] Id at 852.

the availability of abortion in the event that contraception should fail. The ability of women to participate equally in the economic and social life of the Nation has been facilitated by their ability to control their reproductive lives.[96]

What these Justices are saying—what the Court is saying, with this threesome joined by Justices Blackmun and Stevens—is that the right at stake here is not just the right of a woman to act in a particular way. It is her right to control her own identity. Seen in a broader context, it is a right to group status equality, the right of women generally to choose inclusion in the public world, including the world of work.

The three-Justice joint opinion modified the rigid *Roe* formula into an "undue burden" limit on state regulation. This nod to the anti-abortion point of view was seen by some to take a middle path on the constitutionality of government restrictions on abortion.[97] The *Casey* majority may indeed have shaped a doctrinal solution that gave something to each side in a long-standing political dispute. But thus far—and it is now approaching two decades—women's right to abortion choice remains solid, at least as to laws broadly forbidding abortion.[98] The claim to inclusion embraced in *Casey* now has a clearly defined status as an entitlement, a right to equal citizenship.

---

[96] Id at 856.

[97] Neal Devins, *How Planned Parenthood v. Casey (Pretty Much) Settled the Abortion Wars*, 118 Yale L J 1318 (2009).

[98] An overruling of *Roe*, it seems, would terrify strategists for Republican Party candidates outside the South.

The political attack on the right to abortion has moved to other fronts. (i) On laws designed around "the new rhetoric" that women need protection against their own decisions to have abortions, see Reva B. Siegel, *The New Politics of Abortion: An Equality Analysis of Woman-Protecting Abortion Restrictions*, 2007 U Ill L Rev 991. (ii) On TRAP laws (Targeted Regulation of Abortion Providers), see Dawn Johnson, *"TRAP"ing Roe in Indiana and a Common-ground Alternative*, 118 Yale L J 1156 (2009). (iii) Some states are poised to bar insurance companies from covering abortion costs under the recent health insurance legislation. Erik Eckholm, *Across Country, Lawmakers Push Abortion Curbs*, NY Times, Jan 21, 2011 (on line). (iv) Meanwhile, foes of abortion rights have been telling African Americans that supporters of such rights are promoting genocide, seeking to reduce the black population. Shala Dewan, *To Court Blacks, Foes of Abortion Make Racial Case*, NY Times, Feb 26, 2010 (on line). For the moment, one anti-abortion group has specifically recommended a particular form of restriction on abortion, explicitly on the ground that it will appeal to Justice Kennedy. Siegel, 2007 U Ill L Rev at 1028 n 152.

III. On Gay Rights: Inclusion, from Zero to (Almost Complete) Entitlement

The "zero" here refers to the Supreme Court's treatment of this subject up through its 1986 decision in *Bowers v Hardwick*.[99] The modern gay rights movement, of course, was energized in response to the 1969 Stonewall riots. That movement's great success was its persuasion of millions of gay and lesbian Americans to come out of the closet, affirming their sexual orientation. Recognizing each other in significant numbers, they became a potential voting bloc. More importantly, their coming out educated their friends and relatives. By the time *Hardwick* came to the Court, a great many Americans who defined themselves as "straight" had come to see their gay and lesbian acquaintances as individuals, not defining them with labels describing sexual orientations.[100] Even in the Supreme Court, attitudes had shifted; in *Hardwick* the Court initially voted 5–4 to hold that Georgia's law forbidding homosexual sodomy[101] was unconstitutional. When Justice Powell changed his mind, however, the Court's decision changed,[102] and Justice White wrote for the new majority. His harsh opinion suggests that he was bent on inscribing the Court's gay rights score at zero. In *Hardwick*, our group of so-called "centrists" divided 2–2, with Justices Powell[103] and O'Connor voting to uphold the law, and Justices Stevens and Blackmun concluding that it was invalid.[104]

---

[99] 476 US 747 (1986). Up to the time of *Hardwick*, the Court had largely ignored the topic. See William N. Eskridge, Jr. and Nan D. Hunter, *Sexuality, Gender, and the Law* 44–52 (Foundation, 2d ed 2004).

[100] "Before Stonewall, forty-nine states criminalized consensual sodomy, most penalizing it as a serious felony. By 1981, twenty-six states had abrogated their consensual sodomy laws, either by legislative repeal or judicial invalidation, and another eleven had reduced consensual sodomy to a misdemeanor." William N. Eskridge, Jr., *Channeling: Identity-Based Social Movements and Public Law*, 150 U Pa L Rev 419, 461 (2001).

[101] As law students now learn, the law on its face forbade sodomy, without the adjective. But counsel for the state, in oral argument to the Court, said the law would be enforced only against homosexual intimacy.

[102] See Greenhouse, *Becoming Justice Blackmun* at 151 (cited in note 28). After he retired from the Court, Justice Powell publicly stated that he had made a mistake in voting to uphold the sodomy law in *Hardwick*. Nat'l L J, Oct 29, 1990 (on line).

[103] White's harshness of tone was an apt culmination of the harsh treatment given to Michael Hardwick from the time of his arrest. For a good capsule statement, see Nussbaum, *From Disgust to Humanity* at 77–85 (cited in note 7).

[104] Justices Kennedy and Souter had not yet been appointed to the Court. Both of them, as appellate judges, had decided cases that are seen today as raising gay rights issues. Their votes (Kennedy in the Ninth Circuit, Souter in the New Hampshire Supreme Court) had not manifested much concern for this aspect of group status equality. See Mary Anne Case, *Of "This" and "That" in Lawrence v Texas*, 2003 Supreme Court Review 75, 101–05.

Justice Powell suggested that imprisonment for sodomy would be unconstitutional; what he would not accept—at that time—was the conclusion that homosexual conduct deserved generalized protection as a due process liberty.[105] We do not have equally trustworthy evidence of Justice O'Connor's thinking in *Hardwick*. One possibility is that she saw the case mainly as another opportunity to join in Justice White's campaign to set limits on the reach of substantive due process.[106] The two of them had argued for such limits in their separate dissents in *Thornburgh*,[107] an abortion case that was percolating in the Court at the same time as *Hardwick*.[108] Justices Stevens and Blackmun, the remaining two in our group of six, wrote dissents in *Hardwick* that were vigorous and well argued. Their views were eventually vindicated when Justice Kennedy had the opportunity to put his own stamp on gay rights doctrine. Two cases, two Kennedy opinions—and the inclusion of gay and lesbian Americans as equal citizens went from a score of zero to the makings of an almost-complete constitutional entitlement.

In doctrinal terms, *Romer v Evans*[109] was a puzzler. The Court invalidated an amendment of Colorado's state constitution (enacted by initiative) that would (i) repeal all laws and official policies, state and local, forbidding discrimination on the basis of sexual orientation, and (ii) prohibit such laws and policies for the future. It was not hard to find an equal protection violation here; the hard task

---

[105] On Powell's dithering as *Hardwick* was being considered, see John C. Jeffries, Jr., *Justice Lewis F. Powell, Jr.* at 518–28 (cited in note 16); Case, 2003 Supreme Court Review at 107 and n 140 (cited in note 104). Powell did join the opinion of the Court, but he also filed a concurring opinion. 476 US at 95. Noting that no one in *Hardwick* had been convicted of a crime, he said the case would present an Eighth Amendment problem if the state were to imprison someone for sodomy. Thus restricted, of course, the only important effect of the Georgia law would be to impose a stigma on homosexual conduct, inflicting a group status harm. See Kenneth L. Karst, *Constitutional Equality as a Cultural Form: The Courts and the Meanings of Sex and Gender*, 38 Wake Forest L Rev 513, 541–43 (2003). Apparently, at the time of *Hardwick*, Justice Powell was not thinking along such lines.

[106] On White's concern to avoid judicial overreaching, reflected in the *Hardwick* opinion, see Hutchinson, *The Man Who Was Called Whizzer White* at 451–54 (cited in note 32). Adam Winkler has suggested that I identify Justice White as one who disappointed the supporters of President Kennedy, who appointed him. Well, some supporters, certainly. But it is hard to know how President Kennedy himself would have thought about abortion rights or gay rights.

[107] Cited in note 86.

[108] For a fuller statement of this speculation, and its possible connection to a minor squabble between Justices O'Connor and Blackmun, see Karst, 2003 Supreme Court Review at 362–67 (cited in note 11).

[109] 517 US 620 (1996).

would be to square the decision with *Hardwick*—a decision the
Court did not cite in *Romer*.[110] Hypothetical alternative opinions
poured onto the pages of books and law reviews, attempting to
reconcile the two decisions; some were accompanied by guesses
why the *Romer* Court had not cited *Hardwick*.[111] Seven years passed,
and then, in *Lawrence v Texas*,[112] the Court cut through the doctrinal
tangle by overruling *Hardwick* and invalidating the Texas sodomy
law. Again the Court's opinion was written by Justice Kennedy, who
explicitly drew some of its substantive content from the Stevens
dissent in *Hardwick*, and implicitly drew from the Blackmun dissent
in that case. Noting that the Court's due process ground was linked
to equality concerns, Justice Kennedy said:

> When homosexual conduct is made criminal by the law of the State, that
> declaration in and of itself is an invitation to subject homosexual persons
> to discrimination both in the public and in the private spheres. The
> central holding of *Bowers* has been brought in question by this case, and
> it should be addressed. Its continuance as a precedent demeans the lives
> of homosexual persons.[113]

By the time *Hardwick* was overruled, Justices Powell and Blackmun
had retired, but Justices Stevens and Souter joined Justice Kennedy's
opinion. Justice O'Connor concurred in the result on an equal
protection ground,[114] emphasizing that the Texas law, by criminal-
izing homosexual conduct, had picked out an identity group—homosexuals—for discrimination.[115]

What had changed? The composition of the Court, for one thing.
In this doctrinal zone, the substitution of Justice Ginsburg for Justice White was bound to make a difference. But another change,
under way well before *Hardwick* was decided, was now evident in
the public's attitudes. Several years before *Lawrence* came to the
Court, Jay Michaelson wrote, "*Romer* did not overrule *Bowers*, but

---

[110] Cass Sunstein analyzes the theoretical problems in detail. Sunstein, *One Case at a Time* at 137–57 (cited in note 21).

[111] Within two years, a long list of these writings appeared in Daniel A. Farber and Philip B. Frickey, *Cases and Materials on Constitutional Law: Themes for the Constitution's Third Century* 386 (Foundation, 2d ed 1998). Further, on *Romer*, see Tushnet, *A Court Divided* at 164–69 (cited in note 33).

[112] 539 US 558 (2003).

[113] Id at 575. See also Toobin, *The Nine* at 219–22 (cited in note 51).

[114] In *Lawrence* she mentioned her vote in *Hardwick* to reject a due process attack on the Georgia law, and she did not recant. A pity—especially after Justice Powell had done just that.

[115] 539 US at 583.

America did."[116] Of course he was not saying that any of the Justices were going to base their votes in the next sodomy case on an opinion poll or on their guesses about the popularity of a decision one way or another. In terms that were purely doctrinal, *Hardwick*'s denial of group status equality had been a deviation from the nation's inclusionary path since the mid-twentieth century. Still, whatever complaint one may register concerning *Romer*'s failure to deal with *Hardwick* directly, the *Romer* opinion did focus on status equality— on the inclusion of gay and lesbian Americans as equal citizens. In this way, it made a vital contribution to the Court's doctrine by isolating *Hardwick* as an outlier. *Romer*'s theme, after all, is central in the *Lawrence* opinion's broad protection of equal liberty.[117]

With the demise of "Don't Ask, Don't Tell,"[118] the most prominent issue remaining in this field is gay marriage. Without question, one day the Supreme Court will hold that a state's limitation of marriage to the union of a woman and a man violates the Equal Protection Clause.[119] So, why not now? William Eskridge knows as much about gay rights as anyone, and he is one of the nation's leading advocates of equality for lesbians and gay men. In 2000 he said that for the Court to recognize a constitutional right to gay marriage just then would be a "premature termination of public debate about an issue of deep concern to different groups"—indeed, a "train wreck" for the Court.[120] As he pointed out, most gay or lesbian couples could, by contract, make their relationship include most state-law features of marriage. Such a contract would be complex, but surely it lay within the capacity of gay rights organizations to construct basic models for many states.[121] Beyond contract, a

---

[116] Jay Michaelson, *On Listening to the Kulturkampf, or How America Overruled Bowers v. Hardwick, Even Though Romer v Evans Didn't*, 49 Duke L J 1559, 1607 (2000).

[117] Some notably thoughtful scholarship on this theme comes from Pamela Karlan, who was one of Justice Blackmun's clerks at the time of *Hardwick*. See, e.g., Pamela S. Karlan, *Loving Lawrence*, 102 Mich L Rev 1447 (2004); Pamela S. Karlan, *Equal Protection, Due Process, and the Stereoscopic Fourteenth Amendment*, 33 McGeorge L Rev 473 (2002). Along related lines, see William N. Eskridge, Jr., *Destabilizing Due Process and Evolutive Equal Protection*, 47 UCLA L Rev 1183 (2000); Karst, 55 UCLA L Rev (cited in note 93).

[118] See Sheryl Gay Stolberg, *Obama Signs Away "Don't Ask, Don't Tell,"* NY Times, Dec 2010 (on line).

[119] Rights of gay parents are also on the way. See Eskridge and Hunter, *Sexuality, Gender, and the Law* at chap 9 (cited in note 99). In custody contests, however, the "best interests of the child" standard is broad enough to accommodate some exercise of a judge's hostility.

[120] Eskridge, 47 UCLA L Rev at 1262–63 (cited in note 117).

[121] Federal law is another matter. Under the so-called Defense of Marriage Act, 110 Stat 2419 (1996), Congress has denied recognition of gay or lesbian marriages for all

number of states in the West and Northeast had adopted "civil union" legislation providing for other marriage-like rights.[122] What remains in such a state's law is the official insult in the law's premise that a couple's gay or lesbian identities make them unworthy of the status of marriage. This denial of status equality to a social group is not a trivial concern. Still, Eskridge's advice was for a gentle approach, allowing time for the rest of the country to get used to civil unions, thus eroding hostility to the recognition of gay marriage. A decade has now passed, and now "gay people are largely treated as (almost) full and equal citizens."[123] Indeed, Eskridge has reason to be more hopeful for the near term.[124] Before long, the constitutional entitlement of lesbians and gay men to equal citizenship will be fully established—most likely by the time today's teenagers have come to adulthood.[125] In the meanwhile, it remains

federal-law purposes, notably the tax advantages of marriage and states' eligibility for federal grants. One federal judge has held DOMA unconstitutional in two cases. *Gill v Office of Personnel Management*, 699 F Supp 3d 374 (D Mass 2010); *Massachusetts v Dep't of Health and Human Services*, 698 F Supp 2d 234 (D Mass 2010).

[122] Eskridge, 47 UCLA L Rev at 1264 (cited in note 117), noted in 2000 that eleven states and the District of Columbia allowed a surviving partner to sue for his or her own injuries in a tort action. On the inadequacy of civil unions to express society's acceptance of lesbian and gay citizens, see Rachel F. Moran, *Loving and the Legacy of Unintended Consequences*, 2007 Wis L Rev 238, 272–76.

[123] William N. Eskridge, *Foreword: The Marriage Cases—Reversing the Burden of Inertia in a Pluralist Constitutional Democracy*, 97 Cal L Rev 1785, 1787 (2009). On the complicated and painful struggle of gay rights advocates in California—as yet unfinished—see Scott Cummings and Douglas NeJaime, *Lawyering for Marriage Equality*, 57 UCLA L Rev 1235 (2010). For recent clues about gay marriage, see Pamela Karlan's article in this volume.

[124] In the quoted article he set out arguments that could be offered in a constitutional challenge to California's (initiative) Proposition 8, in which a 52 percent majority voted to amend the state constitution, overriding the state supreme court's holding that gay couples had a (state) constitutional right to marry. Soon afterward, two couples filed such a lawsuit in federal court. After a detailed examination of evidence concerning the importance of the marriage status and the asserted justifications for excluding gay and lesbian couples from that status, Judge Vaughn Walker concluded that Proposition 8 violated both the Due Process Clause and the Equal Protection Clause of the Fourteenth Amendment. *Perry v Schwarzenegger*, 591 F Supp 3d 1147 (N D Cal 2010). At this writing, the appellate courts have yet to decide conclusively whether anyone has standing to appeal, now that the defendants (California's governor and attorney general) have declined to do so.

[125] Public opinion on the rights of lesbians and gay men has been changing rapidly, with sympathetic attitudes varying inversely with age. See, e.g., Michael J. Klarman, *Brown and Lawrence (and Goodridge)*, 104 Mich L Rev 431, 484–86 (2005); Andrew Koppelman, *DOMA, Romer, and Rationality*, 58 Drake L Rev 923, 942–43 (2010).

In 2006, the Gallup Poll asked whether homosexual relations should be legal. The answer was "yes" from 34 percent of respondents over 65, 49 percent of those ages 40–49, and 63 percent of those ages 18–39. Official recognition of gay marriage had lower rates of approval, but the 18–39 group was 51 percent in favor. Gallup Brain, May 31, 2006 (on line). "According to a 2009 study underwritten by the Pew Charitable Trusts, fifty-eight per cent of Americans between the ages of eighteen and twenty-nine support gay marriage, compared to twenty-two per cent of Americans sixty-five and over." Margaret Talbot, *A*

to be seen just *when* the Court that gave our civic culture *Romer* and *Lawrence* will be disposed to complete the validation of group status equality—the process of inclusion—it has so nearly fulfilled.

IV. NARROW DOCTRINE WITH BROAD EFFECTS—AND VICE VERSA

"Broad" and "narrow" are opposites in theory—even legal theory. But in the world of things and actions and the humans who observe them, these labels for declarations of law are merely educated guesses. More than a century ago Justice Holmes pointed out that statements of legal right and duty—statements here modified by the adjectives "broad" and "narrow"—are no more than predictions about the likely behavior of state actors to enforce them.[126] Another uncertainty must be added: An observer's published label of "broad" or "narrow" is projected onto a doctrinal reality that may be changed by the observation itself. Even when a decision is expected to have wide-ranging consequences, a good judge will be concerned with the particulars of the case at hand.[127] Even narrow shadings of opinions can have broad-ranging effects on individuals and institutions. Even when a judge considers it vital to treat people as individuals and not as representatives of some social group, that same judge may—quite properly—take into consideration a decision's effects on a group.

Justice Powell's *Bakke* opinion may have been narrow, "mini-

---

Risky Proposal: Is It Too Soon to Petition the Supreme Court on Gay Marriage? New Yorker, Jan 18, 2010 (on line). Business Wire reports a 2008–09 poll supported by the Girl Scouts of the USA: "Most tweens and teens (59%) now feel that 'gay or lesbian relations are OK, if that is the person's choice.' This is a huge increase since 1989, when only 31% believed that 'homosexual relations are OK if that is the person's choice' (a slightly different question.)" Business Editors, *Big Changes in Tweens' and Teens' Attitudes and Values over Two Decades; Biggest Change Is a Greatly Increased Acceptance of Gays and Lesbians*, Business Wire, Feb 17, 2010 (on line). (Thanks here to Jennifer Lentz for her research assistance.)

This "generational divide," as Koppelman calls it, has political implications. See Adam Nagourney, *Signs GOP Is Rethinking Stance on Gay Marriage*, NY Times, April 29, 2009 (on line). More generally, increasing numbers of Republican leaders are coming aboard the gay marriage train. Jon Cowan and Evan Wolfson, *A GOP Surprise*, LA Times, Oct 13, 2010, A 21.

[126] Oliver Wendell Holmes, Jr., *The Path of the Law*, 10 Harv L Rev 457 (1897). This definition is most persuasive from the perspective of a lawyer who is counseling a client. Thomas C. Grey, *Holmes and Legal Pragmatism*, 41 Stan L Rev 787, 826–36 (1989). In 1897 Holmes was a Justice of the Supreme Judicial Court of Massachusetts; his appointment to the U.S. Supreme Court came five years later.

[127] "[W]e have no hope of saving the most exalted without respecting the concrete." Justice David H. Souter, quoted by Heather Gerken, *Clerking for Justice Souter*, 2010 J Sup Ct Hist 4, 6.

malist" in the world of doctrine[128] and even in the world of political discourse. But in the more tangible world of university admissions, *Bakke*'s effects were broad and powerful. Universities all over the land followed Powell's implicit suggestion, modifying admissions systems to diversify their student bodies.[129] The systems did consider race as one aspect of diversification, but also made clear that they were considering many other attributes of individuals. These included some attributes assigned to an applicant at birth (not just age, but ethnicity, geographical origin, poverty, etc.), some the applicant had achieved (such as community service, a background in business, overseas experience), and some that were mixed (such as musical or athletic performance). Each of these attributes might be seen to define a group. By now, American university admissions under "diversity" systems must have numbered in the scores of thousands.[130]

Moving to more recent times, Justice Kennedy's opinion in *Parents Involved* follows Justice Powell's lead in precluding broad-scale official action based solely on racial labeling of individuals. Yet Justice Kennedy explicitly suggests several permissible race-conscious actions by school boards to promote school diversity. It remains to be seen whether he would approve a broadening of this receptivity to other "domains" as well. One can imagine that a city council might offer some degree of hiring preference for applicants who are its residents. In many a city, of course, the municipal population includes higher proportions of members of racial or ethnic minorities than do the suburbs. Indeed, for some city council members, recognition of that disparity might be one consideration in adopting the policy. Even a private employer may find it possible to construct an analogous policy to diversify its work force without pinning a racial or ethnic label on any individual. Would such a purpose put an employer in violation of Title VII? I hope not.[131]

---

[128] Sunstein, *One Case at a Time* at 33–34 (cited in note 21).

[129] I should disclose that I was the principal designer of our law school's diversity admissions program in the fall of 1978.

[130] This is a guess, not a statistically respectable count. Surely the guess is conservative.

[131] However, for companies that adopt explicit programs of hiring individual applicants of identifiable minority status, my estimate is that, in today's Court, there are at least three solid votes to overrule the venerable precedent of *United Steelworkers v Weber*, 403 US 193 (1979). More generally, see Primus, 108 Mich L Rev (cited in note 33); Trina Jones, *Race, Economic Class, and Employment Opportunity*, 72 L & Contemp Probs 57, 82–83 (2009).

As for women's rights, the opening sentence of Justice O'Connor's opinion in *MUW* says the case before the Court raises a "narrow issue." Yet, twice in that opinion, she says that a state may not treat men and women differently unless it has "an exceedingly persuasive justification" for the discrimination.[132] This broadly demanding requirement was reinforced when Justice Ginsburg affirmed it anew in her opinion for the Court in *United States v Virginia*, and the Court has not disavowed it since. Now that three women will be sitting in the conference, it is hard to imagine any backtracking by the Court. Indeed, it may be that the culture has come far enough so that state decision makers can be expected to stop, look, and listen before they adopt any explicit sex discrimination.[133] Justices O'Connor and Ginsburg will not claim credit for this sea change in the public's opinion, but it is certain that they have helped.

The law of abortion regulation is another women's-rights field in which broad effects have outrun the narrow purport of opinions. Consider the joint opinion in *Casey*. It emphasizes continuity, stating that the Court is upholding the essentials of *Roe v Wade*. But the effects of the Court's actions were (and remain) enormous. After all, the Court had nearly—*very* nearly—adopted a decision that would, in effect, undermine *Roe*. (The incident worth notice, said a different Holmes, was that the dog did *not* bark in the nighttime.[134]) If you want to measure the broad importance of *Casey* in relation to the modest language of the opinion of the Court, read Justice Scalia's choleric dissent.

Finally, in the field of gay rights, consider first Justice Kennedy's abstract reasoning in *Romer v Evans*, where he treats Colorado's Amendment 2 as a literal denial of the equal protection of the laws.[135] This language, broad as it might be, seems designed to have effects that were narrow. Such a design is one possible explanation for the opinion's failure even to mention *Hardwick*, let alone offer a distinction. At this point, the notion of gay rights escaped from zero, but the status thus recognized was so closely wrapped in the

---

[132] 458 US at 724, 741.

[133] Women already outnumber men in many positions where male supremacy once prevailed. See Hanna Rosin, *The End of Men*, The Atlantic, July/Aug 2010.

[134] Arthur Conan Doyle, *Silver Blaze*, in *The Memoirs of Sherlock Holmes* (1894).

[135] This argument had been presented in the brief amici curiae of Professors Tribe, Ely, Gunther, Kurland, and Sullivan. (Hi, Phil. It's good to salute you here.)

abstraction of "equal rights" that Court watchers were not sure whether it had generative power of its own.[136] It is only with *Lawrence* that the idea of gay rights is perceived to blossom into broad substantive content. Now the Court is no longer reciting a right of equal citizenship in the abstract; it is enforcing the right of two particular men to act out the intimacy that is seen to identify them as members of a social group. That protection of liberty prompts observers of the Court to recognize a broadened entitlement of gay men and lesbians to group status equality.

As these stories illustrate, judicial decisions—with effects seen as broad or effects seen as narrow—can be reached via paths called narrow or paths called broad. Like art, law reflects life and also finds itself reflected in life. None of this is news, but sometimes a little reflecting of our own is warranted.

V. Saving Grace

The accounts here show our six Justices, singly or in concert, acting to save rights of inclusion from serious threats of abandonment or radical restriction.[137] All six have participated in preserving the validation of one or another version of race-conscious diversity admissions to state universities and schools—that is, preserving moves (or at least gestures) toward integration in the face of repeated assault by the cultural counterrevolutionaries. A similar preservation can be seen in the field of women's rights to inclusion. After Justice Rehnquist's successes in rolling back the Constitution's newly recognized protections against sex discrimination, Justice O'Connor led the Court in saving those rights, ultimately with the support of all the others in our set of six, and even Rehnquist, who was now Chief Justice. That support culminated when, after a near-death experience for *Roe v Wade*, all five surviving Justices in our set joined in saving the basic right of a woman to make her own decision about abortion—thus assuring, for women as a group, the power to make their own choices about inclusion in the world

---

[136] See, e.g., the questions about *Romer* posed in a prominent casebook, five years after *Romer* and two years before *Lawrence*. Jesse H. Choper, Richard H. Fallon, Jr., Yale Kamisar, and Steven H. Shiffrin, *The American Constitution: Cases—Comments—Questions* 1123 (9th ed 2001). On *Romer*'s "subminimalism," see Sunstein, *One Case at a Time* at 138–62 (cited in note 21).

[137] Other such save-the-rights behavior can be found, involving these same Justices. See, for example, the decisions cited in note 11. But the three savings accounts I have offered are the ones that most recently drew my interest. (Sorry, Phil.)

outside the home. The story of gay rights is the most obvious one in which an identity group's claim to inclusion is first threatened and then saved. The dissents of Justices Blackmun and Stevens in *Hardwick* offered doctrinal avenues for that decision's overruling, and in *Romer* Justice Kennedy began with an abstract articulation of the right of gay and lesbian Americans to inclusion as equal citizens. By the time of *Lawrence*, he was able to lead the Court further in the process of recovery, giving the coup de grâce to *Hardwick*, with Justices Stevens and Souter joining him in the majority and Justice O'Connor concurring on her own terms.

Does the participation of our six Justices in these decisions illustrate that they should be called "centrists"? Does the "centrist" label result from their participation in decisions like these? I don't care, and neither should you. What matters is that *these* Justices have saved *these* endangered rights of inclusion in *these* perilous times. The idea of preservation usually is not exciting. But, as the text of our National Anthem reminds us, there are occasions when preservation is an achievement to be celebrated.

MARK TUSHNET

HARRY KALVEN AND KENNETH KARST IN *THE SUPREME COURT REVIEW*: REFLECTIONS AFTER FIFTY YEARS

Reading the articles by Harry Kalven and Kenneth Karst fifty years after their initial publication in *The Supreme Court Review* is invigorating and dispiriting.[1] Invigorating because it reminds a reader in an era of constitutional "theory" how much we can learn from incisive doctrinal analyses that worry Supreme Court opinions one way and another, trying to figure out what the decisions might mean rather than trying to evaluate them by invoking some large interpretive theory or trying to explain them by invoking concepts drawn from what we have come to call "other disciplines." Invigorating, too, because the articles show that the questions that scholars today regard as deep were already present, though sometimes submerged, in those articles. But dispiriting because one wonders how much progress we actually have made in understanding constitutional law over the past fifty years. Perhaps we have merely been rephrasing, in terms we find comforting, the questions—and answers—offered by Kalven and Karst.[2] And dispiriting, too, because Kalven and Karst

---

Mark Tushnet is William Nelson Cromwell Professor of Law at Harvard Law School.

[1] Harry Kalven, Jr., *The Metaphysics of the Law of Obscenity*, 1960 Supreme Court Review 1 (cited below as Kalven); Kenneth L. Karst, *Legislative Facts in Constitutional Litigation*, 1960 Supreme Court Review 75 (cited below as Karst).

[2] I should note that I have the recurrent experience of reading older articles—forty or more years after publication—and being dismayed to learn that insights that I thought had been only recently hard-won were available much earlier. My dismay passes as I come

© 2011 by The University of Chicago. All rights reserved.
978-0-226-36326-4/2011/2010-0002$10.00

write in a style—simultaneously detached from and engaged with the Justices—that has been lost to us.

I. Kalven on the Law of Obscenity

"The Metaphysics of the Law of Obscenity" examines in detail several then-recent Supreme Court decisions. Time has rendered obsolete most of Kalven's specific arguments, but the way he addressed the decisions remains important. Perhaps the most significant feature of his article is its generosity of spirit. While criticizing each of them, Kalven indicates that every Justice made valuable contributions to analyzing the problem of regulating obscenity within the Constitution, although no one solved it. Kalven is clearly sympathetic to the *outcome* reached by Justices Black and Douglas, though he is mildly skeptical about their doctrinal absolutism. He is attracted to Justice Frankfurter's balancing, but he worries that it is too unstructured. Overall, Kalven presents himself as a somewhat detached observer of the Court's work, yet somehow in dialogue with it. He ends his article with a long paragraph about "the extraordinary difficulty" of the Court's task.[3] The task was difficult because of the "freighted" topic of obscenity, because obscenity law raises core issues about freedom of speech, and because "they perform their roles in an institutional context" of extreme complexity.[4] His final words are, "The rest of us are fortunate indeed that our job is so much easier and less responsible."[5]

A. ANALYZING THE OPINIONS

After a brief discussion of *Butler v Michigan*,[6] Kalven turned to the opinions in *Roth v United States* and *Alberts v California*.[7] *Roth* was a prosecution by the federal government for violating a federal statute prohibiting sending obscene publications through the

---

to appreciate that each generation of scholars probably has to discover basic truths for itself. The observation usually attributed to Mark Twain comes to mind: "When I was a boy of fourteen, my father was so ignorant I could hardly stand to have the old man around. But when I got to be twenty-one, I was astonished at how much the old man had learned in seven years." I take this to express an important truth about the relation between experience and knowledge understood as justified true belief.

[3] Kalven at 45.

[4] Id.

[5] Id.

[6] 352 US 380 (1957).

[7] 354 US 476 (1957).

mails. *Alberts* was a state prosecution for publishing obscene materials. Kalven observed that Justice Brennan's opinion for the Court "decisively and unequivocally disposed of doubts as to constitutionality," but "by a route which neatly bypassed all the perplexities" of the problem.[8] The reason was that Justice Brennan treated the question before the Court as whether *any* regulation of obscenity could pass constitutional muster; as we would put it today, the grant of review was limited to a facial challenge to obscenity statutes. Kalven criticized Justice Brennan's apparent assumption that obscenity laws could be unconstitutional only if "under the First Amendment no utterances can be prohibited."[9] In light of *United States v Stevens*, which appears to have held that the categories of "low value" speech are to be determined by a strictly historical test without searching for some underlying principle distinguishing low-value from higher-value speech,[10] we might say today that Justice Brennan was arguing at least implicitly that there was no principled way to distinguish between obscene utterances and other "low-value" utterances. Put in those terms, Justice Brennan's position is more defensible than Kalven suggested.

Kalven then addressed the two-tier theory directly, which he concluded was an approach that "may have unhappy repercussions on the protection of free speech generally."[11] He thought it "difficult to accept as doctrine" even though "it afforded the Court a statesmanlike way around a dilemma."[12] After a long paragraph setting out the doctrinal structure of the two-tier theory, Kalven said that the correct question about low-value speech such as obscenity was, "[W]hat is the social utility of excessively candid and explicit discussions of sex?"[13] The next sentence moved to what Kalven clearly believed was the heart of the problem, the "mixed

---

[8] Kalven at 8.

[9] Id at 9.

[10] *United States v Stevens*, 130 S Ct 1577, 1586 (2010) ("Our decisions . . . cannot be taken as establishing a freewheeling authority to declare new categories of speech outside the scope of the First Amendment. Maybe there are some categories of speech that have been historically unprotected, but have not yet been specifically identified or discussed as such in our case law. . . . We need not foreclose the future recognition of such additional categories to reject the Government's highly manipulable balancing test as a means of identifying them.").

[11] Kalven at 17.

[12] Id at 10.

[13] Id at 12.

utterance," in which such "excessive" candor is "integral" to some "serious view."[14] A solution to that problem would lie in the definition of obscenity, a definition that Justice Brennan's formulation of the issue before the Court avoided.[15]

But, Kalven continued, defining obscenity with reference to its worthlessness exposed "a difficulty" with traditional defenses of fee speech.[16] Focusing on how speech contributes to democratic self-governance does not "help much" in explaining why works of imaginative literature and art were covered by the First Amendment: "The people do not need novels or dramas or paintings or poems because they will be called upon to vote. Art and belles-lettres do not deal in such ideas. . . ."[17] Conceding the obvious, that the Court *would* place art works under the First Amendment's coverage,[18] Kalven found "a hiatus in our basic free-speech theory."[19] In my view the gap has not yet been filled and, despite Kalven's prescience, remains largely unnoticed and discussed only rarely.[20]

Acknowledging that Justice Brennan's opinion "made several major contributions to the law," Kalven still found the opinion "unsatisfactory" because it endorsed the two-tier theory and "appeared to find no difficulties" in addressing the problem.[21] He turned to the other opinions to show how Justice Brennan's opinion was "unpersuasive" and to illuminate the "full complexity of

---

[14] Id.

[15] Kalven suggested a definition quite similar to the one on which the Court eventually settled before giving up on the definitional task in *Miller v California*, 413 US 15 (1973): "Obscenity must be so defined as to save any serious, complex piece of writing or art." Id at 13. Given the importance of Kalven's article, one cannot tell without examining the Justices' papers—which I have not—whether Kalven's formulation influenced the Court's, whether the Court invented its formulation independently, or whether the formulation flowed ineluctably from the Court's logic so that anyone addressing the question of definition would reach the same answer. Justice Brennan provides the only citations in Supreme Court opinions to Kalven's article, in *Ginsberg v United States*, 390 US 629, 637 n 5 (1968), and *Paris Adult Theatres I v Slaton*, 413 US 49, 97 (1973) (Brennan, J, dissenting).

[16] Kalven at 15.

[17] Id at 16.

[18] Cf. *Hurley v Irish-American Gay, Lesbian and Bisexual Group of Boston*, 515 US 557, 569 (1995) (describing the "painting of Jackson Pollock [and] the music of Arnold Schoenberg" as "unquestionably shielded" by the First Amendment).

[19] Kalven at 16.

[20] For a recent treatment, see R. George Wright, *What Counts as "Speech" in the First Place? Determining the Scope of the Free Speech Clause*, 37 Pepperdine L Rev 1217 (2010).

[21] Kalven at 17.

the issue."[22] The "difficulties" that Justice Brennan "so carefully muted exploded" in Justice Douglas's dissent, which rejected the two-tier theory in favor of "a single unified doctrine of free speech" that rejected judicial attention to "the social utility of speech."[23] Rather, doctrine should permit regulation only if "there be evidence of clear danger of action resulting from" any verbal—and, if Kalven was right about art, any symbolic—expression.[24]

Kalven devoted nearly as much space to Justice Harlan's "complex and interesting" opinion as he did to Justice Brennan's. He praised Justice Harlan's perception, not inconsistent with anything in Justice Brennan's opinion, that the question of whether a particular item was obscene was a question of constitutional fact, not to be conclusively determined by juries or trial judges as factfinders but subject to "independent review" by appellate courts and ultimately the Supreme Court.[25] And, he had some striking observations about Justice Harlan's effort to distinguish between the tests to be applied to regulation at the national and state levels. Going beyond the obvious points about federalism, Kalven was struck by the fact that the only free-speech cases in which some Justices had suggested such a distinction were cases invoking the two-tier theory to place some material outside the First Amendment's coverage: "Is this just coincidence or is there a relationship?" he asked.[26] He hinted at an answer, mentioning that an unrestrictive rule on the national level would impose a ban on "the entire country," and the local interest in regulation in restriction was stronger (less "attenuated," in Kalven's words) than the national government's.[27] Earlier Kalven suggested that Justice Brennan's opinion might be statesmanlike even though doctrinally unsatisfactory; the same point is implicit in Kalven's treatment of Justice Harlan's opinion, which, though "elegan[t]," was "full of unresolved difficulties," not unlike Justice Brennan's.[28] In the end,

---

[22] Id.

[23] Id at 18–19.

[24] Id at 19.

[25] Id at 20–21. Kalven was right, although the experience of giving materials an independent review was so distasteful that in the end the Court reformulated the test for obscenity in a way that ultimately led to the law's effective demise. See text accompanying note 41 below.

[26] Id at 23.

[27] Id at 24.

[28] Id at 25.

the opinions gave us "more free-speech doctrine than can be used sensibly," an observation bolstered by Justice Harlan's effort to distinguish between the terms used in the federal statute and the state one, which "reveal a capacity to find satisfying distinctions that seem too fine for the ordinary mind."[29]

Criticizing Justices Brennan and especially Harlan for erecting an unhelpfully complex doctrinal structure, Kalven was plainly sympathetic with Justice Douglas's approach, although in a later passage he referred to "doctrinaire liberalism," which his readers would certainly take as a reference to the constitutional jurisprudence of Justices Douglas and Black. Kalven's sympathy for Justice Douglas's free-speech absolutism suggests a revision in a widespread view about the legal academy and the Court in the 1950s—that academics derided Justices Black and Douglas for their First Amendment absolutism and strongly preferred some form of judicial balancing of competing considerations. Discussing Justice Frankfurter's concurring opinion in *Kingsley Pictures Corp. v Regents*, in which the Court unanimously invalidated New York's system for licensing films, Kalven observed that Frankfurter's opinion had "familiar echoes of his earlier opinions on free speech" in calling for "careful balancing."[30] Kalven observed, "However one may feel about the evils of doctrinaire liberalism against which Mr. Justice Frankfurter has so valiantly fought, one cannot, I think, be happy with this opinion."[31] The other opinions in the case had "made valid general points" that Frankfurter did not deal with: "In his desire to avoid broad libertarian generalizations, Mr. Justice Frankfurter generalized too little."[32] Here Kalven set out the agenda for at least categorical balancing or even absolute (libertarian?) rules, an issue that continues to bedevil First Amendment theory as shown by the *Stevens* decision.[33] In Kalven's words, "The preoccupation with balancing . . . , although it steers clear of the doctrinaire, comes precariously close to the opposite evil of the intuitive, particularized judgment which offers no guidance for the

---

[29] Id at 25, 26.

[30] Id at 31.

[31] Id. See also id at 38 (drawing "the moral" that "there are serious weaknesses in Mr. Justice Frankfurter's favorite doctrine of judicial economy" from his analysis of Justice Frankfurter's criticism of the majority in *Smith v California*, 361 US 147 (1959), for failing to provide adequate guidance to legislative drafters).

[32] Id at 31, 32.

[33] See discussion at note 10 above.

future."[34] This "opened up basic issues transcending the problems of obscenity," the tension between "clear statement[s] of ruling principle[s]" and "a particularized balancing that is inevitably personal."[35]

Kalven's attention to "basic issues" recurred in his briefer discussions of the Court's other obscenity cases. In *Smith v California*, Justice Frankfurter concurred in the result because the trial judge has excluded expert testimony on whether a work's dominant appeal is to "prurient interest measured by prevailing community standards."[36] Again "echo[ing]" Justices Douglas and Black, Kalven "suggest[ed] that heavy reliance on expert testimony to objectivize the obscenity judgment indicates once again how powerful the argument is that obscenity is a fatally ambiguous concept."[37] Kalven wondered why the jury was not the best measure of community standards; one might add that Frankfurter's endorsement of expert judgment on what might appear to be fundamentally normative questions is of a piece with his commitment to the Progressive vision of administrative agencies.[38]

Kalven's article uses the word "metaphysics" in its title, but he offered no extended explanation for that use.[39] My reading of the title makes it compatible with Kalven's attitude of detached sympathy. The problem of obscenity law is metaphysical in the serious sense that it raises fundamental questions about what constitutional law is and can do. It is also metaphysical in the somewhat pejorative sense that the Court's discussions are perhaps inevitably detached from the reality with which it and the law of obscenity—

---

[34] Kalven at 32.

[35] Id at 34. Recurring disagreements between Justice Breyer and some of his colleagues appear to reproduce the tension Kalven identified, but Justice Breyer's "balancing" is more structured than the one Kalven attributed to Justice Frankfurter. For additional discussion, see text at notes 83–89 below.

[36] Kalven at 39, discussing *Smith v California*, 361 US 147 (1959).

[37] Id.

[38] For a discussion of Frankfurter's view on administrative agencies and expertise, see Mark Tushnet, *Administrative Law in the 1930s: The Supreme Court's Accommodation of Progressive Legal Theory*, 60 Duke L J (2011).

[39] Indeed, unless I (and the search function in Hein OnLine) missed it, neither the word nor any variant occurs in the article's text or footnotes. Whether those searches were complete is largely irrelevant to my point here, which is that Kalven did not explain his use of the term in any detail. I am reliably informed that the *Review*'s editor chose the title, which probably explains why the article itself does not explain its own title.

and, who knows, perhaps all constitutional law—must deal.[40]

B. CONTEMPORARY PROBLEMS

For all practical purposes the law of obscenity has disappeared from view. After a decade and a half of grappling with the problem, the Court adopted a test for identifying obscenity that made "contemporary community standards" determinative.[41] First videotapes, then DVDs, and finally the Web made "hard core" obscenity readily available. Community standards changed to the point where prosecutors found it essentially pointless to pursue obscenity charges against sexually explicit material depicting adults. The law of obscenity remains one of the better vehicles for explicating the two-tier theory of free speech, but even for purely pedagogical purposes the subject has become problematic. Aside from the difficulty of discussing obscene material in classes where students may be either unfamiliar with the material or familiar with it but embarrassed about saying so, the subject has been complicated by efforts to regulate the different category of pornography. Though those efforts appear to have peaked in the 1990s, they remain interesting conceptually. They provide a vehicle for exploring the possibility of conflicts between constitutional rights or values (free speech and equality) and the idea that some speech regulations might be defensible as legislative efforts to *increase* the dissemination of speech overall.

The "conflict of rights" problem requires us to distinguish between constitutional rights and constitutional values; the "maximizing speech" problem requires us to worry about the relation between quantity (of speech) and distribution (of speakers). Kalven's analysis of obscenity law does not help us in thinking about these newer arguments, at least directly. The "rights/values" problem raises questions about the state action doctrine and whether we have a constitution of merely negative liberties or one of pos-

---

[40] The pejorative sense comes through in an extended quotation Kalven offered from a brief filed by Thurman Arnold in the Supreme Court, in which Arnold argues, as Kalven put it, that "any fool can quickly recognize hard-core pornography, but it is a fatal trap for judicial decorum and judicial sanity to attempt thereafter to write an opinion explaining why." Kalven at 43 (quotation from Arnold at 44). Kalven added a note expressing skepticism that it is so easy to identify hard-core pornography: "One suspects that the touchstone is more likely to be the social status of the publisher than the content of the item." Id at 43 n 129.

[41] *Miller v California*, 413 US 15 (1973).

itive rights as well.[42] The "quantity/distribution" problem raises questions about the foundations of democracy as a system of government resting on individual autonomy, more openly addressed in the Supreme Court's campaign finance decisions. None of those topics appears in Kalven's article. But, it is perhaps worth noting that in both areas the Court and commentators are often more conclusory than analytical. Addressing the "quantity/distribution" question, for example, the Court curtly observed, "the concept that government may restrict the speech of some elements of our society in order to enhance the relative voice of others is wholly foreign to the First Amendment,"[43] without noting that the argument really is that regulation can increase the net amount of speech disseminated while incidentally altering its distribution among speakers rather than "in order to" alter that distribution. In thinking about the modern versions of the problems Kalven dealt with, we might do well to remember not the specifics of his doctrinal analysis but the generous spirit in which he undertook it.

II. Karst on Legislative Facts

"Legislative Facts in Constitutional Litigation" took off from the observation that many Supreme Court decisions rested on the Justices' assessment of facts—not necessarily the facts of the case at hand, but facts about the way things worked in the society at large. He worried that the Justices' assessments too often rested on assumptions that might not stand up to close examination. The problem has not disappeared.[44] In the *Citizens United* decision, the Court had to address the claim that independent expenditures by corporations that expressly endorsed or opposed identified candidates would lead voters to believe that their votes

---

[42] Legislative regulation of pornography promotes a constitutional value of equality, but the source of the inequality lies not in the government decisions that are the focus of a state-action-oriented account of equality but rather in private decisions. In a constitution of positive rights, the government might be thought to have a duty to address the latter source of inequality. For a discussion, see Frank Michelman, *Conceptions of Democracy in American Constitutional Argument*, 56 Tenn L Rev 291 (1989).

[43] *Buckley v Valeo*, 424 US 1, 48–49 (1976). The sentiment has been repeated. See, e.g., *Davis v Federal Election Comm'n*, 554 US 724, 753 (2008); *Citizens United v Federal Election Comm'n*, 130 S Ct 876, 904 (2010).

[44] For a recent overview, see Timothy Zick, *Constitutional Empiricism: Quasi-Neutral Principles and Constitutional Truths*, 82 NC L Rev 115 (2003).

mattered less than the money spent by corporations. Responding to that claim Justice Kennedy wrote, "The appearance of influence or access . . . will not cause the electorate to lose faith in our democracy."[45] This certainly looks like a factual claim. Justice Kennedy supported it by offering *legal* arguments, the import of which is that it would not be reasonable for people to lose faith in democracy in response to such expenditures—perhaps true, but unresponsive to the apparent factual claim.[46] Perhaps reflecting an optimism about the role of reason in adjudication, Karst offered a series of sensible suggestions for making the Court more familiar with the social facts on which informed constitutional adjudication should rest. Before he did so, though, he developed a description of an adjudicatory approach that retains vitality.

A. ANALYZING THE OPINIONS

Karst began by describing the once-famous "mud flaps" case, where the Court invalidated a state law requiring the use of curved mud flaps on trucks passing through the state.[47] As Karst put it, "everyone connected with the case" understood that the "ultimate question" was, "How much more effective must the new guard be to justify a cost of $30 per truck . . . in light of the fact that other states permit the use of the old-style guards?"[48] Justice Douglas's opinion for the Court characterized the problem as involving "questions of degree,"[49] which led Karst to reflect on the "dispute between the so-called balancers and absolutists."[50] For Karst, de-

---

[45] *Citizens United v Federal Election Comm'n*, 130 S Ct at 910. For another example, see *Purcell v Gonzalez*, 549 US 1, 3 (2006) ("Voter fraud drives honest citizens out of the democratic process and breeds distrust of our government. Voters who fear their legitimate votes will be outweighed by fraudulent ones will feel disenfranchised."), discussed in Richard L. Hasen, *The Untimely Death of Bush v. Gore*, 60 Stan L Rev 1, 35 (2007). (The examples should not be taken to suggest that I believe that election law cases distinctively produce unsupported reliance on empirical claims.)

[46] The remainder of the *Citizens United* paragraph reads, "By definition, an independent expenditure is political speech presented to the electorate that is not coordinated with a candidate. The fact that a corporation, or any other speaker, is willing to spend money to try to persuade voters presupposes that the people have the ultimate influence over elected officials. This is inconsistent with any suggestion that the electorate will refuse "'to take part in democratic governance'" because of additional political speech made by a corporation or any other speaker." 130 S Ct at 910.

[47] *Bibb v Navajo Freight Lines*, 359 US 520 (1959).

[48] Karst at 78.

[49] 359 US at 530.

[50] Karst at 78.

nying that balancing was inevitable was "to strike at the heart of the rule of law."[51]

Responding to the argument that balancing was impossible because the values at stake were incommensurable,[52] Karst launched into his first major analytic effort, aimed at providing a structure for conducting the balancing. He used *Breithaupt v Abram* to focus his discussion.[53] There the Court upheld a conviction based on the administration of a blood alcohol test to a driver rendered unconscious in an automobile collision. Karst asked what the questions of legislative fact were in that case. "First of all, how serious is the invasion of the accused's person?"[54] We might note immediately that characterizing "seriousness of invasion of person" as a question of fact at all is not the obviously correct course. Karst's meaning is clear, though: We can array intrusions on the person along a single dimension, with something like taking fingerprints near one end and performing a risky and non-lifesaving operation to remove a bullet near the other.[55] In performing the required balancing, we will initially ask where on this continuum the intrusion is.

Next, "What is the purpose of this invasion of the body?"[56] This looks like an ordinary adjudicative fact: Did the police take the blood sample because they were investigating a crime or because one of them had a perverted interest in acquiring blood for his collection?[57] Karst, though, saw a question of legislative fact lurking: Assuming that the police are engaged in an investigation, "how effectively will the blood test fulfill" the investigative purpose?[58] Perhaps the tests for determining blood-alcohol levels are quite bad, or though good in principle are routinely done quite badly

---

[51] Id at 80.

[52] Cf. *Bendix Autolite Corp. v Midwesco Enterprises, Inc.*, 486 US 888, 897 (1988) (Scalia, J, concurring in the judgment) ("This process is ordinarily called 'balancing,' but the scale analogy is not really appropriate, since the interests on both sides are incommensurate. It is more like judging whether a particular line is longer than a particular rock is heavy."). (Eccles 1:9: "What has been will be again, what has been done will be done again; there is nothing new under the sun.").

[53] 352 US 432 (1957).

[54] Karst at 82.

[55] For the bullet-extraction example, see *Winston v Lee*, 470 US 753 (1985).

[56] Karst at 82.

[57] The allusion here is to the television series *Dexter* (Showtime, since 2006), based on the novel *Darkly Creaming Dexter* by Jeff Lindsay (Doubleday, 2004).

[58] Karst at 82.

by the laboratories the police use. But, Karst observed, the tests were "almost universally well regarded for their reliability," and "there is widespread scientific agreement" that people with high blood-alcohol levels are physically impaired.[59]

That is not the end of the inquiry, though. Perhaps there is "some alternative way of achieving those same good purposes without causing the same impact on the individual's liberty."[60] Karst catalogued some possibilities—getting evidence about how much liquor the driver had consumed, testimony about smelling liquor on the driver's breath—but observed that they might not be as effective in proving high blood-alcohol levels as the blood test was. Suppose, though, that the police had available a less intrusive technology, perhaps one that could determine blood-alcohol levels from beads of sweat (or could be induced to encourage the development of such a technology were they barred from taking the driver's blood)?[61]

Karst then generalized. The question for balancers will take a common form. "How much will this regulation advance the chosen governmental objective?" taking into account the possibility of "partial success," and "How much more will this regulation advance the objective than some other regulation which might interfere less with constitutionally protected interests?" In addition, "How much will freedom . . . be restricted by this regulation," again considering the probabilities of complete and only partial effectiveness, and "How much more restrictive is this regulation than some other regulation which might achieve the same objective?"[62] Again Karst characterized all these as "questions of fact."[63]

Today this is almost instantly recognizable as the kind of structured proportionality inquiry used by constitutional courts around

---

[59] Id.

[60] Id at 83.

[61] Karst used the example of a "'drunkometer' balloon." Id. Karst repeated this type of analysis in his discussion of *Talley v California*, 362 US 60 (1960), where the Court invalidated a city ordinance prohibiting the distribution of handbills that lacked the names and addresses of the authors. Karst at 92–93 (asking, inter alia, how often had anonymous handbills been used in frauds, how many complaints had there been to the Better Business Bureau, and were there reasons for handbill distributors to be concerned for their safety were their names to appear on the handbills). To the same effect, see his discussion of *Huron Portland Cement Co. v Detroit*, 362 US 440 (1960) at 96 (providing a similar list of questions).

[62] Id at 84.

[63] Id.

the world.[64] If structure is all one is seeking, Karst's or some similar formulation might be entirely adequate. But, we have learned that describing the problem as one involving the assessment of facts, even legislative facts, will not in the end solve the incommensurability problem. The reason is easiest to see in the stage known elsewhere as the application of the test of "proportionality as such" and in Karst's formulation as the determination of the governmental objective. Karst's analysis of *Breithaupt* helps identify the difficulty. The government's primary objective is determining accurately the degree of the driver's impairment, and there may be other less intrusive technologies that do as good a job as the blood test in measuring that. The government has other objectives, though, including a budget constraint: It wants to determine impairment as accurately as it can within some budget for doing so. And, again generalizing, it will almost always be the case that there is a trade-off between the primary objective and other objectives when considering alternative means, one more intrusive than the other.[65]

A section explaining that judicial attention to legislative facts would not be inconsistent with a presumption of constitutionality alluded to differences in the trial records in two First Amendment cases, observing that in one "the Court . . . was here faced with a record almost entirely devoid of consideration of the legislative facts, and with briefs of counsel which only partly filled the void."[66] Karst used those differences to introduce a discussion of what could be done to improve the Supreme Court's ability to determine legislative facts.

Legislative facts, according to Karst, involved "prediction and probability," complex matters for which judges "need[] expert

---

[64] For one widely followed formulation, see *R v Oakes*, [1986] 1 SCR 103 (Sup Ct Canada), ¶ 70: "First, the measures adopted must be carefully designed to achieve the objective in question. They must not be arbitrary, unfair or based on irrational considerations. In short, they must be rationally connected to the objective. Second, the means, even if rationally connected to the objective in this first sense, should impair 'as little as possible' the right or freedom in question. Third, there must be a proportionality between the effects of the measures which are responsible for limiting the Charter right or freedom, and the objective which has been identified as of 'sufficient importance.'"

[65] The point is well known in the literature on proportionality and of course in parallel contexts such as purposive statutory interpretation. For one particularly clear exposition, see Mark Elliott, "Proportionality and Deference: The Importance of a Structured Approach," in Christopher Forsyth et al, eds, *Effective Judicial Review: A Cornerstone of Good Governance* 264, 277–80 (2010).

[66] Karst at 91.

help."[67] Brandeis briefs could do something, but trials at which issues of legislative fact were explored were better because trial judges could sort out and evaluate the complexities. Karst devoted several pages to exploring the conditions under which expert testimony and cross-examination were likely to be better than expert memoranda (and counter-memoranda) in putting the trial judge in a position to determine the legislative facts. Then Karst turned to the ability of judges to evaluate the enhanced records they would have before them. He urged conscientious efforts, but could offer little beyond that other than a reiteration of the "traditional American faith in the value of education."[68] His approach, he wrote, "envisages judges who take a more aggressive role than that which is customary, judges who do not leave to the parties the determination of the issues to be litigated but who actively promote the exploration of issues which the parties might be content to leave untouched."[69] Again, Karst did not explore whether judges in the real world could do that to some reasonably acceptable level of quality. He did observe that because "the presumption of constitutionality is weakest . . . [where] there is the least difference between the competence of lay judgment and that expert judgment,"[70] the presumption could do some work—although precisely because experts and judges could draw on the same general information where the presumption of constitutionality was weak, we can wonder whether enhancing the records makes much difference in this category of cases.

B. CONTEMPORARY PROBLEMS

Some of Karst's proposals for reform are the product of the times. He was committed to the Progressive vision of government and its problems, opening his article with a reference to "the rapidity of contemporary social, technological, political, and economic changes," and in his proposals for reform expressing a confidence in the ability of experts to provide the information needed for courts to address the problems posed by those changes.[71] Some

---

[67] Id at 99–100.

[68] Id at 112.

[69] Id at 109.

[70] Id at 107.

[71] Id at 76.

of the proposals seem in retrospect a bit naive. In part the difficulty is that Karst may have identified primarily failures of advocacy, cases in which lawyers failed to use techniques that were available to them. If such failures are a problem, one would think that reforms lie in the direction of improving attorney quality rather than in providing lawyers unable effectively to use the tools at hand with an additional set of tools, unless there is some reason to think that the new tools are easier for lawyers of unchanged quality to use.[72]

Consider the idea of building better trial records on factual matters. *Powell v Texas* involved a constitutional challenge to then-widespread policies of charging homeless alcoholics with public drunkenness.[73] At trial in a Texas municipal court, Powell's lawyer argued that the charge was a status offense imposing liability on those who because of their medical condition could not control their appearance in public. He supported the argument with testimony from a medical doctor to the effect that alcoholism was a disease. The trial judge made "findings of fact" about alcoholism, including that chronic alcoholics do "not appear in public by [their] own volition."[74] The Supreme Court rejected Powell's claim, with Justice Marshall observing that "the record in this case is utterly inadequate to permit the sort of informed and responsible adjudication which alone can support the announcement of an important and wide-ranging new constitutional principle," and that "[t]he trial hardly reflects the sharp legal and evidentiary clash between fully prepared adversary litigants which is traditionally expected in major constitutional cases."[75]

Perhaps Powell's lawyer did not go far enough in the direction Karst urged. Yet, we can wonder about the effectiveness of trials as venues for exploring the legislative facts on which Karst focused. More extensive trials, of course, but also at much greater expense, with costs borne at least initially by lawyers with other cases to handle.[76] From that perspective, we might be impressed with how

---

[72] Karst referred to "failure[s]" by members of the bar, partly attributable to "judges who do not demand that counsel fulfill their obligations." Id at 99.

[73] 392 US 514 (1968).

[74] Quoted in id at 521.

[75] Id at 521–22.

[76] Karst alluded to the problem in commenting that it might not be "worth the very considerable extra expense and delay" occasioned by remanding a criminal case for further factual development, but he suggested even so that it "may be appropriate" to "put [a

much an ordinary lawyer in a Texas municipal court did to build a record on the nature and effects of alcoholism, and take that to indicate some deeper flaw in Karst's effort to improve the Court's ability to assess legislative facts by developing better records at trial. Supplementing trials with amicus briefs and the like generates information provided by competing—and hired—experts, with "axes to grind," as Karst put it,[77] probably leaving the Justices no better informed about the facts than they would have been without the additional information.[78]

Justice Marshall's observation in *Powell* that "there is no agreement among members of the medical profession about what it means to say that 'alcoholism' is a 'disease'"[79] suggests another, probably larger difficulty. Often legislative facts will be open to reasonable contestation.[80] One expert will say that tires will explode under normal operating conditions at a rate of X blowouts per mile if they are inflated to Y pounds per square inch, another will say that at Y pounds the blowout rate will be Z. Surveys will have to be interpreted, and experts will raise reasonable questions about the effects of the questions' precise phrasing on reported outcomes. Statisticians will question the model specification used to produce epidemiological estimates about some phenomenon important to the factual basis for legislation.[81] We can get reasonably precise estimates of such facts as the rate at which the moon orbits the earth—certainly good enough to support legislation. But, of course, facts of that sort are almost never legislative facts in Karst's sense. Where more contestable facts are involved, which is to say with respect to almost every statute, an approach

---

criminal defendant] through the judicial wringer a second time . . . when large interests are represented as parties or sponsors of the litigation," for example, the context suggests, when the National Association for the Advancement of Colored People or the American Civil Liberties Union was involved. Karst at 95–96. See also id at 101 (noting that "testimony tends to be more costly to the parties").

[77] Id at 105.

[78] Cf. id at 96 (referring to "doubts about the ability of experts to improve on the justices' own efforts").

[79] Id at 522.

[80] For examples from Supreme Court decisions, see *San Antonio Ind. Sch. Dist. v Rodriguez*, 411 US 1, 26–27 (1973) (raising questions about what the statistical material submitted in the lower courts showed about relevant constitutional questions); *McCleskey v Kemp*, 481 US 279, 312 (1987) ("At most, the Baldus study indicates a discrepancy that *appears to correlate* with race") (emphasis added).

[81] For an amusing list of all-purpose objections to empirical studies, see George Stigler, *The Conference Handbook*, 85 J Pol Econ 441 (1977).

to constitutional adjudication that makes choices among such facts important seems misguided.

A more general way of putting this is that legislative "facts" might not really be facts of the sort scientists discover and epistemologists describe. Here the recent trial in California's federal gay-marriage case may be exemplary. The district judge heard extensive testimony and made extensive findings of fact about whether individuals choose their sexual orientation, about whether the availability of same-sex marriage will affect the stability of opposite-sex marriage, and more.[82] There is nothing wrong with calling these facts, but one need not be a postmodernist skeptic to think that they are qualitatively different from facts like the rate at which the moon orbits the earth.

There is, I suggest, a better way of thinking about the legislative facts on which Karst focused. Some of those facts are like the ones physical scientists report, but others are not. They are ways in which people in a scientifically oriented society articulate their competing visions of how a good (or decent, or well-ordered) society operates. Justice Kennedy's seemingly factual assertions about the relation between campaign finance and the American people's confidence in our political system fit this description. I believe—not claims about the way the world is though stated in those terms, but claims about the way the world ought to be.[83] And, Karst's proposed reforms would not provide the Justices much help in figuring out the constitutional questions they face by providing them with the "facts" on which their judgments should rest.

The second theme in Karst's article was structured balancing, a topic that Justice Breyer has addressed recently. In *District of Columbia v Heller*, Justice Breyer supplemented Justice Stevens's account of the original meaning of the Second Amendment with

---

[82] *Perry v Schwarzenegger*, 704 F Supp 2d 921 (ND Cal 2010), question certified, 2011 US App LEXIS 153 (CA9 2011).

[83] Duncan Kennedy, *Distributive and Paternalist Motives in Contract and Tort Law, with Special Reference to Compulsory Terms and Unequal Bargaining Power*, 41 Md L Rev 563, 603 (1982) ("the move to efficiency transposes a conflict between groups in civil society from the level of a dispute about justice and truth to a dispute about *facts*—about probably unknowable social science data that no one will ever actually try to collect but which provides ample room for fanciful hypotheses."), offers a more tempered version of this suggestion. Kennedy suggests that the inevitable ambiguities in the facts conceded to be relevant leave space for a judge acting in good faith to see as "established" those facts that are compatible with his or her vision of the world, which Kennedy calls "ideology."

a detailed examination of whether the challenged restriction on handgun possession in the home was proportional to the problems the district was attempting to address.[84] As noted above, courts around the world have used doctrines of proportionality as well. Scholars have begun to explore whether "it" is a unitary doctrine, a "universal rule of law," as one Canadian scholar puts it,[85] or whether a common language of proportionality and even a seemingly common analytic structure conceal the kinds of variations in legal culture that occur in nearly every comparative study.

Taking Justice Breyer's opinion in *Heller* as their starting point, Moshe Cohen-Eliya and Iddo Porat distinguish between what they call "intrinsic" and "bounded" balancing.[86] The former, characteristic of German constitutional law, "expresses values of compromise, mediation, and pluralism," and "is tied to an organic conception of the state, under which all organs trust one another and cooperate to realize common values that express the spirit of the nation."[87] It is not "a pragmatic enterprise involving some sort of cost-benefit analysis," but rather attempts to "optimize[] the constitutional value order."[88] In contrast, Cohen-Eliya and Porat argue, balancing in U.S. constitutional law accommodates "the suspicion-based American approach to the state," with a "residual and instrumental role" within bounds set by the dominant theory of rights as trumps.[89] It is instrumental and pragmatic rather than "idealistic and formalistic."[90] Certainly Justice Breyer thinks of

---

[84] 128 S Ct 2783, 2852 (2008) (Breyer, J, dissenting) (enumerating cases in which the Court has "applied" proportionality analysis). Justice Breyer elaborated on his approach in Stephen Breyer, *Making Our Democracy Work: A Judge's View* (2010).

[85] David M. Beatty, *The Ultimate Rule of Law* (2004).

[86] Moshe Cohen-Eliya and Iddo Porat, *The Hidden Foreign Law Debate in Heller: The Proportionality Approach in American Constitutional Law*, 46 San Diego L Rev 367 (2009). For a more general treatment of proportionality analysis in a problem of comparative methodology, see Jacco Bomhoff, *Balancing the Global and the Local: Judicial Balancing as a Problematic Topic in Comparative (Constitutional) Law*, 31 Hastings Intl & Comp L Rev 555 (2008).

[87] Cohen-Eliya and Porat at 388 (cited in note 86).

[88] Id at 393, 394. The reference to the "constitutional value order" is to the decision of the German constitutional court in the *Lüth* case, 7 BVerfGe 198 (1958), partially translated in Donald Kommers, *The Constitutional Jurisprudence of the Federal Republic of Germany* 361 (2d ed 1997), whose holding that the German Basic Law enacts an "objective order of values" has become the foundation of the German constitutional law of individual rights.

[89] Cohen-Eliya and Porat at 396, 399.

[90] Id at 399.

himself as a pragmatist, as Cohen-Eliya and Porat would expect.

The use of non-U.S. materials in U.S. constitutional interpretation has of course been quite controversial, but comparisons can be illuminating even if—or perhaps because—they are not used as the basis for interpreting the Constitution. The reappearance of discussions of balancing, now labeled proportionality, provides scholars with opportunities to explore again the territory Karst went over, and in particular to examine how there might be a distinctively American form of structured balancing.

III. CONCLUSION

None of what I have said so far means that the articles are without flaws that later scholarship helps identify. Central to Kalven's article, for example, is the observation that "the evil of arousing revulsion in adults . . . is simply too trivial a predicate for constitutional regulation."[91] Earlier, discussing Justice Harlan's approach to the problem of regulation of obscenity, Kalven quoted Harlan's use of "the familiar" standard, that a legislature's judgment "not be 'irrational,'" in connection with Harlan's treatment of the claim that consumption of obscenity might induce "obnoxious" sexual conduct.[92] Today we would properly not accept the judgment of even as sensible a person as Kalven that a specified "evil" was "too trivial." We would ask whether the legislature's judgment that the evil was worth public regulation was reasonable. And, we would worry about the status of the claim that we can assess a judgment about moral evil—"arousing revulsion"—with criteria of rationality. We might ask whether it is enough that there be a reasonable basis for thinking that moral evils can be determined through rational analysis and then that there be a reasonable basis, from within that way of thinking, for concluding that "arousing revulsion" is a moral evil. Kalven's assessment that the evil was "too trivial" might reflect his judgment that, from some unspecified perspective, the legislative judgment is unrea-

---

[91] Kalven at 42. Although the words are ambiguous, I take "constitutional regulation" to mean, not "regulation by the Constitution," but "statutory regulation that survives constitutional challenge." For confirmation of that interpretation, see id at 4 ("Arousing disgust and revulsion in a voluntary audience seems an impossibly trivial base for making speech a crime.").

[92] Id at 24 (quoting *Roth v United States*, 354 US 476, 501–02 (1957) (Harlan, J, concurring)).

sonable or irrational, but he was so sensible that he did not see that there might be other perspectives that legislatures were entitled to take.

Similarly, Kalven used a familiar trope of raising questions left unresolved by the decisions they analyze. For example, Justice Frankfurter was "silent" about "valid general points" made by his colleagues: "Is thematic obscenity constitutionally subject to state control? . . . Is the . . . statute too vague?"[93] We know that this sort of "twenty questions" criticism is close to vacuous because it is always available and never really cogent.[94] It is always available because no decision can foreclose litigation exploring the contours of the doctrine it articulates, if only because attempts to do so can always be dismissed as dicta unnecessary for the disposition of the case before the Court. And, it is never really cogent because a decision takes on meaning only as later courts use it.[95]

"Well, nobody's perfect,"[96] but Kalven and Karst come close. Their articles stand up extraordinarily well after fifty years. Absolutism versus categorical balancing versus ad hoc balancing: We still worry about these, now calling them rules and standards or proportionality and unguided discretion, and it unclear that we know much more about the problems than when Kalven and Karst illuminated them.[97] Kalven's article ended with a footnote offering "an inventory" of four judicial roles in obscenity cases: "urbane resignation" exemplified by Learned Hand, "irreverent amusement" exemplified by Jerome Frank, "uncompromising concern with free speech," as with Justices Black and Douglas, and the role

---

[93] Id at 31.

[94] For the best recent example of the "twenty questions" approach, see *Caperton v AT Massey Coal Co.*, 129 S Ct 2252, 2269–72 (2009) (Roberts, CJ, dissenting) (listing forty questions unresolved by the majority's holding).

[95] For the most sophisticated exposition of this proposition of which I am aware, see Jan Deutsch, *Precedent and Adjudication*, 83 Yale L J 1553 (1974). As I understand it, Chief Justice Rehnquist's approach to writing decisions rested on a similar view. His opinions were spare in the extreme, describing the case facts, listing the precedents thought relevant, and stating that the precedents supported the conclusion announced. Rehnquist eschewed extended analysis of how one got from the precedents to the result because, I believe, he understood that no matter what he said, later courts would pour content into the result without regard to the proffered reasoning.

[96] Quotation from "Some Like It Hot" (United Artists, 1959), final line.

[97] We talk about the problems in different terms because of the rise of "constitutional theory," but whether the terminology (e.g., of decision costs and error costs in connection with the rules/standards or absolutism/balancing discussions) has added anything significant to our knowledge seems to me an open question.

taken by "the responsible man of affairs who feels that there are
limits to what the public will tolerate a court's saying . . . exemplified by most members of the Court."[98] Kalven was too good
a writer to say so, but this inventory covers a great deal, perhaps
all, of constitutional law, and scholars as well as judges. In his
article Kalven took the first role, of urbane detachment, with a
hint of the second. Yet, I think it reasonably clear that he thought
the fourth, that of the "responsible man of affairs," was the one
our judges should take. As the final line of his article showed, he
believed that the judges' job is different from that of the scholar,
who has the freedom to be irresponsible. And, if scholarship has
its virtues, so does responsibility. We should admire, Kalven suggested, those who take on important public responsibilities, and
not be too harsh in evaluating their work with urbane detachment
and irreverent amusement. Even Kalven's critical comments are
generally offered in subdued tones: An argument "is curious," it
"is unfortunate that the collision of complex analyses . . . could
not have been carried to more explicit resolution."[99]

A few years later Kalven's law school colleague and the founding
editor of the *Supreme Court Review*, Philip Kurland, made what
might have seemed the same point about the burdens of public
responsibility in the concluding paragraph of his foreword to the
Harvard Law Review's annual issue on the Supreme Court: "It
behooves any critic of the Court's performance to close on a note
reminiscent of the wall plaque of frontier times: 'Don't shoot the
piano player. He's doing his best.'"[100] The tone, though, was different and much sharper, hardly sympathetic to the constraints
the "responsible man of affairs" necessarily finds himself under
and properly accommodates. For Kurland's final sentences were,
"It is still possible . . . to wish that he would stick to the piano
and not try to be a one-man band. It is too much to ask that he
take piano lessons."[101]

Kurland's tone foreshadowed a change in the rhetoric in which
academic discourse about the Supreme Court was conducted that,
I suggest, came about because of the rise of "constitutional theory,"

---

[98] Kalven at 45 n 132.

[99] Id at 9, 26.

[100] Philip Kurland, *Foreword: Equal in Origin and Equal in Title to the Legislative and Executive Branches of the Government*, 78 Harv L Rev 143, 196 (1964).

[101] Id.

understood as the enterprise of identifying the single best method of constitutional interpretation that simultaneously licensed judges to find some statutes unconstitutional and constrained them from doing so to advance their mere "policy" preferences. Perhaps it was not inevitable, but the rise of constitutional theory conduced to characterization of those who disagreed with the writer's preferred constitutional theory as either fools or knaves: fools, because they lacked the intellectual capacity to understand the compelling logic of the arguments supporting the theory, or knaves, because, knowing that the theory was the best one available, they willfully disregarded it in the service of their personal projects.[102] The ideas that the constitutional questions the Supreme Court deals with are genuinely difficult and that the Justices, people of varying intellectual ability, can reasonably disagree over, for example, the strength of the originalist evidence for and against the positions taken by the majority and dissent in *District of Columbia v Heller* are almost completely absent from today's constitutional discourse—and those who try to advance *those* ideas are dismissed as naive (fools) or as pursuing a concealed political agenda (knaves).

The issues Kalven and Karst discussed remain with us, but their sensibility has been lost. It would, I think, be good to retrieve it, but I wonder whether that is possible. An intellectually ambitious scholar today who is the same age as Kalven and Karst were when they wrote their articles would be well advised—and I am sure is advised—to avoid doing "mere doctrinal work."[103] Kalven and Karst were engaged with doctrine far more deeply than today's scholars are.[104] For obvious structural reasons those with dual degrees in law and some other discipline are unlikely to, and in my experience do not, achieve the heights that Kalven and Karst

---

[102] I do not exempt myself from participation in the discourse of foolishness and knavery. For the most notorious example, see Mark Tushnet, *Dia-Tribe*, 78 Mich L Rev 694 (1980). I am older and, I hope, wiser now. (For that reason, I refrain from providing examples of the discourse of foolishness and knavery, but I do note that it is not confined to the academy but infects the Supreme Court itself.)

[103] Been there, done that myself.

[104] An example is found in the care Kalven took to distinguish between direct regulation of obscenity—penalties imposed on its dissemination—and indirect regulation through rules that induce self-interested actors to "steer wide[] of the forbidden zone," as Justice Brennan put it in a related context. *Speiser v Randall*, 357 US 513, 526 (1958). Drawing on his wide knowledge in the field, Kalven pointed out that lower courts, with seeming approval from the Supreme Court, "steadfastly rejected" the argument that indirect regulation was to be assessed using the doctrines employed to deal with direct regulations. Kalven at 36–37.

reached.[105] But, only by reaching those heights can one truly appreciate the difficulties faced by "responsible men of affairs," and thereby achieve the detached sympathy that Kalven and Karst had for the Supreme Court and its work. That few scholars today have the capacity to do so is unfortunate.

---

[105] Briefly: Although reasonably smart, well-trained lawyers can do doctrinal analysis to a decent level of sophistication, doing doctrinal analysis at the highest level is difficult indeed, requiring a fair amount of intellectual facility and a wide grasp of doctrine from many fields. Dividing one's intellectual effort between acquiring facility in doctrinal analysis and achieving distinction in another discipline means that one will be unable to reach the heights of doctrinal analysis. And, on the other side, in every "other" discipline of which I am aware, the field "other discipline of law" (legal history, sociology of law, economics of law, and the like) is marginal to the discipline as a whole, which means that the most able graduate students will be drawn to the fields at the discipline's core, leaving the subfield dealing with law populated by perfectly able but not truly exceptional students. (There are of course exceptions, quite rare in my experience.)

BURT NEUBORNE

THE GRAVITATIONAL PULL OF RACE
ON THE WARREN COURT

The fiftieth anniversary of the *Supreme Court Review* lends itself to "looking backward"[1] to the ferment in constitutional law that began in 1952 with the first oral argument in *Brown v Board of Education*,[2] and ended twenty-one years later with the plaintiffs' loss in *San Antonio Independent School District v Rodriguez*[3]—a ferment that led to the founding of this distinguished journal in 1960 and led me to a career at the American Civil Liberties Union (ACLU).[4] Much of my work for the ACLU in those heady days was driven by three concerns: (1) opposition to discrimination against black Americans, especially in the South; (2) a perception that many state judges were unable or unwilling to confront issues of racial injustice; and (3) the spectacle of white bureaucracies, especially white police forces,

Burt Neuborne is Inez Milholland Professor of Civil Liberties, New York University Law School.

[1] Edward Bellamy, *Looking Backward: 2000–1887* (Riverside, 1926) (1887), online at http://www.gutenberg.org/files/25439/25439-h/25439-h.htm. I cannot promise that my exercise in looking backward is more accurate than Bellamy's.

[2] *Brown v Board of Education*, 347 US 483 (1954). The classic history of the *Brown* litigation is Richard Kluger, *Simple Justice: The History of Brown v. Board of Education and Black America's Struggle for Racial Equality* (Knopf, 2d ed 2004).

[3] 411 US 1 (1973) (rejecting Equal Protection challenge to unequal school funding). The refusal to treat education as a "fundamental right," id at 37, or poverty as a "suspect classification," id at 18–19, 40, marked the end of the Warren Court's egalitarian surge.

[4] I served from 1967–74 and 1981–86 as a staff lawyer for the American Civil Liberties Union, the last five years as National Legal Director. Since 1995, I have served as founding Legal Director of the Brennan Center for Justice at NYU Law School.

© 2011 by The University of Chicago. All rights reserved.
978-0-226-36326-4/2011/2010-0003$10.00

interacting with black citizens, condescendingly, at best; violently, too often.

My thesis in this article is that concern over racial injustice and state institutional failure was so intense during these twenty-one "Warren years" that it played a significant role in shaping many of the most important constitutional decisions of the Supreme Court in areas as diverse as federalism; separation of powers; criminal law and procedure; freedom of speech, association, and religion; procedural due process of law; and democracy. I believe, as well, that at least some of the changes in constitutional doctrine that have taken place in the post-Warren era, such as the erosion of the exclusionary rule,[5] the rebalancing of federal-state power,[6] and the easing of restrictions on aid to parochial schools,[7] reflect both a decrease in the intensity of the Court's concern over racial injustice, and an increase in the legal system's confidence in state and local institutions to act fairly in racially charged settings.

I begin with a summary of selected aspects of Warren Court constitutional doctrine having nothing directly to do with race, arguing that the Justices' concerns over racial injustice and regional failure to deal fairly with race exercised a gravitational pull on the evolution of constitutional doctrine. I then turn briefly to whether such a gravitational pull should be cause for celebration, condemnation, or a shrug of the shoulders. Finally, I ask why, once the gravitational pull of race had ebbed, certain Warren Court constitutional precedents that appear to owe their genesis, at least in part, to concern over racial injustice and regional failure have flourished, while others have melted away.

---

[5] See, for example, *United States v Leon*, 468 US 897 (1984) (creating good-faith exception to exclusionary rule).

[6] See, for example, *United States v Lopez*, 514 US 549 (1995) (holding that Commerce Clause did not grant the federal government the power to adopt the Gun-Free School Zones Act of 1990).

[7] See, for example, *Mitchell v Helms*, 530 US 793 (2000) (overruling two prior precedents to find that parochial schools in Louisiana could receive federal aid under Chapter 2 of the Education Consolidation and Improvement Act of 1981).

I. THE GRAVITATIONAL PULL OF RACE ON THE WARREN COURT

Despite the election of President Obama, we do not live in a postracial society.[8] Significant disparities in earnings,[9] employment,[10] criminal convictions,[11] sentencing,[12] health care,[13] infant

---

[8] The election in 2008 of Barack Obama as the nation's first nonwhite president triggered an outpouring of comment and disagreement over whether America has finally moved beyond race. Much of the discussion is deeply emotional and takes place on the Internet. For a sample of this discussion, compare the views of Dr. John H. McWhorter, contributing editor to the Manhattan Institute's *City Journal*, online at http://www.manhattan-institute.org/html/mcwhorter.htm, with views aired at the Aspen Festival Ideas Conference, Ta'Nehisi Coates et al, *Post Racial America: Is Obama a Symbol of the New American Dilemma?* online at http://www.aifestival.org/audio-video-library.php?menu =3&title=603&action=full_info (panel discussion at the 2010 Aspen Ideas Festival), and Lloyd Grove, *We're Not Post-Racial Yet*, Daily Beast (July 8, 2010), online at http://www .thedailybeast.com/blogs-and-stories/2010-07-08/america-not-yet-post-racial-the-verdict-from-the-aspen-ideas-festival/ (summarizing panel discussion).

[9] The average per capita income for blacks, Hispanics, and Native Americans in 2009 was 57.1 percent, 48.3 percent, and 52.1 percent of the average for non-Hispanic whites. See US Census Bureau, *S1902: Mean Income in the Past 12 Months (in 2009 Inflation-Adjusted Dollars)*, online at http://factfinder.census.gov/servlet/STTable?_bm=y&-geo _id=01000US&-qr_name=ACS_2009_1YR_G00_S1902&-ds_name=ACS_2009_1YR _G00_&-_lang=en&-redoLog=false&-CONTEXT=st. In 2009, the median household income of individuals who reported to be white only and non-Hispanic was $54,461, while the median household income of individuals who reported to be black only was $32,584. See Carmen DeNavas-Walt, Bernadette D. Proctor, and Jessica C. Smith, *Income, Poverty, and Health Insurance Coverage in the United States: 2009* (US Census Bureau, Sept 2010), online at http://www.census.gov/prod/2010pubs/p60-238.pdf 35–36.

[10] Unemployment rates for blacks are consistently nearly twice as high as for whites. *Table A-2. Employment Status of the Civilian Population by Race, Sex, and Age* (US Bureau of Labor Statistics, Oct 8, 2010), online at http://www.bls.gov/news.release/empsit.t02 .htm.

[11] Largely because of the nation's drug policies, approximately one-third of all black men in the United States were under the supervision of an aspect of the criminal justice system in 1995. See Marc Maurer and Tracy Huling, *Young Black Americans and the Criminal Justice System: Five Years Later* (Sentencing Project, Oct 1995), online at http://www .sentencingproject.org/doc/publications/rd_youngblack_5yrslater.pdf 3.

[12] As of 2007, 2.1 million men were incarcerated in American prisons: 35.4 percent were black, 32.9 percent were white, and 17.9 percent were Hispanic. The general male population in 2007 was 68 percent white, 12.5 percent black, and 14.5 percent Hispanic. See William J. Sobol and Heather Couture, *Prison Inmates at Midyear 2007*, Bureau of Justice Statistics Bulletin (US Department of Justice, June 2008), online at http://bjs.ojp .usdoj.gov/content/pub/pdf/pim07.pdf. American blacks are imprisoned at nearly six times the rate of whites. Marc Maurer and Ryan S. King, *Uneven Justice: State Rates of Incarceration by Race and Ethnicity* (Sentencing Project, June 2007), http://sentencingproject.org/doc/ publications/rd_stateratesofincbyraceandethnicity.pdf, 3. Nearly 12 percent of the black male population in the United States is currently incarcerated. Id at 4.

[13] In 2009, 12.0 percent of non-Hispanic whites, 21.0 percent of blacks, and 32.4 percent of Hispanics lacked health insurance. DeNavas-Walt et al, *Income, Poverty, and Health Insurance Coverage* at 26 (cited in note 9). American whites have a life expectancy five years longer than that of blacks. See *Health, United States, 2008* (National Center for Health Statistics, March 2009), online at http://www.cdc.gov/nchs/data/hus/hus08.pdf 203 (noting that a white person born in 2005 is expected to live to 78.3 years, while a black person born in 2003 is only expected to live 73.2 years).

mortality,[14] teen pregnancy,[15] and education[16] tell a bleak story of continued racial inequality in America. But, neither do we live in the formally and pervasively racist America that existed in 1952. Remember what our legal world looked like before the Supreme Court intervened in *Brown*.[17] In 1953, the state of Texas forbade

---

[14] According to the Center for Disease Control's National Center for Health Statistics, the black infant mortality rate is nearly 2.4 times higher than white infant mortality. T. J. Mathews and Marian F. MacDorman, *Infant Mortality Statistics from the 2006 Period Linked Birth/Infant Death Data Set*, 58 Natl Vital Statistics Rep 17 (Natl Vital Statistics System, Apr 30, 2010), online at http://www.cdc.gov/nchs/data/nvsr/nvsr58/nvsr58_17.pdf 4 (showing the infant mortality rate is 5.58 percent for babies born to non-Hispanic white mothers but 13.35 percent for babies born to non-Hispanic black mothers). Black infants are almost four times more likely to die from complications associated with low birth weight. Id at 25 (showing a mortality rate related to short gestation and low birthrate of 76.8 per 100,000 live births for babies born to non-Hispanic white mothers and 301.8 per 100,000 live births for babies born to non-Hispanic black mothers). Shockingly, among mothers with at least thirteen years of education, black infant mortality is almost three times as high as comparable white mortality. See *Health, United States, 2008* (cited in note 13) (noting that, in the surveyed states, the infant mortality rate was 4.1 percent for babies born to non-Hispanic whites with at least thirteen years of education but 11.4 percent for babies born to non-Hispanic blacks with at least thirteen years of education). See also Paula Braverman, *Racial Disparities at Birth: The Puzzle Persists*, Issues in Science and Technology (University of Texas at Dallas, Winter 2008), online at http://www.issues.org/24.2/p_braveman.html (discussing possible explanations for why "the black/white birth-outcome disparities have persisted even after taking into account mothers' educational attainment or family income around the time of pregnancy").

[15] Teen pregnancy among blacks decreased more than 45 percent from 1990 to 2005, but was still more than 2.4 times the rate of whites in 2005. See *U.S. Teen Pregnancies, Births and Abortions: National and States Trends and Trends by Race and Ethnicity* (Guttmacher Institute, Jan 2010), online at http://www.guttmacher.org/pubs/USTPtrends.pdf 6 (showing pregnancy rates among women ages 15–19).

[16] As of 2003, there were "racially correlated disparities in K–12 education [for] grades, test scores, retention and dropout rates, graduation rates, identification for special education and gifted programs, extracurricular and cocurricular involvement, and discipline rates." Roslyn Arlin Mickelson , *When Are Racial Disparities in Education the Result of Racial Discrimination? A Social Science Perspective*, 105 Teachers College Record 1052, 1055 (Aug 2003). See also Thomas D. Snyder, Sally A. Dillow, and Charlene M. Hoffman, *Digest of Education Statistics: 2008* (National Center for Education Statistics, March 2009), online at http://nces.ed.gov/pubs2009/2009020.pdf, 25 (showing racial disparity in achievement of bachelor's degrees and high school completion); id at 87 (showing that whites are classified as gifted and talented students more than twice as often); id at 169 (showing a higher black high school dropout rate than white high school dropout rate); id at 178 (showing a higher average reading score for whites than blacks); id at 194 (showing a higher mathematics score for whites than blacks); Susan Aud et al, *The Condition of Education 2010* (National Center for Education Statistics, May 2010), online at http://nces.ed.gov/pubs2010/2010028.pdf, 171, 177 (showing that reading and mathematics gap continued in 2009).

[17] The following description of representative pre-*Brown* state apartheid statutes is drawn from Jesse H. Choper, *Consequences of Supreme Court Decisions Upholding Individual Constitutional Rights*, 83 Mich L Rev 1, 25–26 (1984). I drew heavily on the Choper article for my 2004 speech to the New York State Judiciary on the fiftieth anniversary of *Brown*. Burt Neuborne, *Brown at 50* (American Bar Association), online at http://www.abanet.org/publiced/lawday/finch/2ndplacefinch04.pdf (speech given at the New York State Supreme

interracial boxing matches. In Florida, black and white students were forbidden to use the same edition of a school textbook. In Arkansas, black and white voters could not enter a polling place in each others' company. In Alabama, a white nurse was forbidden to care for a black male patient. Six states required separate bathroom facilities for black and white employees. In six states, black and white prisoners could not be chained together. In seven states, tuberculosis patients of different races could not be treated together. In eight states, all forms of public recreation—from parks to beaches to ball fields to movie theaters—were racially segregated by law. Ten states required segregated waiting rooms for public transportation. Eleven states required blacks to ride in the back of the bus. Fourteen states segregated railroad passengers by race. Seventeen states mandated racial segregation in public education, while four additional states and the District of Columbia permitted it. A black family thinking about a vacation had to buy a guide to local places where they could eat and sleep.[18] Black musicians and baseball players kept lists of restaurants where they could buy food at the back door.[19] Entire categories of employment were closed to blacks.[20] Racially motivated violence directed at blacks was rampant, especially if they sought to vote in the South.[21] Lynchings of blacks

---

Court's Annual Law Day Ceremony on May 7, 2004). For studies of American Apartheid, see generally Jerrold M. Packard, *American Nightmare: The History of Jim Crow* (St. Martin's, 2002); C. Vann Woodward, *The Strange Career of Jim Crow* (Oxford, 1955). For a comprehensive description of the massive segregation of southern society in 1950, where 70 percent of American blacks then lived, see Paul Finkelman, *Civil Rights in Historical Context: In Defense of Brown*, 118 Harv L Rev 973, 986, 1006–29 (2005), refuting the contention in Michael J. Klarman, *From Jim Crow to Civil Rights: The Supreme Court and the Struggle for Racial Equality* (Oxford, 2004), that pre-*Brown* race relations in the South were progressing well and were disrupted by *Brown*.

[18] See *Heart of Atlanta Motel Inc. v United States*, 379 US 241, 252–53 (1964) (describing legislative finding about a special guidebook blacks used to travel); Brief for Appellees, *Heart of Atlanta Motel Inc. v United States*, No 515, *39–46 & n 31 (filed Sept 28, 1964) (describing legislative hearings on the effects of segregation on travelers and noting existence of a guidebook).

[19] Id.

[20] See *Griggs v Duke Power Co.*, 410 US 424 (1971) (describing racially tracked employment categories).

[21] See 1 *1961 Report of the U.S. Commission on Civil Rights* 5 (GPO, 1961), online at http://www.law.umaryland.edu/marshall/usccr/documents/cr11961bk1.pdf ("In some 100 counties in eight Southern States there is reason to believe that Negro citizens are prevented—by outright discrimination or by fear of physical violence or economic reprisal—from exercising the right to vote."); id at 27 (noting threat of violence and activity of the Klan in Monroe County, Alabama); id at 28–29 (describing that "[c]rosses were burned and fire bombs hurled" at registered blacks in Liberty County, Florida); id at 30 (noting "threat of physical violence" in Lee County, Florida); id at 31 (noting "economic or physical

were recorded as late as 1964, bringing the shameful documented total to more than 1,500 during the twentieth century.[22]

For many Americans in 1952, racial discrimination was a cancer threatening to destroy the nation. Some perceived American racism as a betrayal of the generation that had fought Nazism and had sacrificed so much for American ideals. I remember my father and his friends angrily asking each other why they had gone to war if not to end racism. Some correctly perceived pervasive racial injustice as a threat to national security. Domestically, the Communist Party was able to expand its allure by highlighting its stand against racism.[23] With the Cold War, it became clear that the Soviets were willing and able to use American racism as a powerful weapon against the United States in the worldwide struggle for supremacy.[24]

In 1947, Jackie Robinson and Branch Rickey integrated major league baseball.[25] In 1948, President Truman desegregated the armed forces by executive order,[26] and the Supreme Court outlawed

reprisals, or threats of such reprisals" to disenfranchise blacks in Mississippi); id at 180 ("[I]n five of seventeen nonvoting counties there were specific incidents of police brutality against Negroes . . . . [I]n four counties reports were received of incidents involving violence against Negroes in which police (apparently deliberately) refused to take action.").

[22] See Douglas Linder, *Lynchings: By Year and Race* (University of Missouri–Kansas City School of Law), online at http://www.law.umkc.edu/faculty/projects/ftrials/shipp/lynchingyear.html. Some consider these numbers to be "conservative." Robert A. Gibson, *The Negro Holocaust: Lynching and Race Riots in the United States, 1880–1950*, Themes in Twentieth Century American Culture, 1979, vol II (Yale–New Haven Teachers Institute), online at http://www.yale.edu/ynhti/curriculum/units/1979/2/79.02.04.x.html.

[23] The American Communist Party exploited appalling racial incidents like the Scottsboro case to appeal to Americans who had little interest in, or understanding of, the party's economic or revolutionary rhetoric. See generally James Goodman, *Stories of Scottsboro* (Vintage, 1st ed 1995). My experience with representing a number of Communist Party members in the 1960s and 1970s was that militant opposition to domestic racial discrimination was the party's most effective recruiting device.

[24] See generally Mary L. Dudziak, *Cold War Civil Rights: Race and the Image of American Democracy* (Princeton, 2000).

[25] My longtime colleague at the ACLU, Ira Glasser, has prepared a useful summary of the events leading up to Rickey's decision. Ira Glasser, *Branch Rickey and Jackie Robinson: Precursors to the Civil Rights Movement* (The World & I Online, March 2003), online at http://www.worldandi.com/specialreport/2003/March/Sa22948.htm. For a more conventional biography, see Arnold Rampersad, *Jackie Robinson: A Biography* (Borzoi, 1997).

[26] 13 Fed Reg 4313 (1948) (Executive Order 9981). The events leading up to the Executive Order and the struggle to give it effect are usefully captured in a time line prepared by the Harry S. Truman Library and Museum, online at http://www.trumanlibrary.org/whistlestop/study_collections/desegregation/large/index.php?action=chronology. Issuing the Executive Order was the beginning of a fifteen-year effort to provide black servicemen with equal access to voting, housing, and recreation. See generally Morris J. Macgregor, Jr., *Integration of the Armed Forces, 1940–1965* (Center of Military History, United States Army, 1985), online at http://www.history.army.mil/books/integration/iaf-fm.htm, for documentation of the reaction to integration.

the enforcement of racially restrictive real estate covenants.[27] In 1950, the Court outlawed racially segregated state law schools.[28] In 1952, the Supreme Court began the process of ending public school segregation in *Brown*, ushering in an era during which the issues of race and regional failure were catapulted to the center of the nation's consciousness.

Brown triggered an explosion of legal energy that dismantled American apartheid. In 1954, segregated municipal facilities on public land were banned.[29] Segregated public beaches were banned in 1955.[30] Laws requiring blacks to ride in the back of the bus were banned in 1956.[31] Segregated parks and playgrounds were invalidated in 1958,[32] and the Supreme Court (with three new members) formally and unanimously reiterated its commitment to *Brown* in an opinion signed by all nine Justices.[33] In 1959, laws banning interracial boxing were invalidated.[34] In 1962, segregation in airport restaurants was struck down.[35] In 1963, segregated courtrooms were outlawed.[36] In 1964, racial designations on the ballot[37] and separate voting and property tax records were banned.[38] Public libraries were integrated in 1966.[39] Laws banning interracial marriage were banned in 1967.[40] Racial segregation in prisons was banned in

---

[27] *Shelley v Kraemer*, 334 US 1 (1948).

[28] *Sweatt v Painter*, 339 US 629 (1950).

[29] *Muir v Louisville Park Theatrical Association*, 347 US 971 (1954) (remanding for consideration in light of *Brown*). In the months after *Brown*, the Court issued a series of per curiam orders affirming lower court decisions outlawing segregated facilities. See Vincent James Strickler, *Green-Lighting Brown: A Cumulative-Process Conception of Judicial Impact*, 43 Ga L Rev 785, 825–27 (2009), for a description and listing of the per curiam opinions. The last of the per curiam orders was the 1956 order in *Gayle v Browder*, 352 US 903 (1956), ending racial segregation in public transportation in Montgomery, Alabama.

[30] *Mayor of Baltimore v Dawson*, 350 US 877 (1955).

[31] *Gayle*, 352 US at 903.

[32] *New Orleans City Park Improvement Association v Detiege*, 358 US 54 (1958). See also *Holmes v Atlanta*, 350 US 879 (1955) (municipal golf courses).

[33] *Cooper v Aaron*, 358 US 1 (1958).

[34] *State Athletic Commission v Dorsey*, 359 US 533 (1959).

[35] *Turner v Memphis*, 369 US 350 (1962).

[36] *Johnson v Virginia*, 373 US 61 (1963).

[37] *Anderson v Martin*, 375 US 399 (1964).

[38] *Virginia Board of Elections v Hamm*, 379 US 19 (1964).

[39] *Brown v Louisiana*, 383 US 131 (1966).

[40] *Loving v Virginia*, 388 US 1 (1967). See also *McLaughlin v Florida*, 379 US 184 (1964) (invalidating laws banning interracial cohabitation).

1968,[41] and the Court held that the mandate of the post-*Brown* cases was that "racial discrimination would be eliminated root and branch."[42] By the time Earl Warren retired in 1969, Jim Crow was dead.

But the judicial energy released by *Brown* was not confined to ending Jim Crow. *Brown* sparked a remarkable nonviolent movement, centered in the South, aimed at achieving racial equality.[43] Much of the Warren Court's constitutional jurisprudence having nothing formal to do with race was in response to, and in defense of, this struggle for racial justice. When the charismatic influence of the civil rights movement waned—in part, a tribute to its own success;[44] in part, a victim of excesses by others;[45] in part, the result of the assassination of its three great national leaders, John Kennedy, Robert Kennedy, and Dr. King; and in part, a victim of the stubborn persistence of racism[46]—post-Warren Court constitutional doctrine often turned back toward pre-Warren standards.

A. RACE AND FEDERALISM

The gravitational pull of race is nowhere more evident than in

---

[41] *Lee v Washington*, 390 US 333 (1968).

[42] *Green v County School Board of New Kent County*, 391 US 430, 437–38 (1968).

[43] The classic three-volume history of the civil rights movement is Taylor Branch, *Parting the Waters: America in the King Years: 1954–63* (Simon and Schuster, 1988); Taylor Branch, *Pillar of Fire: America in the King Years: 1963–65* (Simon and Schuster, 1998); Taylor Branch, *At Canaan's Edge: America in the King Years: 1965–68* (Simon & Schuster, 2006). See also Juan Williams, *Eyes on the Prize: America's Civil Rights Years, 1954–1965* (Viking, 1987), drawn from the six-hour PBS documentary produced by Henry Hampton chronicling the civil rights movement in the South from 1954 to 1965.

[44] In the wake of President Kennedy's assassination, Congress enacted comprehensive federal laws banning discrimination in employment, housing, voting, and access to federally funded programs. See Civil Rights Act of 1964, Pub L No 88-352, 78 Stat 241, codified as amended at 42 USC §§ 1971, 1975a–1975d, 2000a–2000h–6; Voting Rights Act of 1965, Pub L No 89-110, 79 Stat 437, codified as amended at 42 USC §§ 1971, 1973–1973bb; Fair Housing Act of 1968, Pub L No 90-284, Title VIII, 82 Stat 81, codified as amended at 42 USC §§ 3601–19, 3631. We live in the better world those statutes made.

[45] Urban riots in Harlem (1964), Los Angeles (Watts) (1965), Newark (1967), and Detroit (1967) badly eroded national support for the civil rights movement. Lacking effective national leadership after the assassinations of Dr. King and Robert Kennedy, the movement's political influence waned. For a description of the urban riots, see generally *Report of the National Advisory Commission on Civil Disorders* (GPO, 1968) (Kerner Commission).

[46] See Thomas Powell, *The Persistence of Racism in America* (Littlefield Adams, 1993) (describing connections between bases for American thought and racism); Eduardo Bonilla-Silva, *Racism Without Racists: Color-Blind Racism and the Persistence of Racial Inequality in the United States* (Rowman & Littlefield, 2d ed 2006) (arguing that white articulation of color blindness is a tool to mask and continue white supremacy).

the Warren Court's federalism decisions. In the years after *Brown*, a national consensus emerged that legally reinforced racism was unacceptable; but pockets of intense resistance persisted at the local level, especially in the states of the old Confederacy.[47] Because one of the principal purposes of federalism is to protect local majorities that are out of step with a national majority, the civil rights movement in the South was often on a collision course with federalism. The federalism decisions of the Warren Court, which consistently favored national over state or local institutions, were deeply influenced by the Court's mistrust of the willingness of state and local officials to deal fairly with racially charged issues.

The Warren Court's race-driven federalism cases begin with *Thompson v City of Louisville*,[48] which reversed a Louisville police court loitering conviction because of the absence of any evidence of guilt. While the Court's opinion speaks in the racially anodyne language of the Due Process Clause, the Court knew from the briefs that *Thompson* was a paradigm example of white cops rousting a poor black who then had the effrontery to fight back in court.[49] All too often, state courts were useless in dealing with such race-driven issues—and the Warren Court knew it.

Thompson could be invoked only when there was absolutely no evidence of guilt in the record.[50] When some evidence existed

---

[47] Senator Harry F. Byrd's call for "massive resistance" issued on February 24, 1956, is an example of the intensity of local resistance to *Brown*. See *Brown v. Board. of Education: Virginia Responds: The State Responds: Massive Resistance* (Library of Virginia, Dec 2003), online at http://www.lva.virginia.gov/exhibits/brown/resistance.htm. See also 102 Cong Rec 4460–61 (March 12, 1956) (statement of Sen. George) (reading into the record "The Southern Manifesto," promising defiance of *Brown*, signed by nineteen of twenty-two southern senators and a large majority of representatives); Cong Rec 4515–16 (March 12, 1956) (statement of Rep. Smith of Virginia) (same). Five southern states—Alabama, Georgia, Mississippi, South Carolina, and Virginia—enacted similar resolutions. See 1 Race Rel L Rep 437–47 (1956) (reprinting the material). Southern governors competed with one another in promising defiance.

[48] 362 US 199 (1960).

[49] You can scour the unanimous opinion in *Thompson* in vain for any mention of Sam Thompson's race, but Louis Lusky's elegant Supreme Court brief notes that the incident begins with Thompson's decision to contest two earlier unjustified arrests, including a warrantless arrest for vagrancy and loitering in the "colored" waiting room of a Louisville bus station. Brief for Petitioner, *Thompson v City of Louisville*, No 59, *8–10 (filed Sept 21, 1959) (available on Westlaw at 1959 WL 101527).

[50] The Court invoked *Thompson* to reverse the breach-of-the-peace convictions of lunch-counter sit-in demonstrators in *Garner v Louisiana*, 368 US 157 (1961), noting that there was no evidence of breach of the peace in the record. Id at 163–64, 170–74. See also *Brown v Louisiana*, 383 US 131 (1966) (relying on the framework in *Garner*, which was based on *Thompson*, to invalidate a breach-of-peace conviction for a library sit-in).

supporting the conduct of the police, hostile or indifferent state courts remained free to ignore the racist nature of police behavior, and, too often, that is precisely what they did. Because the Supreme Court's institutional ability to review such fact-bound cases on appeal was limited, *Thompson* was quickly followed in 1961 by *Monroe v Pape*,[51] and, in 1963, by *Townsend v Sain*[52] and *Fay v Noia*,[53] broadly opening the politically-insulated federal district courts to constitutional claims, especially in settings requiring fact-finding. As in *Thompson*, there is no reference to race in the majority opinion in *Monroe v Pape*, other than a discussion of the origins of the Fourteenth Amendment.[54] The majority opinion in the case describes an unlawful Chicago police entry into a home at 4:00 a.m., during which a husband and wife were required to stand naked for an extended period of time, after which the husband was held at the police station for 10 hours on so-called "open" charges.[55] But the briefs (and Justice Frankfurter's dissent) reveal that, while being forced to stand naked, Mr. Monroe was called a "nigger" and was referred to as "black boy."[56]

The petitioners in *Townsend v Sain* and *Fay v Noia* appear to have been white. Noia had been convicted of felony murder in 1942, and had declined to appeal because a retrial might have subjected him to the death penalty.[57] His two codefendants appealed and ultimately secured a federal court ruling that their confessions had been unconstitutionally coerced.[58] New York courts refused to entertain a postconviction application by Noia, holding that his failure to appeal foreclosed state postconviction relief.[59] In the Supreme Court, the Kings County District Attorney conceded that Noia had been convicted on the basis of an unlaw-

---

[51] 365 US 167 (1961).

[52] 372 US 293 (1963).

[53] 372 US 391 (1963).

[54] See, for example, *Monroe*, 365 US at 173–74, 178 (Douglas). Justice Douglas wrote for the Court, with Justices Harlan and Stewart concurring. Justice Frankfurter dissented.

[55] Id at 169 (Douglas).

[56] Id at 203 (Frankfurter); Brief for Petitioners, *Monroe v Pape*, No 39, *4–5 (filed Aug 25, 1960) (available on Westlaw at 1960 WL 63600) ("Monroe Brief"). The brief also notes that the officers hit Mr. Monroe several times and hit four of Monroe's six children. Monroe Brief at *4–5.

[57] *Noia*, 372 US at 394, 396–97 n 3.

[58] Id at 394–95.

[59] Id at 394.

fully obtained confession, but argued that by failing to appeal in 1942, he had waived his right to federal habeas corpus review.[60] While race plays no overt role in the case, it is telling that Justice Brennan's decision relaxing the waiver rules relied on the fact that one of the major aims of the 1867 habeas corpus statute was to protect the constitutional rights of newly freed slaves against hostile state judiciaries.[61] Similarly, after Townsend's apparently drug-induced confession was found voluntary by the Illinois state courts, Chief Justice Warren's opinion opened the door to widespread federal oversight over state court fact-finding in constitutional contexts.[62]

Monroe v Pape, *Townsend v Sain*, and *Fay v Noia* ushered in a judicial version of Reconstruction, during which federal district judges exercised front-line supervisory authority in racially charged settings over state and local institutions including criminal courts, police departments, detention facilities, highway departments, firefighters, transportation facilities, parks, public schools, and public housing authorities.[63]

The Warren Court's extremely broad view of Congress's power to enforce individual rights under the Commerce Clause and to enforce the Reconstruction Amendments was also driven by concerns over race. In 1964, in *Katzenbach v McClung*,[64] the Court employed an expansive vision of the Commerce Clause to uphold the application of the federal ban on racial discrimination in access to public accommodations to a small restaurant (Ollie's Barbecue) located eleven blocks from an interstate highway.[65] Similarly, in *Heart of Atlanta Motel Inc. v United States*,[66] the Court upheld the

---

[60] Id at 395–96; Brief of Attorney General of New York, Amicus Curiae, in Support of Reversal, *Fay v Noia*, No 84, *2–3 (filed Dec 3, 1962) (available on Westlaw at 1962 WL 115489).

[61] *Noia*, 372 US at 415–17.

[62] See *Townsend*, 372 US at 315–18 (discussing when a federal district court will have to have a hearing to review facts from state courts).

[63] In *Adickes v S. H. Kress & Co.*, 398 US 144 (1970), the Court reinforced *Monroe* with generous pleading rules. The crucial role of the federal district courts in the South in the struggle for racial equality is described in J. W. Peltason, *58 Lonely Men: Southern Federal Judges and School Desegregation* (1961).

[64] 379 US 294 (1964).

[65] See id at 298–305 (holding Congress had power under Commerce Clause and Necessary and Proper Clause to pass Title II of the Civil Rights Act of 1964); id at 296 (describing the restaurant).

[66] 379 US 241 (1964).

application of the public accommodations statute to a motel "readily accessible to" two interstate highways and two state highways.[67]
As in *McClung*, the Court in *Heart of Atlanta* relied on the Commerce Clause, rather than taking on the difficult question whether
Section 5 of the Fourteenth Amendment authorized federal legislation against racially discriminatory private action.[68] Two years
later, in *United States v Guest*[69] and *United States v Price*,[70] the
Court upheld indictments charging private persons with interfering with the enjoyment of federal constitutional rights. In *Guest*,
a black Army Reserve officer was murdered in Georgia while returning home to Washington, D.C.[71] The defendants were ac-
quitted of murder in a Georgia court and then indicted under 18
USC § 241 for conspiring to deprive a black citizen of the right
to interstate travel and of equal enjoyment of state-operated facilities.[72] Justice Stewart, writing for the Court, ducked the issue
of Congress's power under Section 5, ruling instead that the indictment adequately charged state involvement by alleging that
the defendants had filed false reports of illegal activities by the
victim.[73] Six Justices held that the allegations implied cooperation
by state officials in acting on the false reports, and the remaining
three were willing to assume state action.[74] I have defended more
than a few criminal cases in my time, but I have never seen a more
generous reading of an indictment.[75]

---

[67] See id at 243 (describing the motel).

[68] See id at 253–38 (determining Commerce Clause gave Congress power to pass Title
II of the Civil Rights Act of 1964). I thought then, and think now, that it was a mistake
to have avoided the Section 5 issues raised in the public accommodations cases. It was a
shame to have wasted the votes when we had them.

[69] 383 US 745 (1966).

[70] 383 US 787 (1966).

[71] Michal R. Belknap, *The Legal Legacy of Lemuel Penn*, 25 Howard L J 467, 467 (1982)
(briefly describing murder victim Penn and his murder). For the factual background of
the case, see generally id.

[72] *Guest*, 383 US at 746–47 (noting indictment); id at 747–48 n 1 (noting that two of
the defendants were found not guilty in state court).

[73] Id at 756–57 (noting that indictment alleges state action strongly enough to prevent
dismissal).

[74] Id (Stewart); id at 761–62 (Clark, J, joining the opinion and agreeing with Stewart's
indictment construction); id at 762 (Harlan, J, concurring and dissenting) (concurring with
Part II in which Stewart found enough state action); id at 776 n 1 (Brennan, J, concurring
and dissenting) (assuming that the entire indictment could "be construed to show discriminatory conduct by state law enforcement officers").

[75] Justice Harlan, who dissented from Part III in *Guest*, agreed that the indictment

In addition, Justice Stewart recognized a constitutional right to interstate travel that was not dependent on the Fourteenth Amendment, and held that a conspiracy formed with the purpose of interfering with interstate travel fell comfortably within Congress's power to regulate private behavior.[76] In separate opinions, six of the Justices went even further, noting that Congress possesses power under Section 5 of the Fourteenth Amendment to enforce Section 1 rights against private interference.[77] Congress subsequently read the six concurring votes in *Guest* as resolving the issue in favor of congressional power.[78]

Price was an easier federalism case, involving indictments of three local law enforcement officials and fifteen private persons for conspiring to murder three young civil rights workers, Andrew Goodman, Mickey Schwerner, and James Chaney, in Philadelphia, Mississippi, in 1964.[79] The conspiracy involved falsely arresting the civil rights workers, releasing them from jail in the middle of the night, and murdering them as they left town.[80] The Court ruled unanimously that joint public-private behavior aimed at denying constitutional rights was both action "under color of law" for the purposes of 18 USC § 242, and satisfied the Fourteenth Amendment's state action requirement.[81] Finally, in *Griffin v*

---

implied cooperation by state officials. See id at 762–63, 774 (Harlan, J, concurring and dissenting).

[76] Id at 757–60 (discussing right to travel, recent cases such as *Heart of Atlanta Motel* and *McClung*, and Congress's power to protect against specific intent to interfere with that right).

[77] Id at 762 (Clark, J, concurring and dissenting) ("[I]t is, I believe, both appropriate and necessary under the circumstances here to say that there now can be no doubt that specific language of § 5 empowers the Congress to enact laws punishing all conspiracies— with or without state action—that interfere with Fourteenth Amendment rights."); id at 782 ("§ 5 authorizes Congress to make laws that it concludes are reasonably necessary to protect a right created by and arising under that Amendment; and Congress is thus fully empowered to determine that punishment of private conspiracies interfering with the exercise of such a right is necessary to its full protection.").

[78] In 1968, Congress enacted the Civil Rights Act of 1968, Pub L No 90-284, Title 1, 82 Stat 73, codified at 18 USC § 245 as amended, explicitly reaching certain private conspiracies to interfere with the enjoyment of rights protected under Section 1 of the Fourteenth Amendment.

[79] Mickey Schwerner was a Cornell classmate. We each graduated in 1961. I went to Harvard Law School. Mickey went to social work school, and, in 1963, headed south to register black voters. I dedicate this piece to his memory.

[80] *Price*, 383 US at 790.

[81] Id at 792–96 (finding the defendants' action would be "under color" of law for § 242 in all counts of the indictment); id at 794–95 n 7 (finding that § 242's "under color" requirement is the same as the Fourteenth Amendment's state action requirement).

Breckenridge[82] a unanimous Court invoked Section 2 of the Thirteenth Amendment to uphold the application of 42 USC § 1985(3) to a conspiracy to deny blacks "basic rights that the law secures to all free men."[83] The case involved a brutal attack on a group of black passengers in a car near the Mississippi-Alabama border.[84]

In *South Carolina v Katzenbach*,[85] the Warren Court relied on Section 2 of the Fifteenth Amendment to uphold the constitutionality of provisions of the Voting Rights Act of 1965. The Court upheld the complex trigger mechanism for the Voting Rights Act,[86] as well as the suspension of literacy tests in covered subdivisions for a five-year period,[87] and the dramatic preclearance remedy requiring a covered subdivision to secure federal permission from the Department of Justice before changing any aspect of its election laws.[88] In effect, the preclearance provisions of Section 5 of the Voting Rights Act declared the southern states to be in moral bankruptcy when it came to allowing blacks to vote, and placed them under federal receivership. The Court went further in *Katzenbach v Morgan*,[89] invoking Section 5 of the Fourteenth Amendment to uphold Congress's suspension of an English-language literacy test in New York that operated to disenfranchise Spanish-speaking voters from Puerto Rico.[90] There is even language in

---

[82] 403 US 88 (1971).

[83] Id at 105. Justice Stewart relied, as well, on the right to interstate travel. Id at 105–07.

[84] Id at 94–96 (quoting petitioners' complaint).

[85] 383 US 301 (1966).

[86] The trigger required recent use of a "test or device" (like a literacy test) to measure the right to vote, coupled with sub-50 percent participation in recent elections. An escape hatch existed permitting a covered subdivision to escape by demonstrating that no taint of racial discrimination in voting was taking place within its borders. See generally *Northwest Austin Municipal Utility District Number One v Holder*, 129 S Ct 2504 (2009) (describing the history of the Voting Rights Act of 1965, Pub L No 89-110, 79 Stat 438, codified at 42 USC 1973 et seq).

[87] *South Carolina v Katzenbach*, 383 US 30 (1966). Justice Douglas, writing for a unanimous Court in *Lassiter v Northampton County Election Board*, 360 US 45 (1959), had upheld the constitutionality of North Carolina's literacy test under the Fourteenth Amendment. In 1970, a fragmented Court unanimously upheld Congress's power to suspend literacy tests throughout the United States. *Oregon v Mitchell*, 400 US 112 (1970). But see *City of Boerne v Flores*, 521 US 507 (1997) (finding that the Religious Freedom Restoration Act exceeded Congressional authority).

[88] See *Allen v State Board of Elections*, 393 US 544, 565–70 (1969), for the Warren Court's broad construction of Section 5.

[89] 384 US 641 (1966).

[90] The Warren Court consistently treated activity harmful to Hispanics as a racial issue. See, for example, *Hernandez v Texas*, 347 US 475 (1954).

Katzenbach v Morgan suggesting a "one way ratchet," enabling Congress to go beyond Section 1 of the Fourteenth Amendment in enacting remedial legislation under Section 5.[91]

In *Jones v Alfred H. Mayer Co.,*[92] and *Sullivan v Little Hunting Park,*[93] the Warren Court ended the decade by construing the Civil Rights Act of 1866[94] broadly to provide federal remedies against private racial discrimination in the sale or lease of housing. The Court upheld the act under Section 2 of the Thirteenth Amendment. In *Runyon v McCrary,*[95] the Court extended the 1866 statute to ban racial discrimination in entry to private, commercially operated nonsectarian schools.[96]

The Warren Court's treatment of "state action" also reflected the gravitational pull of race. Even before Warren's appointment, the Court had adopted a broad view of state action in order to deal with private agreements to exclude blacks from voting and buying a home.[97] In *Evans v Newton,*[98] the Court refused to permit Macon, Georgia, to substitute private trustees to operate a white-only park under a 1911 will. The park had been administered by Macon authorities.[99] In *Burton v Wilmington Parking Authority,*[100] the Court struggled to find state action in routine financial support for private commercial facilities. In *Norwood v Harrison,*[101] the

---

[91] *Katzenbach v Morgan*, 384 US 641, 649 (1966).

[92] 392 US 409 (1968).

[93] 396 US 229 (1969).

[94] Civil Rights Act of 1866, 14 Stat 27 (1866), codified at 42 SC §§ 1981 and 1982.

[95] 427 US 160 (1976).

[96] The *Runyon* Court did not apply the 1866 statute to religiously affiliated white-only schools. See text accompanying notes 109–12 for a discussion of the Supreme Court's refusal of tax deductible status to "charitable" contributions to such schools in *Bob Jones University v United States*, 461 US 574 (1983).

[97] See, for example, *Shelley v Kraemer*, 334 US 1 (1948); *Barrows v Jackson*, 346 US 249 (1953); and *Terry v Adams*, 345 US 461 (1953).

[98] 382 US 296 (1966).

[99] In *Evans v Abney*, 396 US 435 (1970), the Court's ingenuity ran out, and it upheld a Georgia ruling under the *cy pres* doctrine that since the terms of the 1911 bequest had become unenforceable, the property reverted to the heirs of the testator. Given the Court's decision the next term in *Palmer v Thompson*, 403 US 217 (1971), upholding a decision to close a municipal swimming pool rather than operate it on an integrated basis, the final denouement in *Evans* is more properly seen as a substantive judgment than a state action case. See also *Bell v Maryland*, 378 US 226 (1964) (avoiding a ruling on whether the enforcement of trespass laws against sit-in demonstrators constituted state action).

[100] 365 US 715 (1961).

[101] 413 US 455 (1973).

Court struck down Mississippi's provision of free textbooks to all schools, both public and private, noting that the technique imperiled the enforcement of *Brown* by funneling state aid to segregated private schools.[102] In short, the Warren Court's Federalism decisions reflect an unremitting suspicion of state and local institutions in any setting involving race.

B. RACE AND THE SEPARATION OF POWERS

The Warren Court's separation of powers cases also reflect the gravitational pull of race. In *Cooper v Aaron*,[103] confronted by a refusal to desegregate a high school in Little Rock, Arkansas, the Court issued the most sweeping assertion of judicial power in the nation's history, insisting that state officials are obliged to comply with the Supreme Court's reading of the Constitution—even in the absence of a court order directing compliance. In *Cooper*, Little Rock school officials acknowledged a duty to comply with court-ordered desegregation. If, however, a black student sought to enroll without a court order, officials often refused admission because, in their opinion, *Brown* had been wrongly decided. Since, prior to the emergence of the modern class action, it was impossible to supply every black schoolchild with an individual court order, such passive resistance posed a severe hurdle to the implementation of *Brown*. The Warren Court met the challenge by issuing an opinion signed by all nine Justices reaffirming the Court's support for *Brown* and treating its reading of the Fourteenth Amendment as the definitive statement of the Constitution's meaning, denying state officials the authority to justify failure to comply with Supreme Court precedent. The adoption of Rule 23(b)(2)[104] in 1966 solved the *Brown* enforcement problem by authorizing a "civil rights" class action in which one or two students, acting as named plaintiffs, could obtain a court order on behalf of all similarly situated students.[105] But the Court's imperial

---

[102] See also *Gilmore v City of Montgomery*, 417 US 556 (1974) (enjoining exclusive use of public athletic facilities by segregated private schools because it eroded enforcement of *Brown*, 347 US 483 (1954); remand to determine whether nonexclusive use imperiled implementation of *Brown*).

[103] 358 US 1 (1958).

[104] FRCP 23(b)(2).

[105] Certification of a Rule 23(b)(2) class, which does not require notice or an opportunity to opt out, was designed to be virtually automatic to facilitate its use in the South. See John K. Rabiej, *The Making of Class Action Rule 23—What Were We Thinking?* 24 Miss

pronouncement in *Cooper* continues to echo in cases like *City of Boerne*[106] and *Dickerson*.[107]

The Warren Court's decision to dispense with traditional standing requirements in *Flast v Cohen*[108] was also driven, at least in part, by concerns over race. *Flast* authorized a taxpayer to challenge government funding of parochial schools without the necessity of satisfying the usual injury-in-fact requirements. While a principled argument can be made that requiring a plaintiff to allege an injury-in-fact in connection with an Establishment Clause challenge risks pitting religions against each other, the Court's decision to dispense with traditional standing in *Flast* was designed to counter a key strategy in the South's massive resistance campaign, which was to establish and fund private alternatives to integrated public education.[109] While direct government funding of the "white academies" was quickly found unconstitutional, and indirect funding was ended by cases like *Norwood v Harrison*,[110] segregationists had two more government-funding strings to their bow—tax deductible private contributions to segregated educa-

---

Col L Rev 323 (2005). Without the gravitational pull of race, some have suggested that the Due Process Clause requires notice and opt-out in a (b)(2) setting, especially if incidental damages are available. *Phillips Petroleum Co. v Shutts*, 472 US 797 (1985).

[106] *City of Boerne v Flores*, 521 US 507 (1997).

[107] *Dickerson v United States*, 530 US 428 (2000). Once the gravitational pull of race is removed, mutterings of discontent are heard in the land about the scope of the Court's pretension. See, for example, Gary Apfel, *Whose Constitution Is It Anyway? The Authority of the Judiciary's Interpretation of the Constitution*, 46 Rutgers L Rev 771 (1994); Steven G. Calabresi, *Thayer's Clear Mistake*, 88 Nw U L Rev 269, 272–76 (1993); Frank H. Easterbrook, *Presidential Review*, 40 Case W Res L Rev 905 (1990); Michael Stokes Paulsen, *The Most Dangerous Branch: Executive Power to Say What the Law Is*, 83 Georgetown L J 217 (1994); Mark V. Tushnet, *The Hardest Question in Constitutional Law*, 81 Minn L Rev 1 (1996); Larry D. Kramer, *The People Themselves: Popular Constitutionalism and Judicial Review* (Oxford, 2004). At a minimum, the President asserts an independent power to construe the Constitution in deciding whether to veto a bill, issue a signing statement, or decline to enforce an unconstitutional law. See Walter E. Dellinger III, *Memorandum for Bernard Nussbaum, Counsel to the President*, 48 Ark L Rev 333 (1995). More controversially, in areas involving exercise of the Commander-in-Chief power, some argue that there is an independent presidential power to construe relevant provisions of the Constitution. See also *United States v Mendoza*, 464 US 154 (1984) (United States not bound by affirmative nonmutual collateral estoppel). The widespread administrative practice of "respectfully non-acquiescing" in binding circuit precedent is criticized in Joseph E. Weis, *Agency Non-Acquiescence—Respectful Lawlessness or Legitimate Disagreement?* 48 U Pitt L Rev 845 (1986–87). See *Hutchinson for Hutchinson v Chater*, 99 F3d 286 (8th Cir 1996) (criticizing nonacquiescence policy).

[108] 392 US 83 (1968).

[109] See *Allen v Wright*, 468 US 737, 743–45 (1984) (describing establishment of segregated private schools in response to *Brown*).

[110] See note 101.

tional institutions, and government assistance to segregated religious schools.

The battle against tax deductible white academies careened through *Runyon v McCrary*,[111] invalidating racially discriminatory commercial private school admissions criteria; *Bob Jones University v United States*,[112] denying tax deductible status to segregated private schools, and *Allen v Wright*,[113] denying standing to black parents seeking to force the IRS to enforce *Bob Jones* more aggressively.

Government assistance to religiously affiliated white academies was even more difficult to counter because it was bound up with the general question of aid to parochial education, and was often disguised as assistance to the free exercise of religion. *Flast* was designed to make it as easy as possible to challenge state aid to the white religious academies. It turns out that the Catholic parochial schools in *Flast* may have just been in the wrong place at the wrong time.

The scope of judicial oversight by the Warren Court over the internal workings of the legislative branch was also affected by concerns about race. Ordinarily, it is next to impossible to persuade the Court to involve itself in the internal workings of the legislature. That is why it would be so hard to mount a credible legal challenge to current Senate filibuster rules that allow forty-one senators representing approximately 15 percent of the population to block legislation favored by fifty-nine senators representing approximately 85 percent of the population.[114] During the Warren Court years, though, when racial justice was implicated, the Court overturned the refusal of the Georgia legislature to seat a black legislator, Julian Bond, for supporting draft resisters,[115] and blocked Congress's effort to expel Adam Clayton Powell, Jr., a

---

[111] 427 US 160 (1976).

[112] 461 US 574 (1983).

[113] 468 US 737 (1984).

[114] I derive the figures from my approximation of the number of people represented in 2009 by fifty-seven Democratic senators (plus the two independents who usually voted with them) and forty-one Republican senators during the debate over legislation providing for disclosure of corporate campaign expenditures.

[115] *Bond v Floyd*, 385 US 116 (1966). The legislature argued that Bond's opposition to the Vietnam War rendered it impossible for him to swear the loyalty oath required of all Georgia legislators.

black congressman from Harlem, for financial misconduct.[116]

C. RACE AND FREE SPEECH[117]

The Warren Court's race-sensitive First Amendment jurisprudence began in 1958 in *NAACP v Alabama*,[118] with Justice Harlan's
invention of freedom of association in order to protect the vulnerable civil rights movement.[119] In 1928, in *New York v Zimmerman*,[120] a unanimous Supreme Court had upheld New York's demand for the membership list of the Ku Klux Klan. Writing for
a unanimous Court in *NAACP v Alabama*, Justice Harlan distinguished *New York v Zimmerman*[121] and rejected Alabama's insistence that government inspection of the National Association for
the Advancement of Colored People (NAACP) membership list
was needed to assure compliance with the state's foreign corporation registration law. *NAACP v Alabama* was quickly applied by
a unanimous Court in *Bates v Little Rock*[122] to strike down Arkansas's demand for the statewide NAACP membership list in
connection with enforcement of the state's occupational license
tax. In *Louisiana v NAACP*,[123] the Court rejected Louisiana's demand for the NAACP membership list in connection with an
investigation of possible infiltration by the Communist Party.[124]

---

[116] *Powell v McCormack*, 395 US 486 (1969). Powell had been expelled for financial
dishonesty in dealing with Congressional funds. The Court held that Congress lacked
power to add new qualifications to the age, citizenship, and residency requirements set
forth in US Const, Art I, § 2, cl 2.

[117] I am not the first to note the close link between the Warren Court's First Amendment
cases and the civil rights movement. The classic study is Harry Kalven, *The Negro and the
First Amendment* (Ohio State, 1965).

[118] 357 US 449 (1958).

[119] The idea of freedom of association did not spring into being in *NAACP v Alabama*,
id. *DeJonge v Oregon*, 299 US 353 (1937), had prefigured it. But, until *NAACP v Alabama*,
no Supreme Court case had explicitly recognized free association as an independent right.

[120] 278 US 63 (1928).

[121] Justice Harlan was careful not to overturn *New York v Zimmerman*, arguing that the
Klan's penchant for lawless action and its refusal to release any information about its
activities distinguished the case. He noted that the NAACP foreswore violence and was
willing to release the names of its officers and staff members. See *NAACP v Alabama*, 357
US 449 at Part III (1958).

[122] 361 US 516 (1960).

[123] 366 US 293 (1961).

[124] By the time *Louisiana v NAACP*, id, was decided, Justice Harlan was beginning to
waver. He and Justice Stewart declined to join Justice Douglas's opinion for the majority,
concurring only in the result. Justices Frankfurter and Clark also concurred in the result.

In *Shelton v Tucker*,[125] the Court invalidated an effort to require an Arkansas teacher to disclose his membership in the NAACP. In *Gibson v Florida Legislative Investigation Committee*,[126] the Court rejected demands by Florida legislative officials to produce state-wide NAACP membership lists in an effort to determine whether fourteen alleged communists were members of the Miami branch of the NAACP. Finally, in *NAACP v Button*,[127] the Court extended First Amendment associational rights to the NAACP's practice of referring potentially fee-paying civil rights cases to cooperating attorneys.

The gravitational pull of race on the Warren Court's First Amendment cases continued in *Talley v California*,[128] the modern origin of the right to speak anonymously. In *Talley*, the Court invalidated a California law requiring that handbills contain the name of the sponsor. Not coincidentally, the handbill at issue called for a boycott of stores engaging in racial discrimination in hiring.[129] In *Edwards v South Carolina*,[130] the Court upheld the First Amendment right of civil rights marchers to demonstrate, picket, and parade, even in the face of significant hostility by onlookers and the police. The break with the past was dramatic. As recently as 1951, the Court had upheld the conviction of a left-wing speaker who had refused to stop addressing a hostile crowd in upstate New York.[131] In *Edwards*, the Court reversed the conviction of 187 black student demonstrators who had walked along the South Carolina State House grounds carrying signs protesting racial segregation, and who refused to disperse after a large crowd of hostile onlookers had gathered. Two years later, in *Cox v Louisiana I*[132] and *II*,[133] the

---

[125] 364 US 479 (1960).

[126] 372 US 539 (1963).

[127] 371 US 415 (1963).

[128] 362 US 60 (1960).

[129] Id. Justice Harlan concurred, noting the lack of a legislative record indicating a need for the blanket ban on anonymity. Justices Clark, Frankfurter, and Whittaker dissented.

[130] 372 US 229 (1963).

[131] *Feiner v New York*, 340 US 315 (1951).

[132] 379 US 536 (1965). *Cox I* was unanimous in finding the breach-of-the-peace statute facially unconstitutional.

[133] 379 US 559 (1965). *Cox II* was 5–4 in overturning convictions for blocking the public way, with the dissenting Justices stressing the fact-intensive nature of the as-applied issue and the difficulty of substituting the Court's post hoc fact-finding for the reasonable fears of the police.

Court reversed the convictions of 2,000 black student demonstrators who had refused to end a demonstration, in the vicinity
of a courthouse, protesting the arrests of twenty-three students
for picketing stores with segregated lunch counters. In *Gregory v
Chicago*,[134] confronted with a fact pattern considerably more in-
cendiary than in *Feiner*, Chief Justice Warren found it an "easy
case" to reverse the convictions of eighty-five civil rights marchers,
led by comedian Dick Gregory, who peacefully marched in support
of public school desegregation from City Hall to the home of
Mayor Daley, and then refused a police order to disperse when
confronted by a crowd of 1,000 hostile "unruly" onlookers.[135]
These decisions revolutionized First Amendment doctrine.

   New York Times v Sullivan[136] also evidenced the Warren Court's
concern with race and the First Amendment. *Times v Sullivan* dealt
with an Alabama libel judgment arising out of the publication of
an advertisement in the *New York Times* seeking financial support
for Dr. Martin Luther King, Jr. The advertisement contained allegedly false statements about the treatment of civil rights demonstrators by Alabama law enforcement personnel. Libel actions
like *Times v Sullivan*, tried before hostile southern juries, threatened to drive national media from covering the extraordinary
events in the South during the height of the civil rights movement.
As if to bring home the point, Dr. King attended the oral argument. (A star-struck Justice Goldberg asked King to autograph a
recent book.)[137] There is no doubt that one of the Supreme Court's
most important First Amendment decisions, described by Alexander Meikeljohn as a cause for dancing in the streets,[138] was
inspired in no small part by the Court's understanding of the
importance of the decision for the continued viability of the civil
rights movement.[139]

---

[134] 394 US 111 (1969).

[135] As Justices Harlan, Black, and Douglas noted, *Gregory*, id, was an "easy case," not
because the facts could not have supported a conviction, but only because Illinois had not
enacted a law governing refusal to comply with a reasonable order to disperse.

[136] 376 US 254 (1964).

[137] See Seth Stern and Stephen Wermeil, *Justice Brennan: Liberal Champion* 222 (Houghton Mifflin Harcourt, 2010).

[138] See Harry Kalven, *The New York Times Case: A Note of the Central Meaning of the
First Amendment*, 1964 Supreme Court Review 191 (1964) (reporting the Meikeljohn quote
and heaping praise on the opinion).

[139] See also the Court's agonized effort to protect sit-in demonstrators in *Hamm v City
of Rock Hill*, 379 US 306 (1964). See also *Brown v Louisiana*, 383 US 131 (1966) (protecting

In *Street v New York*,[140] the Court stretched the record to protect a black protestor who had burned his American flag on a Brooklyn street corner to protest the shooting of James Meredith. Realizing that there were not yet five votes to treat flag burning as protected First Amendment expression, Justice Harlan converted what had been viewed as a flag-burning case into one dealing with verbal criticism of the flag. The decade ended with the Court's protection of an eighteen-year-old who, during a discussion sponsored by the W. E. B. DuBois Club, had hyperbolically threatened to kill President Johnson for trying to draft him and force him to kill his "black brothers."[141] Can you imagine a similar decision today in a case threatening a terrorist act?

The only significant First Amendment rebuff to the civil rights movement during the Warren Court years was *Walker v City of Birmingham*,[142] in which five members of the Court refused to permit civil rights marchers to violate a facially valid state court injunction. Even then, the majority was at pains to confine *Walker* to good faith, plausible exercises of state judicial power, and had already provided civil rights marchers with a powerful weapon to win the race to the courthouse by obtaining advance federal judicial protection of proposed marches.[143]

Often, a Warren Court First Amendment opinion that appears unconnected to race was actually aimed at making it easier for the Court to protect civil rights demonstrators. For example, in *Coates v City of Cincinnati*[144] and *Gooding v Wilson*,[145] cases having nothing overtly to do with race, the Court laid the foundation for the modern First Amendment vagueness and overbreadth doctrines, which enabled federal district judges to protect civil rights pro-

---

civil rights sit-in at public library). But see *Adderley v Florida*, 385 US 39 (1966) (upholding conviction of demonstrators on jail premises) and *Grayned v City of Rockford*, 408 US 104 (1972) (upholding ban on demonstrating near a school). When the gravitational pull of race was removed, the needle dramatically moved back to protecting property rights. See, for example, *Lloyd Corp. v Tanner*, 407 US 551 (1972), and *United States v Kokinda*, 497 US 720 (1990).

[140] 394 US 576 (1969).

[141] *Watts v United States*, 394 US 705 (1969).

[142] 388 US 307 (1967).

[143] *Dombrowski v Pfister*, 380 US 479 (1965) (allowing pre-event access to federal court to prevent "chilling effect" on civil rights demonstration). When you subtract the gravitational pull of race from *Dombrowski*, you get *Younger v Harris*, 401 US 37 (1971), and its progeny.

[144] 402 US 611 (1971).

[145] 405 US 518 (1972).

testors by invalidating state loitering and disorderly conduct stat-
ues on their face, making it unnecessary for federal judges to engage in battles about state court fact-finding that had proved so
fractious in *Cox II*, and sidestepping the inability of federal courts
to construe state statutes narrowly to protect civil rights demonstrators. *Shuttlesworth v Birmingham*,[146] invalidating a standard-
less local demonstration permit statute on its face, shows the doctrines in action, but the real bite of the vagueness and overbreadth
doctrines was felt in federal district courts throughout the South
where demonstrators, invoking jurisdiction under *Dombrowski v
Pfister*, could seek advance judicial protection for civil rights
marches.

When issues of racial justice were not in the picture, either
directly or indirectly, the Warren Court was somewhat less likely
to strike an aggressive pose in defense of free speech. Justice Brennan's much criticized obscenity opinion in *Roth*,[147] and the Court's
subsequent "keystone cops" effort to define obscenity, is but one
example. Similarly, the Court was unmoved by the associational
rights argument in *Terry v Adams*,[148] and was not particularly zeal-
ous in protecting the associational freedom of radical leftists.[149]
Finally, when you remove the gravitational pull of race, the Warren
Court was much less protective of "speech brigaded with conduct."

---

[146] 394 US 147 (1969).

[147] *Roth v United States*, and *Alberts v California*, 354 US 476 (1957) (defining obscenity
as nonspeech); *Ginzburg v United States*, 383 US 463 (1966) (upholding conviction on
pandering theory).

[148] 345 US 461 (1953). In the absence of the gravitational pull of race, the post-Warren
Court has both accepted and rejected associational claims. Compare *Roberts v United States
Jaycees*, 468 US 609 (1984); *Board of Directors of Rotary International v Rotary Club of Duarte*,
481 US 537 (1987); and *New York State Club Ass'n, Inc. v City of New York*, 487 US 1
(1988) (rejecting associational rights argument); with *Boy Scouts of America v Dale*, 530 US
640 (2000) (accepting associational rights argument).

[149] Compare *Elfbrandt v Russell*, 384 US 11 (1966) (invalidating loyalty oath); and *Key-
ishian v Board of Regents of the University of the State of New York*, 385 US 589 (1967) (same);
with *Konigsberg v State Bar of California*, 366 US 36 (1961) (upholding denial of bar
admission on basis of refusal to answer questions on membership or belief); *In re Stolar*,
401 US 23 (1971) (same); and *Law Students Civil Rights Research Council, Inc. v Wadmond*,
401 US 154 (1971) (same). Perhaps the most striking discontinuity was Justice Brennan's
withdrawal of the offer of a Supreme Court clerkship to Michael Tigar, who had been
active in a number of left-wing student groups at Berkeley. Justice Brennan sought to
defuse criticism of the offer by asking Tigar to list his past political associations. When
Tiger declined as a matter of principle, Brennan withdrew the clerkship offer. Professor
Tigar went on to a distinguished academic and practice career. Many years later, he
graciously acknowledged the institutional dilemma faced by Justice Brennan. The incident
is described in Stern and Wermeil, *Justice Brennan* at 264–74 (cited in note 137).

It is impossible to reconcile the solicitude of the Warren Court for civil rights marchers in *Edwards* and *Cox I* and *II* with its unanimous cavalier treatment of draft-card burners in *United States v O'Brien*.[150]

D. RACE AND THE LAW OF DEMOCRACY

Although the Supreme Court had historically made sporadic efforts to protect black voters from particularly egregious efforts to disenfranchise them,[151] concerns over separation of powers and federalism had rendered judicial protection of the right of blacks to vote in state and local elections largely ineffective.[152] Where racially discriminatory purpose was evident, as in *Terry v Adams*[153] and *Gomillion v Lightfoot*,[154] the Court was able to provide relief. In the many cases where discriminatory racial purpose was not self-evident, however, proving it was virtually impossible, especially in settings where sophisticated officials took pains to cover their tracks.[155] Faced with massive disenfranchisement of blacks in the South, and the difficulty of proving discriminatory purpose, the Warren Court pushed the reset button.[156] In *Carrington v Rash*,[157] Texas forbade soldiers assigned to duty in the state from voting, creating a conclusive presumption that they were not bona fide residents of Texas. It was no coincidence that so many of the

---

[150] 391 US 367 (1968). Justice Douglas's dissent in *O'Brien* questioned the constitutionality of the draft, not the free speech aspects of the case, id at 389 (Douglas, J, dissenting).

[151] *Ex parte Siebold*, 100 US 371 (1879); *Ex parte Yarbrough*, 110 US 651 (1884); *Guinn v United States*, 238 US 347 (1915); *United States v Mosely*, 238 US 383 (1915); *Nixon v Herndon*, 273 US 536 (1927); *Nixon v Condon*, 286 US 73 (1932); *Lane v Wilson*, 307 US 268 (1939); *United States v Classic*, 313 US 299 (1941); *Smith v Allwright*, 321 US 649 (1944); *United States v Saylor*, 322 US 385 (1944).

[152] See, for example, *Giles v Harris*, 189 US 475 (1903); *Giles v Teasley*, 193 US 146 (1904); *Pope v Williams*, 193 US 621 (1904); *Grovey v Townsend*, 295 US 45 (1935); *Breedlove v Suttles*, 302 US 277 (1937).

[153] The gravitational pull of race is particularly obvious in *Terry*, because it was at virtually the same moment that the Court was providing intense associational protection to the NAACP, while denying it to the Texas Jaybirds.

[154] 364 US 339 (1960).

[155] See *Arlington Heights v Metropolitan Housing Development Corp.*, 429 US 252 (1977).

[156] The pre-Warren Court had consistently refused to develop a general right to vote. *Minor v Happersett*, 88 US 162 (1874).

[157] 380 US 89 (1965).

soldiers were black.[158] Lacking proof of discriminatory purpose, it was impossible to bring a successful Fifteenth Amendment challenge to the Texas ban. So, the Warren Court started down the road of "fundamental rights" jurisprudence, enabling the Court to protect minority voting rights by imposing strict scrutiny on any effort to selectively apportion the franchise. The Warren Court repeated the process in *Harper v Virginia Board of Elections*,[159] which invalidated Virginia's $1.50 poll tax. Once again, a Fifteenth Amendment challenge would have failed in the absence of proof of discriminatory purpose. *Harper* was particularly difficult because, in 1937, the Court had unanimously upheld the constitutionality of state poll taxes in *Breedlove v Suttles*,[160] and the Twenty-Fourth Amendment, which abolished poll taxes in federal elections, had refrained from extending the ban to the states, creating an *inclusio unis* textual problem. Indeed, Justice Stewart, who wrote for the Court in *Carrington*, dissented in *Harper*. But the Warren Court's majority sensed a "one-two" punch in *Carrington* and *Harper* that would eliminate the traditional impediments to black voting without requiring proof of discriminatory purpose.[161]

A similar process led to *Baker v Carr*.[162] Although the one-person one-vote cases say nothing explicit about race, the issue that drove the cases was pervasive legislative malapportionment throughout the South—and parts of the North—that dramatically overrepresented rural whites at the expense of underrepresented urban and rural blacks.[163] In *Gomillion*, the Court confronted an obvious racial

---

[158] Once President Truman had desegregated the armed forces, a military career became relatively attractive to many black Americans because civilian employment continued to struggle with racism. Moreover, the military draft during the 1960s tended to overrepresent black youths, since student and other deferments were more easily obtained by middle- and upper-class whites. Jonathan Sutherland, 2 *African Americans at War: An Encyclopedia* 502 (ABC-CLIO, 2006).

[159] 383 US 663 (1966).

[160] 302 US 277 (1937).

[161] The Warren Court quickly built on *Carrington*, 380 US 89 (1965), and *Harper*, 383 US 663 (1966), to announce a general constitutional right to vote and to run for office in *Williams v Rhodes*, 393 US 23 (1968), *Kramer v Union Free School Dist. No. 15*, 395 US 621 (1969), and *Dunn v Blumstein*, 405 US 330 (1972).

[162] 369 US 186 (1962).

[163] See C. Herman Pritchett, *Equal Protection and the Urban Majority*, 58 Am Pol Sci Rev 869, 869–71 (arguing that the Supreme Court's decisions on legislative districting and apportionment must be taken in the context of a predominantly black urban majority and are a continuation of its 1950s decisions on racial inequality). See also Richard C. Cortner, *The Apportionment Cases* (Tennessee, 1970); Robert G. Dixon, Jr., *Democratic*

gerrymander, making it possible to invoke the Fifteenth Amendment. But the facts of *Baker v Carr* made it impossible to apply the Fifteenth Amendment. The result was the development of the doctrine of one-person one-vote, enforceable without any need to prove a racially discriminatory purpose. Indeed, it is the gravitational pull of race that explains why, despite the analogy to the United States Senate, the Court was adamant in *Reynolds v Sims*[164] in denying Alabama's effort to apportion one house of its bicameral state legislature to reflect geographical or other non-population-based factors. The Court's effort to assure black citizens fair legislative representation would have been derailed if one house of the state legislature was permitted to remain a malapportioned bastion of white power.[165]

E. RACE, FREEDOM OF RELIGION, AND DUE PROCESS OF LAW

The Warren Court determination to enforce *Brown* also played a role in shaping its Establishment Clause jurisprudence. As we have seen, *Flast v Cohen* eliminated standing as a barrier to the effective enforcement of the ban on government aid to segregated white academies masquerading as religious parochial schools. Justice Brennan's influential concurring opinion in *Abington v Schempp*[166] sought to build an impermeable wall through which government funds could never pass to a racially segregated private religious school.

Race also may have exercised a gravitational pull on Warren Court Free Exercise jurisprudence. It was no coincidence that the plaintiff in *Sherbert v Verner*[167] was a Seventh Day Adventist from South Carolina seeking employment benefits. *Sherbert* fits closely with *Goldberg v Kelly*,[168] the Warren Court's principal procedural

---

Representation: Reapportionment in Law and Politics (Oxford, 1968); Nelson W. Polsby, ed, *Reapportionment in the 1970s* (California, 1971).

[164] 377 US 533 (1964).

[165] In *Wesberry v Sanders*, 376 US 1 (1964), the one-person one-vote principle was imposed on Georgia's apportionment of Congressional districts through Article 1, Section 2 of the Constitution. It is no coincidence that the first major reapportionment cases emerged from Tennessee, Alabama, and Georgia. Once the Court had the bit between its teeth, the same rules were applied to the North. See *Lucas v 44th General Assembly of the State of Colorado*, 377 US 713 (1964); *Kirkpatrick v Preisler*, 394 US 526 (1969).

[166] 374 US 203 (1963) (Brennan, J, concurring).

[167] 374 US 398 (1963).

[168] 397 US 254 (1970).

due process decision. Both opinions by Justice Brennan were designed to empower a black underclass deeply dependent on government benefits that too often were administered by unsympathetic or even racist white bureaucracies.

The introduction of procedural due process guaranties into school disciplinary proceedings in *Goss v Lopez*[169] was also driven by concerns over race. My first federal trial involved an ugly attempt to prevent the integration of a New York City high school by expelling large numbers of black students for alleged truancy. I could not prove racially discriminatory purpose, although the situation reeked of racism. Instead, I argued successfully that the expelled students had been denied procedural due process of law.[170] This lesson was not lost on the Supreme Court when it decided *Goldberg v Kelley* and *Goss v Lopez*.

F. RACE AND CRIMINAL LAW AND PROCEDURE

Perhaps the clearest evidence of the gravitational pull of race on Warren Court constitutional doctrine was in the areas of criminal law and procedure. It is hard to overstate the sense of urgency driving the Court's concern over racial discrimination in the enforcement of the criminal law. The perception—and, too often, the reality—was of white police forces applying racially discriminatory standards in daily street encounters with black citizens, the widespread discriminatory use of force, and the selective prosecution of crime. The sense of crisis was particularly acute in the urban ghettos, which eventually burst into open rebellion.[171]

We have already seen how the notion of white law enforcement officials unfairly treating black citizens played out in the specialized world of the First Amendment.[172] The Warren Court generalized the response in a series of cases designed to limit the power of the police to initiate street encounters in the absence of a legitimate law enforcement justification. *Thompson v Louisville*[173]

---

[169] 419 US 565 (1975). *Goss* was decided in the shadow of *Dixon v Ala. State Bd. of Education*, 294 F2d 150 (5th Cir 1961) (invoking procedural due process to reverse the expulsion of black students for engaging in civil rights protests).

[170] *Knight v Board of Education*, 48 FRD 108 (EDNY, 1969); *Knight v Board of Education*. 48 FRD 115 (EDNY, 1969).

[171] See note 45.

[172] See text accompanying notes 120–56.

[173] 362 US 199 (1960).

is one example of the Court's response. But *Thompson*, standing alone, was unlikely to make a serious dent in the problem. In cases beginning with *Papachristou v City of Jacksonville*,[174] the Court turned to the Due Process Clause to invalidate vague ordinances that provided the police with carte blanche to stop blacks on the streets, especially in white areas.

The Warren Court's most dramatic responses to law enforcement's interaction with the black population were the Court's efforts in *Mapp v Ohio*[175] to prevent the use of illegally obtained evidence in criminal proceedings, and in *Miranda v Arizona*[176] to impose prophylactic rules on police interrogations. Race was not far from the surface of either case. In *Terry v Ohio*,[177] the Court sought to split the difference between the loitering and vagrancy decisions and the strict Fourth Amendment probable-cause test by authorizing the police to make investigatory street stops on less than probable cause, but only if they can demonstrate an "articulable suspicion" of unlawful activity. Finally, the right to counsel cases from *Gideon* to *Argersinger* were driven, in part, by concern over a criminal justice system where white judges and prosecutors processed poor, unrepresented blacks and Hispanics.[178]

II. Post-Warren Court Jurisprudence: When Gravity Ebbed

In the post-Warren Court years, once the gravitational pull of race and regional institutional mistrust had ebbed, much, but not all, of the jurisprudence described in Part I lost its vitality. In the federalism area, *Thompson v Louisville*[179] became a one-of-a-

---

[174] 405 US 156 (1972). See also *Kolender v Lawson*, 461 US 352 (1983). See generally Anthony G. Amsterdam, *The Void-for-Vagueness Doctrine in the Supreme Court*, 109 U Pa L Rev 67 (1960).

[175] 367 US 643 (1961). In fact, it has been suggested that the real target of the *Mapp* search was Don King, then a prominent black gambling figure who went on to fame and fortune as a boxing promoter. See Leonard A. Stevens, *Trespass! The People's Privacy vs. the Power of the Police: Great Constitutional Issues, the Fourth Amendment* (Coward, McCann & Geoghegan, 1977).

[176] 384 US 436 (1966). Justice Clark, who had written for the Court in *Mapp*, dissented in *Miranda*.

[177] 392 US 1 (1968).

[178] See cases at note 262.

[179] 362 US 199 (1960).

kind curiosity, *Monroe v Pape*[180] found itself enmeshed in a lab-yrinthine procedural morass,[181] and the broad vision of federal supervisory habeas corpus in *Townsend* and *Fay v Noia* was mugged by Supreme Court and Congressional hostility.[182] With-out the gravitational pull of race, state action doctrine largely reverted to pre-Warren Court standards,[183] and the Warren Court's extremely broad vision of Congressional power to protect individual rights contracted in cases like *United Brotherhood of Carpenters v Scott*,[184] *Bray v Alexandria Women's Health Clinic*,[185] and *United States v Morrison*,[186] which resemble pre-Warren Court decisions like *United States v Williams*[187] and *Collins v Har-*

---

[180] 365 US 167 (1961).

[181] While *Monroe v Pape*, id, continues to provide immediate access to a federal court to enforce federal constitutional guaranties against state and local authorities, today's prospective § 1983 plaintiff must survive preclusion (*Allen v McCurry*, 449 US 90 (1980)) and find the narrow space between a sufficiently crystallized controversy satisfying ripeness and standing requirements and the commencement of state or local enforcement pro-ceedings that trigger *Younger* abstention. See Martin A. Schwartz, *Section 1983 Litigation: Claims and Defenses* (Aspen, 2d ed 2008). Qualified immunity and good faith defense often make it virtually impossible to invoke a credible damage remedy. See *Weise v Casper*, 131 S Ct 7 (mem) (Oct 12, 2010) (Justices Ginsburg and Sotomayor dissenting from denial of certiorari).

[182] The Warren Court's initial conception of habeas corpus as a shift of power to federal courts is described in J. Skelly Wright and Abraham D. Sofaer, *Federal Habeas Corpus for State Prisoners: The Allocation of Fact-Finding Responsibility*, 75 Yale L J 895 (1966). The erosion of federal habeas corpus review of state criminal convictions is described in Charles Alan Wright, Arthur Raphael Miller, and Edward H. Cooper, 17 *Federal Practice and Procedure* (West Supp 2010). See generally *Wainwright v Sykes*, 433 US 72 (1977); *Teague v Lane*, 489 US 288 (1989); *McClesky v Zant*, 499 US 467 (1991). Congress reacted in the Anti-Terrorism and Effective Death Penalty Act (AEDPA), Pub L No 104-132, 110 Stat 1214 (1996).

[183] *Moose Lodge No. 107 v Irvis*, 407 US 163 (1972) (grant of liquor license does not generate state action); *Jackson v Metropolitan Edison*, 419 US 345 (1974) (public utility not state action); *Lloyd Corp. v Tanner*, 407 US 551 (1972) (privately owned shopping center not open to First Amendment activity); *Hudgens v NLRB*, 424 US 507 (1976) (privately owned shopping center not open to labor picketing); *Rendell-Baker v Kohn*, 457 US 830 (1982) (private school for maladjusted children not state action despite receipt of substantial public funding); *Blum v Yaretsky*, 457 US 991 (1982) (private nursing home not state action despite pervasive regulation and receipt of federal Medicaid funds); *San Francisco Arts & Athletics, Inc. v United States Olympic Comm.*, 483 US 522 (1987) (United States Olympic Committee not state action). Race, however, still has some bite. See *Edmonson v Leesville Concrete Co.*, 500 US 614 (1991) (private lawyer exercises state action when uses racially driven peremptory challenge in choosing civil jury); *Georgia v McCollum*, 505 US 42 (1992) (private defense attorney in criminal trial an agent of state for purposes of racially driven peremptory challenges).

[184] 463 US 825 (1983).

[185] 506 US 263 (1993).

[186] 529 US 598 (2000).

[187] 341 US 70 (1951).

dyman.[188] Similarly, the post-Warren Court rejected the one-way ratchet concept of *South Carolina v Katzenbach*,[189] returning to the more traditional view that Section 5 enforcement statutes must be closely tethered to Section 1 rights.[190] Several members of the post-Warren Court expressed buyer's remorse about the broad construction of the Civil Rights Act of 1866.[191] Indeed, with the success of the Voting Rights Act in enfranchising and empowering black voters, several members of the current Court have called for a reexamination of the constitutionality of the preclearance rule of Section 5 and the Congressionally imposed effects test of Section 2.[192]

As with the federalism cases, once the gravitational pull of race ebbed, post-Warren Court separation-of-powers decisions tended to revert to pre-Warren Court standards. The Establishment Clause standing rules tightened,[193] and the Court reverted to its traditional "hands off" stance when asked to interfere with the internal workings of the political branches.[194]

In the First Amendment and democracy areas, without the gravitational pull of race, the Court, over Justice Brennan's dissent, declined to extend *Times v Sullivan*[195] to speech about public issues,[196] wobbled on its commitment to anonymity,[197] rediscovered

---

[188] 341 US 651 (1951). Both *Williams*, 341 US 70 (1951), and *Hardyman*, 341 US 651 (1951), evidence the pre-Warren Court's much more equivocal approach to Congress's power to reach private behavior in the absence of a racial component.

[189] 383 US 301 (1966).

[190] See *City of Boerne v Flores*, 521 US 507 (1997); *United States v Morrison*, 529 US 598 (2000).

[191] *General Building Contractor's Ass'n v Pennsylvania*, 458 US 375 (1982) (requiring proof of intentional racial discrimination); *Patterson v McLean Credit Union*, 491 US 164, 171–72 (1989) (expressing doubt concerning correctness of *Runyon*, and declining to recognize claim for racial harassment).

[192] *Northwest Austin Municipal Utility District v Holder*, 129 S Ct 2504, 2511–13 (2009); id at 2519 (Thomas, J, dissenting in part).

[193] See, for example, *Elk Grove Unified School Dist. v Newdow*, 542 US 1 (2004); *Valley Forge Christian College v Americans United for Separation of Church and State, Inc.*, 454 US 464 (1982); *Salazar v Buono*, 130 S Ct 1803 (2010).

[194] *Goldwater v Carter*, 444 US 996 (1979) (declining to decide whether unilateral Presidential abrogation of treaty is constitutional); *United States v Nixon*, 506 US 224 (1993) (refusing to review Senate procedure for impeachment of judges).

[195] 376 US 254 (1964).

[196] *Gertz v Robert Welch, Inc.*, 418 US 323 (1974). See also *Time, Inc. v Firestone*, 424 US 448 (1976); *Hutchinson v Proxmire*, 443 US 111 (1979); *Wolston v Reader's Digest Association Inc.*, 443 US 157 (1979) (narrowly construing "public figure").

[197] *Buckley v Valeo*, 424 US 1 (1976) (rejecting anonymity involving campaign contributions); *Citizens United v FEC*, 558 US 50 (2010) (same); *John Doe No. 1 v Reed*, 130 S

the right of members of a political party to exclude outsiders,[198] declined to consider the constitutionality of massive political gerrymanders,[199] and eased the standards on state and local apportionment.[200] In *Shaw v Reno*,[201] a Supreme Court majority with a very different view of the relationship between constitutional doctrine and the achievement of racial justice forbade the drawing of legislative lines designed to favor formerly disenfranchised black voters. The fault line between the majority and dissent in *Shaw* was whether the effort to achieve racial justice would continue to exercise a gravitational pull on constitutional doctrine. Five Justices in *Shaw* said no.

Without the gravitational pull of race, substantial government aid is now available to religious schools,[202] we are on the cusp of overturning *Flast*,[203] the Court's toleration of vague and arguably overbroad statutes has markedly increased,[204] and the Court has systematically loosened the constitutional bonds limiting search-and-seizure and police interrogation.[205]

Some might object at this point that the Justices' differing perceptions about race and regional failure had little or nothing to do with the shift in constitutional doctrine in the post-Warren years. All that happened, they might argue, was that President Lyndon Johnson and Justice Abe Fortas badly botched the succession when

Ct 2811 (2010) (rejecting facial demand for anonymity by petition signers). But see *McIntyre v Ohio Elections Commission*, 514 US 334 (1995) (protecting anonymity).

[198] See, for example, *Rosario v Rockefeller*, 410 US 752 (1973); *Timmons v Twin Cities Area New Party*, 520 US 351 (1997); *California Democratic Party v Jones*, 530 US 567 (2000); *Clingman v Beaver*, 544 US 581 (2005); *New York State Board of Elections v Lopez-Torres*, 552 US 196 (2008).

[199] *Vieth v Jubelirer*, 541 US 267 (2004); *League of United Latin American Citizens v Perry*, 548 US 399 (2006).

[200] Compare *Burns v Richardson*, 384 US 73 (1966); *Mahan v Howell*, 410 US 315 (1973); and *Brown v Thomson*, 462 US 835 (1983); with *Karcher v Daggett*, 462 US 725 (1983).

[201] 509 US 630 (1993).

[202] *Zelman v Simmons-Harris*, 536 US 639 (2002).

[203] 392 US 83 (1968).

[204] See, for example, *Young v American Mini Theaters*, 427 US 50 (1976); *National Endowment for the Arts v Finley*, 524 US 569 (1998); *Holder v Humanitarian Law Project*, 130 S Ct 2705 (2010).

[205] See, for example, *Stone v Powell*, 428 US 465 (1976) (Fourth Amendment factual issues not reviewable on habeas corpus); *United States v Leon*, 468 US 897 (1984) (recognizing good faith defense to exclusionary rule). *Miranda* survived an effort at Congressional overruling in *Dickerson v United States*, 530 US 428 (2000), but has been narrowly applied once the gravitational pull of race waned. *Beckwith v United States*, 425 US 341 (1976); *Oregon v Mathiason*, 429 US 492 (1977).

Chief Justice Warren announced his resignation in 1968,[206] handing President Nixon four Supreme Court appointments and the chance to reconstitute the Court's political and philosophical underpinnings.[207] That's all true, of course. But it does not alter my point on the shift in the gravitational pull of race and regional failure. A Justice's political orientation and judicial philosophy are, after all, merely shorthands for underlying beliefs (often intuitively held) about things like the relative importance of equality and autonomy, the relative spheres of democratic decision making and principled judicial articulation, the relative risks and benefits of central and local power, the relative effectiveness of collective and individual action, the relative weight of environmental determinism and individual effort, the relative importance of procedural regularity and substantive outcome, and the relative costs and benefits of government and private regulation. When President Nixon appointed four new Justices with new (and mutually different) value orientations, he inevitably changed the intellectual prism through which the gravitational pull of the nation's struggle for racial justice, especially in the South, operated on the Supreme Court. That, in turn, affected the evolution of constitutional doctrine.

By the mid-1970s, many believed that *Brown* and its progeny,[208] coupled with Congressional enactment of much of the civil rights agenda during the 1960s,[209] had ameliorated the worst of the nation's racial crisis, and that generational change had rendered state institutions more willing and able to shoulder the burden of acting responsibly in dealing with racially charged issues. Thus, even if the Supreme Court's membership had remained stable, I suspect that at least several Justices might have become more skeptical over whether the quest for racial justice should continue to play such a dominant role in constitutional analysis across the board.[210] But the

---

[206] The failed effort to elevate Justice Fortas to the Chief Justice position and his forced resignation from the Court is described in Bruce Allen Murphy, *Fortas: The Rise and Ruin of a Supreme Court Justice* (William Morrow, 1988).

[207] President Nixon nominated Warren Burger in 1969 to replace Earl Warren, Harry Blackmun in 1970 to replace Abe Fortas, William Rehnquist in 1972 to replace John Marshall Harlan, and Lewis Powell on the same day in 1972 to replace Hugo Black.

[208] See above at nn 29–42.

[209] See above at n 44.

[210] While Justice Brennan, often joined by Justice Marshall and by one or two other Justices, consistently dissented from the constitutional backsliding, I wonder if they would have been as wedded to the body of 1960s precedent if they had been in a position to tweak it to their liking.

Court's membership did not remain stable. The newly appointed Justices viewed the already somewhat weakened argument for continuing to place racial justice and regional failure at the center of the Court's constitutional agenda through their own political and philosophical filters, and virtually zeroed out the search for racial justice and the fear of regional failure as significant tie-breaking factors in developing new constitutional doctrine. I do not suggest that the new Justices were unconcerned about racial justice; merely that their perception of the diminished intensity of the nation's racial crisis, factored through the new Justices' hierarchically ordered value systems, did not impel them in the direction of shaping constitutional doctrine with an eye to its effect on the civil rights struggle.

Given my value orientation, I think the new Justices gave up too soon on the primacy of achieving racial justice, and overvalued the willingness and ability of local institutions to deal effectively with racially charged issues. The Warren Court repeatedly treated the achievement of equality, principally racial equality, as its prime constitutional value. In the post-Warren era, Justice Brennan's dissents continued to do so, describing a constitutional world that might have been, not just for racial minorities, but for women and other historically subordinated groups—a world in which a benign local majority could actively help the minority to achieve real equality,[211] and where politically weak groups could appeal from hostile or unconcerned local majorities to a more responsive national majority.[212] My disagreement with many of the post-Warren Court decisions rejecting that world, often by narrow 5–4 majorities, does not spring from a belief that Justice Brennan was objectively correct, or that the post-Warren majority Justices were objectively wrong. While Justice Brennan continued to place equality—especially racial equality—at the top of the constitutional tree, the post-Warren Court majority increasingly turned toward autonomy as its prime constitutional value. Both approaches are defensible efforts at con-

---

[211] *Parents Involved in Community Schools v Seattle School District No. 1*, 551 US 701 (2007) (Breyer, J, dissenting); *Shaw v Reno*, 509 US 630, 658 (1993) (White, Blackmun, and Stevens, JJ, dissenting); id at 679 (Souter, J, dissenting); *Gratz v Bollinger*, 539 US 244 (2003); *Metro Broadcasting Co. v FCC*, 497 US 547 (1990), rev'd *Adarand Constructors, Inc. v Pena*, 514 US 200 (1995).

[212] *Morrison v United States*, 529 US 598, 628 (2000) (Souter, Stevens, Ginsburg, and Breyer, JJ, dissenting); *Bray v Alexandria Women's Health Clinic*, 506 US 263, 288 (1993) (Souter, J, dissenting in part); id at 307 (Stevens and Blackmun, JJ, dissenting); id at 345 (O'Connor, J, dissenting).

struing the Constitution. Indeed, over time, one would expect equality and autonomy, two of the leading candidates for prime constitutional value (procedural regularity being the third), to co-exist uneasily with each other. Who is to say for certain which one should trump the other at any given point in the nation's history? As many have noted, since plausible arguments that almost always exist on both sides of a hard constitutional case, insistence on so-called objectively correct answers rooted in textual literalism, or law-office history often do little more than mask a Justice's choice of a prime value. That is why I find shrill assertions that externally mandated, objectively correct "originalist" answers exist in the Constitution's text and history so unpersuasive—and so intellectually dishonest.[213] That is also why winning presidential elections is so important to the evolution of constitutional law.

III. So What?

If I am right that concerns over racial injustice and regional failure significantly influenced the Warren Court's constitutional decision making, at least three reactions are possible[214]—condemnation, praise, or the less elegant "so what." Some observers would undoubtedly condemn the Warren Court's willingness to shape constitutional doctrine in aid of racial justice as an unprincipled exercise in political jurisprudence.[215] Others would view the Court's race-conscious constitutional jurisprudence as judicial statesmanship of the highest order.[216] Most, I believe, would shrug their shoulders

---

[213] For a summary of the seemingly endless debate over originalism, see Steven G. Calabresi, ed, *Originalism: A Quarter Century of Debate* (Regnery, 2007). For a useful recent symposium on originalism, see http://www.harvard.jlpp.com?archive/#313.

[214] Another response, of course, is to reject my hypothesis about the gravitational pull of race as wrong, or, more charitably, unproven. I concede that I have not attempted to control for other variables that might explain changes in constitutional doctrine as the Court's personnel altered, like increases or decreases in legal acumen, changes in judicial philosophy, and shifts in political orientation. I have argued above that the altered political views and judicial philosophies of the new Justices merely provided the intellectual lens through which they measured whether racial injustice and regional breakdown continued to be important enough to outweigh other factors in forging constitutional doctrine. See text accompanying notes 212–15.

[215] Herbert Wechsler, *Toward Neutral Principles of Constitutional Law*, 73 Harv L Rev 1 (1959), is the classic critique. See also Philip Kurland, *Politics, the Constitution, and the Warren Court* (Chicago, 1973); Alexander Bickel, *The Original Understanding and the Segregation Decision*, 69 Harv L Rev 1 (1955); and Robert Bork, *The Tempting of America* (Free Press, 1973).

[216] Charles Black, *The Lawfulness of the Segregation Decision*, 69 Yale L J 421 (1960), is the classic defense. See also Charles Fairman, *The Supreme Court 1955 Term—Foreword:*

at what they would see as the inevitability of this process.[217] This is not the place to rehash either the lament over the decline of "neutral principles" in *Brown* or the defense of the Court's role in helping the nation to begin its redemption from racism. Nor is it the place to rehash the argument over whether the Constitution's text or history actually provide binding commands to the Justices in hard cases. Suffice it to say that, today, even the most committed formalists embrace constitutional doctrine requiring a pragmatic, fact-bound balancing of public need against private right. Whether one looks at the First Amendment's weighted balancing test,[218] the notions of "reasonableness" underlying the Fourth Amendment,[219] or the varying iterations of Equal Protection scrutiny,[220] today's judges are knee deep in factual assessments of the impact of constitutional doctrine on the real world.

Three comparatively recent events must have—and should have—had a significant influence on the Supreme Court's reading of the Constitution. The first was the Great Depression. It is now commonly accepted that constitutional doctrine evolved during the Depression in response to a crisis in which market failure appeared to cry out for federal regulation, in part because of problems of scale, in part because the states were trapped in a regulatory race to the bottom in pursuit of a shrinking pool of jobs and investment. The result was the evolution of constitutional doctrine from *Lochner,*[221] *Hammer v Dagenhart,*[222] and *Carter Coal*[223] to *Jones & Laughlin,*[224] *United States v Darby,*[225] and *Wickard v Filburn.*[226] At the same

---

The Attack on the Segregation Cases, 70 Harv L Rev 83 (1956); Louis H. Pollak, *Racial Discrimination and Judicial Integrity: A Reply to Professor Wechsler,* 108 U Pa L Rev 1 (1959); Edmund Cahn, *Jurisprudence,* 30 NYU L Rev 150 (1955).

[217] Richard Posner has made the classic case for the inevitability of pragmatic judicial reasoning. See Richard A. Posner, *Pragmatism and Democracy* (Harvard, 2003); Richard A. Posner, *How Judges Think* (Harvard, 2008).

[218] Compare *Dennis v United States,* 341 US 494 (1951), with *Brandenburg v Ohio,* 395 US 444 (1969). See *Citizens United v FEC,* 558 US 50 (2010).

[219] See, for example, *Terry v Ohio* 392 US 1 (1968).

[220] See, for example, *Korematsu v United States,* 323 US 214 (1944); *Shaw v Reno,* 509 US 630 (1993).

[221] *Lochner v New York,* 198 US 45 (1905).

[222] 247 US 251 (1918).

[223] 298 US 238 (1936).

[224] 301 US 1 (1937).

[225] 312 US 100 (1941).

[226] 317 US 111 (1942).

time, the old model of strict separation of powers gave way to a crisis-driven embrace of the administrative state.[227] Once the twin pressures of economic crisis and perceived state regulatory incapacity abated, constitutional doctrine began taking federalism, separation-of-powers, and regulatory immunity claims more seriously again.[228]

The second was World War II (WW II) and the Cold War, with the nation struggling, first, for military survival; and, then, for worldwide ascendancy during a half century of almost uninterrupted international conflict that demanded a strong national government and led many to argue for the subordination of individual rights. The result was cases like *Gobitis*,[229] *Korematsu*,[230] *Yakus*,[231] and *Dennis*.[232] It is fashionable today to feign astonishment that the Court could have gotten *Korematsu* so wrong, but that is because the gravitational pull that led Justice Black to write the *Korematsu* opinion, and Justice Douglas to join it, has long since disappeared.[233]

---

[227] Obvious examples are the judiciary's loss of fact-finding power in many settings (*Crowell v Benson*, 285 US 22 (1932)), and Congress's delegation of law-making power to administrative agencies. In the seventy-five years since *Schechter Poultry Corp. v United States*, 295 US 495 (1935), the Court has not invalidated a single Congressional delegation of power to an administrative agency.

[228] For example, *United States v Lopez*, 514 US 549 (1995); *United States v Morrison*, 529 US 598 (2000); *Youngstown Sheet & Tube Co. v Sawyer*, 343 US 579 (1952).

[229] *Minersville School Dist. v Gobitis*, 310 US 586 (1940) (upholding compulsory flag salute). *Gobitis* was overruled by *West Virginia Board of Education v Barnette*, 319 US 624 (1943), largely because recognition of a right not to salute the flag was a virtually costless way to draw a bright line between the nation's commitment to freedom and Nazi totalitarianism. *Barnette* is a magnificent case. It was also excellent propaganda.

[230] *Korematsu v United States*, 323 US 214 (1944) (upholding wartime internment of Japanese Americans).

[231] *Yakus v United States*, 321 US 414 (1944) (upholding denial of judicial review in wartime price stabilization case). See also *Bowles v Willingham*, 321 US 503 (1944). Remove the wartime context and you get cases like *United States v Mendoza-Lopez*, 481 US 828, 839 n 15 (1987), and *Adamo Wrecking Co. v United States*, 434 US 275 (1978).

[232] *Dennis v United States*, 341 US 494 (1951) (upholding imprisonment of leaders of American Communist party).

[233] Black and Douglas were the swing votes in *Korematsu*. Justices Roberts, Murphy, and Jackson dissented. Judge Posner has argued that *Korematsu* was rightly decided. Richard Posner, *Breaking the Deadlock: The 2000 Election, the Constitution, and the Courts* (Princeton, 2001). Judge Posner articulated the gravitational pull of the Cold War on First Amendment cases and the continuing viability of the gravitational pull theory: "[J]udges who in the 1950s believed that the nation was endangered by Communist advocacy of violent revolution did not think themselves compelled by the vague language of the First Amendment. . . . When the danger posed by subversive speech passes, the judges become stricter in their scrutiny of legislation punishing such speech. . . . But they are likely to change their tune when next the country feels endangered." Richard A. Posner, *Pragmatism versus Purposivism in First Amendment Analysis*, 54 Stan L Rev 737, 741 (2002).

The third was the moral crisis over race relations that gripped the nation in the aftermath of WW II. The result was *Brown* and many of the Warren Court's decisions discussed above.

Whether or not one agrees with the Supreme Court's reactions to these three crises, I find it impossible to imagine (much less be part of) a constitutional regime that claims to operate in splendid isolation from the existential crises that swirl about it. Bruce Ackerman has constructed a theory of implied constitutional amendment to explain and legitimate the Court's response to the Depression.[234] My colleagues Richard Pildes and Samuel Issacharoff have suggested the existence of an implied emergency switch in the Constitution, analogous to the explicit emergency clauses in many European constitutions that justify altered constitutional doctrine during a national security crisis.[235] Finally, David Strauss has persuasively argued that the Warren Court's approach to constitutional adjudication was driven by the same forces that cause the common law to evolve.[236]

My "gravitational pull" approach could be shoehorned into either Ackerman's idea of a "constitutional moment," or the Pildes/Issacharoff idea of implied emergency power. I prefer, however, to avoid formal claims that the Constitution itself changes in response to external events in favor of a weaker claim closer to David Strauss's that the Justices' reading of ambiguous constitutional provisions in hard cases will inevitably reflect pragmatic responses to perceived crises. For me, the harder issues raised by the Warren Court's response to racial injustice and regional failure are: (1) how to decide when circumstances or events are sufficiently critical to exert a legitimate gravitational influence on constitutional decision making, (2) how to decide when such a gravitational pull is no longer warranted, and (3) what to do with precedents that have emerged, at

---

[234] Bruce Ackerman, *The Living Constitution*, 120 Harv L Rev 1737 (2007). For the complete theory, see Bruce Ackerman, *We the People, Vol. 1: Foundations* (Belknap, 1993), and Bruce Ackerman, *We the People, Vol. II: Transformations* (Belknap, 2000).

[235] See Samuel Issacharoff and Richard Pildes, *Between Unilateralism and the Rule of Law: An Institutional Process Approach to Rights During Wartime*, 5 Theoret Inq in L 1 (2004); Samuel Issacharoff and Richard Pildes, *Emergency Contexts Without Emergency Powers*, 2 Intl J Const L 296 (2004). See also Richard A. Posner, *Not a Suicide Pact: The Constitution in Time of National Emergency* (Oxford, 2006).

[236] See David A. Strauss, *The Living Constitution* (Oxford, 2010); David A. Strauss, *Common Law Constitutional Interpretation*, 63 U Chi L Rev 877 (1996); David A. Strauss, *The Common Law Genius of the Warren Court*, 49 Wm & Mary L Rev 845 (2007). See also Larry D. Kramer, *Popular Constitutionalism, Circa 2004*, 92 Cal L Rev 959 (2004).

least in part, under the influence of a gravitational pull that has ebbed or ceased entirely.

I find the first two questions fascinating, but ultimately beyond the lawyer's craft. The question of when a national crisis achieves sufficient social mass to justify exerting a significant gravitational pull on constitutional doctrine cannot be reduced to a legal formula. It depends on the perceptions of the Justices and the ethos of the community. Racial discrimination in the 1930s was just as important to the nation and just as morally reprehensible as it was in the 1950s, but it took the psychological impact of a costly war against Nazi racism,[237] a major internal and external threat from the Soviet Union, and the growth of a great national political movement for the concepts of racial injustice and regional failure to coalesce to the point where a national crisis over race exercised a sustained gravitational pull on constitutional doctrine. Most national issues, even when passionately felt and argued, are comparative tempests in teapots, unlikely to generate the sustained public passion and judicial concern that are needed to fuel a significant impact on judge-made constitutional doctrine.[238]

The closely related question of whether (and when) a crisis has ebbed sufficiently to lose its power to influence constitutional doctrine is also incapable of formal legal measurement. I believe passionately that many Justices turned away from the pursuit of racial justice too soon. But the choice between "benign neglect" and affirmative action was, at bottom, fundamentally political. For good or ill (and for many reasons), American society lost its intense focus on racial injustice and its intense mistrust of regional southern justice. Once that happened, the gravitational pull of the quest for racial justice on constitutional doctrine inevitably ebbed in ways that left lawyers like me largely out of the equation.

---

[237] The losses suffered by ordinary Americans in the struggle to defeat Hitler and Imperial Japan were very substantial. The United States suffered 131,000 battle deaths, and an additional 400,000 war-related deaths, to say nothing of the maiming and pain of more than 500,000 battle wounds. See Michael Clodfelter, *Warfare and Armed Conflicts: A Statistical Reference to Casualty and Other Figures, 1500–2000* (McFarland, 2002). A people will seek to give meaning to losses of such magnitude by infusing the struggle with moral teaching that shapes the post-loss society—at least for a while. Witness the post–Civil War fervor that resulted in the Thirteenth, Fourteenth, and Fifteenth Amendments, and the post–Great War idealism that gave rise to the League of Nations.

[238] See generally Barry Friedman, *The Will of the People: How Public Opinion Has Influenced the Supreme Court and Shaped the Meaning of the Constitution* (Farrar, Straus and Giroux, 2009).

But that raises a closely related question—should a Justice acknowledge the influence of a crisis on the decisional process? In those settings where a crisis operates under a Justice's conscious radar, it is meaningless to talk of acknowledgment. There is nothing to acknowledge. In many cases, though, I think that the Warren Court knew exactly what it was doing. The Justices' opinions—especially the factual recitations—occasionally signal to an attentive reader that race and the fear of regional failure are playing roles in the Justices' reasoning.[239] Sometimes, though, the Justices' opinions are completely silent about the racial context of a case, even when the briefs must have made the racial implications clear.[240] Most importantly, almost never does a Justice openly acknowledge that concerns about an opinion's impact on race or regional failure are playing a role in the case's outcome.[241] In retrospect, I believe that the Warren Court's jurisprudence in many areas would have been more convincing and less controversial if the Court had acknowledged a crisis-bound necessity for reading the Constitution to avoid regional breakdown in the struggle for racial justice. During the Depression, the Court explained why it was impossible to retain the old federalism and separation-of-powers models. Candor over the impact of wartime crisis on judicial thinking is the only good thing I can say about *Korematsu*. A little of that candor would have strengthened the Warren Court. Justices who claim the power to construe a "living Constitution" should explain why their Constitution has adopted a particular lifestyle.

The third question—how to deal with constitutional precedent that appears to have been influenced by some event or crisis once the gravitational pull has ebbed—is, however, largely a lawyers' issue. Post-Warren Court decisions in at least five areas—freedom of speech, freedom from religion, federalism, separation of powers, and criminal law and procedure—may shed some light on the issue. While Warren Court free speech doctrine has prospered, going on

---

[239] See, for example, *United States v Price*, 383 US 745 (1966); *United States v Guest*, 383 US 787 (1966).

[240] See, for example, *Thompson v City of Louisville*, 363 US 199 (1960); *Monroe v Pape*, 365 US 167 (1961).

[241] I suspect it is because they were bluffed away from the table by Herbert Wechsler and friends. It is the same self-protective but ultimately hypocritical behavior that has led all Supreme Court nominees since Robert Bork to engage in the charade of the modern Senate confirmation hearing, where the nominees fervently promise to apply the law, but duck questions about how they will determine what the law is in hard cases.

to protect commercial advertisers,[242] flag burners,[243] hate speech,[244] and corporations intent on spending unlimited sums to affect the outcome of elections,[245] the Warren Court's constitutional law of federalism was largely abandoned once the gravitational pull of race was removed from the judicial equation.[246] Establishment Clause doctrine has also seen a marked decrease in the intensity of constitutional protection.[247] Finally, the post-Warren Court years have seen a significant relaxation of the exclusionary rule[248] and *Miranda*,[249] but have also experienced a powerful reaffirmation of the Warren Court's due process, jury trial, right to counsel, and error-deflection norms.[250]

My tentative explanation for the staying power of the free speech and criminal law and procedure precedents and the relative erosion of the Establishment Clause, exclusionary rule, and federalism precedents turns on the nature of the original decisions. I acknowledge, however, a substantial bias in attempting to find a principled explanation for the changes in doctrine other than exclusive reliance on the political preferences of a new Supreme Court majority. While I do not subscribe to the myth that constitutional adjudication is a value-free application of objective commands rooted in text, history, and precedent,[251] I believe that constitutional adjudication in a system genuinely committed to the rule of law cannot simply be a matter of raw judicial preference. Constitutional adjudication in hard cases is an untidy mix of choice and constraint. One of the principal constraints is respect for precedent. Where, however, the most plausible explanation for a Warren Court precedent is an instrumental response to the crisis of race and regional failure, I

---

[242] *Virginia Pharmacy Board v Virginia Citizens Consumer Council*, 425 US 748 (1976).

[243] *Texas v Johnson*, 491 US 397 (1989).

[244] *R.A.V. v City of St. Paul*, 505 US 377 (1992).

[245] *Citizens United v FEC*, 558 US 50 (2010).

[246] See text accompanying notes 184–97.

[247] See text accompanying notes 207–10.

[248] See note 210.

[249] Id.

[250] For example, *Blakely v Washington*, 542 US 296 (2004); *United States v Booker*, 543 US 220 (2005).

[251] A generation of bitterly contested 5–4 decisions disagreeing over which "correct" objective norm to apply in a hard constitutional case has rendered the idea that only one objectively correct norm exists in hard cases transparently false to all but the ideologically deaf and blind.

would neither expect nor wish the precedent to outlive the crisis. Don't get me wrong. I do not suggest that the Warren Court's race-driven decisions were wrong. They were necessary to deal with a genuine breakdown in the rule of law. I do suggest, though, that several were crisis-driven and crisis-bound. Where, however, the Warren Court's intense concern over racial justice and regional failure operated as a magnifying glass,[252] sharpening the Justices' perception of the necessity for principled constitutional protection against government overreaching, the decisions deserve, and have received, respect long after the crisis about race and regional failure that gave them life has subsided.

In the free speech, criminal law, and due process cases, the Justices' concern over race and regional failure often acted as just such a magnifying glass, assisting the Court in recognizing the extent to which government behavior was deviating in important ways from the purpose of a given constitutional provision. In cases like *Times v Sullivan*,[253] *In re Winship*,[254] *Goldberg v Kelly*,[255] *Gideon v Wainwright*,[256] and *Papachristou v Jacksonville*,[257] the Warren Court rooted its race-sensitive decisions in principled and persuasive intellectual models that reflected the underlying purpose of the relevant constitutional text. As a consequence, those opinions have had staying power long after the Court's concern over racial injustice has—rightly or wrongly—passed into history. On the other hand, several federalism and Establishment Clause decisions that appear to have been almost wholly instrumental have lacked sustained staying power once the gravitational pull of race diminished.[258]

For example, *Times v Sullivan*[259] almost certainly was influenced in the short term by a desire to protect the civil rights movement in the South, but was rooted in a free marketplace of ideas model of the First Amendment that, while contestable, resonated with our constitutional traditions and advanced the First Amendment's basic

---

[252] I am grateful to Geoff Stone for the metaphor.

[253] 376 US 254 (1964).

[254] 397 US 358 (1970).

[255] 397 US 254 (1970).

[256] 372 US 335 (1963).

[257] 405 US 156 (1972).

[258] As I have noted, I believe that the Court turned away from the gravitational pull of racial equality much too soon.

[259] 376 US 254 (1964).

purpose. Not surprisingly, long after the short-term need to protect the civil rights movement had passed, *Times v Sullivan* continues to serve as an animating precedent driving First Amendment doctrine toward a free market in ideas.[260] It does not hurt that protection of free speech fits so neatly into the post-Warren Court's embrace of autonomy as its prime constitutional value.

Similarly, long after Rule 23(b)(2) solved the short-term dilemma that precipitated *Cooper v Aaron*,[261] the opinion's wise and pragmatic recognition that a stable theory of separation of powers requires respect for the Supreme Court's reading of the Constitution by state and federal officials continues to dominate the field, especially if you ask the Supreme Court.

Many of the Warren Court's criminal procedure decisions also tapped into a powerful intellectual model embedded in the Constitution. Warren Court opinions (1) assuring indigent defendants a right to appointed counsel in criminal prosecutions,[262] (2) requiring the government to prove guilt beyond a reasonable doubt in a criminal case,[263] (3) preserving a fair and representative jury,[264] (4) assuring a fair hearing before adverse government action,[265] and (5) preventing wholly discretionary arrests and investigatory stops[266] have transcended the crisis over race and regional failure that may have influenced the decisions.

On the other hand, it is very difficult to square certain of the Warren Court's federalism cases with any coherent theory of federalism. They were purely instrumental responses to a crisis about

---

[260] Ironically, while the case's marketplace-of-ideas model has powered First Amendment jurisprudence for almost fifty years, in the absence of the gravitational pull of race, Justice Brennan could not persuade the post-Warren Court to take the opinion to its logical conclusion of protecting speech on public issues. *Gertz v Robert Welch, Inc.*, 418 US 323 (1974). On the other hand, the core holding has survived and prospered. See *Philadelphia Newspapers v Hepps*, 475 US 767 (1986) (plaintiff must bear burden of proving malice); *Anderson v Liberty Lobby, Inc.*, 477 US 242 (1986) (clear and convincing standard applicable at summary judgment stage); *Bose Corp. v Consumers Union*, 466 US 485 (1984) (de novo appellate review of whether malice proved with sufficient clarity).

[261] 358 US 1 (1958).

[262] *Gideon v Wainwright*, 372 US 335 (1963); *Argersinger v Hamlin*, 407 US 25 (1972). See also *Klopfer v North Carolina*, 386 US 213 (1967) (speedy, public trial); *Pointer v Texas*, 380 US 400 (1965) (confrontation); *Washington v Texas*, 388 US 14 (1967) (compulsory process).

[263] *In re Winship*, 397 US 358 (1970).

[264] *Duncan v Louisiana*, 391 US 145 (1968).

[265] *Goldberg v Kelly*, 397 US 254 (1970).

[266] *Papachristou v Jacksonville*, 405 US 156 (1972); *Terry v Ohio*, 392 US 1 (1968).

race and regional failure; rightly decided for their time, but time- and crisis-bound. Once states appeared ready to shoulder the burden of race, the post-Warren Court quickly gave them back many of their traditional powers.[267] Similarly, once the Establishment Clause was no longer seen as necessary to protect *Brown*, it was only a matter of time before *Flast*, which was largely instrumental, was put into play. Finally, as police forces integrated and state judiciaries turned over generationally, the crisis-driven prophylactic norms announced in *Mapp* and *Miranda* evolved. *Mapp* and *Miranda* operate on two levels. As dramatic prophylactic responses to an institutional breakdown in the relationship between local police forces and black citizens, both cases are rooted in a time and place.[268] Both opinions were, however, also rooted in a deeply principled constitutional understanding of the relationship between the state and the individual, an understanding that forbids the state from benefiting from its own wrongdoing. That important constitutional principle fuels the enduring staying power of both cases and explains why, once the gravitational pull of race ebbed, both cases have evolved toward requiring blameworthy conduct by a government official.

IV. Conclusion

I have tried to tell a story of the evolution of race-driven constitutional doctrine during and after the Warren Court in three stages: (1) a fully warranted response to a national crisis about race and regional failure, (2) the time-bound nature of those primarily instrumental decisions seeking to deal with the crisis, and (3) the staying power of constitutionally principled responses. While my story is a far cry from contemporary fantasies of objective commands unambiguously embedded in the constitutional text and history, or overarching theories of constitutional meaning, it reflects my day-to-day experiences as a foot soldier in the constitutional trenches for forty-six years and more than 500 constitutional cases. Of course, my trench-bound perspective may have blinded me to the grand designs of the general staff. But maybe there is no general staff,

---

[267] See text accompanying notes 184–212.

[268] I believe that the Court has seriously underestimated the continuing need for prophylaxis in dealing with police interactions with racial minorities, but that's just me arguing for the continued gravitational pull of race.

and no grand designs. Maybe, just maybe, all there is are lawyers and judges plying their craft, trying to do justice as they see it in an imperfect world.

RICHARD H. PILDES

IS THE SUPREME COURT A "MAJORITARIAN" INSTITUTION?

The birth of *The Supreme Court Review* fifty years ago was accompanied by the publication of two classic, enduring works of scholarship on the relationship of the Supreme Court to the political branches of government and American democracy more broadly. These two works, from within different disciplines, stood in some tension with each other, though neither confronted that tension directly.

On one side, Alexander Bickel in 1962 memorably posed a fundamental moral question concerning the role of the Supreme Court in American democracy: the "countermajoritarian difficulty."[1] Why should a small, nonelected group of nine individuals (a bare majority of five of whom is enough) have the power to decide some of the most profound moral issues for a country of now 308 million people, and to do so in a way that all other actors in the national and state governments have no direct power to override?[2] This moral challenge to judicial review, present in all constitutional democracies in which courts have the final power to decide the meaning of fun-

Richard H. Pildes is Sudler Family Professor of Constitutional Law, NYU Law School.

AUTHOR'S NOTE: I thank Rachel Barkow, Adam Samaha, David Golove, Nate Persily, Rick Hills, Trevor Morrison, and Barry Friedman for many fruitful discussions. For research assistance, I thank Alex Mindlin.

[1] Alexander M. Bickel, *The Least Dangerous Branch* 16–23 (Yale, 1962).

[2] The most powerful moral case against the institution of judicial review in a democracy has been made by my colleague, Jeremy Waldron, in works such as *Law and Disagreement* (Clarendon, 1999).

© 2011 by The University of Chicago. All rights reserved.
978-0-226-36326-4/2011/2010-0004$10.00

damental law, is particularly acute in the United States, because the moral force of the ideas of popular sovereignty and self-government have nowhere been as powerful as in the United States. That American constitutional scholarship since Bickel has been uniquely dominated, compared to that in other countries, by the struggle to rationalize judicial review with democracy is thus no surprise. Indeed, it is not wrong to characterize American legal thought as "obsessed" with the moral problem of judicial review.[3]

On the other side, the empirically minded political scientist Robert Dahl, writing in 1957 a few years before Bickel, concluded that the Supreme Court had not functioned historically as a countermajoritarian institution and, for structural reasons, was unlikely to do so.[4] Dahl argued that "the policy views dominant on the Court are never for long out of line with the policy views dominant among the lawmaking majorities of the United States."[5] In Dahl's analysis, the Court was "inevitably a part of the dominant national [lawmaking] alliance,"[6] because "it would appear, on political grounds, somewhat unrealistic to suppose that a Court whose members are recruited in the fashion of Supreme Court Justices would long hold to norms of Right or Justice substantially at odds with the rest of the political elite."[7] Thus, Dahl's social-scientific study of the Court's decisions suggested that Bickel's concern was misplaced, for as a matter of political realism, the Court had not functioned, and could not function, in the countermajoritarian way that troubled Bickel.

For several decades, Bickel's and Dahl's warring perspectives remained largely cabined within their own respective disciplines. Legal scholars continued to develop normative constitutional theories designed to justify judicial review or specific methods of constitutional interpretation that would accommodate judicial review with democracy in morally acceptable ways. Meanwhile, political scientists continued to test Dahl's original claims, to explore more

---

[3] See, for example, Mark A. Graber, *The Countermajoritarian Difficulty: From Courts to Congress to Constitutional Order*, 4 Ann Rev L & Soc Sci 361, 380 (2008); Barry Friedman, *The Birth of an Academic Obsession: The History of the Countermajoritarian Difficulty, Part Five*, 112 Yale L J 153 (2002).

[4] Robert A. Dahl, *Decision-Making in a Democracy: The Supreme Court as a National Policy-Maker*, 6 J Pub L 279 (1957).

[5] Id at 285.

[6] Id at 293.

[7] Id at 291.

broadly the extent to which the Court's decisions were effective in practice, and to examine the empirical relationship between the Court, public opinion, and the political branches. But in recent years, these two bodies of literature have finally come into more direct conversation and collision. A number of legal scholars and commentators on the Court have rediscovered Dahl's insight and run with it. Engaging directly with Bickel, as Dahl did not, they have sought to dissolve Bickel's question or suggest it is naive and passé. Building on Dahl's purportedly realist conclusions, they argue that there is, as a matter of history and fact, simply no counter-majoritarian difficulty about which to worry. The Supreme Court cannot and does not stray too far from "majoritarian views" (we will soon explore more precisely this concept of "majoritarian views"). If the Court does, larger political forces bring the Court back into line; the Justices, knowing this, do not wander far. As Dahl did, this more recent literature seeks to turn Bickel's premise on its head: far from being a countermajoritarian institution, the Supreme Court primarily functions to enforce and enshrine majoritarian views. For better or worse, the Court does not and cannot protect political minorities, be they the "discrete and insular minorities" of liberal jurisprudential fame, or any other kind of minority. Instead, Court decisions will reflect the preferences and views of what some scholars in this camp call the "national governing coalition." This conception of a Court strongly constrained by political and/or popular majorities I will call the "majoritarian thesis" of judicial review.

Last Term's decision in *Citizens United*, in which a 5–4 Court concluded that corporations (and unions) have a First Amendment right to spend unlimited amounts of money to seek to influence the outcome of national, state, and local elections—and overruled two precedents to do so—provides an apt occasion for assessing this debate between Bickel and his modern challengers.[8] Judged in any number of ways, *Citizens United* appears to be the most countermajoritarian act of the Court in many decades. Indeed, *Citizens United* is perhaps the most visible such act on an issue of high public salience since the Court's brief encounter with the symbolic issue

---

[8] This money must involve "independent expenditures," which cannot be coordinated with a candidate or the candidate's campaign. Coordinated expenditures remain subject to various caps. See *Citizens United v Federal Election Commission*, 130 S Ct 876, 910 (2010).

of flag burning in the late 1980s[9] or the Court's more substantive engagement with the death penalty in its decisions of the 1970s.[10]

Citizens United thus prompts many questions about the majoritarian thesis and the limits on the Court's power. What exactly does the new, majoritarian thesis claim about the constraints on the power of the Court? How powerful a normative response to the "countermajoritarian difficulty" does this new thesis turn out to be? And even if the majoritarian thesis describes much of Supreme Court history in the past, are there reasons to think this past will not be prologue—that the Court of our era might be less constrained in these ways than prior Courts might have been? What, then, is the empirical and moral relationship between the Supreme Court and constitutional law, on the one hand, and political and popular constraints on the Court, on the other?

I. The Citizens United Decision

Like many landmark cases, *Citizens United* arose as a result of bureaucratic tunnel vision. Citizens United (CU) was a small nonprofit corporation with an annual budget of around $12 million; most of its funding came from individuals and a small amount from for-profit corporations.[11] In the period leading up to the 2008 presidential primary process, CU wanted to make available through video-on-demand (VOD) broadcast a ninety-minute documentary film called *Hillary: The Movie.* The movie mentioned Hillary Clinton by name and contained relentlessly negative commentary on her from political commentators and others. For a payment from CU of $1.2 million, a VOD cable channel, "Elections '08," offered to make *Hillary* freely available to viewers who chose to access the movie.

But the Bipartisan Campaign Reform Act of 2002 (BCRA), col-

---

[9] The Court in a controversial 5–4 decision, *Texas v Johnson,* 491 US 397 (1989), initially overturned on First Amendment grounds a criminal prosecution under state law for flag desecration. Congress responded by passing the Flag Protection Act of 1989, which was designed to protect the flag against various acts of desecration. In *United States v Eichman,* 486 US 310 (1990), a 5–4 Court again invalidated on First Amendment grounds a criminal prosecution, this time under the federal statute, for flag desecration.

[10] See *Furman v Georgia,* 408 US 238 (1972). Using popular opinion as the baseline, the Court's most "countermajoritarian" decision upholding legislation, if that is a coherent concept, is surely *Kelo v City of New London,* 545 US 469 (2005). See Nathaniel Persily, Jack Citrin, and Patrick J. Egan, eds, *Public Opinion and Constitutional Controversy* 286–309 (Oxford, 2008).

[11] 130 S Ct at 887.

loquially known as the McCain-Feingold Act, arguably covered the VOD broadcast of *Hillary*. BCRA made it illegal, with civil and criminal sanctions, for corporations and unions to use general treasury funds to finance "electioneering communications."[12] The act's primary definition of electioneering communication was "any broadcast, cable, or satellite communication" that "refers to a clearly identified candidate for Federal office" and that was "made within 30 days of a primary or 60 days of a general election."[13] Regulations of the Federal Election Commission (FEC) elaborated that an electioneering communication was a communication that was "publicly distributed," which was further defined to mean, in the case of a candidate for nomination as President, that the communication "[c]an be received by 50,000 or more persons in a State where a primary election is being held."[14] While direct treasury corporate or union funding for such broadcast ads was banned, corporations (and unions) could establish a "separate segregated fund," or political action committee (PAC), to fund such ads.[15] Money could be contributed to a PAC of this sort only from stockholders or employees of the corporation, or, for unions, from union members.

Because CU was partly corporate funded and wanted to make *Hillary* available through VOD within thirty days of a primary election, CU feared, correctly as it turned out, that the FEC would treat the movie's broadcast as a prohibited corporate electioneering communication. In December 2007, CU therefore brought a declaratory and injunctive action against the FEC, in which CU sought to have the relevant provisions of BCRA held unconstitutional as applied to *Hillary*.

At that point, the FEC could have invoked any of several reasons for concluding that, although the VOD movie might fall literally within the terms of BCRA, the FEC would not construe the act to reach the movie. Most importantly, the FEC could have concluded that the entire focus of Congress in 2002 was on broadcast ads on conventional television, in which election ads bombard a captive audience. That audience has chosen a channel or program for its content, not for the election ads with which it gets bombarded during the height of a competitive race. With VOD, by contrast,

---

[12] 2 USC § 441b (2002).

[13] 2 USC § 434(f)(3)(A) (2002).

[14] 11 CFR § 100.29(a)(2) and § 100.29(b) (2009).

[15] 2 USC § 441b(b)(2) (2002).

viewers have to choose to receive the exact communication at is-sue—in this case, a ninety-minute movie. Viewers who choose to watch a movie like this presumably want to receive the message it conveys, and they can turn the movie off any time otherwise.

This distinction, arguably, is critical to the only purpose that lay behind the ban on corporate electioneering and the only purpose that could, constitutionally, justify that ban: preventing corruption or the appearance of corruption of public officials. The theory be-hind § 441b was that captive viewers flooded with corporate-funded broadcast ads on conventional television might be influenced by ads they were forced to see, and officeholders might thus feel be-holden to these funders. But when viewers are a willing audience, as with VOD, they already want to receive the message because of its content or, at least, are more predisposed to accept the message. Information that viewers must choose to receive is therefore less likely to be influential; officeholders are therefore less likely to be beholden to the funding entities. At a minimum, the FEC could have concluded that, in light of the serious constitutional and policy questions new technologies like VOD presented, the term "elec-tioneering communication" should be construed and enforced so as not to reach these technologies until Congress affirmatively ad-dressed them.[16]

But the FEC would have none of that. A legally sophisticated FEC might have recognized that it was operating in a radically changed constitutional environment in which the Court was deeply skeptical, if not outright hostile, to BCRA's regulation of election-eering spending. Nearly two years before CU filed its complaint against the FEC, the Court had dramatically signaled its discomfort with BCRA in *Federal Election Comm'n v Wisconsin Right to Life*

---

[16] In addition, the FEC could have invoked earlier Supreme Court decisions to conclude that § 501(c)(4) nonprofits that accept only a de minimis amount of money from for-profit corporations, as was allegedly the case for CU, were exempt from BCRA's ban on corporate electioneering. In *FEC v Massachusetts Citizens for Life, Inc.*, 479 US 238 (1986), the Court had held unconstitutional § 441b's restrictions on corporate expenditures as applied to nonprofit corporations that did not engage in business activities, were formed for the sole purpose of promoting political ideas, and did not accept contributions from for-profit corporations or labor unions. Finally, the FEC regulations that require that a commu-nication "[c]an be received by 50,000 or more persons" could have been read to require "a plausible likelihood that the communication will be viewed by 50,000 or more potential voters," rather than being understood to require only that the communication be tech-nologically capable of reaching that many viewers. In the Supreme Court, this suggestion was made in an amicus curiae brief that former officials of the American Civil Liberties Union filed. 130 S Ct at 889.

(*WRTL*).[17] Although a 5–4 Court in the *McConnell*[18] case in 2003 had upheld BCRA's ban on corporate-funded electioneering communications shortly after BCRA was enacted, by the time of *WRTL* in 2007, Justice Alito had replaced Justice O'Connor, one of the authors of *McConnell*. *WRTL* then dramatically cut back on *McConnell*'s holding by concluding that *McConnell* had only addressed a facial challenge to BCRA, that as-applied challenges remained open, and that BCRA's ban on corporate-funded electioneering communications was only valid as applied to ads that involved "express advocacy [of the election or defeat of a specific candidate] or its functional equivalent."[19] Seven Justices—including all those on the Court in *McConnell*—asserted that *WRTL* had effectively overruled *McConnell*'s holding on electioneering communications.[20] Moreover, Justice Alito went out of his way to signal his openness to reconsidering *McConnell*.[21]

In the face of all this, the FEC nonetheless went ahead and took the litigation position that it would apply the full, literal force of BCRA to the facts of *Citizens United*. By the time the case reached a second round of argument in the Supreme Court, the new Solicitor General, Elena Kagan, desperately offered the Court several ways to avoid reaching the merits of the constitutional challenge.[22] But by then it was too late. The FEC had either taken the bait of a litigation strategy CU had cunningly designed or been obtuse about how the FEC's enforcement position on these facts would come across to an already skeptical Court.

The Court concluded, by a 5–4 vote with Justice Alito in the majority, that independent expenditures on election advertising and communication are fully protected by the First Amendment, including when undertaken through general-treasury corporate

---

[17] 551 US 449 (2007).

[18] *McConnell v Federal Election Commission*, 540 US 93 (2003).

[19] *WRTL*, 551 US at 481.

[20] See, for example, id at 499 n 7 (Scalia, J, dissenting) ("This faux judicial restraint [of distinguishing *McConnell*, rather than overruling it] is judicial obfuscation."); id at 525 (Souter, J, dissenting) (concluding that *WRTL* overruled *McConnell*).

[21] Id at 482.

[22] See Supplemental Brief for the Appellee, *Citizens United v FEC*, No 08-205, *2–5 (US S Ct, filed July 4, 2009) (available on Westlaw at 2009 WL 2219300) (arguing that *Citizens United* is "a particularly unsuitable vehicle" for reexamination of *Austin* and *McConnell*); Transcript of Oral Argument, *Citizens United v FEC*, No 08-205 (US S Ct, Sept 9, 2009) (available on Westlaw at 2009 WL 6325467).

funds.[23] The Court also concluded that insufficient justification exists for overcoming this First Amendment protection because independent expenditures, by corporations and others, do not and cannot create the reality or appearance of quid pro quo corruption of officeholders.[24] Corruption, understood in these terms, is the exchange of campaign spending for political favors, such as the enactment of rent-seeking legislation officeholders would not support but for this spending. *McConnell* had invoked a broader conception of political corruption, which included preferred access to policymakers that large campaign spending might secure. In the critical conceptual shift, Justice Kennedy, reviving his own dissenting opinion in *McConnell* but now writing for the majority, expressly rejected the view that differential access, or other forms of differential influence, was a kind of corruption at all.[25] As a result, the Court held that the First Amendment prohibited Congress from banning independent spending on election broadcast ads, including ads involving express advocacy of the election or defeat of candidates that ran close to election day, whether those ads were financed by domestic corporate (or, by implication, union) general-treasury funds or any other domestic source.[26] To reach that conclusion, the Court was required to overrule not just *McConnell*, but also *Austin v Michigan Chamber of Commerce*, a 1990 decision that had upheld a state ban on general-treasury corporate independent expenditures in connection with state elections.[27] Having struck down the ban

---

[23] For my view of the doctrinal questions the case raises, see Frederick Schauer and Richard H. Pildes, *Electoral Exceptionalism and the First Amendment*, 77 Tex L Rev 1803 (1999), and Richard H. Pildes, *Foreword—The Constitutionalization of Democratic Politics*, 118 Harv L Rev 29, 130–53 (2004).

[24] 130 S Ct at 910 ("This confirms *Buckley*'s reasoning that independent expenditures do not lead to, or create the appearance of, *quid pro quo* corruption.").

[25] Justice Kennedy first stated: "The fact that speakers may have influence over or access to elected officials does not mean that these officials are corrupt." 130 S Ct at 910. He then went on to quote from his earlier dissent: "Favoritism and influence are not . . . avoidable in representative politics. It is in the nature of an elected representative to favor certain policies, and, by necessary corollary, to favor the voters and contributors who support those policies. It is well understood that a substantial and legitimate reason, if not the only reason, to cast a vote for, or to make a contribution to, one candidate over another is that the candidate will respond by producing those political outcomes the supporter favors. Democracy is premised on responsiveness." Id (quoting *McConnell*, 540 US at 297 (opinion of Kennedy, J)).

[26] The Court left open the question of foreign spending on election ads. 130 S Ct at 911.

[27] 494 US 652 (1990). The state statute at issue permitted corporate independent expenditures on elections from segregated funds, akin to PACs, to which the corporation

on corporate electioneering, *Citizens United* did go on to uphold BCRA's disclaimer and disclosure provisions, including as applied to *Hillary: The Movie*.[28] And with that, the five-year-old Roberts Court issued by far its most controversial decision.

II. Response to the Decision

Citizens United spawned an immediate torrent of academic and more popular reactions and commentary, surely as much as any Supreme Court decision since *Bush v Gore*. BCRA had been enacted with significant bipartisan support; it passed the House 240–189, the Senate 60–40, and was signed into law by President George W. Bush. Few Court decisions immediately become such pervasive and central features of popular culture and debate, as well as electoral politics, as did *Citizens United*. The public is typically less aware of Court decisions than constitutional scholars assume or would like to believe,[29] but not so with *Citizens United*. Not only did President Obama directly attack *Citizens United* in front of members of the Court during his State of the Union address,[30] but the Democratic Party suggested the decision was turning the 2010 midterm elections in the Republicans' favor.[31] During this first election cycle after the decision, newspapers were filled with almost daily stories suggesting (often, in my view, without an adequate basis in fact) that *Citizens United* had dramatically reshaped the world of election financing and campaigns.[32] Though public opinion polls are no-

could solicit specific contributions from an enumerated list of persons associated with the corporation, such as stockholders, officers, directors, and certain employees. Id at 656.

[28] 130 S Ct at 913–16. The disclaimer provisions require all electioneering communications, among other items, to include a statement that "___ is responsible for the content of this advertisement." The disclosure provisions require any person or entity that spends more than $10,000 in a calendar year on such communications to file forms with the FEC identifying the actor making the expenditure, the election to which the communication is directed, and the names of certain contributors.

[29] See David Adamany and Joel B. Grossman, *Support for the Supreme Court as a National Policymaker*, 5 Law & Policy Q 405, 407 (1983).

[30] President Barack H. Obama, *Remarks by the President in the State of the Union Address*, online at http://www.whitehouse.gov/the-press-office/remarks-president-state-union-address.

[31] Perhaps the most concise expression of this view was the comment of House Speaker Nancy Pelosi, introducing President Barack Obama at a fundraiser, who commented about the 2010 election: "Everything was going great and all of a sudden secret money from God knows where—because they won't disclose it—is pouring in." David Brooks, *No Second Thoughts*, NY Times A29 (Oct 26, 2010).

[32] See, for example, David G. Savage, *Corporate Campaign Spending Still Murky*, LA Times A1 (Oct 27, 2010).

toriously suspect as a gauge of popular views, 80 percent of Americans reportedly oppose the Court's decision, with a strikingly high percentage, 65 percent, reporting that they "strongly oppose" it.[33] To the extent that these numbers are meaningful, *Citizens United* provoked more widespread popular resistance than *Bush v Gore*, to which popular reactions divided more along partisan lines.[34]

In addition, within months of the decision, Congress reacted. The "Disclose Act" would have required organizations financing independent electioneering communications to disclose the source of their largest donors and to reveal their identities in ads.[35] The act passed the House but has succumbed thus far to Republican filibusters in the Senate. Outside Congress, academics and others immediately began generating proposals that the rules of corporate governance be changed in response to *Citizens United*, so that shareholders, for example, be required to approve the amounts and targets of corporate spending on elections and that independent directors be required to oversee this spending.[36]

Fear of the practical consequences of the Court's decision is generated by the amounts of money available, in theory, for corporate general-treasury spending.[37] The fear is that this money will over-

[33] See Gary Langer, *In Supreme Court Ruling on Campaign Finance, The Public Dissents*, online at http://blogs.abcnews.com/thenumbers/2010/02/in-supreme-court-ruling-on-campaign-finance-the-public-dissents.html. See also David Savage, *Most Agree with High Court; Since the Justices' Tilt to the Right, Rulings Appear Largely in Sync with Public Opinion*, LA Times A26 (Oct 17, 2010) (reporting on results of Constitutional Attitudes Survey showing that decision was "very out of step with public opinion" and that 85 percent of those surveyed support requirement of shareholder approval for corporate political electioneering spending).

[34] See Jeffrey Rosen, *A Majority of One*, NY Times Magazine 32 (June 3, 2001) (noting that, after *Bush v Gore*, "[a]mong Republicans, approval of the court between August and January jumped from 60 percent to 80 percent, but among Democrats, it fell from 70 percent to 42 percent.").

[35] See HR 5175, 111th Cong, 2d Sess (Apr 29, 2010), in 156 Cong Rec H4795–4828 (June 24, 2010); S 3295, 11th Cong, 2d Sess (Apr 30, 2010), in 156 Cong Rec S3029–3032 (May 3, 2010).

[36] For one of the leading versions of this proposal, see Lucian A. Bebchuk and Robert J. Jackson, Jr., *Corporate Political Speech: Who Decides*, 124 Harv L Rev 83 (2010).

[37] The Court's decision also had further immediate legal and regulatory consequences. In response to *Citizens United*, an en banc D.C. Circuit held unconstitutional other federal provisions that limited individual contributions made to political action committees (PACs) to $5,000, as applied to PACs that only engage in independent election spending. *SpeechNow.org v FEC*, 599 F3d 686 (DC Cir, 2010) (en banc). The D.C. Circuit rejected the FEC's narrower interpretation of *Citizens United*. In later regulatory rulings, the FEC then concluded that these PACs could also accept unlimited corporate as well as individual contributions. Federal Election Commission, Advisory Opinion 2010–11 (July 22, 2010) (concluding that the "Commonsense Ten" PAC may accept unlimited contributions for

whelm all other sources of election financing, making officeholders, in turn, beholden to corporate interests. The two largest energy companies, Exxon Mobil and Chevron, made more than $120 billion in profits in the last election cycle.[38] If an Exxon CEO decided to commit one week of profits to spending on elections, he would have over $800 million to spend (in the pre-*Citizens United* world in 2008, Exxon's PAC raised only $950,000 in voluntary contributions). The four biggest high-tech companies, Google, Microsoft, Apple, and Intel, have more than $100 billion in cash on hand. These are daunting figures. President Obama, for example, raised around $745 million and spent $730 million in 2008, which itself was more than both major party candidates combined in any previous presidential election.[39] In addition to the fear that the success of corporate rent seeking will skyrocket, there is also the fear that corporate spending will have a partisan skew.

The practical question of how much new corporate—and union—spending the Court's decision will trigger is too uncertain to gauge at this stage. In the short term, media coverage of the issue during the 2010 elections was unreliable; while greatly increased spending by independent groups occurred, stories too casually linked this increase to the Court's decision, without adequate information about the sources funding this spending.[40] In the long term, the

independent expenditures). These rulings gave birth to what quickly came to be known as "Super PACs."

[38] These figures and those concerning other corporate profits and cash are taken from the testimony of Karl J. Sandstrom, former FEC Commissioner and now election-law specialist at Perkins Coie LLP, in Hearing on Corporate Governance After *Citizens United* before the Subcommittee on Capital Markets Insurance and Government Sponsored Enterprises of the House Financial Services Committee, 111th Cong, 2d Sess (2010) (statement of Karl J. Sandstrom).

[39] Samuel Issacharoff, *On Political Corruption*, 124 Harv L Rev 118 (2010).

[40] Spending from all sources—independent groups, the party committees, and candidates—soared dramatically in 2010 compared to prior midterm elections, though the Court's decision had no effect on spending by the latter two entities. See Dan Eggen, *Records Broken for Fundraising*, Wash Post A1 (Oct 26, 2010). The generally high level of spending was driven by the perception that control of one or both chambers of Congress is potentially at stake, as well as reaction to the first two years of President Obama's agenda. Levels of spending by entities independent of the parties and campaigns increased also, though, in both absolute dollar terms and as a percentage of overall spending; about a third of all independent expenditures reported to the FEC as of this writing came from the two major parties, as compared with 54 percent in 2008 and 80 percent in previous cycles. See T. W. Farnamand and Dan Eggen, *Democratic Donors Catch Up*, Wash Post A4 (Oct 28, 2010). To the extent news stories have revealed some of those contributors, they have overwhelmingly been wealthy individuals who had long been free, by virtue of *Buckley v Valeo*, not *Citizens United*, to make such contributions. See Spencer MacColl, *Wealthy Political Bankrollers Favor Conservative 527 Groups*, Open Secrets (Oct 23, 2010), online at

amount of corporate spending will likely be affected by whether
Congress enacts legislation to require adequate disclosure of all
direct and indirect corporate spending. But in striking down a major,
bipartisan act of Congress (passed by a Republican-controlled
House, a 50–50 Senate controlled by the Democratic Party, and
signed into law by a Republican President), and in triggering such
broad public opposition, immediate presidential condemnation, and
congressional legislative response (albeit failed), *Citizens United* provides an appropriate occasion to ask how constrained the modern
Supreme Court is likely to be by the "majoritarian" forces of public
opinion or formal politics.

III. The Majoritarian Thesis and Its Problems

The "majoritarian thesis" was perhaps first put forward in
general form during the New Deal by Dean Alfange, whose 1937
book, *The Supreme Court and the National Will*, asserted that "[n]o
institution can survive the loss of public confidence, particularly
when the people's faith is its only support" (of course, all public
institutions, not just the Court, ultimately exist by virtue of that
support).[41] Thus, he argued, the Court "with but few exceptions,
has adjusted itself in the long run to the dominant currents of public
sentiment."[42] Dahl's work in the late 1950s placed this general historical conclusion on a firmer social-scientific foundation. Dahl examined all cases in which the Court had held a provision of federal
law unconstitutional. He then correlated those decisions with how

---

http://www.opensecrets.org/news/2010/10/top-executives-favor-conservative-5.html. The
one well-documented source of new corporate money is the spending by the Chamber of
Commerce, all of whose funds come from anonymous corporate contributions. But to
determine what percentage of that new spending is due to *Citizens United*, one must know
how much of the Chamber's spending has been on traditional issue ads, to which corporations could contribute before *Citizens United*, how much has been on the kind of
electioneering communications that the Court concluded were constitutionally protected
before *Citizens United*, in the *WRTL* case, and how much is for election ads that is permitted
only by virtue of *Citizens United*. The most intriguing speculation about the practical
consequences of *Citizens United* is that the Court's decision is having an unanticipated
legitimation effect: individuals and groups who were always free to engage in various forms
of contributing and spending before the decision are now doing much more of both because
Citizens United constitutes a kind of cultural endorsement that this activity is a positive,
important First Amendment form of participation. See Michael Luo, *Money Talks Louder
Than Ever in Midterms*, NY Times A13 (Oct 7, 2010).

[41] Dean Alfange, *The Supreme Court and the National Will* 235 (Doubleday, 1937). On
the ultimate dependence of public institutions on the support of public opinion, see Jack
Goldsmith and Daryl Levinson, *Law for States*, 122 Harv L Rev 1791 (2009).

[42] Alfange, *The Supreme Court* at 40 (cited in note 41).

long after the statute's enactment they had occurred; with admirable precision, Dahl defined as countermajoritarian those decisions that came down within four years of a statute's enactment, so that the Court could plausibly be said to be standing against the preferences of the current, national lawmaking institutions.[43] More than fifty years later, Dahl's work still provides a foundation for today's "majoritarian" theorists, many of whom continue to invoke his work as authority for the majoritarian thesis.[44]

Cast carefully enough, an appropriate version of this thesis is surely right: in a sustained conflict between the Court and an overwhelming consensus within the political branches and the public, concerning the most salient and momentous issues of the day, the Court will eventually reflect that broader consensus, if a President gets enough successful appointments to seize control of the Court. It is true that "whenever popular majorities elect an entire government opposed to the direction of recent judicial policymaking, the justices quickly abandon their effort to make those policies."[45] If for no other reason, this is true because the appointments process in the United States is itself controlled by the political branches (unlike in some other countries[46]); it should come as no surprise, then, that nominations and appointments are likely to reflect the median preferences of the relevant political actors. If a coalition governs long enough to make enough appointments to control the Court, the Court is likely to reflect the median preferences of that coalition. Constitutional doctrine obviously changes significantly over periods of time. Those changes reflect shifts in cultural un-

---

[43] According to Dahl's data, the Court had invalidated 86 provisions in federal law, in 78 cases, over the 167 years of the Court's history at the time he wrote. Dahl, 6 J Pub L at 282 (cited in note 4).

[44] See, for example, Gerald Rosenberg, *The Hollow Hope: Can Courts Bring About Social Change?* 16 (Chicago, 1991); Mark A. Graber, *The Nonmajoritarian Difficulty: Legislative Deference to the Judiciary*, 7 Stud Am Polit Dev 35, 38 (1993). Shortly after Dahl, Robert McCloskey' s well-known historical study, *The American Supreme Court*, concluded "it is hard to find a single historical instance when the Court has stood firm for very long against a really clear wave of public demand." Robert McCloskey, *The American Supreme Court* 230 (Chicago, 3d ed 2000).

[45] Graber, 7 Stud Am Polit Dev at 72 (cited in note 44).

[46] In Israel, which has one of the most activist "Supreme Courts" in the world, the judges on the highest court are appointed by a committee consisting of the current president of the Supreme Court, two other Supreme Court Justices, two government ministers, two members of the Knesset, and two members of the Israel Bar Association. Once a candidate has been nominated by this committee, the candidate must then be approved by the prime minister. See Malvina Halberstam, *Judicial Review, a Comparative Perspective: Israel, Canada, and the United States*, 31 Cardozo L Rev 2393, 2396 (2010).

derstandings and political values, and the most direct route by which those changes come to be expressed in doctrine is through appointments that reflect contemporary cultural and political understandings.

Dahl's effort to situate the Court in the larger political context in which it inevitably operates provided a necessary corrective to overly romanticized images of the Court as a wholly autonomous institution capable of protecting any minority interest or group against the forces of majoritarian democracy. But current majoritarians have gone too far in the other direction. In dismissing out of hand Bickel-like concerns as naive or passé, they present the Court as so tightly cabined in by "majoritarian forces" as to be little more than a reflection of preexisting majoritarian preferences. Judicial review can be defended, of course, on many different moral grounds. But today's majoritarians do not mount those kind of defenses; instead, they argue no need for such defenses exist because judicial review, like democracy itself, is essentially a majoritarian institution. In pushing this view as far as they have, today's majoritarians risk complacency about the extent to which judicial review and democratic self-government remain in deep tension, both as a descriptive and a moral matter.

At the descriptive level, today's majoritarians are able to cast the Court as so powerfully constrained by "majoritarian pressures" because they rely on constantly varying and slippery conceptions of "the majority" that purportedly constrains the Court. The lack of a precise conception of the relevant majority enables majoritarians to claim that almost any decision of the Court reflects majoritarian views, since there is almost always some "majority" to which one can appeal in asserting that the Court's decisions reflect "majority" views. Indeed, some modern majoritarians come dangerously close to claiming that Court decisions are not just majoritarian over long enough periods of time, but majoritarian from the moment of birth, taken one by one. Moreover, today's majoritarians are not clear enough about the mechanisms or institutional pressures by which the Court is purportedly constrained; vague appeals to means by which the Court is said to be constrained further enable overly complacent portraits of a tightly hemmed-in Court. But once one actually explores those possible mechanisms, it becomes easier to identify not only the specific conditions under which these mechanisms might actually function (or not), but why these mechanisms might be much weaker today and in the future than in the past. Modern majoritarians often leave behind too quickly all the conditions and qualifications, noted above, that make more nuanced versions of the majoritarian thesis more plausible. As a result, they paint a dangerously misleading picture of how constrained the Court actually is.

Moreover, even assuming the majoritarian thesis correctly describes much of the Court's prior history, past returns are no guarantee of future performance. Structural changes in the appointments process and the Court's perceived authority and support vis-à-vis other institutions suggest the Court might have considerably more freedom of action today than in the past. Finally, Bickel's challenge is fundamentally a moral one. The majoritarian literature offers a descriptive account of purported constraints on the Court, but those constraints cannot answer the moral challenge.

Thus, both descriptively and morally, the modern majoritarian view of the Court has been pushed to unrealistic and troubling extremes. At the least, *Citizens United* is a reminder of how dramatically the Court can stand against "majoritarian views." Whether the decision is a harbinger of a Court that continually does so remains to be seen, but despite the claims of modern majoritarians, that possibility cannot be ignored or dismissed out of hand.

A. WHAT IS THE RELEVANT BASELINE?

In reviewing the modern majoritarian literature, one can become frustrated by the elusiveness of the central claim. Different theorists appeal to different baselines for defining what constitutes the "majoritarian views" that purportedly constrain the Court. Or the same theorists invoke different concepts of "the majority" in different works. Moreover, some of the baselines are so nebulous that it becomes almost impossible to confirm or falsify the theory.

As a social scientist, Dahl recognized these problems and provided an admirably precise definition and test of "majoritarian views." Dahl emphasized that unless "majoritarian" was defined with reference to legislative outcomes, the concept would be difficult, if not impossible, to pin down. Moreover, he understood that legislative majorities can come and go quickly. Thus, Dahl's baseline was actual legislation enacted four years or fewer before the Court's decision (this time frame avoided the problem of defunct legislative majorities). In essence, Dahl treated the Court as acting in countermajoritarian ways only if it invalidated acts of Congress within four years of their enactment. That definition provided a meaningful way to assess how far out of line from current, national lawmaking majorities the Court's decisions might be.

Modern majoritarians are not as precise as Dahl. They appeal to a range of different baselines. To Barry Friedman, the relevant baseline is "mainstream public opinion," or "the popular will," or "the considered judgment of the American people."[47] For Jack Balkin, the theory sometimes is taken to mean that courts work in cooperation with "the dominant national political coalition." They invalidate "statutes passed by older regimes that are inconsistent with the current coalition's values."[48] Here "majoritarian" means the current national lawmaking majority, similar to Dahl's baseline. Yet at other times, Balkin is concerned about the problem of "partisan entrenchment," which he calls the most important factor in understanding how judicial review works.[49] In this view, Justices are responsive not to current lawmaking majorities, but to those that were in power at the time the Justices were appointed. The governing coalition at one point in time appoints Justices who entrench that coalition's preferences long into the future— for individual Justices, eighteen years on average, given the average tenure on the Court.[50] Balkin notes that this might suggest that the Court is indeed a countermajoritarian institution. But he rejects this view and argues that the Court represents "a temporally extended majority rather than a contemporaneous one."[51] Here, the definition of "majoritarian" is the governing coalition at the time a Justice was appointed; the Court is not countermajoritarian

---

[47] Barry Friedman, *The Will of the People: How Public Opinion Has Influenced the Supreme Court and Shaped the Meaning of the Constitution* 368, 369, 370, 371 (Farrar, Straus, 2009). For criticism of whether some of the sources Friedman relies on are adequate measures of "public opinion," see Justin Driver, *Why Law Should Lead*, New Republic (April 2, 2010).

[48] Jack M. Balkin, *Framework Originalism and the Living Constitution*, 103 Nw U L Rev 549, 563 (2009).

[49] See, for example, Jack M. Balkin and Sanford Levinson, *Understanding the Constitutional Revolution*, 87 Va L Rev 1045, 1066 (2001).

[50] Balkin suggests we consider Justices as analogous to senators who are elected once and then serve, on average, for eighteen years. Id at 1076. For the argument that efforts at partisan entrenchment explain the creation of judicial review in several modern contexts, see Ran Hirschl, *Toward Juristocracy: The Origins and Consequences of the New Constitutionalism* (Harvard, 2004).

[51] Balkin and Levinson, 87 Va L Rev at 1076 (cited in note 49).

because it enforces the preferences of the earlier lawmaking majority.

Keith Whittington, whose interdisciplinary work in history and political science has contributed a great deal to understanding the Court within the larger political-institutional environment, argues that the Court reflects the policy preferences, not of national lawmaking institutions, but of the President or "the presidential wing" of the dominant party.[52] Though Mark Graber presents himself as a majoritarian theorist, his argument is that the Court "typically makes policies only in response to legislative stalemates or invitations."[53] But the former acknowledges far more scope for independent Court action than one might think a "majoritarian" view of the Court entails, or that seems implied in other versions of majoritarian theory, while the latter suggests a different set of moral questions about judicial review than other majoritarian theories (or Bickel's book) raise. In other work, Graber offers a particularly thin conception of majoritarian constraint by asserting that the Court is majoritarian in the sense that some "subset of the lawmaking elite supports particular judicial decisions or the trend of judicial decision making"; the key point, for him, is that courts do not protect those who have "no" champions among the power-holding majority.[54] Gerry Rosenberg, often taken to be another majoritarian theorist, actually asks a somewhat different question: whether courts can effectively impose significant social change. His conclusion is that the answer varies, depending on factors such as whether the incentives of private actors align with the courts' objectives (thus he emphasizes market-based constraints on effective implementation of *Roe*).[55] But exploration of the practical effectiveness of Court decisions, though not unrelated to the countermajoritarian debate, pursues somewhat different questions.

---

[52] Keith Whittington, *The Political Foundations of Judicial Supremacy: The Presidency, the Supreme Court, and Constitutional Leadership in U.S. History* (Princeton, 2007).

[53] Graber, 7 Stud Am Polit Dev at 35, 37 (cited in note 44).

[54] Graber, 4 Ann Rev L & Soc Sci at 364 (cited in note 3). Though Friedman generally casts the Court as constrained by "mainstream public opinion," he sometimes suggests that the Court instead reflects "elite voices, rather than the average person" (which he suggests explains the Court's decisions in the school prayer and flag burning cases) or that Justices respond to their peer groups, so that if a Justice's "peers have elite views not shared by most of the country, the justice will seem to be going his own way." Friedman, *Will of the People* at 378 (cited in note 47).

[55] Rosenberg, *Hollow Hope* at 195 (cited in note 44).

It is easy to assume that all these theorists are "majoritarians" who share a common view and whose work collectively establishes a common point. But different work of this sort appeals to quite different conceptions of the relevant majority. Some of these conceptions envision the Court as much less constrained than others. Some of these conceptions are so nebulous as to make the theory difficult to confirm or falsify. These differences matter in assessing "majoritarian" theories. For example, the *Lochner* era's activism might have reflected majority popular opinion even as the Court overturned lawmaking majorities.[56] The same might have been true of the Rehnquist Court's cases holding unconstitutional all or parts of thirty-one statutes between 1995 and 2002.[57] These different baselines also have different implications both for the descriptive issue of how constrained the Court is in fact, and by what means, as well as for the moral issue of how to reconcile judicial review with democracy.

B. WAS BROWN MAJORITARIAN OR COUNTERMAJORITARIAN?

These different definitions of "the majority" come into play when majoritarians contend with one of the most important decisions of the twentieth century, *Brown*.[58] The views of "majoritarian" theorists about the extent to which *Brown* and related cases reflected majoritarian preferences at the national level reflect a wide range of different conclusions. These divergences cast doubt on the cogency of the underlying theoretical claim.

Dahl, the founding father of the theory, did not directly address Court decisions striking down state laws; yet he said enough to suggest that he viewed *Brown* as at odds with his claim about the highly constrained Court. For Dahl, *Brown* illustrated that the Court *can* successfully act, "and may even succeed in establishing national policy," when the governing national coalition in Con-

---

[56] For the claim that popular opinion supported the *Lochner* Court's substantive decisions, see Barry Cushman, *Mr. Dooley and Ms. Gallup: Public Opinion and Constitutional Change in the 1930s*, 50 Buff L Rev 7 (2002).

[57] See Neal Devins, *The Majoritarian Rehnquist Court?* 76 L & Contemp Probs 63, 64 (2004).

[58] The substantive conception of equality reflected in *Brown* can, of course, be considered a required aspect of a morally thick conception of "democracy." But these kinds of justifications for *Brown* as consistent with a certain substantive, moral conception of democracy are not what the modern majoritarians I discuss have in mind when they argue that *Brown* reflected the "majority's preferences."

gress and the White House is "unstable with respect to certain policies," as Dahl thought the national government was with respect to civil rights in this period.[59] Dahl thus saw *Brown* and the Court's civil rights decisions of the prior thirty years as an exception to his thesis (one might think this is a rather large, significant exception).[60] Such exceptions were possible, in his view, whenever a powerful enough legislative-executive coalition did not exist to *overturn* the Court, as did not with respect to *Brown*. In those contexts, Dahl argued, the Court would have a wide berth for freedom of action.

But of course, by this standard, the Court will have vast scope to act in ways that do not reflect majority views, if "majority" is understood in certain plausible ways. There is a world of difference in viewing the Court as likely to act consistently with the general preferences of the national lawmaking institutions, and viewing the Court as free to act up to the point at which those institutions are able to muster an effective response. Congress in the 1950s could not act either to legislate to require segregation or to require the end of segregation. The "gridlock interval," as political scientists call it, can be vast on certain issues—indeed, the more salient and controversial the issue, perhaps the larger. In our modern world of hyperpolarized parties and routine filibusters, marshaling effective legislative responses to Court decisions will be all the more daunting.

In contrast to Dahl, other "majoritarian theorists" view *Brown* as consistent with their theory. Despite the more conventional view of *Brown* as the paradigmatic instance of countermajoritarian Court decision making that nonetheless justifies judicial review, these theorists rescue *Brown* for the majoritarian cause by asserting that "a national majority favored the result in *Brown*, as did foreign policy elites."[61] This view sometimes rests *Brown*'s majoritarianism on appeals to national public opinion at the time. But among all the familiar problems with relying on polls as evidence of public

---

[59] Dahl, 6 J Pub L at 294 (cited in note 4).

[60] Id (noting that legislative gridlock "is probably the explanation for the relatively successful work of the Court in enlarging the freedom of Negroes to vote during the past three decades and in its famous school integration decisions.").

[61] Balkin, 103 Nw U L Rev at 576 (cited in note 48). See also Friedman, *Will of the People* at 245 (cited in note 47) (national majority in public opinion polls favored *Brown*). Balkin also cites the same polls, but his primary evidence that national majorities supported *Brown* is that twenty-seven states had abolished de jure segregation.

opinion, on this issue, those data are even more suspect: the only polls available were taken after *Brown* was decided, and there is no way of knowing whether their results were influenced by *Brown* itself.[62]

Yet still other majoritarians argue that *Brown* was ineffective precisely because it was countermajoritarian in a different sense than what public opinion polls expressed: it did not have the support of Congress or the executive branch. In one of the canonical works in this literature, Gerald Rosenberg's *The Hollow Hope: Can Courts Bring About Social Change?* Rosenberg famously argues that *Brown* was too countermajoritarian to be effective.[63] Only when Congress and the President were prepared to support *Brown*'s principles wholeheartedly did *Brown* have any practical effect.[64] Still other majoritarians hedge their bets regarding whether *Brown* stood against national political opinion or not.[65] Thus, the majoritarian theory has no settled view about the monumentally significant *Brown* decision. Slipping back and forth between appeals to a vaguely defined and deeply divided "national opinion," and appeals to majorities in lawmaking bodies which did not support the Court but were not coherent or large enough to overturn the Court, the theory fails to make any clear sense of whether one of the most significant decisions in the Court's history is consistent with the theory's claims or not.

C. THE WHOLESALE-RETAIL CONFUSION

The reality that the Court acts within a larger political and institutional context that shapes and constrains the Court to some

---

[62] See Thomas A. Schemling, *Supreme Court Counter-Majoritarianism Revisited: Warren Court Cases Invalidating State Laws, 1954–1969* (paper prepared for delivery at the annual meeting of the Midwest Political Science Association, April 7–10, 2005).

[63] Rosenberg, *Hollow Hope* at 46–54 (cited in note 44).

[64] More recent work argues that the courts were effective in implementing major social changes, such as the integration of labor unions, that national lawmaking majorities were not prepared to adopt. See Paul Frymer, *Black and Blue: African Americans, the Labor Movement, and the Decline of the Democratic Party* (Princeton, 2007).

[65] Thus, Michael Klarman is appropriately cautious in his conclusion: "during the time period covered by this book, not a single Court decision involving race clearly contravened national public opinion. *Brown* was the closest to doing so, but half the country supported it from the day it was decided." Michael J. Klarman, *From Jim Crow to Civil Rights: The Supreme Court and the Struggle for Racial Equality* 450 (Oxford, 2004). For a similarly nuanced view, see also Michael Klarman, *Rethinking the Civil Rights and Civil Liberties Revolution*, 82 Va L Rev 1 (1996) (arguing that the scope of the Court's autonomy lies somewhere between the countermajoritarian and the majoritarian views).

extent need not lead to the view that the Court's decisions, taken one by one, are likely or structurally predetermined to reflect current "majoritarian" preferences. That over broad enough swaths of time the Court's decisions eventually reflect that larger political and cultural context does not entail the quite different claim that individual Court decisions are destined to reflect current "majoritarian" views.

Some majoritarian theorists are careful to note and honor this distinction.[66] Yet others push the majoritarian view all the way to the point of insisting, or strongly suggesting, that the Court's individual decisions necessarily reflect majoritarian views.[67] Thus, in calling the Supreme Court "the most democratic branch," for example, Jeffrey Rosen argues that on "a range of issues during the 1980s and 1990s, the moderate majority on the Supreme Court represented the views of a majority of Americans more accurately than the polarized party leadership in Congress."[68] That might or might not be true as a contingent, factual matter, but the thrust of Rosen's book is that it is in the nature of the Court's place within the larger political environment that the Court will reflect this kind of "majority view."

To illustrate his general point, Rosen offers specific recent examples. In the area of race and equal protection, he notes that the Court seemed to flirt with the idea of holding that the Fourteenth Amendment banned race-conscious affirmative action in settings like academic institutions, only to back away in the 2003 case testing the constitutionality of affirmative action in law school admissions, *Grutter v Bollinger*.[69] In Rosen's portrayal, the Court backed down in the face of the endorsement of affirmative action by the President, Congress, and the military. But to insist that individual 5–4 decisions, such as *Grutter*, "had" to come out the

---

[66] See, for example, Whittington, *Political Foundations* at 288 (cited in note 52) ("It is certainly not the case that every decision rendered by the Supreme Court and every aspect of its jurisprudence can be reduced to the political interests of the party in power, but in understanding how the Court has successfully claimed and exercised the power of constitutional interpretation and judicial review, it is fruitful to understand the ways in which that power can coexist with the demands of political leadership.").

[67] Although these theorists typically nod to the point that the majoritarian constraints on the Court apply over long periods of time, they quickly leave this acknowledgment behind in arguing that virtually every decision of the Court does so.

[68] Jeffrey Rosen, *The Most Democratic Branch: How the Courts Serve America* 3 (Oxford, 2006).

[69] 539 US 306, 326 (2003).

way they did, because the Court inevitably reflects majoritarian pressures, is to cede too little to randomness and fortuity, at the very least.[70] Had *Grutter* reached the Court three years later, or had Justice O'Connor retired three years earlier, it seems clear that Justice Alito would have been a fifth vote for the opposite result in *Grutter*.[71] *Grutter* also reached the Court at the same time as a constitutional challenge to affirmative action in undergraduate admissions; and the Court held the latter unconstitutional even as it upheld the law school program in *Grutter*.[72] Had the Court not been able to "split the baby" by deciding the two cases at the same time, who knows whether the result in *Grutter* would have been affected? Of course, if the Court had banned all affirmative action in public institutions, it is possible that political and other institutions would have responded in some way that would have tested the Court's commitment to this principle. But to maintain that individual 5–4 decisions necessarily reflect "majoritarian views"— whether majority here refers to national lawmaking majorities or national "popular" majorities or a majority of "the elite" or the views of the President as the relevant baseline—is to push a deterministic view of the Court too hard. Even if the general thrust of the Court's decisions over extended periods of time tends to come into line with dominant views, each and every decision need not do so.

Similarly, Barry Friedman comes close to suggesting that the Court's decisions, one by one, necessarily will reflect "majoritarian views" by insisting that now "the system [of judicial review and politics] tends to rest in a relatively quiet equilibrium."[73] Invoking the concept of anticipated reaction, Friedman argues that the Court has so internalized the disciplining power of Congress or

[70] The claim that the Court backed down is also at odds with the fact that Justice O'Connor had taken this intermediate position on affirmative action cases for years, as had Justice Powell, a figure she greatly admired, in the *Bakke* case itself. Nothing in Justice O'Connor's jurisprudence indicated agreement with the strict colorblindness position. See Reva Siegal, *From Colorblindness to Antibalkinization: An Emerging Ground of Decision in Race Equality Cases*, 120 Yale L J 1278 (2010); Richard H. Pildes and Richard G. Niemi, *Expressive Harms, "Bizarre Districts," and Voting Rights: Evaluating Election-District Appearances After Shaw v. Reno*, 92 Mich L Rev 483 (1993).

[71] See *Parents Involved in Community Schools v Seattle School District No. 1*, 551 US 701 (2007) (rejecting 5–4, with Justice Alito in the majority, local school district's affirmative action plan and distinguishing *Grutter*).

[72] *Gratz v Bollinger*, 539 US 244 (2003).

[73] Friedman, *Will of the People* at 376 (cited in note 47).

popular opinion that the Court senses trouble in advance and avoids it by rendering only opinions that will have majoritarian support. Congress has not retaliated in any significant way against the Court in many decades.[74] Nonetheless, Friedman believes that the Court has absorbed the much longer history of its relationship to the political branches and popular opinion, so that the shadow of this retribution, however dim, is enough to keep the Court in line. This view, too, leads majoritarians too close to the view that all Court decisions reflect the Court's calculation as to where the (relevant) "majority" view lies.

This deterministic vision leads majoritarians sometimes to sound like Ptolemaic cosmologists, adding epicycle upon epicycle in an effort to sustain their theory (or whichever versions of it the particular theorist happens to hold). Indeed, Friedman recognizes that the Court's decision in *Citizens United* to free up corporate electoral speech at a moment of enormous public anger and hostility to Wall Street and financial institutions was particularly poor timing if the Court cared deeply about public opinion. His conclusion is that the Court simply made a mistake: it misjudged what the reaction to the decision would be.[75] Friedman similarly suggests that the explanation for the Court's highly unpopular school-prayer decisions of the 1960s, which unleashed a "gale of disagreement,"[76] was that the Court failed to anticipate public reaction correctly. If it had, the implication runs, it would have decided differently.

Most of the time, majoritarians view the Court as a savvy judge of the political environment and public opinion. Thus, these *deus ex machina* appeals to mistake seem particularly odd. Moreover, as a factual matter, the appeal to mistake is particularly hard to credit regarding *Citizens United* (or the school-prayer decisions[77]). Cam-

---

[74] See infra Section III.D.2.

[75] Barry Friedman and Dahlia Lithwick, *Speeding Locomotive: Did the Roberts Court Misjudge the Public Mood on Campaign Finance Reform?* Slate (Jan 25, 2010), online at http://www.slate.com/id/2242557/pagenum/all/#p2.

[76] Friedman, *Will of the People* at 264 (cited in note 47).

[77] That the Court wrongly guessed at what public reaction to these decisions would be is belied by the historical record. *Engel* involved a prayer actually written by public officials, which was not a common practice, and the Court's 6–1 decision was written in such a way that it could have been confined to that context. Public disagreement over *Engel* was widespread and intense. Id at 263. But the Court then went ahead and decided *School District v Schempp*, 374 US 203 (1963), which invalidated in an 8–1 decision the more common practice of Bible readings that included the Lord's Prayer. Nor did the Court

paign finance, particularly the issue of corporate speech, is one of the issues on the Court's docket that regularly generates front-page news coverage. Public support for campaign finance reform (other than public financing) has been extremely high for many years.[78] When the Court announced after the first *Citizens United* argument that it would hear argument on the question whether to overrule its precedents on corporate speech, the very announcement triggered a flood of media coverage. The Court received over forty amicus briefs in the case, an exceptionally large number. That the Court did not realize *Citizens United* was one of the most high-profile cases it would hear, or that a 5–4 decision holding unconstitutional one of the two central features of the McCain-Feingold Act, overturning two precedents along the way, including one only four years old, would be noticed and greatly controversial is hard to credit. What seems more likely is that the decision was a matter of deep conviction for the majority who believed it correct; indeed, three of those Justices had endorsed that position for many years.

Of course, there is no need to claim that every Court decision is predetermined by larger structural forces to be a "majoritarian one," whatever the baseline that a particular theorist uses to define "majoritarian." Nearly all majoritarians acknowledge that at least some of the time.[79] Yet having made this formal acknowledgment, many modern majoritarians nonetheless quickly return to theoretical accounts that suggest the Court's decisions nearly always do reflect majoritarian views and to demonstrating, case by case, that the Court's decisions do so.

D. WHAT IS THE MECHANISM BY WHICH THE COURT IS
   CONSTRAINED?

To evaluate the extent to which the Court is constrained by

---

back away from its stance on prayer in the public schools in later cases. I am indebted to Adam Samaha for these observations. Of course, there is a great deal of noncompliance with these decisions, according to many studies. Friedman, *Will of the People* at 266–67 (cited in note 47).

[78] A compendium of public-survey data on popular views on campaign-finance regulation at the time BCRA was enacted is contained in *Public Opinion & Campaign Finance, Expert Report Prepared for Congress* by Robert Y. Shapiro, professor and chair, Department of Political Science, Columbia University (Sept 18, 2002) (on file with author).

[79] See, for example, Friedman, *Will of the People* at 14 (cited in note 47) (acknowledging that " [i]t is hardly the case that every Supreme Court decision mirrors the popular will—even less so that it should.").

"majoritarian pressures," one wants to understand the mechanism by which this constraint is supposed to work. Similarly, to predict whether this constraint is likely to operate in the future with the same force it has in the past, one would like to know what this mechanism is supposed to be. Because different "majoritarians" appeal to different conceptions of the "majority" that constrains the Court, they rely on different mechanisms, explicitly or implicitly, to explain how the Court comes to be constrained. In working through the various mechanisms that might be involved, most appear to be rather weak, at least at this stage of American institutional development. Moreover, the one mechanism that does seem most plausibly effective—the appointments process—is likely to be less effective in the future than in the past.

1. *"Public opinion."* Majoritarians like Friedman and Rosen, among others, rely primarily on "public opinion" as the principal constraint that requires the Court to reflect majoritarian views. As Friedman puts it, this mechanism purportedly works because Justices "are no less vain than the rest of us, and it is human nature to like to be liked or even applauded and admired."[80] Perhaps. Testing this claim is difficult, not just because public opinion polls are notoriously sensitive to subtle wording and framing differences, but because data are available only for a relatively small number of issues that historically have come before the Court.[81]

In addition, we live in a more fragmented "public opinion culture" than in the past, which heightens the possibility for Justices, like the rest of us, to exist in a cultural and news environment preselected to confirm prior beliefs. At one time, it was thought (some) Justices might be particularly responsive to elite academic legal opinion; but here, too, there has been fragmentation of authority and perceived authority. Justices can more readily find confirming academic views for a wide range of opinions than fifty years ago. Friedman himself acknowledges that Justices might be more influenced (if influenced at all) by a narrow segment of the opinion, the opinion of their "peers," rather than some more gen-

---

[80] Id at 374. Interestingly, Friedman alone among majoritarians disclaims strong reliance on the appointments process as the mechanism by which the Court is constrained to reflect public opinion. Id.

[81] Gregory Caldeira, *Courts and Public Opinion*, in J. B. Gates and C. A. Johnson, eds, *The American Courts* (CQ Press, 1991).

eral "public."[82] He offers the example of Justice Scalia, who Friedman suggests remains popular with the Federalist Society even when his votes depart from "mainstream public opinion."[83] But this acknowledgment undermines the notion that the latter will necessarily function as a substantial constraint; those in power have always found it easy to exist in an echo chamber of supporters.

In addition, a considerable difference exists between views that "the public" loosely holds, as revealed in public opinion polls, for example, and views of sufficient moment and intensity as to mobilize the kind of concerted, organized, and effective public response necessary to generate action, particularly legislative action. Not only must the issues the Court decides be of sufficient salience to motivate public action, but the intensity of feeling and belief about the substantive issue must be strong enough to overcome the "diffuse support"[84] that the American public has for the Court as an institution. Though some predicted that the Court's legitimacy or public support would be drastically eroded by its intervention in the 2000 presidential election, for example, the empirical evidence refutes the view that the Court suffered any long-term drop in support.[85] Indeed, as one major study concludes, the aggregate level of public confidence in the Court has remained largely unchanged for several decades despite the range of contentious issues the Court has addressed.[86] Similarly, the Court's approval ratings since the early 1970s have been consistently stronger than those for Congress or the President.[87]

The mechanism by which public opinion is supposed to constrain the Court is not always clearly identified in majoritarian theories. But if the issue is whether public disapproval of specific

---

[82] Friedman, *Will of the People* at 378 (cited in note 47).

[83] Id.

[84] See Gregory A. Caldeira and James L. Gibson, *The Etiology of Public Support for the Supreme Court*, 36 Am J Pol Sci 640 (1992) (finding strong diffuse support for the Court).

[85] Six months after the decision, one major poll concluded public support for the Court was at the 80 percent level. See Devins, 76 L & Contemp Probs at 76 n 88 (cited in note 57) (citing Gallup poll conducted June 8, 2001). See also Stephen P. Nicholson and Robert M. Howard, *Framing Support for the Supreme Court in the Aftermath of Bush v. Gore*, 65 J Pol 676 (2003).

[86] See Persily et al, *Public Opinion and Constitutional Controversy* at 14 (cited in note 10).

[87] See Frank Newport, *Trust in Legislative Branch Falls to Record Low*, Gallup (Sept 24, 2010), online at http://www.gallup.com/poll/143225/Trust-Legislative-Branch-Falls-Record-Low.aspx. At the time of this recent survey, the Court's approval rating was 66 percent, the President's was 49 percent, and Congress's was 36 percent.

decisions in survey-type settings is likely to translate into meaningful public action, such as defiance of the decision or pressure being brought to bear on political actors to resist the decision,[88] then the extent to which "the public" is prepared to challenge the Court, or support challenges to the Court, must be taken into account—not just "public opinion" in the abstract. Nowhere are these hurdles better illustrated than in the Court's battle with FDR over the New Deal.

In the American context, majoritarians have always offered up the Court's dramatic confrontation with the New Deal, in which the Court eventually bowed in the face of the New Deal's transformative constitutional vision, as the most compelling illustration of how public opinion constrains the Court.[89] Thus, "the lesson of 1937" is central to modern American constitutional history, as well as to the understanding of constitutional law and theory today. But what exactly is that lesson?

The conventional takeaway is that public opinion controls the Court.[90] As I have noted throughout, I would build in many more qualifications in characterizing the conditions under which the Court's decisions are likely to reflect "majoritarian views." But it is these qualifications that majoritarians too quickly leave behind. Indeed, properly viewed, "the lesson of 1937" might well be precisely the opposite of the conventional understanding of majoritarians: judicial review can remain remarkably independent and countermajoritarian, for only a concatenation of the most extraordinary circumstances will provoke politics and public opinion into imposing major constraints on the modern Court.

First, the Court's challenge to the political branches was far more breathtaking than many recall. We are all aware of the major highlights—the Court's invalidation of the National Industrial Recovery Act (NIRA) and the Agricultural Adjustment Act (AAA).[91]

---

[88] Kevin T. McGuire and James A. Stimson, *The Least Dangerous Branch Revisited: New Evidence on Supreme Court Responsiveness to Public Preferences*, 66 J Pol 1018, 1019 (2004).

[89] This and the next six paragraphs are slightly modified versions of an online essay I published for Jotwell, the Journal of Things We Like (Lots). See Richard H. Pildes, *The Court and Politics: What Is the Lesson of FDR's Confrontation with the Court*, Jotwell (Sept 23, 2010), online at http://conlaw.jotwell.com/the-court-and-politics-what-is-the-lesson-of-fdrs-confrontation-with-the-court/.

[90] See, for example, Friedman, *Will of the People* at 4 (cited in note 47); McCloskey, *American Supreme Court* at 177–78 (cited in note 44).

[91] *Schechter Poultry Corp. v United States*, 295 US 495 (1935) (NIRA), and *United States v Butler*, 297 US 1 (1936) (AAA).

But consider the range of national and state legislation and presidential action the Court held unconstitutional in one seventeen-month period starting in January 1935: the NIRA, both its Codes of Fair Competition and the President's power to control the flow of contraband oil across state lines;[92] the Railroad Retirement Act;[93] the Frazier-Lemke Farm Mortgage Moratorium Act;[94] the effort of the President to get the administrative agencies to reflect his political vision (*Humphrey's Executor*);[95] the Home Owners' Loan Act;[96] a federal tax on liquor dealers;[97] the AAA; the new SEC's attempts to subpoena records to enforce the securities laws;[98] the Bituminous Coal Conservation Act;[99] the Municipal Bankruptcy Act, which Congress passed to enable local governments to use the bankruptcy process;[100] and, perhaps most dramatically, in *Morehead v Tipaldo*,[101] minimum-wage laws on the books in a third of the states, in some cases, for decades. Some of these decisions have withstood the test of time, but most, of course, have not.

In the summer of 1935, more than 100 district judges held acts of Congress unconstitutional, issuing more than 1,600 injunctions against New Deal legislation.[102] Moreover, at least some of these issues cut to the bone of the average person; a window into the salience of the Court's actions is provided in the comments of the founder of the ACLU, at a town meeting, who said: "Something is seething in America today. . . . We are either going to get out of this mess by a change in the Court or with machine guns on street corners."[103] What would the modern Court have to do, and in what context, that would come close to all this?

Yet even so, from the moment it was announced, the resistance to FDR's legislative assault on the Court—the Court-packing

---

[92] *Panama Refining Co. v Ryan*, 293 US 388 (1935).

[93] *Railroad Retirement Bd. v Alton R. Co.*, 295 US 330 (1935).

[94] *Louisville Joint Stock Land Bank v Radford*, 295 US 555 (1935).

[95] *Humphrey's Executor v United States*, 295 US 602 (1935).

[96] *Hopkins Federal Savings & Loan Ass'n v Cleary*, 296 US 315 (1935).

[97] *United States v Constantine*, 296 US 287 (1936).

[98] *Jones v SEC*, 298 US 1 (1936).

[99] *Carter v Carter Coal Co.*, 298 US 238 (1936).

[100] *Ashton v Cameron County Water Improvement District No. One*, 298 US 513 (1936).

[101] 298 US 587 (1936).

[102] Jeff Shesol, *Supreme Power: Franklin Roosevelt vs. The Supreme Court* (Norton, 2010).

[103] Id at 387–88.

plan—was vehement, geographically widespread, and bipartisan. This resistance is all the more remarkable, for FDR did not propose the use of a new, controversial type of power. Congress has always had the power to decide the size of the Court and, of course, had used that power in the past to increase and decrease the size of the Court. The controversy was over whether FDR was asking Congress to use a power it clearly possessed for purposes that were perceived to undermine the Court's independence.[104]

Yet FDR's Court-packing plan was in dire shape politically long *before* the Court's "switch in time" took the last wind out of that effort—despite the fact, as well, that the plan was the first piece of legislation FDR put forward after having just won the biggest landslide in American history. Two-thirds of the newspapers that had *endorsed* FDR came out immediately and vociferously against the plan.[105] The most common charge was that FDR was seeking "dictatorial powers," a particularly resonant charge.[106] Telegrams to Congress, a leading gauge of public opinion at the time, flowed overwhelmingly, and with passionate intensity, against the plan.[107] Some leading Progressive Democrats in the Senate, like Hiram Johnson and George Norris, quickly bolted from FDR and defended the Court's independence; conservative Democrats wanted no part of the plan; a leading western Democrat, Senator Burton Wheeler, announced he would lead the fight against the plan; FDR's vice president did little to conceal his disdain for Court packing; Republicans sat silently and let the Democratic Party tear itself apart.[108] And the Court, too, has tools to fight back: Chief Justice Hughes sent a letter, with devastating effect, to the Senate Judiciary Committee that took apart FDR's justifications for Court packing.[109]

We cannot know, of course, whether FDR would ultimately have prevailed, had the Court's decisions not started to change course.

---

[104] The Judiciary Act of 1789 called for the appointment of six Justices. The court was expanded to seven members in 1807, nine in 1837, ten in 1863, and then stabilized at nine in 1869.

[105] Shesol, *Supreme Power* at 301 (cited in note 102).

[106] Id at 303.

[107] Id at 305.

[108] Id at 307–49. See also William Leuchtenburg, *The Supreme Court Reborn* 134 (Oxford, 1995) (noting that the plan immediately generated more intensity and controversy than any other legislative proposal "in the century," other than the League of Nations issue).

[109] Id at 393–94.

But more remarkably, here was the most popular President in history, with a Congress his party controlled overwhelmingly, confronted by the most aggressive Court in American history—and yet, it is entirely plausible that FDR's legislative challenge to the authority of the Court would have failed, given how deep the cultural and political support was for the Court's institutional authority, even as the Court issued one unpopular decision after another.

And, finally, consider the aftermath of the confrontation: who won the Court-packing fight? The conventional wisdom among constitutional academics, focused narrowly on the Court itself, is that FDR lost the battle, but won the war, since the Court (assisted by seven FDR appointments between 1937 and 1943) acceded to the New Deal's constitutionality. But FDR's legislative assault on the Court destroyed his political coalition, in Congress and nationally, and ended his ability to enact major domestic policy legislation, despite his huge electoral triumph in 1936.[110] As a *Fortune* magazine poll in July 1937 put it: "The Supreme Court struggle had cut into the President's popularity as no other issue ever had."[111] National health care, the next major item on FDR's agenda, faded away. The progressive domestic policy agenda did not recover until 1964. Reflecting back, FDR's second vice president, Henry Wallace, observed: "The whole New Deal really went up in smoke as a result of the Supreme Court fight."[112] No rational politician, looking back at FDR's attempt to bring the Court into line, other than through the ordinary appointments process, is likely to repeat FDR's efforts.

Thus, one can read the 1937 experience as suggesting that, for better or worse, judicial independence and the authority of the Court have become so entrenched in America that even the most popular politicians play with fire if they seek too directly to take on the power of the Court. If a President is lucky to have enough appointments to control the Court, the Court will likely come to reflect the President's agenda; but that is a matter of luck, not inevitability, and short of that, it is far from clear how likely or effective any other political attempts to hold the Court to account will be. Indeed, by the 1940s, the Court was already striking down or limiting more federal statutes than it had before the burst of

---

[110] Leuchtenburg, *Reborn* at 156–61 (cited in note 108).

[111] Shesol, *Supreme Power* at 458 (cited in note 102).

[112] Id at 158.

extreme activism of 1919 to 1937; by the late 1990s, it was doing so even more often than during the New Deal, though with far less political or public pushback.[113] Put back in the actual historical context, "the lesson of 1937" might be taken to pose a sobering challenge to the view that the Court is inevitably constrained to be a "majoritarian" institution.

2. *Political institutions.* The New Deal history suggests how difficult it now is to marshal effective political responses to the Court. It has been many generations since Congress retaliated against the Court through measures such as eliminating the Court's Term, expanding or shrinking the size of the Court, impeaching a Justice, or stripping the Court of jurisdiction over major areas. Indeed, when Congress has attempted to remove the Court's jurisdiction over specific issues in the modern era, the Court has found ways to reassert its power.[114] The most recent example involves judicial oversight of detentions at Guantánamo. Each time the Court asserted a role for federal court oversight, Congress responded with legislation aimed at reducing or eliminating the courts' role. Yet each time, the Court responded by finding ways to construe the statutes, and ultimately to invoke the Constitution, to fend off Congress's attempts and to reassert the Court's role.[115] Far from being cowed, the modern Court has stood its ground.

But perhaps Congress does not need to act decisively to bend the Court to its will. Perhaps a credible congressional threat is sufficient. Thus, we should look to the general history of congressional threats to curb the Court's powers. Only a few studies of congressional Court-curbing efforts exist. In an important one, Gerald Rosenberg concludes that only nine periods have been characterized by high levels of such efforts, defined as eras with a large number of proposed bills that can be cataloged as major institutional challenges to the Court, rather than as case-specific efforts to reverse a particular decision.[116] Four of these nine periods lasted two years;

---

[113] Tom S. Clark and Keith E. Whittington, *Ideology, Partisanship, and Judicial Review of Acts of Congress, 1789–2006* (unpublished manuscript, Nov 1, 2010) (on file with author).

[114] See Vicki C. Jackson, *Introduction; Congressional Control of Jurisdiction and the Future of the Federal Courts,* 86 Georgetown L J 2445 (1998).

[115] The culminating act in this drama, for now, which summarizes the history of the Court-Congress struggle, is *Boumediene v Bush,* 553 US 723 (2008).

[116] Gerald N. Rosenberg, *Judicial Independence and the Reality of Political Power,* 54 Rev Pol 369 (1992). Rosenberg builds on an earlier study. See Stuart S. Nagel, *Court-Curbing Periods in American History,* 18 Vand L Rev 925 (1965). The periods Rosenberg identifies

two more lasted four years; only three extended longer. During the rest of American history, Congress undertook no sustained effort to rein in the Court.

Rosenberg concludes that in three of these periods, the Court backed down and was effectively constrained by the threat of congressional response (1802 to 1804, 1858 to 1869, and 1935 to 1937). But is it the shadow of congressional retaliation or the appointments process that accounts for the shift in decisions? In at least one of these periods, the change is probably best attributed to changes in personnel; between 1858 and 1869, six Justices retired and Lincoln appointed five. In my view, the appointments process might well have been a crucial element in the Court's New Deal transformation as well; it is difficult to know whether the "switch in time" would have been enduring had FDR not been able to appoint seven Justices from 1937 to 1943. Drawing any conclusions for modern contexts from the weakness of the fledgling Court in 1802 and 1804 seems hazardous. Whether it is Court-curbing legislation or the appointments process that accounts for the Court's change in direction in even these periods of a clear judicial shift, then, remains indeterminate. That uncertainty is important, if there are reasons to argue, as I do below, that the appointments process is unlikely to be as significant a means in the future of constraining the Court as in the past.

In three of the other nine periods of congressional Court-curbing efforts, Rosenberg concludes that the Court was unaffected and stayed on the same decisional path (1893 to 1897, 1922 to 1924, and 1963 to 1965). The political assault on the Court in these periods dissipated of its own accord. In the other three periods, he finds the Court neither acquiesced strongly in the face of congressional pushback nor maintained its same decisional path wholly unaffected by the congressional action. In these three indeterminate periods, he notes, the congressional opposition to the Court could

---

are 1802–04, 1823–31, 1858–69, 1893–97, 1922–24, 1935–37, 1955–59, 1963–65, and 1977–82. Id at 379. These periods do not correspond exactly to those identified in the one other major study of Court-curbing bills. See Tom Clark, *The Separation of Powers, Court Curbing, and Judicial Legitimacy*, 53 Am J Pol Sci 971, 979 (2009). Borrowing from others, Rosenberg defined a relevant congressional bill as legislation introduced in the Congress having as its purpose or effect, either explicit or implicit, Court reversal of a decision or line of decisions, or Court abstention from future decisions of a given kind, or alteration in the structure or functioning of the Court to produce a particular substantive outcome. Rosenberg, 54 Rev Pol at 377 (cited above in this note). His data appear to terminate in 1984.

not effectively coalesce into an effective, unified opposition.

This analysis of Court-curbing efforts in Congress does not seem to support a particularly strong version of the majoritarian thesis.[117] Even if one accepts that the Court might be constrained when Congress manages credibly to threaten to curb the Court, there have been only three periods in which we can conclude unequivocally that the Court actually backed down in any significant manner. One of those is of little modern relevance; in the other two periods, the key factor might well have been, not congressional resistance, but the President's ability to reshape the Court through the appointments process. But if that process no longer provides as effective a means for Presidents to bring the Court into line, as I argue below, it is unclear what relevance even these periods hold going forward.[118]

If congressional efforts have been of only moderate effect, how can majoritarian theorists appeal to political mechanisms as an important mode of Court constraint? The classic source of this claim, Dahl, seems to have implicitly envisioned two distinct configurations of national politics within which the Court might operate. His theory applied to the first, but not the second. In that first configuration, "[n]ational politics in the United States, as in other stable democracies, is dominated by relatively cohesive alliances that endure for long periods of time."[119] In noting this structure of politics, Dahl referred to the Jeffersonian alliance, the Jacksonian era, the "extraordinary long-lived Republican dominance of the post-Civil War years," and the New Deal alliance FDR shaped. It was with respect to *these* alliances that Dahl concluded—in a famous line often taken out of context—that "the Supreme Court is in-

---

[117] Rosenberg himself concludes otherwise, but it is not clear that his data justify that conclusion, unless the hypothesis being tested is that the Court is always fully independent of the political branches and their responses to Court decisions, including through the appointments process. Indeed, a recent study concludes that from 1875 to the present, a large enough political faction or coalition has always existed to block any major congressional effort to curb federal court jurisdiction. See Tara Leigh Grove, *The Structural Safeguards of Federal Jurisdiction*, 124 Harv L Rev 869, 874 (2011).

[118] A comprehensive, recent statistical analysis examines not just discrete periods of intense Court-curbing efforts in Congress, but the entire history of Court-curbing efforts since 1877. See Clark, 53 Am J Pol Sci at 971 (cited in note 116). That study concludes that an increase in year 1 of congressional Court-curbing efforts results in a statistically significant decrease in the number of federal laws held unconstitutional the following year. Id at 981.

[119] Dahl, 6 J Pub L at 293 (cited in note 4).

evitably part of the dominant national alliance."[120] Indeed, dominant political coalitions of the duration of these past alliances will naturally see their preferences reflected in the Court, in no small part because they are in control long enough to appoint controlling Justices who share that coalition's general views.

When Dahl wrote, he was able to look back on long stretches of American politics in which such enduring, dominant governing coalitions had existed. During his lifetime and for the first half of the twentieth century, divided government hardly existed. From 1900 to 1952, twenty-two out of twenty-six national elections (85 percent) produced unified party control, with the Republicans dominating in the first quarter of the century (with an interlude during the Wilson administration) and the Democrats in the second quarter. In only four midterm elections in these years (two of them at the end of wars) did the President's party temporarily lose control of one house of Congress (1910, 1918, 1930, 1946). In each case, unified party control was restored in the next election.[121]

But American politics has not existed in such a period for some time now. We have not had the kind of dominant governing coalition that was critical to Dahl's theory of the Court since, perhaps, the 1960s. Indeed, we live in an era in which the country has remained almost evenly divided over more election cycles in a row than at any time since the 1880s, if then;[122] we thus experience exceptional volatility in partisan control of the national institutions of government. The parties have alternated in control of the House and Senate more in recent years than at any time since the late nineteenth century. We have now had three shifts in partisan control of the House in sixteen years, beginning with the 1994 Republican takeover after forty years of continuous Democratic control; not since the late nineteenth century have partisan turnover rates been

---

[120] Id.

[121] For the data in this paragraph, see Daryl J. Levinson and Richard H. Pildes, *Separation of Parties, Not Powers*, 119 Harv L Rev 2311, 2330 (2006).

[122] The data evidencing these patterns are in Samuel Merrill III et al, *Cycles in American National Electoral Politics, 1854–2006: Statistical Evidence and an Explanatory Model*, 102 Am Pol Sci Rev 1 (2008). In particular, see Figure 1D, at 4, which averages for each election year the Democratic seat share for the House, Senate, and presidency; since around 1992, that percentage has consistently hovered in a narrow range close to 50 percent, longer than in any period reflected in the figure, which dates back to the formation of the modern two-party system in 1854. This pattern appears to have begun, arguably, in 1976, with a brief spike of Democratic preferences around 1992, but not for a sustained period.

as high.[123] Similarly, the Senate has changed party control five times since 1985, again a more rapid rate of partisan turnover than at any time in the twentieth century.[124]

If these patterns continue, they suggest two implications for the Court's freedom of action. First, it becomes unlikely that any electoral coalition would control the presidency and Senate over long enough periods of time to be certain to put its imprint on the Court through the appointments process. FDR succeeded in taming the Court because his coalition governed long enough to dominate that process. Second, this partisan volatility, which also makes divided government more likely, will make it much more difficult to enact specific laws to curb the Court.

Dahl himself recognized a second kind of configuration of politics, one more akin to recent American experience, in which no dominant and sustained national coalition exists. In these periods, Dahl argued, the coalition in power would be "unstable with respect to certain key policies" and the Court could "succeed in establishing policy" of its own.[125] This suppressed strain in Dahl's work is the relevant one for contemporary American politics. As Mark Tushnet has noted, in periods of divided government (or perhaps periods of rapid partisan turnover in control) judges have substantial freedom to enforce their own constitutional visions because any particular vision will be shared by enough elected officials to block legislative response to the Court.[126] In an era of unified political parties and routine Senate filibusters, the system will function like divided government most of the time, absent dramatic change (the last time one party had more than sixty seats, enough to block filibusters regularly, was the 96th Congress in 1979 to 1981).[127] The Court's freedom of action, accordingly, will be considerable, as *Citizens United* perhaps signals.

Mark Graber illuminates still another reason why the Court can

---

[123] These calculations are based on data taken from http://clerk.house.gov/art_history/house_history/partyDiv.html.

[124] These calculations are based on data taken from http://www.senate.gov/pagelayout/history/one_item_and_teasers/partydiv.htm.

[125] Dahl, 6 J Pub L at 294 (cited in note 4).

[126] Mark Tushnet, *Political Power and Judicial Power: Some Observations on Their Relation*, 75 Fordham L Rev 755, 768 (2006).

[127] Harold W. Stanley and Richard G. Niemi, *Vital Statistics on American Politics, 2005–2006* 38–39 (CQ Press, 2006).

often act with relative autonomy.[128] In an effort to avoid responsibility for issues that risk fracturing their supporting coalition, political leaders will defer at times to the Court's power to resolve
the issue. Graber sees these situations as ones in which the political
branches "invite" the Court in.[129]

Because there is no effective congressional majority on the issue,
perhaps these are situations in which the Court's decision to invalidate national action cannot be considered either majoritarian or
countermajoritarian with respect to the political branches. Even so,
here too the Court has considerable latitude and power, and hence
the moral questions about why the Court ought to have this power
cannot be dismissed by casting the Court as doing no more than
implementing "majoritarian views."[130]

Finally, some majoritarians view the President rather than Congress as the most likely source of political constraint. But if presidential leadership is supposed to be a major or contributing force
driving political responses to the Court, it is significant that the
most thorough study of the relationship between Presidents and
the Court concludes that only five Presidents have directly challenged the authority of the Court: Jefferson, Jackson, Lincoln,
Franklin Roosevelt, and Reagan.[131] Only during these "reconstructive" presidencies, as Keith Whittington characterizes them, do
Presidents want to fight constitutional battles with the Court and
enjoy enough public support to be capable of waging a credible
battle. Only these few reconstructive Presidents have sought to
challenge the fundamental interpretive authority of the Court—to
split the constitutional atom, as he nicely puts it—and separate
judicial supremacy from constitutionalism.[132] But these periods of
reconstructive presidencies do not endure for long. During the rest
of American history, Presidents have had neither the ambition nor

---

[128] Graber, 7 Stud Am Polit Dev at 35 (cited in note 44).

[129] Graber has good evidence to support the claim that Congress did affirmatively invite
the Court into the slavery issue in the 1850s, which led to *Dred Scott*, and the antitrust
issues of the late nineteenth and early twentieth centuries. Id at 46–53. In other contexts,
it might be more appropriate to see Congress as acquiescing in the Court's power, rather
than affirmatively inviting the Court in.

[130] Graber thinks that because there is a dominant majority whose preferences the Court
is frustrating, the Court cannot be said to be countermajoritarian in these contexts. But
that is not enough to dismiss the moral concerns about judicial review: the Court is
exercising an important form of political power, and the question is what justifies that.

[131] Whittington, *Political Foundations* at 30–31 (cited in note 52).

[132] Id at 286.

the support to challenge the Court in any fundamental way. And as "presidential authority to interpret the Constitution wanes, judicial authority waxes."[133] In addition, Whittington concludes that the reduced ability of Presidents since the New Deal to control Congress, even a same-party Congress, and the greater frequency of divided government mean that the power of Presidents to pursue constitutionally reconstructive visions that challenge the Court has diminished; while visions of this sort might continue to exist, Presidents are less able to muster effective support for them.[134] This, too, enables Courts to act with greater autonomy.[135] Indeed, though Whittington's work is sometimes invoked as support for the majoritarian view of the Court, his analysis is actually more complex and subtle. His view is that the Court should be understood within the larger framework of national political institutions, especially the presidency, but that within that framework the Court often has a great deal of semiautonomous space within which it can act.

In sum, the constraints political institutions impose on the Court today might be much less than some majoritarian theorists suggest. None of this is to say that the Court will necessarily challenge the central political commitments of a dominant governing coalition, particularly an enduring one. But Congress has not effectively retaliated or even credibly threatened to retaliate against the Court in generations; even when Congress has done so, it has had only sporadic success. Only two Presidents in the twentieth century have directly challenged the authority of the Court. And whatever power dominant, enduring governing coalitions have to constrain the Court, we have not had such coalitions for many years. The political branches today are less likely effectively to resist the Court. History suggests the most effective means of doing so is through the appointments process. But for reasons to which I now turn, that process is likely to be a much weaker mechanism than it has been in the past.

3. *The appointments process.* The one powerful mechanism for ensuring that the Court is in line with majoritarian views is the appointments process, which in the United States is more politically structured than in some countries. Indeed, most majoritarians rely

---

[133] Id at 287.

[134] Id at 273–74.

[135] Id at 274.

centrally on this mechanism to explain how the Court purportedly comes to reflect national political majorities.[136] If the cycle of appointing Justices tracked the cycles of electoral politics, there would be strong reason to expect the Court continually to reflect the dominant views of the President and Senate. But the life-tenure system has always made the appointments process more random than that; moreover, that randomness has increased dramatically over recent decades. The majoritarian thesis depends heavily on the appointments mechanism, but that mechanism is much weaker now than in the past.

The role of luck in the extent to which Presidents and their governing coalition can shape the Court is illustrated by the contrast between the Nixon and Clinton presidencies. Nixon had the opportunity to make four appointments (Burger, Blackmun, Powell, and Rehnquist) between 1969 and 1972. Those appointments defined the character of the Burger Court until at least the mid-1980s. Yet while serving two full terms, Clinton was able to appoint only two Justices (Ginsburg and Breyer), with only modest effect on the Court's substantive positions. Power to shape the Court through the appointments process does not always correlate with electoral success.

Moreover, Justices these days serve longer, on average, than in the past; they leave the Court at much older ages; and they therefore create vacancies at much lower rates. As Steven Calabresi and James Lindgren have documented, the average tenure of a Justice from 1941 to 1970 was 12.2 years.[137] But from 1971 to 2000, retiring Justices spent an average of 26.1 years on the Court. In that first period, Justices retired at an average age of 67.6 years; in the latter period, they did so on average at 78.7 years. These patterns then show up in vacancy rates; from 1881 to 1970, the average number

---

[136] See, for example, Dahl, 6 J Pub L at 284–85 (cited in note 4); Graber, 4 Ann Rev L & Soc Sci at 366–67 (cited in note 3); Balkin, 103 Nw U L Rev at 22 (cited in note 48).

[137] The data in this and the following paragraph are taken from Steven G. Calabresi and James Lindgren, *Term Limits for the Supreme Court: Life Tenure Reconsidered*, 29 Harv J L & Pub Pol 769 (2006). Calabresi and Lindgren characterize the change since 1970 as "dramatic and unprecedented." Id, *passim*. In an important rejoinder, David Stras and Ryan Scott argue that this characterization is an artifact of the way Calabresi and Lindgren have chosen the time intervals they use. Instead, Stras and Scott conclude that there has been "slow and steady growth in length of tenure over time." David R. Stras and Ryan W. Scott, *An Empirical Analysis of Life Tenure: A Response to Professors Calabresi and Lindgren*, 30 Harv J L & Pub Pol 791, 830 (2007).

of years between appointments was 1.7, with that rate fairly consistent throughout these years. Since 1970, it has increased to 3.1 years.[138] Put differently, in that earlier era, a two-term President appointed on average 4.7 Justices (more than half the Court), while today such a President would appoint only 2.7 Justices.

This change has a dramatic effect on the opportunity of Presidents to shape the Court. For example, Jimmy Carter was the only President in American history to complete one term yet never make an appointment to the Court. The same would have happened to George W. Bush had he not been reelected. Another telling fact: from 1994 to 2005, the Court went nearly eleven years without a vacancy, the longest such period since the Court's size was fixed at nine Justices in 1869. Indeed, three of the five longest periods between vacancies since the Court went to nine members have occurred in the last thirty years.

In addition, over the last generation American political parties have become more ideologically unified and more sharply polarized and differentiated from each other than at any time since the late nineteenth century.[139] Thus, "in 1970, moderates constituted 41% of the Senate; today, they are 5%."[140] The center "has all but disappeared."[141] The effects of this transformed party structure on the appointments process remain to be seen in full. As Geoffrey Stone reports, even before this transformation, no nominee of a President whose party controls the Senate has been denied confirmation in a full Senate vote in more than eighty years; only one has been so denied in the last 140 years. Stone reports that from 1964 to 1986, around 91 percent of Senators voted to confirm a nominee chosen by a same-party President, and since then that figure has gone up to around 99 percent.[142] With such unified, lock-step parties, we do not know how far a President with a same-party Senate can go toward appointing Justices with more extreme views, should a President choose to head in that direction. Of course, this partisan

---

[138] By my own calculations, it has been slightly lower, 2.5 years between appointments, on average, since 1980, taking into account the most recent appointment of Justice Elena Kagan.

[139] Richard H. Pildes, *Why the Center Does Not Hold: Hyperpolarized Democracy in America*, 99 Cal L Rev 273 (forthcoming 2010).

[140] Id.

[141] Id.

[142] Geoffrey R. Stone, *Understanding Supreme Court Confirmations*, 2010 Supreme Court Review (in this volume).

configuration might spawn more contested nominations (as it already has, though with little effect on outcomes)[143] or more filibusters of Supreme Court nominations. The equilibrium that these competing pushes and pulls from highly unified and polarized parties will generate for the kinds of Justices who will be nominated and confirmed in the future is unknown. But the emergence of "hyperpolarized democracy in America" over the last generation further suggests that predicting how the increasingly random timing of appointments will play out in constraining or liberating the Court cannot necessarily be predicted from the past.

E. THE DATA

Surprisingly little data have been collected to test empirically any of the (many) versions of the majoritarian thesis. Many of the works seeking to demonstrate this thesis take the form of historical Court narratives,[144] but works of this sort, while valuable, always run the risk of selection bias and do not provide the systematic and comprehensive quantitative data on which we can base robust judgments about patterns of Court-Congress-President relationships over time. For empirical support, these works often refer back to Dahl's original, pioneering study.

But Dahl's work, pathbreaking in 1957, has not stood up over time. Parts of it come across as quaint. Dahl, for example, noted that there was not a single case in the Court's history in which the Court had held federal legislation unconstitutional on First Amendment grounds.[145] In the years since, of course, it has become commonplace for the Court to do so. Whether with respect to Congress's efforts to regulate flag burning, child pornography, sexually explicit material, funding to legal services organizations, commercial advertisements, government-employee receipt of honoraria, or speech in public spaces, the Court has struck down numerous federal statutes on the basis of the First Amendment.[146]

---

[143] Id.

[144] See, for example, Alfange, *The Supreme Court* (cited in note 41); McCloskey, *American Supreme Court* (cited in note 44); Friedman, *Will of the People* (cited in note 47); Graber, 7 Stud Am Polit Dev 35 (cited in note 44).

[145] Dahl, 6 J Pub L at 292 (cited in note 4).

[146] See, for example, *United States v Stevens*, 130 S Ct 1577 (2010); *Ashcroft v American Civil Liberties Union*, 542 US 656 (2004); *Legal Services Corp. v Velazquez*, 531 US 533 (2001); *Sable Communications of California v FCC*, 492 US 115 (1989); *Regan v Time, Inc.*, 468 US 641 (1984); *Bolger v Youngs Drug Products Corp.*, 463 US 60 (1983).

And in the context of campaign-finance regulation, Dahl's observation is particularly ironic. Ever since the beginning of modern congressional efforts in the 1970s to regulate financing of national elections, the Court—starting with *Buckley v Valeo*—has invalidated national legislation time and time again, culminating in *Citizens United*. But beyond the specific example of the First Amendment, a series of empirical studies starting in the mid-1970s have undermined Dahl's general findings.[147] As Whittington notes, "[s]ubsequent empirical analyses of Dahl's thesis have generally failed to confirm his findings."[148]

The most comprehensive study of these questions appears in recent unpublished work by Clark and Whittington.[149] As they point out, most empirical work in "attitudinal studies" of judicial decision making focuses on correlating votes of individual judges or Justices with outcomes, rather than on the behavior of multi-member judicial institutions, like the Supreme Court, as a whole.[150] They constructed a data set that includes every Supreme Court decision from 1789 to 2006 in which the Court addressed a substantial question concerning the constitutionality of federal legislation. By examining not just cases in which the Court holds legislation unconstitutional, but also cases in which the Court upholds legislation against constitutional challenge, their study is the first to offer a comprehensive view of the Court's treatment of federal legislation. Surprisingly, they conclude that the Court over its history has struck down or constitutionally limited federal legislation in 25 percent of the cases involving a constitutional challenge.[151] To my mind, that is an unexpectedly high rate, particularly because the rate in the modern era must be much higher

---

[147] See generally Richard Funston, *The Supreme Court and Critical Elections*, 69 Am Pol Sci Rev 795 (1975); Jonathan D. Casper, *The Supreme Court and National Policy Making*, 70 Am Pol Sci Rev 50 (1976); Bradley C. Canon and S. Sidney Ulmer, *The Supreme Court and Critical Elections: A Dissent*, 70 Am Pol Sci Rev 1215(1976); Roger Handberg and Harold F. Hill Jr., *Court Curbing, Court Reversals, and Judicial Review: The Supreme Court versus Congress*, 14 L & Society Rev 309 (1980); Gregory A. Caldeira and Donald J. McCrone, *Of Time and Judicial Activism: A Study of the U.S. Supreme Court, 1800–1973*, in Stephen Halpern and Charles Lamb, eds, *Supreme Court Activism and Restraint* (Lexington, 1982); William Lasser, *The Supreme Court in Periods of Critical Realignment*, 47 J Pol 1174 (1985); John B. Taylor, *The Supreme Court and Political Eras: A Perspective on Judicial Power in a Democratic Polity*, 54 Rev Pol 345(1992).

[148] Whittington, *Political Foundations* at 42 (cited in note 52) .

[149] Clark and Whittington, *Ideology* (cited in note 113).

[150] Id at 35.

[151] Id at 12.

than that, given that judicial review has become more assertive over time. If accurate, their analysis suggests that the Court stands up against national lawmaking majorities at much higher rates than many majoritarian theorists (and others) have assumed. Their findings also portray a Court characterized by sustained periods of "activism" (defined as invalidating federal legislation), rather than a Court defined by brief outbursts of activism, followed by long periods of deference.[152]

Moreover, Clark and Whittington find that the Court's decisions are not, in the aggregate, correlated with partisan alignments between the Justices and Congress. The Court has been no more likely to invalidate congressional statutes of the Court's partisan opponents than the Court's partisan allies. That is, using the party of the appointing President as the party affiliation of a Justice, a Republican-dominated Court has historically been no more likely to strike down statutes enacted by a Democratic Congress than a Republican one, and so too for a Democratic-dominated Court. As they note, this finding runs counter to much of the received wisdom on the perceived relationship of the Court, the political process, and partisanship. The Court is somewhat more likely to invalidate laws passed at moments of divided government.[153]

Turning to more refined measures of judicial ideology than the party of the appointing President,[154] Clark and Whittington then find that the more ideologically distant the enacting Congress is from the ideology of the Court (using their measure), the more likely the Court is to invalidate a statute on its face. But these ideological differences have no effect when it comes to decisions invalidating statutes as applied; the Court is no more or less likely to invalidate federal statutes as applied based on whether the enacting Congress is ideologically close or distant to the Court.[155]

---

[152] Id at 13.

[153] Id at 34.

[154] Having rejected the view that the partisan identity of the Court's majority affects whether the Court is more or less likely to invalidate congressional legislation enacted by the same party, Clark and Whittington then construct a different measure of judicial "ideology." To construct this measure of ideology, Clark and Whittington attempt to replicate the now familiar DW-NOMINATE scores used for votes in Congress. Thus, for Justices who served in Congress, they use the actual DW-NOMINATE scores from their votes. For Justices who did not, they average the DW-NOMINATE scores of the appointing President and the same-party home-state senators of the appointed Justice. Id at 16. Whether these are useful measures of judicial "ideology" I leave to others to assess.

[155] Id at 20.

The Court invalidates statutes as applied more often than on their face (58 percent of federal statutes invalidated were invalidated as applied). Finally, contrary to one of Dahl's claims, Clark and Whittington do not find that important legislation is invalidated any more quickly than less important legislation (they also find important legislation to be upheld at higher rates than other legislation).[156] These findings suggest, at the least, that considerably more refined conclusions than Dahl's original ones are required to understand the relationship between partisan and ideological preferences, on the one hand, and Court decisions on the other.

F. THE CHANGING POWER OF THE COURT OVER TIME

The perceived legitimacy and authority of the Court are not constant or static, but dynamic. That the power and stature of the Court have increased dramatically over time is widely recognized. In the 1820s and 1830s, for example, state officials regularly denied the authority of the Court. They refused to appear before the Court, ignored Court decisions, contested the authority of the Court to review state court decisions, and even executed a defendant in the face of Court orders to the contrary.[157] In 1831, the House Judiciary Committee went so far as to report out a bill to repeal Section 25 of the Judiciary Act of 1789, which would have eliminated the Court's power over the state courts.[158] But much as the Civil War settled the question of whether states can secede from the Union—the ultimate question to which all these forms of state defiance of the Court in the antebellum period were leading—American constitutional and political development have effectively settled these related questions concerning the Court's authority over state officials and institutions. The forms of state defiance of the Court from this earlier era are virtually inconceivable today.

Similarly, when faced in 1903 with constitutional challenges to the massive disfranchisement of black voters in the South after Reconstruction had died, the Court confessed impotence, declaring that any order on its part to counter disfranchisement "would

---

[156] Id at 21.

[157] See generally Friedman, *Will of the People* at 72–105 (cited in note 47).

[158] Id at 88.

be an empty form."[159] In language shocking to a modern ear, the Court, per Justice Holmes, wrote that the Court had:

> little practical power to deal with the people of the State in a body. The bill imports that the great mass of the white population intends to keep the blacks from voting. To meet such an intent something more than ordering the plaintiff's name to be inscribed upon the lists of 1902 will be needed. If the conspiracy and the intent exist, a name on a piece of paper [issued by the Court] will not defeat them. Unless we are prepared to supervise the voting in that State by officers of the court, it seems to us that all that the plaintiff could get from equity would be an empty form.[160]

Giles's language and result is consistent with the majoritarian thesis, in that the Court had no reason to believe the national political branches in that era would support and effectively enforce a Court decision to hold disfranchisement unconstitutional.[161] But the Court's language is shocking today precisely because these words are so alien to widely shared and deeply entrenched modern cultural and political understandings. Today, the Court can force a President to commit political suicide, by requiring him to turn over evidence that will inexorably drive him out of office,[162] and can help put a President in office by resolving a disputed presidential election.[163] It is difficult to conceive of the Court contemplating such actions in the nineteenth century, let alone being confident that its decisions on such issues would be honored and enforced. That is not to say that *any* decision of the Court today will be obeyed and enforced; surely limits exist. But the capacity of the Court to bend political actors and institutions, state and national, to the Court's judgments has increased dramatically.

A dynamic appreciation of the Court's authority over time requires caution about concluding that the deep history of political control over the Court is predictive of the Court's freedom of action today. The authority of the Court over time is also relational: as the authority of competing institutions, such as Congress or the presidency, wax and wane, the Court's autonomy will also

---

[159] *Giles v Harris*, 189 US 475 (1903).

[160] Id at 488.

[161] For fuller discussion of the context and aftermath of the case, see Richard H. Pildes, *Keeping Legal History Meaningful*, 19 Const Comm 645 (2002), and Richard H. Pildes, *Democracy, Anti-Democracy, and the Canon*, 17 Const Comm 295 (2000).

[162] *United States v Nixon*, 418 US 683 (1974).

[163] *Bush v Gore*, 531 US 908 (2000).

ebb and flow. But as noted above, since the 1970s, the Court has consistently been the most trusted institution in the national government; in recent years, public trust in the Court has vastly exceeded that in Congress or the President.[164] These long-term patterns give the Court additional space for autonomous action.

Majoritarians sometimes diminish the force of these contextual considerations and take too static or isolated a view of the Court's freedom of action. They suggest, for example, that the Court has internalized this deep history of state defiance of, or legislative assaults on, the Court, even if no effective major national or state efforts to cabin in the Court have occurred for generations.[165] Yet the more recent history of failed political attempts to rein in the Court should give the Court more, not less, confidence in its independent authority.

Indeed, the modern Congress typically treats the Court as the exclusive authority over constitutional issues. As Neal Devins has pointed out, one expression of this legislative deferral is the growing prevalence of statutes creating expedited Supreme Court review for statutes whose constitutionality is subject to debate.[166] Not only does Congress willingly invite the Court in, or prefer that the Court take responsibility for constitutional issues, but today's Congress "rarely casts doubt on either the correctness of the Court's ruling or, more fundamentally, the Court's power to authoritatively interpret the Constitution."[167]

Nonetheless, we are told, the institutional memory of the Court has absorbed this deeper history, which disciplines the Court to avoid countermajoritarian decisions. But why should the Court feel any more threatened by the history of antebellum attacks on it, for example, than Congress is today by the threat of secession? Why should the Court fear retaliatory Court-packing or Court-reducing plans, given the history of FDR's failed and self-destructive efforts? Norms about the legitimate role of the Court could change again—even secession could, in theory, become a viable option again—but the Court can safely discount to almost zero

---

[164] See note 87.

[165] See, for example, Friedman, *Will of the People* at 376 (cited in note 47) (arguing that, although "it has been a long time since the justices were disciplined in any significant way," nonetheless "anticipated reaction" keeps the Justices in line with public opinion).

[166] Devins, 76 L & Contemp Probs at 70 (cited in note 57).

[167] Id.

the risk that the most extreme political responses against it from the past will emerge again if the Court pursues its convictions about constitutional law too aggressively. The modern Court has considerably more latitude to depart from "majoritarian preferences," however defined, and the Court knows it. For prudential reasons, the Court might conclude that it is healthier for the country if particularly explosive cultural issues are handled legislatively or in the state courts—same-sex marriage might be a test case of this proposition—but that would not be because the Court feared it would be institutionally self-destructive for the Court to engage the issue.

One final response from majoritarians to the obviously greater autonomy of the modern Court is that this autonomy exists only because the American people continue to grant it. But this move radically shifts the grounds for the majoritarian thesis and transforms it into something else altogether; it now offers a second-order, rather than first-order, definition or conception of "majoritarian." This shift salvages the majoritarian thesis by asserting that even if the Court defies majorities (whatever the conception of "majorities" might be) on particular substantive issues, those same majorities still support the Court's legitimacy and authority to defy them. That argument turns the majoritarian thesis into a theory of Burkean consent or acquiescence in the status quo; the public's inaction in the face of a Court decision means, on this view, that whatever the Court decides is accepted by "the majority." In other words, by definition the Court can never get away with actions that are countermajoritarian, in this sense (nor can any other public institution, I suppose).

At this point, it is not clear what the majoritarian thesis is supposed to be illuminating. It is true of all public institutions, of course, that in some sense they continue to exist and maintain their authority only because "the people" are willing to accept that authority (or, the perceived costs of destroying that authority are greater than the harms imposed from particular decisions). At the descriptive level, this argument raises several questions, many of them familiar. How would the withdrawal of this second-order consent to the Court's authority have to manifest itself to be effective in bringing the Court to heel? Would it be enough for public support for the Court to drop dramatically? Or would that withdrawal of diffuse support and consent have to be expressed

through actual legislative withdrawal of powers from the Court—
in which case, all the familiar collective-action problems of organizing and mobilizing a discontented public into concerted political action would arise, as well as the familiar realities of many
veto gates within legislative bodies and the need to construct an
effective supermajority to overcome the inertial forces internal to
Congress.

In addition, we would now want to know what the parameters
of this second-order or diffuse support for the Court might be.
On this view, the Court can in fact go some distance toward creating law that runs counter to the substantive preferences of (political or public) majorities. Of course, this autonomy is not lim-
itless. But how far can the Court deviate from majoritarian
preferences (public or political) before its second-order support
dissolves? That is a rather different question from the claim that
the Court's decisions are substantively strongly constrained by
first-order "majoritarian" pressures. And from a moral perspective,
if one thought judicial review were a kind of oligarchic rule or a
form of despotism, as Bickel suggested and as some modern critics
of judicial review, such as Jeremy Waldron, argue, this second-
order consent argument would raise familiar moral questions
about the status of consent to despotism.

G. MORAL ISSUES: STATE LAWS AND TIME

Most of the laws the Court invalidates are state laws. By
one count, for example, the Burger Court struck down ten times
as many state as federal laws; the Warren Court, seven times as
many.[168] The Court's review of state law was the context in which
Bickel wrote in 1962; his aim was to confront moral questions the
Court's recent civil rights decisions, starting with *Brown*, had
spawned. Moreover, even a brief list provides a reminder of how
much of the most significant and most controversial work of the
Court involves constitutional invalidation of state, not national,
laws: the reapportionment revolution, *Brown* and civil rights,[169]
the development of a constitutional code of criminal procedure,

---

[168] See Bernard Schwartz, *The Ascent of Pragmatism: The Burger Court in Action* 408
(Addison, 1990).

[169] Richard Primus has pointed out that the Court has never invalidated a federal law
as a race-based violation of equal protection, even as the Court has invalidated many state
laws on this basis. Richard A. Primus, *Bolling Alone*, 104 Colum L Rev 975 (2004).

the right to privacy and *Roe v Wade*, issues concerning religion, obscenity, sexual orientation, and so on.

The classic majoritarians, such as Dahl, did not address this aspect of the Court's work at all. Dahl examined only the relationship between the Court and federal statutes.[170] Thus, Dahl had nothing to say about whether the Court did or could act as a countermajoritarian institution in the most important arena in which the Court acts, its review of state laws, or even what this question might mean.[171]

Modern majoritarians are more imperialistic than Dahl. They seek to extend the majoritarian thesis to state laws as well. Their response is that when the Court strikes down state laws, it often invalidates laws that are "outliers"—because few states have similar laws—or reflects the preferences of a national *popular* majority.[172] The Court's decisions are thus "majoritarian" in one or the other or both of these senses. Thus, we are told that *Brown* reflected the views of a national majority,[173] or that many seemingly controversial decisions of the Warren and Burger Courts were supported by half the public or more in polls, or that *Roe v Wade*[174] "followed social trends," because "polls suggested strong support for leaving the decision to women and their doctors"[175]—although

---

[170] Dahl, 6 J Pub L at 282 (cited in note 4).

[171] Nonetheless, legal scholars sometimes cite Dahl as if his analysis applied not only to national laws, but to the Court's more significant role: its relationship to state lawmaking institutions. See, for example, Rosen, *Most Democratic Branch* at 6 (cited in note 68); Balkin, 103 Nw U L Rev at 561 n 32 (cited in note 48).

[172] See, for example, Adam Samaha, *Low Stakes and Constitutional Interpretation* (unpublished manuscript, 2010) (arguing that debates over judicial review involve low stakes, in part because "much of the Warren Court's constitutional work policed local or regional outlier policies without contradicting anything approaching a national consensus") (citing Lucas A. Powe, Jr., *The Warren Court and American Politics* 34–37, 376, 379–80, 396, 489–94 (2000)); Balkin, 103 Nw U L Rev at 565 (cited in note 48).

[173] Friedman, *Will of the People* at 297 (cited in note 47). On state statutes concerning abortion at the time of *Roe*, see Jack M. Balkin, *What Brown Teaches Us About Constitutional Theory*, 90 Va L Rev 1537, 1545 (2004).

[174] 410 US 113 (1973).

[175] More refined breakdowns in the questions polled suggest that support for abortion in extreme circumstances, such as serious danger to the woman's health or pregnancy due to rape, received 75 percent support in polls, while support for abortion dropped to less than 50 percent if the reasons for it were that the woman could not afford more children, was not married and did not want to marry the man, or the woman was married and did not want any more children. Thomas A. Schmeling, *Supreme Court Counter-Majoritarianism Revisited: Warren Court Cases Invalidating State Laws, 1954–1969* at 20 (paper for delivery at the annual meeting of the Midwest Political Science Association, April 7–10, 2005). These divergences illuminate the notoriously elusive nature of polling data on these kinds of questions.

Roe had the effect of invalidating abortion laws in forty-six states, and ten months after *Roe*, thirty-two states had adopted new abortion restrictions, most of which were clear attempts to cabin in *Roe*.[176]

This "outlier" claim, however, should not be overstated. Many of the Court's most well-known decisions holding state laws unconstitutional did not involve state "outliers." In addition to *Roe*'s invalidation of forty-six state laws, *Reynolds v Sims*[177] invalidated the structure of every state senate, *New York Times v Sullivan*[178] invalidated the libel laws of every state, *Miranda*[179] held unconstitutional state laws in nearly every state, *Engel v Vitale*[180] invalidated at least thirty states' statutes, *Mapp v Ohio*[181] struck down laws in twenty-four states (though the trend was moving toward state adoption of the exclusionary rule).[182] One major empirical study on this question concludes that 36 percent of the Warren Court's "most significant decisions" struck down state laws in a majority of states.[183] Even at the descriptive level, then, it is important not to overstate the extent to which the Court's constitutional veto extends only to aberrational state laws.

More profoundly, the facts about how common a particular state law is, or how much national "opinion" supports or opposes that law, cannot answer the moral question Bickel raised. Yet modern majoritarians sometimes assert that facts like these do provide an answer, so that the concerns about judicial review can be dismissed.[184] But even assuming that "majoritarian" views can adequately be measured by polling data, rather than actual state laws, or even assuming most state laws the Court invalidates are outliers,

---

[176] See Barry Friedman, *Mediated Popular Constitutionalism*, 101 Mich L Rev 2596 (2003); Barry Friedman, *Dialogue and Judicial Review*, 91 Mich L Rev 577 (1993).

[177] 377 US 533 (1964).

[178] 376 US 254 (1964).

[179] *Miranda v Arizona*, 384 US 436 (1966).

[180] 370 US 421 (1962).

[181] 367 US 643 (1961).

[182] Schmeling, *Supreme Court Counter-Majoritarianism* at 25 (cited in note 175).

[183] Id at 39.

[184] See, for example, Graber, 7 Stud Am Polit Dev at 35–36 (cited in note 44) ("Indeed, the claim that independent judicial policymaking is rarely legitimate in a democracy is not wholly compatible with the claim that independent judicial policymaking seldom takes place in a democracy."); Friedman, *Will of the People* at 372 (cited in note 47) (concluding that "the close relationship between popular opinion and judicial review goes a long way toward addressing Bickel's 'counter-majoritarian difficulty.'").

these facts do not answer the moral question. If the appropriate level of democratic self-government for a certain issue is the state level (based on American political practices and culture, or a view of the Constitution, or more general theoretical considerations), the Court is overturning a judgment of the relevant lawmaking majority. The question of what level of self-government, national or state, is appropriate for various issues is itself a moral question. Yet the Court's decision imposes a national rule for the issue. Simply to say that the rule reflects national majority preferences, or the preferences of other states, is to beg this moral question. That the Court has concluded that the Constitution mandates a particular result cannot answer this question, of course, since we need a theory that stands outside the Court's action to evaluate whether the Court's action is correct. Put another way, those who are inflamed by the Court's decisions, on the ground that the Court is running roughshod over the preferences of state lawmaking majorities, have every reason to express outrage at the Court's actions, even if those actions reflect the views of a national majority. The moral force behind Bickel's challenge to judicial review still requires a morally adequate answer.

In addition, the Court's decisions in these areas are often outcome determinative: these decisions change public policy in ways it would not have otherwise changed. National popular opinion majorities in opinion polls might agree with the Court's decisions, but those free-floating majority opinions would never have been translated into national lawmaking outcomes. Would Congress have legislated a national code of proper police conduct even if national majorities agreed with the substantive content of the rules in cases like *Miranda*? At the time of *Roe*, is it conceivable that Congress would have enacted national legislation on abortion, regardless of what national popular opinion polls might have shown? Apart from whatever issues might exist about Congress's formal power to legislate in such areas, American political practices and understandings would have made it seem inappropriate, if even conceivable, for Congress to legislate in these ways. Thus, the Court's decisions overturning state laws, particularly on some of the most controversial issues the Court has addressed, effectively change policy on these issues. Why the Court should have the power to do so is a moral question that cannot be dismissed by appeals to how popular the Court's decisions might be.

Finally, the majoritarian thesis should not underestimate the moral concerns that time imposes. Over long enough periods of time, if enough vacancies on the Court occur, the Court will come into line with a dominant national lawmaking coalition. But temporal lags still implicate moral concerns about judicial power.

Thus, Court decisions left the income tax unconstitutional for eighteen years, the time between *Pollock*[185] and ratification of the Sixteenth Amendment. More broadly, the Court was able to exercise considerable independence from 1912 to 1937 because opposition to its aggressive judicial role was too fragmented to cohere into an effective national lawmaking majority to resist the Court. As Keith Whittington puts it, progressives were successful enough in some states and in Congress to generate a flow of laws that the Court regarded as unconstitutional, but not strong enough to be able to marshal sufficient internal agreement or control of the presidency to be able to push back effectively at the Court.[186] To take one powerful example, the Court forestalled the implementation of child labor laws for a quarter century; Congress first enacted legislation on the issue in 1916, then again in 1919, then pursued a failed effort in the 1920s at a constitutional amendment, before enacting legislation in 1938 that the Court finally upheld in 1941.[187] To the extent majoritarians implicitly or explicitly rely on lawmaking action as the key mechanism by which the Court is constrained, the inability of nominal political majorities to translate their power into the effective majorities needed to constrain the Court should be sobering.

In the modern era, Congress is more likely to accept Court decisions as final and less likely to continue to challenge the Court than in the child labor saga. Thus, once the Court struck down restrictions on independent election spending in *Buckley v Valeo*,[188] Congress did not seek to reenact those restrictions in other forms or directly challenge the Court, even though public opinion has always strongly supported spending restrictions and most other

---

[185] *Pollock v Farmers' Loan & Trust Co.*, 157 US 429 (1895).

[186] Whittington, *Political Foundations* at 264–65 (cited in note 52).

[187] For the Court decisions, see *Hammer v Dagenhart*, 247 US 251 (1918) (holding unconstitutional act of Congress that prohibited interstate transportation of goods made with child labor), *Bailey v Drexel Furniture Co.*, 259 US 20 (1922) (holding unconstitutional Child Labor Tax Law of 1919), and *United States v Darby*, 312 US 100 (1941) (overruling *Hammer*).

[188] 424 US 1 (1976) (per curiam).

Western democracies impose such limits.[189] Although those restrictions had strong bipartisan legislative and public support at
the time, the Court's 1976 decision has essentially ended debate
on that option for the last forty years, giving the United States
the most unique system of election financing among democracies.
The Court's decisions can involve consequential and enduring
changes to the legislatively and popular preferred status quo, and
to the extent the modern majoritarian thesis (or a certain version
of it) obscures that truth, it should be resisted.

IV. THE SEMIAUTONOMOUS COURT

Nearly fifty years after Dahl first presented his argument
and empirics to suggest a Court strongly constrained by national
lawmaking institutions when reviewing national legislation, the
legal academy has rediscovered Dahl's vision and run with it. The
modern "majoritarian" scholarship has made many important contributions. For those still inclined toward a romanticized image
of the Court as a regular protector of the powerless, the outcast,
and the minority against the forces of majoritarian democracy, this
literature provides a sobering dose of realism. The Court inevitably exists and works within a larger cultural and political context.
Constitutional doctrine has changed over time, often in dramatic
ways, and the Court's decisions are not purely a matter of autonomous legal reasoning, of the law working itself "pure" in a wholly
internal process of distinctly legal reasoning. Viewed over longer
periods of time, rather than case by case, the development of
constitutional doctrine is driven by some mix, perhaps ineffable,
of external changes in politics and culture, as reflected particularly
in appointments to the Court, and internal legal analysis.

Moreover, those who hold political power, whether Presidents
or legislative-executive coalitions, sometimes have rationally self-
interested reasons on some occasions to prefer that courts resolve
certain issues.[190] In these contexts, political leaders might be conceived as willingly delegating power to courts. Thus, decisions
that appear countermajoritarian at one level, because they invoke

---

[189] On public opinion support for spending restrictions, see note 78 above. For comparative perspective on campaign finance laws, see Keith Ewing and Samuel Issacharoff,
eds, *Party Funding and Campaign Financing in International Perspective* (Oxford, 2006).

[190] Two important sources presenting this view are Graber, 7 Stud Am Polit Dev 35
(cited in note 44), and Whittington, *Political Foundations* (cited in note 52).

the Constitution to invalidate enacted laws, might better be understood as majoritarian (or better, not so obviously countermajoritarian) at a deeper level. We can always question, as well, the extent to which the elected branches of government accurately reflect "the majority's" preferences, as some of this literature reminds us.[191] Thus, in a variety of ways, the majoritarian literature has contributed to a much richer descriptive understanding of the dynamic relationship between judicial and political power.[192]

Yet if the majoritarian thesis was born in reaction to overly inflated conceptions of the Court's autonomy, that literature risks overreaction. Both descriptively and morally, the majoritarian thesis has been pushed beyond where it can be supported. To the extent some majoritarian theories now lapse into suggesting that virtually all individual Court decisions reflect "majoritarian positions," they go too far.

At the descriptive level, this literature slips back and forth between ill-defined and imprecise conceptions of the "majority" by which the Court is purportedly constrained: public opinion, or the current governing national lawmaking coalition, or the coalition that existed at the time individual Justices were appointed, or the President, or some segment of "elite" public opinion, or some faction within the governing coalition. This looseness risks making the theory a tautology. There is always some conception of "the majority" to which the Court's decisions can be said to cohere. And moral judgments about the institution of judicial review will vary depending on "the majority" by which the Court is constrained. These elusive and constantly changing conceptions of "the majority" are particularly likely to infect historical narratives of the Court's relationship to larger political forces. Yet surprisingly little comprehensive empirical work exists on the issue. Modern majoritarians often look back to Dahl for empirical support, yet within his own discipline, more recent investigations are recognized as having cast substantial doubt on his conclusions.

A clearer sense of which external constraints can plausibly be claimed to cabin in the Court would also enable better evaluation of the mechanisms by which the Court is purportedly kept within

---

[191] The first to press this point was probably Richard Parker, *The Past of Constitutional Theory—and Its Future*, 42 Ohio St L J 223 (1981). For a recent expression, see Graber, 4 Ann Rev L & Soc Sci (cited in note 3).

[192] See also Tushnet, 75 Fordham L Rev 755 (cited in note 126).

certain bounds. Is the Court constrained only when national law-making majorities are able to legislate to cut back on the Court's powers? Or is the mere credible threat that they will do so sufficient to cause the Court to pull back? Does the Court consistently respond to widespread public criticism of its actions? Or only if that challenge finds voice through the President? Or through Congress? Alternatively, perhaps it is only the appointments process that provides a robust means by which majoritarian values, as refracted through the White House and the Senate, effectively shape the Court's direction. In that case, does the Court continue to reflect the values of the coalition that appointed (the median Justice on) it? Or does it nonetheless reflect the current coalition in power? More precise argument and analysis concerning the mechanisms by which the Court is constrained is important not only to understand and assess majoritarian theories, but to gauge whether the key mechanisms are likely to remain as robust going forward as they purportedly have been in the past. Majoritarian theories at this stage thus raise as many questions as they answer.

As a moral matter, the majoritarian thesis also does not dissolve Bickel's countermajoritarian concern. Even assuming the thesis is descriptively true, it cannot and does not answer the moral question. The Court does have the power to change the rules under which we live by imposing national solutions to issues the national political process would never address—out of widespread judgment that the issue is not appropriately addressed at the national level. Many of the state laws the Court strikes down are not outliers, but even when they are, the moral question remains: why should this unelected institution have the authority to override the preferences and judgments of the representative institutions of state governments? In addition, once the majoritarian theory is limited to the more defensible position that, over long enough periods of time, with enough appointments available to Presidents, the Court will come into line with "majoritarian views," it is easier to remember the periods in which the Court managed to delay major national policies for a significant time. There are moral defenses of judicial review, of course, which seek to answer these kind of questions. But the majoritarian theories cannot answer these kind of questions.

Finally, the majoritarian theories can easily suggest a false inevitability about the limited power of judicial review. But the past

might well not be prologue. Even if the Court has been as constrained in the past as the strongest versions of the majoritarian
thesis suggest, the Court going forward might not be. If the appointments process is the key means of popular or political control
of the Court, the fact that vacancies occur much less frequently
than in the past (if that pattern continues) inevitably means that
the linkage between presidential electoral success and the opportunity to shape the Court will be weakened. In addition, to the
extent the success of that linkage in the past depended on regularly
recurring successful electoral coalitions dominating American politics and government for extended periods of time, if we continue
to experience the opposite structure of politics—frequent shifts in
partisan control over national political institutions and no governing coalitions that dominate over many years—the ability of
the appointments process to control the Court will be even further
diminished. If another key mechanism for constraining the Court
is Congress's ability to enact, or credibly threaten to enact, laws
to rein in the Court, that constraint, too, will be diminished if we
continue to experience the kind of deeply divided political system
that has characterized American politics since the 1980s. In addition to more frequent shifts in partisan control over parts of the
national government, that system is also more likely to generate
divided government; even when it produces unified government,
the hyperpolarized political parties that define our era, combined
with the routine use of Senate filibusters, will make effective legislative action ever more difficult. The more paralyzed the political
process, the greater the space for Supreme Court independence
(if the threat of political response is what constrains the Court).
Moreover, political paralysis and hyperpolarized parties and politics are almost certain to diminish the stature of Congress and
the President, relative to that of the Court, in public opinion—
as we have seen in recent decades. To the extent public opinion
is offered as the constraint on judicial review, that constraint too
might well diminish over time if the configuration of politics remains as it has been over the last generation or more.

Citizens United is the most countermajoritarian decision invalidating national legislation on an issue of high public salience in
the last quarter century.[193] The decision's practical consequences

---

[193] For national legislation, one probably has to go back to the flag burning decisions
to find an even faintly analogous circumstance. See note 9.

remain to be seen, but the Court can hardly be said to have acted on a misunderstanding of the likely political reaction. Striking down legislation that had been bipartisan when enacted, the Court's decision was also issued in the teeth of Democratically controlled executive and legislative institutions with larger partisan majorities more likely to be hostile to the decision than at any time in the last thirty or so years. Though the decision has been intensely criticized in some quarters, there has been virtually no suggestion of any legislative effort to retaliate against the Court or bring it to account, nor to challenge the ruling directly by enacting new legislation that tests the Court's commitment to the decision.

Under more extreme versions of today's majoritarian understanding, the Court would never have issued *Citizens United* (except as a mistake). Under other versions, Congress would have effectively threatened or enacted legislation to defang the Court. Still other versions of the thesis would predict that the Court will back down in the face of the reaction to *Citizens United*. Yet other versions rest on the view that over the "long run," new appointments to the Court will eventually bring the Court into line with "majoritarian" views about corporate spending in elections.

Judicial review, perhaps America's most distinctive and enduring contribution to the design of democratic self-government, exists somewhere between a realm in which judges are free to reach any outcome, regardless of the likely public or political response, and a world in which judicial decisions are so heavily constrained by the power of other institutions and actors that those decisions simply mirror the preferences of these other actors. *Citizens United* is a powerful reminder that, despite the best efforts of modern majoritarian theorists, Bickel's countermajoritarian difficulty endures. *Citizens United* may prove to be an isolated but important reminder—or a harbinger of an assertive new era of judicial review.

PAMELA S. KARLAN

THE GAY AND THE ANGRY: THE
SUPREME COURT AND THE BATTLES
SURROUNDING SAME-SEX MARRIAGE

Marriage is in the air at One First Street, N.E., and thoughts about it pop up in the oddest places. Like discussions over whether the Constitution confers a right to postconviction DNA testing.[1] Faced with that issue, a majority of the Court found no "freestanding, substantive due process right."[2] But in the course of his dissent, Justice David Souter, who was to leave the Court a fortnight later, included the following extraordinary passage about "the right moment for a court to decide whether substantive due process requires recognition of an individual right unsanctioned by tradition (or the invalidation of traditional law)":[3]

> [It is] essential to recognize how much time society needs in order to work through a given issue before it makes sense to ask whether a law

Pamela S. Karlan is Kenneth and Harle Montgomery Professor of Public Interest Law, Stanford Law School.

AUTHOR'S NOTE: I thank Viola Canales, Vince Chhabria, Walter Dellinger, Sam Issacharoff, Rick Pildes, Jane Schacter, Teresa Stewart, and Robert Weisberg for helpful suggestions during our many conversations about the issues I discuss here. I also presented portions of this article at Stanford Law School's faculty workshop and as the Central Valley Foundation/James D. McClatchy Lecture at UC Davis School of Law and each time benefited greatly from comments and questions. Finally, Adam Samaha's deft editing dramatically improved my understanding of the issues I discuss.

[1] *District Attorney's Office v Osborne*, 129 S Ct 2308 (2009).

[2] Id at 2312.

[3] Id at 2340 (Souter, J, dissenting) (internal citations omitted).

© 2011 by The University of Chicago. All rights reserved.
978-0-226-36326-4/2011/2010-0005$10.00

or practice on the subject is beyond the pale of reasonable choice, and subject to being struck down as violating due process. . . .

Changes in societal understanding of the fundamental reasonableness of government actions work out in much the same way that individuals reconsider issues of fundamental belief. We can change our own inherited views just so fast, and a person is not labeled a stick-in-the-mud for refusing to endorse a new moral claim without having some time to work through it intellectually and emotionally. Just as attachment to the familiar and the limits of experience affect the capacity of an individual to see the potential legitimacy of a moral position, the broader society needs the chance to take part in the dialectic of public and political back and forth about a new liberty claim before it makes sense to declare unsympathetic state or national laws arbitrary to the point of being crunconstitutional.[4]

It is hard to read Justice Souter's observations as a commentary on whether convicted criminals should be able to gain access to physical evidence within the state's control for the purpose of running scientific tests designed to establish their innocence. What individual even *has* an "inherited view" on that question, let alone a view, however obtained, involving "issues of fundamental belief"? And postconviction DNA testing hardly seems the kind of question that society needs to "work through" in some therapeutic or "dialectic" way. It is a discrete, albeit important, issue of criminal justice policy.

But if the question is whether the Supreme Court should recognize a constitutional right to marriage for same-sex couples—well, then, this passage makes much more sense. That issue does involve moral claims, inherited views, societal understandings, and questions of timing. Social scientific evidence regarding changes in popular opinion and demography suggests that marriage equality is coming,[5] and coming more quickly than anyone might have hoped or feared eight years ago when the Supreme Court held, in *Lawrence v Texas*,[6] that "[t]he liberty protected by the Constitution" as a matter of substantive due process protects gay people's intimate

---

[4] Id at 2340–41 (Souter, J, dissenting) (internal citations omitted).

[5] See Nathaniel Persily and Patrick J. Egan, *Court Decisions and Trends in Support for Same-Sex Marriage*, Polling Report (Aug 17, 2009), online at http://www.pollingreport.com/penp0908.htm; Pew Research Center, *Support For Same-Sex Marriage Edges Upward* (Oct 6, 2010), online at http://pewforum.org/Gay-Marriage-and-Homosexuality/Support-For-Same-Sex-Marriage-Edges-Upward.aspx.

[6] 539 US 558 (2003).

sexual relationships.[7] Five states plus the District of Columbia now issue marriage licenses to same-sex couples.[8] Three other states recognize same-sex marriages performed elsewhere.[9] California exists in an uneasy state of suspended animation.[10] Overall, when newly created institutions like civil unions and registered domestic partnerships are taken into account as well, we have moved in roughly a generation from a nation in which no state provided legal recognition to same-sex couples to one in which two in five Americans live in states that do.[11]

The question whether the Constitution requires such recognition will, at some point in the foreseeable future, arrive at the Supreme Court,[12] since it is unlikely that we will achieve national legal uni-

---

[7] Id at 567.

[8] See National Conference of State Legislatures, *Same Sex Marriage, Civil Unions, and Domestic Partnerships* (Apr 2010) (showing that Connecticut, Iowa, Massachusetts, Vermont, New Hampshire, and the District of Columbia issue licenses), online at http://www.ncsl.org/default.aspx?tabid=16430.

[9] Id (showing that Maryland, New York, and Rhode Island will recognize same-sex marriages performed elsewhere).

[10] In May 2008, the California Supreme Court struck down the state's then-existing law restricting marriage to opposite-sex couples. See *In re Marriage Cases*, 43 Cal 4th 757 (2008). In November 2008, California voters approved an amendment to the state constitution (known colloquially as "Proposition 8") reinstating the restriction of marriage to opposite-sex couples. See Cal Const, Art I, § 7.5. Between those two events, over 18,000 same-sex couples obtained marriage licenses in California. In *Strauss v Horton*, 46 Cal 4th 364 (2009), the California Supreme Court held that these marriages remain valid. See id at 475. And in *Perry v Schwarzenegger*, 704 F Supp 2d 921 (ND Cal 2010), a federal district court struck down Art. I § 7.5 as a violation of the Due Process and Equal Protection Clauses of the Fourteenth Amendment. The court of appeals stayed the district court's judgment pending review. See *Perry v Schwarzenegger*, No 10-16696 (9th Cir Aug 16, 2010), online at http://www.ca9.uscourts.gov/datastore/general/2010/08/16/order_motion_stay.pdf.

[11] See Andrew Koppelman, *Twenty-Eight Percent*, Balkinization (Dec 2, 2010), online at http://balkin.blogspot.com/. Koppelman calculates that 28 percent of the American population "now lives in a jurisdiction that recognizes same-sex marriage or its functional equivalent." He identifies five jurisdictions that currently allow same-sex marriage (Connecticut, District of Columbia, Iowa, Massachusetts, New Hampshire, and Vermont) and six states that currently provide for civil unions or domestic partnerships (California, Illinois, Nevada, New Jersey, Oregon, and Washington). Those jurisdictions contain slightly more than 28 percent of the U.S. population.

In addition, according to the National Conference of State Legislatures, three other states (Maryland, New York, and Rhode Island) recognize same-sex marriages from other states and a further three (Hawaii, Maine, and Wisconsin) have "[s]tatewide law providing some state-level spousal rights to unmarried couples." National Conference of State Legislatures, *Same-Sex Marriage, Civil Unions and Domestic Partnerships* (2010), online at http://www.ncsl.org/default.aspx?tabid=16430. When those six states are added to Koppleman's total, 39.7 percent of Americans live in a jurisdiction which provides some legal recognition.

[12] There are at least two major marriage-related cases in the federal courts of appeals. *Perry v Schwarzenegger*—the case challenging California's restriction of marriage to op-

formity regarding same-sex marriage through the political process any time soon.[13] When the issue does arrive at the Court, the Justices will have to choose sides on an issue about which many Americans care passionately. They have, of course, done that before. In *Loving v Virginia*,[14] the Court recognized a constitutional right for interracial couples to marry even though sixteen states still forbade it. Yet there was nearly a generation between when the California Supreme Court became the first court to reach that conclusion[15] and when the United States Supreme Court so held. In the meantime, the Court dodged the issue for a decade, apparently because it feared that a decision striking down state bans on interracial marriage would imperil its recent decision in *Brown v Board of Education*.[16]

Moreover, by the time the Supreme Court decided *Loving*, it had

---

posite-sex couples—is before the Ninth Circuit. That appeal may be delayed by the court's recent decision certifying to the California Supreme Court the question whether, under California law, the official proponents of Proposition 8 "possess either a particularized interest in the initiative's validity or the authority to assert the State's interest in the initiative's validity" sufficient to permit them to defend the restriction given the decision of the state defendants not to appeal. See *Perry v Schwarzenegger*, 628 F3d 1191 (9th Cir 2011). In the companion cases of *Massachusetts v Dept of Health and Human Services*, 698 F Supp 2d 234 (D Mass 2010), and *Gill v Office of Personnel Management*, 699 F Supp 2d 374 (D Mass 2010), a federal district court held that section 3 of the federal Defense of Marriage Act—which provides, with respect to federal law, that "the word 'marriage' means only a legal union between one man and one woman as husband and wife, and the word 'spouse' refers only to a person of the opposite sex who is a husband or a wife," 1 USC § 7 (2006)—is unconstitutional as applied to deny federal benefits to same-sex couples who are married under Massachusetts law. Those cases are currently on appeal to the First Circuit.

[13] In recent years, there has been a widespread reaction to the prospect of swift social change occasioned by the Supreme Court's decisions in *Romer v Evans*, 517 US 620 (1996), and *Lawrence v Texas*, 539 US 558 (2003), and the Massachusetts Supreme Judicial Court's decision in *Goodridge v Dep't of Public Health*, 798 NE2d 941 (Mass 2003). See Jane S. Schacter, *Courts and the Politics of Backlash: Marriage Equality Then and Now*, 82 S Cal L Rev 1153, 1155 (2009) ("In all, forty-one states and the U.S. Congress have enacted measures restricting the protections afforded same-sex couples since 1995, and twenty-six states have passed constitutional bans just since the *Goodridge* decision in 2003."). In the states that have constitutionalized the nonrecognition of same-sex marriage, it seems plausible to assume that it may be harder to achieve marriage equality through the political process than would otherwise be the case.

[14] 388 US 1 (1967).

[15] See *Perez v Sharp*, 32 Cal 2d 711 (1948).

[16] 347 US 483 (1954). For discussion of the Court's evasiveness, see Philip Elman, *The Solicitor General's Office, Justice Frankfurter, and Civil Rights Litigation, 1946–1960: An Oral History*, 100 Harv L Rev 817, 845–47 (1987) (discussing the Court's decision to dodge the question in *Naim v Naim*, 350 US 891 (1955) and 350 US 985 (1956)); Pamela S. Karlan, *Loving Lawrence*, 102 Mich L Rev 1447, 1459 (2004) (same).

For a fascinating comparative history of public reactions to the California Supreme Court's decision legalizing interracial marriage, and the recent same-sex marriage cases, see Schacter, 82 S Cal L Rev (cited in note 13).

largely completed the project of dismantling formal Jim Crow. During the Warren Court years, the Supreme Court clearly took sides, embracing African Americans' constitutional claims for equality, striking down every formal racial distinction that came before it, and rejecting white litigants' constitutional challenges to the Second Reconstruction across the board.[17] Summing up this position in *Norwood v Harrison*,[18] Chief Justice Burger wrote that the "the Constitution . . . places no value on discrimination," and therefore even if some private discrimination "may be characterized as a form of exercising freedom of association protected by the First Amendment . . . it has never been accorded affirmative constitutional protections."[19]

When it comes to gay rights, the Court's approach has been more equivocal. On the one hand, in *Romer v Evans*[20] and *Lawrence v Texas*,[21] a majority of the Justices recognized gay litigants' claims for equal treatment and equal dignity under the law. On the other hand, in cases like *Hurley v Irish-American Gay, Lesbian, and Bisexual Group of Boston*[22] and *Boy Scouts v Dale*,[23] a majority of the Justices accorded First Amendment protection to groups that sought to exclude gay people from participating in their activities. Chief Justice Rehnquist's opinion for the Court in *Dale* drew a direct link between changes in social understandings and constitutional protection for the cultural rear guard:

> [I]t appears that homosexuality has gained greater societal acceptance. But this is scarcely an argument for denying First Amendment protection to those who refuse to accept these views. The First Amendment protects expression, be it of the popular variety or not. And the fact that an idea may be embraced and advocated by increasing numbers of people is all

---

[17] See, for example, the Court's decision in *Heart of Atlanta Motel v United States*, 379 US 241, 258–62 (1964) (rejecting the defendant's claims that forcing it to provide services to black patrons violated various constitutional provisions). Burt Neuborne's contribution to this volume, *The Gravitational Pull of Race on the Warren Court*, explores in detail the ways in which the Court shaped constitutional law across a wide range of domains to serve its overarching commitment to racial equality.

[18] 413 US 455 (1973) (striking down a Mississippi program providing textbooks to private schools).

[19] Id at 469, 470.

[20] 517 US 620 (1996).

[21] 539 US 558 (2003).

[22] 515 US 557 (1995).

[23] 530 US 640 (2000).

the more reason to protect the First Amendment rights of those who wish to voice a different view.[24]

In fundamental ways, the question of marriage equality per se more closely resembles *Romer* and *Lawrence* than it does *Hurley* and *Dale*. Gay people are seeking access to a state-created institution, and not a privately run activity. And whatever the merits of the metaphysical assertion that marriage equality somehow dilutes the value of opponents' own marriages,[25] no one has seriously suggested that opposite-sex couples in states that have recognized same-sex marriage have a constitutional claim against their states' extension of marriage to gay couples. That being said, constitutional claims on behalf of marriage traditionalists can arise in a range of contexts. Whether, and how, to respect those claims is likely to confront the Court repeatedly.

Last Term, the Court got a taste of what is to come in a trilogy of cases. In *Hollingsworth v Perry*,[26] the Court overturned a district court's decision to allow closed-circuit televising of the trial challenging California's ban on same-sex marriage. In *Doe v Reed*,[27] the Court rejected a challenge to Washington State's Public Records Act by opponents of Washington's domestic partnership law who wanted to keep private their signatures on a referendum petition. And in *Christian Legal Society v Martinez*,[28] the Court upheld a public law school's refusal to fund a student group that restricted its membership to individuals who agreed that sexual intimacy was permissible—and that they would engage in it—only within a "marriage between a man and a woman."[29] Each time, the Court was sharply, indeed angrily, divided. In contrast to the *Loving* Court, on the

---

[24] Id at 660 (citations omitted). One wonders what to make of the fact that the Chief Justice chose to illustrate his assertion that unpopular views must be protected by citing *Texas v Johnson*, 491 US 397 (1989) (protecting flag burning), and *Brandenburg v Ohio*, 395 US 444 (1969) (protecting speech by leaders of the Ku Klux Klan). It can hardly have gratified the Boy Scouts to travel in such company.

[25] I describe and reject the argument that recognizing same-sex marriage will somehow dilute the value of opposite-sex marriages in Pamela S. Karlan, *Constitutional Law as Trademark*, 43 UC Davis L Rev 385, 405–09 (2009).

[26] 130 S Ct 705 (2010).

[27] 130 S Ct 2811 (2010).

[28] 130 S Ct 2971 (2010).

[29] Id at 2980.

Roberts Court partisans of the cultural rear guard are within the building as well as outside.

Precisely because the marriage issue will be in the background of a range of constitutional issues, it may come to inflect a range of constitutional doctrines. Unlike the "gravitational pull" that race exercised over the Warren Court,[30] where the Court's overarching and unanimous commitment to racial equality shaped the development of doctrine on issues ranging from constitutional criminal procedure to the state action doctrine to the scope of libel law under the First Amendment, how the Justices' views of marriage equality will influence the development of doctrine in other areas is less certain, at least for now.

Moreover, at the same time that the Justices are confronting rapid cultural change with respect to marriage, they are also confronting rapid cultural change with respect to methods of expression and association, and understandings of privacy, more generally. The rights to communicate about political issues, to associate with like-minded people, and to retain one's decisional and informational privacy touch core constitutional values. The internet has transformed the nature of information, simultaneously enhancing and threatening these values and posing new problems for constitutional interpretation. The interaction of rapid social and technological change makes it quite plausible that many, perhaps most, of the gay-rights-related constitutional cases the Supreme Court will see over the coming decades will involve the claims of gay-rights opponents.[31] What makes this phenomenon particularly interesting is that, perhaps because of the sheer speed of political and social change, the Court is confronting the claims of opponents before it has confronted, let alone worked out, the primary rights claim itself. In this article, I suggest that much of the conservative Justices' apparent agitation in last Term's cases comes from their sense that they are fighting a rearguard action to protect traditionalists against an emerging mainstream.

---

[30] See Neuborne, *Gravitational Pull of Race* (cited in note 17).

[31] I say "constitutional" here because I expect that once Congress passes antidiscrimination legislation protecting individuals on the basis of sexual orientation—for example, something like the proposed Employment Non-Discrimination Act, which would provide Title VII-style protection—that legislation will generate litigation as well. To be sure, even some of that litigation will raise constitutional questions.

I. HOLLINGSWORTH V PERRY: A PRELIMINARY SKIRMISH IN THE CALIFORNIA MARRIAGE CASE

In the years following *Lawrence*—where Justice Kennedy's opinion for the Court and Justice O'Connor's concurrence in the judgment bracketed same-sex marriage rights, while Justice Scalia's dissent thundered that the Court had irretrievably set off down that road[32]—it became virtually an article of faith within the gay-rights bar that the time for mounting a federal constitutional challenge to state laws restricting marriage to opposite-sex couples had not yet come.[33] The leading organizations litigating marriage-equality cases (Lambda Legal, the Gay & Lesbian Advocates & Defenders, the National Center for Lesbian Rights, and the American Civil Liberties Union) adopted a carefully calibrated strategy of challenging marriage laws on state-law grounds before relatively liberal state courts. While there were significant defeats in states like New York[34] and New Jersey,[35] there also was a countervailing string of victories in states like Massachusetts,[36] Connecticut,[37] Iowa,[38] and California.[39]

---

[32] See *Lawrence*, 539 US at 578 (stating that the Court's decision "does not involve whether the government must give formal recognition to any relationship that homosexual persons seek to enter"); id at 585 (O'Connor, J, concurring in the judgment) (reserving the question whether "other laws distinguishing between heterosexuals and homosexuals would similarly fail under rational basis review" and describing "preserving the traditional institution of marriage" as a "legitimate" state interest); id at 590 (Scalia, J, dissenting) (declaring that state laws against same-sex marriage are "called into question by today's decision").

[33] See, for example, Mary Bonauto, *Goodridge in Context*, 40 Harv CR-CL L Rev 1, 21–31 (2005); Patricia A. Cain, *Contextualizing Varnum v Brien: A "Moment" in History*, 13 J Gender Race & Just 27, 32–33 (2009); Darren Hutchinson, *Sexual Politics and Social Change*, 41 Conn L Rev 1523 (2009).

[34] *Hernandez v Robles*, 7 NY3d 338 (2006).

[35] *Lewis v Harris*, 188 NJ 415 (2005). But note that although the New Jersey Supreme Court refused to recognize a right to marry, it did hold, as the Vermont Supreme Court had held in *Baker v State*, 170 Vt 194 (1999), that the state constitution required the state to provide some legal structure for providing same-sex couples "on equal terms, the rights and benefits enjoyed and burdens and obligations borne by married couples." *Lewis*, 188 NJ at 423.

[36] *Goodridge v Dept of Pub. Health*, 798 NE2d 941 (Mass 2003).

[37] *Kerrigan v Comm'r of Pub. Health*, 957 A2d 407 (Conn 2008).

[38] *Varnum v Brien*, 763 NW2d 862 (Iowa 2009). In the 2010 election, all three of the Iowa Supreme Court justices who were facing a retention vote were defeated after groups opposing marriage equality poured huge amounts of resources into the election. See A. G. Sulzberger, *In Iowa, Voters Oust Judges Over Marriage Issue*, NY Times, Nov 3, 2010 (web edition).

[39] *In re Marriage Cases*, 43 Cal 4th 757 (2008).

California, however, differed from these other states in one critical respect: Like many of its western neighbors, California had adopted the initiative as a Progressive Era constitutional reform. With the requisite number of signatures, voters could put nearly any constitutional or statutory question up for popular vote.[40] In the wake of the California Supreme Court's decision that restriction of marriage to opposite-sex couples violated the state constitution, opponents of marriage equality gathered the nearly 700,000 signatures required to put an initiative (Proposition 8) on the November 2008 ballot. The initiative proposed a constitutional amendment reinstating the restriction of marriage to opposite-sex couples.[41] The election was hotly contested, breaking every record for expenditures on an initiative and garnering national attention. Proposition 8 passed with 52.3 percent of the vote. The California Supreme Court subsequently rejected a state constitutional challenge to the initiative,[42] although it did hold that marriages entered into prior to passage of Proposition 8 would remain valid.[43]

The same week that the California Supreme Court issued its decision on Proposition 8, two gay couples filed suit in federal district court in the Northern District of California challenging California's marriage restriction under both the Due Process and the Equal Protection Clauses of the Fourteenth Amendment. The plaintiffs in *Perry v Schwarzenegger* were represented by a legal odd couple: Theodore Olson and David Boies, whose last joint appearance had been before the Supreme Court, arguing on opposite sides in *Bush v Gore*.[44] The case was assigned to Chief Judge Vaughn R. Walker. Coincidentally, one of the most well-known cases in the judge's career as a private attorney had involved a different struggle

---

[40] I say "nearly any" because California constitutional law did impose one important substantive restriction (along with more quasi-procedural restrictions, such as the requirement that any initiative deal with only a single subject). Voters could only "amend," but not "revise," the state constitution through the initiative. A constitutional "revision"—which involved a more fundamental change in the constitution—could be accomplished only through a more deliberative process. See *Strauss v Horton*, 46 Cal 4th 364 (2009) (explaining the amendment/revision distinction and holding that Proposition 8's restriction of marriage to only opposite-sex couples constituted an amendment).

[41] Under California law, a constitutional initiative, as opposed to a statutory one, requires a number of signatures equal to 8 percent of the votes cast in the prior gubernatorial election. See Cal Const, Art II, § 8. Roughly 8.6 million votes had been cast in the 2006 gubernatorial race.

[42] See *Strauss*, 46 Cal 4th at 391.

[43] See id at 392.

[44] 531 US 98 (2000) (per curiam).

over gay people's right to use a value-laden term controlled by the government. Walker had represented the U.S. Olympic Committee in its efforts to keep an athletic event from using the phrase "Gay Olympics."[45]

While the nominal defendants in *Perry* were state officials, it was immediately evident that the state would not mount a full-scale defense of Proposition 8. Most of the government defendants "refused to take a position on the merits of plaintiffs' claims and declined to defend Proposition 8."[46] The governor's answer actively invited judicial resolution, stating that the complaint "presents important constitutional questions that require and warrant judicial determination" because "[i]n a constitutional democracy, it is the role of the courts to determine and resolve such questions."[47] The attorney general (who was subsequently elected governor) went further, conceding the proposition's unconstitutionality.[48] Thus, the substantive defense of Proposition 8 fell to a group of defendant-intervenors consisting of the five California voters who had acted as the "official proponents" of Proposition 8 along with ProtectMarriage.com-Yes on 8, which was the ballot measure committee that proponents had formed to receive contributions and disburse expenditures in support of the measure.[49]

In October 2009, the district court denied the defendant-intervenors' motion for summary judgment, holding that a trial would be necessary to resolve disputed factual and legal issues.[50] It set the date for the trial in early January 2010.

---

[45] *International Olympic Comm. v San Francisco Arts & Athletics*, 781 F2d 733 (9th Cir 1986), aff'd, 483 US 522 (1987).

[46] *Perry v Schwarzenegger*, 2010 US Dist LEXIS 78817 at *14 (ND Cal 2010).

[47] See Administration's Answer to Complaint for Declaratory, Injunctive, or Other Relief at 2, 9, 49, *Perry v Schwarzenegger*, Case 3:09-cv-02292-VRW (ND Cal June 16, 2009) (Doc 46).

[48] *Perry*, 2010 US Dist LEXIS 78817 at *14.

[49] See id at *14–*15.

[50] See Tr 75–90, *Perry v Schwarzenegger*, Case 3:09-cv-02292-VRW (ND Cal Oct 15, 2009) (Doc 228).

This being the fiftieth anniversary of the *Supreme Court Review*, it is worth noting Kenneth Karst's wonderful article in the first: *Legislative Facts in Constitutional Litigation*, 1960 Supreme Court Review 75. Karst begins his article—which discusses, among other things, cases involving what he terms "political privacy," id at 90, a concept central to *Doe v Reed*—with the following observation: "Judges makes constitutional law as they make other kinds of law, on the basis of facts proved and assumed. They are likely to do a better job when their assumptions rest on information rather than hunch." Id at 75. Although it is beyond the scope of this article, one of the distinctive features of the *Perry* litigation

Public interest in the case was intense. At the end of a hearing on a discovery dispute in September 2009, the district judge called the lawyers for the parties into chambers to notify them that he planned to "relay" some of the proceedings from his own courtroom to a larger ceremonial courtroom in order to accommodate the public and the press.[51] The lawyers responded in unison that they had "[n]o objection at all" to that proposal.[52] The judge also raised the prospect that he might arrange to "broadcast" the proceedings beyond the overflow room, asking the parties to respond to that possibility and noting that the issue of televising federal judicial proceedings was "in flux."[53]

Shortly thereafter, the chief judge of the Ninth Circuit appointed a three-judge committee to consider amending the Circuit's pre-existing 1996 policy prohibiting television or radio coverage of district court proceedings. (During roughly the same time period, the Ninth Circuit, which had no categorical ban, had released video or audio recordings in approximately 200 appellate oral arguments.[54]) The committee recommended to the Circuit's Judicial Council that district courts be permitted to experiment with broadcasting court proceedings on a trial basis. On December 17, the Circuit's Public Information Office issued a press release announcing that the council had voted unanimously to allow district courts within the Circuit "to experiment with the dissemination of video recordings in civil non-jury matters only."[55]

Following the December 17 announcement, the district court "indicated on its Web site that it had amended Civil Local Rule 77-3, which had previously banned the recording or broadcast of court proceedings" to create an exception allowing "'for participation in a pilot or other project authorized by the Judicial Council of the Ninth Circuit.'"[56] The defendant-intervenors objected to the

---

was Chief Judge Walker's insistence on holding a full-scale trial and issuing lengthy findings of fact rather than treating the issue before him as entirely a question of law.

[51] See Tr 69, *Perry v Schwarzenegger*, Case 3:09-cv-02292-VRW (ND Cal Sept 25, 2009) (Doc 212).

[52] Id at 70.

[53] Id at 72.

[54] See Public Information Office, United States Courts for the Ninth Circuit, *Ninth Circuit Judicial Council Approves Experimental Use of Cameras in District Courts* 2 (Dec 17, 2009), online at http://www.ce9.uscourts.gov/cm/articlefiles/137-Dec17_Cameras_Press %20Relase.pdf.

[55] Id at 1.

[56] *Hollingsworth v Perry*, 130 S Ct 705, 708 (2010) (quoting the district court's website).

rule revision on procedural grounds, arguing that any change to the rules required a notice-and-comment period. Initially, the district court responded by revising its website to provide notice that the court only intended to make the proposed rule change, and that there would be an eight-day period for public comment—which ultimately produced "138,574 comments, all but 32 of which favored transmitting the proceedings."[57] But midway through the comment period, the district court changed course and announced that it was adopting the revised rule effective retroactively "pursuant to the 'immediate need' provision of Title 28 Section 2071(e)."[58]

On January 6, 2010, following a hearing, the district court announced its intention to permit live streaming of the trial to federal courthouses in several other cities, along with slightly delayed access to the proceedings through a government-provided YouTube channel. In the course of its ruling, the district court identified several reasons why the case was an appropriate one for audiovisual access, ranging from the intense public interest to the educative function that observing the trial process would have.[59] The court pointed out that "today we have the capability of providing that kind of widespread distribution through, essentially, the Internet."[60]

On January 7, 2010, the district court filed a notice to the parties that it had formally requested that the Chief Judge of the Ninth Circuit "approve inclusion of the trial" in the Circuit's pilot program permitting broadcast coverage.[61] The next day, the Chief Judge approved the decision to allow real-time streaming to a handful of federal courthouses both within and outside California.[62] But

---

[57] Id at 716 (Breyer, J, dissenting).

[58] Id at 708 (opinion of the Court). Section 2071 contains the general rulemaking powers of the federal courts. Subsection (a) authorizes the Supreme Court "and all courts established by Act of Congress" to "prescribe rules for the conduct of their business." Subsection (b) requires that such rules "shall be prescribed only after giving appropriate public notice and an opportunity for comment," but subsection (e) provides that "[i]f the prescribing court determines that there is an immediate need for a rule, such court may proceed under this section without public notice and opportunity for comment, but such court shall promptly thereafter afford such notice and opportunity for comment."

[59] See Tr 40, *Perry v Schwarzenegger*, Case 3:09-cv-02292-VRW (ND Cal Jan 6, 2010) (Doc 363).

[60] Id at 41.

[61] Notice to Parties 2, *Perry v Schwarzenegger*, Case 3:09-cv-02292-VRW (ND Cal Jan 7, 2010) (Doc 358).

[62] See Public Information Office, United States Courts for the Ninth Circuit, *Federal Courthouses to Offer Remote Viewing of Proposition 8 Trial* 1 (Jan 8, 2010), online at http://www.ca9.uscourts.gov/datastore/general/2010/01/08/Prop8_Remote_Viewing_Locations.pdf.

he postponed ruling on the request for dissemination over the internet in light of technical difficulties.[63] That same day, the Ninth
Circuit denied a petition for a writ of mandamus ordering the district court to withdraw its order.

On January 9, 2010, the Saturday before the trial was to begin,
the defendant-intervenors filed an application with the Supreme
Court for a stay of the plan for closed-circuit dissemination. On
January 11, the Court issued a one-paragraph order temporarily
staying the streaming "except as it permits streaming to other rooms
within the confines of the courthouse in which the trial is to be
held."[64] The order was to remain in effect until January 13. Only
Justice Breyer dissented. And on January 13, the Court ordered a
halt to any remote streaming of the trial.[65] The expressed basis for
the Court's ruling was that "the courts below did not follow the
appropriate procedures set forth in federal law before changing their
rules to allow such broadcasting."[66]

It is hard to escape the whiff of *Bush v Gore* that hangs over the
case, and not only because the respondents were represented by
Messrs. Olson and Boies and the case was resolved on an exceptionally expedited basis. As in *Bush v Gore*, the Court seemed motivated to intervene because of the importance of the ultimate issue—there, the presidential election and, here, the constitutionality
of restrictions on marriage—rather than the need to resolve the
specific legal question presented. The result in both cases was a
sharply divided per curiam opinion that resolved virtually nothing
except the outcome of an individual case.[67] Also as in *Bush v Gore*,

---

[63] See *Hollingsworth*, 130 S Ct at 709.

[64] Order in No 09A648 at 469, *Hollingsworth v Perry* (Jan 11, 2010), online at http://
www.supremecourt.gov/orders/journal/jnl09.pdf.

[65] To be precise, the Supreme Court continued the earlier-ordered stay, which was to
remain in effect "pending the timely filing and disposition of a petition for a writ of
certiorari or the filing and disposition of a petition for a writ of mandamus." *Hollingsworth*,
130 S Ct at 715. Given that the trial lasted only a few weeks, the stay had the practical
effect of being a permanent injunction. While the defendant-intervenors did file a petition
for a writ of certiorari in mid-April, that petition was dismissed by stipulation a month
later. See *Hollingsworth*, 130 S Ct 2432 (2010).
    In response to the Supreme Court's decision, a troupe of actors set about doing a
reenactment of the trial and subsequent proceedings on You Tube. See MarriageTrial.com.
Going beyond verisimilitude, the troupe also had an actor read the district court's decision
on the merits aloud—a five-hour undertaking.

[66] *Hollingsworth*, 130 S Ct at 706.

[67] Compare *Bush v Gore*, 531 US 98, 109 (2000) (per curiam) (stating that the Court's
decision was "limited to the present circumstances, for the problem of equal protection
in election processes generally presents many complexities"), with *Hollingsworth*, 130 S Ct

the five Justices who joined the unsigned opinion seemed motivated
to intervene by an almost personal distaste for what they saw as
result-oriented procedural irregularities in the lower courts' actions.[68] This played out in an unusual feature of the opinion: its
repeated references to Chief Judges Walker and Kozinski by name
rather than simply by position, as if to announce that the Court
was watching them personally, and skeptically.

Finally, as in *Bush v Gore*, there was an odd mismatch between
the identity of the claimant and the nature of the legally cognizable
injury on which the majority fastened. In *Bush v Gore*, George W.
Bush, the Republican candidate for president, invoked the equal
protection rights of individual voters and alleged that those voters'
ballots were being counted under different standards in different
parts of the state. The most plausible remedy for a voter to seek
in such a case would have been an order that the ballots be reviewed
uniformly. Instead, because his real interest was winning the election
quickly, Bush argued for a halt to the recount that left ballots un-
counted, basing his arguments on the lateness of the hour. In *Hollingsworth*, the rights ostensibly being vindicated were also only
indirectly those of the parties. The defendant-intervenors claimed
that streaming the trial posed a risk of intimidation to potential
witnesses who might thereby decline to testify or modify their conclusions, presumably to the disadvantage of the defendant-intervenors' case. But if the risk to their case had been the defendant-
intervenors' sole basis for relief, they might have faced a serious
problem obtaining a stay. Presumably, they would have needed to
show a real additional risk to the witnesses from streaming their

---

at 709 (declining to "here express any views on the propriety of broadcasting court proceedings generally" and declaring that its review was "confined to a narrow legal issue:
whether the District Court's amendment of its local rules to broadcast this trial complied
with federal law"), and id at 717 (Breyer, J, dissenting) (stating that "this legal question
is not the kind of legal question that this Court would normally grant certiorari to
consider," given that there was no conflict among the lower courts over the procedures
by which district courts change their rules and that "[t]he technical validity of the procedures followed below does not implicate an open 'important question of federal law'")
(citing Sup Ct R 10(c)).

[68] Compare *Hollingsworth*, 130 S Ct at 714–15 (characterizing the district court's action
as having "attempted to change its rules at the eleventh hour to treat this case differently
than other trials in the district" and declaring that "[i]f courts are to require that others
follow regular procedures, courts must do so as well"), with *Bush*, 531 US at 105–09
(criticizing various aspects of the Florida state courts' attempts to handle the recount),
and id at 119–20 (Rehnquist, CJ, joined by Scalia and Thomas, JJ, concurring) (using
words like "absurd," "peculiar," and "inconceivable" to refer to the Florida Supreme
Court's interpretations of Florida law).

testimony over and above whatever risk might come from their appearance in a courtroom already otherwise open to the public. And it would have been especially hard to identify that risk with respect to expert witnesses or official ballot proponents (the two categories of witnesses they planned to call), since those individuals had sought substantial publicity for their views in a variety of settings already. Had the defendant-intervenors based their arguments against televising the trial solely on how it might affect their defense at trial, they could well have found themselves saddled with a factual finding from the district court that there was no risk they would be deprived of due process.

So the defendant-intervenors instead invoked procedural claims about the adequacy of the process by which the decision to televise the trial had been made—essentially pressing the rights of those members of the public whose ability to participate in the rulemaking process had been short-circuited by precipitous adoption of the rule. This had the benefit of framing the issue more as a question of law that could be litigated before the Court de novo. But as Justice Breyer's dissent observed, the defendant-intervenors were in an awkward position to claim lack of adequate notice. Whatever the general public's awareness of the possibility of trials being televised, the parties actually complaining about it in court had known for months that Chief Judge Walker was considering doing so in their case.

As a question of law, moreover, the adequacy of the notice-and-comment process was a close one. The relevant statute provided that a rule for the conduct of business in the federal courts "be prescribed only after giving appropriate public notice and an opportunity for comment."[69] The statute nowhere defined "appropriate"; it certainly set no specific length for an appropriate comment period. To be sure, there are situations in which a lengthy comment period would be appropriate, both to ensure that relevant stakeholders become aware of the proposed change and have time to evaluate it and to enable the preparation of comments dependent on extensive empirical or legal analysis. The Supreme Court pointed to two court of appeals cases that had suggested, in response to the fact that the Administrative Procedure Act similarly contained no specific time period, that administrative agencies should "'usually'

---

[69] 28 USC § 2071(b) (2006).

provide a comment period of 'thirty days or more.'"[70] But *Hollingsworth* seemed an odd case in which to announce a rule of general applicability about the length of a legally required period. For one thing, the district court received 138,574 comments during the week-long comment period it provided,[71] and it is hard to imagine that another three weeks would have changed anything about the overall tenor of the comments. More fundamentally, more or better public comments about the change to the Northern District of California's Civil Local Rule 77-3 would not, in any event, have directly addressed the Supreme Court's real concerns, which were quite specific to the California marriage litigation. The rule change did not require that trials be broadcast. It simply created a potential exception to the preexisting ban on broadcasting trial-level proceedings for cases in the Ninth Circuit's pilot program.[72] Even had the rule been in place for years, after months of public comment, nearly all of the Supreme Court's declared problems with the district court's decision to permit remote streaming in *this* case would presumably have been the same. None of those complaints had anything to do with novelty per se.[73]

The crux of the Supreme Court's concern was not really a failure to provide a sufficient notice-and-comment period for a local rule that would permit district judges to decide on a case-by-case basis whether to permit broadcasts. Rather, as the per curiam opinion acknowledged, even "[i]f Local Rule 77-3 had been validly revised, questions would still remain about the District Court's decision to

---

[70] *Hollingsworth*, 130 S Ct at 711 (quoting *Riverbend Farms, Inc. v Madigan*, 958 F2d 1479, 1484 (9th Cir 1992), and citing *Petry v Block*, 737 F2d 1193, 1201 (DC Cir 1984)).

Curiously, the Court failed to cite Executive Order 12866, 58 Fed Reg 51735 (Oct 4, 1993), which might have provided more systematic support for its position. That order provides, in pertinent part, that a "meaningful opportunity to comment on any proposed regulation" from an administrative agency "in most cases should include a comment period of not less than 60 days." Id at 51740.

[71] *Hollingsworth*, 130 S Ct at 716 (Breyer, J, dissenting).

[72] See ND Cal Local R 77-3, online at http://www.cand.uscourts.gov/cand/LocalRul.nsf/fec20e529a5572f0882569b6006607e0/7f39eafb2106e6db882569b4005a23f1/$FILE/Civ4-10.pdf (published April 2010).

[73] And had the rule been amended significantly earlier—for example, before the passage of Proposition 8 or before the filing of the complaint in *Perry*—it seems implausible that the defendant-intervenors or the witnesses who felt chilled would have participated in any notice-and-comment rulemaking. They would have had no reason to anticipate that at some point in the future they would be participants in a case to whose broadcast they would object. Thus, the defendant-intervenors were injured not so much by the truncated opportunity to comment on the proposed amendment of the local rule as by the substance of the amendment.

allow broadcasting of this particular trial, in which several of the witnesses have stated concerns for their own security."[74] The Court declared the California marriage case "not a good one for a pilot program," precisely because it "involve[d] issues subject to intense debate in our society."[75] The Court pointed with approval to the kinds of proceedings that had been televised in other federal district courts—ones that "were not high profile or did not involve witnesses."[76]

The Court's position raises two related questions. The first goes to the nature of the interest in televising trials. It seems paradoxical to broadcast trials only in cases where the public has little desire to watch them—what we might call the "low-profile" rationale. Remote public access to judicial proceedings, like other First Amendment-inflected interests, should not be "limited to things that do not matter much. That would be a mere shadow of freedom. The test of its substance," as the Court once reminded us in the free speech setting, is access to cases "that touch the heart of the existing order."[77] The streaming of a trial can serve its educative function only if people care enough to watch.

That the trial in question involved witnesses actually offers additional reasons why audiovisual distribution might serve important functions. Direct and cross-examination provide a mechanism for the "dialectic" and "back and forth" that Justice Souter urged in his *Osborne* dissent. While not all of the beliefs that underpin individuals' views on access to marriage rest on empirical claims, many do. And while the trial process is hardly the only way to evaluate the truth value of such claims, it happens to be one traditional and

---

[74] *Hollingsworth*, 130 S Ct at 714.

[75] Id.

[76] Id (internal citations omitted).

[77] *West Va State Bd of Educ. v Barnette*, 319 US 624, 642 (1943). See also Tr 41–42, *Perry v Schwarzenegger*, Case 3:09-cv-02292-VRW (ND Cal Jan 6, 2010) (Doc 363) (doubting that "a run-of-the-mill is the kind of case that will provide the civic lesson that might be helpful," and adding that "the only time that you're going to draw sufficient interest in the legal process is when you have an issue such as the issues here, that people think about, talk about, debate about and consider").

The Supreme Court's own practice seems in some tension with its position here. Traditionally, the Supreme Court generally did not release the audiotapes of oral arguments until years afterward. But in certain cases of intense public interest—for example, *Bush v Gore* and the University of Michigan affirmative action cases—the Court released the tapes within a few minutes after the argument ended. And this Term, the Supreme Court began releasing the tapes of *all* oral arguments on the Friday of the week in which they occurred. See http://www.supremecourt.gov/oral_arguments/argument_audio.aspx.

important way to do so in our society. Citizens' ability to observe for themselves how well witnesses defend views on empirical questions when those witnesses cannot escape cross-examination and must answer under oath might influence their own answers to those questions. The Confrontation Clause of the Constitution rests on a similar intuition that jurors can better assess the merits of a witness's assertions if they have the ability to see the witness, rather than simply read his testimony or a third party's account of what the witness said.[78]

Moreover, the Court's approving reference to Congress's authorization of closed-circuit off-site broadcasting in one very high profile case (the federal prosecution of the Oklahoma City bombing[79]) failed to recognize relevant parallels to the California marriage case. The trial court in the bombing case had granted a motion for a change of venue. Congress then enacted a statute that required trial courts to "order closed circuit televising" of proceedings back to the original venue "for viewing by such persons the court determines have a compelling interest in doing so and are otherwise unable to do so by reason of the inconvenience and expense caused by the change of venue."[80] Congress's clear intent was to enable survivors and relatives of individuals killed by the bombing to observe the trial. By the time *Perry* reached the Supreme Court, it too involved only closed-circuit televising of judicial proceedings to other courthouses. To be sure, four of those courthouses were outside California. The individuals who might attend those venues would generally not have a direct personal stake in the question whether California's marriage statute was unconstitutional, although they might well have a direct interest in the broader question of what the Due Process and Equal Protection Clauses have to say about marriage equality generally. But individuals who would have attended the closed-circuit broadcast at the Pasadena federal courthouse were almost certain to be Californians. And they might well have had a compelling interest in the trial. The trial proceedings were set to determine whether some potential audience members would be allowed to marry the person of their choice, or whether the state would be required to abandon a definition of marriage

---

[78] In recent Terms, the Supreme Court has reaffirmed that this rationale applies even in the case of expert witnesses. See *Melendez-Diaz v Massachusetts*, 129 S Ct 2527 (2009).

[79] *Hollingsworth*, 130 S Ct at 713–14.

[80] 42 USC § 10608(a) (2006).

central to the moral beliefs of other potential viewers. The majority's offhanded dismissal of any substantial public interest in permitting real-time audiovisual access in a single phrase—"respondents have not alleged any harm if the trial is not broadcast"[81]—completely missed this point.

Having found no public interest on the side of permitting remote audiovisual distribution, an equities balancing was almost an afterthought. Indeed, the per curiam's view was foreshadowed in the way the opinion started its statement of the facts. After noting that Proposition 8 was designed to overturn the California Supreme Court's decision giving same-sex couples the right to marry, the opinion launched immediately into an account of the plight of Proposition 8 supporters who alleged "harassment as a result of public disclosure of their support."[82] That account elided completely the distinction between criminal conduct and constitutionally protected activity. It is one thing to use death threats, vandalism, or physical violence against potential witnesses as a justification for limitations on the degree of public access courts should provide. It is quite another to privilege the First Amendment activity of Proposition 8's proponents over its opponents.

But that is what the Court implicitly did when it included, in its litany of "harassment," the allegation that opponents "compiled 'Internet blacklists' of pro-Proposition 8 businesses and urged others to boycott those businesses in retaliation for supporting the ballot measure."[83] In *NAACP v Claiborne Hardware Company*,[84] the Court had held that a boycott of white merchants by black residents of Port Gibson, Mississippi, involved protected First Amendment activity to the extent that the boycott was designed to put pressure on local businesses to support demands for equal treatment by the government. Like blacks in Port Gibson, the gay community can understandably view Proposition 8 as designed to reinstate "a social

---

[81] *Hollingsworth*, 130 S Ct at 713.

[82] Id at 707. Because of the procedural posture of the case, none of the allegations of harassment had been subject to any adversarial testing. Compare Cal Dept Justice, *Hate Crime in California 2008* at ii, 20 (Aug 2009) (reporting 403 hate crimes against LGBT individuals, as opposed to three incidents of "anti-heterosexual crime" and 21 incidents targeting Christian denominations), online at http://www.ag.ca.gov/cjsc/publications/hate crimes/hc08/preface08.pdf.

[83] *Hollingsworth*, 130 S Ct at 707.

[84] 458 US 886 (1982).

order that had consistently treated them as second-class citizens."[85] In *Claiborne Hardware*, the Court held that "[s]peech does not lose its protected character . . . simply because it may embarrass others or coerce them into action."[86] And the picketing and boycott activity did not lose its First Amendment protection because some episodes of violence undeniably occurred.[87] The *Hollingsworth* Court offered no explanation for why the balance between protest and protection should be struck differently for the proponents of Proposition 8 and their retained experts than it had been for the white merchants and opinion leaders of Mississippi.[88]

Although the Court did not focus directly on the issue here—leaving that discussion for *Doe v Reed*—technological innovation played some role in the adverse treatment of Proposition 8 supporters. The Court's account suggests it may have played some role in its decision, as well. Websites like eightmaps.com—which, overlaid onto a Google map, shows the names of individuals who donated to pro-Proposition 8 campaign committees along with their approximate location, the size of their contribution, and sometimes their employer—made it far easier for harassers or attackers to locate and contact their targets,[89] as well as for neighbors, colleagues, and customers to conduct unwanted yet constitutionally protected conversations. But these technologies were independent of the remote streaming of trial testimony to a handful of federal courthouses at issue in *Hollingsworth*, and the Court made no serious effort to explain any connection.[90] Instead, it uncritically adopted the defendant-intervenors' contention that some witnesses might decline to participate if the proceedings were televised.

---

[85] Id at 912.

[86] Id.

[87] See id at 903–06.

[88] While percipient witnesses may have distinctive interests that come from their being required to participate in trials as a civic duty, the witnesses in the *Perry* litigation were far closer to the merchants in *Claiborne Hardware*: Some of them were retained experts who, like the white merchants, were seeking (or having others seek) to dampen public criticism of their positions and who objected to having their livelihoods affected, and others were aspiring civic leaders who had devoted their efforts to seeking changes in public policy.

[89] See Brad Stone, *Prop 8 Donor Web Site Shows Disclosure Is a 2-Edged Sword*, NY Times BU3 (Feb 8, 2009) (New York edition) (discussing eightmaps.com).

[90] One of my colleagues has told me that, after an early internet case led Chief Justice Rehnquist to discover that his home address could be obtained on the internet, he suggested the Court's computers be disconnected—apparently not realizing that it was not the Court's computers that were providing the information.

The Court indicated its concern for three types of witnesses—
"members of same-sex couples," "academics" (by which it seemed
to mean expert witnesses), and "those who participated in the campaign leading to the adoption of Proposition 8" (which seemed a
reference to the defendant-intervenors).[91] But, in reality, the Court's
entire analysis boiled down to a claim about testimony by inter-
venor-retained expert witnesses. It would make no sense to take the
defendant-intervenors' word on whether the same-sex couples (that
is, the plaintiffs) or *their* "academics" would be chilled from testifying; the plaintiffs were represented by high-powered counsel who
were entirely capable of protecting their clients' interest, and those
counsel had consistently supported the district court's intention to
broadcast the trial to the public at large. Even with respect to a
potential chilling effect on the defendant-intervenors or their witnesses, there was a real question about the plausibility of any claimed
chill. The defendant-intervenors had turned themselves into public
figures through pervasive media appearances during the Proposition
8 campaign and had already mounted "their own videos on You
Tube."[92] It was not at all clear what marginal contribution streaming
would make to whatever risk of harassment they already faced, nor
what marginal deterrent effect it would have on individuals who
had already received intensive media coverage.

The Court's authority for the proposition that "witness testimony
may be chilled if broadcast"[93] was a single, decades-old decision in
Estes v Texas.[94] The Court's discussion there, however, had focused
on the effects of commercial broadcasting on percipient witnesses
in a criminal trial.[95] The Court did not consider the fact that in

---

[91] *Hollingsworth*, 130 S Ct at 712–13.

[92] Tr 39, *Perry v Schwarzenegger*, Case 3:09-cv-02292-VRW (ND Cal Jan 6, 2010) (Doc
363).

[93] *Hollingsworth*, 130 S Ct at 713.

[94] 381 US 532 (1965).

[95] Id at 547 (stating that "[t]he quality of the testimony in criminal trials will often be
impaired" if the trial is televised).
Moreover, the technology available at the time of *Estes* was dramatically more intrusive
than the technology for capturing an audiovisual feed today. The Court actually included
photographs of the scene at the pretrial proceedings in an appendix to convey its sense
that the proceedings were bound to be shaped by the noise and bustle caused by broadcast
media. See also id at 551–52 ("It is said that the ever-advancing techniques of public
communication and the adjustment of the public to its presence may bring about a change
in the effect of telecasting upon the fairness of criminal trials. But we are not dealing here
with future developments in the field of electronics. Our judgment cannot be rested on
the hypothesis of tomorrow but must take the facts as they are presented today.").

the intervening years, many courts had televised their proceedings without constitutional objection. Many of the factors identified in *Estes* as problematic seemed inapposite to *Perry*. The risk that "memories may falter, as with anyone speaking publicly,"[96] does not apply to expert witnesses, who are not generally testifying on the basis of memories to begin with. Unlike percipient witnesses, experts are generally *expected* to "shape their own testimony as to make its impact crucial" in light of the other testimony being offered.[97] Moreover, expert witnesses, unlike percipient ones, are seldom involuntary participants in the trial process; they agree to appear in full awareness of the potential for "withering cross-examination."[98] In *Hollingsworth*, the Court brushed these distinctions aside, writing that its concerns "are not diminished by the fact that some of applicants' witnesses are compensated expert witnesses" because "[t]here are qualitative differences between making public appearances regarding an issue and having one's testimony broadcast throughout the country."[99] The Court gave no hint as to what those qualitative differences might be. Testifying at a trial is, of course, not the same as making a public appearance, where one can refuse to go before a hostile audience or to answer uncomfortable questions. But isn't that the point?

Across a variety of dimensions, the Supreme Court remains a holdout in an era of immediate information. For many years, the Court released transcripts of oral arguments that failed to indicate the name of the Justice asking a question. Even now, the Court delays release of audio recordings of oral arguments,[100] for no apparent technological reason. Many observers attribute the delay to the Court's desire that news outlets not have snippets of oral arguments available for their regular coverage. And Justice Souter famously told a congressional committee that "the day you see a camera coming into our courtroom it is going to roll over my dead body."[101] The Court's visceral distaste for televised judicial pro-

---

[96] Id at 547.

[97] Id.

[98] Id.

[99] *Hollingsworth*, 130 S Ct at 713.

[100] See note 77.

[101] Departments of Commerce, Justice, and State, the Judiciary, and Related Agencies Appropriations for 1997: Hearings Before a Subcommittee of the House of Representatives Committee on Appropriations, 104th Cong, 2d Sess 31 (1996).

ceedings perhaps combined with its sensitivity about the issues involved in the marriage equality case to prompt its unusual intervention into an ongoing district court case.

The upshot of *Hollingsworth* was that the California marriage trial
was not televised and, one might think, essentially nothing else.
Despite their victory in preventing live streaming, the defendant-
intervenors nevertheless "elected not to call the majority of their
designated witnesses to testify at trial and called not a single official
proponent of Proposition 8."[102] The Northern District of California
ultimately adopted a revision to its local rule that permits participation in the Ninth Circuit's pilot program to broadcast judicial
proceedings. And the Supreme Court issued very little guidance to
lower courts going forward, save for (perhaps) a thirty-day requirement for notice-and-comment judicial rulemaking.

From another angle, though, *Hollingsworth* revealed something
significant about the Supreme Court and the Justices' view of the
marriage issue. The decision marked the Court's first articulation
of the view that supporters of traditional marriage are at substantial
risk of unfair treatment and therefore deserving of special judicial
solicitude. Indeed, this sentiment reverberated through the Term
with discussions in *Citizens United v Federal Election Commission*,[103]
Doe v Reed,[104] and *Christian Legal Society*.[105] By the time the Term
ended, with *Christian Legal Society*, four members of the *Hollingsworth* majority—the Chief Justice and Justices Scalia, Thomas, and
Alito—had expressed their view that "prevailing standards of political correctness" threatened cultural conservatives with "marginalization."[106]

If the California marriage case ever arrives at the Supreme Court,
it may well reinforce their belief. After the district court held that
California's restriction of marriage to opposite-sex couples violates
the Due Process and Equal Protection Clauses of the Fourteenth

---

[102] *Perry v Schwarzenegger*, 2010 US Dist LEXIS 78817 at *58 (ND Cal 2010). Whatever
the deterrent factor—and the defendant-intervenors claimed that some witnesses were
concerned for their personal safety, see id at *59—audiovisual dissemination of their testimony did not contribute to their reluctance to appear.

[103] 130 S Ct 876, 980–81 (2010) (Thomas, J, dissenting).

[104] 130 S Ct at 2823 (Alito, J, concurring in the judgment).

[105] 130 S Ct at 3000, 3010, 3019–20 (Alito, J, dissenting).

[106] *Christian Legal Soc'y v Martinez*, 130 S Ct 2971, 3000, 3019 (2010) (Alito, J, dissenting).

Amendment,[107] the state governmental defendants all declined to appeal, and the state courts rebuffed various efforts to force the government to defend the marriage restriction.[108] The only appellants who remain are the defendant-intervenors.[109] If they ultimately seek the Supreme Court's assistance in reinstating Proposition 8, the conservative Justices will face a strong temptation to relax the restrictive standing doctrines they have adopted over the past several Terms.[110] In the interim, the Court's decision in *Hollingsworth* may reflect five Justices' sense that decorum and restraint are particularly critical when courts are on the verge of adjudicating contentious social issues—and that cultural conservatives should have their day in court conducted in the traditional way.

II. Doe v Reed: Popular Lawmaking and Unpopular Positions

Given the Court's solicitude for the fears of potential expert witnesses in *Hollingsworth*, its decision later in the Term permitting Washington State to release the names of people who petitioned to put its domestic partnership law up for popular vote was perhaps a bit surprising. The fractured nature of the Justices' analysis (the case produced seven opinions) reflects the fact that however divided the Court may turn out to be on questions of gay rights and marriage equality, it is already splintered on questions about the constitutional structure of the political process. The position of mar-

---

[107] *Perry v Schwarzenegger*, 704 F Supp 2d 921 (ND Cal 2010).

[108] *Beckley v Schwarzenegger*, Case No S186072 (Sept 8, 2010), online at http://appellatecases.courtinfo.ca.gov/search/case/mainCase-Screen.cfm?dist=0&doc_id=1954641&doc_no=S186072; see Bob Egelko, *High Court Won't Order a Defense of Prop. 8*, San Francisco Chronicle A1 (Sept 9, 2010) (describing the unsuccessful litigation to force the state to appeal).

[109] The Ninth Circuit rebuffed an attempt by Imperial County and some of its officials to intervene as defendants to prosecute the appeal. See *Perry v Schwarzenegger*, 630 F3d 898, 904–06 (9th Cir 2011).

[110] In *Arizonans for Official English v Arizona*, 520 US 43, 66 (1997), the Justices unanimously expressed "grave doubts" as to whether proponents of an initiative have the right to defend the ensuing law if the state declines to do so. The Roberts Court has taken a restrictive view of access to the courts across a broad range of cases. See, for example, *Hein v Freedom from Religion Found.*, 127 S Ct 2553 (2007) (narrowing taxpayer standing); see also David Franklin, *The Roberts Court, the 2008 Election, and the Future of the Judiciary*, 6 DePaul Bus & Comm L J 513 (2008) (discussing a range of access to the courts decisions). But see Maxwell L. Stearns, *Standing at the Crossroads: The Roberts Court in Historical Perspective*, 83 Notre Dame L Rev 875 (2008) (suggesting that once the conservative members of the Court perceive a stable conservative judiciary, they may expand standing doctrine to enable them to adjudicate cases).

riage traditionalists within that process simply adds another layer
of complexity.

In 2009, Washington State adopted a new domestic partnership
law. Referred to as the "everything but marriage act,"[111] the law
expanded the rights and responsibilities of state-registered domestic
partners to make them largely equivalent to those of married couples. In response, opponents of the new law formed a political
committee—Protect Marriage Washington—and sought to hold a
referendum. In order to force one, they were required to obtain
valid signatures from slightly more than 120,000 voters.[112] Protect
Marriage and its allies collected over 137,000 signatures, which they
submitted to the secretary of state in July 2009.[113] He certified the
measure, commonly referred to as "R-71." As a result, the law was
suspended pending the results of the referendum.[114]

Within a month, several supporters of the domestic partnership
law had filed requests with the secretary for copies of the R-71
petitions. They invoked the state's Public Records Act, which generally permits public access to "any writing containing information
relating to the conduct of government."[115] In recent years, the secretary of state's office had released a number of petitions connected
with initiatives, but it had never before received a request for a

---

[111] *Doe v Reed*, 586 F3d 671, 675 (9th Cir 2009).

[112] Under Washington Revised Code § 29A.72.150, they were required to obtain a
number of signatures of registered voters equal to 4 percent of the votes cast in the prior
gubernatorial election. See Washington Secretary of State, *Verifying Signatures for Referendum* 71 (2009) (stating that 120,577 signatures were required for ballot measures at the
2009 general election), online at http://wei.secstate.wa.gov/osos/en/initiativesReferenda/
Pages/R-71SignatureStats.aspx.

[113] *Doe v Reed*, 130 S Ct 2811, 2816 (2010).

[114] Wash Const, Art 2, § 1(d).

[115] See Wash Rev Code §§ 42.56.70, 42.56.010(2) (defining "public record"). The act
further provides that "[i]n the event of conflict between the provisions of [the act] and
any other act, the provisions of [the Public Records Act] shall govern." Id § 42.56.030.
Exceptions must either appear in the act itself or be expressly included in another statute.
Id § 42.56.070(1).

The Public Records Act itself was the product of an initiative. Another provision of the
act makes explicit its populist cast:

> The people of this state do not yield their sovereignty to the agencies that serve
> them. The people, in delegating authority, do not give their public servants the
> right to decide what is good for the people to know and what is not good for
> them to know. The people insist on remaining informed so that they may
> maintain control over the instruments that they have created. This chapter shall
> be liberally construed and its exemptions narrowly construed to promote this
> public policy and to assure that the public interest will be fully protected.

Id § 42.56.030.

referendum petition.[116] Moreover, two of the requesters issued a press release announcing their intention to post the signatories' names "online, in a searchable format."[117]

Seeking to prevent the disclosure of signatories' names, Protect Marriage Washington and two anonymous voters filed suit in federal district court. They alleged that the Public Records Act involved "compelled political speech" by requiring the public disclosure of petition signers' names and addresses and "infringe[d] on privacy of association and belief guaranteed by the First Amendment."[118] Their complaint contained two counts. Count I alleged that the Public Records Act was "unconstitutional as applied to referendum petitions."[119] Count II alleged that the act was "unconstitutional as applied to the Referendum 71 petition because there is a reasonable probability of threats, harassment, and reprisals."[120] Addressing only Count I, the district court granted the R-71 proponents a preliminary injunction, which the Ninth Circuit stayed and ultimately reversed. Justice Kennedy, acting as the Circuit Justice, then stayed the Ninth Circuit's stay, and his decision was confirmed by the full Court.[121] The election went forward without the signatories' names being disclosed and the voters approved the new domestic partnership law.[122]

Following the election, the Supreme Court granted certiorari,[123] and Chief Justice Roberts delivered the opinion of the Court.[124] Despite the language of the pleadings, he recast Count I as a facial challenge to the Public Records Act, rather than an as-applied challenge. The explanation he gave was that the relief the petitioners

---

[116] See Joint Appendix 26, *Doe v Reed*, 130 S Ct 2811 (2010).

[117] *Doe*, 130 S Ct at 2816.

[118] Joint Appendix 14, *Doe v Reed*, 130 S Ct 2811 (2010) (quoting *Davis v FEC*, 128 S Ct 2759, 2774–75 (2008), and *Buckley v Valeo*, 424 US 1, 64 (1976)).

[119] Joint Appendix 16, *Doe v Reed*, 130 S Ct 2811 (2010) (capitalization altered).

[120] Id at 17 (capitalization altered).

[121] See *Doe*, 586 F3d at 676 n 8.

[122] See Washington Secretary of State, *November 3, 2009 General Election Results*, online at http://vote.wa.gov/Elections/WEI/Results.aspx?RaceTypeCode=M&JurisdictionType ID=-2&ElectionID=32&ViewMode=Results (showing that 53.15 percent of the votes cast favored approval of the domestic partnership law).

[123] 130 S Ct 1133 (2010).

[124] Justices Kennedy, Ginsburg, Breyer, Alito, and Sotomayor joined the Chief Justice's opinion—although each of them (save Justice Kennedy) also wrote or joined another opinion as well, some of those opinions in substantial tension with the approach taken by the Chief Justice.

sought—an injunction preventing the release of referendum petitions—"reach[ed] beyond the particular circumstances" of their
case.[125]

At first blush, it is not entirely clear why the Court felt the need
to classify Count I as a facial challenge, which is the sort of claim
the Roberts Court has generally frowned upon.[126] After all, the
Court itself recognized that the claim straddled the line: "The claim
is 'as applied' in the sense that it does not seek to strike the [Public
Records Act] in all its applications, but only to the extent it covers
referendum petitions. The claim is 'facial' in that it is not limited
to plaintiffs' particular case, but challenges application of the law
more broadly to all referendum petitions."[127] While the first of those
two sentences is clearly true, the second seems to expand the category of facial challenges significantly. If as-applied challenges are
restricted to cases where the relief extends no further than the
"particular circumstances" of the plaintiffs themselves, a significant
number of constitutional challenges that have until now been understood to be as-applied challenges will be treated as facial attacks
instead. Countless plaintiffs seek injunctive relief that will benefit
others whose particular circumstances differ along at least some
dimensions.[128] Even in class actions, for example, courts permit

---

[125] *Doe*, 130 S Ct at 2817.

[126] In recent Terms, the Court had indicated a general antipathy to facial challenges.
For comprehensive treatments of the Roberts Court's approach, see David L. Franklin,
Through Both Ends of the Telescope: Facial Challenges and the Roberts Court, 33 Hastings Const
L Q 689 (2009), and Gillian Metzger, *Facial and As-Applied Challenges Under the Roberts
Court*, 36 Fordham Urban L J 773 (2009).
  The Court's approach has been a little more mixed when it comes to the electoral arena.
In *Washington State Grange v Washington State Republican Party*, 552 US 442 (2008), the
Court rejected a facial challenge to Washington State's new blanket primary law, and in
Crawford v Marion County Election Board, 553 US 181 (2008), it rejected a facial challenge
to Indiana's voter identification law. By contrast, in the campaign finance arena, while the
late Rehnquist Court seemed similarly hostile to facial challenges, see *McConnell v FEC*,
540 US 93 (2003) (rejecting a facial challenge to the Bipartisan Campaign Reform Act),
the Roberts Court seems to have shifted ground, see *Citizens United v FEC*, 130 S Ct 876
(2010) (striking down several provisions of the Bipartisan Campaign Reform Act); *Davis
v FEC*, 128 S Ct 2759 (2008) (striking down the so-called "millionaires' provision" of the
act).

[127] *Doe*, 130 S Ct at 2817.

[128] For example, consider what this might mean in the context of an as-applied challenge
to voter ID laws—the availability of which the Court expressly recognized in *Crawford*.
Could a court certify a class of voters for whom the law posed an unjustifiable burden?
Compare *Crawford*, 553 US at 200 (opinion of Stevens, J) (suggesting that voters who
faced such a burden could challenge the ID law as applied to them). Or would individual
classes of such voters—the elderly who lack access to birth certificates, impoverished voters
who lack the resources to obtain documentation, and individuals with a religious objection—each have to bring suit?

named representatives to seek relief under a typicality standard.[129] Recasting the dividing line between facial and as-applied challenges as one that turns on the nature of the relief requested makes little sense given the spillover consequences of many constitutional adjudications.

Given that at least five Justices were prepared to reject an as-applied challenge, as well,[130] it was unclear why the Court postponed that issue. Moreover, as members of the Court had previously recognized, relegating election-related litigation to as-applied challenges poses serious problems if one element of a successful as-applied challenge is a showing of how the practice operated in a particular instance.[131] Justice Thomas's solo dissent and Justice Alito's solo concurrence picked up on this point.[132] Circulators of

---

[129] Federal Rule of Civil Procedure 23(a) provides, in pertinent part, that a court can permit class actions in cases involving "questions of law or fact common to the class" where "the claims or defenses of the representative parties are typical of the claims or defenses of the class." While a plaintiff cannot represent a class of people whose factual circumstances or interests differ in material respects, see *Gen. Tel. Co. of Southwest v Falcon*, 457 US 147 (1982), the typicality test does not require an absolute identity of circumstances, either.

[130] Justice Scalia, as we shall see, saw no First Amendment right implicated to begin with. Justice Sotomayor, joined by Justices Stevens and Ginsburg, and Justice Stevens, joined by Justice Breyer, each issued concurrences that made it quite plain that they would apply a test that could not be met in this case. Only the Chief Justice, who delivered the opinion for the Court, and Justice Kennedy, who joined that opinion and was otherwise uncharacteristically silent (along with Justice Ginsburg, he was the only Justice who did not write), provided no insight into how they would have approached an as-applied challenge.

[131] As Justice Scalia observed in his concurrence in the judgment in *Crawford v Marion County Election Board*, 553 US 181 (2008):

> This is an area where the dos and don'ts need to be known in advance of the election, and voter-by-voter examination of the burdens of voting regulations would prove especially disruptive. A case-by-case approach naturally encourages constant litigation. Very few new election regulations improve everyone's lot, so the potential allegations of severe burden are endless. . . . That sort of detailed judicial supervision of the election process would flout the Constitution's express commitment of the task to the States. See Art I, § 4. It is for state legislatures to weigh the costs and benefits of possible changes to their election codes, and their judgment must prevail unless it imposes a severe and unjustified overall burden upon the right to vote, or is intended to disadvantage a particular class. Judicial review of their handiwork must apply an objective, uniform standard that will enable them to determine, *ex ante*, whether the burden they impose is too severe.

Id at 208.

[132] Interestingly, Justice Thomas agreed with the Court that the petitioners had brought a facial challenge. But unlike the majority, he would have applied the *Salerno* "no set of circumstances" standard. See *Doe*, 130 S Ct at 2838 (Thomas, J, dissenting). Or, rather, having invoked *Salerno*, he then applied the test only to the subset of cases involving

a petition, Justice Thomas explained, will be unable to provide
evidence of risk "specific to signers or potential signers of *that
particular referendum*" at the time they decide to circulate a petition.[133] If voters demand public anonymity as a condition of signing
petitions, permitting circulators to challenge disclosure at some later
date by showing that some signatories have faced harassment will
do nothing to protect either the circulators' or the signers' interests:
Without the ability to promise anonymity, circulators will be unable
to persuade some voters to sign. As Justice Alito put it, an "as-
applied exemption becomes practically worthless if speakers cannot
obtain the exemption quickly and well in advance of speaking."[134]
Having agreed on the problem, Justices Thomas and Alito diverged
on the solution. For Justice Thomas, the "significant practical problems" with requiring as-applied challenges led him to address the
claim as a facial challenge, and ultimately to conclude that disclosure
regimes are facially unconstitutional—a result consistent with his
dissent in *Citizens United v Federal Election Commission*,[135] where he
was the lone Justice who would have struck down the disclosure
provisions regarding corporate and union electioneering communications. For Justice Alito, the evidentiary difficulties associated
with timely as-applied challenges led to a remarkably relaxed burden
of proof for plaintiffs seeking exemption from disclosure regimes.[136]

After categorizing the challenge as a facial one, however, the
Court declined to apply the test articulated in *United States v Salerno*.[137] Under that test, a plaintiff bringing a facial challenge must
show that "no set of circumstances exists under which the [chal-
lenged] Act would be valid."[138] Instead, along with the Court's decision earlier in the Term in *United States v Stevens*,[139] *Doe* formalized
a distinct test for First Amendment-based facial attacks. In this
category, plaintiffs are required to show only that "a substantial
number of [the act's] applications are unconstitutional, judged in

---

application of the Public Records Act to ballot measure petitions, thereby also blurring
the facial/as-applied line.

[133] *Doe*, 130 S Ct at 2844 (Thomas, J, dissenting) (emphasis in original).

[134] Id at 2822 (Alito, J, concurring).

[135] 130 S Ct 876 (2010).

[136] See text accompanying notes 189–93 (describing the evidence Justice Alito found
sufficient).

[137] 481 US 739 (1987).

[138] Id at 745.

[139] 130 S Ct 1577 (2010).

relation to the statute's plainly legitimate sweep."[140] That substantive standard shares some features with First Amendment overbreadth doctrine. The unifying idea is the fear that if courts wait to adjudicate claims of constitutional infringement until individuals facing "particular circumstances" experience feared injuries, there will be no cases to adjudicate. Individuals will forgo exercising their rights rather than risk the consequences of the offending statute.[141]

The blurring of categorical lines continued when the Justices turned to the merits of Protect Marriage's constitutional challenge. The starting point for the majority's analysis was the holding that petition signers are engaged in First Amendment-protected expression. At the very least, by signing a referendum petition, a signer is indicating a belief that the issue in question ought to be put up for popular vote; presumably, most signatories also are expressing their opposition to the law being subject to the referendum.[142]

Regulations targeting political speech generally trigger the most searching judicial scrutiny. Indeed, the Court had long ago determined that "the circulation of a petition [to place an issue on the ballot] involves the type of interactive communication concerning political change that is appropriately described as 'core political speech.'"[143] A decade earlier, the Court had therefore struck down a Colorado statute that required signature gatherers to wear name badges on the grounds that such a disclosure requirement might deter their participation.[144] And earlier in the Term, the Court had reiterated that "[l]aws that burden political speech are 'subject to strict scrutiny,' which requires the Government to prove that the

---

[140] Id at 1587 (quoting *Washington State Grange v Washington State Republican Party*, 552 US 442, 449 n 6 (2008)) (internal quotation marks omitted); see *Doe*, 130 S Ct at 2817 (citing *Stevens*).

[141] See *City of Lakewood v Plain Dealer Publ'g Co.*, 486 US 750, 757 (1988) ("Self-censorship is immune to an 'as-applied' challenge, for it derives from the individual's own actions, not an abuse of government power.").

There are also some differences between the Court's approach in *Doe* and conventional overbreadth doctrine. In the mine-run overbreadth case, the plaintiff before the Court invokes the effect of the challenged law on other, more sympathetic parties; the doctrine functions as a sort of third-party standing device. Here, by contrast, the plaintiffs were seeking to focus the Court's attention on the risk that *they*, and their allies, would be treated unfairly or chilled from participating fully in the political process.

[142] See *Meyer v Grant*, 486 US 414, 421 (1988).

[143] Id at 421–22.

[144] *Buckley v American Constitutional Law Foundation*, 525 US 182 (1999).

restriction 'furthers a compelling interest and is narrowly tailored to achieve that interest.'"[145]

But Chief Justice Roberts's opinion in *Doe* adopted a decidedly more deferential approach. He pointed to "a series of precedents considering First Amendment challenges to disclosure requirements in the electoral context" that had, he wrote, "reviewed such challenges under what has been termed 'exacting scrutiny.'"[146] The "exacting scrutiny" standard, he explained, "requires a 'substantial relation' between the disclosure requirement and a 'sufficiently important' governmental interest. To withstand this scrutiny, 'the strength of the governmental interest must reflect the seriousness of the actual burden on First Amendment rights.'"[147] In short, "exacting scrutiny" was less exacting than strict scrutiny, which would have required a compelling, rather than a merely "important," government interest and would have required narrow tailoring, rather than simply a "substantial relation" between the disclosure regime and that governmental end.[148] Thus, "exacting scrutiny" resembled most closely the sliding scale the Court had already adopted for a variety of other election-related regulations—such as limitations on write-in voting[149] or voter identification requirements[150]—that did not implicate core political speech at all.

The Court's prior decisions had not squarely stated that the phrase "exacting scrutiny" constituted a term of art—like "strict scrutiny" or "rationality review"—with a distinct framework for assessing whether the government's interest was sufficiently weighty or the fit between the statute and that interest was sufficiently tight. Rather, cases often used the phrase in an offhanded way that suggested it was a description of conventional strict scrutiny.[151] By

---

[145] *Citizens United v FEC*, 130 S Ct 876, 898 (2010) (quoting *FEC v Washington Right to Life, Inc.*, 551 US 449, 464 (2007) (opinion of Roberts, CJ)).

[146] *Doe*, 130 S Ct at 2818.

[147] Id (quoting *Citizens United*, 130 S Ct at 914, and *Buckley v Valeo*, 424 US at 64).

[148] See id at 2820 n 2 (explaining that Justice Thomas's "contrary assessment" of the fit between disclosure and the state's interests was "based on his determination that strict scrutiny applies, . . . rather than the standard of review that we have concluded is appropriate").

[149] See *Burdick v Takushi*, 504 US 428, 433–34 (1992) (upholding a ban on write-in voting) (cited in *Doe*, 130 S Ct at 2818).

[150] See *Crawford*, 553 US at 190–91 (opinion of Stevens, J).

[151] For example, in *McConnell v FEC*, 540 US 93 (2003), Justice Kennedy wrote an opinion that the Chief Justice joined in which he pointed to the Court's "ample precedent affirming that burdens on speech necessitate strict scrutiny review," id at 312, and sup-

turning "exacting scrutiny" into a technical standard of review, *Doe* marked another stage in the ongoing splintering of the seemingly rigid system of tiered scrutiny erected during the latter years of the Warren Court and cemented into place by the Burger Courts.[152]

The spate of separate opinions took wildly different positions on the nature of the First Amendment interest at stake and therefore, not surprisingly, on the framework for analyzing the petitioners' claims. At one end of the spectrum, Justice Scalia, concurring in the judgment, denied that petition signers had any First Amendment right to "partial anonymity" at all.[153] His approach was avowedly historical: "Our Nation's longstanding traditions of legislating and voting in public refute the claim that the First Amendment accords a right to anonymity in the performance of an act with governmental effect."[154] As a matter of Washington constitutional law, voters within the referendum process are exercising legislative power. Such power, Justice Scalia explained, was traditionally exercised publicly. Indeed, the United States and many state constitutions expressly require recording legislative action, including the votes of individual legislators. To be sure, the referendum was a turn-of-the-twentieth-century device,[155] and the only direct evidence we had of the Framers' views was that they structured the federal government to avoid it altogether. But, in keeping with his professed commitment to original public meaning originalism, Justice Scalia pointed out that the town hall meeting of the eighteenth century was a precursor to popular lawmaking. At the time of the framing (and since, for that matter), participation in town hall meetings was always public. More expansively, Justice Scalia argued that even if participation in the referendum process were treated simply as voting, rather than legislating, there was no originalist support for anonymity as a con-

---

ported that statement with a citation and quotation of a passage from *Buckley v Valeo*, 424 US 1, 44–45 (1976) (per curiam), stating that "exacting scrutiny [applies] to limitations on core First Amendment rights of political expression."

[152] For comprehensive discussions of the nuanced ways in which the tiers of scrutiny now operate, see Adam Winkler, *Fatal in Theory and Strict in Fact: An Empirical Analysis of Strict Scrutiny in the Federal Court*, 59 Vand L Rev 793 (2006); Suzanne B. Goldberg, *Equality Without Tiers*, 77 S Cal L Rev 481 (2004) (arguing that the three-tier system has outlived its usefulness).

[153] *Doe*, 130 S Ct at 2832 (Scalia, J, concurring in the judgment).

[154] Id at 2832–33 (Scalia, J, concurring in the judgment).

[155] See generally Nathaniel Persily, *The Peculiar Geography of Direct Democracy: Why the Initiative, Referendum and Recall Developed in the American West*, 2 Mich L & Pol'y Rev 11 (1997).

stitutional requirement. Vive voce voting was commonplace at the time the First Amendment was ratified and for years thereafter. And the adoption of secret ballots in the latter part of the nineteenth century apparently rested on arguments about ordinary policy—most notably, concerns with vote buying and corruption—rather than on appeals to constitutional privacy concerns.[156]

Four other Justices assigned the First Amendment interests more weight, but not by much. Justice Sotomayor, in a concurrence joined by Justices Stevens and Ginsburg, pointed to the public nature of "the process of legislating by referendum" as a reason for treating any First Amendment-based interest in nondisclosure as relatively slight.[157] Justice Stevens, in his opinion concurring and concurring in the judgment, which was joined by Justice Breyer, likewise downplayed any strong First Amendment interest in participating anonymously. Although the "democratic act" of signing a petition "does serve an expressive purpose, the act . . . is 'not principally'" one of individual expression; rather, it serves the public function of "sorting those issues that have enough public support to warrant limited space on a referendum ballot."[158] As a result, both Justice Sotomayor and Justice Stevens concluded that Washington State was entitled to considerable deference in applying the Public Records Act to the R-71 petitions. Justice Sotomayor found it "by no means necessary" for a state to show that its restrictions "are narrowly tailored to its interests."[159] Because Justice Scalia had found no First Amendment rights implicated at all, it seems as if five Justices actually would not have applied "exacting scrutiny" if that term really means anything. Justice Sotomayor denominated her opinion a concurrence, rather than a concurrence in the judgment. Justice Stevens did not expressly identify the parts of the opinion of the Court he found inconsistent with his concurrence in part and in the judgment. So while there was technically an opinion for the Court, it is not entirely clear that all the analysis in that opinion in fact garnered support from a majority of the Justices.

At the other end of the spectrum, Justices Alito (in a solo con-

---

[156] See *Doe*, 130 S Ct at 2836 (Scalia, J, concurring in the judgment).

[157] Id at 2828 (Sotomayor, J, concurring).

[158] Id at 2829 & n 1 (Stevens, J, concurring in part and concurring in the judgment) (quoting *Timmons v Twin Cities Area New Party*, 520 US 351, 373 (1997) (Stevens, J, dissenting)).

[159] Id at 2828 (quoting *Anderson v Celebrezze*, 460 US 780, 788 (1983)).

currence) and Thomas (in a solo dissent) saw the case as implicating core constitutional principles of privacy. Particularly in light of their extensive invocations of history four days later in *McDonald v City of Chicago*,[160] it is striking that they did not engage, let alone dispute, Justice Scalia's account of the original understanding of the First Amendment. Justice Alito repeatedly described the circulators and signers of petitions as "speakers,"[161] and also referred to their "right to privacy of belief and association."[162] In contrast to the majority, who treated the act of signing a petition as an individual act of expression, Justice Thomas characterized signers as engaging in First Amendment-protected "political association."[163] And unlike the Court, he believed that the appropriate standard was conventional "strict scrutiny," which would require the state to show that disclosure under the Public Records Act was "narrowly tailored— *i.e.*, the least restrictive means—to serve a compelling state interest."[164]

In fact, Justices Thomas and Alito were strikingly nonoriginalist in their approach to Protect Marriage Washington's claim, perhaps because their substantive sympathies pushed in the opposite direction. The next Term, during oral argument over a California statute restricting the sale of violent video games to minors, Justice Alito interrupted Justice Scalia's questioning regarding the original understanding of the First Amendment to joke that "I think what Justice Scalia wants to know is what James Madison thought about video games."[165] Of course, he thought nothing ("Grand Theft Horse and Buggy"?). Modern technology inflects privacy in a number of ways, and Justices Alito and Thomas seemed strongly influenced by those considerations. The "state of technology today," Justice Thomas declared, "creates at least *some* probability that signers of every referendum will be subjected to threats, harassment, or reprisals if their personal information is disclosed. [T]he advent of the Internet enables rapid dissemination of the information

---

[160] 130 S Ct 3020 (2010).

[161] *Doe*, 130 S Ct at 2822, 2823, 2825 (Alito, J, concurring).

[162] Id at 2824 (Alito, J, concurring).

[163] Id at 2389 (Thomas, J, dissenting) (quoting *Citizens Against Rent Control/Coalition for Fair Housing v Berkeley*, 454 US 290, 295 (1981), and *Buckley v Valeo*, 424 US 1, 15 (1976) (per curiam)).

[164] Id at 2839 (Thomas, J, dissenting).

[165] Tr 16, *Schwarzenegger v Entertainment Merchants Association*, No 08-1448 (Nov 2, 2010).

needed to threaten or harass every referendum signer."[166] Justice Alito emphasized that if signers' names were posted on the internet, "then anyone with access to a computer could compile a wealth of information about all of those persons."[167] He detailed the information retrievable through on-line links, ranging from the amount of their mortgage to newspaper articles about their children's athletic activities before concluding that "[t]he potential that such information could be used for harassment is vast."[168]

Regardless of how they characterized the right at issue, the eight Justices who agreed that some First Amendment-based interest was at stake were faced with the need to balance those interests against the state's countervailing considerations.[169] Washington had asserted two justifications for its disclosure regime: first, an electoral integrity rationale focused on combating fraud and promoting governmental transparency; second, an informational rationale focused on giving voters information about the source of a petition's support.[170] The most remarkable aspect of the Court's brief discussion of the integrity rationale was just how unexacting "exacting scrutiny" turned out to be—something more akin to rationality review than to strict scrutiny. In rationality review cases, courts do not ask about a law's actual purpose. Rather, they often hypothesize some purpose that fits the challenged classification. They require only the most relaxed fit between the challenged law and a permissible government purpose. Nor do they require much empirical evidence of such a link, instead asking whether "any state of facts reasonably may be conceived to justify [the challenged law]."[171] I think it is a fair bet that when Washington's voters enacted the state's Public Records Act, they were not thinking of how disclosure of ballot petitions would combat fraud in the electoral process. But on the basis of relatively thin evidence, the Court hypothesized that disclosure would enable the public to backstop the secretary of state's verification process, enable individuals to discover that their names

---

[166] *Doe*, 130 S Ct at 2845 (Thomas, J, dissenting) (brackets in the original; internal quotation marks omitted).

[167] Id at 2825 (Alito, J, concurring).

[168] Id.

[169] Justice Breyer offered a one-paragraph separate concurrence devoted entirely to this point. See *Doe*, 130 S Ct at 2822 (Breyer, J, concurring).

[170] See id at 2819.

[171] *McGowan v Maryland*, 366 US 420, 426 (1961).

had been forged on petitions, and deter bait-and-switch fraud in which voters are induced to sign petitions based on misrepresentations about the nature of the ballot measure. Finding that concerns with electoral integrity provided a sufficient basis for disclosure, Chief Justice Roberts's opinion declined to address the informational rationale. The Court discussed the case as if disclosure would lead only to more accurate signature verification, and thereby enhance public confidence in the electoral process.

But had the Court addressed the informational rationale, it would have had to confront more directly the range of uses to which electoral information can be put and where to draw the line between legitimate and unacceptable uses. At a wholesale level, aggregated information about a measure's supporters serves long-recognized legitimate purposes. Such information can provide voters with a useful cue in deciding how to vote on a ballot measure. For example, if the bulk of a petition's signatures are gathered in heavily Democratic or heavily Republican neighborhoods or from relatively wealthy or relatively less affluent parts of the state, this can tell a voter something about the predicted impact of a particular measure.[172] By contrast, both the groups requesting the petitions and the petitioners in *Doe* seemed more focused on the retail use of information—namely, the identification of individual signatories for the purpose of enabling opponents of the referendum to contact them. The opponents hoped that voters supporting same-sex couples' rights would engage in core political speech with neighbors, coworkers, relatives, and acquaintances who had signed the petition.[173] The proponents feared that signatories would be subjected to harassment and retaliation by strangers. As I have already sug-

---

[172] Only Justice Thomas contested this point. See *Doe*, 130 S Ct at 2843 (Thomas, J, dissenting) (stating that "'[t]he inherent worth of the speech in terms of its capacity for informing the public does not depend upon the identity of its source'" and that "[p]eople are intelligent enough to evaluate the merits of a referendum without knowing who supported it") (quoting *First Natl Bank of Boston v Bellotti*, 435 US 765, 777 (1978)). But even Justice Thomas has never questioned such voting cues as party identification.

[173] See KnowThyNeighbor.org, *Whosigned.org Refutes Intimidation Charges; Will Post Names of Petition Signers as Planned* (June 9, 2009), online at http://knowthyneighbor .blogs.com/home/2009/06/whosignedorg-refutes-intimidation-charges-will-post-names-of-petition-signers-as-planned.html (stating that the group did not anticipate an "organized plan to confront petition signers" but rather anticipated that "conversations are triggered between people that already have a personal connection like friends, relatives, and neighbors" and describing such conversations, while potentially "uncomfortable for both parties," as being "desperately needed to break down stereotypes and to help both sides realize how much they actually have in common").

gested,[174] the line between protected First Amendment activity and retaliation can be hazy. Would refusal to associate with a measure's supporters, for example, be an instance of the former or of the latter? And can that question necessarily be answered in the abstract? On top of the conceptual haziness rest challenging empirical questions. What is the likelihood that disclosure will produce valuable robust debate as opposed to impermissible harassment or intimidation? If it produces both, in what proportions will they occur?

More fundamentally, because none of the other Justices engaged Justice Scalia's originalist account, they did not grapple with another potential justification for requiring participants in the referendum process to act publicly. As Justice Scalia described, historically one rationale for requiring citizens to cast their votes publicly was precisely its effect on their decision making. Vive voce voting required a voter to "show at the hustings the courage of his personal conviction."[175] It forced the voter, in short, to be accountable. This loss of accountability was precisely why the English political philosopher John Stuart Mill opposed the adoption of the secret ballot:

> The best side of their character is that which people are anxious to show, even to those who are no better than themselves. People will give dishonest or mean votes from lucre, from malice, from pique, from personal rivalry, even from the interests or prejudices of class or sect, more readily in secret than in public. And cases exist . . . in which almost the only restraint upon a majority of knaves consists in their involuntary respect for the opinion of an honest minority.[176]

The practice of direct democracy itself, and not only disclosure laws regulating it, "significantly implicates competing constitutionally protected interests in complex ways."[177] On the one hand, it allows greater public participation in the lawmaking process. On the other hand, as many scholars have noted, direct democracy lacks many

---

[174] See text accompanying notes 83–90.

[175] *Doe*, 130 S Ct at 2837 (Scalia, J, concurring in the judgment) (quoting James Schouler, *Evolution of the American Voter*, 2 Am Hist Rev 665, 671 (1897)).

[176] John Stuart Mill, *Considerations on Representative Government* 210 (2d ed, Parker, Son, & Bourne 1861).

[177] *Doe*, 130 S Ct at 2822 (Breyer, J, concurring).

of the braking features that protect minorities in republican, representative politics.[178]

One way to get a handle on the possible effect of public accountability on voter decision making is to think about the "Bradley effect." The idea is that the votes actually cast for minority candidates lag behind the estimates derived from survey data—including exit polls, which involve voters being asked not to predict how they may vote but to report how they actually voted, generally within minutes of doing so.[179] The conventional explanation for the effect centers on voters' unwillingness to be thought to have cast their votes on the basis of a candidate's race.[180] Most recently, the 2008 presidential primaries may have involved a refinement of the Bradley effect: The gap between survey data and actual vote totals for Barack Obama was lower in caucus states, where voters must indicate their preference publicly, than in primary states with secret ballots.[181] The Bradley effect raises the question whether a state might permissibly balance its competing desires to permit direct public input into the legislative process and to reduce the discriminatory potential of direct democracy by instituting a disclosure regime.

The countervailing argument, of course, is that the electoral system is supposed to report voters' preferences, and not to shape them, or at least not to shape citizens' fundamental beliefs about critical issues of public policy.[182] In some ways, the contemporary

[178] See, for example, Julian N. Eule, *Judicial Review of Direct Democracy*, 99 Yale L J 1503 (1990); Clayton P. Gillette, *Plebiscites, Participation, and Collective Action in Local Government Law*, 86 Mich L Rev 930, 944 (1988) ("The requirement of public voting and public explanation restricts the capacity of legislators to vote either their own dark urges or those of their constituents."); see also Sylvia R. Lazos Vargas, *Judicial Review of Initiatives and Referendums in Which Majorities Vote on Minorities' Democratic Citizenship*, 60 Ohio St L J 399, 409 (1999) (noting that, from 1960 to 1998, minorities "'lost' over 80% of the time" on initiatives or referenda dealing with "the content of minorities' citizenship").

[179] The "Bradley effect" is named for Tom Bradley. Bradley, an African American, ran for governor of California in 1982. "Surveys up to and including exit polls" reported that Bradley had a substantial lead on the Republican candidate, who was white. Nevertheless, Bradley lost. William Safire, *The Bradley Effect*, NY Times, Sept 26, 2008, online at http://www.nytimes.com/2008/09/28/magazine/28wwln-safire-t.html?_r=1&ref=magazine.

[180] When Bradley lost, "[s]peculation ranged from inaccurate sampling, to last-minute mind-changes, to latent racism, to freely lying voters, to the reluctance of those being polled to admitting a preference that may be socially unacceptable—anti-black—in talking to interviewers." Id.

[181] See Gregory S. Parks and Jeffrey J. Rachlinski, *Implicit Bias, Election '08, and the Myth of a Post-Racial America*, 37 Fla St U L Rev 659, 708 (2010).

[182] A central premise of the casebook I wrote along with Sam Issacharoff and Rick Pildes is the idea that "[b]efore the first vote is cast or the first ballot counted, the possibilities

understanding that voters are free to cast their ballots on whatever basis they choose may explain why none of the other Justices took an originalist approach. Public voting occurred in an era when voting itself was not yet viewed as a fundamental constitutional right.[183] In such a world, states' control over the electoral process would have been virtually plenary.[184] Thus, when it came to voting and views on marriage, the Supreme Court in 1885 upheld the disenfranchisement of polygamists because states should be entitled to "withdraw all political influence from those who are practically hostile" to "the basis of the idea of the family, as consisting in and springing from the union for life of one man and one woman in the holy estate of matrimony."[185] If the state could outright disenfranchise such citizens, then a disclosure rule that deterred individuals from expressing those views might be less problematic than it would be today. Once the Court had held that "'[f]encing out' from the franchise a sector of the population because of the way they may vote is constitutionally impermissible,"[186] there is a strong argument that a voter's choices should be protected, not only from illegal acts, but from other forms of pressure as well.

The *Doe* Court's decision to address only the facial challenge—leaving the petitioners' as-applied claim to be litigated in the first instance before the district court—enabled the Court essentially to sidestep the petitioners' relatively case-specific predictions of harassment and intimidation. The Court emphasized that the question before it was not whether disclosure of the R-71 petitions, or even other controversial ballot measures more generally, posed a "rea-

---

for democratic politics are already constrained and channeled" by the institutional structures within which voting takes place. Samuel Issacharoff, Pamela S. Karlan, and Richard H. Pildes, *The Law of Democracy: Legal Structure of the Political Process* 1 (Foundation, 3d ed 2007). Thus, for example, voters who prefer third-party candidates may often feel impelled to vote for a major party candidate instead because the current structure means voting for a minor party candidate will often be fruitless.

[183] See, for example, *Minor v Happersett*, 88 US 162, 178 (1875) (announcing that the Supreme Court was "unanimously of the opinion that the Constitution of the United States does not confer the right of suffrage upon any one"); compare *Bush v Gore*, 531 US 98, 104 (2000) (per curiam) (declaring that "[t]he individual citizen has no federal constitutional right to vote for electors for the President of the United States unless and until the state legislature chooses a statewide election as the means to implement its power to appoint members of the Electoral College").

[184] See generally Pamela S. Karlan, *Convictions and Doubts: Retribution, Representation, and the Debate over Felon Disenfranchisement*, 56 Stan L Rev 1147, 1151–53 (2004) (comparing the nineteenth- and twentieth-century treatments of the right to vote).

[185] *Murphy v Ramsey*, 114 US 15 (1885).

[186] *Carrington v Rash*, 380 US 89, 94 (1965).

sonable probability" of impermissible action against signatories.[187]
Rather, the petitioners had to show that across the broad range of
ballot measures, including the arcane and the mundane, there was
a significant risk of harassment or intimidation. This they could not
do. Washington and other states had disclosed petitions regarding
a variety of issues in recent years "without incident"[188]—indeed,
apparently without objection. And the steady stream of citizen-
driven ballot measures on controversial issues further suggests that
the prospect of disclosure (if in fact voters are even aware of the
possibility) seems not to have chilled petitioning activity. Although
Chief Justice Roberts's opinion for the Court suggested that signers
who demonstrated a "reasonable probability of harassment" might
prevail in an as-applied challenge, what constitutes such a probability is unclear.

Justice Alito, in his separate opinion, claimed that Protect Marriage Washington had a "strong argument" that disclosure violated
the First Amendment "as applied to the Referendum 71 petition."[189]
The evidentiary basis for his argument was the assertion of "widespread harassment and intimidation suffered by supporters of California's Proposition 8."[190] The source for that claim was in turn
the Court's earlier statements to that effect in *Hollingsworth v Perry*
and Justice Thomas's dissent in *Citizens United*. But those statements
in turn were based on *allegations* of intimidation and harassment,
rather than evidence subjected to any official assessment or adversarial testing. To be sure, several of the allegations involved criminal
behavior, such as threats or vandalism. Some of that vandalism,
however, was the sort of near-universal behavior that attends nearly
all heated elections—for example, the destruction or removal of
campaign yard signs. Nothing about that activity suggests what the
comparable activity would be against petition signatories, whose
political speech is further removed from opportunities for retaliation.

Moreover, other allegations characterized as "threats and harassment" in the complaint on which Justice Thomas had relied[191]

---

[187] *Doe*, 130 S Ct at 2820 (quoting *Buckley v Valeo*, 424 US 1, 74 (1976) (per curiam)).

[188] Id at 2821.

[189] Id at 2822 (Alito, J, concurring).

[190] Id at 2823.

[191] See *Citizens United*, 130 S Ct at 980–81 (Thomas, J, dissenting) (citing the complaint
in *ProtectMarriage.com–Yes on 8 v Bowen*, Case No 2:09-cv-00058-MCE-DAD, filed in the
Eastern District of California).

may fall within the boundaries of protected speech and association: for example, the distribution of a flyer in one individual's hometown calling him a "bigot" for having made a four-figure financial contribution to Proposition 8 and identifying him as a Catholic deacon; and emails sent to another contributor stating that "I am boycotting your organization as a result of your support of Prop 8" and that "I will tell all my friends not to use your business. I will not give you my hard earned money knowing that you think I don't deserver [*sic*] the same rights as you do. This is a consequence of your hatred."[192] Justice Alito claimed that "if the evidence relating to Proposition 8 is not sufficient to obtain an as-applied exemption in this case, one may wonder whether that vehicle provides any meaningful protection for the First Amendment rights of persons who circulate and sign referendum and initiative petitions."[193] But if this evidence *is* sufficient, one may wonder whether there are any as-applied challenges that would fail. There may be little daylight in practice between Justice Alito and Justice Thomas.

In contrast, Justices Sotomayor and Stevens announced standards for assessing as-applied challenges that made it unlikely that any plaintiff will ever prevail in preventing disclosure of his signature on an initiative or referendum petition. Justice Stevens observed that "[a]s a matter of law, the Court is correct to keep open the possibility" that a plaintiff could challenge disclosure, but almost immediately shut the door to claims about disclosure regimes like the Public Records Act. Even "a significant threat of harassment" would not be enough, in his view, unless that threat "cannot be mitigated by law enforcement measures."[194] This could mean that absent conditions like those in the mid-century American South, whence came the anonymity cases like *NAACP v Alabama*[195]—and which hardly describe life in even the bluest of states today—a challenge to general disclosure requirements will fail. Justice Sotomayor similarly announced the view that "any party attempting to challenge particular applications of the State's regulations will bear a heavy burden," and would limit as-applied challenges to the

---

[192] Complaint ¶ 34, in *ProtectMarriage.com–Yes on 8*, online at http://docs.justia.com/cases /federal/district-courts/california/caedce/2:2009cv00058/186477/1/ (capitalization altered).

[193] *Doe*, 130 S Ct at 2823–24 (Alito, J, concurring).

[194] Id at 2831 (Stevens, J, concurring in part and concurring in the judgment).

[195] 357 US 449 (1958).

"rare circumstance in which disclosure poses a reasonable probability of serious and widespread harassment that the State is unwilling or unable to control."[196]

The various opinions' invocations of *NAACP v Alabama* and *Bates v Little Rock*[197] may indicate something about how they view the struggle over marriage equality. Justice Sotomayor's and Stevens's use of those cases suggests they saw a clear distinction between the difficulties faced by (largely African American) civil rights activists in the 1950s and 1960s and the situation confronting marriage traditionalists today.[198] In Alabama and Arkansas, not only were African Americans pervasively excluded from the formal political process altogether, but they faced official suppression, pervasive private violence to which the government never responded, and discrimination across the entire range of civic life. In distinguishing *NAACP v Alabama*, the more liberal wing of the Court implicitly rejected the claim that marriage traditionalists were a group needing such special solicitude from the courts. By contrast, Justices Alito and Thomas seemed to see a kinship between two sets of movement activists subject to reprisals and needing judicial protection from (or even within) majoritarian political processes. That perception of kinship was to play out more fully in *Christian Legal Society*, where questions of First Amendment association were more directly at stake than in the fleeting association attached to signing a petition circulated by an evanescent group. In their solicitude for opponents of marriage equality, the conservative Justices seemed not to notice another, ironic, historical parallel: Opponents of marriage equality were essentially complaining about being "outed" by gay people and their supporters who had come out of the closet to participate actively in politics.

---

[196] *Doe*, 130 S Ct at 2829 (Sotomayor, J, concurring) (adding a "cf." citation for *NAACP v Alabama ex rel Patterson*, 357 US 449 (1958)).

[197] 361 US 516 (1960).

[198] Justice Sotomayor cited *NAACP* as an example of the "rare circumstance" in which "[c]ase specific relief" might be available, *Doe*, 130 S Ct at 2829 (Sotomayor, J, concurring), implicitly suggesting that the cultural rear guard was in no such danger. Similarly, Justice Stevens cited *Bates* in a context that made clear that he saw no danger in the present situation that there was any substantial burden on the rear guard's speech rights. See id at 2831 n 6 (Stevens, J, concurring in part and concurring in the judgment).

III. Christian Legal Society v Martinez: Sexual Orientation, Religion, and the Relationship Among Status, Conduct, and Belief

Herbert Wechsler infamously identified the central question in *Brown v Board of Education* as a "conflict in human claims of high dimension, not unlike many others that involve the highest freedoms."[199] He asked,

> Given a situation where the state must practically choose between denying the association to those individuals who wish it or imposing it on those who would avoid it, is there a basis in neutral principles for holding that the Constitution demands that the claims for association should prevail?[200]

At least with respect to the claims of African Americans, that conflict was resolved during the 1960s and 1970s by the political process and judicial acquiescence. The antidiscrimination statutes of the Second Reconstruction, upheld by the Supreme Court, came down heavily on the side of nondiscrimination and full inclusion.[201]

This past Term saw a reprise of the conflict, this time involving sexual orientation rather than race. The University of California Hastings College of the Law (UC Hastings) denied official recognition to a student organization that excluded gay students from membership. The organization sued, claiming a violation of its First Amendment rights to freedom of speech, freedom of association, and free exercise of religion. Ultimately, the Court upheld the law school's decision. Along the way, the Justices revealed vastly different worldviews when it comes to what Justice Scalia years ago referred to as the "culture wars" over gay rights.[202] The barely

---

[199] Herbert Wechsler, *Toward Neutral Principles of Constitutional Law*, 73 Harv L Rev 1, 34 (1959). For a more extensive discussion of Wechsler and his influence on contemporary constitutional argument, see Pamela S. Karlan, *What Can Brown® Do for You? Neutral Principles and the Struggle over the Equal Protection Clause*, 58 Duke L J 1049 (2009).

[200] Wechsler, 73 Harv L Rev at 34 (cited in note 199).

[201] In *Heart of Atlanta Motel v United States*, 379 US 241 (1964), for example, the Court brusquely rejected a motel owner's claim that it had a cognizable liberty interest in "select[ing] its guests as it sees fit." Id at 259. Similarly, in *Runyon v McCrary*, 427 US 160 (1976), the Court rejected the freedom-of-association claim of racially exclusive private schools, holding that 42 USC § 1981 prohibited racial discrimination in private contracts. Id at 176.

[202] *Romer v Evans*, 517 US 620, 652 (1996) (Scalia, J, dissenting). Earlier in his dissent, Justice Scalia more stridently termed the disagreement a Kulturkampf. Alluding to the nineteenth-century Prussian effort to bring the Roman Catholic Church under state control provides the unspoken parallel to the University of California's efforts in *Christian Legal Society*. See id at 636.

suppressed rage in Justice Alito's dissent supporting the Christian Legal Society may reflect the Justices' sense of who's winning that battle.

The Christian Legal Society (CLS) is a national association of Christian lawyers and law students. It had long required all members to sign a Statement of Faith embracing the group's principles. In early 2004, the society adopted a resolution declaring that engaging in "acts of sexual conduct outside of God's design for marriage between one man and one woman" was "inconsistent" with the society's foundational belief "and consequently may be regarded by CLS as disqualifying such an individual from CLS membership."[203]

At the beginning of the 2004–05 academic year, the leaders of a preexisting and officially recognized Christian students' group at UC Hastings decided to affiliate the group with CLS.[204] Shortly thereafter, the students applied to the law school for travel funds to attend a national CLS conference. The law school provided such funding only to registered student organizations (RSOs). Accordingly, the Hastings CLS submitted a copy of its new bylaws as part of the registration process.

That was where the trouble began. The UC Hastings administration determined that the group's bylaws did not comply with the school's Nondiscrimination Policy, which provided in pertinent part that school-sponsored activities would not "discriminate unlawfully on the basis of race, color, religion, national origin, ancestry, disability, age, sex or sexual orientation."[205] After some back and forth, the school denied the group RSO status. This meant the group was ineligible for certain financial benefits and access to certain law school facilities.

Hastings CLS sued. Both the society and the law school moved for summary judgment. In a fairly lengthy opinion, the district court granted the school's motion, concluding that UC Hastings' "uni-

---

[203] *Christian Legal Soc'y v Martinez*, 130 S Ct 2971, 3001 (2010) (Alito, J, dissenting) (quoting the resolution).

[204] Id at 2980 (opinion of the Court). The predecessor group's bylaws provided that the Hastings Christian Fellowship (which apparently also sometimes called itself the Hastings Christian Legal Society) "welcomes all students of the University of California, Hastings College of law." The predecessor group, which had official student organization status, "did not exclude members on the basis of religion or sexual orientation." *Christian Legal Soc'y v Kane*, 2006 US Dist LEXIS 27347 at *8 (ND Cal 2006).

[205] *Christian Legal Soc'y*, 130 S Ct at 2979.

form enforcement of its Nondiscrimination Policy"[206] passed constitutional muster as a regulation of conduct whose incidental effects on First Amendment rights were justified by the school's "compelling interest in prohibiting discrimination on its campus."[207] The Ninth Circuit affirmed in a one-paragraph, unpublished opinion that stated, in its entirety,

> The parties stipulate that Hastings imposes an open membership rule on all student groups—all groups must accept all comers as voting members even if those individuals disagree with the mission of the group. The conditions on recognition are therefore viewpoint neutral and reasonable.[208]

The arguments before the Supreme Court concerned, to an unusual degree, a factual question: What precisely was the UC Hastings policy at issue?[209] Justice Ginsburg, in her opinion for the Court, relied on a stipulation between the parties to describe the regulation as "an all-comers policy."[210] UC Hastings required RSOs to open their membership to all students, subject to "neutral and generally applicable membership requirements unrelated to 'status or beliefs,'" such as paying dues, refraining from misconduct, or achieving distinction on a skill-based test such as a journal writing competition.[211] By contrast, Justice Alito's dissent insisted that the school's actual policy was not an all-comers rule. As he saw it, groups were entitled to exclude students on any basis other than those listed in the school's Nondiscrimination Policy, which proscribed exclusion on only a "limited number of specified grounds."[212] He further claimed that the school's actual practice was more arbitrary. Although UC Hastings had denied CLS's application for RSO status, it had granted that status to other groups that discriminated on bases enumerated in the Nondiscrimination Policy—most no-

---

[206] *Christian Legal Soc'y*, 2006 US Dist LEXIS 27347 at *17.

[207] Id at *78.

[208] *Christian Legal Soc'y v Kane*, 319 Fed Appx 645, 645–46 (9th Cir 2009) (citing *Truth v Kent Sch. Dist.*, 542 F3d 634, 649–50 (9th Cir 2008)).

[209] More than half of the petitioner's oral argument was consumed by questions relating to the nature of the policy. See Tr of Oral Arg 2–13, *Christian Legal Soc'y v Martinez*, No 08-1371 (Apr 19, 2010).

[210] *Christian Legal Soc'y*, 130 S Ct at 2984. Her opinion for the Court was joined by Justices Stevens, Kennedy, Breyer, and Sotomayor.

[211] Id at 2979 (quoting from Hastings' brief).

[212] Id at 3003 (Alito, J, dissenting). Justice Alito's dissent was joined by the Chief Justice and Justices Scalia and Thomas.

tably La Raza, which Justice Alito claimed had limited membership to Latino students.[213]

The heated language surrounding this factual disagreement[214] raises the question why the Justices cared so much about the precise contours of the UC Hastings policy. Some part of the disagreement seemed to center on the school's bona fides. The dissenters, in particular, hinted that the school's refusal to recognize the Christian Legal Society reflected little more than antireligious bigotry—"prevailing standards of political correctness," Left Coast-style.[215] The majority, by contrast, criticized the dissent for "impugning the veracity of a distinguished legal scholar and a well respected school administrator."[216] It credited the law school's account of its policy as designed to provide equal educational opportunities to all students, encourage interaction among students, and vindicate state antidiscrimination principles.

But both an all-comers and a nondiscrimination policy forbidding exclusion on only specified bases would serve the school's goals, at least to some extent. In fact, one of the justifications for the all-comers policy was its utility in enforcing the overarching Nondiscrimination Policy. The main consequence of characterizing UC Hastings' policy as an all-comers rule was to relieve the Court of the need to address CLS's claim that a nondiscrimination policy *itself* constitutes a form of impermissible viewpoint discrimination. That claim has some intuitive appeal: A nondiscrimination policy permits groups formed around criteria not enumerated in the policy to exclude students on the basis of viewpoint—for example, Silenced Right, a pro-life group, could exclude students who favored abortion rights, and the Hastings Democratic Caucus could reject students who were Republicans—while not according groups identified in terms of the enumerated criteria, such as religion, the right to re-

---

[213] See id at 3004 (Alito, J, dissenting).

[214] See, for example, id at 2982 n 6, 2983, 2983 n 7 (opinion of the Court) (accusing the dissent of "spill[ing] considerable ink attempting to create uncertainty" about the policy, "time and again ⋯ . rac[ing] away from the facts to which CLS stipulated," and "indulg[ing] in make-believe" about the Court's view of the facts); id at 3001, 3005 (Alito, J, dissenting) (accusing the majority of "provid[ing] a misleading portrayal" of the facts and "distort[ing]" the record).

[215] Id at 3000 (Alito, J, dissenting).

[216] Id at 2995 n 29 (opinion of the Court). For a more extensive discussion of the Court's complicated relationship to law schools as litigants in constitutional cases, see Pamela S. Karlan, *Compelling Interests/Compelling Institutions: Law Schools as Constitutional Litigants*, 54 UCLA L Rev 1613 (2007).

strict membership to people who share their beliefs.[217]

All nondiscrimination rules are, as Wechsler observed, nonneutral in at least one sense: They identify particular reasons or motivations as illegitimate bases for a decision, while leaving actors free to act on the basis of other characteristics.[218] In this sense, nondiscrimination law is viewpoint based because it treats the view that an individual's religion or his sexual orientation is relevant to whether he should be accorded a benefit differently from views, for example, that his test scores or his political affiliation can be taken into account.[219] But unless the entire edifice of modern antidiscrimination law is to be declared unconstitutional, a government's decision not to permit public discrimination on the basis of religion or sexual orientation cannot really be understood as viewpoint discrimination of the type the First Amendment disfavors. Indeed, in his *Romer* dissent, Justice Scalia recognized this point, writing that "homosexuals are as entitled to use the legal system for reinforcement of their moral sentiments" through enactment of antidiscrimination laws "as is the rest of society."[220]

Focusing on an all-comers rule also enabled the Court to sidestep the question whether CLS was seeking to exclude gay students based on those students' belief, their conduct, or their status.[221] For tactical

---

[217] The dissent pressed quite hard on this point, claiming that the Nondiscrimination Policy "singled out one category of expressive associations for disfavored treatment: groups formed to express a religious message. Only religious groups were required to admit students who did not share their views." *Christian Legal Soc'y*, 130 S Ct at 3010 (Alito, J, dissenting). The dissent was mistaken. While it would be true under the Nondiscrimination Policy that "[a]n environmentalist group was not required to admit students who rejected global warming," any ideological group whose views centered on a protected category would be required to admit students who did not share its views. For example, a black separatist group would be required to admit white students. Compare *Christian Legal Soc'y*, 2006 US Dist LEXIS 27347 at *82–*83 (pointing out that Hastings had required La Raza to repudiate a passage in its bylaws that could have been read to suggest that only Latino students could be members). Religion was no more singled out than race or sex.

[218] For a fuller discussion of this point, see Karlan at 1024 (cited in note 199).

[219] Even an all-comers policy might not avoid viewpoint discrimination under a robust version of this approach, since such a policy gives official benefits to groups whose membership policies express an inclusive approach while denying those benefits to groups whose membership rules profess exclusive criteria.

[220] *Romer v Evans*, 517 US 620, 646 (1996) (Scalia, J, dissenting). In *Christian Legal Society*, Justice Stevens termed any such attack on antidiscrimination law an "unsound," "counterintuitive theory." 130 S Ct at 2996 (Stevens, J, concurring).

[221] Interestingly, all the Justices focused their attention on Hastings' refusal to recognize CLS because of its exclusion of gay students. There was little discussion of the perhaps thornier question whether CLS's refusal to admit, say, avowedly Christian, straight students who were unwilling to subscribe to one or more of the organization's Statements of Faith would violate school rules.

reasons, CLS had argued that it was not engaged in status-based discrimination. It claimed that it excluded students not because they were gay, but rather because of "a conjunction of conduct and the belief that the conduct is not wrong."[222] Had CLS not qualified its policy in this respect, it would have faced the unappealing prospect of having to explain how its status-based membership restrictions could be sustained without also compelling official recognition and support of student groups that discriminated on the basis of race or gender. CLS hoped to avoid that problem by claiming that while race or gender are matters of status, homosexuality (and religion) are not.[223]

The Court's opinion rejected CLS's attempted framework with the observation that "[o]ur decisions have declined to distinguish between status and conduct" when it comes to gay people.[224] But in quoting *Lawrence v Texas*[225] to support this proposition, the Court subtly reframed that decision as an antidiscrimination case. In *Lawrence* itself, the Court had rejected a call to ground its decision striking down Texas's homosexual sodomy statute in the Equal Protection Clause as well as in substantive due process.[226] To be sure, as I have explained elsewhere,[227] *Lawrence* should be understood as *more* than just a decision about conduct: "Protecting gay people's choices within the intimacy of their homes serves essentially as a

---

[222] *Christian Legal Soc'y*, 130 S Ct at 2990 (quoting CLS's brief).

[223] Compare *McDaniel v Paty*, 435 US 618 (1978), in which the Court unanimously struck down a Tennessee statute that disqualified members of the clergy from serving as delegates to a state constitutional convention. Chief Justice Burger's plurality opinion treated the disqualification as being "directed primarily at status, acts, and conduct" rather than "*belief*." Id at 627. Justice Brennan declared that "[t]he characterization of the exclusion as one burdening appellant's 'career or calling' and not religious belief cannot withstand analysis." Id at 631 (Brennan, J, concurring in the judgment). Justice Stewart saw any distinction between belief and an individual's "decision to pursue a religious vocation as directed by his belief" as "without constitutional consequence." Id at 643 (Stewart, J, concurring in the judgment). Justice White avoided the inquiry altogether: Seeing no way in which the law interfered with a clergy member's "ability to exercise his religion as he desires," id at 644 (White, J, concurring in the judgment), he located the constitutional infirmity in the way the state law deprived voters of the right to elect the delegates of their choice, see id at 645–46.

[224] Id at 2990.

[225] 539 US 558 (2003).

[226] The quoted passage from *Lawrence*—"[w]hen homosexual conduct is made criminal by the law of the State, that declaration in and of itself is an invitation to subject homosexual persons to discrimination," id at 575—appeared within the Court's explanation for why it was grounding its decision in the Liberty Clause of the Fourteenth Amendment, rather than the Equal Protection Clause.

[227] See Karlan, 102 Mich L Rev (cited in note 16).

safeguard of their dignity in a more public sphere. That, whatever the Court chooses to call it, is as much a claim about equality as it is a claim about liberty."[228] By quoting *Lawrence* in the context of explaining the nature of discrimination against gay people, and by juxtaposing the Court's statement with Justice O'Connor's concurrence in the judgment, which had expressly relied on the Equal Protection Clause rather than substantive due process,[229] the Court may have signaled a new willingness to scrutinize claims by gay people under the Equal Protection Clause.

That possibility is reinforced by the Court's reference, in the course of upholding UC Hastings' policy as "reasonable,"[230] to California's treatment of discrimination on the basis of sexual orientation on the same terms as discrimination on the basis of gender, race, or religion.[231] Although the Court referred only to California's statutory antidiscrimination requirement, it may well have been aware also of the California Supreme Court's recent decisions holding that, under the state constitution's equal protection clause, discrimination on the basis of sexual orientation should be subjected to the same heightened scrutiny accorded to discrimination on the basis of race or gender.[232]

In his concurrence, Justice Stevens drew the parallel between various protected aspects of personal identity even more tightly. "A person's religion," he observed, "often simultaneously constitutes or informs a status, an identity, a set of beliefs and practices, and

---

[228] Id at 1459.

[229] See *Christian Legal Soc'y*, 130 S Ct at 2990 (quoting *Lawrence*, 539 US at 583 (O'Connor, J, concurring in judgment) ("While it is true that the law applies only to conduct, the conduct targeted by this law is conduct that is closely correlated with being homosexual. Under such circumstances, [the] law is targeted at more than conduct. It is instead directed toward gay persons as a class.")).

[230] *Christian Legal Soc'y*, 130 S Ct at 2991.

[231] See Cal Educ Code § 66270 (providing that "[n]o person shall be subjected to discrimination on the basis of disability, gender, nationality, race or ethnicity, religion, sexual orientation," among other characteristics, "in any program or activity conducted by any postsecondary educational institution that receives, or benefits from, state financial assistance or enrolls students who receive state student financial aid").

[232] See *Strauss v Horton*, 46 Cal 4th 364, 412 (2009) (reaffirming, after the passage of Proposition 8, the "general principle that sexual orientation constitutes a suspect classification and that statutes according differential treatment on the basis of sexual orientation are constitutionally permissible only if they satisfy the strict scrutiny standard of review"); see also *In re Marriage Cases*, 43 Cal 4th 757, 840–41 (2008) (holding that "sexual orientation should be viewed as a suspect classification for purposes of the California Constitution's equal protection clause and that statutes that treat persons differently because of their sexual orientation should be subjected to strict scrutiny under this constitutional provision").

much else besides. (So does sexual orientation for that matter, notwithstanding the dissent's view that a rule excluding those who engage in 'unrepentant homosexual conduct' does not discriminate on the basis of status or identity.)"[233] And he followed by criticizing the dissent for "see[ing] pernicious antireligious motives and implications where there are none," while failing to recognize "the fact that religious sects, unfortunately, are not the only social groups who have been persecuted throughout history simply for being who they are."[234]

Perhaps the fervor of the dissent stems from the dissenters' sense that public opinion—or, as they might resentfully frame it, "the views and values of the lawyer class from which the Court's Members are drawn"[235]—is coming to view sexual orientation as an aspect of personhood as central and as worthy of protection as race, gender, or religion. The dissenters, by contrast, seem to view religion—and traditional religious beliefs in particular—as uniquely worthy of protection and respect. (Given the dissent's dismissive treatment of La Raza, a Latino-oriented student group, it is hard to imagine that the dissenters would have sided with a racial minority group's attempt to obtain official recognition while excluding white students.)[236] A particularly strong illustration of their perspective was the fact that the only "claim of unlawful discrimination" they saw implicated by UC Hastings' policy belonged to CLS.[237] The dissenters never stopped to consider why UC Hastings might have adopted a Nondiscrimination Policy in the first place; they ignored entirely the problem of discrimination against groups other than religious traditionalists. For the dissenters, religious conservatives seemed to be the most marginalized and victimized group within

---

[233] *Christian Legal Soc'y*, 130 S Ct at 2996 n 1 (Stevens, J, concurring).

[234] Id at 2997 n 3.

[235] *Romer v Evans*, 517 US 620, 652 (1996) (Scalia, J, dissenting).

[236] There are many points of resemblance between Justice Alito's dissent in *Christian Legal Society* and his concurring opinion in *Ricci v DeStefano*, 129 S Ct 2658 (2008), the case in which the Court held that New Haven's decision to discard the results of a promotional exam because of the test's disparate impact violated Title VII. There, too, he criticized Justice Ginsburg for her version of the facts. See id at 2683. There, too, he described the justifications offered by government officials who claimed to be concerned with discrimination as disingenuous or pretextual. See id at 2687–88. And there, too, he expressed his sympathy for individuals who challenge the principles of contemporary antidiscrimination law. See id at 2689.

[237] *Christian Legal Soc'y*, 130 S Ct at 3006.

the legal academy.[238] Left unsaid, but perhaps in the back of their minds, is the sense that nowhere is the process of full inclusion for gay people, even at the cost of overriding religious objections, further along than in San Francisco, where UC Hastings is located.[239]

The dissent's near-paranoia came through most clearly in its claim that Hastings' policy rendered groups like CLS vulnerable to infiltration or hijacking. Justice Alito expressed the fear that "[a] true accept-all-comers policy permits small unpopular groups to be taken over by students who wish to change the views that the group expresses."[240] He was not reassured by the absence of any example in the record of "RSO-hijackings at Hastings."[241] Nor did he offer any plausible explanation for why students would join a group for the purpose of destroying it. His hypothetical example of how such a "threat" might play out was itself telling:

> Not all Christian denominations agree with CLS's views on sexual morality and other matters. During a recent year, CLS had seven members. Suppose that 10 students who are members of denominations that disagree with CLS decided that CLS was misrepresenting true Christian doctrine. Suppose that these students joined CLS, elected officers who shared their views, ended the group's affiliation with the national organization, and changed the group's message. The new leadership would likely proclaim that the group was "vital" but rectified, while CLS, I assume, would take the view that the old group had suffered its "demise." Whether a change represents reform or transformation may depend very much on the eye of the beholder.[242]

---

[238] See, for example, id at 3000 (Alito, J, dissenting) (claiming that the Court had declared there to be "no freedom for expression that offends prevailing standards of political correctness in our country's institutions of higher learning"); id at 3019 (warning that the consequence of an all-comers policy would be "marginalization" for religious groups acting "in good conscience").

[239] The city's then-mayor (now California's lieutenant governor) sparked California's current encounter with same-sex marriage during the winter of 2004, when he requested the city and county's clerk to alter the official marriage forms to permit same-sex couples to marry. For a brief account of that history, see *Lockyer v City and County of San Francisco*, 33 Cal 4th 1055, 1069–72 (2004). For another example of the city's commitment to full equality for gay citizens, even when that equality runs up against religious beliefs, see *Catholic League for Religious and Civil Rights v City and County of San Francisco*, 624 F3d 1043 (9th Cir 2010) (en banc) (affirming dismissal of a challenge by a Catholic advocacy group and several Catholic residents of San Francisco to a city board of supervisors' resolution declaring it "an insult to all San Franciscans when a foreign country, like the Vatican, meddles with and attempts to negatively influence this great City's existing and established customs and traditions such as the right of same-sex couples to adopt and care for children in need" by directing the Catholic Charities of the Archdiocese of San Francisco to cease placing children with same-sex couples).

[240] *Christian Legal Soc'y*, 130 S Ct at 3019 (Alito, J, dissenting).

[241] Id at 2992 (opinion of the Court).

[242] Id at 3019 (Alito, J, dissenting).

What the dissent seemed not to notice was that a similar dynamic, only in reverse, produced—and rather recently, at that—the Hastings CLS whose views the dissent saw as entitled to protection from change. From the 1994–95 academic year through the 2003–04 academic year, UC Hastings had several avowedly Christian RSOs (including one that had called itself "Hastings Christian Legal Society"[243]) whose expressed objectives were "to encourage those who identify themselves as followers of Jesus Christ to more faithfully live out their commitment in their personal and academic lives, to prepare members for future lives as Christian attorneys, and to provide a witness and outreach for Jesus Christ in the Hastings community."[244] At the same time, those RSOs each agreed in their bylaws to comply with UC Hastings' Nondiscrimination Policy. In the two years prior to the emergence of the current group, the Hastings Christian Fellowship's bylaws provided that the organization "welcomes all students of the University of California, Hastings College of law" and the organization admitted members without regard to religion or sexual orientation.[245] Hastings CLS emerged from this inclusive organization[246] through a "takeover." Three students became the leaders of the small group (around a dozen members) at the end of the 2003–04 academic year and "decided to affiliate their student organization officially" with CLS, thereby triggering the adoption of the exclusionary membership rules to which UC Hastings objected.[247]

But the central point—which the dissent never confronts—is that it is in the nature of student groups to change. If the next cohort of Christian students to enroll at UC Hastings were to join CLS and then decide to "end[] the group's affiliation with the national organization, and change[] the group's message," why should anyone care? To be sure, the national Christian Legal Society must remain free to disaffiliate student chapters that do not hew to its policies. But that group is not entitled itself to participate in UC Hastings' limited public forum, because that forum is limited to

---

[243] *Christian Legal Soc'y*, 2006 US Dist LEXIS 27347 at *8.

[244] Id (quoting from the bylaws used for seven of those years).

[245] Id at *9.

[246] According to the district court, during the 2003–04 academic year, one of the participants in the five- to seven-member group "was an openly lesbian student and two were students who held beliefs inconsistent with what CLS considers to be orthodox Christianity." Id at *9–*10.

[247] Id at *10.

groups comprised entirely of current students. I cannot see anyone with a legally cognizable interest in cementing into place a set of bylaws that do not attract support from the existing cohort of students. In a sense, UC Hastings' all-comers policy adopts John Hart Ely's anti-entrenchment principle: By requiring that groups remain open to all students, the policy keeps the current officers or membership from "choking off the channels of political change to ensure that they [or their values] will stay in and the outs will stay out."[248] The dissent's fear, by contrast, almost seems to presuppose that it is entirely sensible for a Christian legal society (with a lower-case "l" and "s") to exclude gay students. It is clear with which "beholder" the dissent has aligned its eyes. And the dissent in *Christian Legal Society* reflects the same sense underlying the per curiam in *Hollingsworth v Perry* as well as Justice Alito's concurrence and Justice Thomas's dissent in *Doe v Reed*—the sense that traditionalists face distinctive threats demanding special judicial solicitude.

IV. CONCLUSION

The Court ended its foundational opinion in *Griswold v Connecticut*[249] by declaring that marriage "is an association that promotes a way of life, not causes; a harmony in living, not political faiths; a bilateral loyalty, not commercial or social projects. Yet it is an association for as noble a purpose as any involved in our prior decisions."[250] *Griswold* was a case about both marriage and privacy: the defendants sought to keep the government out of their marriage. Today, however, the fundamental legal question about marriage involves assertions of positive rights rather than negative liberties: Same-sex couples demand not that the state stay out of their marriages, but that the state admit them to a civic institution.

The struggle over marriage equality *is* a cause. How to referee that struggle poses profound questions of political and jurisprudential faith. Along the way, as this Term shows, there will be a series of subsidiary disputes that raise issues of method, as well as marriage. Standing, the distinction between facial and as-applied challenges, the scope of rationality review and of "exacting scrutiny,"

---

[248] John Hart Ely, *Democracy and Distrust: A Theory of Judicial Review* 103 (Harvard, 1980).

[249] 381 US 479 (1965).

[250] Id at 486.

adherence to originalism in the face of rapid social and technological change, and the continuing vitality of antidiscrimination law—each involves questions likely to dog the Court for years to come. If this Term's cases are any indication, the Court will divide along a variety of dimensions.

But the Court must confront more than doctrinal complexities. The marriage cases raise anew the recurring question of when the Court should intervene to declare that a contested social or political issue has been resolved as a matter of constitutional law, and how it should deal with the losing side. Few institutions are more deeply rooted in the popular consciousness than marriage. That is why it always appears, regardless of the Justice writing the opinion, in the list of fundamental rights protected by the substantive due process principle.[251] But in asking what that tradition means today, the Court is being called upon to police an "evolving boundary"[252] between marriage as it used to be and marriage as it is becoming. Obviously, litigation—albeit litigation in state courts raising state constitutional claims—has played a significant role, not only in achieving marriage equality directly but also in changing the context of the national debate. The Supreme Court's decisions, when they come, will do the same. How the Justices answer the marriage question may influence the Court's political and moral capital with future generations in the way that the Court's substantive due process decisions in *Dred Scott v Sandford*,[253] *Loving v Virginia*,[254] and *Roe v Wade*[255] have done for previous generations. And so, precisely because feelings about marriage are so fundamental to so many people, there may be *two* institutions whose future is on the line: marriage and the Court.

---

[251] See, for example, *Glucksberg*, 521 US at 723 (opinion for the Court by Chief Justice Rehnquist); *Loving v Virginia*, 388 US 1, 12 (1967) (opinion for the Court by Chief Justice Warren).

[252] *Glucksberg*, 521 US at 770 (Souter, J, concurring in the judgment).

[253] 60 US 393 (1857).

[254] 388 US 1 (1967).

[255] 410 US 113 (1973).

CURTIS A. BRADLEY AND LAURENCE R. HELFER

INTERNATIONAL LAW AND THE U.S. COMMON LAW OF FOREIGN OFFICIAL IMMUNITY

In *Samantar v Yousuf*,[1] the Supreme Court unanimously held that the Foreign Sovereign Immunities Act (FSIA) does not apply to lawsuits brought against foreign government officials for alleged human rights abuses.[2] The Court did not necessarily clear the way for future human rights litigation against such officials, however, cautioning that such suits "may still be barred by foreign sovereign immunity under the common law."[3] At the same time, the Court provided only minimal guidance as to the content and scope of common law immunity. Especially striking was the Court's omission of any mention of the immunity of foreign officials under customary international law (CIL), the body of international law that "results from a general and consistent practice of states followed by them

Curtis A. Bradley is the Richard A. Horvitz Professor of Law, Duke Law School, and Laurence R. Helfer is the Harry R. Chadwick, Sr. Professor of Law, Duke Law School.

AUTHORS' NOTE: For their helpful comments and suggestions, we thank John Bellinger, Tai-Heng Cheng, Chimène Keitner, Michael Ramsey, Anthea Roberts, Paul Stephan, Beth Stephens, the participants in an international law workshop at Hebrew University in Jerusalem, and the participants in the annual workshop of the American Society of International Law's Interest Group on International Law in Domestic Courts. David Riesenberg and Adam Schupack provided excellent research assistance.

[1] 130 S Ct 2278 (2010).

[2] Id at 2282.

[3] Id at 2289–92.

© 2011 by The University of Chicago. All rights reserved.
978-0-226-36326-4/2011/2010-0006$10.00

from a sense of legal obligation."[4] Not only were international law issues extensively briefed by the parties and amici, but the question of whether foreign officials are immune from suits alleging human rights violations had recently been extensively litigated in other national courts and international tribunals, and these decisions were brought to the Court's attention.

Notwithstanding the Supreme Court's inattention to the international law backdrop in *Samantar*, CIL immunity principles are likely to be relevant to the development of the common law of foreign official immunity. The Court has taken account of CIL in related contexts and has endorsed a canon of statutory construction designed to avoid unintended breaches of CIL. Both Congress and the Executive Branch have also indicated that they consider CIL to be relevant to immunity, and the judiciary is usually attentive to the views and actions of the political branches when developing common law relating to foreign affairs.

There is also a rich and growing body of CIL materials that courts can draw upon. As we will explain, these materials show that CIL traditionally extended immunity to individual officials in proceedings in foreign courts for actions taken on behalf of their state. In the criminal context, this immunity has eroded over the past decade, with national courts outside of the United States increasingly exercising criminal jurisdiction over former officials, including heads of state, charged with human rights violations. No comparable erosion has yet occurred, however, in the civil context. Although a few decisions have embraced a human rights exception to immunity, the courts of several other countries have expressly declined to adopt such an exception. At the same time, the relationship between immunity and human rights law is still very much in flux, and international tribunals currently are considering cases that concern this relationship.

The unsettled state of CIL raises important issues concerning the role and competence of U.S. courts as they develop the common law of foreign official immunity. On the one hand, they have an opportunity to participate in a global judicial dialogue over the proper balance between immunity and accountability and to shape international law's future trajectory. On the other hand, the uncertain state of the law may indicate that U.S. courts should exercise

---

[4] Restatement (Third) of the Foreign Relations Law of the United States § 102(2) (1987).

caution before advancing an interpretation of CIL that may offend foreign governments or create foreign relations difficulties for the Executive Branch. Ultimately, as we will discuss, a variety of institutional and policy considerations are likely to shape the relevance of CIL to the post-*Samantar* common law of immunity.

The development of this body of common law immunity also implicates long-standing debates over the incorporation of CIL into federal common law. In the past, scholars who argued for such incorporation did so primarily to promote accountability for past human rights abuses and to expand the opportunities for litigating human rights claims in U.S. courts. Other scholars, however, challenged the federal adjudication of customary human rights norms on the basis of domestic considerations such as separation of powers. There may be a reversal of positions in the wake of *Samantar*. Commentators who previously opposed adjudication of CIL in U.S. courts may be favorably disposed to incorporating international immunity rules into the common law—a doctrinal move that could significantly narrow the scope of international human rights litigation. Conversely, commentators who previously supported application of CIL by U.S. courts may now oppose the incorporation of CIL in this context, or argue that it is too indeterminate, and urge courts to apply instead the immunity principles of domestic civil rights law—principles that may facilitate holding foreign government officials accountable for human rights abuses.

This article self-consciously avoids taking a position on these theoretical debates or on the ultimate question of the proper scope of foreign official immunity. Instead, we seek to make three contributions. First, we set forth a case for CIL's relevance to the post-*Samantar* common law of immunity that is not dependent on a single theoretical perspective regarding the domestic status of CIL. Second, we present what we believe is a relatively dispassionate assessment of the evolving CIL landscape, an assessment that is aided by the fact that we ourselves have somewhat differing perspectives about the proper role of international law in general and in human rights litigation in U.S. courts in particular. Third, by emphasizing institutional considerations, we are able to isolate particular variables—such as the views of the Executive Branch and the policies embodied in domestic statutes—that will shape how CIL affects the common law of immunity after *Samantar*.

The article proceeds as follows. Part I briefly discusses the history of foreign sovereign immunity in the United States. It then reviews the facts, procedural history, and decision in *Samantar*, highlighting the international law backdrop of the case. Part II reviews the CIL of foreign official immunity and recent national and international court rulings. Part III returns to the United States. It explains how the relevance of CIL immunity rules will depend not only on international law's relationship to federal common law, but also on other considerations such as the degree to which U.S. courts should be active players in the development of CIL, the authority of the Executive Branch to affect ongoing litigation, and the policies reflected in existing statutes.

I. SAMANTAR AND THE INTERNATIONAL LAW ROAD NOT TAKEN

In this part, we begin by describing the historical background and text of the FSIA, as well as the lower court precedent that had developed prior to *Samantar* concerning suits against foreign officials. We then describe the facts and proceedings in *Samantar*. Finally, we consider the Court's decision and explain why, regardless of whether the Court reached the right conclusion, it is noteworthy that its analysis takes no direct account of international law.

A. FOREIGN SOVEREIGN IMMUNITY

The application of foreign sovereign immunity in U.S. courts is usually traced to the Supreme Court's early nineteenth-century decision in *Schooner Exchange v McFaddon*.[5] In that case, two individuals brought a "libel" action against a French naval vessel that had docked in Philadelphia, claiming that they were the original owners of the vessel and that it had been seized from them unlawfully. In upholding a dismissal of the action, the Court, in an opinion by Chief Justice Marshall, began by noting that "[t]he jurisdiction of the nation within its own territory is necessarily exclusive and absolute" and "is susceptible of no limitation not imposed by itself."[6] As a result, said the Court, "[a]ll exceptions . . . to the full and complete power of a nation within its own

---

[5] 11 US (7 Cranch) 116 (1812); see also *Republic of Austria v Altmann*, 541 US 677, 688 (2004) ("Chief Justice Marshall's opinion in *Schooner Exchange* . . . is generally viewed as the source of our foreign sovereign immunity jurisprudence.").

[6] *Schooner Exchange*, 11 US (7 Cranch) at 136.

territories, must be traced up to the consent of the nation itself."[7] The Court found, however, based on "common usage" and "common opinion," that there was "a principle of public law, that national ships of war, entering the port of a friendly power open for their reception, are to be considered as exempted by the consent of that power from its jurisdiction."[8] In reaching this conclusion, the Court analogized to the well-settled immunity under CIL for both heads of state and foreign ministers.[9] The Court also appears to have been influenced by the fact that the Executive Branch had intervened in the case to support a grant of immunity.[10]

Although *Schooner Exchange* specifically addressed only the immunity of foreign warships, over time U.S. courts applied a doctrine of absolute immunity in suits brought against foreign states and their instrumentalities, a doctrine that was viewed as stemming from considerations of both international law and international comity.[11] The courts also developed an "act of state" doctrine that barred U.S. courts from judging the validity of the acts of foreign governments taken within their own territory.[12] As originally developed, the act of state doctrine was intertwined with considerations of immunity.[13] Eventually, however, it evolved into a distinct doctrine that was grounded in considerations of separation of powers.[14]

---

[7] Id.

[8] Id at 136, 145–46.

[9] See id at 137–38.

[10] See *Schooner Exchange*, 11 US (7 Cranch) at 147 ("There seems to be a necessity for admitting that the fact [of immunity] might be disclosed to the Court by the suggestion of the Attorney for the United States.").

[11] See Gamal Moursi Badr, *State Immunity: An Analytical and Prognostic View* 9–20 (Martinus Nijhoff, 1984); Restatement (Third) of Foreign Relations Law, pt IV, ch 5, Introductory Note at 390–91 (cited in note 4). See also, for example, *Wulfsohn v Russian Socialist Federated Soviet Republic*, 138 NE 24, 26 (NY Ct App 1923) ("[Courts] may not bring a foreign sovereign before our bar, not because of comity, but because he has not submitted himself to our laws. Without his consent he is not subject to them."); *Hassard v United States of Mexico*, 29 Misc 511, 512 (NY Sup Ct 1899) ("It is an axiom of international law, of long-established and general recognition, that a sovereign State cannot be sued in its own courts, or in any other, without its consent and permission."), aff'd, 46 AD 623 (1899).

[12] See, for example, *Underhill v Hernandez*, 168 US 250, 252 (1897).

[13] See id ("The immunity of individuals from suits brought in foreign tribunals for acts done within their own States, in the exercise of governmental authority, whether as civil officers or as military commanders, must necessarily extend to the agents of governments ruling by paramount force as matter of fact.").

[14] See *Banco Nacional de Cuba v Sabbatino*, 376 US 398, 438 (1964) ("The act of state doctrine . . . although it shares with the immunity doctrine a respect for sovereign states,

From the earliest days of the nation, the Executive Branch expressed the view that the immunity of a foreign state also extended to officials acting on its behalf, at least when the conduct in question occurred outside the United States.[15] The Supreme Court endorsed this proposition in *Underhill v Hernandez*.[16] In that case, a U.S. citizen sued a Venezuelan military commander, whose revolutionary government had been recognized by the United States, for unlawful assault and detention in Venezuela. The decision is most famous for its articulation of the act of state doctrine, pursuant to which "the courts of one country will not sit in judgment on the acts of the government of another done within its own territory."[17] The Supreme Court also recognized, however, that individual officials have "immunity . . . from suits brought in foreign tribunals for acts done within their own States, in the exercise of governmental authority, whether as civil officers or as military commanders."[18] Similarly, the Second Circuit in *Underhill* had concluded that a foreign state's immunity extends to suits against the state's officials for actions carried out on behalf of the state. "[B]ecause the acts of the official representatives of the state are those of the state itself, when exercised within the scope of their delegated powers," the Second Circuit explained, "courts and publicists have recognized the immunity of public agents from suits brought in foreign tribunals for acts done within their own states in the exercise of the sovereignty thereof."[19]

concerns the limits for determining the validity of an otherwise applicable rule of law."); see also *Altmann*, 541 US at 700 ("Unlike a claim of sovereign immunity, which merely raises a jurisdictional defense, the act of state doctrine provides foreign states with a substantive defense on the merits.").

[15] See Curtis A. Bradley and Jack L. Goldsmith, *Foreign Sovereign Immunity and Domestic Officer Suits*, 13 Green Bag 2d 137, 141–44 (2010); see also Brief for the United States of America as Amicus Curiae in Support of Affirmance, *Matar v Dichter*, No 07-2579-cv, *7 (2d Cir, filed Dec 19, 2007) ("United States *Matar* Brief") (available on Westlaw at 2007 WL 6931924) ("The immunity of a foreign sovereign was, early on, generally understood to encompass not only the state, heads of state, and diplomatic officials, but also other officials insofar as they acted on the state's behalf."); Statement of Interest of the United States of America, *Yousuf v Samantar*, at 4, No 1:04 CV 1360 (LMB) (ED Va, Feb 14, 2011) ("The immunity of a foreign state was, early on, generally understood to extend not only to the state, heads of state, and diplomatic officials, but also to other officials acting in an official capacity.").

[16] 168 US 250, 252 (1897).

[17] Id.

[18] Id. See also *Sabbatino*, 376 US at 430 (noting that "sovereign immunity provided an independent ground" in *Underhill*).

[19] *Underhill v Hernandez*, 65 F 577, 579 (2d Cir 1895). See also John Bassett Moore, 2

Starting in the late 1930s, U.S. courts began to give absolute deference to suggestions from the State Department about whether to grant immunity in particular cases.[20] If the department did not take a position on immunity, courts attempted to decide the issue "in conformity to the principles accepted by the department."[21] In 1952, the department issued the Tate Letter, which announced an important shift in the U.S. approach to sovereign immunity.[22] Addressed from the State Department's Acting Legal Adviser to the Acting Attorney General, the Tate Letter asserted that, consistent with the practice of a number of other countries, the department now supported only a "restrictive" approach to immunity, pursuant to which "the immunity of the sovereign is recognized with regard to sovereign or public acts (*jure imperii*) of a state, but not with respect to private acts (*jure gestionis*)."[23] Among other things, the letter explained that "the widespread and increasing practice on the part of governments of engaging in commercial activities makes necessary a practice which will enable persons doing business with them to have their rights determined in the courts."[24] The letter concluded with this observation: "It is realized that a shift in policy by the executive cannot control the courts but it is felt that the courts are less likely to allow a plea of sovereign immunity where the executive has declined to do so."[25]

Despite the letter's modesty about its potential impact on judicial decision making, courts followed the department's new re-

---

A Digest of International Law § 179 (1906) (collecting authorities from the late 1700s through *Underhill*).

[20] See *Compania Espanola de Navegacion Maritima, SA v The Navemar*, 303 US 68, 74 (1938); *Ex parte Republic of Peru*, 318 US 578, 588–89 (1943). Consider also *Berizzi Bros. Co. v The Pesaro*, 271 US 562, 574 (1926) (granting immunity even though the State Department had argued in the lower court that immunity should not be granted). For discussion, see Curtis A. Bradley and Jack L. Goldsmith, *Pinochet and International Human Rights Litigation*, 97 Mich L Rev 2129, 2161–65 (1999); G. Edward White, *The Transformation of the Constitutional Regime of Foreign Relations*, 85 Va L Rev 1, 27–28, 134–45 (1999).

[21] *Republic of Mexico v Hoffman*, 324 US 30, 35 (1945).

[22] See Letter from Jack B. Tate, Acting Legal Adviser, U.S. Dept. of State, to Acting U.S. Attorney General Philip B. Perlman (May 19, 1952), reprinted in 26 Dept State Bull 984 (1952).

[23] Id at 984.

[24] Id at 985.

[25] Id.

strictive immunity approach.[26] They also continued to defer to the department's case-by-case suggestions about whether to grant immunity, in those cases in which the department made such suggestions,[27] even where such suggestions were arguably contrary to the Tate Letter.[28] These suggestions sometimes included suggestions of immunity for foreign officials.[29] In the absence of a State Department suggestion, courts attempted to decide the immunity issue in a manner that was consistent with the Tate Letter, although that letter did not provide much guidance about how to distinguish between a foreign state's public and private acts.[30] A two-track system eventually developed, in which in some cases a foreign state would seek an immunity determination from the State Department and in other cases the state would ask the court to make its own determination.[31] The result was that "sovereign immunity determinations were made in two different branches, subject to a variety of factors, sometimes including diplomatic considerations."[32] Perhaps not surprisingly, this regime did not always produce consistent decisions. The State Department also found itself acting as an adjudicative body, a role that it was ill equipped to perform, and it was frequently lobbied and pressured by foreign states to support their requests for immunity.[33]

---

[26] See Restatement (Third) of Foreign Relations Law, pt IV, ch 5, Introductory Note at 392 (cited in note 4) (noting that after the Tate Letter the "courts in the United States also adopted the restrictive theory and developed criteria for its application").

[27] See, for example, *Spacil v Crowe*, 489 F2d 614, 616–17 (5th Cir 1974); *Isbrandtsen Tankers, Inc. v President of India*, 446 F2d 1198, 1201 (2d Cir 1971).

[28] See, for example, Monroe Leigh, *Sovereign Immunity—The Case of the "Imias,"* 68 Am J Intl L 280, 281 (1974), citing *Rich v Naviera Vacuba, SA*, 295 F2d 24 (4th Cir 1961), and *Chemical Natural Resources, Inc. v Republic of Venezuela*, 215 A2d 864 (Pa 1966).

[29] See, for example, *Greenspan v Crosbie*, No 74 Civ 4734 (GLG), 1976 WL 841, at *2 (SDNY, Nov 23, 1976) ("The Suggestion of Immunity removes the individual defendants from this case.").

[30] See, for example, *Victory Transport, Inc. v Comisaria General de Abastecimientos y Transportes*, 336 F2d 354, 360 (2d Cir 1964).

[31] See id at 358 ("A claim of sovereign immunity may be presented to the court by either of two procedures. The foreign sovereign may request its claim of immunity be recognized by the State Department, which will normally present its suggestion to the court through the Attorney General or some law officer acting under his direction. Alternatively, the accredited and recognized representative of the foreign sovereign may present the claim of sovereign immunity directly to the court.").

[32] *Verlinden BV v Central Bank of Nigeria*, 461 US 480, 487 (1983).

[33] For discussion of some of the problems posed by the Tate Letter regime, see Leigh, 68 Am J Intl L at 281–82 (cited in note 28), and Andreas F. Lowenfeld, *Litigating a Sovereign Immunity Claim—The Haiti Case*, 49 NYU L Rev 377, 389–90 (1974).

In 1976, with the State Department's support, Congress enacted the FSIA.[34] The statute comprehensively regulates the issue of foreign sovereign immunity in U.S. courts and provides the exclusive basis for jurisdiction over civil suits against foreign states.[35] The FSIA's legislative history makes clear that the statute was designed to "codify the so-called 'restrictive' principle of sovereign immunity, as presently recognized in international law."[36] Indeed, the statute's findings and declaration of purpose specifically provide that "[u]nder international law, states are not immune from the jurisdiction of foreign courts insofar as their commercial activities are concerned, and their commercial property may be levied upon for the satisfaction of judgments rendered against them in connection with their commercial activities."[37] The FSIA also reflected an effort by Congress to transfer immunity determinations solely to the judiciary and away from the Executive Branch. As noted in the legislative history, under the FSIA "sovereign immunity decisions [would be] made exclusively by the courts and not by a foreign affairs agency."[38]

The FSIA provides that foreign states "shall be immune" from the jurisdiction of U.S. courts except as provided in certain specified exceptions.[39] Consistent with the restrictive theory of immunity, the FSIA has a broad exception to immunity for cases involving commercial activity.[40] It also has an exception to immunity for tort claims, but this exception applies only if the damage or injury from the tort occurs within the United States.[41] There is no express reference in the FSIA to suits against individual

---

[34] See Foreign Sovereign Immunities Act (FSIA), Pub L No 94-583, 90 Stat 2891 (1976), codified at 28 USC §§ 1330, 1602–11.

[35] See *Republic of Argentina v Weltover, Inc.*, 504 US 607, 610 (1992); *Argentine Republic v Amerada Hess Shipping Corp.*, 488 US 428, 434–39 (1989).

[36] Foreign Sovereign Immunities Act of 1976, HR Rep No 94-1487, 94th Cong, 2d Sess 6 (1976), reprinted in 1976 USCCAN 6604, 6605.

[37] 28 USC § 1602.

[38] HR Rep No 94-1487 at 7 (cited in note 36); see also *Altmann*, 541 US at 691 (noting that the FSIA "transfers primary responsibility for immunity determinations from the Executive to the Judicial Branch").

[39] See 28 USC § 1604.

[40] 28 USC § 1605(a)(2).

[41] See 28 USC § 1605(a)(5). Since 1996, the FSIA has had an exception for certain egregious torts committed by designated "state sponsors of terrorism," but this exception currently applies to only four nations: Cuba, Iran, Sudan, and Syria. For the latest version of this exception, see 28 USC § 1605A.

officials. The statute applies to suits against "foreign state[s]," which is defined to "include[] a political subdivision of a foreign state or an agency or instrumentality of a foreign state."[42] An "agency or instrumentality" is in turn defined as "a separate legal person, corporate or otherwise . . . which is an organ of a foreign state or political subdivision thereof, or a majority of whose shares or other ownership interest is owned by a foreign state or political subdivision thereof."[43]

B. HUMAN RIGHTS LITIGATION

As a result of its limited exception for tort claims, the FSIA generally does not permit suits in U.S. courts against foreign states for human rights abuses committed abroad. International human rights litigation has nevertheless flourished in the United States during the last thirty years. The foundational decision was the Second Circuit's 1980 decision in *Filartiga v Peña-Irala*.[44] That case involved a suit by two Paraguayan citizens against a former Paraguayan police inspector for allegedly torturing and killing their family member in Paraguay. For subject matter jurisdiction, the plaintiffs relied on the Alien Tort Statute (ATS), a provision that dates back to the First Judiciary Act of 1789 and states that "[t]he district courts shall have original jurisdiction of any civil action by an alien for a tort only, committed in violation of the law of nations or a treaty of the United States."[45] In allowing the case to proceed, the court in *Filartiga* famously held that foreign victims of human rights abuses committed abroad could use this statute to sue for violations of CIL, including violations of customary human rights norms.[46] Since this decision, numerous suits have been brought under the ATS concerning human rights abuses from around the world.[47]

---

[42] 28 USC § 1603(a).

[43] See 28 USC § 1603(b)(1), (2). In addition, to qualify as an agency or instrumentality of a foreign state, the entity must be neither a U.S. citizen as defined in provisions governing diversity jurisdiction involving corporations nor created under the laws of a third country. 28 USC § 1603(b)(3).

[44] 630 F2d 876 (2d Cir 1980).

[45] Alien Tort Statute (ATS), 28 USC § 1350.

[46] See *Filartiga*, 630 F2d at 887–88 ("This is undeniably an action by an alien, for a tort only, committed in violation of the law of nations.").

[47] The Second Circuit assumed for the sake of argument that the ATS is only a jurisdictional statute that does not create any substantive rights. See id at 887. In 2004, the

Even though the defendant in *Filartiga* was a state official at the time of the alleged acts, and even though most violations of international law (including torture) require state action, there was no discussion in *Filartiga* of whether the suit implicated Paraguay's sovereign immunity.[48] The court's only mention of immunity was an observation that the defendant had not claimed *diplomatic* immunity.[49] Nor did the parties, or the United States as amicus curiae, raise the sovereign immunity issue.[50]

Ten years after *Filartiga*, the Ninth Circuit issued what was to become an influential decision holding that suits against foreign officials, for actions taken in their official capacity, constitute suits against the foreign state for purposes of the FSIA. In *Chuidian v Philippine National Bank*,[51] the Marcos government of the Philippines had issued a letter of credit to Chuidian, payable through the Philippine National Bank, as part of a litigation settlement. An official in the new Aquino government stopped payment on the letter of credit out of a concern that the former government might have given it to Chuidian to keep him quiet about its wrongdoing. Chuidian sued both the national bank and the official. The national bank obviously was an agency or instrumentality of the Philippines for purposes of the FSIA. The issue was whether the individual official was also covered by the FSIA. The Ninth Circuit considered three possibilities: the official was entitled to no im-

---

Supreme Court confirmed this assumption, while also holding that courts are authorized to recognize a modest number of common law causes of action for violations of international law when exercising jurisdiction under the ATS. See *Sosa v Alvarez-Machain*, 542 US 692, 713–14, 724 (2004).

[48] The court did "note in passing," however, that it doubted that the suit was barred by the act of state doctrine, given that the alleged conduct was "in violation of the Constitution and laws of the Republic of Paraguay, and wholly unratified by that nation's government." *Filartiga*, 630 F2d at 889.

[49] See id at 879.

[50] See Appellants' Brief, *Filartiga v Pena-Irala*, No 79-6090 (2d Cir, filed July 25, 1979) (available on Westlaw at 1979 WL 200205); Defendant-Appellee's Brief in Support of Judgment of Dismissal, *Filartiga v Pena-Irala*, No 79-6090 (2d Cir, filed Sept 19, 1979) (available on Westlaw at 1979 WL 200206); Memorandum for the United States as Amicus Curiae, *Filartiga v Pena-Irala*, No 79-6090 (2d Cir, filed June 6, 1980) (available on Westlaw at 1980 WL 340146). One amicus brief discussed the FSIA and argued that it was inapplicable because the defendant had not shown that he was "invested with sovereign authority" to carry out the acts alleged by the plaintiff, and because the Paraguayan government had not asserted immunity on his behalf. See Brief of the International Human Rights Law Group, the Council on Hemispheric Affairs, and the Washington Office on Latin America as Amici Curiae Urging Reversal, *Filartiga v Pena-Irala*, No 79-6090, *30 (2d Cir, filed July 23, 1979) (available on Westlaw at 1979 WL 200209).

[51] 912 F2d 1095 (9th Cir 1990).

munity whatsoever; the official was covered by the FSIA as an agency or instrumentality of a foreign state; or the official was not covered by the FSIA but was entitled to immunity under common law principles.

The Executive Branch filed an amicus curiae brief supporting the third, common law approach. The Ninth Circuit, however, adopted the second approach and applied the FSIA to the claim against the official.[52] The court noted that neither the text of the FSIA nor its legislative history specifically excluded individuals, and it reasoned that failing to apply the statute to these sorts of suits would undermine the policies of the act.[53] If no immunity were allowed in this situation, the court reasoned, the act's limitations could be circumvented by pleading: litigants could "accomplish indirectly what the [FSIA] barred them from doing directly."[54] Alternatively, if immunity were to be determined by the common law, the court reasoned, Congress's effort in the FSIA to regulate foreign sovereign immunity and its exceptions comprehensively would be undermined.[55] The Ninth Circuit also noted that under a common law approach courts likely would feel obligated to defer to the case-by-case views of the State Department, as they had done before the enactment of the FSIA, even though one of the purposes of the statute was to shift immunity determinations away from the Executive Branch.[56]

Over time, most circuit courts that considered the issue agreed with the reasoning in *Chuidian*.[57] At first, these decisions had little effect on international human rights litigation. The court in *Chuidian* had noted that the FSIA applied only to actions taken by officials in their official rather than personal capacity,[58] and most

---

[52] Id at 1103.

[53] Id at 1102–03.

[54] Id at 1102.

[55] See *Chuidian*, 912 F2d at 1102.

[56] See id at 1102–03.

[57] See *In re Terrorist Attacks on Sept. 11, 2001*, 538 F3d 71, 81 (2d Cir 2009); *Keller v Central Bank of Nigeria*, 277 F3d 811, 815–16 (6th Cir 2002); *Byrd v Corporacion Forestal y Industrial de Olancho, SA*, 182 F3d 380, 388–89 (5th Cir 1999); *El-Fadl v Central Bank of Jordan*, 75 F3d 668, 671 (DC Cir 1996). Courts concluded, however, that the FSIA did not apply to suits against heads of state and that such suits were instead governed by the pre-FSIA immunity regime, including deference to the Executive Branch. See, for example, *Ye v Zemin*, 383 F3d 620, 625 (7th Cir 2004); *United States v Noriega*, 117 F3d 1206, 1212 (11th Cir 1997); *Lafontant v Aristide*, 844 F Supp 128, 136–37 (EDNY 1994).

[58] See *Chuidian*, 912 F2d at 1106 ("Plainly [the defendant] would not be entitled to sovereign immunity for acts not committed in his official capacity.").

courts concluded that, when officials committed human rights abuses, they were not acting in an official capacity. The rationales for this conclusion were somewhat unclear. Several courts referred to foreign law to determine the scope of the official's authority and found, without extended analysis, that the alleged human rights violations exceeded anything that could plausibly be considered within that authority. Other courts appear to have assumed that human rights abuses are per se unauthorized acts. In general, these decisions did not consider the CIL of foreign official immunity.[59]

Two years after *Chuidian*, Congress legislated in the area of human rights litigation by enacting, in 1992, the Torture Victim Protection Act (TVPA).[60] Subject to certain limitations, the TVPA, codified as a note to the ATS, creates a cause of action for damages against individuals who, "under actual or apparent authority, or color of law, of any foreign nation," commit acts of torture or "extrajudicial killing."[61] Although the text of the TVPA does not mention immunity, there are several ambiguous references to immunity in its legislative history.[62]

Eventually, greater conflict developed between the *Chuidian* line of decisions and human rights litigation. In several cases alleging war crimes and human rights violations by Israeli officials, courts held that suits against foreign officials for their official acts, even if those acts constituted human rights abuses, were covered by the FSIA.[63] As one court explained, "[a]ll allegations stem from actions taken on behalf of the state and, in essence, the personal capacity

---

[59] See, for example, *Hilao v Estate of Marcos*, 25 F3d 1467, 1471 (9th Cir 1994); *Trajano v Marcos*, 978 F2d 493, 498 (9th Cir 1992); *Doe I v Qi*, 349 F Supp 2d 1258, 1282, 1287 (ND Cal 2004); *Cabiri v Assasie-Gyimah*, 921 F Supp 1189, 1198 (SDNY 1996); *Xuncax v Gramajo*, 886 F Supp 162, 175–76 (D Mass 1995); *Paul v Avril*, 812 F Supp 207, 212 (SD Fla 1993); *Forti v Suarez-Mason*, 672 F Supp 1531, 1546 (ND Cal 1987). But see *Matar v Dichter*, 563 F3d 9, 15 (2d Cir 2009) ("A claim premised on the violation of *jus cogens* does not withstand foreign sovereign immunity.").

[60] See Torture Victim Protection Act of 1991 (TVPA), Pub L No 102-256, 106 Stat 73 (1992), codified at 28 USC § 1350 note.

[61] 28 USC § 1350 note.

[62] These references are discussed below in Section C of Part III.

[63] See *Belhas v Ya'alon*, 515 F3d 1279, 1284 (DC Cir 2008); *Matar v Dichter*, 500 F Supp 2d 284, 291 (SDNY 2009), aff'd on other grounds, 563 F3d 9 (2d Cir 2009); *Doe I v State of Israel*, 400 F Supp 2d 86, 104–05 (DDC 2005). The Second Circuit also applied the reasoning of *Chuidian* to a suit brought against (among others) four Saudi Arabian princes in which it was alleged that the princes had facilitated the September 11 terrorist attacks. See *Terrorist Attacks on Sept. 11, 2001*, 538 F3d at 83–85.

suits amount to suits against the officers for being Israeli government officials."[64] The Seventh Circuit interpreted the FSIA differently, however, in a case brought against a former Nigerian general for acts of torture and killing in Nigeria. This court reasoned that "[i]f Congress meant to include individuals acting in the official capacity in the scope of the FSIA, it would have done so in clear and unmistakable terms."[65] The court also noted that it had held in another case that the FSIA did not apply to suits against heads of state, and it asked rhetorically, "[h]ow much less, then, could the statute apply to persons, like [the general in this case], when he was simply a member of a committee, even if, as seems likely, a committee that ran the country?"[66]

C. THE SAMANTAR CASE

The conflict among the courts of appeals deepened with the Fourth Circuit's decision in *Samantar*. The plaintiffs in that case were members of the Isaaq clan in Somalia. They alleged that the defendant, Mohamed Ali Samantar, a former Prime Minister and Minister of Defense of Somalia, was responsible for human rights abuses perpetrated against the Isaaq and other Somali clans who opposed the country's Supreme Revolutionary Council. The council, which seized power in a 1969 coup in which Samantar participated, responded to growing political opposition in the 1980s by "terroriz[ing] the civilian population" with "widespread and systematic use of torture, arbitrary detention and extrajudicial killing."[67] The plaintiffs and their family members were victims of this policy. In 2004, they filed a complaint in a federal district court in Virginia, alleging that Samantar was responsible for these human rights violations because, in his capacity as Prime Minister (a position he held from January 1987 to September 1990) and Minister of Defense (an office he occupied from January 1980 to December 1986), "he knew or should have known about this conduct and, essentially, gave tacit approval for it."[68] The plaintiffs sought damages under the ATS and the TVPA.

---

[64] *Doe I v Israel*, 400 F Supp 2d at 105, citing *El-Fadl*, 75 F3d at 671.

[65] *Enaboro v Abubakar*, 408 F3d 877, 881–82 (7th Cir 2005).

[66] Id at 881, citing *Ye*, 383 F3d at 625.

[67] *Yousuf v Samantar*, 552 F3d 371, 373–74 (4th Cir 2009).

[68] Id. Samantar fled to the United States in 1991 after the Council's fall from power and was living in Virginia at the time of suit. See id.

Samantar moved to dismiss the complaint, arguing that the FSIA provided him with immunity from suit and deprived the district court of subject matter jurisdiction. The district court agreed, adopting the reasoning of the *Chuidian* line of cases that the FSIA applies to suits against foreign officials for actions taken in their official capacity. The court then considered the plaintiffs' argument that Samantar's conduct could not be considered official for these purposes because it violated international norms. In rejecting this argument, the court noted that the complaint "does not allege that Samantar was acting on behalf of a personal motive or for private reasons."[69] The court also assigned "great weight" to two letters sent to the U.S. Department of State by the Prime Minister and Deputy Prime Minister of the Somali Transitional Federal Government,[70] which asserted that Samantar was "acting within the scope of his authority during the events at issue" and that his actions were "taken . . . in his official capacities."[71] The court further reasoned that allowing the lawsuit to proceed would effectively abrogate Somalia's sovereign immunity by enabling the plaintiffs to achieve "indirectly what the [FSIA] barred them from doing directly."[72]

The plaintiffs appealed the dismissal to the Fourth Circuit, which reversed the district court's immunity ruling. The court of appeals analyzed the text of the FSIA's "agency or instrumentality" provision as well as the statute's overall structure, purpose, and legislative history. It reasoned that, in choosing the words "separate legal person" in the FSIA, Congress intended to include within the statute's ambit only organizations and corporate entities, not individuals.[73] The court also agreed with the plaintiffs

---

[69] *Yousuf v Samantar*, 2007 WL 2220579, *11 (ED Va 2007). Each count of the complaint contained the following statement: "Defendant Samantar's acts or omission described above and the acts committed by his subordinates against [plaintiffs] were committed under actual or apparent authority, or color of law, of the government of Somalia." First Amended Complaint, *Yousuf v Samantar*, No 1:04 CV 1360 (LMB/BRP) ¶ 99 (ED Va, filed Jan 27, 2005) (available on Westlaw at 2005 WL 6382922).

[70] *Samantar*, 2007 WL 2220579 at *11. The district court had previously stayed the proceedings "to determine whether the State Department planned to provide a Statement of Interest" as the Somali officials had requested. Id at *6. When, after two years, the officials' request was "still under consideration," the court reinstated the case to the active docket and ruled on the defendant's motion to dismiss. Id.

[71] Id at *11.

[72] Id at *14, quoting *Chuidian*, 912 F2d at 1102.

[73] *Samantar*, 552 F3d at 379–80.

that "even if an individual foreign official could be an 'agency or instrumentality under the FSIA,' sovereign immunity would be available only if the individual were still an 'agency or instrumentality' at the time of suit," which Samantar clearly was not.[74] Having concluded that the FSIA did not bar the plaintiffs' ATS and TVPA claims, the Fourth Circuit declined to address Samantar's alternative argument that he was "shielded from suit by a common law immunity doctrine such as head-of-state immunity."[75] Instead, it directed the district court to consider that issue on remand.

The Supreme Court affirmed. While acknowledging that the petitioner's interpretation of the FSIA as extending to suits against foreign officials for their official acts was "literally possible," the Court said that its "analysis of the entire statutory text persuades us that petitioner's reading is not the meaning that Congress enacted."[76] "Reading the FSIA as a whole," said the Court, "there is nothing to suggest we should read 'foreign state' in [the statute] to include an official acting on behalf of the foreign state, and much to indicate that this meaning was not what Congress enacted."[77] The Court also considered the background, purposes, and legislative history of the FSIA and concluded that, although Congress had in that statute attempted to codify the common law governing *state* sovereign immunity, it had not attempted to codify the separate common law "field" of foreign official immunity.[78]

Finally, the Court disagreed with the petitioner's contention that, unless the FSIA applied to suits against foreign officials, plaintiffs could easily circumvent the FSIA's immunity protections by suing responsible officials rather than the state. Among other things, the Court noted that, "[e]ven if a suit is not governed by the [FSIA], it may still be barred by foreign sovereign immunity

---

[74] Id at 383. In *Dole Food Co. v Patrickson*, 538 US 468 (2003), the Supreme Court held that the determination of whether an entity qualifies as an "instrumentality" of a foreign state for purposes of the FSIA should be based upon the facts that exist at the time of the lawsuit rather than at the time of the defendant's conduct. See id at 478–80.

[75] *Samantar*, 552 F3d at 383; see also id at 383–84 (noting Samantar's reliance on an "immunity doctrine arising under pre-FSIA common law").

[76] *Samantar*, 130 S Ct at 2286.

[77] Id at 2289 (footnote omitted).

[78] Id at 2289–90.

under the common law."[79] The Court did not, however, provide any guidance about the contours of this possible common law immunity. Emphasizing the "narrowness" of its holding, the Court observed that, "[w]hether petitioner may be entitled to immunity under the common law, and whether he may have other valid defenses to the grave charges against him, are matters to be addressed in the first instance by the District Court on remand."[80]

D. LACK OF CONSIDERATION OF INTERNATIONAL LAW

Although seemingly straightforward, the *Samantar* decision is noteworthy for what is missing from the Court's analysis, namely, any consideration of what international law might have to say about immunity in suits brought against foreign officials. This omission is significant for a number of reasons.

First, as explained above, the FSIA was intended to codify principles of international law relating to sovereign immunity. Indeed, the Court had acknowledged only a few years before *Samantar* that the FSIA had "two well-recognized and related purposes"— the "adoption of the restrictive view of sovereign immunity and codification of international law at the time of the FSIA's enactment."[81] Although the Supreme Court has sometimes stated that sovereign immunity "is a matter of grace and comity on the part of the United States, and not a restriction imposed by the Constitution,"[82] it has never denied that immunity also implicates principles of international law, and that is also the widespread view of commentators and of courts in other nations.[83] In light of this,

---

[79] Id at 2292. The Court also described two other limitations that mitigated "the risk that plaintiffs may use artful pleading to attempt to select between application of the FSIA or the common law." Id. First, "the foreign state itself, its political subdivision, or an agency or instrumentality [may be] a required party," a result that might result in dismissal of the suit "regardless of whether the official is immune or not under the common law." Id. Second, "some actions against an official in his official capacity should be treated as actions against the foreign state itself, as the state is the real party in interest." Id. In both of these instances, the FSIA would presumably be brought back into play and determine whether the district court had subject matter jurisdiction.

[80] Id at 2292–93.

[81] *Permanent Mission of India to the United Nations v City of New York*, 551 US 193, 199 (2007). The Court in *Samantar* acknowledged this point, noting further that it had previously "examined the relevant common law *and international practice* when interpreting the [FSIA]." *Samantar*, 130 S Ct at 2289 (emphasis added).

[82] *Verlinden*, 461 US at 486.

[83] See, for example, Hazel Fox, *The Law of State Immunity* 13 (Oxford, 2d ed 2008) ("That immunity is a rule of law is generally acknowledged by States."); Restatement

one might have expected the Court to consider what international law had to say—at least as of 1976—about whether and to what extent the immunity of a state was triggered by a suit against the state's officials.

Second, many of the briefs submitted to the Court in *Samantar* discussed international law. The petitioner devoted several pages of his brief to the topic, contending that "international law in 1976 extended the state's immunity to its officials for the obvious reason that, since the state can only act through its officials, those officials are indistinguishable from the state itself, so stripping their immunity would substantially undermine the state's immunity."[84] Several of the amicus briefs submitted in support of the petitioner, especially the brief submitted by the American Jewish Congress, elaborated in detail on the contours of foreign official immunity under international law.[85] On the other side of the case, the respondents, while emphasizing the FSIA's text, argued at length that international law did not require immunity in damages suits brought against individual officials.[86] Some of the amicus briefs in support of the respondents, most notably the brief submitted on behalf of a group of international law professors, elaborated on this argument.[87]

Third, there is a well-settled canon of construction pursuant to which courts will interpret federal statutes, when reasonably possible, in a manner that avoids violations of international law.[88]

(Third) of Foreign Relations Law, pt IV, ch 5, Introductory Note at 390 (cited in note 4) ("The immunity of a state from the jurisdiction of the courts of another state is an undisputed principle of customary international law."); Green Haywood Hackworth, 2 *Digest of International Law* § 169 (1941) ("While it is sometimes stated that [jurisdictional exemptions for sovereigns] are based upon international comity or courtesy, and while they doubtless find their origin therein, they may now said to be based upon generally accepted custom and usage, i.e. international law.").

[84] Brief of Petitioner, *Samantar v Yousuf*, No 08-1555, *21–*22 (filed Nov 30, 2009) ("Brief of Petitioner") (available on Westlaw at 2009 WL 4320417); see also id at *35–*41.

[85] See Amicus Curiae Brief of the American Jewish Congress in Support of Petitioner, *Samantar v Yousuf*, No 08-1555, *10–*28 (filed Dec 4, 2009) (available on Westlaw at 2009 WL 4709540).

[86] Brief for the Respondents, *Samantar v Yousuf*, No 08-1555, *39–*48 (filed Jan 20, 2010) (available on Westlaw at 2010 WL 265636).

[87] See Brief of Professors of Public International Law and Comparative Law as Amici in Support of Respondents, *Samantar v Yousuf*, No 08-1555, *14–*34 (filed Jan 27, 2010) (available on Westlaw at 2010 WL 342033).

[88] See Restatement (Third) of Foreign Relations Law, § 114 (cited in note 4); *Murray v Schooner Charming Betsy*, 6 US (2 Cranch) 64, 118 (1804).

Samantar invoked this *"Charming Betsy"* canon and argued that a denial of immunity in the case would violate CIL.[89] This invocation of the *Charming Betsy* canon prompted the decision's only reference to international law. In a short footnote, the Court stated:

> We find similarly inapposite petitioner's invocation of the canon that a statute should be interpreted in compliance with international law, see Murray v. Schooner Charming Betsy, [6 U.S.] 2 Cranch 64, 118 (1804), and his argument that foreign relations and the reciprocal protection of United States officials abroad would be undermined if we do not adopt his reading of the Act. Because we are not deciding that the FSIA bars petitioner's immunity but rather that the Act does not address the question, we need not determine whether declining to afford immunity to petitioner would be consistent with international law.[90]

Technically, the Court was correct. Even if CIL requires the conferral of immunity in suits against foreign officials, the United States would still be in compliance with international law if it conferred this immunity through application of the common law rather than through a statute. As a result, the Court's interpretation of the FSIA—whereby the statute does not address the issue of immunity in suits against foreign officials but instead leaves that issue to be resolved through the common law—does not necessarily place the United States in breach of international law. Nevertheless, the Court has at other times assumed that Congress has not left open the issue of international law compliance. Perhaps most notably, the Court in *Hamdan v Rumsfeld*,[91] in construing the references in the Uniform Code of Military Justice to the use of military commissions, assumed that Congress intended to require compliance with international law.[92] The Court's opinion in *Hamdan*, moreover, was authored by Justice Stevens, the same Justice who wrote the opinion in *Samantar*.[93]

A final reason why the omission of international law in *Samantar*

---

[89] See Brief of Petitioner at *40 (cited in note 84).

[90] *Samantar*, 130 S Ct at 2290 n 14.

[91] 548 US 557 (2006).

[92] See id at 625–35.

[93] The comprehensive nature of the FSIA, and Congress's desire to shift immunity determinations away from the Executive Branch, might also have weighed against the conclusion that Congress had allowed the pre-1976 common law regime to continue. Consider also *Altmann*, 541 US at 699 (noting that "Congress established a comprehensive framework for resolving any claim of sovereign immunity").

is noteworthy concerns recent judicial rulings from other countries that *have* taken account of the CIL of immunity when construing similar statutory provisions. For example, the British House of Lords, in a 2006 decision that was discussed extensively in the briefs, relied heavily on international law in construing the word "State" in Britain's State Immunity Act to encompass foreign officials acting in an official capacity.[94] The structure of the British statute is similar to that of the FSIA and, like the FSIA, does not expressly cover suits against individual officials. Nevertheless, in large part because of what it believed international law to require, the House of Lords concluded that the statute should be construed to apply to such suits.[95]

Regardless of whether foreign court decisions such as this one correctly assessed the current state of CIL immunity for foreign officials (an issue we address below in Part II), they demonstrate the potential relevance of international law to the construction of foreign sovereign immunity statutes. It is unclear why the Justices in *Samantar* did not at least consider whether those decisions or other sources of international law might be instructive. By contrast, only three years earlier, in *Permanent Mission of India to the U.N. v City of New York*,[96] the Court considered "international practice at the time of the FSIA's enactment" when construing an ambiguity in the statute.[97] The authorities that the Court referenced there included a multilateral treaty on diplomatic immunity, a report of the International Law Commission, and judicial decisions from the United Kingdom and the Netherlands.[98]

Of course, even if the Court had taken account of international law in *Samantar*, it might still have reached the same conclusion as a matter of statutory interpretation. Regardless of whether international law requires the conferral of immunity in suits alleging

[94] See *Jones v Saudi Arabia*, 129 Intl L Rep 713 (House of Lords 2006).

[95] See, for example, id at 717–18, ¶ 10 (Lord Bingham) (reasoning that when a foreign state's officials are sued for acts taken within the foreign state, there is a "wealth of authority" in support of allowing the foreign state to "claim immunity for its servants as it could if sued itself"). See also, for example, *Zhang v Zemin*, NSWSC 1296, ¶¶ 20–23 (New South Wales S Ct), online at http://www.lawlink.nsw.gov.au/scjudgments/2008nswsc.nsf/2008 nswsc.nsf/WebView2/716C1BB1E68711A3CA25751500191BE0?OpenDocument (construing the Foreign States Immunities Act of Australia, in light of international law, as extending immunity "to members of the foreign government through whom the State acts").

[96] 551 US 193 (2007).

[97] Id at 200.

[98] Id at 201.

human rights violations by foreign officials, the Court could reasonably have concluded that Congress did not address that issue in the FSIA. There were, after all, relatively few suits against foreign officials prior to the FSIA's enactment in 1976, and there is no mention of them in the FSIA's legislative history.[99] In subsequent years, the *Filartiga* line of cases and other developments have made the issue much more salient, but Congress probably did not anticipate that development.

Seen in this light, the case might have raised the question of whether the Court should, in effect, adjust or update the FSIA to address an issue not specifically considered by Congress. There are institutional arguments against such judicial updating, although these considerations may have been tempered by the long-standing nature of the *Chuidian* line of cases and Congress's failure to overturn those cases' construction of the statute. Moreover, in other contexts, the Court has attempted to translate statutory purposes to take account of current conditions; indeed, the Court expressly did so when interpreting the ATS to allow for modern human rights litigation.[100] In any event, the Court in *Samantar* never addressed this question because it did not expressly consider the international law backdrop of the case.

II. The Immunity of Foreign Officials Under Customary International Law

In this part, we consider the extent to which foreign officials are entitled to immunity in other nations' courts as a matter of

[99] See *Samantar*, 130 S Ct at 2291 n 18 (noting that "[a] study that attempted to gather all of the State Department decisions related to sovereign immunity from the adoption of the restrictive theory in 1952 to the enactment of the FSIA reveals only four decisions related to official immunity, and two related to head of state immunity, out of a total of 110 decisions"). Mark Feldman, a participant in the drafting of the FSIA, explained the statute's silence on the issue of head-of-state immunity (a status immunity under international law for certain high-level officials) as follows: "Frankly, we forgot about it, or didn't know enough about it at the time, during those two or three critical years when the statute was being formulated." Panel, *Foreign Governments in United States Courts*, 85 Am Socy Intl L Proc 251, 276 (1991).

[100] See *Sosa v Alvarez-Machain*, 542 US 692, 725 (2004); see also Curtis A. Bradley, Jack L. Goldsmith, and David H. Moore, *Sosa, Customary International Law, and the Continuing Relevance of Erie*, 120 Harv L Rev 869, 873 (2007) (explaining that *Sosa* "was, in effect, a translation of the specific intentions of the [Alien Tort Statute] framers to the regime of post-*Erie* federal common law"); Richard H. Fallon, Jr. et al, *Hart and Wechsler's The Federal Courts and the Federal System* 682–83 (Foundation, 6th ed 2009) (discussing the translation issue presented in *Sosa*).

CIL. As noted above, CIL arises from state practice that is followed out of a sense of legal obligation. For the issue of foreign official immunity, the most relevant state practice will likely be the decisions of national courts.[101] The decisions of international tribunals, even if not technically part of state practice,[102] will also be relevant, in that they may reflect consensus or create expectations about the relevant legal principles.[103]

A review of these materials shows that CIL has long distinguished between immunity based on the status of a government official and immunity based on the subject matter of an official's conduct. With respect to the first type of immunity, referred to as "status immunity" or "immunity *ratione personae*," certain officials such as diplomats and "heads of state" (a category that includes presidents, prime ministers, monarchs, and foreign ministers) are immune from the civil and criminal jurisdiction of other nations' courts.[104] The rationales for granting status immunity are threefold: "to ensure the effective performance of [the officials'] functions on behalf of their respective States";[105] to facilitate "the proper functioning of the network of mutual inter-State relations";[106] and to preserve the sovereign equality and dignity of the state itself, which

---

[101] See International Law Association, Committee on Formation of Customary (General) International Law, *Statement of Principles Applicable to the Formation of General Customary International Law* § 9, cmt d (2000) ("Domestic courts, too, are organs of the State, and their decisions should also be treated as part of the practice of the State. . . . [such as with] a determination that international law does or does not require State immunity to be accorded in a particular case . . . .").

[102] See id at § 10.

[103] Although there is general agreement on the definition of CIL, there are many theoretical debates and uncertainties surrounding its application. These include how extensive and widespread state practice must be, how quickly CIL can develop, and the circularity of requiring nations to act out of a sense of legal obligation (*opinio juris*) before they are bound to an emerging custom. See Curtis A. Bradley and Mitu Gulati, *Withdrawing from International Custom*, 120 Yale L J 202, 210–11 (2010). We do not engage with these debates in this article, but the materials that we rely on in discussing the CIL of foreign official immunity are relatively standard for this topic.

[104] In addition to diplomatic and head-of-state immunity, foreign officials who participate in task-specific visits to other states may enjoy "special mission immunity," a doctrine recognized in CIL and in the Convention on Special Missions, Dec 8, 1969, 1410 UNTS 231. See, for example, *Li v Bo*, 568 F Supp 2d 35 (DDC 2008) (deferring to Executive suggestion of special mission immunity).

[105] *Case Concerning the Arrest Warrant of 11 April 2000 (Democratic Republic of the Congo v Belgium)* (merits), 2002 ICJ Rep 3, 22 at ¶ 53.

[106] *Immunity of State Officials from Foreign Criminal Jurisdiction: Memorandum Prepared by the Secretariat*, International Law Commission, 60th Sess (Mar 31, 2008), UN Doc A/CN.4/596 36 at ¶ 148 ("ILC Secretariat Memorandum").

the official embodies. Status immunity is substantively broad; it applies to all claims against the official, regardless of whether they concern public or private acts or whether the acts took place during the official's time in office. But status immunity is also temporary; it ends when the official leaves office.

The second type of immunity is "conduct immunity" or "immunity *ratione materiae*." Unlike status immunity, conduct immunity "covers only official acts, that is, conduct adopted by a State official in the discharge of his or her functions."[107] The rationales for conduct immunity are linked to its scope. Since a state can only act through its officials, the state's immunity would be undermined if those officials could be sued for acts carried out on the state's behalf. A related justification is that "a state official is not accountable to other states for acts that he accomplishes in his official capacity and that therefore must be attributed to the state" under the international law of state responsibility.[108] Inasmuch as conduct immunity is based on the individual's actions and not his personal status, it extends to all government officials who carry out state functions. For the same reason, conduct immunity does not depend on whether the official is currently in office and thus applies equally to former officials.[109]

Traditionally, CIL has extended immunity *ratione materiae* to officials sued or prosecuted in foreign courts for conduct that is imputable to their state. Hazel Fox, a leading expert on foreign sovereign immunity, describes this traditional view:

> An individual enjoys no immunity in his or her own right. But a State as an artificial person created by the law can act only by means of individual human beings. Under municipal law acts performed by an agent on behalf of another may give rise to liability on behalf of both principal and agent or, where the agent is understood purely as a conduit, a means of communication, give rise to sole liability on the part of the principal. The doctrine of imputability of the acts of the individual to the State has in classical law assumed the second analysis to be correct and con-

---

[107] Id at ¶ 154; see also *Case Concerning Certain Questions of Mutual Assistance in Criminal Matters (Djibouti v France)* (merits), 2008 ICJ 177, 243 at ¶ 191 (indicating that immunity *ratione materiae* extends only to "acts within the scope of [officials'] duties as organs of State").

[108] See Antonio Cassese, *When May Senior State Officials Be Tried for International Crimes? Some Comments on the Congo v. Belgium Case*, 13 Eur J Intl L 853, 862 (2002).

[109] As this description indicates, the two types of immunities sometimes overlap, such as when a high-ranking official performs acts in the exercise of his or her official functions. See id at 864.

sequently imputes the act solely to the state, who alone is responsible for its consequence. In consequence any act performed by the individual as an act of the State enjoys the immunity which the State enjoys.[110]

This view that the conduct immunity of foreign officials derives from the CIL of foreign state immunity was understood as a general rule, "any exception [to which] must be based on a special rule of customary or conventional international law."[111] This approach is also reflected in the UN Convention on Jurisdictional Immunities of States and their Property ("UN Immunities Convention"), a proposed multilateral treaty that was endorsed by the UN General Assembly in 2004.[112] The Convention—which defines a "State" to include "representatives of the State acting in that capacity"[113]— provides as one of its "general principles" that "[a] State enjoys immunity . . . from the jurisdiction of the courts of another State," and it expressly enumerates the limited exceptions to immunity in "the provisions of the present Convention."[114]

Over the last decade, however, a growing number of domestic and international judicial decisions have considered whether a foreign official acts as an arm of the state, and thus is entitled to conduct immunity, when that official allegedly violates a *jus cogens* norm of international law or commits an international crime. A *jus cogens* norm is a rule of international law that has been "accepted and

---

[110] Fox, *The Law of State Immunity* at 455 (cited in note 83). See also, for example, Hans Kelsen, *Principles of International Law* 235 (Rinehart, 1952) (explaining that "no state has jurisdiction over another state . . . not only in case a state as such is sued in a court of another state but also in case an individual is the defendant or the accused and the civil or criminal delict for which the individual is prosecuted has the character of an act of state"); *Underhill*, 168 US at 252.

[111] Hans Kelsen, *Collective and Individual Responsibility in International Law with Particular Regard to the Punishment of War Criminals*, 31 Cal L Rev 530, 551 (1943).

[112] UN Convention on Jurisdictional Immunities of States and their Property, Resolution 59/38, UN General Assembly, 59th Sess (Dec 2, 2004), UN Doc A/Res/59/38 Annex. Although the Convention had not entered into force as of early 2011, many commentators consider it as "the most authoritative restatement of current customary law on state immunity." Thilo Rensmann, *Impact on the Immunity of States and Their Officials*, in Menno T. Kamminga and Martin Scheinin, eds, *The Impact of Human Rights Law on General International Law* 151, 153 (Oxford, 2009).

[113] UN Convention on Jurisdictional Immunities, Art 2(b)(iv) (cited in note 112); see also id at Art 6(2)(b) ("A proceeding before a court of a State shall be considered to have been instituted against another State if that other State . . . is not named as a party to the proceeding but the proceeding in effect seeks to affect the property, rights, interests or activities of that other State").

[114] Id at Art 5; see also Christopher Keith Hall, *UN Convention on State Immunity: The Need for a Human Rights Protocol*, 55 Intl & Comp L Q 411, 415 (2006) ("The Convention establishes a broad general rule of immunity, subject to a number of limited exceptions.").

recognized by the international community of states as a whole as a norm from which no derogation is permitted and which can be modified only by a subsequent norm of general international law having the same character."[115] Norms commonly said to qualify as *jus cogens* include the prohibitions on genocide, slavery, and torture.[116] International crimes include genocide, war crimes, and crimes against humanity.[117] (For ease of reference, we label all of these acts as *jus cogens* violations.)

The cases addressing the relationship between *jus cogens* norms and immunity are numerous and varied. They include both criminal prosecutions and civil suits for damages; complaints against both serving and former heads of state, military officers, and lower-level government officials; litigation in domestic courts; and proceedings before international tribunals and review bodies. A review of this burgeoning case law, as well as the drafting history of international conventions, studies of expert bodies such as the International Law Commission,[118] and the writings of commentators that have interpreted these developments, suggests the following propositions.

First, sitting heads of state are entitled to status immunity in both criminal investigations and prosecutions and in civil suits for damages in the domestic courts of other countries, including in cases alleging violations of *jus cogens*.[119] The International Court of Justice (ICJ) reaffirmed this principle in its 2002 judgment in the *Arrest*

---

[115] Vienna Convention on the Law of Treaties, Art 53, 1155 UN Treaty Ser 332, 8 Intl Leg Mat 679 (1969). The *jus cogens* category of international law is not free from controversy. See, for example, A. Mark Weisburd, *The Emptiness of the Concept of Jus Cogens, as Illustrated by the War in Bosnia-Herzegovina*, 17 Mich J Intl L 1 (1995).

[116] See Restatement (Third) of Foreign Relations Law § 702, cmt n (cited in note 4).

[117] See, for example, Rome Statute of the International Criminal Court, Art 5, 2187 UN Treaty Ser 90 (1998).

[118] The International Law Commission (ILC) is a body composed of twenty-four international law experts elected by the General Assembly to promote the codification and progressive development of international law, including by proposing draft conventions. In 2007, the ILC began a study of the "immunity of State officials from foreign criminal jurisdiction" with the aim of making a contribution to ensuring a proper balance between combating impunity for human rights abuses and stable and predictable interstate relations. See *Preliminary report on immunity of State officials from foreign criminal jurisdiction*, International Law Commission (Roman Anatolevich Kolodkin, Special Rapporteur), 60th Sess (May 29, 2008), UN Doc A/CN4/601 9 at ¶ 17–18. In 2008, the ILC Secretariat published a detailed analysis of state practice and national and international court decisions. ILC Secretariat Memorandum (cited in note 106).

[119] Immunity does not apply to international prosecutions for violations of *jus cogens* norms because the treaties and statutes of international courts and tribunals expressly abrogate both status and conduct immunity. See Robert Cryer et al, *An Introduction to International Criminal Law and Procedure* 550–56 (Cambridge, 2d ed 2010).

Warrant Case,[120] which concerned a warrant for the arrest of the foreign minister of the Democratic Republic of Congo issued by a magistrate judge in Belgium pursuant to that country's "universal jurisdiction" statute.[121] The ICJ held that the warrant violated the status immunity of incumbent foreign ministers, whose functions as state representatives entitle them to "full immunity from criminal jurisdiction and inviolability" during their term of office even against allegations "of having committed war crimes or crimes against humanity."[122] National courts have consistently followed the ICJ's analysis and dismissed suits against sitting heads of state alleging *jus cogens* violations.[123]

Second, a growing number of international and national courts have abrogated the conduct immunity of former heads of state as well as current and former lower-level officials from *criminal* investigations and prosecutions for *jus cogens* violations, especially where international law provides a basis for exercising universal jurisdiction. This trend can be traced to the *Pinochet* case,[124] a watershed 1999 decision in which the British House of Lords held that Chile's former head of state could be extradited to Spain to stand trial for torture. The majority opinions relied heavily on the Convention Against Torture, in particular the provision authorizing states parties to exercise universal criminal jurisdiction. According to Lord Brown-Wilkinson, "the whole elaborate structure of universal jurisdiction over torture committed by officials [would be] rendered abortive and one of the main objectives of the Torture Convention—to provide a system under which there is no safe haven for torturers—[would be] frustrated"[125] if former officials charged

---

[120] *Case Concerning the Arrest Warrant of 11 April 2000 (Democratic Republic of the Congo v Belgium)* (merits) 2002 ICJ 3.

[121] When an offense falls within universal jurisdiction, all nations of the world are said to have the authority to prosecute the offense. See Restatement (Third) of Foreign Relations Law § 404, cmt a (cited in note 4).

[122] *Arrest Warrant Case*, 2002 ICJ 3, at 22–24, ¶¶ 54, 58.

[123] See, for example, *Re General Shaul Mofaz*, 128 Intl L Rep 709 (Dist Ct, Bow Street 2004) (Israeli Minister of Defense); *Re Bo Xilai*, 128 Intl L Rep 713 (Dist Ct, Bow Street 2005) (Chinese Minister for Commerce and International Trade); *SOS Attentats et Béatrice Castelnau d'Esnault c Gadafy*, 125 Intl L Rep 490 (French Court of Cassation) (Mar 13, 2001) (Libyan head of state); *Auto del Juzgado Central de Instrucción No. 4* (Spanish Audiencia Nacional 2008), at 151–57 (granting immunity to the President of Rwanda and noting similar grants of immunity to Cuban President Fidel Castro, the King of Morocco, and the President of Equatorial Guinea).

[124] *Regina v Bartle*, ex parte *Pinochet*, 38 Intl Legal Mat 581 (House of Lords 1999).

[125] Id at 595 (Lord Brown-Wilkinson).

with torture were accorded conduct immunity. Consistent with this reasoning, the court limited Pinochet's extradition to allegations that occurred after Chile, Spain, and the United Kingdom had all ratified the Convention and after the United Kingdom had enacted legislation making torture an extraterritorial crime.

In the decade following *Pinochet*, courts and prosecutors across Europe and elsewhere have commenced criminal proceedings against former officials of other nations for torture and other violations of *jus cogens*.[126] In Spain, criminal investigations are under way against former heads of state, government ministers, and high-level military officials from Argentina, China, El Salvador, Guatemala, Israel, Morocco, Rwanda, and the United States.[127] In France, prosecutors obtained convictions for torture *in absentia* against a former Mauritanian army officer[128] and *in personam* against a Tunisian ex-police chief.[129] After the Netherlands amended its criminal code to recognize status but not conduct immunity for *jus cogens* violations,[130] a former head of Afghan intelligence and his deputy and a former Zairian army colonel were tried and convicted of torture.[131] A judge in Argentina is investigating the torture and disappearances of political opponents of the Franco regime in Spain.[132] And in Italy, a Nazi army sergeant was convicted *in absentia*

---

[126] For a review of recent cases in Europe, see ILC Secretariat Memorandum (cited in note 106). See also *The AU-EU Expert Report on the Principle of Universal Jurisdiction*, Council of the European Union, Council Secretariat (Apr 16, 2009), EU Doc 8672/1/09 Rev 1 24–26 at § 24(vii). For a thoughtful analysis of these cases, see Ed Bates, *State Immunity for Torture*, 7 Hum Rts L Rev 651 (2007).

[127] See Ignacio de la Rasilla del Moral, *The Swan Song of Universal Jurisdiction in Spain*, 9 Intl Crim L Rev 777, 778–80, 785–86 (2009); see also Naomi Roht-Arriaza, *Making the State Do Justice: Transnational Prosecutions and International Support for Criminal Investigations in Post-Armed Conflict Guatemala*, 9 Chi J Intl L 79 (2008).

[128] *Fédération Internationale des Ligues des Droits de l'Homme v Ould Dah* (Nîmes Assize Ct 2005).

[129] *Gharbi v Ben Saïd* (Strasbourg Assize Ct 2008); see also *France Jails Tunisian Diplomat for Torture*, AFP, Dec 15, 2008, online at http://www.google.com/hostednews/afp/article/ALeqM5gTIWQI7cr9uGHdU-0zW5gfr0mjxA.

[130] International Crimes Act 2003, Art 16 (excluding prosecutions of *jus cogens* violations committed by "foreign heads of state, heads of government and ministers of foreign affairs, *as long as they are in office*") (emphasis added); see also M. Boot-Matthijssen and R. van Elst, *Key Provisions of the International Crimes Act 2003*, 35 Neth YB Intl L 251, 286–88 (2004) (analyzing the influence of the ICJ's *Arrest Warrant Case* on the Act).

[131] See Naomi Roht-Arriaza, *Guatemala Genocide Case*, 100 Am J Intl L 212, 213 & n 32 (2006).

[132] Giles Tremlett, *Argentinian Judge Petitions Spain to Try Civil War Crimes of Franco*, The Guardian (Oct 26, 2010), online at http://www.guardian.co.uk/world/2010/oct/26/argentina-spain-general-franco-judge.

of war crimes against Italian civilians during World War II.[133] International courts and treaty bodies have also consistently upheld assertions of criminal jurisdiction by domestic courts over former officials charged with torture.[134] There are a few exceptions to this trend,[135] and several countries have recently narrowed their universal jurisdiction statutes in response to controversies engendered by criminal complaints against foreign officials.[136] But these developments are unlikely to prevent the formation of a CIL exception to conduct immunity in criminal proceedings involving alleged *jus cogens* violations.[137]

Third, there has been less erosion to date of foreign official immunity in the civil context. Most noteworthy is a series of rulings by the Court of Cassation of Italy asserting jurisdiction over civil suits against Germany and German military officers alleging *jus cogens* violations committed in part on Italian territory during World War II.[138] But a number of other jurisdictions have rejected a *jus*

---

[133] *Criminal Proceedings Against Milde*, 92 Rivista di diritto internazionale 61 (Italian Ct of Cassation 2009), reprinted and translated in Oxford Rep Intl L in Dom Cts 1224 (discussing conviction *in absentia* by Military Court of First Instance of La Spezia and subsequent civil proceedings).

[134] See, for example, *Case Concerning Questions Relating to the Obligation to Prosecute or Extradite (Belgium v Senegal)*, ICJ Order No 144 (May 28, 2009) (criminal proceedings against ex-President of Chad for torture), online at http://www.icj-cij.org/docket/files/144/15149.pdf; *Communication No. 181/2001: Senegal*, Committee Against Torture, 36th Sess (May 19, 2006), UN Doc CAT/C/SR.646/Add.1 ¶¶ 9–11 (same); *Ould Dah v France*, App No 13113/03 (Eur Ct Hum Rts 2009) (admissibility decision) (dismissing Mauritanian ex-army officer's challenge to a conviction for torture by a French court and affirming France's authority to exercise universal criminal jurisdiction over allegations of torture).

[135] The two most prominent examples are a French prosecutor's refusal, in 2008, to investigate torture allegations against former U.S. Secretary of Defense Donald Rumsfeld, Letter from Public Prosecutor (Procureur général), Court of Appeal of Paris, to Patrick Baudouin (Feb 27, 2008), online at http://ccrjustice.org/files/Rumsfeld_FrenchCase_ProsecutorsDecision_02_08.pdf, and a German federal prosecutor's decision in 2005 to recognize the conduct immunity of former Chinese President Jiang Zemin. See Human Rights Watch, *Universal Jurisdiction in Europe: The State of the Art* 64 (2006).

[136] See, for example, de la Rasilla del Moral, 9 Intl Crim L Rev at 804 (cited in note 127) (discussing 2009 revision of Spain's universal jurisdiction statute); Steven R. Ratner, *Belgium's War Crimes Statute: A Post-Mortem*, 97 Am J Intl L 888 (2003) (discussing 2003 revision of similar statute in Belgium); see also Police Reform and Social Responsibility Bill, UK House of Commons (Nov 30, 2010), online at http://www.publications.parliament.uk/pa/cm201011/cmbills/116/11116.i-v.html (proposing amendment to the United Kingdom's universal jurisdiction statute to remove the exclusive power of local magistrates to grant arrest warrants and require that all such warrants be approved by the Director of Public Prosecutions).

[137] The precise contours of this exception could be affected by the views of the ILC, which has been studying the immunity of state officials from foreign criminal jurisdiction since 2007. See explanation and sources cited in note 118.

[138] The leading Italian case is *Ferrini v Germany*, 87 Rivista di diritto internazionale 539

cogens exception to foreign official immunity in civil cases, including appellate court decisions from Australia,[139] New Zealand,[140] and the United Kingdom.[141] Although not directly on point, the reasoning of a decision from Canada is also consistent with this pro-immunity position.[142] Furthermore, although a decision from Greece seemed to accept a *jus cogens* limitation on immunity, a subsequent decision from another court in Greece reached the opposite conclusion.[143]

Jones v Saudi Arabia,[144] a 2006 ruling of the British House of Lords, is the leading case for the pro-immunity view. The plaintiffs in *Jones* sued Saudi Arabia and several Saudi officials (a colonel in

---

(Italian Ct of Cassation 2004), reprinted and translated in Oxford Rep Intl L in Dom Cts 19. For further analysis, see Andrea Gattini, *War Crimes and State Immunity in the Ferrini Decision*, 3 J Intl Crim Just 224, 230 (2005). In addition, a few domestic courts in Europe reviewing criminal prosecutions for *jus cogens* violations appear to have awarded damages to victims. See Written Comments by Redress, Amnesty International, Interights, and Justice, *Jones v UK*, App No 34356/06; *Mitchell v UK*, App No 40528/06, *6, at ¶ 21 (Eur Ct Hum Rts, filed Feb 24, 2010), online at http://www.interights.org/jones.

[139] See *Zhang v Zemin*, NSWSC 1296, at ¶¶ 20–23 (New S Wales S Ct 2008), online at http://www.austlii.edu.au/au/cases/nsw/supreme_ct/2008/1296.html; see also *Habib v Commonwealth of Australia*, FCAFC 12, at ¶¶ 85, 115 (Fed Ct of Austl 2010) (in a suit against Australian government for aiding and abetting torture by foreign officials, the court stated that it was "common ground" that "if the agents of Pakistan, Egypt and the USA were sued directly in an Australian court for the alleged acts . . . those agents would be entitled to invoke sovereign immunity," citing *Jones*), online at http://www.austlii.edu .au/au/cases/cth/FCAFC/2010/12.html.

[140] See *Fang v Jiang*, NZAR 420, ¶ 62 (High Ct of NZ 2007), reprinted in Oxford Rep Intl L in Dom Cts 1226.

[141] See *Jones*, 129 Intl L Rep 713, 726 at ¶ 24 (House of Lords 2006).

[142] In *Bouzari v Islamic Republic of Iran*, 71 OR (3d) 675, at ¶ 95 (Ontario Ct of App 2004), the Court of Appeal concluded that Canada's State Immunity Act, Section 2 of which defines "foreign state" to include "any sovereign or other head of the foreign state or of any political subdivision of the foreign state while acting as such in a public capacity," applied even to claims of torture. It should be noted, however, that the Committee Against Torture—the body of human rights experts that reviews implementation of the Convention Against Torture and issues nonbinding recommendations to states parties—expressed concern over this interpretation of the State Immunity Act when reviewing Canada's periodic report in 2005. See *Fourth and Fifth Periodic Reports of Canada*, Committee Against Torture, 34th Sess (May 13, 2005), UN CAT/C/SR.646/Add.1.

[143] In *Prefecture of Voiotia v Federal Republic of Germany*, Case No 11/2000 (Greek Ct of Cassation 2000), the Greek Court of Cassation adopted an implied waiver theory to deny immunity to Germany in a case alleging *jus cogens* violations by the German military in Greece during World War II. See Maria Gavouneli and Elias Bantekas, *Case Report: Prefecture of Voiotia v. Federal Republic of Germany*, 95 Am J Intl L 198 (2001). The Greek Special Supreme Court—convened to decide cases involving the interpretation of international law—later disagreed with the Court of Cassation and rejected the plaintiffs' attempt to enforce the judgment against Germany. See *Margellos v Federal Republic of Germany*, Case No 6/2002 (Greek Special S Ct 2002). For a discussion, see Elena Vournas, Comment, *Prefecture of Voiotia v. Federal Republic of Germany: Sovereign Immunity and the Exception for Jus Cogens Violations*, 21 NY L Sch J Intl & Comp L 629, 648 (2002).

[144] 129 Intl L Rep 713 (House of Lords 2006).

the Ministry of Interior, a deputy prison governor, and two police officers), whom they alleged were responsible for torture that oc- curred "in discharge or purported discharge of [their] duties."[145] As with its earlier *Pinochet* decision, the House of Lords gave careful consideration to the Convention Against Torture. It first rejected the plaintiffs' contention that "torture . . . cannot attract immunity *ratione materiae* because it cannot be an official act,"[146] reasoning that this contention was inconsistent with the treaty's definition of torture: acts "inflicted by or with the connivance of a public official or other person acting in an official capacity."[147] The court also reasoned that whereas the Convention implicitly abrogated im- munity in criminal cases by authorizing universal jurisdiction, no similar jurisdictional grant existed for civil suits.[148] The court further expressed the view that "[t]he foreign state's right to immunity cannot be circumvented by suing its servants or agents."[149] Finally, the House of Lords denied that the recognition of immunity con- flicted with torture's unquestioned status as a *jus cogens* norm. By refusing to allow the suit, the court asserted that it was not "jus- tifying the use of torture"; rather, it was giving effect to "a pro- cedural rule going to the jurisdiction of a national court" and "di- vert[ing] any breach of [*jus cogens*] to a different method of settlement."[150]

The leading decision supporting a *jus cogens* exception to im- munity in civil suits is *Ferrini v Germany*,[151] a case involving the Nazi military's deportation of the plaintiff from Italy to a German

---

[145] Id at 714–18, ¶¶ 2–3, 11 (Lord Bingham).

[146] Id at 744, ¶ 85 (Lord Hoffman).

[147] Id at 723–24, ¶ 19 (Lord Bingham); see also id at 744, ¶¶ 83–84 (Lord Hoffman).

[148] Id at ¶ 25 (Lord Bingham); id at 733–37, ¶¶ 46, 57 (Lord Hoffman).

[149] Id at ¶ 10 (Lord Bingham); see also Bates, 7 Hum Rts L Rev at 655 (noting "the Law Lords' clear conclusion that the immunity *ratione materiae* that attached to the State could not be circumvented by claims being brought against individuals who acted on behalf of the State") (cited in note 126); United States *Matar* Brief at 23 (statement by Executive Branch that "there is broad agreement in international law that, where a foreign state is immune, '[t]he foreign state's right to immunity cannot be circumvented by suing its servants or agents.'") (quoting *Jones*).

[150] See *Jones*, 129 Intl L Rep at 726, ¶ 24 (Lord Bingham); id at 732, ¶ 44 (Lord Hoffman) (both quoting Hazel Fox, *The Law of State Immunity* 525 (Oxford, 1st ed 2004)). For criticism of the court's reasoning on this point, see Alexander Orakhelashvili, *State Immunity and Hierarchy of Norms: Why the House of Lords Got It Wrong*, 18 Eur J Intl L 965 (2007).

[151] 87 Rivista di diritto internazionale 539 (Italian Ct of Cassation 2004), reprinted and translated in Oxford Rep Intl L in Dom Cts 19.

concentration camp. The Italian Court of Cassation characterized the actions as "an expression of [Germany's] sovereign power since they were conducted during war operations."[152] But it refused to recognize "the functional immunity of foreign state organs"[153] for acts that violate *jus cogens,* which stand "at the apex of the international system [and] tak[e] precedence over all other norms whether of conventional or customary nature and therefore also over those norms governing immunity."[154] In 2008 and 2009, the Court of Cassation exercised jurisdiction over more than a dozen additional complaints seeking damages for the German military's actions during World War II.[155] The court reaffirmed that the clash between *jus cogens* and immunity should be resolved on the basis of "value judgments" and a "balancing of interests" that gives primacy to legal principles of higher rank,[156] and it deemphasized the fact that the challenged conduct occurred partly in Italy.[157]

International tribunals have yet to take a definitive position on whether there is a *jus cogens* exception to foreign official immunity in civil cases. In *Al-Adsani v United Kingdom,*[158] a Grand Chamber of the European Court of Human Rights (ECHR) held, by a sharply divided 9–8 vote, that recognizing the immunity of foreign states from civil suits alleging torture did not violate the right of access to the courts protected by the European Convention on Human Rights.[159] Interpreting the Convention "in harmony with other rules of international law . . . , including those relating to the grant of

---

[152] Id at ¶ 7.

[153] Id at ¶ 11.

[154] Id at ¶ 9 (citations and internal quotations omitted). In support of this conclusion, the Court of Cassation cited the International Criminal Tribunal for the Former Yugoslavia (ICTY) Trial Chamber's decision in *Prosecutor v Furundzija,* IT-95-17/I-T 59 at ¶ 155 (ICTY 1998), which "lists the possibility of victims 'bringing civil suits for compensation before Courts of a foreign state' among the effects of the violation of [*jus cogens* norms] at 'an inter-State level.'" Id ¶ 155.

[155] See, for example, *Germany v Mantelli,* 45 Rivista di diritto internazionale privato e processuale 651 (Italian Ct of Cassation 2009), and *Milde,* Oxford Rep Intl L in Dom Cts at 1224. For analysis of these decisions, see Annalisa Ciampi, *The Italian Court of Cassation Asserts Civil Jurisdiction over Germany in a Criminal Case Relating to the Second World War: The Civitella Case,* 7 J Intl Crim Just 597 (2008); Carlo Focarelli, *Case Report: Federal Republic of Germany v. Giovanni Mantelli and Others, Order No. 14201,* 103 Am J Intl L 122 (2009).

[156] Ciampi, 7 J Intl Crim Just at 603–04 (cited in note 155).

[157] See Focarelli, 103 Am J Intl L at 126 (cited in note 155).

[158] App No 35763/97 (Grand Chamber, Eur Ct Hum Rts 2001), online at http://www.unhcr.org/refworld/docid/3fe6c7b54.html.

[159] Id at 20.

State immunity,"[160] the ECHR concluded that, notwithstanding "the special character of the prohibition of torture in international law," it was "unable to discern in the international instruments, judicial authorities or other materials before it any firm basis for concluding that, as a matter of international law, a State no longer enjoys immunity from civil suit in the courts of another State where acts of torture are alleged."[161] The dissenting judges, in contrast, reasoned that the *jus cogens* character of torture overrides immunity, which does not share its hierarchically superior status.[162] Although the majority rejected this view, it left open the possibility that CIL might evolve to abrogate immunity from such suits.[163]

The conduct immunity of foreign officials was not at issue in *Al-Adsani*, but it has been raised in a pending ECHR challenge to *Jones*.[164] The key issue before the ECHR is whether the House of Lords' grant of immunity to the Saudi officials violated the right of access to the courts under the European Convention, even if the recognition of Saudi Arabia's immunity did not.[165] In addition, Germany recently challenged the *Ferrini* line of cases before the ICJ, asking the court to declare that, "by allowing civil claims based on violations of international humanitarian law by the German Reich during World War II," Italy had "failed to respect the jurisdictional immunity which . . . Germany enjoys under international law."[166] The CIL of foreign official immunity from civil damage claims is

---

[160] Id at 16, ¶ 55.

[161] Id at 18, ¶ 61.

[162] See *Al-Adsani*, App No 35763/97 at 26, ¶ 3 (joint dissenting opinion).

[163] See id at 19, ¶ 66.

[164] See *Jones v United Kingdom*, App No 34356/06 (Eur Ct Hum Rts, filed on July 26, 2006); *Mitchell v United Kingdom*, App No 40528/06 (Eur Ct Hum Rts, filed on Sept 22, 2006).

[165] Application Statement of Facts and Questions to the Parties, *Jones v UK* and *Mitchell v UK* (Eur Ct Hum Rts, filed on Sept 18, 2009). The ECHR also asked the parties to address whether European countries "allow civil proceedings to be brought against officials of another State and/or for compensation to be awarded to victims in criminal proceedings brought against those officials." Id.

[166] *Jurisdictional Immunities of the State (Germany v Italy)*, ICJ Press Release no 2008/44 (Dec 23, 2008) at 1, online at http://www.icj-cij.org/. In June 2010, the Italian Parliament adopted a law that suspends until the end of 2011 the execution and enforcement of judgments against a foreign state that has filed a complaint with the ICJ against Italy on matters relating to immunity. The law was "adopted in order to stop the enforcement of proceedings pending before the Italian courts against Germany" during the pendency of the ICJ proceedings in *Germany v Italy*. Andrea Atteritano, *Immunity of States and Their Organs: The Contribution of Italian Jurisprudence over the Past Ten Years*, 19 Ital YB Intl L 33, 46 (2009).

likely to remain unsettled at least until the ECHR and ICJ have issued judgments in these cases.

A fourth principle that is emerging from recent national court decisions—both those that uphold immunity and those that abrogate it—is that *jus cogens* violations committed by officials are governmental rather than private acts.[167] The rationales for this conclusion are first, that illegal and *ultra vires* acts by officials can be attributable to the state under the international law of state responsibility,[168] and, second, that proceedings against officials for acts carried out in an apparently official capacity are equivalent to proceedings against the foreign state itself.[169] However, several international law expert groups and commentators have advanced proposals to disaggregate conduct immunity from state attribution in the case of *jus cogens* violations.[170] Such proposals would enable

---

[167] See ILC Secretariat Memorandum at 116, ¶¶ 180–83 (reviewing authorities) (cited in note 106).

[168] See id at 102, ¶ 156 ("[T]here appear to be strong reasons for aligning the immunity regime with the rules on attribution of conduct for purposes of State responsibility."); id at 105, ¶ 160 ("If unlawful or criminal acts were considered, as a matter of principle, to be 'non-official' for purposes of immunity *ratione materiae*, the very notion of 'immunity' would be deprived of much of its content."); International Law Commission, *Draft Articles on Responsibility of States for Internationally Wrongful Acts, with commentaries* Art 7, cmt 8 (2001) ("*Articles on States' Responsibility*") (acts of a state official or organ in excess of authority or in contravention of instructions is nonetheless attributable to the state provided that the organ or official was "purportedly or apparently carrying out official functions"), online at http://untreaty.un.org/ilc/texts/instruments/english/commentaries/9_6_2001.pdf; id at Art 4, cmt 13 ("[T]o determine whether a person who is a State organ acts in that capacity . . . [i]t is irrelevant . . . that the person concerned may . . . be abusing public power."). But see id at Art 7, cmt 8 (distinguishing "between unauthorized but still 'official' conduct, on the one hand, and 'private' conduct on the other," and indicating that "isolated instances of outrageous conduct on the part of persons who are officials" should be treated as private conduct not attributable to the state).

[169] See *Ferrini*, Oxford Rep Intl L in Dom Cts at ¶ 11; *Jones*, 129 Intl L Rep at 744, ¶ 84 (Lord Hoffman); id at 723–24, ¶ 19 (Lord Bingham); see also *Articles on States' Responsibility* at Art 4, cmt 13 (cited in note 168) ("Where [a government official] acts in an apparently official capacity, or under colour of authority, the actions in question will be attributable to the State."). To be sure, the Draft Articles are "without prejudice to any question of the individual responsibility under international law of any person acting on behalf of a State." Id at Art 58. The commentary makes clear, however, that "[s]o far this principle has operated in the field of [individual] criminal responsibility," although "it is not excluded that *developments may occur* in the field of individual civil responsibility." Id at Art 58, cmt 2 (emphasis added). The commentary also reiterates that "[w]here crimes against international law are committed by State officials, it will often be the case that the State itself is responsible for the acts in question or for failure to prevent or punish them." Id at Art 58, cmt 3.

[170] See, for example, Hazel Fox, *Imputability and Immunity as Separate Concepts: The Removal of Immunity from Civil Proceedings Relating to the Commission of an International Crime*, in Kaiyan Homi Kaikobad and Michael Bohlander, eds, *International Law and Power: Perspectives on Legal Order and Justice* 165 (Brill, 2009).

domestic courts to assert both criminal and civil jurisdiction over former officials alleged to have committed such violations without, at the same time, implicating the responsibility of the foreign state itself.[171]

Two additional considerations are also relevant. First, the UN Immunities Convention, discussed above, does not contain an exception to immunity for civil suits alleging violations of *jus cogens*. In fact, the Convention's drafters twice rejected proposals to adopt such an exception, both because there was no settled state practice to support it and because "any attempt to include such a provision would almost certainly have jeopardized the conclusion of the Convention."[172] As a result, even commentators critical of this omission concede that "state officials and other state agents may benefit from the immunity of the state afforded by the Convention, even with respect to civil suits seeking to recover pecuniary compensation for crimes under international law."[173] This conclusion is reinforced by declarations that Norway and Sweden filed when ratifying the Convention in 2006 and 2009, respectively, which assert that the Convention is "without prejudice to any *future* international legal development concerning the protection of human rights."[174]

A second consideration relates to the persuasiveness of distinguishing between civil and criminal cases. If *jus cogens* are higher-order legal norms, they should arguably negate immunity "in relation to any legal liability whatsoever," whether civil or criminal.[175]

---

[171] See, for example, Rosanne Van Alebeek, *The Immunities of States and Their Officials in International Criminal Law and International Human Rights Law* (Oxford, 2008); Fox, *The Law of State Immunity* at 699–700, 750 (cited in note 83) (reviewing a proposal by the Institut de Droit International); Donald Francis Donovan and Anthea Roberts, *The Emerging Recognition of Universal Civil Jurisdiction*, 100 Am J Intl L 142 (2006); Stacy Humes-Schulz, *Limiting Sovereign Immunity in the Age of Human Rights*, 21 Harv Hum Rts J 105 (2008).

[172] Hall, 55 Intl & Comp L Q at 412 & n 5 (internal quotations omitted) (cited in note 114).

[173] Id at 416; see also Lorna McGregor, *State Immunity and Jus Cogens*, 55 Intl & Comp L Q 437, 438 (2006).

[174] UN Convention on Jurisdictional Immunities of States and Their Property, Declarations of Norway and Sweden (emphasis added), online at http://treaties.un.org/pages/ViewDetails.aspx?src=TREATY&mtdsg_no=III-13&chapter=3&lang=en; see also id, Declaration of Switzerland (asserting that the Convention "is without prejudice to developments in international law" regarding "pecuniary compensation for serious human rights violations which are alleged to be attributable to a State").

[175] See, for example, *Al-Adsani*, App No 35763/97 at 34 (Grand Chamber) (Loucaides dissenting); see also Fox, *Imputability and Immunity* at 167 (proposing "an extension of the removal of functional immunity to civil proceedings in respect of the commission of . . . an international crime") (cited in note 170).

One might also argue that immunity should be determined by the nature of the underlying acts rather than the type of proceeding involved.[176] This claim is supported by the fact that many civil law countries allow victims to recover damages as part of a criminal proceeding.[177] Lastly, abrogating the immunity *ratione materiae* of foreign officials in criminal cases may result in a conviction that deprives the official of his or her liberty for many years. In civil suits, by contrast, lifting immunity may result in an award of monetary damages against the official that, in some instances, may be paid or reimbursed by the foreign state. If immunity is abrogated in criminal proceedings where the penalties are greater, it might seem to follow a fortiori that it should also be disregarded in civil suits.

There are a number of potential responses to these arguments. First, the abrogation of immunity in criminal proceedings has a long pedigree, one that dates back at least to the Nuremberg trials of Nazi officials after World War II and that is more recently reflected in multilateral conventions that impose a duty on states parties to exercise universal criminal jurisdiction over the alleged perpetrators of *jus cogens* violations, and in international criminal tribunals whose statutes expressly override the immunity of government officials charged with those violations.[178] Second, domestic criminal proceedings are subject to screening mechanisms and procedural safeguards that do not exist in civil suits, most notably review by public prosecutors or government agencies that are authorized

---

[176] See, for example, Humes-Schulz, 21 Harv Hum Rts J at 118–19 (cited in note 171); McGregor, 55 Intl & Comp L Q at 444 (cited in note 173).

[177] See, for example, Written Comments by Redress et al at 6 (cited in note 138). See also Beth Stephens, *Translating Filartiga: A Comparative and International Law Analysis of Domestic Remedies for International Human Rights Violations*, 22 Yale J Intl L 1, 19 (2002) (noting that "[m]any civil law systems permit civil claims to be filed as an adjunct to a criminal prosecution").

[178] See, for example, Cryer et al, *An Introduction to International Criminal Law and Procedure* at 531–60 (cited in note 119); William Schabas, *Genocide in International Law: The Crimes of Crimes* 316–24 (2000). The General Assembly adopted the UN Immunities Convention with the understanding that it did not apply to criminal proceedings "out of concern that the availability of immunity in [such] proceedings would conflict with the duty to prosecute certain crimes under international law." McGregor, 55 Intl & Comp L Q at 444 (cited in note 173). The trend toward accountability and monetary reparations in civil cases is more recent and less well developed. See, for example, Dinah Shelton, *Remedies in International Human Rights Law* 10–12, 291–353 (Oxford, 2d ed 2006); UN Basic Principles and Guidelines on the Right to a Remedy and Reparation for Victims of Gross Violations of International Human Rights Law and Serious Violations of International Humanitarian Law, Resolution 60/147, UN General Assembly, 60th Sess (Mar 21, 2005), UN Doc A/Res/60/147.

to dismiss complaints on various grounds.[179] Third and relatedly, the permissive approach to civil litigation in the United States—including broad personal jurisdiction rules, contingent attorneys' fees, expansive discovery, and punitive damages—is controversial in many other countries, whereas the exercise of U.S. criminal jurisdiction is much less so.[180]

* * *

The foregoing overview reveals that, although CIL traditionally conferred immunity on foreign officials for actions taken on behalf of their state, this immunity has eroded over the past decade, although primarily in the criminal rather than civil context. It is difficult, however, to reach firm conclusions about the current state of the CIL of foreign official immunity because the law in this area is unsettled and rapidly evolving. This has implications for whether and how U.S. courts apply CIL in shaping the common law of foreign official immunity after *Samantar*, a subject we address below.

Before turning to this issue, we first bracket the ongoing debate among scholars of U.S. foreign relations law over the proper relationship between CIL and federal common law. There are three basic positions in this debate. One position is that, at least in the absence of a directive by Congress to the contrary, CIL automatically has the status of federal common law.[181] At the other end of the spectrum is the view that CIL should never operate as federal law unless and until it is affirmatively incorporated as such by the political branches.[182] An intermediate position (of which there are

[179] The universal jurisdiction statutes in Spain and Belgium were amended to incorporate such procedural safeguards, and a similar proposal is pending in the United Kingdom. See citations in note 136.

[180] See, for example, Paul B. Stephan, *A Becoming Modesty: U.S. Litigation in the Mirror of International Law*, 52 DePaul L Rev 627 (2002).

[181] See, for example, Louis Henkin, *International Law as Law in the United States*, 82 Mich L Rev 1555, 1561 (1984); Harold Hongju Koh, *Is International Law Really State Law?* 111 Harv L Rev 1824, 1835 (1998); Gerald L. Neuman, *Sense and Nonsense About Customary International Law: A Response to Professors Bradley and Goldsmith*, 66 Fordham L Rev 371, 373 (1997); Beth Stephens, *The Law of Our Land: Customary International Law as Federal Law After Erie*, 66 Fordham L Rev 393, 397 (1997).

[182] It is not clear whether there are currently any academic proponents of this view, although it is possible to read some critiques of CIL as having this implication. See, for example, John O. McGinnis and Ilya Somin, *Should International Law Be Part of Our Law?* 59 Stan L Rev 1175 (2007), and J. Patrick Kelly, *The Twilight of Customary International Law*, 40 Va J Intl L 449 (2000); see also *Al-Bihani v Obama*, 619 F3d 1, 16 (DC Cir 2010) (Kavanaugh concurring in the denial of rehearing en banc) ("[I]nternational-law principles found in non-self-executing treaties and customary international law, but not incorporated into statutes or self-executing treaties, are not part of domestic U.S. law.").

many variants) is that CIL can inform federal common law in select instances, but only if it is applied interstitially in a manner consistent with the policy choices made by the political branches.[183]

Although one of us has written extensively on the topic, we do not take a position here on which of these views is correct. For present purposes, it is sufficient to note two points. First, CIL is potentially relevant to the post-*Samantar* common law of immunity under each of these three views, since even those who contend that CIL should not be applied absent incorporation by the political branches might accept that statutes such as the ATS or TVPA have incorporated principles of CIL or have delegated to courts some authority to incorporate them. Second, one of the paradigmatic cases cited by proponents of the view that CIL applies automatically as federal common law is the issue of foreign official immunity,[184] and even skeptics of that view have acknowledged that CIL may be relevant to judicial development of this area of law.[185]

III. International Law and the Post-Samantar Common Law of Immunity

In this part, we consider the potential relevance of the international law discussed in the last part to the post-*Samantar* common law of foreign official immunity. Our goal here is to frame the possible judicial choices in this area rather than argue for a particular approach. As we will explain, CIL's relevance is likely to

---

[183] See, for example, Bradley, Goldsmith, and Moore, 120 Harv L Rev at 904–05 (cited in note 100); see also Curtis A. Bradley and Jack L. Goldsmith, *Federal Courts and the Incorporation of International Law*, 111 Harv L Rev 2260, 2270 (1998) ("When the political branches cannot plausibly be viewed as having authorized the incorporation of CIL, and especially when they have explicitly precluded incorporation, federal courts cannot legitimately federalize CIL."). For somewhat similar views, see Anthony J. Bellia Jr. and Bradford R. Clark, *The Federal Common Law of Nations*, 109 Colum L Rev 1, 76–90 (2009) (arguing that, although CIL is not automatically part of federal common law, courts should apply some rules derived from CIL as a means of implementing the Constitution's assignments of authority to the federal political branches), and Daniel J. Meltzer, *Customary International Law, Foreign Affairs, and Federal Common Law*, 42 Va J Intl L 513, 536, 550 (2002) (arguing that federal courts have some authority to develop federal common law "interstitially in the area of foreign affairs to serve important federal interests," while also noting that such federal common law "should take its cue from congressional enactments").

[184] See, for example, Koh, 111 Harv L Rev at 1829 (discussing head-of-state immunity) (cited in note 181); Neuman, 66 Fordham L Rev at 382–83 (discussing consular immunity) (cited in note 181).

[185] See Bellia and Clark, 109 Colum L Rev at 90 (cited in note 183); Bradley and Goldsmith, 111 Harv L Rev at 2270 (cited in note 183); Bradley, Goldsmith, and Moore, 120 Harv L Rev at 922–24 (cited in note 100).

depend in part on institutional considerations relating to the proper role of U.S. courts in the area of foreign affairs, the authority of the Executive Branch to affect pending litigation, and the congressional policies reflected in existing statutes.

A. CUSTOMARY INTERNATIONAL LAW

For several reasons, we believe that courts will take account of CIL when developing the post-*Samantar* common law of foreign official immunity. As explained in Part I, the Supreme Court has recognized that sovereign immunity is governed by principles of international law and that the FSIA codified some of those principles.[186] The Court's conclusion in *Samantar* that the statute codified only principles relating to suits against foreign states and not those against foreign officials does not suggest that the Court believed that international law was irrelevant to the latter suits. Indeed, in rejecting the assertion that its interpretation of the FSIA might create a conflict with international law, the Court did not deny CIL's relevance, but rather noted that common law immunity could protect against a breach of international law.[187]

The Court has also looked to international law for guidance in other related contexts. A good example is *First National City Bank v Banco Para El Comercio Exterior de Cuba*.[188] In that case, a Cuban government-owned instrumentality sued to recover on a letter of credit, and the issue was whether the defendant could assert a counterclaim against the instrumentality for the value of assets that the Cuban government had expropriated. In allowing the counterclaim (and thus piercing the veil between the instrumentality and the state), the Court applied principles "common to both international law and federal common law, which in these circumstances is necessarily informed both by international law principles and by articulated congressional policies."[189] As part of its analysis, the Court considered the history and purposes of the

---

[186] See, for example, *Permanent Mission of India*, 551 US at 200 (considering "international practice at the time of the FSIA's enactment" when construing an ambiguity in the statute).

[187] See *Samantar*, 130 S Ct at 2290 n 14.

[188] 462 US 611 (1983).

[189] Id at 623.

FSIA, judicial decisions from the United States and other countries, and general principles of equity.[190]

Assuming that international law is relevant, there are a number of ways that U.S. courts could interpret and apply CIL immunity rules when developing the common law. We begin with the easiest case: sitting heads of state. With regard to ATS and TVPA suits against these national leaders, we foresee at least three reasons that federal courts will follow the ICJ's *Arrest Warrant* judgment and interpret CIL to require dismissal on status immunity grounds.[191] First, as Part II reveals, the immunity *ratione personae* of officials that international law recognizes as "heads of state"— presidents, prime ministers, monarchs, and foreign ministers—has become more rather than less entrenched over the last decade. Second, actions against serving heads of state are the closest that litigants can come to suing the foreign state itself. Such suits thus raise serious foreign relations concerns that weigh heavily against adjudication. Finally, interpreting CIL as mandating status immunity is consistent with pre-*Samantar* decisions that dismissed suits alleging even *jus cogens* violations by heads of state.[192]

With regard to the immunity *ratione materiae* of lower-level officials and all officials no longer in office, the key issue that U.S. courts will face is whether CIL includes a *jus cogens* exception to conduct immunity. As discussed in Part II, a growing number of national and international courts recognize such an exception in criminal proceedings against former officials who served at all levels of government. In civil suits for damages, by contrast, there has been less recognition of such an exception. Below, we identify a number of competing legal and policy considerations that U.S.

---

[190] Although more controversial, a majority of the Court has even looked to international law when interpreting certain provisions of the U.S. Constitution that have an exclusively domestic application. See, for example, *Graham v Florida*, 130 S Ct 2011, 2033–34 (2010); *Roper v Simmons*, 543 US 551, 575–78 (2005). A fortiori, the Court is likely to view CIL as germane to developing common law doctrines that are closely related to foreign affairs, such as the common law governing foreign official immunity.

[191] A potential exception would be where the Executive suggests nonimmunity, an issue we discuss in Section B below.

[192] See *Ye v Zemin*, 383 F3d 620, 624–30 (7th Cir 2004); *Lafontant v Aristide*, 844 F Supp 128, 131–39 (EDNY 1994) (recognizing head-of-state immunity of exiled Haitian President in suit under TVPA alleging extrajudicial killing); *Tachiona v Mugabe*, 169 F Supp 2d 259, 294–97 (SDNY 2001) (recognizing head-of-state immunity of President of Zimbabwe in a suit alleging numerous human rights violations), aff'd in part and rev'd in part on other grounds, 386 F3d 205 (2d Cir 2004).

courts should take account of when addressing this question of CIL.

We begin with a general point about the relationship between immunity and human rights. As we explained in Part II, the erosion of conduct immunity during the decade since the House of Lords' *Pinochet* decision represents a striking shift from the traditional approach to the CIL immunity of foreign officials. This erosion serves an important international interest—expanding domestic accountability mechanisms for individuals responsible for human rights abuses. To date, however, these accountability mechanisms are mandatory only where states have a treaty- or CIL-based obligation to extradite or criminally prosecute the perpetrators of *jus cogens* violations. In civil suits relating to those same violations, by contrast, efforts to promote accountability outside a government official's home country must be consistent with CIL immunity rules.[193] Stated differently, the recent narrowing of conduct immunity has not (or at least not yet) created a concomitant CIL obligation that *requires* national courts to exercise jurisdiction in civil cases.[194]

This fact has important implications for which approach U.S. courts follow. A court that interprets immunity broadly will not violate CIL, whereas a court that interprets immunity narrowly may. To avoid the risk of foreign relations frictions and accusations that the United States is disregarding international law, U.S. courts may decide to follow the reasoning of their colleagues in Australia, New Zealand, and the United Kingdom and hold that CIL presumptively shields former government officials from suits alleging human rights violations.

The arguments in favor of adopting this approach to conduct

---

[193] The Grand Chamber of the European Court of Human Rights has emphasized this point, reasoning that the rights protected in the European Convention—including the *jus cogens* ban on torture—must be interpreted "in harmony with other rules of international law . . . , including those relating to the grant of State immunity." *Al-Adsani*, App No 35763/97 at 16, ¶ 55; see also *Kalogeropoulou v Greece and Germany*, App No 59021/00 (Eur Ct Hum Rts 2002) (inadmissibility decision) (unreported) (rejecting the petitioners' argument that "international law on crimes against humanity was so fundamental that it amounted to a rule of *jus cogens* that took precedence over all other principles of international law, including the principle of sovereign immunity").

[194] The hierarchy argument adopted by the Italian Court of Cassation in *Ferrini* arguably imposes an obligation to assert jurisdiction in civil cases. Although such an obligation has been endorsed by a number of commentators, see, for example, Orakhelashvili, 18 Eur J Intl L at 967 (cited in note 150), it has received little support in state practice or the decisions of domestic and international courts.

immunity are especially strong where a foreign state asserts either that the official's actions were carried out on its behalf or that it is willing to assume responsibility for his or her conduct. In both instances, dismissal can be seen as furthering the policy rationale of aligning CIL immunity principles with the international law of state responsibility.[195] As the ICJ indicated in *Djibouti v France*,[196] a case involving the immunity *ratione materiae* of two Djiboutian officials, a "State notifying a foreign court that judicial process should not proceed, for reasons of immunity, against its State organs, is assuming responsibility for any internationally wrongful act in issue committed by such organs."[197]

Interpreting CIL to require conduct immunity for foreign officials in civil cases would not completely bar ATS or TVPA suits against such officials. A court adopting this approach could continue to assert jurisdiction over ATS and TVPA complaints against foreign officials in at least two instances: first, where the foreign state waives immunity;[198] and second, where the foreign state indicates that the defendant's actions were unauthorized or not within the scope of his or her authority.[199] As discussed below in Section B, it is also possible that the Executive Branch may have some case-specific authority to override an official's immunity even where CIL recognizes it.

Nevertheless, the recognition of CIL conduct immunity for foreign officials is in tension with the approach that U.S. courts

---

[195] See discussion and authorities in notes 168–69 and accompanying text.

[196] *Case Concerning Certain Questions of Mutual Assistance in Criminal Matters (Djibouti v France)* (merits), 2008 ICJ 177.

[197] Id at 244, ¶ 196.

[198] Where a state has recently undergone a regime change, for example, the new government may favor human rights litigation in the United States against its former officials. See, for example, *In re Grand Jury Proceedings*, 817 F2d 1108, 1110–11 (4th Cir 1987) (giving effect to the Philippine government's waiver of head-of-state immunity claimed by the former President and his wife).

[199] Prior to *Samantar*, courts gave considerable weight to the views of foreign governments on these issues. See, for example, *Belhas v Ya'alon*, 515 F3d 1279, 1283 (DC Cir 2008) ("In cases involving foreign sovereign immunity, it is also appropriate to look to statements of the foreign state that either authorize or ratify the acts at issue to determine whether the defendant committed the alleged acts in an official capacity."); *Hilao v Estate of Marcos*, 25 F3d 1467, 1472 (9th Cir 1994) (citing a letter from the Philippine government urging the court to exercise jurisdiction over its former President for "acts of torture, execution, and disappearance [that] were clearly acts outside of his authority"); see also *Kline v Kaneko*, 685 F Supp 386, 389–90 (SDNY 1988) (deferring to submission of Mexican government that defendant was acting "within the scope of his official duties" for purposes of the FSIA).

followed during the thirty years between *Filartiga* and *Samantar*. During that period, most courts held that suits against former government officials were covered by the FSIA. Courts also concluded, however, that *jus cogens* violations were not official acts and, as a result, that the individuals who committed such violations were not entitled to immunity.[200] In the wake of the Court's holding in *Samantar* that federal common law now controls these issues, a judge that endorses the pro-immunity view may, in effect, be conceding that many of the cases decided during those three decades were in violation of CIL. Indeed, the House of Lords in *Jones* suggested precisely this conclusion, as did the separate opinion in the *Arrest Warrant Case*, albeit using more diplomatic language.[201]

In light of the division in foreign court decisions, and the lower court precedents that have built up since *Filartiga*, U.S. courts could plausibly hold that conduct immunity is unavailable to foreign officials in civil suits alleging *jus cogens* violations. This approach would advance important international interests that are in tension with immunity, such as expanding domestic accountability mechanisms for *jus cogens* violations and providing damage remedies to victims.[202] The U.S. political branches have expressed support for these interests, albeit not always consistently, during the three decades of domestic human rights litigation since *Filartiga*.[203]

In choosing between these positions, U.S. courts will need to

---

[200] See citations in note 59.

[201] *Jones*, 129 Intl L Rep at 724–25, ¶20 (Lord Bingham) (describing the TVPA as not "express[ing] principles widely shared and observed among other nations"); id at 737, ¶ 58 (Lord Hoffman) (labeling the TVPA as "not required and perhaps not permitted by customary international law"); *Arrest Warrant Case* (Joint Separate Opinion of Higgins, Kooijmans, and Buergenthal), 2002 ICJ at 77, ¶ 48 (characterizing the ATS as a "unilateral exercise of the function of guardian of international values [that] has not attracted the approbation of States generally").

[202] See, for example, Shelton, *Remedies in International Human Rights Law* at 10–12, 291–353 (cited in note 178); UN Basic Principles and Guidelines on the Right to a Remedy and Reparation for Victims of Gross Violations of International Human Rights Law and Serious Violations of International Humanitarian Law (cited in note 178).

[203] For example, the Carter administration submitted an amicus brief in support of the plaintiffs in *Filartiga*, and the Clinton administration submitted an amicus brief in support of the plaintiffs in *Kadic v Karadžić*, 70 F3d 232 (2d Cir 1995). In addition, Congress in 1992 enacted the TVPA, which was signed by the first President Bush (although he articulated some concerns about the statute in a signing statement). Both the Reagan administration and the second Bush administration, however, argued for curtailing ATS litigation.

take account of the fact that CIL immunity rules are unsettled. The leading national exemplars of the two contending approaches have both been challenged before international courts. As noted in Part II, the ECHR is considering whether the British House of Lords' decision in *Jones* is contrary to the European Convention, and the ICJ is reviewing Germany's challenge to the *Ferrini* line of cases from Italy. At least until the ECHR and ICJ have issued their judgments in these cases, the international law of foreign official immunity will remain in flux.

This uncertainty raises difficult issues concerning the institutional competence of U.S. courts to interpret and apply CIL. On the one hand, the unsettled content of international law provides a unique opportunity for federal judges to participate in the global judicial dialogue over the proper balance between immunity and accountability and shape CIL's future trajectory.[204] But this uncertainty also suggests that U.S. courts should exercise caution before advancing an interpretation of CIL that may offend foreign governments or create foreign relations difficulties for the Executive.

The Supreme Court sounded a similar note of caution in what is arguably the leading decision concerning the role of federal common law in the area of foreign affairs, *Banco Nacional de Cuba v Sabbatino*.[205] In that case, the Cuban government attempted to recover proceeds from the sale of a shipment of sugar and the issue was whether it should be barred from recovery because it had violated CIL in expropriating the sugar factory. In holding that the expropriation did not bar recovery, the Court relied on the act of state doctrine, pursuant to which U.S. courts will not

---

[204] See generally Anne-Marie Slaughter, *A Typology of Transjudicial Communication*, 29 U Richmond L Rev 99 (1994). Many of the foreign and international court decisions cited in Part II refer to U.S. statutes and judicial decisions when canvasing state practice regarding the immunity of foreign officials, sometimes characterizing the same evidence in conflicting ways. Compare *Ferrini*, Oxford Rep Intl L in Dom Cts at ¶ 10.2 (interpreting 1996 amendment to FSIA authorizing certain suits against foreign states designated as sponsors of terrorism as evidence of "the priority importance that is now attributed to the protection of basic human rights over the interests of the State in securing recognition for its own immunity from foreign jurisdiction"), with *Al-Adsani*, App No 35763/97 at 19, ¶ 64 (interpreting the same amendment as "confirm[ing] that the general rule of international law remain[s] that immunity attache[s] even in respect of claims of acts of official torture" in civil suits for damages). By participating in the global judicial dialogue on CIL immunity issues, U.S. courts could help to resolve these differences and clarify the implications of recent developments in the United States.

[205] 376 US 398 (1964).

question the validity of the acts of foreign governments taken within their own territory, a doctrine that the Court made clear had the status of federal common law.[206]

In applying the act of state doctrine even in the face of an alleged violation of CIL, the Court reasoned that the propriety of federal judicial involvement in interpreting and applying CIL was directly proportional to how widely accepted it was,[207] and it concluded that "[t]here are few if any issues in international law today on which opinion seems to be so divided as the limitations on a state's power to expropriate the property of aliens."[208] The Court also characterized as "quite unpersuasive" the countervailing argument in favor of judicial review—that "United States courts could make a significant contribution to the growth of international law."[209] At the same time, the Court made clear that it was "in no way intimat[ing] that the courts of this country are broadly foreclosed from considering questions of international law" in "areas . . . in which consensus as to standards is greater and which do not represent a battleground for conflicting ideologies."[210]

Although there are similarities between the expropriation issues in *Sabbatino* and the immunity issues in ATS and TVPA suits against foreign officials, there are also important differences. First, U.S. courts have been contributing, albeit indirectly, to the erosion of CIL immunity principles for more than three decades. Second, all states, or nearly all, are participants in the international human rights system and have recognized, via treaty ratifications and state practice, the importance of abrogating official immunity for *jus cogens* violations in at least some contexts. The divisions in CIL are thus less "a battleground for conflicting ideologies" than a debate over how to strike a proper balance between two widely shared international values. Third, the U.S. political branches (as well as the Supreme Court) have sanctioned at least some forms of judicial interpretation and application of CIL in litigation under the ATS and TVPA. Taken together, these distinguishing factors

---

[206] See id at 432–33.

[207] Id at 428 (explaining that "the greater the degree of codification or consensus concerning a particular area of international law, the more appropriate it is for the judiciary to render decisions regarding it").

[208] Id.

[209] *Sabatino*, 376 US at 434.

[210] Id at 430 n 34.

suggest that *Sabbatino* is not a categorical bar to a more assertive judicial role in the development of CIL immunity principles. Finally, a key consideration in *Sabbatino* was the need to protect the institutional prerogatives of the Executive Branch, an issue to which we now turn.

B. ROLE OF THE EXECUTIVE

There are a number of reasons to believe that the views of the Executive Branch will be relevant to the development and application of the post-*Samantar* common law of immunity. As discussed above, courts gave absolute deference to Executive suggestions of immunity and non-immunity prior to the enactment of the FSIA in 1976.[211] Since that time, courts have continued to defer to Executive suggestions of immunity for heads of state—including in suits alleging violations of *jus cogens*.[212] Furthermore, in *Samantar*, the Supreme Court observed that it had "been given no reason to believe that Congress saw as a problem, or wanted to eliminate, the State Department's role in determinations regarding individual official immunity."[213] It is also arguable that the Executive's interpretation of CIL is entitled to some deference, just as it is with respect to treaty interpretations,[214] in which case its views regarding the scope of the CIL of foreign official immunity would likely be influential. Finally, in the context of both the FSIA and the ATS, the Supreme Court has suggested (albeit cryptically) that the Executive's views concerning whether particular cases should proceed might be a relevant consideration for the courts.[215]

There are, to be sure, countervailing considerations. Courts have addressed the immunity of foreign officials (other than heads

---

[211] See text accompanying notes 20–28.

[212] See citations in note 57.

[213] 130 S Ct at 2291 (footnote omitted).

[214] See Restatement (Third) of Foreign Relations Law § 112, cmt c ("Courts give particular weight to the positions taken by the United States Government on questions of international law because it is deemed desirable that so far as possible the United States speak with one voice on such matters. The views of the United States Government, moreover, are also state practice, creating or modifying [customary] international law.") (cited in note 4); consider also *Medellín v Texas*, 552 US 491, 513 (2008) ("It is . . . well settled that the United States' interpretation of a treaty 'is entitled to great weight.'"), quoting *Sumitomo Shoji America, Inc. v Avagliano*, 457 US 176, 184–85 (1982).

[215] See *Republic of Austria v Altmann*, 541 US 677, 702 (2004) (FSIA); *Sosa v Alvarez-Machain*, 542 US 692, 733 n 21 (2004) (ATS).

of state) for over thirty years without deferring to the Executive. Moreover, as discussed above, one of the principal reasons for the FSIA's enactment was to shift immunity determinations away from the Executive Branch.[216] Furthermore, the constitutional rationale for the pre-FSIA deference regime is under-theorized and thus may be open to challenge. The Constitution assigns to the President the authority to receive foreign ambassadors, and the Supreme Court has plausibly interpreted this authority to include the power to determine which governments and heads of state should be recognized by the United States.[217] It is not clear, however, why that recognition power encompasses a power to decide whether particular officials of a recognized government are entitled to immunity, which turns on questions of law rather than status. For a sitting head of state, an Executive recognition might *in effect* determine immunity, assuming CIL gives absolute immunity to sitting heads of state (as it probably does). But for other officials as well as all former officials, immunity does not automatically follow from recognition.

As for the implications of *Samantar*, although the Court referred to the pre-FSIA deference regime, it also repeatedly suggested that foreign official immunity is governed by the common law, and it did not direct the courts on remand to solicit or consider the Executive Branch's views in determining the content of the common law. Moreover, in a closely analogous context—judicial development of the common law governing the act of state doctrine—the Supreme Court has declined to treat as dispositive the Executive's views concerning the contours of that law,[218] and a majority of Justices have also balked at the idea of giving absolute deference to the Executive in the case-specific applications of the doctrine.[219]

After *Samantar*, the question of whether federal courts should defer to the Executive's views regarding immunity will be a key point of contention in many ATS and TVPA suits. In particular,

---

[216] See text accompanying note 38.

[217] See *Sabbatino*, 376 US at 410.

[218] See *W.S. Kirkpatrick & Co., Inc. v Environmental Tectonics Corp., Intl.*, 493 US 400, 408 & n * (1990) (rejecting the Executive Branch's proposed multifactored approach to the act of state doctrine).

[219] See *First National City Bank v Banco Nacional de Cuba*, 406 US 759 (1972), in which six Justices rejected the "*Bernstein* exception" to the act of state doctrine that would have allowed the Executive Branch to turn the doctrine off on a case-by-case basis.

the Court's conclusion that the FSIA does not apply to individuals may lead the State Department to reconsider its prior practice as to when it suggests immunity in suits against foreign officials.[220] The Executive Branch had previously expressed the view that foreign officials were protected by immunity for acts taken on behalf of their state and that "customary international law does not recognize any *jus cogens* exception to foreign official immunity."[221] That view was expressed during the Bush administration, however, and it is possible that the current administration or future administrations will adopt a different position.

At a minimum, foreign governments are likely to pressure the State Department to suggest immunity in a nontrivial number of cases, much as they did in the years prior to the FSIA's adoption. Conversely, U.S. human rights advocates may urge the department to intervene on behalf of plaintiffs by indicating that immunity would not be appropriate.[222] This raises the question of what process the department should employ in deciding how to respond to these competing pressures.

There are several ways in which the Executive Branch might express its views regarding the common law of foreign official immunity. First, the State Department might suggest immunity in individual cases, just as it did before the FSIA's enactment. Such suggestions are likely to reflect the foreign policy interests of the United States and thus may not track perfectly the contours of CIL. Nevertheless, because international law does not require that U.S. courts hear civil suits against foreign officials, such suggestions pose little risk of placing the United States in breach of CIL.

---

[220] The State Department "has a longstanding practice of affirmatively 'suggesting' head-of-state immunity to our courts when a person who enjoys the immunity has been served with judicial process." John Bellinger, *Immunities* (Opinio Juris, Jan 18, 2007), online at http://opiniojuris.org/2007/01/18/immunities/. Less frequently, the department has expressed a position on the immunity of other foreign officials. See, for example, Statement of Interest of the United States of America, *Matar v Dichter*, 05 Civ 10270 (WHP) (SDNY, filed Nov 17, 2006), online at http://ccrjustice.org/files/StatementofInterestDichter 11.17.06.pdf. As a procedural matter, "suggestions of immunity normally respond to requests from a foreign government made after its official has been served with a complaint in a civil action. [The Department] usually asks that the request be conveyed through a diplomatic note, with all relevant information and documents . . . ." Bellinger, *Immunities* (cited in this note).

[221] United States *Matar* Brief at *22 (citation omitted) (cited in note 15).

[222] See John B. Bellinger III, *Ruling Burdens State Dept.*, Natl L J (June 28, 2010), in which the former State Department Legal Adviser predicts that, as a result of *Samantar*, the department "will be subject in the future to intensive lobbying by both plaintiffs and defendants."

At worst, if courts defer to these suggestions, the United States might provide more immunity than international law requires. The decision whether to defer to such suggestions, therefore, will primarily be informed by domestic separation of powers considerations, even for courts that might otherwise conclude that CIL conduct immunity does not protect foreign officials from civil suits alleging violations of *jus cogens*.

Second, the State Department might make suggestions of *non-immunity* in particular cases. Since the enactment of the FSIA, the Executive Branch has not made such suggestions, although in two cases courts relied on what they perceived as de facto Executive opposition to immunity.[223] Suggestions of non-immunity pose a greater risk of conflict with international law than suggestions of immunity, since, as discussed above in Part II, CIL can still reasonably be interpreted as providing officials with conduct immunity from civil suits in foreign courts, even for alleged *jus cogens* violations. The Supreme Court has indicated, however, that CIL should not be applied by U.S. courts in the face of a "controlling executive or legislative act" to the contrary.[224] Even putting to one side whether a suggestion of non-immunity qualifies as such an act, if the Executive Branch argues that CIL does not require immunity in a particular situation, courts are likely to give that view some weight, as noted above. So, once again, the issue of deference to these suggestions is likely to turn more on domestic rather than international law considerations.[225]

---

[223] See *United States v Noriega*, 117 F3d 1206, 1212 (11th Cir 1997) (rejecting claim of head-of-state immunity in part because the government's decision to prosecute constituted implicit rejection of immunity); *Kadic v Karadžić*, 70 F3d 232, 248–50 (2d Cir 1995) (rejecting head-of-state immunity in part because the State Department had filed a Statement of Interest in favor of allowing the plaintiffs' ATS claims to proceed).

[224] See *The Paquete Habana*, 175 US 677, 700 (1900); see also, for example, *Gisbert v U.S. Attorney General*, 988 F2d 1437, 1447 (5th Cir 1993).

[225] On remand in *Samantar*, the Department of Justice filed a Statement of Interest with the district court explaining that "[u]pon consideration of the facts and circumstances of this case, as well as the applicable principles of customary international law, the Department of State has determined that Defendant enjoys no claim of official immunity from this civil suit." "Particularly significant among the circumstances of this case and critical to the present Statement of Interest," the Justice Department further stated, "are (1) that Samantar is a former official of a state with no currently recognized government to request immunity on his behalf, including by expressing a position on whether the acts in question were taken in an official capacity, and (2) the Executive's assessment that it is appropriate in the circumstances here to give effect to the proposition that U.S. residents like Samantar who enjoy the protections of U.S. law ordinarily should be subject to the jurisdiction of our courts, particularly when sued by U.S. residents." Finally, the statement asserted that "[b]ecause the Executive Branch is taking an express position in this case, the Court should

A third way that the Executive Branch might express its view would be through a document akin to the Tate Letter. Such a document would likely describe a variety of factors that the State Department considers relevant to determinations of immunity. Indications of what such a document might contain are found in the government's amicus brief in *Samantar*. Emphasizing the "complexities that could attend the immunity determination in this and other cases," the brief explained that "the Executive might find it appropriate to take into account [1] issues of reciprocity, [2] customary international law and state practice, [3] the immunity of the state itself, and, when appropriate, [4] domestic precedents."[226] Additional considerations mentioned in the brief include [5] "the nature of the acts alleged—and [6] whether they should properly be regarded as actions in an official capacity," [7] whether the United States has recognized the foreign government at issue, [8] "the foreign state's position on whether the alleged conduct was in an official capacity," [9] whether the foreign state has "waive[d] the immunity of a current or former official," [10] whether the suit "relie[s] on the ATS to assert a federal common law cause of action" or "the statutory right of action in the TVPA," [11] whether one or more plaintiffs or defendants reside in the United States, [12] "fidelity to international norms," and [13] the consequences of immunity or non-immunity for "the protection of United States officials abroad."[227]

By itself, a list of such numerous and diverse factors is unlikely to provide much guidance to courts attempting to decide whether to recognize immunity in particular ATS or TVPA cases. As Judge Easterbrook remarked in a somewhat different context, such a list does little more than "call[] on the district judge to throw a heap of factors on a table and then slice and dice to taste."[228] If the letter were to closely track the government's brief in *Samantar*, it would likely leave considerable freedom to courts to apply the

---

accept and defer to the determination that Defendant is not immune from suit." Statement of Interest, *Yousuf v Samantar* at 6–7 (cited in note 15).

[226] Brief for the United States as Amicus Curiae Supporting Affirmance, *Samantar v Yousuf*, No 08-1555, *24–*25 (filed Jan 27, 2010) (available on Westlaw at 2010 WL 342031) (enumeration added).

[227] Id at *25–*27 (enumeration added).

[228] *Reinsurance Co. of America, Inc. v Administratia Asigurarilor de Stat*, 902 F2d 1275, 1283–284 (7th Cir 1990) (Easterbrook concurring) (criticizing the creation of a federal common law of privileges based on the indeterminate multifactor balancing test in the Restatement (Third) of Foreign Relations Law).

CIL principles discussed in Part II above or the domestic statutory policies reviewed in Section C below.[229]

The State Department may, however, attempt to distill these factors into a more coherent set of legal and policy guidelines that explain the types of suits, claims, and contexts in which recognition of immunity for foreign officials would or would not be appropriate. For example, the department might identify specific situations in which immunity would be recognized or abrogated, presumptions that could be rebutted by particular factual showings, and inferences courts should draw from the department's failure to express a position. Immunity *ratione personae* for sitting heads of state and foreign ministers (and perhaps for other high-level officials), and non-immunity for officials whose immunity has been waived by a foreign government that the United States has recognized, are two obvious candidates for categorical rules. A presumption against conduct immunity might apply to suits against former officials for alleged torture or extrajudicial killing, unless the foreign state indicates that the officials were acting in the scope of their authority or otherwise agrees to accept responsibility for the officials' acts.[230] Such a presumption would arguably be consistent with Congress's intent in enacting the TVPA,[231] and with a recent ICJ judgment linking state responsibility to immunity *ratione materiae*.[232] It would also provide a rationale for U.S. courts to dismiss cases where the alleged human rights violations are

---

[229] On remand in *Samantar*, the Executive Branch said the following about the list of factors it had recited in its Supreme Court brief: "The identification of certain considerations that the Executive could or might find it appropriate to take into account served to underscore the range of discretion properly residing in the Executive under the Constitution to make immunity determinations in particular cases. It did not reflect a judgment by the Executive that the considerations mentioned were exhaustive or would necessarily be relevant to any particular immunity determination if, as the United States argued to the Supreme Court, the responsibility for doing so was vested in the Executive and not governed by the FSIA." Statement of Interest, *Yousuf v Samantar*, at 5 n 2 (cited in note 15).

[230] Although the Transitional Federal Government of Somalia did request immunity for the defendant in *Samantar*, the Supreme Court noted that the United States does not currently recognize this government. See *Samantar*, 130 S Ct at 2283 and n 3.

[231] See the Torture Victim Protection Act of 1991, S Rep No 102-249, 102d Cong, 1st Sess 8 (1991) (explaining that, to successfully assert immunity from suit under the TVPA, "a former official would have to prove an agency relationship to a state, which would require that the state 'admit some knowledge or authorization of relevant acts'").

[232] *Djibouti v France*, 2008 ICJ at 244, ¶ 196 ("[T]he State notifying a foreign court that judicial process should not proceed, for reasons of immunity, against its State organs, is assuming responsibility for any internationally wrongful act in issue committed by such organs.").

inextricably linked to de jure or de facto government policies—such as in the suits against high-level Israeli officials involved in authorized military operations—and where, in addition, the foreign state is prepared to officially and publicly identify the defendant's conduct as linked to those policies.

A remaining question is how much deference U.S. courts should give to a letter that contains such rules and presumptions. The answer may turn on several factors, such as whether the document explains the Executive's views as to the scope of CIL immunity for foreign officials and the extent to which it is consistent with the policies of Congress as reflected in statutes such as the FSIA, ATS, and TVPA, an issue discussed in the next section.

C. DOMESTIC LAW CONSIDERATIONS

In developing the common law of immunity, courts are also likely to take into account the policies reflected in U.S. domestic law. As Justice Jackson has explained, "[f]ederal common law implements the federal Constitution and statutes, and is conditioned by them."[233] As illustrated by the *Sabbatino* and *First National City Bank* decisions discussed in Section A, this is true even of federal common law that relates to CIL.

Foreign official immunity does not directly implicate the Constitution, although the role of the judiciary in developing this body of law may be affected by the separation of powers considerations discussed above in Sections A and B. More immediately relevant are four federal statutes: the FSIA, the ATS, the TVPA, and 42 USC § 1983. We discuss below how the policies of each statute intersect with the common law of foreign official immunity.

Although the Court in *Samantar* held the FSIA generally inapplicable to suits against foreign officials,[234] this does not mean that the statute is irrelevant to the development of common law immunity. In *First National City Bank*, the Court concluded that the FSIA did not address when it is appropriate to pierce the veil

---

[233] *D'Oench, Duhme & Co., Inc. v FDIC*, 315 US 447, 472 (Jackson concurring) (footnote omitted). See also, for example, Thomas W. Merrill, *The Common Law Powers of Federal Courts*, 52 U Chi L Rev 1 (1985) (discussing the circumstances under which federal common law is legitimate).

[234] For discussion of how the FSIA may continue to apply in some cases involving suits against foreign officials, see generally Ingrid Wuerth, *Foreign Official Immunity Determinations in U.S. Courts: The Case Against the State Department*, 51 Va J Intl L 1 (2011).

of a state-owned corporation, but it nevertheless relied in part on the statute's policies in fashioning a common law rule.[235] Moreover, in an important domestic federal common law decision, *Boyle v United Technologies Corp.*,[236] the Court concluded that, although the Federal Tort Claims Act did not address the immunity of U.S. government contractors, its policies were relevant to the development of a federal common law of government contractor immunity.[237]

The FSIA is likely to cast a shadow in a variety of contexts. For example, the FSIA generally limits tort suits against foreign states and their instrumentalities to situations in which the damage or injury occurs in the United States.[238] In developing the common law of foreign official immunity, courts may seek to avoid a regime that allows for circumvention of this limitation by simply naming responsible foreign officials rather than the state itself. The Court in *Samantar* did not think this concern compelled application of the FSIA to suits against foreign officials, but this was in part because, as the Court noted, "[e]ven if a suit is not governed by the [FSIA], it may still be barred by foreign sovereign immunity under the common law."[239] The Court also noted that "some actions against an official in his official capacity should be treated as actions against the foreign state itself, as the state is the real party in interest," distinguishing those actions from suits against an official "in his personal capacity and [that] seek[s] damages from his own pockets."[240]

A related issue concerns the governmental character of abusive police conduct, including torture. When interpreting the FSIA, the Supreme Court has explained that "however monstrous such abuse undoubtedly may be," it is a "peculiarly sovereign" activity shielded by immunity.[241] Similarly, a number of circuit courts have

---

[235] See *First National City Bank*, 462 US at 627–28.

[236] 487 US 500 (1988).

[237] See id at 511–12.

[238] See 28 USC § 1605(a)(5). Suits against state sponsors of terrorism are a narrow exception. See 28 USC § 1605A.

[239] 130 S Ct at 2292.

[240] Id.

[241] See *Saudi Arabia v Nelson*, 507 US 349, 361 (1993) ("[T]he intentional conduct alleged here [the wrongful arrest, imprisonment, and torture of Nelson] . . . boils down to abuse of the power of its police by the Saudi Government, and however monstrous such abuse undoubtedly may be, a foreign state's exercise of the power of its police has long been

held that even *jus cogens* violations by a state fall within the immunity provided for in the FSIA and have rejected arguments that a state constructively waives its immunity when it engages in such conduct.[242] These conclusions are in tension with the holdings of several lower federal courts, which, prior to *Samantar*, held that torture and other *jus cogens* violations are not official acts and that, as a result, the individuals who commit them were not entitled to immunity under the FSIA or to dismissal under the act of state doctrine.[243]

As for the ATS, the Supreme Court discussed its policies at length in *Sosa v Alvarez-Machain*.[244] The Court unanimously concluded that the ATS was by its terms "only jurisdictional."[245] That holding suggests that the ATS should not be construed as affecting issues of immunity—issues that the Court has in other contexts distinguished from issues of jurisdiction.[246] The Court in *Sosa* proceeded, however, to construe the ATS as also "underwrit[ing] litigation of a narrow set of common law actions derived from the law of nations."[247] That conclusion would not necessarily affect immunity, since even statutory causes of action—such as the domestic civil rights statute, 42 USC § 1983—have been construed as not overriding common law immunities.[248]

Of greater potential relevance are the reasons for "judicial caution" recited by the Court in *Sosa* for deciding whether to allow claims under the ATS. Included among these is the Court's "general practice . . . to look for legislative guidance before exercising

---

understood for purposes of the restrictive theory as peculiarly sovereign in nature."); see also *Abiola v Abubakar*, 267 F Supp 2d 907, 916 (ND Ill 2003) (recognizing common law immunity of former head of state of Nigeria for *jus cogens* violations, including torture, and quoting *Saudi Arabia v Nelson*, 507 US at 361), aff'd on other grounds, *Enahoro v Abubakar*, 408 F3d 877 (7th Cir 2005).

[242] See *Sampson v Federal Republic of Germany*, 250 F3d 1145, 1152 (7th Cir 2001); *Smith v Socialist People's Libyan Arab Jamahiriya*, 101 F3d 239, 242–45 (2d Cir 1996); *Princz v Federal Republic of Germany*, 26 F3d 1166, 1174 (DC Cir 1994); *Siderman de Blake v Republic of Argentina*, 965 F2d 699, 714–19 (9th Cir 1992).

[243] See citations in note 59.

[244] 542 US 692 (2004).

[245] Id at 729.

[246] See, for example, *Verlinden BV v Central Bank of Nigeria*, 461 US 480, 496–97 (1983).

[247] *Sosa*, 542 US at 721.

[248] See, for example, Jack M. Beermann, *Common Law Elements of the Section 1983 Action*, 72 Chi Kent L Rev 695, 698 (1997) (noting that the Supreme Court has "presumed that Congress intended to incorporate well-established common law rules that were in operation at the time the statutes were passed into the causes of action created by the statutes").

innovative authority over substantive law," as well as the "risks of adverse foreign policy consequences."[249] These factors could be read to suggest that the judiciary should not take the lead in expanding the civil liability of foreign officials beyond what is generally accepted under CIL. On the other hand, although the Court in *Sosa* was not focused on the issue of foreign official immunity, it seemed to endorse *Filartiga* and other lower court decisions that had allowed ATS suits against former government officials for alleged *jus cogens* violations.[250]

The third statute—the TVPA—likely provides the strongest domestic law argument for limiting immunity in at least some human rights cases. The TVPA provides a cause of action for damages for acts of torture or "extrajudicial killing" done "under actual or apparent authority, or color of law, of any foreign nation."[251] By its terms, the statute focuses on what are typically the actions of foreign government officials. If such officials were entitled to immunity for *jus cogens* violations, including acts of torture or extrajudicial killings, the statute might be rendered largely a nullity.

To be sure, the TVPA would still apply when a foreign government waived the official's immunity. In addition, if the Executive Branch has the ability to make binding suggestions of nonimmunity (an issue discussed above in Section B), the statute would still be effective in that circumstance.[252] Nothing in the TVPA's text or legislative history, however, indicates that it was intended to be limited to these situations. As a result, it is possible to construe the TVPA as a "controlling legislative act" that would override the CIL of immunity that might otherwise apply to these claims, although the *Charming Betsy* canon of construction might require that Congress's intent to override CIL be manifest.[253] Presumably this construction would apply only to conduct rather than status immunity.

The legislative history is unclear about the TVPA's relationship to foreign official immunity. It suggests that the statute was not designed to override either diplomatic immunity or head-of-state immunity—which are both forms of status immunity—but it does

---

[249] *Sosa*, 542 US at 726, 728.

[250] See id at 725, 730.

[251] 28 USC § 1350 note.

[252] See *Matar v Dichter*, 563 F3d 9, 15 (2d Cir 2009) (making this point).

[253] For discussion of this canon, see text accompanying notes 88–90.

not mention conduct immunity.[254] Complicating matters further, the TVPA was enacted after the *Chuidian* decision, and Congress appears to have assumed that suits against foreign officials (other than heads of state) would fall under the FSIA. In this respect, the House Report states that the TVPA is "subject to the restrictions" of the FSIA, but it also expresses the view that "sovereign immunity would not generally be an available defense."[255] The Senate Report elaborates as follows:

> To avoid liability by invoking the FSIA, a former official would have to prove an agency relationship to a state, which would require that the state "admit some knowledge or authorization of relevant acts." 28 USC § 1603(b). Because all states are officially opposed to torture and extrajudicial killing, however, the FSIA should normally provide no defense to an action taken under the TVPA against a former official.[256]

It is difficult to know how to interpret this passage, both because relying on legislative history to establish propositions not addressed in the text of a statute is hazardous, but also because the legislative history appears to be premised on an assumption—the suits against foreign officials are covered by the FSIA—that the Supreme Court has now rejected.[257] In any event, whatever the implications of the TVPA for foreign official immunity, by its terms it only covers claims for torture or extrajudicial killing and does not apply to other human rights violations.[258]

In addition to these three statutes, human rights advocates are likely to urge courts to look to domestic civil rights litigation as a model for the proper scope of official immunity. In this litigation, such as in suits brought under 42 USC § 1983, government officials can often be sued for violating federal rights, especially constitutional rights, even if the government itself would have

---

[254] See Torture Victim Protection Act of 1991, HR Rep No 102-367(I), 102d Cong, 1st Sess 5 (1991), reprinted in 1992 USCCAN 84, 87–88.

[255] Id.

[256] S Rep No 102-249 at 8 (cited in note 231).

[257] Consider also *Belhas v Ya'alon*, 515 F3d 1279, 1293 (DC Cir 2008) (Williams concurring) (finding "the overall message of the legislative history [of the TVPA] to be mixed—and thus ultimately not that helpful").

[258] See *Sosa*, 542 US at 728 (explaining that the "affirmative authority [in the TVPA] is confined to specific subject matter, and although the legislative history includes the remark that [the ATS] should 'remain intact to permit suits based on other norms that already exist or may ripen in the future into rules of customary international law,' . . . Congress as a body has done nothing to promote such suits").

sovereign immunity from the suit. This is true even though most constitutional violations require state action.

In the famous *Ex parte Young*[259] decision, for example, the Supreme Court permitted a suit for injunctive relief against a state attorney general for violating the Fourteenth Amendment in enforcing allegedly confiscatory railroad rates on behalf of the state, even though the state itself was protected by Eleventh Amendment immunity. The Court reasoned that, when an official acts contrary to the "superior authority" of the federal Constitution, the official is "stripped of his official or representative character and is subjected in his person to the consequences of his individual conduct."[260] Some federal courts scholars have described this reasoning as a "fiction," since it envisions that an official can simultaneously engage in state action for purposes of constitutional liability but act in a personal capacity for purposes of immunity,[261] and the Supreme Court has itself described the doctrine this way.[262] Whether fictional or not, the Court has defended the *Ex parte Young* idea as "necessary to permit the federal courts to vindicate federal rights and hold state officials responsible to 'the supreme authority of the United States.'"[263]

Ex parte Young applies only to suits for prospective relief. The rules for suits seeking monetary damages are more complex, although mainly in form rather than in substance. The Supreme Court has held that sovereign immunity applies in damages suits brought against state officers in their "official" capacity, but not when the suit is brought against the officers in their "personal" capacity. However, in distinguishing between official and personal capacity suits, the Court has, at least for tort suits, allowed plaintiffs to decide how the case should be characterized: if the plaintiff pleads against an official in their personal capacity, the court will accept that characterization, but the plaintiff will be allowed to seek damages only from the official, not the state.[264] Thus, the bottom line in many damages suits, just as with claims for injunctive relief, is

---

[259] 209 US 123 (1908).

[260] Id at 159–60.

[261] See, for example, Peter W. Low and John C. Jeffries, Jr., *Federal Courts and the Law of Federal-State Relations* 1021 (Foundation, 6th ed 2008) ("However desirable the result in *Ex parte Young*, the Court's theory rests on a fictional tour de force.").

[262] See, for example, *Idaho v Coeur d'Alene Tribe of Idaho*, 521 US 261, 270 (1997).

[263] *Pennhurst State School & Hospital v Halderman*, 465 US 89, 105 (1984), quoting *Ex parte Young*, 209 US at 160.

[264] See, for example, *Hafer v Melo*, 502 US 21, 27 (1991).

that plaintiffs can avoid sovereign immunity by suing state officials rather than the state itself. With some minor complications, a similar regime applies to suits against federal officials for constitutional violations.

Some scholars have urged courts to adopt a similar approach to foreign official immunity after *Samantar*.[265] This approach would be consistent with the pre-*Samantar* lower court decisions that concluded that *jus cogens* violations cannot be official acts.[266] Suits under the ATS are all tort suits, so the argument would be that, as long as the plaintiff is seeking damages only from the foreign officials personally, the suits should be deemed to be brought against the defendants in their personal capacity. This is true even though the official was a state actor when violating the international law norm in question. In this way, the proponents of this approach would contend, U.S. courts can vindicate the supremacy of international human rights law in the same way that they vindicate the supremacy of the Constitution under cases such as *Ex parte Young*.

As one of us has argued, however, there are a number of complications associated with applying the domestic civil rights regime to suits brought against foreign officials.[267] First, the domestic regime is premised on the idea that the federal courts have the role of ensuring that federal and state actors comply with the supreme federal Constitution. It is not clear, however, that the federal courts do or should have a comparable role of ensuring that foreign officials comply with international human rights law. As the Court noted in *Sosa*:

> It is one thing for American courts to enforce constitutional limits on our own State and Federal Governments' power, but quite another to consider suits under rules that would go so far as to claim a limit on the power of foreign governments over their own citizens, and to hold that a foreign government or its agent has transgressed those limits.[268]

That said, there are arguments, as discussed in Part II, that inter-

---

[265] See, for example, Chimène I. Keitner, *The Common Law of Foreign Official Immunity*, 14 Green Bag 2d 61 (2010); Beth Stephens, *The Modern Common Law of Foreign Official Immunity*, 79 Fordham L Rev (forthcoming 2011).

[266] See cases cited in note 59.

[267] See generally, Bradley and Goldsmith, 13 Green Bag 2d at 137 (cited in note 15).

[268] *Sosa*, 542 US at 727.

national law increasingly provides national courts with just this sort of authority with respect to *jus cogens* violations.[269]

Second, in the domestic immunity context, the Supreme Court has based its approach on a balancing of competing policy considerations. But it is not clear that courts can or should engage in comparable balancing in the international context. For example, the Supreme Court in the domestic context has developed a "qualified immunity" doctrine that shields domestic officials from damages claims unless it is shown that they violated "clearly established" federal rights "of which a reasonable person would have known"[270]—a doctrine that the Court has described as resulting from "the balancing of 'fundamentally antagonistic social policies.'"[271] These polices include, on the one hand, the vindication of federal law, the compensation of victims, and the deterrence of future misconduct, and, on the other, the promotion of vigorous public decision making without fear of harassing litigation.[272]

There has been much scholarly debate in the domestic context about whether it is proper for the judiciary to attempt to balance such complicated social trade-offs. Regardless of how that debate is resolved, U.S. courts may face greater challenges in identifying and resolving the relevant social trade-offs for other countries, given that foreign nations have different legal and political cultures, different attitudes toward spreading risk through civil damages, and different degrees of wealth (and thus different capacities to pay or indemnify civil damages). At the same time, when U.S. courts apply *jus cogens* norms, they can be seen as vindicating fundamental international human rights norms that all nations, including the United States, have endorsed. Courts could thus reasonably conclude that less policy balancing is required to adjudicate complaints alleging violations of *jus cogens*, at least absent additional guidance from the political branches.

---

[269] There is also growing evidence that national courts are actually exercising this authority in a variety of contexts. See generally Eyal Benvenisti, *Reclaiming Democracy: The Strategic Uses of Foreign and International Law by National Courts*, 102 Am J Intl L 241 (2008) (analyzing national courts' increasing reliance on international law to "challeng[e] executive unilateralism in what could perhaps be a globally coordinated move").

[270] *Harlow v Fitzgerald*, 457 US 800, 818 (1982).

[271] *United States v Stanley*, 483 US 669, 695 n 13 (1987), quoting *Barr v Mateo*, 360 US 564, 576 (1959) (plurality).

[272] See, for example, *Harlow*, 457 US at 807; *Gregoire v Biddle*, 177 F2d 579 (2d Cir 1949) (L. Hand).

Third, suits against foreign officials implicate international law and foreign relations considerations that do not apply to domestic officer suits. The international law of immunity has nothing to say about whether a state allows suits against or prosecutions of its own officials, but, as discussed in Part II, it long ago developed rules to limit the power of one nation's courts to sit in judgment on the officials of other states. There can be reasonable debates, of course, about the contours of the CIL of immunity, but there is no question that it introduces a factor wholly absent from the civil rights context. In addition, even apart from the specific question of what international law requires, suits against foreign officials present issues of foreign relations friction and reciprocity that are not posed by domestic suits.[273] Of course, if CIL continues to evolve toward greater accountability, the adjudication by U.S. courts of at least certain human rights claims against foreign officials in at least some contexts (for example, those encompassed by the hypothetical State Department letter discussed in Section B above) might become less contentious. Such adjudication would also enable U.S. courts to further a basic principle of international human rights law—"the recognition that the treatment by a state of its own citizens is a legitimate matter of international concern and thus of import to its fellow states."[274]

Finally, we note that the critiques of the civil rights paradigm have less force in cases brought under the TVPA. As noted above, the TVPA might have little effect if foreign officials could claim immunity for acts of torture or extrajudicial killing. Moreover, unlike the ATS, which is written only in jurisdictional terms, the TVPA creates a cause of action, its language is similar to the language used in Section 1983, and its legislative history also contains references to that statute.[275]

---

[273] For a discussion of potential foreign relations friction posed by ATS litigation, see John B. Bellinger III, *Enforcing Human Rights in U.S. Courts and Abroad: The Alien Tort Statute and Other Approaches*, 42 Vand J Transnatl L 1, 9 (2009); Curtis A. Bradley, *The Costs of International Human Rights Litigation*, 2 Chi J Intl L 457 (2001). For discussion of concerns expressed by the U.S. government concerning the broad exercise of criminal jurisdiction by Belgium over U.S. and other officials, see Ratner, 97 Am J Intl L at 890–91, 893 (cited in note 136).

[274] Anne-Marie Burley (now Slaughter), *The Alien Tort Statute and the Judiciary Act of 1789: A Badge of Honor*, 83 Am J Intl L 461, 490 (1989); consider also *Filartiga*, 630 F2d at 890 ("Our holding today . . . is a small but important step in the fulfillment of the ageless dream to free all people from brutal violence.").

[275] See HR Rep No 102-367(I) at 5 (cited in note 254); S Rep No 102-249 at 8 (cited in note 231).

IV. CONCLUSION

This article has examined the relevance of CIL to the common law of foreign official immunity that U.S. courts will now develop in the wake of *Samantar v Yousuf*. The immunity of states and their representatives from the judicial process of other nations has been a central concern of international law since its inception. The last decade, however, has seen an erosion of international immunity protections for government officials who are criminally prosecuted for their alleged involvement in genocide, torture, war crimes, and other grave human rights abuses. In their place, international and national mechanisms of accountability are expanding. Thus far, however, there has not been a general trend outside the United States to extend the erosion of foreign official immunity to civil suits in domestic courts, even in suits for alleged violations of *jus cogens*.

These evolving CIL immunity rules have important implications for U.S. courts as they develop the common law of foreign official immunity. Although the decision in *Samantar* did not analyze CIL, the Court was aware of the international backdrop of the case, and it has emphasized international law's relevance in a variety of related contexts. As a result, it is likely that CIL will influence judicial assessments of common law immunity claims raised in human rights litigation after *Samantar*.

The precise influence of CIL will be affected by three considerations: the proper institutional role of U.S. courts in the area of foreign affairs, the weight that should be given to the views of the Executive Branch, and the congressional policies embodied in domestic statutes. In analyzing each variable, we have intentionally held the other two variables constant to highlight the relevant legal and policy choices within that variable. We recognize, of course, that the variables will often overlap. For example, if the State Department favors abrogating the conduct immunity of former officials for *jus cogens* violations in certain circumstances, courts that would otherwise interpret CIL to afford immunity to such officials will need to consider how much weight to give to the department's views.

This article has not attempted to advocate particular answers to these interconnected questions. Nor has it purported to address all of the conceptual and doctrinal debates implicated by *Samantar*. We have focused instead on other important issues—such as the evolution of CIL immunity rules and their relevance to human rights litigation—to isolate the key decisional choices that U.S. courts will face and to clarify points of uncertainty that other scholars may wish to explore in the future.

JONATHAN S. MASUR

REGULATING PATENTS

Imagine the following scenario: In 1972, instead of creating the Environmental Protection Agency,[1] Congress passes the Environmental Pollution Act, which states that "no person shall be permitted to emit any pollutant in a manner that unreasonably endangers human health" and provides for civil penalties and injunctive relief against violators. After the statute takes effect, eager plaintiffs begin filing cases against industries that they believe are breaking the law. The courts are then faced with the task of sorting out which suits are meritorious and which are not, a process that naturally involves interpreting what it means for a pollutant to "unreasonably" endanger human health.

Immediately, of course, the courts run into significant difficulties. A factory that is emitting significant amounts of mercury directly into a source of drinking water is obviously in violation, but what about a factory that emits smaller amounts of mercury into the ocean? What about a factory that emits substantial quantities of carbon monoxide, a known carcinogen, but has installed cutting-edge technology to mitigate these emissions as much as possible?

Jonathan S. Masur is Assistant Professor, University of Chicago Law School.

AUTHOR'S NOTE: I thank Daniel Abebe, John Bronsteen, Jake Gersen, Todd Henderson, Aziz Huq, Jeff Lefstin, Mark Lemley, Saul Levmore, Michael Schill, and Lior Strahilevitz for helpful comments, and Karen Bradshaw, Hanna Chung, Mark Geiger, Thomas Haley, Faye Paul, Anthony Sexton, and Nathan Viehl for excellent research assistance. I would especially like to thank Adam Samaha for excellent comments, suggestions, and edits. This work was supported by the David and Celia Hilliard Fund.

[1] To be precise, President Nixon formed the EPA by reorganizing a number of different subagencies that Congress had created. See note 113.

© 2011 by The University of Chicago. All rights reserved.
978-0-226-36326-4/2011/2010-0007$10.00

Or consider a third factory that produces water bottles made with BPA, a chemical that may (or may not) cause adverse health effects in humans.[2] This factory could cease using BPA in its manufacturing processes, but that would mean inferior bottles, perhaps without any environmental benefit.

Not surprisingly, courts find themselves poorly equipped to evaluate the relevant scientific and economic questions. They cannot determine consistently or reliably how harmful a particular pollutant really is, and in what doses. They struggle with the inevitable economic trade-offs involved in banning environmental pollutants. If restricting the emission of a chemical will save one life but lead to the loss of 10,000 jobs, does that chemical pose an "unreasonable" threat to human health? The courts have no workable metric for deciding. The result is a patchwork of environmental prohibitions that may not do much to protect humans or the environment, and may involve counterproductive and costly economic trade-offs that few people would be willing to accept.

The institutional arrangement described in this scenario will likely strike most readers as inadvisable. It makes little sense to entrust generalist judges with a task as technically complicated as determining which environmental emissions are dangerous, and at what economic cost they should be regulated. The courts have limited technical expertise and little institutional ability to conduct the necessary studies and analyses. If it is necessary to regulate environmental pollutants, better to delegate regulatory authority to the Environmental Protection Agency than the courts. Congress has indeed taken this approach.

As ill-conceived as judge-driven environmental policy might seem, a similar arrangement prevails in the equally technocratic field of patent law. The Patent Act is written in broad terms, permitting patents on any "new and useful process, machine, manufacture, or composition of matter." Congress has not significantly amended the Patent Act since 1952, and the Patent and Trademark Office (PTO) has never had substantive rule-making authority.[3]

---

[2] See Adam Hinterthuer, *Just How Harmful Are Bisphenol A Plastics?* Scientific American (Aug 26, 2008), online at http://www.scientificamerican.com/article.cfm?id=just-how-harmful-are-bisphenol-a-plastics.

[3] See Clarisa Long, *The PTO and the Market for Influence in Patent Law*, 157 U Pa L Rev 1965, 1968 (2009); *Animal Legal Defense Fund v Quigg*, 932 F2d 920, 930 (Fed Cir 1991) (interpreting the Patent and Trademark Office's rule-making authority as extending only to the procedures used in the course of examination).

Courts, therefore, have taken center stage. In particular, the Federal
Circuit has assumed near-total authority over patent policy and
doctrine, which is a position held by no other appellate court over
any area of law. The result has not been felicitous. The Federal
Circuit has been roundly criticized for promulgating overly formalistic doctrines that ignore pragmatic considerations, tolerating
uncertainty and confusion on key points of law, enhancing the power
of patent holders to the point of diminishing innovation, and failing
to distinguish technological fields in which patents are necessary
from those in which they are not.[4]

In recent years, the Supreme Court has intervened to address
some of the Federal Circuit's more glaring faults. Since 2005, the
Court has decided seven patent cases[5]—a startling number given
the Court's traditional reluctance to involve itself in patent matters.[6]
The most recent and most important of these forays came during
the October 2009 Term, in *Bilski v Kappos*.[7] The case posed the
question whether inventors could patent "business methods" (that
is, processes for running a business that do not necessarily involve
any physical product) or other similarly intangible processes. *Bilski*
held potentially enormous economic significance. Thousands of
patents on business methods and other intangible processes are
granted each year, even though the Supreme Court had never before
passed on their validity. Moreover, many scholars now believe that
these types of patents are counterproductive: By increasing transaction costs and creating anticommons problems, they might well

[4] See generally Dan L. Burk and Mark A. Lemley, *The Patent Crisis and How the Courts Can Solve It* 21 (Chicago, 2009); James Bessen and Michael J. Meurer, *Patent Failure* (Princeton, 2008); Adam B. Jaffe and Josh Lerner, *Innovation and Its Discontents: How Our Broken Patent System Is Endangering Innovation and Progress, and What to Do About It* (Princeton, 2004).

[5] See *Bilski v Kappos*, 130 S Ct 3218, 3225 (2010); *Quanta Computer, Inc. v LG Electronics, Inc.*, 553 US 617, 625 (2008); *Microsoft Corp. v AT&T Corp.*, 550 US 437, 447 (2007); *KSR Intern Co. v Teleflex Inc.*, 550 US 398, 407 (2007); *MedImmune, Inc. v Genentech, Inc.*, 549 US 118, 122 (2007); *eBay Inc. v MercExchange, LLC*, 547 US 388, 391 (2006); *Merck KGaA v Integra Lifesciences I, Ltd.*, 545 US 193, 202 (2005). The Court has also granted certiorari in three more patent cases for the 2010 Term. See *Microsoft Corp. v i4i Limited Partnership, et al*, 2010 WL 3392402 (2010); *Board of Trustees of the Leland Stanford Junior University v Roche Molecular Systems, Inc.*, 131 S Ct 501 (2010); *Global-Tech Appliances, Inc. v SEB S.A.*, 131 S Ct 458 (2010).

[6] See John M. Golden, *The Supreme Court as "Prime Percolator,"* 56 UCLA L Rev 657, 658 (2009) ("[T]he Supreme Court has, in the past six years, asserted its dominion over patent law with frequency and force.").

[7] 130 S Ct 3218 (2010).

discourage innovation more than they encourage it.[8] Many commentators thus hoped that the Court would use *Bilski* to limit the sorts of intangible processes that can be patented.

As it turned out, the Supreme Court did no such thing. Rather, *Bilski* merely reaffirmed the well-known principle that "abstract ideas" cannot be patented, without providing guidance on whether business methods and software algorithms are abstract ideas, or even explaining how to define abstract ideas in the first instance.[9] It is easy to view this outcome as a lost opportunity for the Court to correct the Federal Circuit's excesses.

But it is worth pausing to consider more thoroughly what, precisely, the Supreme Court could or should have done. Whether to allow patents on business methods is a highly complex economic question, one that requires balancing the incentives for innovation provided by patents against the costs that monopoly rights impose upon innovators and market entrants. These issues are layered upon the technological complexity that surrounds patent law. To make sensible judgments, courts must first understand the technology and markets involved, and then parse the economic details.

These are tasks to which courts have never been well suited. Indeed, the courts themselves have implicitly recognized this fact— including prominently in *Bilski*. There, the Court acknowledged that questions of patentability should be resolved with reference to economics, with patents granted only where they will promote, rather than hinder, innovation.[10] Yet the majority did not attempt any such analysis. Instead the Justices fell back on traditional tools of statutory interpretation: text, doctrine, and history. Perhaps likewise recognizing their own limitations, the judges on the Federal Circuit have appeared equally unwilling to engage the key economic issues at anything other than a doctrinal level, in *Bilski* or elsewhere.

These are not earthshaking revelations. In areas of regulation ranging from securities, to pharmaceutical drugs, to transportation, to the environment, policymakers have turned instead to expert administrative agencies, perhaps because they understood the institutional deficiencies of courts. This general trend toward agency policymaking in technical fields comes with good reason. Absent

---

[8] See Burk and Lemley, *The Patent Crisis* at 31 (cited in note 4).

[9] See *Bilski*, 130 S Ct at 3225.

[10] See id at 3228–29.

input from an agency or the legislature, the federal courts have repeatedly proved inadequate to the task of setting sound patent policy. Yet the institutional design for patent law remains an outlier. Patent law is a highly technically complex regulatory field controlled entirely by the courts. Similarly, the PTO is one of the only federal administrative agencies to lack any semblance of substantive rule-making authority.

The time has come to consider reorienting patent law's institutional arrangements to bring them more into line with the rest of the administrative state. And the most straightforward means of achieving this would be for Congress to endow the PTO with substantive rule-making authority.

Such a change could produce significant benefits for patent law. A properly empowered PTO could bring expertise and institutional resources to bear on complex questions of patent policy to a degree unthinkable within the federal courts. In addition, the patent office currently produces enormous quantities of useful information but has no reliable mechanism for transmitting that information to the Federal Circuit, in part because the Federal Circuit does not have the proper incentives to accept and utilize that information. Substantive rule-making power would allow the PTO to utilize its substantial informational resources in crafting intelligent patent policy and would permit the agency to design rules that respond to particular technological developments in specific fields. Where Federal Circuit hegemony has failed to generate sensible patent policy, intervention by the PTO may yet succeed.

My argument is comparative, first and foremost. It may be that patent questions should be decided with respect to moral or deontological considerations, not economic ones. However, modern theories of patent law center almost entirely around economic considerations.[11] Economics plays as large a role in contemporary understandings of the shape and scope of patent law as it does in nearly any other field. Accordingly, I simply adopt an economic perspective here while recognizing that some observers may favor a different approach. Similarly, I do not argue that all or even most areas of regulation should be entrusted to agencies rather than

---

[11] See, for example, Burk and Lemley, *The Patent Crisis* at 66 (cited in note 4) ("It is true that there have been a few theories of patent law based in moral right, reward, or distributive justice, but to be blunt they are hard to take seriously as explanations for the actual scope of patent law.").

courts. Rather, the point is that the case for agency authority is at least as strong for patent law as it is in environmental law, securities law, food and drug law, or any other major area of regulation.[12] Agencies have long held primary substantive rule-making authority in those fields and many others. Unless one believes that the administrative state should be dismantled wholesale, there is no compelling reason to resist granting substantive rule-making authority to the PTO.

This article proceeds in three parts. Part I describes the *Bilski* decision and explains how it exposes courts' fundamental inability to solve the technically complex problems that surround patent law. Part II explores the reasons behind the courts' historical dominance of patent law in contrast to the power of agencies in other fields, and concludes that it is little more than a historical accident. Part III lays out the affirmative case for granting substantive rule-making authority to the PTO and addresses possible objections to that new institutional arrangement. There is no reason, modern or historical, for allowing the judiciary to continue as the sole steward of patent law and policy.

I. Bilski and the Failure of the Courts

At the most basic level, the objective of the patentability doctrines—those legal rules that govern which inventions can be patented and which cannot—is to allow patents on inventions that would not otherwise be created (or disseminated) without the incentive provided by a monopoly right.[13] It is for this reason that an invention must be novel[14] and nonobvious[15] in order to be pat-

---

[12] See Part II.F.

[13] See Robert Patrick Merges and John Fitzgerald Duffy, *Patent Law and Policy: Cases and Materials* 253–56 (LexisNexis, 3d ed 2007) (describing the incentive systems meant to drive the patent law); Donald S. Chisum et al, *Principles of Patent Law* 6 (West, 1998). There are other potential objectives behind the rules governing patentability, including reducing transaction costs for follow-on inventors, see Michael A. Heller and Rebecca S. Eisenberg, *Can Patents Deter Innovation? The Anticommons in Biomedical Research*, 280 Science 698, 700 (1998), avoiding rent-dissipating races, see Mark F. Grady and Jay I. Alexander, *Patent Races and Rent Dissipation*, 78 Va L Rev 305, 317 (1992), and avoiding duplicative research, see generally Edmund W. Kitch, *The Nature and Function of the Patent System*, 20 J L & Econ 265 (1977). I do not pause to dwell on these additional goals because they are essentially aligned with the objective of dynamic efficiency: the production of the greatest amount of innovation at the lowest economic cost.

[14] 35 USC § 102.

[15] 35 USC § 103.

entable. It is not necessary to provide inventors with incentives to create or disclose an invention that is already in the public domain.[16]

In addition to these limitations, patent law also imposes the baseline requirement that an invention comprise "patentable subject matter." That is, the invention must be a "process, machine, manufacture, or composition of matter."[17] Courts and commentators have understood this language to mean that there are some types of inventions (and perhaps even some fields of endeavor) that cannot be patented even if they are novel and nonobvious.[18]

What could be the purpose of barring patents on certain types of inventions, even if they are novel and not obvious? If there is a basis for doing so, it must be that certain types of patents will be more harmful than beneficial—that the inefficiencies caused by allowing patents on these inventions will exceed the benefits of providing additional inducement for their development.[19] Indeed, it is now clear that patents function very differently in different industries.[20] In some industries they are almost certainly essential to incentivizing innovation; in others they likely inhibit research and development more than they promote it.[21]

The reasons are multiple. In industries where up-front innovation costs are high but copying costs are low, firms would lack the proper incentives to innovate without the ability to acquire patents.[22] For instance, no pharmaceutical company will attempt to bring a drug to market without a patent for fear that a generic competitor will simply appropriate the idea.[23] On the other hand, in other industries first-mover advantage and other nonpatent business strategies can be enough to encourage firms to proceed with research and development, even where patent protection is uncertain.[24] In these

---

[16] See Chisum et al, *Principles of Patent Law* at 335 (cited in note 13).

[17] 35 USC § 101.

[18] See Michael Abramowicz and John F. Duffy, *Intellectual Property for Market Experimentation*, 83 NYU L Rev 337, 344 (2008).

[19] See Burk and Lemley, *The Patent Crisis* at 31 (cited in note 4).

[20] See id at 27–40.

[21] See id at 40.

[22] See, for example, id at 66–68; see also Mark A. Lemley, *The Economics of Improvement in Patent Law*, 75 Tex L Rev 989, 994–95 (1997); Rebecca S. Eisenberg, *Patents and the Progress of Science: Exclusive Rights and Experimental Use*, 56 U Chi L Rev 1017, 1024–28 (1989).

[23] See Burk and Lemley, *The Patent Crisis* at 143–44 (cited in note 4).

[24] See, for example, Dennis D. Crouch, *The Patent Lottery: Exploiting Behavioral Economics*

industries, competition is the best catalyst of invention. The soft-ware, computer, and semiconductor industries appear to fit this mold.[25]

At the same time, the proliferation of patents almost certainly threatens greater economic harm in some industries than in others.[26] For instance, some industries are characterized by patent thickets[27] and anticommons problems.[28] Firms that wish to innovate must negotiate licenses on large numbers of extant patents and conse-quently face high transaction costs.[29] The software and semicon-ductor industries are widely believed to suffer from these prob-lems.[30] Conversely, the biotechnology industry may be much less susceptible to growth in transaction costs, as each pharmaceutical compound is typically covered by only one patent.[31] Under these circumstances, a sensible patent policy would prohibit, or at least limit, patents within certain technological fields while allowing them in others.

A. JUDICIAL MANAGEMENT OF PATENT POLICY

It was within this context that *Bilski* reached the Supreme Court. The case concerned a patent on a method for hedging risk in the

---

for the Common Good, 16 Geo Mason L Rev 141, 145–46 (2008) ("Many non-patent factors drive innovation and can in some instances make patents irrelevant. These include the desire for a first-mover advantage. . . ."); Burk and Lemley, *The Patent Crisis* at 72–73 (cited in note 4).

[25] See Burk and Lemley, *The Patent Crisis* at 82–85 (cited in note 4).

[26] See Mark A. Lemley, *Industry-Specific Antitrust Policy for Innovation* (Stanford Law and Economics Olin Working Paper No 397, Sept 2010), online at http://www.ssrn.com/abstract_id=1670197.

[27] "Patent thickets" arise in industries in which multiple overlapping patents cover a single invention. See Burk and Lemley, *The Patent Crisis* at 77–78 (cited in note 4). For instance, there might be hundreds of patents that read on a single integrated circuit design, many of them on the same parts of the circuit.

[28] A patent anticommons is a situation in which multiple patents cover sequential parts of an invention. See Burk and Lemley, *The Patent Crisis* at 75–77 (cited in note 4). For instance, there might be a patent on a purified DNA sequence, a patent on the protein that this DNA sequence codes for, a patent on a process for artificially manufacturing this protein, a patent on a pharmaceutical compound incorporating this protein, and a patent on a means for delivering this compound to a patient (such as a pill). A pharmaceutical company that wished to manufacture this pill would be forced to license all of these patents. The threat of an anticommons is the explanation usually offered for the prohibition on patenting abstract ideas. See *Diamond v Diehr*, 450 US 175, 185 (1981).

[29] See Heller and Eisenberg, 280 Science at 700 (cited in note 13).

[30] See Burk and Lemley, *The Patent Crisis* at 86–92 (cited in note 4).

[31] See Mark A. Lemley, *Ten Things to Do About Patent Holdup of Standards (and One Not to)*, 48 BC L Rev 148, 149 (2007).

movement of commodities prices, which is a prototypical method for doing business. Over the past several decades, business methods,[32] tax methods,[33] software algorithms,[34] and other intangible processes have been patented in increasing numbers.[35] Yet the Court had never before considered whether these types of inventions were patentable. Meanwhile, some scholars have suggested that patents in many of these fields were unnecessary, or even counterproductive. Many observers believed that the Supreme Court agreed and would impose significant limits on patents in these fields.[36]

In *Bilski*, the Court acknowledged the role that subject matter limitations should play in restricting patenting where it might be harmful. As Justice Kennedy explained for the Court, "[i]f a high enough bar is not set . . . patent examiners and courts could be flooded with claims that would put a chill on creative endeavor and dynamic change."[37] For all intents and purposes, however, the Court stopped there. It resisted calls for categorical limitations on patents for business methods and similar inventions,[38] and it refused to provide guidance on how patent law should "strik[e] the balance between protecting inventors and not granting monopolies over procedures that others would discover. . . ."[39] The Court's only instructions for the rest of us were a generic reaffirmation that abstract ideas cannot be patented and a declaration that Bernard Bilski's particular patent was invalid on that ground. The Court's opinion did not specify any helpful legal standard to

---

[32] See *State Street Bank v Signature Financial Group*, 149 F3d 1368, 1375 (Fed Cir 1998).

[33] See, for example, *Transamerica Life Ins. Co. v Lincoln Nat. Life Ins. Co.*, 597 F Supp 2d 897 (ND Iowa 2009).

[34] See generally *In re Beauregard*, 53 F3d 1583 (Fed Cir 1995) (allowing software patent); *In re Alappat*, 33 F3d 1526, 1544 (Fed Cir 1994) (en banc) (same).

[35] See Justin M. Lee, *The Board Bites Back: Bilski and the B.P.A.I.*, 24 Berkeley Tech L J 49, 49 (2009) (describing the "period of considerable expansion in subject-matter eligibility").

[36] See, for example, Joe Mullin, *Supreme Skepticism Over Bilski Claims Puts Method Patents on Shaky Ground*, AmLaw Daily (Nov 9, 2009), online at http://amlawdaily.typepad.com/amlawdaily/2009/11/bilski.html; Tony Mauro, *Bilski Case Provokes Patent Skepticism from Justices*, BLT: The Blog of Legal Times (Nov 9, 2009), online at http://legaltimes.typepad.com/blt/2009/11/bilski-case-provokes-patent-skepticism-from-justices.html.

[37] *Bilski*, 130 S Ct at 3229.

[38] See id at 3227.

[39] Id at 3229.

employ when determining whether an invention constitutes an abstract idea.[40]

Justice Stevens's concurrence fared slightly better. The majority of the concurrence is a lengthy analysis of text, precedent, and history—the standard tools of statutory interpretation.[41] However, at the end of his opinion Justice Stevens explained that patents should be granted only when "a patent monopoly is necessary to motivate the invention" and attempted to determine whether business methods qualify under that standard.[42] After canvassing some of the scholarly literature on business method patents, Stevens concluded that they did not.[43]

This is an improvement on the majority, but it demonstrates the limitations of judicial analysis. Stevens cites many leading patent scholars,[44] but he does not so much as mention any of the scholars who support business method patents.[45] The concurrence does not grapple with the competing positions; the case against business methods is stated in conclusory fashion.[46] Accordingly, it is difficult to have much confidence in Justice Stevens's analysis, even if one were inclined to credit the Supreme Court for an approach that could not garner five votes.[47]

1. *Patent economics in the courts.* To some, the Court's general unwillingness to analyze came as a disappointment. But it is easy to understand the Supreme Court's reticence. Suppose that the Court was willing to consider the possibility that patents should

---

[40] See id at 3226–27.

[41] See id at 3231–52 (Stevens, J, concurring in the judgment).

[42] Id at 3253 (Stevens, J, concurring in the judgment) (quotation marks omitted).

[43] See id at 3252–56.

[44] See id.

[45] See, for example, Richard A. Epstein, *The Disintegration of Intellectual Property? A Classical Liberal Response to a Premature Obituary*, 62 Stan L Rev 455, 484 (2010); Brief of Dr. Ananda Chakrabarty as Amicus Curiae in Support of Petitioners, *Bilski v Kappos*, No 08-964, at *15–*23 (filed Aug 6, 2009) (available on Westlaw at 2009 WL 2481328) (written by Richard A. Epstein and F. Scott Kieff).

[46] Notably, the only concession Justice Stevens makes to countervailing argument is one sentence buried in a footnote: "Concededly, there may be some methods of doing business that do not confer sufficient first-mover advantages." *Bilski*, 130 S Ct at 3254 n 51 (Stevens, J, concurring in the judgment), citing Abramowicz and Duffy, 83 NYU L Rev at 337, 340–42 (cited in note 18).

[47] I mean to take no position on the underlying question of whether business methods should be patentable. But I hasten to add that if I were forced to choose a side I would most likely agree with Justice Stevens. My criticism of his analysis has nothing to do with my view of his ultimate conclusion.

not be allowed in certain technological fields, or at least that the bar to them should be raised substantially. How was the Court to judge whether it should reduce patenting of business methods, or tax strategies, or software, or any number of other possible fields of endeavor? These are complicated economic questions with difficult empirical dimensions, precisely the type of questions that courts are not well positioned to answer. Courts have no resources to conduct economic studies and no staff qualified to interpret them.[48] Typically, a court is limited to perusing the amicus briefs filed by outside parties, most of whom have a vested interest in the outcome of the case.[49] These are not reliable, neutral sources of information, much less comprehensive examinations of such complicated issues. Nor do courts have the capacity to compare and evaluate competing technical arguments, which the two sides to an issue will inevitably provide.[50] The shortcomings of even the *Bilski* concurrence lay bare these limitations. Not surprisingly, then, evidence indicates that the Federal Circuit is not significantly influenced by amicus briefs.[51] This may very well be for the best.

This issue is not limited to business method patents. For instance, a district court recently declared that isolated and purified gene sequences are unpatentable as "products of nature."[52] This would be a momentous ruling were it to stand. Molecular genetics is a multi-billion-dollar industry in the United States alone, and many firms have business models dependent largely on obtaining patents on gene sequences. Eliminating gene patents might dampen important innovation. On the other hand, doing so might reduce the transaction costs involved in developing pharmaceuticals and gene therapies.[53] Not surprisingly, the district court

---

[48] See Peter Lee, *Patent Law and the Two Cultures*, 120 Yale L J 2, 20–25 (2010).

[49] In some cases a court could retain a special master to evaluate the economic issues presented by a particular case. This might well be an improvement on typical judicial decision making. At the limit, however, it reduces to ad hoc expert decision making—a less desirable version of typical agency action. I discuss this point further below.

[50] See Richard Posner, *The Law and Economics of the Economic Expert Witness*, 13 J Econ Persp 91, 96 (1999).

[51] See Colleen V. Chien, *Patent Amicus Briefs: What the Courts' Friends Can Teach Us About the Patent System*, U Cal Irvine L Rev (forthcoming) (manuscript at 25–28) (finding that amicus briefs exert very little influence on the Federal Circuit), online at http://www.ssrn.com/abstract_id=1608111.

[52] See *Association for Molecular Pathology v U.S. Patent and Trademark Office*, 702 F Supp 2d 181, 222 (SDNY 2010).

[53] See Heller and Eisenberg, 280 Science at 700 (cited in note 13).

opinion mentioned none of these possible economic consequences. Instead the judge presented a straightforward doctrinal analysis of whether "purification" was enough to transform a natural product into a patentable invention.[54]

The result of *Bilski* is to return the issue to the Federal Circuit and allow that body to develop the law further. But it is hard to imagine that court faring much better. With the same lack of resources and absence of staff expertise, the Federal Circuit is no better equipped to make difficult economic judgments than the Supreme Court. The Circuit decides a large number of patent cases every year, but those cases only represent a small fraction of the economic activity involving patents in any given industry. While any court will struggle with complex economic issues, it is particularly difficult for a court to ascertain the answer to questions such as whether patents are harmful or beneficial within a given field. The problem is that the vast majority of the relevant economic action takes place outside of the courtroom. Patents will be harmful where they create thickets or anticommons and raise transaction costs for new innovators;[55] they will be beneficial where they incentivize invention that would not otherwise occur. Courts cannot observe either activity.

It is certainly not news that courts struggle with difficult economic questions. Scholars have recognized this issue most prominently within the field of antitrust—the other area of federal law in which judges are the primary policymakers.[56] Yet this criticism has largely been confined to antitrust law. The likely explanation is that the Sherman Antitrust Act explicitly calls for an economic judgment: any contract "in restraint of trade" is illegal.[57] Patent law, by contrast, embeds its economic judgments within doctrine. An invention is only patentable if it is novel, nonobvious, and

---

[54] See *Association for Molecular Pathology*, 702 F Supp 2d at 226–27.

[55] See Ian Ayres and Paul Klempere, *Limiting Patentees' Market Power Without Reducing Innovation Incentives: The Perverse Benefits of Uncertainty and Non-Injunctive Remedies*, 97 Mich L Rev 985, 1018–20 (1999); Heller and Eisenberg, 280 Science at 698–99 (cited in note 13).

[56] See Richard Posner, *Economic Analysis of Law* 249 (Aspen, 7th ed 2007); Michael R. Baye and Joshua D. Wright, *Is Antitrust Too Complicated for Generalist Judges?* J L & Econ (forthcoming 2010), online at http://www.ssrn.com/abstract_id=1319888; William Kovacic and Carl Shapiro, *Antitrust Policy: A Century of Economic and Legal Thinking* (U of Cal–Berkeley, Center for Competition Policy Working Paper No CPC99-09, October 1999), online at http://www.ssrn.com/abstract_id=506284.

[57] 15 USC § 1.

involves a "process, machine, manufacture, or composition of matter," and none of these doctrinal elements overtly demands an economic analysis. Patent judges have thus clung tenaciously to the legal language of patent law, refusing to engage directly with the economic issues at hand.

This arrangement would be suitable if there were reason to believe that the Patent Act already incorporated sound economic judgment on the part of Congress. While such a claim might have been sustainable fifty years ago, it no longer appears plausible. The Patent Act was last amended in 1952, a time that precedes almost all business method, software, and tax patents, and even the modern computer and semiconductor industries.[58] These industries may very well have different market structures than other major areas of patenting such as machinery and pharmaceuticals, and those different market structures may dictate divergent reactions to the availability of patents. If patents diminish innovation and social welfare in some of these fields more than they increase it, as critics of expansive patent rights maintain, then the patent system ought to adjust accordingly. It makes no sense to pretend that Congress somehow managed to embed the proper rules into the act's terse language in 1952 (and before), and that the courts need merely divine Congress's intent. If courts are not well equipped to make economic judgments, there is no reason to believe that decades-old verbal formulations provide the answers.

2. *The particular problems with subject matter distinctions.* These problems are endemic to any situation involving complex empirical questions. But the difficulties the Supreme Court would face in formulating a sensible doctrine of patentable subject matter run even deeper. Suppose that the Court wished to wall off business methods as unpatentable. Consider the various verbal formulations that the Court might have adopted. The Federal Circuit's original test asked whether an invention created a "useful, concrete, and tangible result."[59] This is far too permissive. Nearly any type of business method—a method of sale, a means of organizing a business, or a strategy for structuring taxable income—creates a tangible result of one type or another, if only indirectly, simply by altering the way in which people exchange goods or services.

---

[58] See Long, 157 U Pa L Rev at 1968 (cited in note 3).

[59] *In re Alappat*, 33 F3d 1526, 1544 (Fed Cir 1994) (en banc).

In *Bilski*, the Federal Circuit settled on what is known as the "machine-or-transformation test": an invention is patentable if it involves a machine or transforms matter.[60] But this test might itself be dramatically under- or overinclusive, depending upon how capaciously it is understood. The principal issue is whether a general-purpose computer, appended to a claim, would constitute a machine for purposes of the test. If it did not, the test would likely exclude a host of inventions not commonly thought of as business methods, including software. This may be undesirable. And if the machine-or-transformation test *did* permit the patenting of abstract process claims to which a general-purpose computer had been attached, it would likely have little or no force. A large proportion of modern business methods require a computer to run. (Consider Amazon.com's archetypal "one-click" patent.[61]) Requiring a computer as an element would not greatly limit the scope of patent claims.

Finally, the Court could have declared as a matter of doctrine that "business methods cannot be patented." But precisely defining "business method" is not a trivial exercise. After all, most inventions—from farm machinery to pharmaceuticals to industrial processes—are "methods of running a business" in the most general sense. Business methods are defined most prominently by what they are *not*, namely, tangible objects. Similar problems of definition will plague attempts to flesh out the Supreme Court's prohibition on "abstract ideas" as well, especially considering that the Court rejected the machine-and-transformation test as the sole guide for determining whether a patent was merely an abstract idea.[62]

The courts could commence the laborious process of drawing a boundary around the concept of business methods, but they would face a patent bar working to find new ways to draft patents to evade the courts' rules. The result would be a flood of litigation on the issue and a substantial degree of uncertainty regarding what is patentable. While the Federal Circuit is in the process of deciding which inventions are business methods and which are not, the PTO might well be making its own errors of under- and

---

[60] See *In re Bilski*, 545 F3d 943, 957 (Fed Cir 2008) (en banc).

[61] See *Amazon.com, Inc. v Barnesandnoble.com, Inc.*, 239 F3d 1343 (Fed Cir 2001).

[62] *Bilski*, 130 S Ct at 3226.

overinclusion—issuing patents that are later understood to be invalid, or refusing to grant patents that it should. These errors create significant social costs.[63]

Eventually, the courts likely would settle upon a workable understanding of business methods and the number of difficult cases would diminish. Yet this would only return to the earlier problem: in the course of finding a common-law solution to the question of what constitutes a business method patent, there is no reason to believe that the Federal Circuit would have the ability or the inclination to evaluate the difficult economic issues involved. Indeed, there is evidence that the Federal Circuit relies even more heavily on doctrine and is even more reticent than the Supreme Court to address patent questions in economic terms.[64]

B. OTHER PATENT DOCTRINES

Bilski lays bare the courts' ultimate unsuitability in deciding the complex economic questions that underlie patent law. But the issue of patentable subject matter is hardly the only area in which the courts' shortcomings are manifest. In a number of areas, courts struggle badly with the trade-off between allowing too few patents and too many.

There are more optimistic views. In their recent book, *The Patent Crisis and How the Courts Can Solve It*, Dan Burk and Mark Lemley offer the most sustained and cogent defense to date of the role of courts in managing the patent system. Burk and Lemley advance and defend the idea, described earlier, that patents function differently across industries. Certain industries will benefit from broader patents and others from narrower ones; some from compulsory licensing and others from stronger patent remedies; some from higher barriers to patenting (utility, nonobviousness, or written description[65]) and others from lower. Burk and Lemley argue that courts already possess the tools to fine-tune the rules governing patents in various industries. They point to a variety of doctrines—"patent levers"—that courts can employ to adjust

---

[63] See Mark A. Lemley, *Rational Ignorance at the Patent Office*, 95 Nw U L Rev 1495, 1503–08 (2001); Christopher R. Leslie, *The Anticompetitive Effects of Unenforced Invalid Patents*, 91 Minn L Rev 101 (2006).

[64] See Lee, 120 Yale L J at 25–35 (cited in note 48).

[65] The more demanding the requirements of utility and nonobviousness, the fewer the patents, and the later they will be granted in the life cycle of an invention.

the power or scope of patents from industry to industry, and they argue that the federal courts have in effect already created different patent rules for different types of technology.[66]

Although Burk and Lemley's argument is nuanced and thorough, and they leave little doubt that these patent levers exist,[67] their analysis does not indicate that courts are using them properly in most circumstances. To the contrary, Burk and Lemley describe industry after industry in which the Federal Circuit has failed to select what the authors believe to be the proper rule, leading to patents that may do more harm than good.[68] After all, their book is titled *The Patent Crisis*. They obviously agree with the broad consensus that the patent system is functioning very poorly.[69]

Burk and Lemley are also forthright in admitting that scholars may disagree about the rules that should govern each of these industries.[70] They characterize the outstanding questions as difficult economic issues that remain to be resolved by experts, and quite rightly so.[71] Yet there is no reason to believe—and every reason to doubt—that courts could play that expert role. A number of recent cases have grappled with the doctrines of utility and nonobviousness in ways that could significantly alter the numbers and timing of patent grants.[72] But courts deciding those cases have little idea whether they are balancing properly between these competing concerns. In general, they hardly appear to be trying. The cases are largely bereft of any indication that economic concerns played a role in the judges' decision making; their decisions are driven by text, precedent, and other traditional legal tools.

This sketch of some of the economic questions that courts have

---

[66] See Dan L. Burk and Mark A. Lemley, *Policy Levers in Patent Law*, 89 Va L Rev 1575, 1674–75 (2003).

[67] See Burk and Lemley, *The Patent Crisis* at 109–30 (cited in note 4).

[68] See, for example, id at 116 (describing Federal Circuit misuse of person having ordinary skill in the art); id at 148–49 (describing numerous ways in which the courts have formulated poor patent policy to govern the biotechnology industry); id at 159 (stating, with respect to software patents, "[u]nfortunately, the Federal Circuit's current standard seems to be precisely backwards"); id at 160 (criticizing courts' awards of excessive damages in software cases).

[69] See generally Jaffe and Lerner, *Innovation and Its Discontents* (cited in note 4) (describing the ways in which the patent system is functioning poorly); Bessen and Meurer, *Patent Failure* (cited in note 4) (same).

[70] See Burk and Lemley, *The Patent Crisis* at 169 (cited in note 4).

[71] See id.

[72] See, for example, *KSR Intern Co. v Teleflex Inc.*, 550 US 398 (2007) (revising the standard for obviousness).

left unanswered does not even touch upon the technical and scientific issues that judges are asked to decide in the course of nearly every patent case, issues that they are equally poorly prepared to handle. In the regular course of litigation, generalist judges must determine whether a patent describes a technically complex invention sufficiently well that a person skilled in the relevant technology could recreate it, or whether an invention is obvious in light of two or more prior inventions in related fields. It is almost to state the obvious to observe that untrained judges cannot perform these tasks well. Even the Federal Circuit is little better off: of the twelve active judges on the court, only five of them had practiced or taught patent law before joining the court, only six have even undergraduate degrees in technical fields, and none has an advanced degree in economics.[73] It is thus puzzling that the Federal Circuit has managed to acquire a reputation as an expert court.

Of course, it is possible that even after sustained examination some of these patent questions will not yield economic answers. The economics of innovation are hardly straightforward. But if any institutional actor is capable of providing such answers, it is not likely to be the federal courts.

C. OBJECTIONS AND CAVEATS

1. *The judicial role.* Some scholars and judges—indeed, many members of the current Supreme Court—might sidestep the foregoing critique on the ground that it misunderstands the judicial role. On one view, deciding which inventions represent "patentable subject matter" simply involves interpreting section 101 of the Patent Act. Judges, on this account, are meant to decide questions of statutory interpretation with reference only to traditional legal materials (such as statutory text, structure, judicial precedent, and legislative history), and not economic theory or empirics.[74]

---

[73] See *Federal Circuit—Judicial Biographies*, available online at http://www.cafc.uscourts.gov/judgbios.html.

[74] See, for example, Anthony J. Bellia, *State Courts and the Interpretation of Federal Statutes*, 59 Vand L Rev 1501, 1513 (2006), quoting 1 William Blackstone, *Commentaries on the Laws of England* 59 (1765) ("The fairest and most rational method to interpret the will of the legislator, is by exploring his intentions at the time when the law was made, by signs the most natural and probable. And these signs are either the words, the context, the subject matter, the effects and consequence, or the spirit and reason of the law."); William N. Eskridge, *All About Words: Early Understandings of the "Judicial Power" in Statutory Interpretation, 1776–1806*, 101 Colum L Rev 990, 1000 (2001).

Accordingly, this story goes, a critique of judges as incapable of addressing such complex economic or technical issues misses the mark.

It may be precisely *because* courts are ill-equipped to delve into complicated economic matters that they are best advised to adhere closely to traditional legal materials when interpreting statutes. This is only a possibility; a full theory of statutory interpretation is well beyond the scope of this article. Regardless of the proper theory, however, the point is the same: there is no reason to have a patent system that does not structure incentives to promote innovation. If courts, as a matter of institutional role, should not be taking such considerations into account, then responsibility for setting baseline patent rules should be transferred to an institution that can address such questions.

2. *The uniqueness of patent law?* If the foregoing argument regarding the comparative disadvantage of courts is correct, it raises a separate issue: why should it apply only to patent law? Many if not all common-law doctrines—such as the judge-made elements of contract and tort law—produce significant economic consequences. Courts may be unable to address competently the economic issues presented by, for instance, the choice between negligence and strict liability in tort, or various treatments of liquidated damages clauses in contract. Early law and economics scholarship maintained that the common law would naturally evolve toward efficient rules,[75] but that theory remains unsupported.[76]

Some readers might recoil against any argument suggesting that classic common-law fields are better handled by institutions other than courts. Even if that reaction turns out to be correct, however, it would not necessarily defeat the argument presented here. There are several reasons to believe that judges are especially ill-suited to setting the rules of patent law.

First of all, the existing rules of patent law have been roundly criticized, and to a degree currently unequaled within the common

---

[75] See Posner, *Economic Analysis of the Law* at 249–50 (cited in note 56).

[76] See Paul H. Rubin, *Why Is the Common Law Efficient?* 6 J Legal Stud 51, 61–63 (1977) (criticizing the notion that the common law necessarily evolves toward efficiency and offering a more realistic account of legal change); Nicola Gennaioli and Andrei Shleifer, *Overruling and the Instability of the Law*, 35 J Comp Econ 309, 323–25 (2007) (arguing that overruling precedent leads to instability and prevents the common law from evolving toward efficiency).

law.[77] If judges appear to be performing adequately, there seems little reason to reallocate responsibilities. The indictment of judges as stewards of the patent law is driven by the fact that patent law seems to have strayed far from its optimal course.

Second, the economic questions underlying patent law may simply be more difficult for judges than those involved in typical common-law rules. According to Richard Posner, "Many common law doctrines are economically sensible but not economically subtle. . . . Their articulation in economic terms is beyond the capacity of most judges and lawyers, but their intuition is not."[78] (Posner contrasts common-law doctrines with antitrust law, which he argues has been handled inadequately by judges.[79]) In addition, patent law requires navigating an additional layer of technical complexity above and beyond the selection of an economically efficient rule. Even if it is equally difficult for a court to judge the economic consequences of allowing patents on gene sequences and deciding tort liability on a negligence standard, a court must attempt the former while simultaneously grappling with the technical specifics of gene sequences and the question of how they are different from other types of biotechnology.[80]

Another possible reason lies with the objectives embodied in these areas of law. While contract and tort law may seek to balance a variety of consequentialist and deontological considerations—welfare maximization, efficiency, fairness, distributive justice, and so on[81]—the objectives of patent law are potentially more straight-

---

[77] See, for example, Burk and Lemley, *The Patent Crisis* at 21 (cited in note 4) (cataloging the various criticisms directed at patent law); Jaffe and Lerner, *Innovation and Its Discontents* (cited in note 4) (same); Bessen and Meurer, *Patent Failure* (cited in note 4) (same).

[78] Posner, *Economic Analysis of Law* at 252 (cited in note 56).

[79] See id at 300 (stating that the courts' "touch has been less sure in antitrust cases than in common law cases").

[80] Of course, some tort cases might also involve technical questions that are difficult for nonexperts. The point here is again comparative: patent cases will raise these types of issues on a much more frequent basis than typical common-law cases.

[81] See, for example, Eyal Zamir and Barak Medina, *Law, Morality, and Economics: Integrating Moral Constraints with Economic Analysis of Law*, 96 Cal L Rev 323, 388 (2008) ("The extent to which existing contract law deviates from the efficient breach doctrine by 'excessively' deterring breaches may reflect a deontological constraint against promise breaking."); Jody S. Kraus, *Transparency and Determinacy in Common Law Adjudication: A Philosophical Defense of Explanatory Economic Analysis*, 93 Va L Rev 287, 322–23 (2007) ("[T]ort law in fact cognizes claims in corrective justice for the violation of a type of individual duty which cannot be reconstructed in consequentialist terms and so cannot be accounted for by the economic analysis of tort law. These duties are ones that are necessarily correlative to individual rights and so allow a plaintiff to claim compensation only

forward. As I note above, patent law appears to involve only consequentialist, economic considerations.[82] If courts are particularly
adept at achieving fairness or justice, that may be a reason to
continue delegating contract and tort cases to them irrespective
of their economic shortcomings. But if those types of deontological considerations are not present in patent law, the argument for
vesting the power to make rules with a more expert technocratic
body is strengthened.

Finally, institutions other than the judiciary have already intervened significantly in typical common-law fields. State legislatures
frequently pass laws governing contracts, torts, and property.[83] A
substantial number of states have adopted the Uniform Commercial Code, a model law drafted by a panel of experts, though
not precisely an administrative agency.[84] States have also borrowed
liberally from the Uniform Electronic Transaction Act and other
similar model codes drafted by expert institutions.[85] An even more
extreme example is criminal law, frequently thought of as a com-

---

from the individual who violated the plaintiff's right."); Kenneth W. Simons, *The Hand
Formula in the Draft Restatement (Third) of Torts: Encompassing Fairness as Well as Efficiency
Values*, 54 Vand L Rev 901, 908 (2001) ("A balancing approach to negligence that explicitly
considers tradeoffs can indeed accommodate an economic efficiency approach. As we shall
see, however, it can also accommodate broader social welfare and nonutilitarian approaches, though these other approaches will trade off different competing interests and
values, or will trade them off differently.").

[82] See Burk and Lemley, *The Patent Crisis* at 66 (cited in note 4); Michael Abramowicz,
The Uneasy Case for Patent Races Over Auctions, 60 Stan L Rev 803, 809–10 (2007) ("This
trade-off between static and dynamic efficiency is familiar to patent scholarship."); Note,
*Limiting the Anticompetitive Prerogative of Patent Owners: Predatory Standards in Patent Li-
censing*, 92 Yale L J 831, 836 (1983) ("The patent system that Congress created reflects a
tradeoff between dynamic and static efficiency."); Chisum et al, *Principles of Patent Law* at
6 (cited in note 13); Merges and Duffy, *Patent Law and Policy* at 253–56 (cited in note 13)
(describing the incentive systems meant to drive the patent law).

[83] See, for example, 735 Ill Ann Stat § 2-1207 (Smith-Hurd) (allowing judges to apportion punitive damages to the Department of Human Services); NY Pers Prop Law §
252(1) (McKinney) (creating a duty to return found property valued above twenty dollars
to the police); Or Rev Stat § 646.557 (West) (requiring specific disclosures by telephonic
sellers in Oregon).

[84] See, for example, Ariz Rev Stat Ann § 47-9315 (West) (UCC § 9-315 (ALI 1999));
Ohio Rev Code Ann § 1302.10 (Baldwin) (UCC § 2-207 (ALI 1961)). All fifty states have
adopted some form of the UCC. See Richard B. Amandes, *The Uniform Land Transactions
Act and the Uniform Simplification of Land Transfers Act Twenty Years Later: Why Have There
Been No Adoptions?* 20 Nova L Rev 1033, 1034 (1996).

[85] The Uniform Electronic Transaction Act (NCCUSL 1999) has been adopted in forty-
seven states. A complete list is posted online at http://www.ncsl.org/IssuesResearch/
TelecommunicationsInformationTechnology/UniformElectronicTransactionsActs/tabid/
13484/Default.aspx. The Uniform Trade Secrets Act (NCCUSL 1986) has been adopted
by forty-six states. See, for example, The Uniform Trade Secrets Act, Cal Civil Code §
3426 et seq (Deering); 12 Pa Cons Stat Ann § 5301 et seq (Purdon).

mon-law field but actually dominated by statutes and administrative rules. Nearly every crime is delineated by a statute.[86] In many states those statutes are based in whole or in part upon the Model Penal Code, another model statute drafted by a panel of criminal law experts. Sentencing decisions, long the province of the judiciary, had been placed largely under the control of administrative sentencing commissions at both the federal and state levels until the Supreme Court struck down the arrangement.[87] Even so, sentencing statutes still matter and sentencing guidelines can still be used for guidance.

Patent law is thus striking for the confluence of an overmatched judiciary and an absent legislature. It has been more than fifty years since Congress substantially revised the Patent Act, and the types of patents granted now bear little resemblance to those that existed in 1952. There are few areas of law, traditional common-law fields included, that have involved less extrajudicial management in the past half century. Patent law has suffered as a result.

II. EXPLAINING THE PTO's PUZZLING LACK OF AUTHORITY

If judges are ill-equipped to manage patent policy, why has Congress not delegated substantive rule-making authority to the PTO, as it has to so many other administrative agencies? Patent law is one of the few areas of federal law that receives no meaningful input from an administrative agency. With the exception of the length of the patent term, a single core issue over which Congress has maintained authority, Congress has effectively handed full control over the patent system to the Federal Circuit. Congress has, on occasion, considered vesting the PTO with the power to make substantive patent rules, but authorizing legislation has never made it out of either House. In this part, I consider several possible explanations. The objective is both positive and normative. If Congress has refrained from delegating authority to the PTO for some intelligible reason, that might cast doubt on the wisdom or likelihood of future action. However, I conclude that the most likely

---

[86] Most states do not allow courts to create new crimes, see, for example, 18 Pa Cons Stat Ann § 107(b) (Purdon), though a few still do, see Fla Stat § 775.01. Similarly, federal judges are not permitted to create new federal crimes via common law. See *U.S. v Hudson & Goodwin*, 1 US (7 Cranch) 32 (1812).

[87] See *Blakely v Washington*, 542 US 296, 305 (2004); *U.S. v Booker*, 543 US 220, 226 (2005).

explanation is the least satisfying one: the PTO's lack of authority is likely a historical accident.

A. RENT-SEEKING

It is conceivable that Congress has failed to grant the PTO substantive rule-making authority due to a desire to continue collecting rents from interest groups concerned with changes in patent law.[88] On this theory, these interest groups would direct their lobbying efforts at the PTO if that body possessed substantive authority, and hence campaign contributions to Congress would diminish.

As an initial matter, theory seems to have very little general explanatory power, regardless of context. One could ask why Congress ever delegates authority, if delegating means sacrificing the opportunity to collect rents. Equally and oppositely, one could ask why Congress would be sacrificing any opportunity by delegating if it could simply threaten to change the law or reclaim power at a moment's notice. There is little indication that a theory of rent-seeking could explain Congress's pattern of delegation or non-delegation in any set of contexts, much less this one in particular. The theory is essentially nonfalsifiable.

Here, moreover, the evidence against the rent-seeking explanation is even stronger. In the context of patent law, Congress has evinced comparatively little interest in collecting rents. Congress adjusts the patent law very rarely—the only significant amendment to the Patent Act since 1952 was the Hatch-Waxman Act.[89] Nor has Congress shown any particular interest in "rattling the cages" of its patent constituencies: patent reform bills rarely make it out of committee. It is thus hard to imagine that Congress has refrained from granting rule-making authority to the PTO in order

---

[88] See Richard L. Hasen, *Clipping Coupons for Democracy: An Egalitarian/Public Choice Defense of Campaign Finance Vouchers*, 84 Cal L Rev 1, 10 (1996); Nathaniel O. Keohane, Richard L. Revesz, and Robert N. Stavins, *The Choice of Regulatory Instruments in Environmental Policy*, 22 Harv Envir L Rev 313, 323 (1998), citing Jose Edgardo L. Campos, *Legislative Institutions, Lobbying, and the Endogenous Choice of Regulatory Instruments: A Political Economy Approach to Instrument Choice*, 5 J L Econ & Org 333, 348–49 (1989) ("[T]he choice of regulatory instrument is the equilibrium of a game between interest groups (who choose how much to allocate to lobbying in support of their preferred instrument) and legislators (who vote for the instrument that maximizes their support, taking into account the contributions from the interest groups.").

[89] Drug Price Competition and Patent Term Restoration Act, Pub L No 98-417, 98 Stat 1585 (1984).

to maximize its rent-seeking opportunities. Of course, this would not be a normatively defensible rationale for withholding rule-making power, anyway, even if it were a descriptively accurate one.

B. PROPERTY RIGHTS

Another potential explanation for congressional inaction is the nature of the rights that the PTO confers. Congress might believe that the patent system should be governed by a different set of rules than other regulatory areas because patents are property rights, and thus potentially more valuable or harmful than the standard subjects of regulation.[90]

Yet there is nothing talismanic about the notion of property. Whether or not patents are in fact "property" in the traditional sense—and there is considerable debate on this point[91]—does not change the set of rights and entitlements they convey. Patents are alienable, tradable rights to exclude other parties from making, using, or selling a particular invention—nothing more and nothing less. In a variety of other contexts, Congress has delegated authority to administrative agencies to issue permits or award rights that may be equally valuable (or equally harmful). For instance, the Environmental Protection Agency (EPA) issues permits that authorize firms to pollute, and the FCC awards broadcast licenses to firms that allow them to operate radio and television stations (to name just two of many possible examples). These permits are not necessarily property rights or rights to exclude per se, but they have many of the same effects. They convey private benefits and (in many cases) negative externalities, and they offer business advantages to the firms that possess them.[92] Under some conditions these types of permits can be as valuable as formal property rights to the firms that possess them, and equally socially wasteful if they are allocated improperly.

---

[90] For a sample of scholars who believe patent rights are property in the classical sense, see Adam Mossoff, *The Use and Abuse of IP at the Birth of the Administrative State*, 157 U Pa L Rev 2001, 2014 (2009) (describing patents as property rights); Epstein, 62 Stan L Rev at 455, 520–21 (cited in note 45) (same).

[91] Burk and Lemley, *The Patent Crisis* at viii (cited in note 4).

[92] In some cases, these permits do function as rights to exclude. For instance, if pollution is an essential by-product of a particular business, and if a limited number of pollution permits are available, a permit to pollute may function effectively as a right to exclude. Similarly, if there are only a limited number of broadcast licenses available in a particular market, a broadcast license is effectively a right to exclude.

Moreover, administrative agencies frequently make rules governing classical property rights of other types. For instance, in many localities zoning boards have extensive authority to determine how private parties may use real property. Environmental laws also often have substantial effects on property usage.[93] It would be peculiar to argue that zoning boards should be abolished simply because property rules should never be determined by administrative agencies. At bottom, there is very little that differentiates regulation of property (if that is indeed what patents are) from the regulation of any other area of private behavior. As in any area, the institution charged with regulating should be the one best positioned to create productive incentives and minimize externalities and social costs. There is no reason to believe that the label of "property" is determinative of which institution that is.

C. STATUTORY VAGUENESS

The Patent Act sets the boundaries of what inventions are patentable in very general terms. Any "new and useful process, machine, manufacture, or composition of matter" can be patented, provided that no other inventor has beaten the patentee to the invention.[94] This lack of specificity affords an interpreter a variety of possibilities for including or excluding various classes of inventions or discoveries that are not obviously addressed by the plain terms of the act itself. Perhaps Congress has shied away from granting substantive rule-making authority to the PTO because it fears that the agency will take undue liberties with such a vague statutory grant—and for some reason this fear is less serious with respect to the Federal Circuit.[95]

At the outset, it is difficult to understand as a policy matter why Congress would be reluctant to delegate a broad swath of authority to an agency (rather than the Federal Circuit) absent some independent substantive or procedural concern about how the agency might use that authority. If an agency is superior to a court

---

[93] See, for example, Lior Jacob Strahilevitz, *Informational Asymmetries and the Rights to Exclude*, 104 Mich L Rev 1835, 1843 (2006) (describing "zoning laws and environmental regulations" as typical land use governance mechanisms).

[94] 35 USC §§ 101 & 102.

[95] Compare *Industrial Union Department, AFL-CIO v American Petroleum Institute*, 448 US 607 (1980).

at managing smaller regulatory responsibilities, it is not clear why the agency would not be similarly superior at handling larger responsibilities. In fact, the broader the grant of authority from Congress, the more that the exercise of delegated power will resemble genuine policymaking, as opposed to mere implementation of the law. The procedural and structural advantages (described below) that agencies possess in comparison to courts are most significant when deployed in the formulation of policy, rather than the mere execution of it.

Moreover, the Patent Act is no broader or less well defined than a panoply of administrative statutes under which agencies currently regulate. For instance, the Occupational Health and Safety Act instructs the Occupational Safety and Health Administration (OSHA) to adopt regulations of all potential workplace hazards "which most adequately assure[], to the extent feasible . . . that no employee will suffer material impairment of health or functional capacity."[96] The regulations adopted must be "reasonably necessary or appropriate to provide safe or healthful employment and places of employment."[97] The Clean Air Act authorizes the EPA to regulate "any air pollutant."[98] And the Endangered Species Act makes it illegal to "harass [or] harm" any endangered animal.[99] Based on this language the Secretary of the Interior successfully asserted authority to prohibit modifications to those animals' habitats.[100] The notion that statutory vagueness could provide a rationale for refusing to delegate to an agency fails not only as a matter of logic, but as a matter of historical practice as well.

D. PTO EXPERTISE

A number of scholars have suggested that the PTO cannot be trusted to employ substantive rule-making authority competently, even if Congress were to repose it in the agency.[101] These scholars

---

[96] 29 USC § 655(b)(5).

[97] 29 USC § 652(8).

[98] 42 USC § 7521(a)(1).

[99] 16 USC § 1532(19).

[100] See *Babbitt v Sweet Home Chapter of Communities for a Great Oregon*, 515 US 687, 700 (1995).

[101] See Rochelle Dreyfuss, *Pathological Patenting: The PTO as Cause or Cure*, 104 Mich L Rev 1559, 1575–78 (2004); Arti Rai, *Engaging Facts and Policy: A Multi-Institutional Approach to Patent System Reform*, 103 Colum L Rev 1035, 1132–33 (2003); John R.

point out that the PTO has been roundly criticized for lackluster performance of its current task of examining patents. They note as well that the PTO traditionally has had no policy or economic staff, though it has recently hired a chief economist.[102] By these measures, the PTO appears far from prepared to assume any sort of meaningful substantive authority.

But this argument does not account for the fact that the PTO is a creature of its circumstances. In any administrative agency—indeed, in any organization—form follows function. The PTO can hardly be expected to assemble an economic staff if that staff would play no meaningful role, limited to releasing guidance documents to which the Federal Circuit would not defer. The PTO operates under conditions of limited resources; it would be folly for the organization to expend resources on extraneous staff and activities at the expense of its core mission of examination. This is not to say that it would be costless for the PTO to assemble a full policymaking staff and transform itself into a regulatory entity along the lines of EPA or OSHA. There would be significant transition costs, among them the hiring of staff and the restructuring of the office to emphasize the collection and transmission of information from patent examination. But this cost should be no greater than the costs borne by any other administrative agency, costs which hardly hindered their creation.[103]

Furthermore, the current system supplies the PTO with ample incentives to deliberately grant too many invalid patents. The PTO is funded entirely by the fees that it generates from examining patents,[104] and thus the organization benefits when it can induce private actors to file for patents in ever greater numbers. In addition, only applicants who have been denied patents can ever appeal to the Federal Circuit; if the PTO grants a patent, the matter is over. Accordingly, the PTO has an incentive to err on the side of granting too many patents in order to avoid appeals and reversals.[105] Yet these problems are hardly of the PTO's own

Thomas, *The Responsibility of the Rulemaker: Comparative Approaches to Patent Administration Reform*, 17 Berkeley Tech L J 727, 742 (2002).

[102] See Arti K. Rai, *Growing Pains in the Administrative State: The Patent Office's Troubled Quest for Managerial Control*, 157 U Pa L Rev 2051, 2054 (2009).

[103] See Part III.

[104] See Rai, 157 U Pa L Rev at 2057 & n 24 (cited in note 102).

[105] See generally Jonathan S. Masur, *Patent Inflation* (U of Chicago, Public Law Working Paper No 316, U of Chicago Law & Economics, Olin Working Paper No 529), online at http://www.ssrn.com/abstract_id=1623929.

making. It is Congress that sets the agency's funding, and Congress that created one-way incentives for the agency to grant patents. Endowing the PTO with substantive authority would likely alleviate these shortcomings, not exacerbate them.[106]

There is little wrong with the patent office as a regulatory body that time and resources cannot cure.[107] The relatively minor investments necessary provide no rationale for eschewing the institutional and structural advantages that a regulatory agency could supply.

E. PTO CAPTURE

Finally, it is possible that Congress has shied away from granting substantive rule-making authority to the PTO for fear that the agency will be captured by private interests. A number of scholars have voiced similar concerns, in some cases claiming that the PTO has already been captured, despite its currently limited role.[108] Courts are generally thought to be more resistant to capture,[109] and Congress might have delegated primary policymaking authority to the Federal Circuit (rather than the PTO) for this reason.

This is a reasonable argument in favor of trusting courts, rather than an agency, but it is no stronger in the context of the PTO and patent law than it is with respect to the EPA and environmental law, or the Department of Labor and workplace safety law, or any of the other myriad areas of regulation that have come to be dominated by agency rule making.[110] There is no reason to believe that the PTO is particularly susceptible to capture or likely to cause particular harm if captured. Indeed, even critics of the PTO have suggested that it may be *less* vulnerable to capture than the

---

[106] See Part III.B.1.

[107] It is worth noting that the Federal Circuit has failed to develop meaningful expertise despite being endowed with resources typical to an appellate court since 1982.

[108] See Burk and Lemley, *The Patent Crisis* at 106–07 (cited in note 4) (arguing that the PTO is subject to capture); Michael J. Meurer, *Patent Examination Priorities*, 51 Wm & Mary L Rev 675, 686 (2009) (same); Long, 157 U Pa L Rev at 1984 (cited in note 3) (suggesting that the PTO has invited capture in order to increase its own stature); R. Polk Wagner, *Understanding Patent Quality Mechanisms* 25 (Jan 6, 2009), online at http://www.ftc.gov/bc/workshops/ipmarketplace/apr17/docs/rwagner2.pdf (suggesting the influence that repeat players can have on PTO behavior).

[109] See Burk and Lemley, *The Patent Crisis* at 106–07 (cited in note 4).

[110] See Part III.

typical administrative agency.[111] At the same time, other scholars have argued that the Federal Circuit itself may have been captured by private interests.[112] As with the issue of agency expertise, I develop the capture analysis further in Part III.

The foregoing discussion was principally normative, but there is a related positive possibility that is worth considering. It is entirely possible that Congress has refrained from delegating substantive authority to the PTO because of various interest-group forces (or a lack thereof). It may be that powerful patent interest groups are united in preferring the status quo to a shift in regulatory authority even though they disagree about the substantive content of patent law. Or it may be that Congress has had little incentive to change the law absent strong private preferences. It is impossible to rule out these possibilities, though there is no particular evidence in support. But it is worth noting that they are not normative arguments against vesting regulatory authority in the PTO. If interest-group dynamics have prevented Congress from reallocating powers, that might indicate that any proposal for reform is unlikely to succeed. (I return to this point in greater detail below.) But it is not a reason for disfavoring that reform.

F. PATH DEPENDENCE

What then is left to explain the patent office's puzzling deficiency of substantive authority? The most likely remaining possibility is the least satisfying if the objective is crafting sound patent policy. The fact that Congress has never vested the PTO with substantive rule-making power may be nothing more than a historical accident—a path-dependent relic of early American government.

The vast majority of administrative agencies that possess regulatory authority were created during the New Deal era or later. For instance, Congress created the EPA and OSHA in 1970;[113] the Securities and Exchange Commission (SEC) and National La-

---

[111] See Burk and Lemley, 89 Va L Rev at 1640 and n 226 (cited in note 66).

[112] See John R. Thomas, *Formalism at the Federal Circuit*, 52 Am U L Rev 771, 792–94 (2003).

[113] See Occupational Safety and Health Act of 1970, Pub L No 91-596, 84 Stat 1590 (1970); Jack Lewis, *The Birth of EPA*, EPA J (1985), online at http://www.epa.gov/history/topics/epa/15c.htm. The so-called EPA Reorganization Plan Number 3, dated July 9, 1970, can be found in the *Congressional Record*, Vol 116, H 6523, 91st Cong, 2d Sess.

bor Relations Board (NLRB) in 1934;[114] and the Food and Drug Administration (FDA) in 1930, though it only assumed its modern form in 1938.[115] These agencies were born during the modern era of technocratic bureaucracy. The rapid growth of the American economy, coupled with increasing faith in the scientific and policy judgments of experts, led Congress to assign vast swaths of regulatory authority to executive-branch agencies as it came to realize that it could not adequately manage the economy on its own accord.[116] The powers held by these agencies are very much a product of the time they came into existence.

By contrast, the first Patent Act was passed in 1790,[117] and the Patent and Trademark Office was created in 1836.[118] In the much smaller and economically less complex United States of that period, regulatory agencies (as we understand them today) were essentially unknown.[119] Congress and the courts were then the major engines of national policymaking, and an extensive federal common law of patents has developed in the two centuries since. Accordingly, in the modern era there has never been a moment at which patent law was in need of wholesale development. Patent law, however flawed it may be, has always existed in common-law form. This is unlike, for instance, environmental law and food and drug law, which sprang into existence at the federal level nearly coextensively with the EPA and FDA, respectively.

Of course, Congress could have later recognized the inadequacies of the Federal Circuit and redistributed authority to the PTO. But this type of reallocation of institutional control is extremely rare. Congress's creation of the United States Sentencing Commission may be the only significant instance in which Congress has delegated power previously held by the judiciary to an administrative agency.[120] Where judicially made rules already exist,

---

[114] Securities Exchange Act of 1934, Pub L No 73-291, 48 Stat 881 (enacted June 6, 1934), codified at 15 USC § 78a et seq.

[115] Food, Drug and Cosmetic Act, 21 USC § 301 et seq.

[116] See generally Stephen G. Breyer et al, *Administrative Law and Regulatory Policy* 14–29 (Aspen, 6th ed 2006).

[117] Act of April 10, 1790, 1 Stat 109. A pdf is available online at http://www.ipmall.info/hosted_resources/lipa/patents/Patent_Act_of_1790.pdf.

[118] Patent Act of 1836, ch 357, 5 Stat 117, online at http://www.ipmall.info/hosted_resources/lipa/patents/Patent_Act_of_1836.pdf.

[119] See generally Breyer et al, *Administrative Law* at 14–15 (cited in note 116).

[120] See Sentencing Reform Act of 1984, Pub L No 98-473 § 212, 98 Stat 1987 (1984).

Congress very rarely revisits delegations of authority.[121] With the federal courts firmly ensconced as the expositors of patent law, Congress may not have understood the need for another institutional actor to play a role in the formation of patent policy.

It is beyond the scope of this article to conduct a full analysis of the relationship between regulatory authority and the year an agency was formed, and the examples proffered here are by no means conclusive proof of that relationship. But they suggest a strong role for happenstance and inertia in the institutional assignment of policy responsibilities, one that may have been determinative in the case of the PTO. At the same time, this might indicate that Congress is unlikely to take action in the future if it did not do so in the past. This is a problem for all proposals for legal reform, and one that I address below.

III. Administrative Authority

In light of the courts' failings, this part suggests that Congress should consider delegating substantive rule-making authority to the PTO.[122] That is not to suggest that the federal courts would

---

[121] Congress frequently provides existing agencies with additional authority. And on some occasions Congress will bestow substantive rule-making power on an agency that did not previously possess it, but only with respect to newly created federal law. For instance, in 1991 the Americans with Disabilities Act granted the Equal Employment Opportunity Commission rule-making authority regarding discrimination on the basis of disability. See 42 USC § 12117 (West 2011). But it did not give the EEOC rule-making authority over previously existing federal law. Other than the creation of the Sentencing Commission, I have not been able to locate an instance in which Congress granted an agency power to make rules concerning an extant body of federal law that had previously been controlled by the courts, but it is possible that one or more exists. (For that matter, I was also unable to find any area of law in which Congress has dissolved an agency with substantive rule-making authority and returned the federal courts to a position of singular authority over the law.)

[122] I mean to distinguish this from the thoughtful suggestion, offered by some commentators, that the PTO be afforded *Chevron* deference when it examines patents. See, for example, Stuart Minor Benjamin and Arti K. Rai, *Who's Afraid of the APA? What the Patent System Can Learn from Administrative Law*, 95 Georgetown L J 269, 297–98 (2007); Dreyfuss, 104 Mich L Rev at 1577 (cited in note 101) ("Congress should expressly instruct courts to afford the PTO the deference given to federal agencies generally."). This kind of *Chevron* deference is probably a good idea, but it would be largely limited to protecting PTO examination decisions and according its ad hoc views some modicum of respect. It would not make the PTO into the primary patent policymaker. Accordingly, it is notable that proponents of *Chevron* deference oppose—or at least stop short of supporting— delegating substantive rule-making power to the PTO. See Rai, 103 Colum L Rev at 1132–33 (cited in note 101) ("Moreover, there are reasons to be wary about granting the PTO substantive rulemaking authority."); Dreyfuss, 104 Mich L Rev at 1577 (cited in note 101) (treating the PTO's "absence of explicit rulemaking authority" as fixed). Rai and Dreyfuss's work is impressive and important, but it does not go as far as the argument advanced here.

have no role in patent policy. They would still be involved in overseeing the PTO's regulatory actions, adjudicating infringement actions and appeals from the PTO, and making policy where the PTO has not yet acted. In short, they would play the same role as the federal courts currently do in environmental law, securities law, and many other areas of federal regulation.

The literature on congressional delegation is replete with analyses of the strengths and weaknesses of courts and agencies as potential recipients of legal and policy authority.[123] Indeed, this question encapsulates the *Chevron* inquiry—to what extent courts should defer to an agency's statutory interpretation—and all of its attendant intellectual baggage.[124] Arguments regarding the choice of institutional actor have coalesced around the following finite set of issues: comparative expertise,[125] responsiveness to public opinion,[126]

---

[123] See generally Matthew C. Stephenson, *Legislative Allocation of Delegated Power: Uncertainty, Risk, and the Choice Between Agencies and Courts*, 119 Harv L Rev 1036 (2006); Frank B. Cross, *Shattering the Fragile Case for Judicial Review of Rulemaking*, 85 Va L Rev 1243 (1999) (arguing for the complete abandonment of judicial review of agency rule making); Cynthia R. Farina, *Statutory Interpretation and the Balance of Power in the Administrative State*, 89 Colum L Rev 452 (1989) (arguing that judicial deference to agencies is unconstitutional); Cass R. Sunstein, *On the Costs and Benefits of Aggressive Judicial Review of Agency Action*, 1989 Duke L J 522 (1989) (evaluating the costs and benefits of courts as legal authority); Colin S. Diver, *Statutory Interpretation in the Administrative State*, 133 U Pa L Rev 549 (1985) (concluding that courts should defer to agencies where Congress has endowed the agency with significant policymaking responsibility); F. Scott Kieff, *The Case for Preferring Patent-Validity Litigation Over Second-Window Review and Gold-Plated Patents: When One Size Doesn't Fit All, How Could Two Do the Trick?* 157 U Pa L Rev 1937, 1943–45 (2009) (cataloging the strengths and weaknesses of agencies with particular reference to the patent context).

[124] *Chevron USA, Inc. v Natural Res. Def. Council, Inc.*, 467 US 837 (1984). See generally Linda Jellum, *Chevron's Demise: A Survey of Chevron from Infancy to Senescence*, 59 Admin L Rev 725 (2007) (analyzing the first prong of the *Chevron* test); Evan J. Criddle, *Chevron's Consensus*, 88 BU L Rev 1271 (2008) (synthesizing the various *Chevron* rationales and proposing a new rationale); Cass R. Sunstein, *Law and Administration after Chevron*, 90 Colum L Rev 2071 (1990) (examining the rationale and reach of *Chevron*); Thomas W. Merrill and Kristin E. Hickman, *Chevron's Domain*, 89 Georgetown L J 833 (2001) (analyzing the scope of the *Chevron* doctrine).

[125] See, for example, Ronald J. Krotoszynski, Jr., *Why Deference? Implied Delegations, Agency Expertise, and the Misplaced Legacy of Skidmore*, 54 Admin L Rev 735, 737 (2002) (arguing that administrative expertise provides the best rationale for judicial deference to administrative agencies). See also Einer Elhauge, *Preference-Estimating Statutory Default Rules*, 102 Colum L Rev 2027, 2135 (2002) ("The legal realists' hope that legal ambiguities could be resolved by objective policy expertise has long ago grown quaint. . . . In practice, it is rare to find a field of social policy where there are not experts on opposing sides of an issue, . . . undermining any claim to an objective expert resolution.").

[126] See, for example, William N. Eskridge, Jr. and Kevin S. Schwartz, *Chevron and Agency Norm-Entrepreneurship*, 115 Yale L J 2623, 2626 (2006) (arguing that agencies are more democratically accountable than judges); Cass R. Sunstein, *Beyond Marbury: The Executive's Power to Say What the Law Is*, 115 Yale L J 2580, 2587 (2006) (noting the executive branch's

procedural advantages,[127] and political insulation and susceptibility to capture.[128] However, these various arguments have hardly produced agreement. Perhaps the most that can be said is that there are some circumstances under which delegations to agencies will be superior, and others under which delegations to courts will produce better outcomes.

I endeavor here to avoid wading into that analytical mire. Rather, this part aims to demonstrate that the affirmative case for delegating substantive rule-making authority over the law of patents to the PTO is at least as strong, if not stronger, than the typical case for administrative delegation; and that the drawbacks to delegating rule-making authority to the PTO are no more significant, and likely less so, than in the typical administrative case.

My point is not that the current allocation of powers between courts, Congress, the president, and federal agencies (other than the PTO) is ideal. It may be that some agencies should be stripped of their authority with the power returned to the courts; it may be that agencies should be afforded even greater power. One can easily name administrative agencies that most likely should be disbanded immediately.[129] It is well beyond the scope of this article to defend the status quo fully. Rather, I mean to argue that if one accepts the status quo as reasonably approximating when delegation is appropriate or desirable, the case for delegation to the PTO is compelling.

This part proceeds in two sections. The first section analyzes the PTO's capacity to effectively implement substantive regulations according to standard administrative law metrics. The second section describes a set of particular advantages that rule-making authority would provide for the patent system. The patent system faces a

political responsiveness and accountability); Charles H. Koch, Jr., *Judicial Review of Administrative Discretion*, 54 Geo Wash L Rev 469, 485 (1986) (arguing that agencies are better than courts at distilling public opinion).

[127] See, for example, Richard J. Pierce, Jr., *Reconciling Chevron and Stare Decisis*, 85 Georgetown L J 2225, 2239 (1997) (noting the superiority of the notice and comment procedure over judicial decision-making procedures); Diver, 133 U Pa L Rev at 575 (cited in note 123) (noting that agency members are often involved in creating legislation, and therefore have a better understanding of legislative intent).

[128] See, for example, Jonathon T. Molot, *Reexamining Marbury in the Administrative State: A Structural and Institutional Defense of Judicial Power over Statutory Interpretation*, 96 Nw U L Rev 1239, 1276 (2002) (arguing that judicial power is superior for its political insulation); Thomas W. Merrill, *Capture Theory and the Courts*, 72 Chi Kent L Rev 1039, 1054 (1997) (discussing the role of public choice in deciding between institutional actors).

[129] See, for example, Ian Urbina, *Inspector General's Inquiry Faults Regulators*, NY Times (May 24, 2010), online at http://www.nytimes.com/2010/05/25/us/25mms.html (describing the failings of the Minerals Management Service).

unique set of institutional problems, but the solution lies with a familiar tool of administrative policymaking.

A. COMPARATIVE INSTITUTIONAL COMPETENCE

1. *Expertise.* That agencies possess greater technical expertise than courts and are better positioned to address scientifically complex questions is by now a shibboleth of administrative theory. Judges are legal generalists, unskilled in the policy nuances of the cases that come before them;[130] agencies are staffed by economists and experts in the substantive field[131] who have the benefit of years of education, training, and experience.[132] Moreover, agencies have substantial budgets with which they can research particular problems in depth,[133] while courts must rely upon amicus briefs and the rare appointment of a special master.[134]

This is the conventional wisdom, and it holds true for the PTO as much as for the typical agency. Even low-level employees in the PTO are experts in their technical fields. Patent examiners are divided by technical specialty (certain examiners scrutinize only

---

[130] See Sheila Jasanoff, *Science at the Bar: Law, Science, and Technology in America* 43 (1997) ("[L]egal institutions and procedures for dealing with technical evidence have remained remarkably static. Most U.S. judges are still generalists, without any special schooling in the sciences, and practices such as random assignment of cases prevent judicial specialization in areas requiring technical knowledge."); David L. Schwartz, *Practice Makes Perfect? An Empirical Study of Claim Construction Reversal Rates in Patent Cases,* 107 Mich L Rev 223 (2008) (describing the problems that district judges face in performing claim construction).

[131] Along with deadwood, incompetents, zealots, turf warriors, cronies, sycophants, and overconfident experts. See William N. Eskridge, Jr., *No Frills Textualism,* 119 Harv L Rev 2041, 2058–61 (2006). The point is not that agencies are models for ideal governance, but that they include *at least some* technical experts, to a greater extent than courts. I thank Adam Samaha for this point.

[132] See Rai, 103 Colum L Rev at 1069 (cited in note 101) (noting the abundant resources of the PTO as compared to the district courts and Federal Circuit; in biotechnology, for example, the PTO employs 150 people with Ph.D.'s); Benjamin and Rai, 95 Georgetown L J at 310 (cited in note 122) (discussing the institutional advantages of administrative agencies over courts, including abundant resources).

[133] For instance, the budget for all federal agencies combined was $1.174 trillion in 2010. See Office of Mgmt and Budget, Budget of the U.S. Government: Fiscal Year 2010 at 28, online at http://www.whitehouse.gov/omb/budget/fy2010/assets/summary.pdf.

[134] See Paul R. Michel, *Introduction—The Challenge Ahead: Increasing Predictability in Federal Circuit Jurisprudence for the New Century,* 43 Am U L Rev 1231, 1244 (1994) (discussing the limited resources of the court); Adrian Vermeule, *Should We Have Lay Justices?* 59 Stan L Rev 1569, 1601 (2007) (same); see also Michael Rustad and Thomas Koenig, *The Supreme Court and Junk Social Science: Selective Distortion in Amicus Briefs,* 72 NC L Rev 91, 128 (1993) (examining the distorted nature of Supreme Court amicus briefs).

biotechnology patents, certain work only on semiconductor patents, and so forth), and each examiner must have at least a bachelor's degree in the relevant field.[135] In the course of her training
and employment, each examiner also becomes proficient in the
details of patent law. In addition, PTO examiners benefit from
the sheer volume of applications. The typical examiner reviews
dozens of patent applications in a typical year, all falling within
the same technological field.[136] Consequently, the examiner is afforded a representative snapshot of both developments in technology and developments in patenting practices; the lowly examiner is most likely expert in contemporary trends in patent
writing and prosecuting.[137] And these are merely the lowest rung
of employees at the PTO; higher-ups possess even greater experience.

What the PTO currently lacks are staffs of economists[138] who
would be indispensable in formulating broader patent and competition policy, as well as disposable funds that could be used to
conduct broader research. However, as I noted above, these shortcomings are endogenous to the fact that the PTO has no need
for such staff members or such resources because it lacks substantive authority over the law. Were Congress to endow the Patent Office with greater regulatory power, it would be a comparatively trivial matter for it to provide it with the funds to hire
professional staff and conduct research at the same moment. Indeed, the PTO has already hired a chief economist,[139] and more
staff need not be far behind.

Compare the Federal Circuit. Because it was created as a specialized court, the Federal Circuit is usually credited with greater

---

[135] See *General Requirements Bulletin to the Examination for Admission for Registration to Practice in Patent Cases before the United States Patent and Trademark Office* 4–9, online at http://www.uspto.gov/web/offices/dcom/olia/oed/grb.pdf (detailing the degrees or extent of scientific background necessary to sit for the examination).

[136] There are 6,242 patent examiners, see online at http://www.uspto.gov/web/offices/com/annual/2009/oai_05_wlt_28.html, and 485,500 patents were filed in 2009, see online at http://www.uspto.gov/web/offices/com/annual/2009/oai_05_wlt_02.html. Each exam-iner is thus charged with examining approximately seventy-eight patents per year.

[137] "Patent prosecution" is the process of applying for a patent and seeing that application through examination to the granting of the patent. The lawyers who shepherd patents through PTO examination are known as "patent prosecutors."

[138] See Rai, 103 Colum L Rev at 1113 (cited in note 101) (noting that until very recently the PTO employed no economists).

[139] See Rai, 157 U Pa L Rev at 2054 (cited in note 102).

expertise than the typical judicial body. Judges on the Federal Circuit are fed a steady diet of patent cases and have ample opportunity to develop a detailed understanding of patent law, unlike a judge on a typical circuit who may see one or fewer of many types of cases each year.

But this regularly accepted perception of expertise is misleading. The Federal Circuit has great experience with patent *law*—not patent *policy*, much less patent *economics*. Judges on the Circuit possess a detailed understanding of the workings of patent doctrine and the interrelation of various pieces of the patent law,[140] but this is far from equivalent to the ability to design a sensible patent system that provides the correct incentives for inventors and market participants. In fact, it is not even clear that the Federal Circuit is trying. Patent law is now notoriously formalistic[141]—precisely what one might expect when a court attempts to establish judicially manageable rules in the absence of expertise or agency input.[142] Not surprisingly, many extant doctrines seem significantly flawed from the perspective of economic theory. And because every patent

---

[140] Nevertheless, they manage to err in formulating doctrine at an alarming rate. The Federal Circuit could not coalesce around a single methodology for interpreting claims for decades, until *Phillips v AWH Corp.*, 415 F3d 1303 (Fed Cir 2005). Even now it does not adhere to its own doctrinal prescriptions. See R. Polk Wagner and Lee Petherbridge, *Is the Federal Circuit Succeeding? An Empirical Assessment of Judicial Performance*, 152 U Pa L Rev 1105, 1179 (2004) (finding that the Federal Circuit has been only mildly successful in promulgating a coherent and predictable doctrine of claim construction). The Federal Circuit has also become notorious for resurrecting old doctrines and applying them in novel, unnecessary ways. See Merges and Duffy, *Patent Law and Policy* at 299–327 (cited in note 13) (describing this phenomenon with respect to the written description requirement); Mark D. Janis, *On Courts Herding Cats: Contending with the "Written Description" Requirement (and Other Unruly Patent Disclosure Doctrines)*, 2 Wash U J L & Pol 55, 60–61 (2000) (same); *Lizardtech, Inc. v Earth Resource Mapping, Inc.*, 424 F3d 1336 (Fed Cir 2005) (developing the doctrine). To say that the Federal Circuit is adept even with patent law doctrine is to afford it the benefit of the doubt.

[141] See, for example, Thomas, 52 Am U L Rev at 792 (cited in note 112) (describing a trend of formalism in five areas of patent law jurisprudence); Timothy R. Holbrook, *The Supreme Court's Complicity in Federal Circuit Formalism*, 20 Santa Clara Computer & High Tech L J 1, 1 (2003) (noting that the Federal Circuit has recently formulated rules to promote predictability and certainty at the expense of fairness, specifically in the areas of patent claim construction and the doctrine of equivalents). This formalism may be due in part to the Federal Circuit's early reliance on the decisions of one of its predecessor courts, the Court of Customs and Patent Appeals. See generally Jeffrey A. Lefstin, *The Constitution of Patent Law: The Court of Customs and Patent Appeals and the Shape of the Federal Circuit's Jurisprudence*, 43 Loyola LA L Rev 843 (2010).

[142] See Lee, 120 Yale L Rev at 25–30 (cited in note 48); Thomas, 52 Am U L Rev at 793 (cited in note 112) (attributing the formalistic trend to a preference for rules over standards); Rai, 103 Colum L Rev at 1115 (cited in note 101) (noting the decrease in decision-making costs and the increase in predictability from the use of formalistic rules).

case must be appealed to the Federal Circuit, there is no juris-dictional competition and thus no mechanism that might induce patent doctrine to evolve in beneficial directions.[143]

The Federal Circuit suffers from many of the same limitations as any court. As a group, Federal Circuit judges had insignificant relevant experience, either with patent law or with the technical disciplines that surround it, before they were elevated to the court. Of the twelve active judges on the court, only five of them prac-ticed or taught patent law before joining the court, only six have even undergraduate degrees in technical fields, and none has an advanced degree in economics.[144] The court may be "expert" in some limited, legalistic sense, but that expertise is a poor substitute for genuine administrative competence. It goes almost without saying that the district courts and the Supreme Court are no better off.[145]

In place of true expertise, courts have expert witnesses. The reliability and usefulness of expert witnesses is of course limited by the fact that they are paid advocates for a position, not dis-interested observers.[146] This disadvantage is exacerbated when the expert witness must be relied upon to opine on an issue well outside of the judge's area of competence. The large-scale eco-nomic questions involved in patent law are precisely those sorts of issues. Determining whether the benefits of patents on business methods outweigh the costs, or how stringent the utility require-ment should be for gene patents, will inevitably require extensive empirical analysis. Promising research is already under way.[147] But it is unrealistic to believe that judges will ever be able to accurately comprehend expert testimony on these points. As one economi-cally proficient federal judge put it, "econometrics is such a dif-ficult subject that it is unrealistic to expect the average judge or

---

[143] Consider notes 75–78 and accompanying text.

[144] See *Federal Circuit—Judicial Biographies*, available online at http://www.cafc.uscourts.gov/judgbios.html.

[145] The Supreme Court can attempt to mitigate its inadequacies by only granting cer-tiorari in cases that do not involve difficult technology. However, that would mean forgoing any opportunity to pass on issues involving genetics, pharmaceuticals, semiconductors, or any other innovation at the forefront of modern technology. Because these types of tech-nology raise particular, and particularly important, questions, this would be a significant detriment to the Court's proper functioning.

[146] See Lee, 120 Yale L J at 18 (cited in note 48).

[147] See, for example, David S. Abrams, *Did TRIPS Spur Innovation? An Analysis of Patent Duration and Incentives to Innovate*, 157 U Pa L Rev 1613 (2009).

juror to be able to understand all the criticisms of an econometric study, no matter how skillful the econometrician is in explaining the study to a lay audience."[148]

2. *Procedural advantages.* Agencies are commonly understood to possess a variety of "procedural" advantages over courts—particularly Article III federal courts—stemming from the manner in which they may engage with questions of policy. Agencies can initiate regulatory action when they choose, on the subjects they select. They need not wait for private parties to bring a case appropriate for policymaking, as would a court. Notice-and-comment rule-making authority also permits agencies to solicit opinions from a broad spectrum of interested parties, and to test preliminary regulatory proposals against outside objections.[149] Courts, by contrast, must rely predominantly upon the parties' and amici's briefs and reports, supplemented only occasionally by special masters and outside experts. Here again the supposedly expert Federal Circuit possesses no special advantages; it functions like any other federal appellate court. The tools that accompany typical administrative rule making are thus more adaptable, and more comprehensive, than the typical ad hoc systems upon which courts are forced to rely. A reformed PTO, imbued with substantive rule-making authority, would possess this range of procedural tools.

This discussion illustrates a more general point regarding the PTO's procedural capabilities and patent policy. Over the past several centuries, patent lawmaking has proceeded incrementally, as might be expected from a common-law system.[150] This might have been adequate in some contexts and as applied to some doctrines, but just as surely it must be suboptimal or ill-suited in others.[151] It makes little sense to consign an entire field of law to

[148] Posner, 13 J Econ Persp at 96 (cited in note 50).

[149] See 5 USC § 553 (2008) (setting forth the procedural requirements for notice-and-comment or "informal" rule making).

[150] Compare David A. Strauss, *Common Law Constitutional Interpretation*, 63 U Chi L Rev 877 (1996) (analyzing the process of common-law rule making in constitutional law).

[151] Indeed, it is conceivable that the present shape of patent law has been determined in part by the procedural shortcomings of the federal courts as patent policymakers. Even if the Federal Circuit (for instance) were to believe a putative change in the law beneficial, it might nonetheless shy away from initiating such a change if it believed its own institutional tools inadequate to the task of legal reform. Compare *Warner-Jenkinson Co., Inc. v Hilton Davis Chemical Co.*, 520 US 17, 28 (1997) ("Congress can legislate the doctrine of equivalents out of existence any time it chooses. The various policy arguments now

one mode of development and reform when others are available.[152]

3. *Political responsiveness and agency capture.* The final two canonical institutional design considerations—an agency's responsiveness to public opinion, and the extent to which an agency is subject to outside "capture" and therefore biased decision making—are essentially two sides of the same coin. On the one hand, an advantage typically ascribed to agencies over courts is the political nature of the former: their connection to the elected branches of government.[153] If regulation involves political considerations or trade-offs, then they are best delegated to an institutional actor, such as an agency, over which the political branches can exercise authority.[154] It is difficult to hold judges accountable if their decisions cease to serve the public interest. *Chevron* deference is frequently defended on these terms. Because regulatory choices are, at their core, discretionary matters of policy and politics, silences and ambiguities in statutes are best read as invitations for agencies, not courts, to make law.[155]

At the same time, a court's insulation from ordinary political processes and from the actors who might seek to influence it can provide certain advantages. Like any politically influenced organ of government, administrative agencies are subject to inducements and pressures from private outside actors who may have preferences that diverge widely from the best interests of society at large.[156] This problem can be exacerbated for agencies, which deal repeatedly with the same industries and often the same firms in the course of regulating a single field or area of the economy. The fear is that repeated lobbying, along with the movement of staff members between the private and public sector, will leave agencies beholden to the industries they are meant to regulate or inculcated

made by both sides are thus best addressed to Congress, not this Court."); Owen M. Fiss, *Foreword: The Forms of Justice*, 93 Harv L Rev 1 (1979) (analyzing courts' suitability as venues for "structural" litigation in pursuit of broad and ongoing social reform).

[152] Compare Rai, 103 Colum L Rev 1035 (cited in note 101) (suggesting collaboration between Congress, the courts, and the PTO).

[153] See Mark Seidenfeld, *The Psychology of Accountability and Political Review of Agency Rules*, 51 Duke L J 1059, 1068–93 (2001) (describing and assessing executive and legislative oversight of agency rule making).

[154] See Matthew C. Stephenson, *Optimal Political Control of the Bureaucracy*, 107 Mich L Rev 53 (2008) (arguing that the optimal arrangement may be some type of power sharing between agencies and the President); Jonathan S. Masur and Jonathan Remy Nash, *The Institutional Dynamics of Transition Relief*, 85 NYU L Rev 391, 435–440 (2010).

[155] See *Chevron*, 467 US at 843–44.

[156] Masur and Nash, 85 NYU L Rev at 445–47 (cited in note 154).

with those industries' own preferences and priorities.[157]

Courts are not entirely immune from capture, however. Judges operate within an elite legal community and seek reputational benefits and status within that community,[158] and most judges are former lawyers drawn from that community. Occasionally judges retire and resume careers as lawyers.[159] Conceivably, then, courts are subject to a similar type of capture by actors within the legal community. This possibility grows as the size of the relevant community shrinks and the frequency of judges' interactions with the same attorneys increases.[160]

This is the terrain on which the battles over choice of institutional actor are fought, and thus far these arguments have neither dissuaded Congress from vesting agencies with tremendous regulatory power nor convinced proponents of agency capture theories. On this ground, at least, the PTO fares no worse than the typical administrative agency. There is no reason to believe that it is less politically responsive or more subject to capture than the EPA, FDA, or any other of its peers. On the usual administrative law terms, the PTO can make out at minimum a prima facie case for regulatory authority commensurate with similarly situated agencies.

In fact, however, the case for the PTO is stronger than even this first-order picture would indicate. Structural features of the market for patents should render the PTO less susceptible to capture than many other typical agencies, and better situated vis-à-vis the federal courts than most agencies. The regulated community that must deal with the PTO is larger than for nearly any other administrative agency. The PTO's ambit includes every private entity that engages in any sort of research or development, a larger cohort than the class of firms that release pollutants (EPA), or produce consumables (FDA), or engage in collective bargaining

---

[157] See generally Nicholas Bagley and Richard L. Revesz, *Centralized Oversight of the Regulatory State*, 106 Colum L Rev 1260, 1284–92 (2006); Kieff, 157 U Pa L Rev at 1949–50 (cited in note 123).

[158] See Richard A. Posner, *What Do Judges and Justices Maximize? (The Same Thing Everybody Else Does)*, 3 Sup Ct Econ Rev 1, 13 (1993).

[159] See, for example, Jerry Markon, *Appeals Court Judge Leaves Life Appointment for Boeing*, Wash Post (May 1, 2006), online at http://www.washingtonpost.com/wp-dyn/content/article/2006/05/10/AR2006051000929.html (describing the resignation of Judge Michael Luttig, formerly of the Court of Appeals for the Fourth Circuit).

[160] See Thomas, 52 Am U L Rev at 792–94 (cited in note 112) (suggesting that the Federal Circuit has been captured).

(NLRB). Because the PTO interacts with a broader and more diverse regulated community, it will be more difficult for any single firm or industry to gain sway over the agency.

Moreover, many of the parties that interact with the PTO lack strong interests either for or against stringent patent protection. Most high-technology firms both hold patents and face competitors with their own overlapping patent portfolios. Accordingly, it is uncertain whether these firms would benefit or be harmed if patents were strengthened or weakened.[161] In any event, without decisive lobbying objectives, these parties should have little interest in even attempting to capture the PTO.

Of course, as with any agency, there are firms with divergent private interests before the PTO. In particular, the brand-name pharmaceutical industry is viewed as the primary modern beneficiary of powerful patent protection and the industry most likely to invest resources in lobbying for greater patent rights.[162] There has been movement toward extending patent rights for drug companies,[163] but those trends are, by and large, neither significant nor contemporary. The explanation for the pharmaceutical industry's general failure to secure most extensive patent rights is likely found in the fact that it is opposed by powerful interests as well: consumer groups—including such dominant national orga-

---

[161] See Burk and Lemley, *The Patent Crisis* at 160–64 (cited in note 4) (arguing that the software industry's patent crisis is due to the ill-defined scope of software patents and the lax standards with which they are issued); Leon Radomsky, *Sixteen Years After the Passage of the U.S. Semiconductor Chip Protection Act: Is International Protection Working?* 15 Berkeley Tech L J 1049, 1054 (2000) (asserting that patents are not useful in the semiconductor industry because the complexity of the technology makes obtaining a patent impractical); Robert L. Risberg, Jr., Comment, *Five Years Without Infringement Litigation Under the Semiconductor Chip Protection Act: Unmasking the Spectre of Chip Piracy in an Era of Diverse and Incompatible Process Technologies,* 1990 Wis L Rev 241, 252 ("[T]he design that makes one chip's layout better than another's is generally not patentable."); Clarisa Long, *Institutions and Interest Groups in Patent and Copyright Law* 10 (unpublished manuscript, 2007). Long ascribes the lack of congressional attention to patents, as a historical matter, to this phenomenon.

[162] See Bessen and Meurer, *Patent Failure* at 88–89 (cited in note 4) (noting the high value of patent protection to the pharmaceutical industry compared to most other industries); Jaffe and Lerner, *Innovation and Its Discontents* at 39–41 (cited in note 4) (asserting that patent protection provides incentives for drug development that would otherwise be uneconomical).

[163] The Hatch-Waxman Act is an example of this movement, though it involved trade-offs and was not entirely beneficial to the prescription drug industry. See generally Henry Grabowski, *Patents and New Product Development in the Pharmaceutical and Biotechnology Industries,* 8 Georgetown Pub Pol Rev 7 (2003) (describing the trade-offs involved in that legislation); Scott Hemphill, *Paying for Delay: Pharmaceutical Patent Settlement as a Regulatory Design Problem,* 81 NYU L Rev 1553 (2006) (same).

nizations as the AARP, which is concerned about rising prices of drugs for senior citizens—and generic pharmaceutical companies.[164] The presence of these countervailing forces places the PTO in a situation far different from, for instance, the EPA. That agency regulates vast numbers of businesses, all of whom would likely prefer a slackening in regulation, counterbalanced only by a handful of comparatively weaker environmental groups.[165] There is little reason to suspect that the PTO will have as much difficulty evading improper outside influence as the canonical administrative body.

B. THE ADVANTAGES OF PTO INVOLVEMENT

As the previous section argued, there seems little reason to favor administrative involvement in highly technical regulatory fields such as environmental and securities law while simultaneously disfavoring it for patent law. Yet there are advantages to bestowing substantive rule-making authority upon the PTO that transcend that meager justification. This section sketches out two of the most important.

1. *Substantive rules and information gathering.* One of the principal goals of any organized system is to ensure that information flows to the decision makers most in need of it, or best positioned to make use of it. Achieving this goal is a matter of bureaucratic structure and incentives. The parties with the capacity to gather information must have the proper incentives to invest in obtaining it and passing it along to the higher-value users, and they must have the capacity to do so. This problem is difficult enough to solve within a government bureaucracy that lacks any market pricing mechanism that could set incentives. But the problem becomes even more difficult when the institution positioned to gather information and the institution in need of that information are housed under separate organizational roofs.

This is the state of play in patent law. The PTO grants approximately 200,000 patents per year, and in doing so accumulates vast amounts of information on a variety of topics integral to the patent law. To name just a few examples, the PTO is positioned

---

[164] Long, *Institutions and Interest Groups* at 10 (cited in note 161).

[165] Nonetheless, over the EPA's lifetime, a period of intense industry lobbying, the agency's trend has been toward more extensive and stricter regulation of pollutants, not a loosening of its grip.

to learn what the state of the art is in any given industry, and thus what sorts of inventions would be truly novel and nonobvious; the level of technical expertise of a person of ordinary skill in a given field, which is the standard upon which much of the patent law is based; and the ways in which patent drafters in various fields employ particular terms of art and describe particular types of inventions. Yet the PTO cannot make use of this information directly because it lacks control over the substantive patent law.

The Federal Circuit, by contrast, sees only a very small fraction of all patents—it decided fewer than 300 patent cases in 2008,[166] for instance—and nothing approaching a representative sample. In addition, whereas patent applications come into the PTO's hands immediately upon filing, the Federal Circuit typically sees a patent only years after it was filed. The patent must first wend its way through the PTO, be allegedly infringed by another party, and then progress through lengthy litigation at the district court level. This process takes more than twelve years on average.[167] Accordingly, the Federal Circuit possesses very little information regarding the current state of technology in any field, and its level of knowledge is particularly lacking in the quickly developing technological fields where it might be most useful.

This lack of information hamstrings the Federal Circuit's efforts at formulating sound policy. As an initial matter, the Federal Circuit undoubtedly makes significant errors when deciding difficult technical questions. Without a current, ongoing understanding of the state of a given technological field, the Federal Circuit can hardly be expected to ascertain how a person of ordinary skill in the art would understand a patent, or whether that person would have found a particular invention obvious. And these deficiencies do not touch on even more complex questions involving the doctrines of utility and obviousness, for example.

This is not to say that the Federal Circuit has no means of obtaining information from the patent office. The PTO regularly produces nonbinding guidelines for its examiners, to which the Federal Circuit could defer if it so chose. Or the court could simply solicit information and guidance from the PTO in particular cases

---

[166] This is based on a search of the Westlaw database using the word "patent." The results were then culled to remove any cases that did not involve the decision of any patent-related issue.

[167] Burk and Lemley, *The Patent Crisis* at 57 (cited in note 4).

or in the course of formulating particular doctrines. Generally speaking, however, the Federal Circuit has done neither of these things. It grants no deference to PTO guidelines, and it does not ask for the PTO's advice or guidance. *In re Fisher*[168] is illustrative of this attitude. In that case, the PTO rejected a patent filing pursuant to its own examination guidelines, and the patentee appealed to the Federal Circuit. The court eventually upheld the PTO's decision and validated the agency's approach in the guidelines, but it granted no particular deference to the patent office— not even weak *Skidmore* deference, much less genuine *Chevron* deference.[169] The Federal Circuit treated the PTO as merely another litigant.

It is worth pausing to note that there is one respect in which courts would seem better institutionally situated than agencies in this field. The federal courts adjudicate issues related to both patent validity and patent infringement, while the PTO encounters only questions of patent validity.[170] This might seem to provide the courts with at least one informational advantage.[171] But again, the PTO's singular focus on validity is an artifact of the PTO having never been delegated any authority over issues of infringement. Moreover, the issues surrounding infringement—determining when injunctions are appropriate,[172] calculating reasonable royalties,[173] etc.—are no less technically complex than other patent questions.[174] If the PTO were tasked with setting rules to govern

---

[168] 421 F3d 1365 (Fed Cir 2005).

[169] See id at 1372 (noting only that "[t]he PTO's standards for assessing whether a claimed invention has a specific and substantial utility comport with this court's interpretation of the utility requirement of § 101"). Under the *Chevron* line of cases, agency actions that are not entitled to *Chevron* deference frequently receive deference "according to [their] persuasiveness," which is known as *Skidmore* deference. *U.S. v Mead Corp.*, 533 US 218, 221 (2001).

[170] Burk and Lemley, *The Patent Crisis* at 107 (cited in note 4).

[171] Nonetheless, it is worth noting that the most important infringement doctrines have direct analogues in doctrines of patent validity: literal infringement parallels novelty, while the doctrine of equivalents is very similar to obviousness. See Merges and Duffy, *Patent Law and Policy* at 781–877 (cited in note 13).

[172] 35 USC § 283.

[173] 35 USC § 284.

[174] Burk and Lemley, *The Patent Crisis* at 129 (cited in note 4) (suggesting that a reasonable royalty should be determined by "the profit margin that a company might expect and the royalty rate common in licenses in that industry"); id at 160 (suggesting that the likelihood of holdup problems should drive decisions regarding injunctions).

infringement, there is similar reason to believe that it would out-perform the courts.[175]

It is something of a puzzle that the Federal Circuit has not made better use of the PTO as an informational resource. Why, after all, should it not avail itself of all available means of improving its jurisprudence? The answer likely lies with the political economy of patent law, and in particular the institutional rivalry between the Federal Circuit and the PTO. The Federal Circuit is, first and foremost, a patent court. The remainder of its docket is compar-atively insignificant. It was created to function as an expert over-seer of the patent law, and undoubtedly its judges continue to understand their roles very much in those terms.[176] Consequently, the Federal Circuit has been loath to cede any authority or even any hint of primacy to the PTO, its main institutional competi-tor.[177] In addition to refusing to afford any deference to the PTO's view of the law, the Federal Circuit notably declined to review even the PTO's findings of fact with the level of deference man-dated by the Administrative Procedure Act,[178] until the Supreme Court finally forced it to do so.[179]

For its part, the PTO has little incentive to invest in infor-mation. It has nothing to gain from plying the Federal Circuit

---

[175] It is possible that the PTO should also be granted the authority to hear suits for patent infringement in the first instance, just as administrative law judges currently ad-judicate regulatory cases across a wide variety of federal agencies (with parties holding rights of appeal to the federal courts). See the Federal Administrative Law Judges Con-ference, *FALJC's Mission, Constitution, and Bylaws*, online at http://005754d.netsolhost.com/faljc1.html. Full consideration of this possibility is both beyond the scope of this article and somewhat to the side of it; the argument here principally concerns which institution will determine substantive patent law rules, and the PTO need not have adjudicative authority to fulfill that role. I pause only to note that a shift to agency adjudication is not inconsistent with the approach advocated here.

[176] See the Federal Courts Improvement Act of 1982, Pub L No 97-164, 96 Stat 25 (1982) (codified in various sections of Title 28) (establishing the Federal Circuit); Harry F. Manbeck Jr., *The Federal Circuit—First Ten Years of Patentability Decisions*, 14 Geo Mason U L Rev 499, 499 (1992) ("It was expected that the Federal Circuit would provide uniform application and interpretation of the patent law."); Robert L. Harmon, *Patents and the Federal Circuit* 1162 (BNA Books, 8th ed 2007) ("The Federal Circuit was created, in part, for the purpose of achieving uniformity in the exposition and application of substantive patent law.").

[177] See Jonathan Masur et al, *Who Defines the Law? USPTO Rulemaking Authority*, 8 Nw U J Tech & Intell Prop 410 (2010), online at http://www.law.northwestern.edu/journals/njtip/v8/n3/5.

[178] 5 USC § 706(2)(A).

[179] See *Dickinson v Zurko*, 527 US 150, 163 (1999) (holding that the Federal Circuit must review PTO findings of fact with deference).

with knowledge that the court will not use. Even if the Federal Circuit were to make use of the information, it surely would not credit the PTO with having provided it. Nor can the PTO realize any advantage by challenging the Federal Circuit directly. Absent intervention from Congress or the Supreme Court, two parties that rarely engage with the patent law, the PTO holds no playable cards. The PTO typically behaves accordingly: nearly all of its guidance documents merely parrot Federal Circuit caselaw.[180] Independent PTO efforts to shape the law are extremely rare and nearly always unsuccessful. By consequence, the large quantities of information generated in the PTO sit uncollected and unutilized.

If the PTO disagrees with the courts as to the appropriate content of patent law, it is almost certainly best for the patent system and for society if the PTO simply states (and acts upon) its preferences directly. This would allow information to reach the public. The PTO has strong incentives not to pursue this course, however, because to do so would invite reversal and its attendant costs.[181]

Accordingly, the PTO might well attempt to accomplish effectively the same substantive ends through more sub rosa means. In particular, the PTO may attempt to use its control over patent examinations to enforce a de facto substantive law that is opaque and effectively unreviewable.

Imagine, for example, that the PTO does not believe that strands of the human genome should be patentable. The patent office can raise the costs of obtaining a patent on this type of invention in a variety of ways. It can allocate resources away from the relevant technological field and reduce the number of working examiners, causing applications to pile up and lengthening the time it takes for them to be granted. It can instruct its examiners to search more diligently for prior art, raising the probability that an application will be rejected and an inventor will be forced to redraft claims. And it can use what little discretionary authority it has in extending deadlines or granting additional leave to file to discrim-

---

[180] See Megan E. Lyman, *Judicial Fitness for Review of Complex Biotechnology Issues in Patent Litigation: Technical Claim Interpretation*, 23 J NAALJ 503, 509 (2003) (noting that PTO guidelines incorporate Federal Circuit opinions and do little else).

[181] See Masur, *Patent Inflation* at 17–18 (cited in note 105).

inate among technological fields.[182] These mechanisms will increase the transaction costs of getting a patent, and in some cases they may even serve to block a patent from issuing. Even where the patent eventually issues and where the transaction costs are insignificant,[183] the delay itself can be extremely costly for a patentee. Delay reduces the effective length of the patent term because the twenty-year term begins running when the application is first filed, and it can result in millions or billions of dollars in lost revenues for patentees.[184]

These sorts of pathologies are neither unique to the PTO nor necessarily rare within the administrative state. Nearly any executive-branch organization possessing enforcement power but not lawmaking power may use its enforcement discretion to affect the de facto content of the substantive law. This phenomenon has been observed most notably in the criminal law,[185] and it may exist in a variety of other legal fields as well.[186] Yet its operation in patent law is different for one important reason: unlike other fields of law, there is no explicit element of discretion vested in the PTO. Unlike any prosecutor, the PTO must accept every filed application and is *obligated* to grant every patent that is valid under the Patent Act. The PTO is expected to function, ideally, as an automaton. Accordingly, the PTO possesses no official policymaking space; there is no sense in which the patent office's ability to promote or delay certain applications could be understood or justified as a purposeful, systemic means of agenda setting. When the PTO subverts the Federal Circuit's intentions regarding the

---

[182] The PTO's recent efforts to limit the number of continuation applications that a patentee can file *as a matter of right* can be understood in this vein. Under the PTO's final rules, the office retained discretion to allow parties leave to file additional continuation applications under certain sets of circumstances. The PTO may well have envisioned this additional discretion as another mechanism for selecting among types of technology and fields of potentially patentable subject matter.

[183] See Jonathan S. Masur, *Costly Screens and Patent Examination*, 687 J Legal Analysis (2011), online at http://www.ssrn.com/abstract_id=1105184 (comparing the low cost of obtaining a patent with the value of a profitable invention).

[184] This is a particularly pressing issue for pharmaceutical companies, which frequently reap substantial income throughout the life of a patent and depend upon a lengthy patent term to fund the expensive clinical trials required to bring a patent to market. See Benjamin N. Roin, *Unpatentable Drugs and the Standards of Patentability*, 87 Tex L Rev 503, 504–05 (2009); see also note 162.

[185] See William J. Stuntz, *The Pathological Politics of Criminal Law*, 100 Mich L Rev 505, 506 (2001).

[186] See Adam B. Cox and Cristina M. Rodriguez, *The President and Immigration Law*, 119 Yale L J 458, 520 (2009).

patent law, it is acting beyond the contemplated boundaries of the patent system.

By contrast, a PTO imbued with the authority to make substantive legal rules would possess both the ability and the incentive to draw upon the information it is positioned to gather. The PTO could collect information from both outsiders and its own examiners. It could conduct studies analyzing the types of patents filed and the state of the art in various technological fields. And it could even enlist economists in performing larger-scale studies to determine the economic value of particular doctrines.

Importantly, these PTO policy innovations would be substantially resistant to Federal Circuit intervention. If the PTO were to employ notice-and-comment rule making, like any other similarly situated administrative agency, it would be entitled to *Chevron* deference in its interpretations of the Patent Act. Because the act is phrased in such general, ambiguous terms,[187] in most cases this deference should be decisive. This is not to say that the Federal Circuit would have no oversight role; PTO regulations would still undergo arbitrary and capricious review in the Circuit. But for the most part the PTO would be able to implement policy without fear of being summarily overturned by the Federal Circuit. Accordingly, the PTO would have the proper motivation to challenge the Federal Circuit where appropriate.

2. *Particularized patent advantages.* Armed with this information, the PTO could conceivably adjust a variety of patent doctrines with greater precision than an inexpert court can achieve. Patent law differs importantly from other legal fields because of the scope and specificity of the technologies involved. One case may require detailed scrutiny of semiconductor designs; another may demand an analysis of gene sequencing. In response to this great variety of technological issues, and because judges are not skilled in the relevant technologies, patent law has officially embraced a doctrine of technological neutrality: patent doctrines should not differentiate between technologies. Accordingly, courts have constructed

---

[187] See, for example, 35 USC § 101 (2009) ("Whoever invents or discovers any new and useful process, machine, manufacture, or composition of matter, or any new and useful improvement thereof, may obtain a patent therefor, subject to the conditions and requirements of this title."). The statute does not define "new," "useful," "composition of matter," or any of its other relevant terms.

a number of general rules that operate across technological fields.[188]

Yet this is despite the fact that there is little reason to believe that all fields should be treated equivalently. Moreover, each new patent case demands that the courts reapply this general standard to the relevant technology, which is a difficult and time-consuming exercise. Some scholars believe that the courts have already attempted to design field-specific patent rules, though frequently without success.[189] The PTO could improve upon these doctrines by drafting technology-specific rules that more accurately reflect the state of the art and reduce the decision costs of courts that must comb through the technologies. This section highlights three particular areas in which PTO rule making could lead to marked improvements.

First, consider the role of the "person having ordinary skill in the art" (the "PHOSITA") in patent law. Much like the "reasonable person" in tort law, the PHOSITA is a construct used to define a variety of patent doctrines. An invention is obvious if a PHOSITA would find it obvious;[190] a patent sufficiently enables the underlying invention (per section 112 of the Patent Act) if it would teach a PHOSITA how to create the invention.[191] The PHOSITA allows courts to decide patent cases without assembling any systematic understanding of the state of the art in any technological field—they need only decide what a PHOSITA would have understood regarding the technology at issue.[192] A consequence of this approach is that no case creates meaningful precedent regarding skill in the art. Courts' conclusions as to how a given PHOSITA would treat a particular technology are of essentially no use beyond the four corners of the opinions in which they are issued. Far preferable would be particular legal findings regarding the state of the art or the level of available knowledge in a given field, findings that could govern future cases and allow private

---

[188] See Burk and Lemley, 89 Va L Rev at 1630–75 (cited in note 66).

[189] See Burk and Lemley, *The Patent Crisis* at 109–30 (cited in note 4).

[190] See, for example, *Geo M. Martin Co. v Alliance Machine Systems Intern LLC*, 618 F3d 1294, 1302–03 (Fed Cir 2010).

[191] See, for example, *Forest Laboratories, Inc. v Ivax Pharmaceuticals, Inc.*, 501 F3d 1263, 1266 (Fed Cir 2007).

[192] It is worth noting that the PHOSITA must be defined not just by technological field but by time: a person with ordinary skill in the art would know more about computers in 2010 than in 1960.

parties to adjust their patenting behavior accordingly. For reasons likely related to its lack of information, the Federal Circuit has shied away from this course.

By contrast, the PTO could employ the expertise of its examiners directly to determine the level of ability and knowledge of a person having ordinary skill in the art in any number of technical fields. It could then incorporate this information into a set of regulations, updated regularly, which would govern the many PHOSITA-related questions arising in patent cases in those fields.[193] Note that the PTO already is forced to ascertain the level of skill of the PHOSITA in the course of assessing essentially every patent application for obviousness. It seems absurd to waste the enormous amounts of information generated through this process, rather than standardizing it and applying it to both examinations and court cases. Moreover, a consistently updated set of regulations would create a permanent record of the changing level of skill in the art over time. Courts could draw upon this database when adjudicating infringement actions that arise years after a patent has issued, rather than having to rely upon experts and guesswork to ascertain the appropriate level of skill in the art in a bygone era.

Second, the PTO could issue a set of rules for construing patent claims. These rules could take into account the specifications, prosecution history, and available extrinsic evidence based on the PTO's broad-based knowledge, acquired in the course of examining hundreds of thousands of patents, regarding how patent drafters commonly employ language and structure. The Federal Circuit's efforts in this area have been halting and uncertain. Current law is little more than an admonition to consider a variety of factors in turn, and to an unspecified extent.[194] Not surprisingly, the Federal Circuit's jurisprudence is viewed as largely unsuc-

---

[193] If this seems too rigid, these regulations could be structured instead as rebuttable presumptions. The PHOSITA would be presumed to have the knowledge and skill embodied in the relevant PTO regulation unless a litigant demonstrated otherwise with expert testimony. The PTO could even select the proper evidentiary standard: a preponderance of the evidence, clear and convincing evidence, or something in between.

[194] See *Phillips v AWH Corp.*, 415 F3d 1303, 1314–18 (Fed Cir 2005) (en banc) (explaining that district court judges should consider the language of the claims themselves, the specifications, the prosecution history, and also extrinsic evidence when construing patent claims).

cessful.[195] The rate of reversal of district court opinions is very high, and district court judges do not appear to improve with experience.[196] It would not be difficult for the PTO to improve upon this record.

Third, at the outer reaches of possibility, a properly empowered patent office could consider varying the length of the patent term among different industries.[197] It is entirely likely that the standard twenty-year term is inappropriate for all patents in all fields; it persists in part because Congress and the courts lack the resources and skill necessary to adjust it. The PTO could combine the expertise of its examiners in understanding how research is conducted in various fields with the analysis of economists to determine whether deviations from the standard term are warranted.

C. PROSPECTS FOR REFORM

Irrespective of the wisdom of delegating substantive rule-making authority to the PTO, it might appear unlikely that Congress will act simply because it has not done so thus far. The very fact that the allocation of institutional authority remains unchanged, despite the Federal Circuit's documented failings, might be taken as evidence that Congress will not alter it in the future. In addition, if Congress does grant the PTO rule-making authority and the agency misuses that power, it might be advisable for Congress to strip the PTO of authority and return to the status quo ante. Yet

---

[195] See Wagner and Petherbridge, 152 U Pa L Rev (cited in note 140) (illustrating the failings of Federal Circuit claim construction doctrine and the Federal Circuit's own treatment of that doctrine).

[196] See Schwartz, 107 Mich L Rev (cited in note 130) (noting the low rate at which the Federal Circuit affirms claim construction judgments and the fact that district judges do not appear to improve their success rates with experience). This is not even to speak of the mind-bending contradictions inherent to Federal Circuit doctrine, such as the mutually contradictory notions that claims "must be read in view of the specification, of which they are a part," *Markman*, 52 F3d at 978, on the one hand, and that the courts "should not import limitations from the specifications into the claims." *ICU Medical, Inc. v Alaris Medical Systems, Inc.*, 558 F3d 1368, 1375 (Fed Cir 2009). Not to mention the fact that the written description requirement demands that the specification "describe the manner and process of making and using . . . the *full scope* of the invention," *Lizardtech, Inc. v Earth Resources Mapping, Inc.*, 424 F3d 1336, 1344–45 (Fed Cir 2005), which also seems inconsistent with the admonition against reading limitations from the specification into the claims.

[197] This might run afoul of the Agreement on Trade-Related Aspects of Intellectual Property Rights (TRIPS) and might thus be unworkable absent an internationally negotiated amendment to that treaty. See Burk and Lemley, *The Patent Crisis* at 20 (cited in note 4). It is in that sense in particular that this option is especially far-fetched.

if it is difficult to persuade Congress to make one change, it might be impossible to convince it to make a second.

This is a type of objection that might be raised against any proposal for legislative reform—if the idea is so beneficial, why has Congress not acted upon it already? But it is strengthened somewhat in the context of patent law, where Congress has not enacted *any* significant legal change in more than fifty years. It is possible that a powerful coalition of patent interest groups favor the status quo, or that interest in legal change is simply too minimal to spur congressional action.[198] This may also be a particularly difficult type of reform to enact. As I note above, Congress very rarely (if ever) grants an agency authority to make rules concerning a judge-made body of law.[199]

At the same time, there has never been any serious attempt to transfer substantive rule-making authority to the PTO or any strong advocate for such a move. It may simply be an idea whose time has not yet arrived. A transfer of institutional authority also involves different political dynamics than a substantive change in the law. It is clearer who the winners and losers will be from a substantive change than from a reallocation of decisional authority, and thus perhaps easier to reallocate authority when private parties have entrenched interests. Congress is also likelier to grant power to an agency when it is uncertain as to the proper policy course.[200] If Congress is dissatisfied with the Federal Circuit but lacks the information necessary to make sound substantive patent judgments, it might turn instead to the PTO.

In the end, it may well be that the prospects for institutional change are slim. But given the failings of the current system, there is little reason not to try.

IV. Conclusion

For years, federal judges have decided patent cases pursuant to doctrine and precedent without any clear indication as to the wisdom of the policies they were attempting to promote. The

---

[198] See Part II.E.

[199] See Part II.F.

[200] See generally David Epstein and Sharyn O'Halloran, *Delegating Powers: A Transaction Cost Politics Approach to Policy Making Under Separate Powers* 34–38 (Cambridge, 1999) (describing Congress as facing a decision whether to "make" policy through substantive legislation or "buy" it through delegation).

result is a set of patent rules that in many contexts appears broken. Yet the courts can hardly be blamed for the mess; they were never meant to manage policy in an area as fraught with technological and economic complexity as patent law. *Bilski* lays bare this fundamental institutional weakness. Faced with a crucial issue of patentability that might affect the shape of several major areas of economic activity, the Supreme Court had no choice but to fall back upon doctrine and precedent, legal tools that have proven entirely inadequate to the task at hand. For its part, Congress has played no meaningful role in managing the patent system for more than half a century.

Because the courts have appeared incapable—and the legislature uninterested—it is time to consider other institutional arrangements. Rather than continuing to rely upon the federal courts to fumble toward a workable patent policy, Congress should authorize the Patent and Trademark Office to make rules with the force of law. The case for vesting substantive regulatory authority in the PTO is perhaps even stronger than for the typical administrative agency. Unlike the Federal Circuit, the PTO would be able to muster resources and expertise in addressing the crucial economic and technical issues that underlay patent law. The PTO could even innovate further, creating field-specific rules of patent scope, interpretation, or even duration. There is no principled justification for the arrangement that has left patent law governed by the courts while other similarly technical areas such as environmental law or securities law are run by agencies. It is merely a historical accident—and one that Congress should rectify.

ALISON SIEGLER AND BARRY SULLIVAN

"'DEATH IS DIFFERENT' NO LONGER": GRAHAM v FLORIDA AND THE FUTURE OF EIGHTH AMENDMENT CHALLENGES TO NONCAPITAL SENTENCES

In *Graham v Florida*,[1] a Florida state prisoner asked the Supreme Court to hold that the Cruel and Unusual Punishments Clause of the Eighth Amendment categorically precludes the imposition of life-without-parole sentences for any juvenile offender who has committed a nonhomicide offense.[2] There was no Supreme Court

Alison Siegler is an Assistant Clinical Professor and Director of the Federal Criminal Justice Project of the Mandel Legal Aid Clinic at the University of Chicago Law School. Barry Sullivan is Cooney & Conway Chair in Advocacy and Professor of Law at the Loyola University Chicago School of Law.

AUTHORS' NOTE: The authors would like to thank Richard Mrizek, Winnifred Fallers Sullivan, and Robin Walker Sterling for helpful comments and Molly Booth, Hyeng Kim, and Michael Kuppersmith for exceptional research assistance.

[1] 130 S Ct 2011 (2010).

[2] The Supreme Court originally granted certiorari in two Florida cases in which two defendants had been sentenced to life without parole for nonhomicide offenses committed while they were juveniles. In *Graham v Florida* the defendant was sixteen years old when he was arrested with three other juveniles for the bungled robbery of a barbecue restaurant. Id a 2018. "No money was taken" but one of the other youths "struck the manager in the back of the head with a metal bar." Id. Graham was prosecuted as an adult and pled guilty to attempted armed robbery and to armed burglary with assault or battery, the latter of which carried a maximum possible penalty of life without parole. Graham was sentenced to probation. At the age of seventeen, Graham was arrested in connection with a home invasion robbery. A different judge revoked his probation and sentenced him to life without

© 2011 by The University of Chicago. All rights reserved.
978-0-226-36326-4/2011/2010-0008$10.00

precedent to support such a holding. Indeed, the relevant Supreme Court jurisprudence seemed clearly to preclude Graham's argument. The Court had previously held in *Roper v Simmons*[3] that the Eighth Amendment categorically prohibits capital sentences for offenders who were below the age of eighteen when they committed their crimes, but the Court did so for the expressed reason that death is different.[4] Members of the Court had long explained the uniqueness of capital cases by intoning the mantra "death is different" in countless cases since at least 1972.[5] Remarkably, however, the Court accepted Graham's invitation and left behind more than thirty years of consistent Supreme Court jurisprudence, seemingly without a second thought or backward glance. Indeed, the Court did not even acknowledge that the law had changed, still less that it had changed substantially and dramatically. The result reached in *Graham* was consistent with sound constitutional policy and could have been supported with many good reasons, but the Court failed to provide a candid explanation for its decision. Death was different no longer, but the Court did nothing to explain why that was the case.

In the thirty-year period preceding *Graham*, the Supreme Court had developed two clear and distinct lines of precedent.[6] The Court had enforced the Cruel and Unusual Punishments Clause in capital

---

parole on the original case. See id at 2018–20. Graham framed his question presented broadly to cover all juveniles: "Whether the Eighth Amendment's ban on cruel and unusual punishments prohibits the imprisonment of a juvenile for life without the possibility of parole as punishment for the juvenile's commission of a non-homicide." Petition for Writ of Certiorari, *Graham v Florida*, No 08-7412, *i (filed Nov 20, 2008) (available on Westlaw at 2008 WL 6031405). In *Sullivan v Florida*, 130 S Ct 2059 (2010) (dismissing writ of ceriorari as improvidently granted), the defendant presented a question that was narrowly tailored to his own circumstances: Whether "imposition of a life-without-parole sentence on a thirteen-year-old for a non-homicide violates . . . the Eighth and Fourteenth Amendments, where the freakishly rare imposition of such a sentence reflects a national consensus on the reduced criminal culpability of children." Petition for Writ of Certiorari, *Sullivan v Florida*, No 08-7621, *i (filed Dec 4, 2008) (available on Westlaw at 2008 WL 6031406).

[3] 543 US 551 (2005).

[4] Id at 568 (describing the Court's special treatment of death penalty cases).

[5] See, for example, *Furman v Georgia*, 408 US 238, 290 (1972) (Brennan, J, concurring) ("Death is a unique penalty."); id at 306 (Stewart, J, concurring) ("[P]enalty of death differs from all other forms of criminal punishment, not in degree but in kind."). See also *Graham*, 130 S Ct at 2046 (Thomas, J, dissenting) ("Until today, the Court has based its categorical proportionality rulings on the notion that the Constitution gives special protection to capital defendants because the death penalty is a uniquely severe punishment that must be reserved for only those who are most deserving of execution.") (citations omitted).

[6] See Rachel E. Barkow, *The Court of Life and Death: The Two Tracks of Constitutional Sentencing Law and the Case for Uniformity*, 107 Mich L Rev 1145, 1146 (2009) (describing a "stark two-track system for sentencing").

cases by applying a two-step test to decide when to create categorical rules which prohibited the imposition of the death sentence for certain crimes and certain classes of offenders. For example, the death penalty could not be imposed for rape; nor could it be imposed on offenders who were mentally retarded. By contrast, the Court did not articulate categorical rules for noncapital cases; it required those sentences to be evaluated on a case-by-case basis under a balancing test. Because this balancing test caused courts to focus on the nature and specifics of the offense, before *Graham* it was virtually impossible for juvenile offenders in noncapital cases to prove that their sentences were unconstitutional. In *Graham*, however, the Court adopted a variation of the categorical rule that it had most recently applied in *Roper* to prohibit the imposition of the death penalty based on age. The Court thus took the radical step of announcing a categorical rule applicable to noncapital cases. By a 6-to-3 vote, the Court held that the life-without-parole sentence in *Graham* violated the Eighth Amendment. Five Justices held that the imposition of life-without-parole sentences for nonhomicide crimes committed by juvenile offenders categorically violates the Eighth Amendment.[7] Because the majority opinion provided scant explanation for switching to a categorical rule, it is not clear how the Court will treat future cases. The Court's decision prompted Justice Thomas, one of the three dissenters, to observe: "'Death is different' no longer."[8]

The Court's decision to abandon the balancing test in this context had an important practical effect: it ensured that no juvenile would ever be subject to a life-without-parole sentence for a crime short of homicide.[9] The decision had immediate and profound effects for

---

[7] *Graham*, 130 S Ct at 2034. Chief Justice Roberts expressly rejected the majority's categorical rule, but concluded in a separate concurrence that Graham had shown that his sentence violated the Eighth Amendment under the traditional proportionality test applicable to noncapital cases. Id at 2042 (Roberts, CJ, concurring).

[8] Id at 2046 (Thomas, J, dissenting).

[9] The Court dismissed the *Sullivan* petition as improvidently granted, presumably because of certain procedural defects identified by the state. Sullivan, who was thirteen years old at the time he committed his crimes, was convicted in 1989 for the brutal rape and robbery of a seventy-nine-year-old woman in her home. Brief for Respondent, *Sullivan v Florida*, No 08-7621, *4 (filed Sept 4, 2009) (available on Westlaw at 2009 WL 2954164) ("Sullivan Res Brief"). Sullivan was sentenced to serve a term of life imprisonment without possibility of parole. Following the Supreme Court's decision in *Roper*, Sullivan filed a successive postconviction petition under Florida law, contending that the Supreme Court's decision in *Roper* applied to his case, and entitled him to relief, even though he had not been sentenced to death. The Florida trial court held that Sullivan was not entitled to

that admittedly small subset of juveniles. Before, when the offender's culpability was simply one factor to be considered in the sentencing decision, juvenile offenders had little hope of proving that their sentences should be set aside: juveniles lacking in genuine culpability, and fully capable of rehabilitation, might well receive sentences that made it impossible for them ever to redeem themselves or lead productive lives. That danger existed because judges applying a fact-dependent balancing test on a case-by-case basis were likely to place too much weight on the nature and specifics of the offense, while giving too little attention to the diminished culpability of juvenile offenders. There was reason to be concerned about whether the balancing test was capable, as a practical matter, of accomplishing what must be accomplished if the Eighth Amendment is to be given effect in this area.[10]

file a successive petition under Florida law because such otherwise time-barred petitions could be filed, as a matter of state law, only in cases in which a new, applicable constitutional right had been established. Id at *8. According to the trial court, that exception did not apply because *Roper* did not create a new constitutional right that was applicable to Sullivan's case. Id at *12–*13. The state appellate court affirmed without opinion, and the Florida Supreme Court, as a matter of Florida law, lacked jurisdiction to hear a further appeal. Id at *1. Although the Supreme Court of the United States granted review, the state argued that the Court lacked jurisdiction because Sullivan's claims were time-barred under state law. At oral argument, the state continued to press that point, but conceded that Sullivan would be entitled, as a matter of state law, to file a new postconviction petition in the event that the Court reversed the decision in *Graham*. Thus, following its decision in *Graham*, the Court dismissed the petition in *Sullivan*, and thereby avoided having to deal with both the nettlesome procedural issues and the unsavory facts presented in *Sullivan*.

[10] The decision to alter course also situated the Court within a larger debate. Some of the most fundamental questions for theories of adjudication involve locating the proper line between issues of fact and questions of law, the division of authority between factfinder and expositor of law, and the proper role of discretion in legal decision making. These issues arise in different forms in many areas of law, the most notable, perhaps, involving the proper division of authority between judge and jury in cases in which a jury trial is guaranteed by either the Sixth or Seventh Amendment to the Constitution. See US Const, Amend VI; US Const, Amend VII. However, these issues also arise in somewhat different form in other areas. They arise, for example, in administrative law, where, even absent the possibility of a trial by jury, the choice between rulemaking and adjudication is often thought to have significant practical consequences. See generally *United States v Storer Broadcasting Company*, 351 US 192 (1956) (holding that applicants for an FCC license to operate a broadcasting station must be given a "full hearing" if they have reached their existing limit of stations and presented adequate reasons to justify why the FCC's regulations should be changed or waived upon their application). One particularly important situation in which this issue arises is when the Supreme Court identifies a constitutional violation, defines its limits, and prescribes how it is to be proved. Compare *Swain v Alabama*, 380 US 202 (1965), with *Batson v Kentucky*, 476 US 79 (1986). Sometimes the Court provides for enforcement of a particular constitutional value by announcing a balancing test, which necessarily requires case-by-case adjudication, close attention to particular factual circumstances, and the exercise of discretion. At other times, the Court simply prescribes a categorical rule, which takes one or another factor to be dispositive, and effectively dictates the outcome once that factor has been established. The Court

The first part of this article will discuss the evolution of the Court's two lines of Eighth Amendment jurisprudence leading up to *Graham*, those relating to noncapital and capital cases, respectively, and will discuss the two distinct frameworks the Court has applied to the two categories: a balancing test for noncapital cases and a categorical approach for capital cases. It will also distill three factors that underlie both tests. The second part will discuss the Court's decision to apply the categorical approach to *Graham*, even though it was a noncapital case. The second part will then analyze the Court's holding and the principal alternative opinions (authored by Chief Justice Roberts and Justice Thomas) to determine why the Court was willing to break so fundamentally with its prior jurisprudence. The third part will consider the ramifications of *Graham* and will make some predictions about where the doctrinal innovation of *Graham* may lead. In particular, the third part will consider what *Graham* bodes for three subsets of offenders: juvenile offenders who commit homicides, mentally retarded defendants, and adult defendants who commit nonhomicides.

I. The Court's Cruel and Unusual Punishment Jurisprudence

Until *Graham*, the Court had drawn a clear and unmistakable line down the middle of its Eighth Amendment Cruel and Unusual Punishments Clause jurisprudence. Capital cases were analyzed under a "categorical" test, and all punishments of imprisonment for a term of years, even those that might seem to be functionally indistinguishable from capital sentences, were analyzed under a "balancing" test.[11] Specifically, in capital cases, the Court had used a multipart test to decide whether to formulate a categorical rule binding on the lower courts that would prohibit the death penalty with respect to an entire class of offenses or offenders. In noncapital (or term-of-years) cases, by contrast, the Court had engaged in a multipart, case-by-case analysis to determine whether, in light of all the circumstances, a particular sentence was constitutionally dis-

---

presumably chooses one approach or the other depending on what work needs to be done and how well the Court thinks one or the other approach will facilitate that work. At times, these practical considerations are strong enough to compel the Court to deviate from precedent.

[11] See generally Kathleen M. Sullivan, *The Supreme Court 1991 Term: Foreword: The Justices of Rules and Standards*, 106 Harv L Rev 22 (1992) (discussing categorical and balancing tests).

proportionate to the particular crime that the offender had committed. Before discussing the categorical-balancing distinction between the Court's capital and noncapital jurisprudence and the way in which that distinction was elided in *Graham*, it is useful to note that the two lines of jurisprudence share certain underlying commonalities; three common factors run through both tests.

A. THE THREE UNDERLYING FACTORS

The three factors that can be distilled from the Court's capital and noncapital Cruel and Unusual Punishments Clause jurisprudence are: the nature and seriousness of the offense (Factor 1), the culpability of the offender (Factor 2), and the nature and harshness of the penalty (Factor 3). The Court has focused on these three factors in determining whether a particular punishment is prohibited by the Eighth Amendment, and has incorporated these factors at different stages of its analysis depending on whether it is reviewing a capital or noncapital case. It is necessary to flesh out these factors before showing how they are manifested in the very different legal tests that have evolved in capital and noncapital cases.

First, the Court has considered offense-related considerations, which can be grouped together as Factor 1. These include the nature of the offense, the number of crimes committed by the defendant, and "the harm caused or threatened to the victim or society."[12] The Court has essentially divided the universe of crimes into three categories for purposes of proportionality analysis: murder, other crimes against individuals (including rape of a child), and certain crimes thought to constitute crimes against society, such as treason, terrorism, and drug trafficking. In the capital context, the Court has deemed the death penalty to be categorically impermissible for certain crimes (e.g., the crime of rape). In reviewing the imposition of life-without-parole sentences under recidivism statutes, the Court also has looked to the nature of the predicate crimes on which eligibility depends.

Second, the Court has focused on the culpability of the offender. We call this offender-related consideration Factor 2. At the threshold, the Court has distinguished among defendants with presumptively full adult capacity and culpability, those with severely

---

[12] *Graham*, 130 S Ct at 2042 (Roberts, CJ, concurring).

diminished culpability due to mental retardation, and those with presumptively diminished culpability by virtue of their youth. With respect to defendants with presumptively full adult capacity and culpability, the Court has found that the proportionality principle requires individualized consideration of the offender's "mental state and motive in committing the crime," as well as his or her criminal history, including prior convictions and such collateral matters as probation or parole violations.[13] The Court has constitutionally excluded from some punishments for some crimes those with severely diminished culpability by virtue of actual mental defect, as well as those who are categorically deemed to have constructive diminished culpability because of their membership in a particular age group. Presumably, special factors such as somewhat diminished mental capacity, psychological problems, and extraordinary emotional immaturity might also be considered. In general, however, the case law has suggested that offenders with full adult culpability will be eligible for the imposition of any punishment that is theoretically available with respect to the crime charged.

Third, the Court has considered the nature and harshness of the penalty. We call this consideration Factor 3. This factor also breaks down into three categories: capital sentences, noncapital sentences that may be deemed functionally similar to the death penalty (e.g., life without parole), and ordinary noncapital sentences. Despite the Court's repeated incantation that "death is different," the *Graham* Court acknowledged that some noncapital sentences are sufficiently like a capital sentence (either categorically or in particular circumstances) that they should be evaluated on that basis.[14] There also seems to be considerable disagreement within the Court as to whether such a realist or functional view of sentences is justified, and, if so, how far it should be permitted to affect the substance of the Court's Eighth Amendment jurisprudence.

B. THE TWO TESTS FOR CRUEL AND UNUSUAL PUNISHMENT CHALLENGES

The three factors we have distilled are evident in the very dif-

---

[13] Id at 2037.
[14] Id at 2027.

ferent tests the Court has formulated in noncapital and capital cases to determine whether a particular penalty is unconstitutionally cruel and unusual. In noncapital cases before the *Graham* decision, the Court applied what began as a three-part balancing test and evolved into a two-stage balancing test. The two stages are as follows. At Stage 1, the Court and lower courts engage in a threshold analysis to determine whether the defendant has established "an inference of gross disproportionality."[15] This threshold analysis requires an inquiry into "the gravity of the offense," which encompasses both the nature of the offense (Factor 1) and the culpability of the offender (Factor 2). To complete the threshold analysis, the gravity of the offense (Factors 1 and 2) is then weighed and balanced against the type of sentence imposed (Factor 3). Not every showing of disproportionality is sufficient to warrant further constitutional scrutiny; only in the "rare case"[16] in which the court determines that the defendant has indeed established an inference of *gross* disproportionality is the court required to proceed to the second stage. At Stage 2, the court considers "sentences imposed on other criminals in the same jurisdiction" ("intrajurisdictional" analysis) and "sentences imposed for commission of the same crime in other jurisdictions" ("interjurisdictional" analysis).[17] For both analyses, the court looks both to the legislatively available sentencing possibilities and to actual sentencing outcomes within the jurisdiction.[18]

The Court has applied a very different test to determine whether the Eighth Amendment categorically prohibits imposition of the death penalty for a particular kind of offense or class of offender. The Court's test in capital cases is a two-step categorical test. At Step 1 of the test, the Court determines whether "objective indicia of society's standards"[19] demonstrate a national consensus against the death penalty. (This part of the test is based on the notion that the Eighth Amendment "must draw its meaning from the evolving standards of decency that mark the progress of a maturing

---

[15] *Harmelin v Michigan*, 501 US 957, 1005 (1991) (Kennedy, J, concurring).

[16] Id.

[17] Id, quoting *Solem v Helm*, 463 US 277, 291–92 (1983).

[18] *Solem*, 463 US at 298–300.

[19] *Roper*, 543 US at 563. This aspect of the test derives originally from *Gregg v Georgia*, 428 US 153, 173 (1976) (discussing the importance of "objective indicia that reflect the public attitude toward a given sanction").

society.")[20] The Court determines whether a national consensus exists by looking to the number of jurisdictions in which legislation authorizes the death penalty for a particular category of offender or offense,[21] and by looking as well to how often, if at all, a legislatively authorized sentencing option has been utilized with respect to the particular offense or class of offender.[22] In examining sentencing outcomes, the Court may consider the total number of individuals within that class of offender who have received the death penalty for that offense in each jurisdiction.[23] At Step 2 of the test, the Court makes a "subjective,"[24] "independent judgment"[25] about whether capital punishment for the particular type of crime or class of offenders violates the Eighth Amendment. The Court does so by considering the same factors it considers at the threshold first stage of the balancing test in noncapital cases: It weighs the seriousness of the crime or class of crime at issue (Factor 1) and the culpability of the offender or class of offenders (Factor 2) against the severity of the punishment (Factor 3).[26] At this second step of the test, the Court also considers the "penological justifications" for the death penalty,[27] and especially whether it serves the goals of retribution and deterrence.[28] In addition, "the Court has referred to the laws of other countries

---

[20] *Trop v Dulles*, 356 US 86, 101 (1958).

[21] *Atkins v Virginia*, 536 US 304, 312 (2002).

[22] See *Roper*, 543 US at 567 (including among "objective indicia of consensus" "the infrequency of [a punishment's] use even where it remains on the books"). See also *Kennedy v Louisiana*, 554 US 407, 433 (2008) (noting the importance of examining "statistics about the number of executions" in addition to legislation).

[23] See, for example, *Kennedy*, 554 US at 433–34. Although this analysis is clearly a type of interjurisdictional analysis, the Court has never termed it such in its death penalty jurisprudence. Nor has the Court even analogized the interjurisdictional analysis used in noncapital cases to the national consensus analysis used in death cases.

[24] *Gregg*, 428 US at 173; *Coker v Georgia*, 433 US 584, 592 (1977).

[25] *Roper*, 543 US at 564.

[26] This subjective and independent comparative analysis goes back to *Gregg*, in which the Court held that "the imposition of capital punishment for the crime of murder" was not "invariably disproportionate to the crime." 428 US at 187. The Court engaged in the same analysis in its later capital cases. See, for example, *Enmund v Georgia*, 458 US 782, 797 (1982) ("the death penalty [Factor 3] . . . is an excessive penalty for the robber who, as such, does not take human life [Factor 1]"); *Atkins*, 536 US at 320–21 (concluding that especially in light of the "reduced capacity" of mentally retarded offenders (Factor 2), the death penalty is an "excessive" punishment (Factor 3)).

[27] *Roper*, 543 US at 571.

[28] See, for example, *Gregg*, 428 US at 183; *Coker*, 433 US at 592; *Edmund*, 458 US at 798–801; *Atkins*, 536 US at 318–21; *Roper*, 543 US at 571–75.

and to international authorities as instructive for its interpretation of the Eighth Amendment's prohibition of 'cruel and unusual punishments.'"[29] The international consensus is not a formal part of the test; the Court deems it to be "instructive" but "not . . . controlling."[30]

C. THE EVOLUTION OF THE COURT'S NONCAPITAL AND CAPITAL TESTS

A review of the Court's precedents demonstrates the evolution of the balancing test in the noncapital cases and the categorical test in the capital cases, and shows that until *Graham*, the Court had never imported the test for one type of case into the other context.

1. *The noncapital cases.* The Court's modern Eighth Amendment noncapital sentencing jurisprudence dates to 1980. In dissent in *Rummel v Estelle*,[31] Justice Powell laid out the first incarnation of what would become the Court's standard cruel and unusual test for noncapital cases. In *Rummel*, the Court faced the first proportionality challenge to a state noncapital sentence since the Court's 1962 holding that the Cruel and Unusual Punishments Clause of the Eighth Amendment applied to the states.[32] By a 5-to-4 vote, the Court rejected the challenge, holding that Texas had not violated the Eighth Amendment when, in accordance with its recidivism statute, it imposed a life sentence on a defendant who had been convicted of a series of three offenses—credit card fraud, passing a forged check, and obtaining money by false pretenses—which netted him a total of $229.11.[33] The Court held that "the length of the sentence actually imposed is purely a matter of legislative prerogative,"[34] and that Texas, "having twice imprisoned him for felonies, . . . was entitled to place upon Rummel the onus of one who is simply unable to bring his conduct within the social norms prescribed by the criminal law of the State."[35]

---

[29] *Roper*, 543 US at 575. See also *Coker*, 433 US 596 n 10 ("[T]he climate of international opinion" is "not irrelevant."); *Enmund*, 458 US at 796 n 22; *Atkins*, 536 US at 318–20.

[30] *Roper*, 543 US at 575.

[31] 445 US 263 (1980).

[32] See *Robinson v California*, 370 US 660, 667 (1962).

[33] *Rummel*, 445 US at 285.

[34] Id at 274.

[35] Id at 284.

However, the Court acknowledged that it had "on occasion stated that the Eighth Amendment prohibits imposition of a sentence that is grossly disproportionate to the severity of the crime"[36] and conceded in a footnote that a proportionality principle might come into play "in the extreme example mentioned by the dissent, . . . if a legislature made overtime parking a felony punishable by life imprisonment."[37]

In his dissent, Justice Powell suggested a test for determining unconstitutional disproportionality in a noncapital case. Powell's test had three steps, the first of which rested on one of the three factors we have distilled: First, courts should consider the nature of the offense (Factor 1); second, courts should examine the penalties imposed within the jurisdiction for similar crimes (intrajurisdictional analysis); and third, courts should look to penalties imposed in other jurisdictions for the same crime (interjurisdictional analysis).[38]

Three years later, in *Solem v Helm*,[39] another 5-to-4 decision, the Court specifically adopted the three-part test that the *Rummel* Court had rejected.[40] Justice Powell, writing for the Court, articulated Step 1 of the test as comparing "the gravity of the offense" (which could be discerned by evaluating "the harm caused or threatened to the victim or society" (Factor 1) as well as "the culpability of the offender" (Factor 2)) with "the harshness of the penalty."[41] Steps 2 and 3 remained the intrajurisdictional and interjurisdictional analyses.[42] Because of Helm's six prior nonviolent felony convictions, the court had sentenced him to life imprisonment without parole under South Dakota's recidivism statute.[43]

---

[36] Id at 271.

[37] Id at 274.

[38] Id at 295 (Powell, J, dissenting).

[39] 463 US 277 (1983).

[40] Id at 290–92.

[41] Id at 291–92.

[42] Id ("the sentences imposed on other criminals in the same jurisdiction; and . . . the sentences imposed for commission of the same crime in other jurisdictions.").

[43] Helm had committed a series of relatively minor offenses over a fifteen-year period, culminating in a drunken episode in which he uttered a "no account" check for $100 in circumstances he could not later recall. Helm was convicted of three third-degree burglaries, one each in 1964, 1966, and 1969. He was convicted of obtaining money by false pretense in 1972 and of grand larceny in 1973. In 1975, he was convicted of driving while intoxicated. Finally, in 1979, he pleaded guilty to the offense of uttering a "no account" check for $100. At the time of his guilty plea, Helm explained that he had been drinking

In view of Helm's record as a "habitual criminal," the trial judge thought that "the only prudent thing . . . is to lock you up for the rest of your natural life."[44] The *Solem* Court set aside the sentence as unconstitutionally disproportionate.[45] A proportionality challenge would not succeed in another noncapital case until *Graham*.

In 1991, the Court was asked in *Harmelin v Michigan*[46] to hold that the imposition of a mandatory life-without-parole sentence, without consideration of mitigating factors (such as the absence of prior felony convictions), violated the Cruel and Unusual Punishments Clause.[47] Harmelin was a first-time offender who had been convicted of simple possession of 672 grams of cocaine.[48] The relevant statute required imposition of a life-without-parole sentence for possession of 650 or more grams of a narcotic mixture, without regard to its purity.[49]

In an opinion by Justice Scalia, the Court in *Harmelin* declined to find that the mandatory life-without-parole sentence was unconstitutional, holding, again by a 5-to-4 vote, that severe mandatory penalties may be cruel, but that such penalties are not "unusual in the constitutional sense."[50] Justice Scalia, joined by Chief Justice Rehnquist, would have gone on to hold that the Eighth Amendment contains no proportionality requirement in noncapital cases.[51] While Justice Scalia acknowledged that "one can imagine extreme examples that no rational person, in no time or place, could accept," such examples are both "easy to decide" and "certain never to occur."[52] While acknowledging that the

---

and that he knew that he had ended up with more money than he had started out with, but he could not otherwise recall the circumstances. The maximum sentence for uttering a "no account" check was five years' imprisonment and a $5,000 fine. Id at 279–83.

[44] Id at 282–83.

[45] Id at 303. The Court reasoned that Helm had "received the penultimate sentence for relatively minor criminal conduct," had "been treated more harshly than other criminals in the state who have committed more serious crimes," and had "been treated more harshly than he would have been in any other jurisdiction, with the possible exception of a single state." Id.

[46] 501 US 957 (1991).

[47] Petition for Writ of Certiorari, *Harmelin v Michigan*, No 89-7272, *I (filed Aug 13, 1990) (available on Westlaw at 1990 WL 515104).

[48] *Harmelin*, 501 US at 961.

[49] Id.

[50] Id at 994–95.

[51] See generally *Harmelin*, 501 US 957.

[52] Id at 985–86.

Court previously had applied a proportionality principle in capital cases, Justice Scalia presumably found no constitutional basis for that practice either.[53] Justice Scalia stated that he would not over-rule that line of cases, but neither would he "extend it further."[54]

Justice Kennedy, writing for himself and two other members of the Court, concurred in the judgment, but rejected Justice Scalia's general views with respect to proportionality, on the ground that "stare decisis counsels our adherence to the narrow proportionality principle that has existed in our Eighth Amendment jurisprudence for 80 years."[55] Justice Kennedy also asserted that *Solem* "did not announce a rigid three-part test."[56] Instead, according to Justice Kennedy, it established a "threshold" inquiry into whether a "comparison of the crime committed and the sentence imposed leads to an inference of gross disproportionality."[57] "[O]nly in the rare case" in which such an inference was created was it appropriate to engage in "intrajurisdictional and interjurisdictional analyses."[58] The *Harmelin* plurality thereby redefined Justice Powell's three-part test as a two-stage test, consisting of a difficult-to-meet threshold gross disproportionality inquiry at Stage 1, followed at Stage 2 by intrajurisdictional and interjurisdictional analyses.

The four dissenting Justices would have held that Harmelin's sentence was cruel and unusual.[59] Particularly noteworthy was Justice White's emphasis on the limited universe of sentences available in Michigan. He found significance in the fact that "[t]he mandatory sentence of life imprisonment without possibility of parole 'is the most severe punishment that the State could have

---

[53] Id at 965.

[54] Id at 995.

[55] Id at 996 (Kennedy, J, concurring). Justice Kennedy's reference to "80 years" is a reference to *Weems v United States*, 217 US 349 (1910), in which the Court held that a noncapital sentence violated the Cruel and Unusual Punishments Clause because it was excessive compared to the crime. The case involved a criminal conviction from the Philippines, which was then subject to federal jurisdiction. The defendant had been convicted of falsifying pay records and sentenced to fifteen years' hard labor, permanent deprivation of civil rights, and lifetime surveillance. Although this "narrow proportionality principle" has "existed in our Eighth Amendment jurisprudence" since *Weems*, its routine application in capital cases dates only to 1977, when the Court decided *Coker v Georgia*, 433 US 584 (1977), and in noncapital cases to 1980, when the Court decided *Rummel v Estelle*, 445 US 63 (1980).

[56] *Harmelin*, 501 US at 1004 (Kennedy, J, concurring).

[57] Id at 1005.

[58] Id.

[59] Id at 1027 (White, J, dissenting).

imposed on any criminal for any crime,' for Michigan has no death penalty."[60] The *Graham* Court would later justify its holding by reference to a similar consideration, noting that its decision in *Roper* had left life without parole as the most severe penalty any juvenile could receive.

Finally, in 2003, the Court decided two noncapital proportionality cases involving California's "three strikes" recidivism law.[61] In the first case, *Ewing v California*,[62] a defendant with two prior felony convictions was sentenced to a term of twenty-five years to life imprisonment as an enhanced penalty for shoplifting three golf clubs valued at $399 each.[63] The Court upheld the sentence by a 5-to-4 vote. In a plurality opinion for herself, the Chief Justice, and Justice Kennedy, Justice O'Connor held, "The proportionality principles in our cases distilled in Justice Kennedy's concurrence [in *Harmelin*] guide our application of the Eighth Amendment" in noncapital cases.[64] Specifically, the *Ewing* Court held that *Solem* "did not *mandate*" comparative analysis "within and between jurisdictions."[65] *Ewing* thus solidified the transformation of *Solem*'s three-part test into a two-stage test with an onerous threshold inquiry. Justice Scalia and Justice Thomas each separately concurred in the judgment on the ground that the Eighth Amendment contains no proportionality principle.[66]

---

[60] Id at 1022. In addition, because of the mandatory life sentence imposed for mere possession, and the absence of any more punitive penalty, the same sentence would be imposed for the crime of possession with intent to distribute.

[61] Under that law, a defendant who previously had been convicted of one "serious" or "violent" felony would be subject, when later convicted of a felony, to a mandatory sentence "twice the term otherwise provided." Cal Penal Code § 667(e)(1) (West). A defendant who had two or more prior convictions for "serious" or "violent" felonies would receive a mandatory "indeterminate term of life imprisonment" as a sentence for a new felony conviction. Cal Penal Code § 667(e)(2)(A) (West).

[62] 538 US 11 (2003).

[63] Id at 19–20.

[64] Id at 23.

[65] Id (emphasis added).

[66] Justice Scalia reiterated the substance of his opinion in *Harmelin*, that is, that the Eighth Amendment's prohibition of cruel and unusual punishments "was aimed at excluding only certain modes of punishment, and was not a 'guarantee against disproportionate sentences.'" Id at 31. Justice Scalia went on to state that the "narrow proportionality principle" which had evolved from the majority's footnote concession in *Rummel*, and had been articulated at length in *Solem*, was incapable of coherent application and thus not entitled to stare decisis effect. Id. Justice Scalia argued that "the notion that the punishment should fit the crime . . . is inherently . . . tied to the penological goal of retribution," whereas, as the plurality concedes, a "sentence can have a variety of justifications, such

Justices Stevens, Breyer, Souter, and Ginsburg dissented. The dissenters would have held that Ewing's sentence was unconstitutionally disproportionate.[67] Among other things, Justice Breyer noted in his dissent that "Ewing's sentence, unlike Rummel's (but like Helm's sentence in *Solem*), is long enough to consume the productive remainder of almost any offender's life. (It means that Ewing himself, seriously ill when sentenced at age thirty-eight, will likely die in prison.)."[68]

In *Lockyer v Andrade*,[69] a federal habeas case that was decided the same day, the Court held, by the same 5-to-4 vote, that the California Court of Appeals had not ruled "contrary to" or unreasonably applied "clearly established" Supreme Court precedent when it rejected a disproportionality attack on the two consecutive twenty-five-year terms the sentencing court had imposed for two counts of petty theft by a person with a prior conviction.[70] The two counts of petty theft involved two instances of shoplifting videos with a total combined value of $150.[71] The majority found that the "clearly established" test (applicable to habeas cases because of the limitations on federal review mandated by the Antiterrorism and Effective Death Penalty Act of 1996)[72] was not met because the Court's jurisprudence was unclear: "In most situations, the task of determining what we have clearly established will be straightforward. The difficulty with Andrade's position, however, is that our precedents in this area have not been a model of clarity."[73]

Justice Souter, writing for the four dissenting Justices, would have found that the law was "clearly established" because Andrade's case was virtually identical to Helm's.[74] In addition, Justice Souter made the common-sense point that, practically speaking, a sentence of fifty years (for what he characterized as two trivial

---

as incapacitation, deterrence, retribution, or rehabilitation"—none of which logically can be evaluated in terms of proportionality. Id.

[67] Id at 35 (Breyer, J, dissenting).

[68] Id at 39.

[69] 538 US 63 (2003).

[70] Id at 77.

[71] Id at 66.

[72] Antiterrorism and Effective Death Penalty Act of 1996 (AEDPA), Pub L No 104-132, 110 Stat 1214 (1996).

[73] *Lockyer*, 538 US at 72.

[74] Id at 78 (Souter, J, dissenting).

offenses) imposed on an ill thirty-seven-year-old man "amounts to life without parole."[75] The majority responded:

> Justice Souter's position would treat a sentence of life without parole for the 77-year-old person convicted of murder as equivalent to a sentence of life with the possibility of parole in 10 years for the same person convicted of the same crime. Two different sentences do not become materially indistinguishable based solely upon the age of the persons sentenced.[76]

2. *The capital cases.* In its death penalty jurisprudence, the Court has employed a two-step test to determine when to adopt categorical, bright-line rules holding that the imposition of the death penalty could never be justified for a particular offense or category of offender. While the categorical test itself has changed little since its earliest articulation, defendants have had substantial success in convincing the Court that they have met the test's criteria, and, as a result, the number of circumstances in which the Court categorically prohibits capital punishment has grown.

As noted above, to determine whether there is a national consensus against the imposition of the death penalty for a particular crime (e.g., rape) or a particular class of offender (e.g., the mentally retarded), the Court first examines "objective" criteria (Step 1 of the test), and then brings to bear its own "subjective" judgment about whether the imposition of the death penalty for that same crime or on that same class of offenders constitutes cruel and unusual punishment (Step 2 of the test).[77] If both steps of the test are met, the Court categorically prohibits the imposition of the death penalty for the type of crime or class of offender at issue. The Court also considers whether there is an international consensus on the issue, although that inquiry is not formally one of the steps of the test.

The Court's categorical rules in capital cases have been based on two of the factors we have distilled. Sometimes the Court imposes a categorical rule based on "the nature of the offense" (Factor 1), prohibiting the death penalty for a particular crime; sometimes the Court imposes a categorical rule based on "the

---

[75] Id at 79.

[76] Id at 74.

[77] *Gregg*, 428 US at 173; *Coker*, 433 US at 592; *Enmund*, 458 US at 788–89; *Thompson v Oklahoma*, 487 US 815, 821–23 (1988); *Atkins*, 536 US at 312–13; *Kennedy*, 554 US at 421. See also Part I.B above.

characteristics of the offender" (Factor 2), prohibiting the death penalty for a particular class of defendants.[78] The cases in which the Court has categorically prohibited the imposition of death based on the nature of the offense include *Coker v Georgia*[79] (rape of an adult), *Enmund v Florida*[80] (felony murder), and *Kennedy v Louisiana*[81] (rape of a child), while the Court has prohibited the death penalty based on the characteristics of the offender in cases such as *Thompson v Oklahoma*[82] (youth under sixteen), *Atkins v Virginia*[83] (mental retardation), and *Roper v Simmons*[84] (youth under eighteen).

The modern development of proportionality analysis in capital cases begins after the Court's 1976 reinstatement of the death penalty in *Gregg v Georgia*.[85] In 1977, the Court ruled in *Coker v Georgia*[86] that the Cruel and Unusual Punishments Clause categorically prohibited the imposition of the death penalty for the crime of rape of an adult woman. Four Justices applied the two-step test and concluded that the punishment was grossly disproportionate to the severity of the crime.[87] The plurality determined that Step 1 of the test was satisfied because "the objective evidence of the country's present judgment"[88] demonstrated that death was not an acceptable penalty for the crime at issue.[89] In reaching this determination, the plurality focused on three facts: no other state authorized the death penalty for rape of an adult, only two other states authorized the death penalty for rape of a child, and Georgia juries had not imposed the death penalty in 90 percent of rape convictions.[90] Step 2 of the test was satisfied because, in the Court's independent judgment, comparing the seriousness of the crime of

---

[78] *Graham*, 130 S Ct at 2022.

[79] 433 US 584 (1977).

[80] 458 US 782 (1982).

[81] 554 US 407 (2008).

[82] 487 US 815 (1988).

[83] 536 US 304 (2002).

[84] 543 US 551 (2005).

[85] 428 US 153 (1976).

[86] 433 US 584 (1977).

[87] Id at 592.

[88] Id at 593.

[89] Id at 596.

[90] Id at 586–600.

rape (Factor 1) with the harshness of capital punishment (Factor 3) leads to the conclusion that "the death penalty . . . is an excessive penalty for the rapist who, as such, does not take human life."[91] According to these four Justices, mere aggravating circumstances could not justify imposition of the death penalty on a defendant whose victim did not die.[92] Two Justices would have held that the death penalty violates the Eighth Amendment in all circumstances.[93]

Several members of the *Coker* Court rejected the appropriateness of a categorical rule. Justice Powell concurred in the judgment, but he would have upheld the imposition of the death penalty in a case in which the rape was committed with "excessive brutality" or resulted in "serious or lasting injury" to the victim.[94] In a dissent joined by Justice Rehnquist, Chief Justice Burger also rejected the appropriateness of a categorical rule.[95] They suggested that imposition of the death penalty would be constitutionally permissible, for example, in the case of "a person who has, within the space of three years, raped three separate women, killing one and attempting to kill another, who is serving prison terms exceeding his probable lifetime and has not hesitated to escape confinement at the first available opportunity."[96]

The Court continued to recognize additional categorical exclusions from capital punishment through the late 1980s. In 1983, in *Enmund v Florida*,[97] the Court again applied the two-step test and adopted another bright-line rule, holding that the death penalty could not be imposed for felony murder, where the defendant had not committed the actual murder and lacked intent to kill.[98] The *Enmund* Court referred back to *Gregg* to add an additional consideration to the Court's Step 2 subjective analysis: To pass constitutional muster, capital punishment must contribute to the penological purposes of retribution and deterrence.[99] Four Justices

---

[91] Id at 598.

[92] Id at 599.

[93] Id at 600.

[94] Id at 604.

[95] See id at 606–07 (Burger, CJ, dissenting).

[96] Id at 607.

[97] 458 US 782 (1982).

[98] Id at 801.

[99] Id at 798–99.

dissented.[100] In 1986, in *Ford v Wainwright*,[101] the Court held that the Eighth Amendment categorically prohibited the execution of prisoners who were insane at the time of execution.[102] Five Justices held that the Eighth Amendment prohibited the execution of the insane. Two Justices joined in the judgment on the narrow ground that Florida had deprived the defendant of a state-created liberty interest without affording due process of law, and two other Justices dissented.[103] In 1988, the Court held in *Thompson v Oklahoma*,[104] by a vote of 5-to-3, that juveniles under the age of sixteen could not be executed pursuant to death penalty statutes that did not specify any minimum age.[105] Four Justices would have held that the Eighth Amendment categorically prohibited the execution of people younger than sixteen, regardless of what the statute provided.[106]

The next year, the Court declined to extend categorical protection from capital punishment to mentally retarded persons and to juveniles who commit capital crimes while under the age of seventeen. In *Penry v Lynaugh*,[107] the Court was asked to hold that executing mentally retarded persons categorically violated the Eighth Amendment.[108] The Court held that the Eighth Amendment was violated because the trial court failed to instruct the jury that it could consider and give effect to mitigating evidence of the defendant's mental retardation and abused background, but only four Justices would have held that the Eighth Amendment categorically prohibited the execution of the mentally retarded.[109] Also in 1989, in *Stanford v Kentucky*,[110] the Court declined to adopt a bright-line rule prohibiting the execution of persons who com-

---

[100] See generally id at 801–31 (O'Connor, J, dissenting).

[101] 477 US 399 (1986).

[102] Id at 410.

[103] See id at 399.

[104] 487 US 815 (1988).

[105] Id at 838 (Stevens, J) (plurality).

[106] Id.

[107] 492 US 302 (1989).

[108] Id at 307.

[109] See generally id.

[110] 492 US 361 (1989).

mitted capital crimes while sixteen or seventeen.[111] Four Justices would have adopted that rule.[112]

Penry and *Stanford* proved to be short-lived. In 2002, the Court decided *Atkins v Virginia*,[113] holding, by a 6-to-3 vote, that the Eighth Amendment categorically prohibited the execution of the mentally retarded.[114] Three years later, in *Roper*, the Court held, by a 5-to-4 vote, that the Cruel and Unusual Punishments Clause prohibited the execution of persons whose offenses were committed before the age of eighteen.[115]

In *Atkins*, the Court reconfirmed its two-step test for determining whether the Eighth Amendment categorically prohibits imposition of the death penalty for a particular kind of offense or class of offender. With regard to Step 1 of the test, the Court emphasized that "[p]roportionality review under . . . evolving standards [of decency] should be informed by objective factors to the maximum extent possible,"[116] and "the clearest and most reliable objective evidence of contemporary values is the legislation enacted by the country's legislatures."[117] Recent legislation and the trend of legislation are particularly important.[118] The Court also looked to other indicia of consensus, such as the frequency with which an authorized penalty has been used,[119] evidence of a "broader social and professional consensus,"[120] and the practice of other countries.[121] Once the Court determined that a consensus existed, the Court moved on to Step 2 of the test and brought its "own judgment . . . to bear on the acceptability of the death penalty under the Eighth Amendment."[122] The Court decided that executing the mentally retarded did not meet the goals of retribution

---

[111] Id at 380.

[112] Id at 382.

[113] 536 US 304 (2002).

[114] Id at 321.

[115] *Roper*, 543 US at 578.

[116] 536 US at 312 (citations omitted).

[117] Id, citing *Penry*, 492 US at 331.

[118] *Atkins*, 536 US at 313–16.

[119] Id at 316.

[120] Id at 316 n 21.

[121] Id ("[W]ithin the world community, the imposition of the death penalty for crimes committed by mentally retarded offenders is overwhelmingly disapproved.").

[122] Id at 312, quoting *Coker*, 433 US at 597 (1977).

and deterrence,[123] and that there was therefore no "reason to disagree with the judgment reached by the citizenry and its legislators."[124] Applying this analysis, the *Atkins* Court held that the Eighth Amendment categorically prohibits the execution of the mentally retarded.[125]

In *Roper*, the Court revisited the juvenile death penalty issue. Using the same two-step test, the Court, in an opinion by Justice Kennedy, held that the Eighth Amendment categorically precludes the imposition of the death penalty for any crime committed before the age of eighteen.[126] As in *Atkins*, the Court in *Roper* looked to "the opinion of the world community" as "not controlling [the] outcome" but "provid[ing] respected and significant confirmation of [the Court's] own conclusions."[127]

Finally, in 2008, the Court decided *Kennedy v Louisiana*,[128] in which the Court again applied its two-step test and held, by a 5-to-4 vote, that the Eighth Amendment categorically precludes the imposition of the death penalty for the rape of a child where the crime did not result, and was not intended to result, in the victim's death.[129] Effectively, the Court answered the question left open in *Coker* and thus expanded the prohibition against the imposition of capital punishment for rape to include all rape cases not resulting in the victim's death. Justice Kennedy, again writing for the majority, distinguished the crime of rape (including the rape of a child) from the crime of murder, holding that the Eighth

---

[123] *Atkins*, 536 US at 321.

[124] Id at 313. See also id at 321.

[125] Id at 321.

[126] *Roper*, 543 US at 568. Justice O'Connor, one of the four dissenters, observed: "The Court's decision today establishes a categorical rule forbidding the execution of any offender for any crime committed before his eighteenth birthday, no matter how deliberate, wanton, or cruel the offense. Neither the objective evidence of contemporary societal values, nor the Court's moral proportionality analysis, nor the two in tandem suffice to justify this ruling." Id at 587 (O'Connor, J, dissenting).

[127] Although Justice Kennedy has been criticized for considering the international perspective in *Roper*, Erwin Chemerinsky believes that "the criticism is misplaced because Justice Kennedy did not base his decision on the law in other countries. Instead, he pointed to it as an indication of evolving standards of decency." Erwin Chemerinsky, *The Rehnquist Court and the Death Penalty*, 94 Georgetown L J 1367, 1372 (2006); see also Barry Sullivan, *The Irish Constitution: Some Reflections from Abroad*, in Oran Doyle and Eoin Carolan, eds, *The Irish Constitution: Governance and Values* (Thompson Round Hall, 2008) (discussing controversy regarding citation of foreign law).

[128] 554 US 407 (2008).

[129] Id at 413.

Amendment never permitted the imposition of the death penalty for rape.[130] However, Justice Kennedy specifically left open the possibility that other crimes—such as drug trafficking, treason, and terrorism—might well warrant the death penalty.[131]

Pre-*Graham* precedent thus demonstrates that the Court has historically applied the two-stage balancing test in noncapital cases to determine, on a case-by-case basis, whether a given term-of-years punishment violates the Eighth Amendment, and has applied the two-step categorical test in capital cases to determine whether to categorically prohibit the imposition of the death penalty for a particular type of crime or class of offender.[132] Precedent also shows that defendants have fared far better in capital cases than in noncapital cases. While the Court has expanded categorical prohibitions on the death penalty for particular types of crimes and particular classes of defendants, the Court has narrowed the relief available to defendants challenging their noncapital sentences.

II. The Radical Result in Graham v Florida

A. THE DEFENDANTS' BOLD LITIGATION STRATEGY

The *Graham* and *Sullivan* defendants adopted a litigation strategy that appeared risky at first blush. Although the defendants were challenging a noncapital sentence rather than the imposition of the death penalty, they shied away from the traditional case-by-case balancing test used in noncapital cases and instead asked the Court to analogize their cases to the capital case of *Roper*, in which the Court had announced a categorical rule that imposing the death penalty on juveniles violated the Eighth Amendment.[133]

---

[130] Id at 446.

[131] Id at 437.

[132] The case law also reflects a great deal of struggle within the Court over the legitimacy and application of the Eighth Amendment's proportionality principle, as well as strong disagreement over the legitimacy of limiting the discretion of the sentencing authority through constitutionally based, bright-line rules that require issues to be decided as a matter of law.

[133] See, for example, Brief for Petitioner, *Sullivan v Florida*, 08-7621, *5 (filed July 16, 2009) (available on Westlaw at 2009 WL 2159656) ("Sullivan Pet Brief") (stating from the outset of the summary of the argument: "The constitutional logic of *Roper v Simmons* controls this case."); Reply Brief, *Graham v Florida*, 08-7412, *2 (filed October 14, 2009) (available on Westlaw at 2009 WL 3340114) ("Graham Rep Brief") ("*Roper*'s rationale cannot be cabined solely to capital cases.").

Indeed, Sullivan articulated and applied only the categorical test from *Roper* and the other death penalty cases[134] and made no mention whatever of the traditional noncapital test. Graham paid slightly more attention to the noncapital test. He first articulated three "factors" that included only the threshold analysis portion of the noncapital test ("a comparison of the gravity of the offense with the harshness of the punishment imposed")[135] and then spent the bulk of his brief focusing on *Roper* and applying *Roper*'s categorical test to the facts of his case.[136] Only toward the end of the brief did Graham apply the traditional two-stage noncapital test and engage in intrajurisdictional and interjurisdictional analyses.[137] Clearly, the defendants thought it virtually impossible that they could prevail under the balancing test traditionally used in noncapital cases and therefore wanted the Court to abandon (or ignore) that test for purposes of evaluating their claims.

Given that the Court had applied some species of the balancing test for nearly thirty years in noncapital cases, it seemed unlikely that the Court would simply abandon that test, abandon the notion that "death is different," and apply the alternative test that the defendants proposed. On the other hand, if the Court used the traditional noncapital proportionality test, the defendants had virtually no chance of winning. The Court had not sustained a single Eighth Amendment challenge in a noncapital case since 1983, the year Helm convinced a bare majority of the Court that the imposition of a sentence of life imprisonment without parole was a constitutionally disproportionate punishment for the offense of issuing a "no account" check.

The defendants in *Graham* and *Sullivan* fortified their position by arguing that their cases fit into both subsets of prior jurisprudence subject to categorical rules. As discussed above, the Court's capital jurisprudence covers cases in which the death penalty is categorically prohibited based on the nature of the offense (Factor

---

[134] Sullivan Pet Brief at *8–*11.

[135] Brief for Petitioner, *Graham v Florida*, 08-7412, *31 (filed July 16, 2009) (available on Westlaw at 2009 WL 2159655) ("Graham Pet Brief"). The other two "factors" Graham articulated came from the categorical test: "whether the particular sentence would serve a legitimate penological purpose" and "a comparison of the sentence imposed to evolving standards of decency as reflected in the laws and practices of the States and the international community." Id.

[136] Id at *36–*53. Part II of the brief applies the categorical test.

[137] Id at *56–*64.

1), as well as cases in which it is categorically prohibited based on the characteristics of the offender (Factor 2). Graham argued that he was part of a class defined by both factors: his crimes had not resulted in death (Factor 1), and his juvenile status constituted a constructive diminution of his culpability (Factor 2). The defendant also argued that Factor 3 (the harshness of the penalty) was especially salient for his particular class, because, after *Roper*, life without parole was the most severe penalty that any juvenile under the age of eighteen could face. Thus, Graham argued that because the Court had held in *Enmund* that the death penalty was disproportionate to nonhomicide crimes, "[i]t logically follows . . . that the harshest juvenile punishment (life without parole) is disproportionate when it is imposed on a juvenile offender, like Graham, who did not take life, attempt to take life, or intend to take life."[138] The defendants' primary argument in support of applying the categorical test hinged on the characteristics and culpability of juvenile offenders.[139] In essence, they argued that "youth is different"—so much so that it is a controlling factor analogous to "death," and thus one that justifies application of a categorical prohibition by analogy to the Court's capital jurisprudence.

B. THE REASONS BEHIND THE GRAHAM MAJORITY'S BREAK WITH
PRECEDENT

Remarkably, the *Graham* majority accepted the defendants' argument, thereby breaking with the Court's prior Eighth Amendment jurisprudence, even as the Court feigned adherence to precedent. Although Chief Justice Roberts claimed in his concurrence

---

[138] Id at *55. One significant question raised in both the *Graham* and *Sullivan* cases was the precise age at which the Court should draw the line if it chose to formulate a categorical rule prohibiting the imposition of life-without-parole sentences on juveniles. In one sense, there was an easy solution, that is, for the Court simply to adopt the same age that it had adopted for purposes of the death penalty in *Roper*. On the other hand, perhaps there was a point below eighteen at which there was, as a general matter, sufficient culpability to warrant imposition of a sentence that was not entirely indistinguishable from death. The matter was discussed extensively at oral argument in both cases. Given his age at the time of his crimes, Graham was required to argue that the cutoff should be eighteen. Given his own circumstances, Sullivan would have been content with an earlier age being designated as the cutoff, but he offered no advice to the Court as to where the line should be drawn, except to say that it should be a line that included him within the protection of the rule. The Court ultimately drew the line at eighteen without any real explanation, but presumably because that is where it had drawn the line with respect to the death penalty in *Roper*.

[139] Graham Pet Brief at *32–*43; Sullivan Pet Brief at *11–*30. Part A of the Brief applies the categorical test.

that the Court would have reached the same result under the balancing test traditionally employed in noncapital cases, a closer analysis of the three principal opinions in *Graham* (Justice Kennedy's opinion for the majority, Chief Justice Roberts's concurrence, and Justice Thomas's dissent) shows that the Court's adoption of the defendants' proffered test was far from gratuitous in terms of the result it permitted the Court to reach. Indeed, the adoption of a categorical test prohibiting life-without-parole sentences for juveniles was essential if the Court was to ensure that Graham and other juvenile offenders who commit nonhomicide crimes would not be subject to a punishment that was thought to be unconstitutional by a majority of the Court.[140]

Justice Kennedy began his opinion for the Court by explaining that the Court's Eighth Amendment proportionality jurisprudence could be divided into "two general classifications," namely, challenges to sentences of imprisonment, which require an analysis of "all the circumstances of the case," and challenges to capital sentences, which require the application of "categorical restrictions."[141] After elaborating at some length on the legal test ap-

---

[140] Justice Thomas's dissent was joined in whole by Justice Scalia and in part by Justice Alito. In addition to the three principal opinions, there was a brief concurring opinion by Justice Stevens (joined by Justices Ginsburg and Sotomayor) and a brief dissenting opinion by Justice Alito. In his concurring opinion, Justice Stevens took issue with Justice Thomas's assertion that the majority opinion was in error because it was unfaithful to the Court's earlier decisions in *Lockyer, Ewing, Harmelin*, and *Rummel*. Justice Stevens responded that, "Given 'evolving standards of decency' have played a central role in our Eighth Amendment jurisprudence for at least a century, see *Weems v United States*, 217 US 349, 373–78 (1910), this argument suggests that the dissenting opinions in those cases more accurately describe the law today than does Justice Thomas' rigid interpretation of the Amendment." *Graham*, 130 S Ct at 2036 (Stevens, J, concurring). Justice Stevens concluded his opinion with the observation that "[w]hile Justice Thomas would apparently not rule out a death sentence for a $50 theft by a 7-year-old, . . . the Court wisely rejects his static approach to the law. Standards of decency have evolved since 1980. They will never stop doing so." Id. Justice Alito wrote separately to make three points. First, Justice Alito joined only in Parts I and III of Justice Thomas's opinion, and thus did not join in three other parts. Those were Part II, in which Justice Thomas argued that the Court's decision in *Weems*, as well as the Court's more recent jurisprudence, were unfaithful to the language and history of the Eighth Amendment; Part IV, in which Justice Thomas attempted to show that the result was not even warranted under *Solem* and would create serious problems of application; and Part V, in which Justice Thomas stated that the decision as to whether the punishment fit the crime was one for the Florida legislature, not the Supreme Court. Justice Alito made two other points: First, "Nothing in the Court's opinion affects the imposition of a sentence to a term of years without the possibility of parole." *Graham*, 130 S Ct at 2058 (Alito, J, dissenting). Second, "the question whether petitioner's sentence violates the narrow, as-applied proportionality principle that applies to noncapital sentences is not properly before us in this case," because Graham had not sufficiently preserved that issue. Id.

[141] *Graham*, 130 S Ct at 2021.

plicable to each class of cases, however, Justice Kennedy quickly and deftly abandoned that well-established distinction, and applied the test for capital cases to a noncapital case. He largely accomplished this sleight-of-hand in a single paragraph.[142] Justice Kennedy's opinion attempted to mask the Court's departure from precedent by (1) distinguishing *Graham* from the noncapital cases the Court previously had considered, and (2) claiming that the Court's prior jurisprudence left it with a legitimate choice between the categorical approach and the balancing approach in the context of life-without-parole sentences for juveniles, when, in fact, the Court had never previously recognized the categorical approach as an available option in the noncapital context.[143]

In a move that deeply troubled the dissenters, the Court first endorsed Graham's grounds for distinguishing his case from the noncapital cases previously considered by the Court, thus allowing the defendants, by pursuing a novel litigation strategy, to redefine the legal issue presented for the Court's decision: "The present case involves an issue the Court has not considered previously: a categorical challenge to a term-of-years sentence."[144] The majority explained that it was not using the case-by-case balancing approach it had used in the noncapital cases of *Harmelin* and *Ewing* because those defendants had simply challenged their own individual sentences under the traditional test. Graham, by contrast, was challenging the constitutionality of a sentence as applied to an entire class of persons, namely, to all juveniles who had committed nonhomicide offenses.[145] According to the majority, the Court's balancing approach was "suited [only] for considering a gross proportionality challenge to a particular defendant's sentence, but here a sentencing practice itself is in question. This case implicates a particular type of sentence as it applies to an entire class of offenders who have committed a range of crimes."[146] Without further analysis, the majority then held that because Graham's

---

[142] Id at 2022–23.

[143] The Court's pretense of adherence to precedent calls to mind Justice Scalia's criticism of the majority in *Federal Election Commission v Wisconsin Right to Life*, 551 US 449 (2007), that the Court had "effectively overrule[d]" precedent while pretending its new test was compatible with its old test; Justice Scalia pronounced that "[t]his faux judicial restraint is judicial obfuscation." Id at 498.

[144] *Graham*, 130 S Ct at 2022.

[145] Id.

[146] Id at 2022–23.

challenge questioned the appropriateness of a particular penalty for a class of people who had committed various crimes, rather than for a particular individual who had committed a particular crime, Step 1 of the traditional noncapital test, which requires a threshold comparison of the severity of the penalty and the gravity of the offense, "does not advance the analysis."[147]

The majority's attempt to conceal its deviation from precedent is unpersuasive. First, it is unclear why a defendant's framing of the issue presented should ever be sufficient by itself to dictate the Court's approach to the substantive issues presented by a case, much less to persuade the Court to depart from precedent and abandon its customary mode of analysis.[148] Moreover, the challenges in *Harmelin* and *Ewing*, no less than the challenge mounted in *Graham*, could be said to "implicate[] a particular type of sentence as it applies to an entire class of offenders who have committed a range of crimes," even though they were not styled as categorical challenges. It could easily be said that *Harmelin* involved the "sentencing practice" of giving an entire class of offenders (adult defendants) life-without-parole sentences for fairly minor crimes. It could likewise be said that *Ewing* involved the sentencing practice of giving the class of adult defendants with prior criminal histories sentences of twenty-five years to life for even more minor crimes. While it is true that the Court had recently given juveniles class treatment in capital cases and had never treated adult defendants writ large as a class in such cases, that difference alone would not explain the Court's application of the categorical test to a noncapital case, especially considering the Court's repeated admonition that death is different.

The Court also attempted to mask its departure from relevant precedent by claiming that it was simply choosing between two equally legitimate tests when it decided to evaluate Graham's case under the categorical approach. But that was not the case. Notwithstanding the Court's failure to acknowledge it, the Court's prior jurisprudence recognized no such choice in the noncapital context. Instead of applying the balancing approach that the Court

---

[147] Id at 2023.

[148] Justice Thomas observed in dissent: "The Court asserts that categorical proportionality review is necessary here merely because Graham asks for a categorical rule and because the Court thinks clear lines are a good idea. I find those factors wholly insufficient to justify the Court's break from past practice." Id at 2047 (Thomas, J, dissenting) (citations omitted).

traditionally had applied in noncapital cases (or explaining its decision not to do so), the majority simply stated that "the appropriate analysis is the one used in cases that involved the categorical
approach, specifically *Atkins, Roper,* and *Kennedy*."[149] By citing
these three decisions in this way, the Court gave the impression
that *Graham* followed naturally from established case law. But
Atkins, Roper, and *Kennedy* were all capital cases, and, given the
Court's "death is different" mantra, there was no basis for assuming that the approach used in those cases provided an available
option in a noncapital case. Later in the opinion, the majority
referred to the traditional balancing test for noncapital cases, stating: "Another possible approach would be to hold that the Eighth
Amendment requires courts to take the offender's age into consideration as part of a case-specific gross disproportionality inquiry."[150] But of course that traditional balancing test was not
merely "[a]nother possible approach"; it was the only approach
that found support in the Court's noncapital jurisprudence. In
sum, the majority attempted to mask the radical nature of its
opinion by alternately pretending either to be responding to a new
permutation of Eighth Amendment challenge or to be choosing
between two relevant, established, equally available analytical tests.
Notwithstanding the Court's protestations to the contrary, *Graham* marked a clear break with precedent.

Chief Justice Roberts, in a concurring opinion, twice called the
categorical test that the Court announced in *Graham* "a new constitutional rule,"[151] adding in one instance that the new rule was
"of dubious provenance."[152] He also accused the majority of "using
this case as a vehicle for unsettling our established jurisprudence,"[153] and further observed that the Court's holding "is at
odds with our longstanding view that 'the death penalty is different
from other punishments in kind rather than degree.'"[154] Justice
Thomas, in dissent, criticized the majority opinion on the more

---

[149] Id at 2023. Since *Atkins* and *Roper* belong to the subset of categorical cases that
focuses on the characteristics of the offender, while *Kennedy* belongs to the subset that
focuses on the nature of the offense, the majority thus acknowledged that *Graham* straddled
both subsets.

[150] Id at 2031.

[151] Id at 2041 (Roberts, CJ, concurring).

[152] Id at 2037.

[153] Id at 2042.

[154] Id at 2038–39, citing *Solem,* 463 US at 294.

fundamental ground that the Court's gross disproportionality jurisprudence itself "lacks a principled foundation" in the Eighth Amendment, but he also criticized the Court for "remarkably expand[ing] [the] reach" of that standard.[155] In addition, Justice Thomas pointed out the unprecedented nature of the Court's decision to abandon the traditional balancing test in favor of a categorical rule: "For the first time in its history, the Court declares an entire class of offenders immune from a noncapital sentence using the categorical approach it previously reserved for death penalty cases alone. . . . 'Death is different' no longer."[156]

The *Graham* Court's decision to adopt a categorical test is especially noteworthy because that decision also deviated from the Court's recent tendency to favor the use of balancing tests, especially in criminal procedure cases. Although the Warren Court often decided constitutional issues by adopting categorical rules, the Court more recently has shifted its approach to favor the use of balancing tests, both in the constitutional criminal procedure arena and elsewhere.[157] As Jeffrey Fisher has suggested, "the Burger and Rehnquist Courts made the balancing revolution complete," particularly in the criminal procedure context.[158] Moreover, Fisher has observed that "modern balancing tends to work against individual rights in the realm of criminal procedure, where the consideration of governmental interests most often is used to create exceptions to previously firm protections for the accused."[159] Fisher points out that the Court has abandoned a balancing test in favor of a categorical test in only two criminal procedure cases in the past decade, namely, *Crawford* and *Blakely*.[160]

---

[155] Id at 2046 (Thomas, J, dissenting).

[156] Id.

[157] Jeffrey L. Fisher, *Categorical Requirements in Constitutional Criminal Procedure*, 94 Georgetown L J 1493, 1498–1502 (2006). See generally Sullivan, 106 Harv L Rev at 22 (cited in note 11); T. A. Alenikoff, *Constitutional Law in the Age of Balancing*, 96 Yale L J 943 (1987).

[158] Fisher, 94 Georgetown L J at 1502 (cited in note 157).

[159] Id at 1505. See also Kathleen M. Sullivan, *Post-Liberal Judging: The Roles of Categorization and Balancing*, 63 U Colo L Rev 283, 307 (1992) ("[A]fter a period in which liberals have been using categorical approaches to favor rights and limit government, conservatives have advocated a shift to balancing approaches in order to limit rights and liberate government. A rich vein of examples may be found in contemporary criminal procedure law.").

[160] Fisher, 94 Georgetown L J at 1502 (cited in note 157) (discussing *Crawford v Washington*, 541 US 36 (2004) and *Blakely v Washington*, 542 US 961 (2005)).

The three principal opinions in *Graham* (the majority opinion, Chief Justice Roberts's concurrence, and Justice Thomas's dissent) provide significant insight into the reasons the Court departed from precedent, broke with the general trend identified by Fisher, and abandoned the traditional noncapital balancing test for a categorical formulation in the context of life-without-parole sentences for juveniles who commit nonhomicide crimes. If the Court's prior jurisprudence were truly controlling in *Graham*, the Court faced no "choice" of methodology; it was required to analyze Graham's claims under the traditional balancing test. Nonetheless, the majority perceived an alternative method of analysis and chose to adopt it.

The majority offered some insight into why it had exercised its "choice" in favor of the categorical approach by stating: "The [traditional] case-by-case approach to sentencing must . . . be confined by some boundaries."[161] The majority then provided three justifications for employing a categorical approach with respect to juveniles who are eligible for life-without-parole sentences. The majority's first justification rested on institutional competencies. The majority took from *Roper* the general proposition that juvenile offenders on the whole are less culpable and more capable of reform than adult offenders, and concluded that sentencing authorities lack the means for identifying "with sufficient accuracy" the "few incorrigible juvenile offenders" who might theoretically deserve the ultimate punishment a juvenile can receive.[162] The majority's second justification was that juveniles are generally less able than adults to assist their counsel to an extent that is "likely to impair the quality" of their representation, and that "a case-by-case approach . . . does not take account of [these] special difficulties encountered by counsel in juvenile representation."[163] The third justification was that "a categorical rule gives all juvenile nonhomicide offenders a chance to demonstrate maturity and reform."[164]

Underlying each of the majority's justifications for preferring a categorical rule over the traditional balancing approach is a normative judgment based on a factual conclusion: although a cate-

---

[161] *Graham*, 130 S Ct at 2031–32.

[162] Id at 2032.

[163] Id.

[164] Id.

gorical rule may allow a few truly culpable (and irredeemable) juvenile offenders to escape a life-without-parole sentence, the balancing test undoubtedly will impose life-without-parole sentences on other offenders who are not sufficiently culpable to warrant it, or who are at least capable of maturing and being rehabilitated—issues which, as a practical matter, are extremely difficult to predict.[165] The Court therefore concluded that it is better that those who do deserve the sentence should escape it than that those who do not deserve the sentence should have it imposed on them.[166] As a matter of constitutional policy, the Court's choice could be justified on the ground that an overinclusive rule provides more effective enforcement of Eighth Amendment values than an underinclusive balancing test.

The majority's justifications tell only part of the story. Scholars have identified a number of reasons to explain why courts might favor categorical tests over balancing tests.[167] Several of those reasons resonate here, specifically the reviewing courts' interest in formulating a test that is easy to administer and the desirability of reducing the possibility of bias on the part of the initial decision maker. Fisher has observed that "concerns regarding administrability . . . appear quite properly to propel various coalitions within the Court to favor categorical rules over balancing tests."[168] Fisher shows that the Court, both in *Crawford* and in *Blakely*, adopted a categorical approach based on the Court's stated view that such a rule would lead to more predictable outcomes.[169] Although the *Graham* majority did not explicitly cite predictability and administrative ease as justifications for its adoption of the bright-line rule, it seems clear that its sense of administrative convenience

---

[165] Id at 2029.

[166] Categorical tests are easier to administer because, as Kathleen Sullivan has observed, "When categorical formulas operate, all the important work in litigation is done at the outset. Once the relevant right and mode of infringement have been described, the outcome follows, without any explicit judicial balancing of the claimed right against the government's justification for the infringement." Sullivan, 63 U Colo L Rev at 293 (cited in note 159).

[167] For a discussion of why the Court should not have developed two different Eighth Amendment tests in the first place, see generally, Barkow, 107 Mich L Rev at 1145 (cited in note 6) (arguing that there is no justifiable reason for the Court to analyze death sentences differently than other sentences, and the Court's practice of doing so has produced regrettable consequences).

[168] Fisher, 94 Georgetown L J at 1521 (cited in note 157).

[169] Id at 1521–22.

was a driving force behind its departure from precedent in this context as well. The Eighth Amendment concern at issue in *Graham* will not arise as frequently as the Sixth Amendment jury trial issue in *Blakely* or the Confrontation Clause concern in *Crawford*, but it will certainly arise too frequently for the Court to "be reasonably confident it will have room on its docket to review [each problematic lower court] case and modify or reverse the decision."[170] Particularly given the present Court's apparent understanding of its role in the judicial system, as evidenced by the greatly reduced size of its merits docket, it seems unlikely that the Court would ever choose to take enough cases to afford relief to juveniles who have been erroneously sentenced to life without parole under the balancing test. Nor would that be a wise use of the Court's limited resources in any event.[171]

Kathleen Sullivan has observed that another reason courts might favor categorical tests is that they "reduce the danger of official arbitrariness or bias by preventing decisionmakers from factoring the parties' particular attractive or unattractive qualities into the decisionmaking calculus."[172] The *Graham* majority's adoption of a categorical approach likewise reflects this "distrust for the decisionmaker."[173] That distrust, which is one that goes beyond the question of institutional competencies, is evident from the majority's juxtaposition of its own stated concern, that courts might not be able to tell the difference between the corrigible and the incorrigible juvenile, with the *Roper* Court's observation that "the brutality or cold-blooded nature of any particular crime" might lead a judge to sentence to death a juvenile who is not sufficiently culpable to warrant that punishment.[174] That concern is also evident from the Court's conclusion that "this clear [categorical] line is necessary to prevent the possibility that life without parole sentences will be imposed on juvenile nonhomicide offenders who are not sufficiently culpable to merit that punishment."[175] In both of those statements the majority subtly acknowledged its concern

---

[170] Id.

[171] See, for example, Antonin Scalia, *The Rule of Law as a Law of Rules*, 56 U Chi L Rev 1175 (1989).

[172] Sullivan, 106 Harv L Rev at 62 (cited in note 11).

[173] Id at 64.

[174] *Roper*, 543 US at 553.

[175] *Graham*, 130 S Ct at 2030.

that the traditional balancing test might lead certain sentencing judges astray in some cases, particularly at the all-important first stage of the test. If the sentencing judges were to engage in balancing in such cases, the nature of the offense (Factor 1) might impermissibly cloud the judge's analysis of the culpability of the offender (Factor 2), so that the judge would determine, erroneously, that the punishment of life without parole (Factor 3) was not grossly disproportionate to the gravity of the offense. Here, as elsewhere, "Law triumphs when the natural impulses aroused by a shocking crime yield to the safeguards which our civilization has evolved for an administration of criminal justice at once rational and effective."[176] The Court seemed to recognize that the need to overcome such "natural impulses" presents a challenge for overworked and overconditioned judges as well as for lay juries.

In "choosing" the categorical approach over the balancing approach, the *Graham* majority also rejected what it termed a second "alternative approach[]."[177] Florida raised that alternative by claiming that state criminal procedure took sufficient account of the age of juvenile offenders to satisfy any possible constitutional concern. The Court's rejection of that approach likewise reflects a distrust of the decision maker and a concern that the sentencing authority's natural inclination to overvalue Factor 1 in its calculus will lead to a substantial distortion in its application of the balancing test. The Court in *Graham* dismissed the state's argument, finding that Florida law did not meet Eighth Amendment requirements because it failed to prevent the state from "sentencing a juvenile nonhomicide offender to life without parole based on a subjective judgment that the defendant's crimes demonstrate an 'irretrievably depraved character.'"[178] To support that conclusion, the majority emphasized that the sentencing judges in both *Graham* and *Sullivan* had reached "discretionary, subjective judgment[s] that the offender[s] [were] irredeemably depraved," without fully considering the possibility that they "lack[ed] the moral culpability" to justify the imposition of life-without-parole sentences.[179]

Chief Justice Roberts's concurrence and Justice Thomas's dis-

---

[176] *Watts v Indiana*, 338 US 49, 55 (1949) (Frankfurter, J) (plurality).

[177] *Graham*, 130 S Ct at 2030.

[178] Id at 2031.

[179] See id.

sent both demonstrate the validity of the Court's concern that judges might overvalue the nature of the offense (Factor 1) and undervalue the degree to which an offender's youth lessened his culpability (Factor 2). Both show that the greatest flaw in the traditional balancing test is that it provides overworked and over-conditioned criminal court judges with an easy way to rule against the defendant every time. To apply the test with ease and speed, judges simply need to rely on Factor 1, the nature of the offense, to trump Factor 2, the culpability of the offender. Not only is that route the easiest one, but it may also seem the most natural and even the most just result to a judge who is charged with sentencing a young offender for a truly horrific crime. Indeed, it seems natural to expect that the horror of a particular crime will always appear in more graphic detail to the sentencing judge than will the offender's more elusive characteristics—his culpability and possible amenability to rehabilitation. Those characteristics may not have been explored and developed fully by defense counsel, and in any event their details necessarily will lack the same tangibility and immediacy as those of the crime. Those details simply cannot be ascertained, communicated, or understood with the same degree of certainty.[180] That flaw is surely the central concern that caused the majority to depart from precedent.

In his concurrence, Chief Justice Roberts insisted that the Court could have ruled in favor of Graham under the traditional balancing test applicable to noncapital cases. According to the Chief Justice, "existing precedent already provides a sufficient framework for assessing the concerns outlined by the majority."[181] His argument depended on an amalgam of the traditional test and the Court's treatment of juveniles in *Roper*. The Chief Justice did not adopt the categorical rule articulated in *Roper*, but he relied on *Roper* to incorporate age into the traditional test, which he did in a very robust way that was aimed at showing that Graham could win. He viewed this approach as preferable to the Court's because it retained the case-by-case analysis, and thus provided the promise of a benefit only to deserving members of the class (those who actually lacked culpability by virtue of their youth and immaturity), while retaining the possibility of life-without-parole sentences for

---

[180] See id at 2032.

[181] Id at 2039.

those whose crimes were so heinous that their youth could not translate as a matter of fact into a lack of culpability.[182] In other words, the Chief Justice thought that Graham should prevail on the facts of his case, but the Chief Justice also wished to avoid formulating a categorical rule that he considered overbroad insofar as it would provide relief to both deserving and undeserving members of the class.

The Chief Justice's application of his more robust formulation of the balancing test to Graham's case proceeded as follows. He first conducted the threshold inquiry at Stage 1 of the balancing test, comparing the gravity of Graham's conduct to the harshness of the penalty. As discussed above, the "gravity of the conduct" prong requires an analysis of the nature of the offense (Factor 1) and the characteristics of the offender (Factor 2). With regard to Factor 1, the Chief Justice noted that Graham's crimes were serious, but less serious than murder or rape.

It was the Chief Justice's analysis of offender-focused Factor 2, however, that enabled Graham to prevail under his formulation, where the defendants in all Supreme Court cases since *Solem* had failed.[183] The Chief Justice first noted that the traditional balancing test "itself takes the personal 'culpability of the offender' into account in examining whether a given punishment is proportionate to the crime."[184] He then showed that Graham's status as a juvenile was relevant to the characteristics of the offender prong of the test in part because "*Roper*'s conclusion that juveniles are typically less culpable than adults has pertinence beyond capital cases."[185]

---

[182] Id at 2041–42 (Roberts, CJ, concurring).

[183] See generally, *Gonzalez v Duncan*, 551 F3d 875 (9th Cir 2008) (reversing district court and awarding habeas relief to petitioner who was sentenced to twenty-eight years to life under California's three-strikes law for failing to update his annual sex offender registration within five days of his birthday); *Ramirez v Castro*, 365 F3d 755 (9th Cir 2004) (holding unconstitutional a mandatory life sentence for theft of a VCR under California's three-strikes law); *Henderson v Norris*, 258 F3d 710 (8th Cir 2001) (invalidating a life sentence for first-offense delivery because "the amount of drugs that Mr. Henderson sold was extraordinarily small: The three 'rocks' of cocaine base, or crack, weighed less than one-quarter of a gram, which is less than a hundredth of an ounce"); *State v Davis*, 79 P3d 64 (Ariz 2003) (holding unconstitutional a mandatory fifty-two-year sentence for a twenty-year-old convicted of four counts of sexual misconduct with a minor with two postpubescent teenage girls); *State v Bruegger*, 773 NW2d 862 (Iowa 2009) (finding twenty-five-year sentence for statutory rape violated the Eighth Amendment).

[184] *Graham*, 130 S Ct at 2039 (Roberts, CJ, concurring), citing *Solem*, 463 US at 292.

[185] *Graham*, 130 S Ct at 2039 (Roberts, CJ, concurring). See also id at 2040 (Graham "committed the relevant offenses when he was a juvenile—a stage at which, *Roper* emphasized, one's culpability or blameworthiness is diminished, to a substantial degree, by

In addition to Graham's juvenile status, two other aspects of his history rendered him "markedly less culpable than a typical adult who commits the same offenses": (1) he had no prior convictions,[186] and (2) he had a difficult upbringing.[187] The Chief Justice then determined that the harshness of the penalty (Factor 3) also favored Graham, because a sentence of life imprisonment without parole is "the most severe sanction available for a nonhomicide offense."[188] Next, he concluded that a threshold comparison of the gravity of the offense (Factors 1 and 2) with the harshness of the penalty (Factor 3) created "a strong inference that Graham's sentence . . . was grossly disproportionate in violation of the Eighth Amendment."[189] Once the Chief Justice had enabled Graham to surmount the previously insurmountable threshold analysis, he made short work of the intra- and interjurisdictional analyses at Stage 2 of the test and found that those analyses also dictated an outcome in Graham's favor.[190] Despite Graham's apparent success under the Chief Justice's application of his modified balancing test, a close reading of the concurring opinion demonstrates that the Chief Justice did not support retention of the balancing test only out of respect for precedent; he clearly also wanted judges to retain the discretion to assess the particulars of the crime for which the defendant was convicted, and he was opposed to having a categorical rule that would apply regardless of the nature of the crime. The Chief Justice stated the true basis for his preference for a more robust application of the balancing test (as opposed to a categorical rule) when he emphasized, both at the outset and in closing, that "successful challenges to noncapital sentences under the Eighth Amendment have been—and, in my view, should continue to be—exceedingly rare."[191]

reason of youth and immaturity."); *Roper*, 543 US at 591 (holding that because juveniles are "typically less blameworthy than adults, . . . an offender's juvenile status can play a central role in the inquiry.").

[186] *Graham*, 130 S Ct at 2040.

[187] Id.

[188] Id.

[189] Id.

[190] For his intrajurisdictional analysis, the Chief Justice made these observations: "Graham's sentence was far more severe than that imposed for similar violations of Florida law . . . and more severe than the sentences typically imposed for murder." Id at 2041. Similarly, his interjurisdictional analysis consisted of the observation that "Florida is an outlier in its willingness to impose sentences of life without parole on juveniles convicted of nonhomicide crimes." Id.

[191] Id at 2042. See also id at 2037.

The Chief Justice evidently was more disturbed by what he perceived to be the practical consequences of the majority's holding than by the fact that the Court had deviated from precedent to reach that holding. In most cases involving juveniles, it is clear that the Chief Justice's application of Factors 1 and 2 of the traditional balancing test would result in a ruling adverse to the defendant. He repeatedly criticized the majority's adoption of a categorical test on the ground that it prevents judges from taking into account the relevant characteristics of the particular offender and the particular crime under Factors 1 and 2, and from determining based on those characteristics that the gravity of the offense justifies Factor 3, the harshness of the penalty of life without parole. One of his observations is especially telling: "Some crimes are so heinous [Factor 1], and some juvenile offenders so highly culpable [Factor 2], that a sentence of life without parole may be entirely justified under the Constitution."[192] In calling the majority's new test "unwise," he said: "Most importantly, it ignores the fact that some nonhomicide crimes . . . are especially heinous or grotesque [Factor 1], and thus may be deserving of more severe punishment [Factor 3]."[193] Moreover, the Chief Justice considered the new test to be "unnecessary" because "there is nothing *inherently* unconstitutional about imposing sentences of life without parole on juvenile offenders," as evidenced by the fact that the Court admits there is no constitutional problem with sentencing a juvenile who commits murder to life without parole. "[R]ather, the constitutionality of such sentences depends on the particular crimes for which they are imposed."[194]

Justice Thomas's dissent further demonstrates the ease with which a judge can rule against a defendant under the traditional balancing test. Applying the balancing test to the facts of Graham's case, Justice Thomas easily concluded that Graham's challenge to his sentence lacked merit and should be rejected. In addressing the threshold analysis at Stage 1, Justice Thomas determined that Factor 1, the nature of the offense, weighed against Graham; he

---

[192] Id at 2042.

[193] Id at 2041.

[194] Id. Presumably, the Chief Justice did not share the majority's skepticism about the judicial system's ability to distinguish those juveniles who were truly culpable and irredeemable from those who had done truly horrible things, but were less culpable and redeemable.

reasoned that Graham's "actual violent felony is surely more severe than" the nonviolent drug crime committed by the adult defendant in *Harmelin*.[195] The dissent next rejected the Chief Justice's robust formulation of Factor 2 for juveniles, contending that juveniles should not be afforded a "general presumption of diminished culpability."[196] If Factors 1 and 2, which together comprise the "gravity of the offense" element of the test, weigh against the offender, then the offender certainly will not satisfy the threshold first stage, and it will not be necessary to reach Stage 2. Sure enough, the dissent concluded that Graham had not established an "'inference' of gross disproportionality" as a threshold matter.[197]

Chief Justice Roberts's concurrence and Justice Thomas's dissent both demonstrate how easy it is for a judge to reject all juvenile nonhomicide offenders' Eighth Amendment claims under the traditional test. At a minimum, the judge would simply need to find, when conducting the threshold analysis, that offense-focused Factor 1 weighs against the defendant. The judge could do so by taking Chief Justice Roberts's approach and finding that the particular crime is "especially heinous and grotesque" in the abstract. Alternatively the judge could follow the dissent and compare the defendant's particular crime with the fairly minor and nonviolent crimes in *Harmelin*, *Ewing*, and *Andrade*. As the majority fears, it is always possible to overvalue—and thus give dispositive weight to—"the brutality or cold-blooded nature of any particular crime." The subjectivity and flexibility of the balancing test enables Factor 1 to trump Factor 2 and render the offense sufficiently grave that no inference of gross disproportionality can be established at Stage 1; thus, the defendant loses at that stage, obviating any need to proceed to the intra- and interjurisdictional analyses of Stage 2. Accordingly, it does not matter whether all juveniles are afforded a rebuttable presumption of diminished culpability under Factor 2, as the Chief Justice proposed, or that no such presumption applies, as the dissent preferred. If Factor 1 can cancel out Factor 2, a robust formulation of Factor 2 in the juvenile

---

[195] Id at 2056 (Thomas, J, dissenting).

[196] Id at 2056–57.

[197] The dissent then moved to the second and third steps of the test and concluded that the intra- and interjurisdictional analyses did not weigh in Graham's favor. The dissent again relied on post-*Solem* precedents in support of its conclusion, noting that Graham's sentence was "certainly less rare than the sentences upheld in" *Harmelin* and *Ewing*. Id at 2057.

context would not enable juvenile defendants to win any more frequently.

Because a sufficiently heinous or grotesque offense can always trump the generally diminished culpability of juveniles, maintaining the balancing test would result in a whole cadre of juvenile offenders being subjected to life-without-parole sentences despite a lessened culpability which (by the majority's lights) should have saved them from that fate. After all, in the nearly thirty years since *Solem*, no defendant until Graham had met the threshold aspect of the balancing test, let alone won a noncapital Eighth Amendment challenge, in the Supreme Court. During the same time, only a handful of the countless defendants who challenged their sentences as cruel and unusual in state and federal appellate courts won relief under the balancing test.[198] Moreover, the Supreme Court could never take a sufficient number of cases to grant relief to all of the juveniles who had been incorrectly sentenced to life without parole under the traditional test. Thus, the Court recognized that the only effective alternative to the balancing test (which was "fatal in fact" to the defendant's claim) was a categorical test which gave no discretion to sentencing authorities and required that everyone eighteen and under would win if the test were met.

While it is not surprising that four members of the Court did not want to subject juvenile offenders to a test that was fatal in fact, the outcome of *Graham* surely hinged on the fact that Justice Kennedy, the Court's lone remaining swing voter in the death penalty arena,[199] is troubled by punitive sentencing in general and by harsh sentencing of juveniles in particular.[200] Without Justice Kennedy, the Chief Justice's approach would have carried the day. Graham might still have won, but the future would look bleak for

[198] See note 185.

[199] See Joseph E. Kennedy, *Cautious Liberalism*, 94 Georgetown L J 1537, 1539 (2006) (identifying Justices Kennedy and O'Connor as issuing more "pro-defendant decisions" than their "fellow conservatives"); id at 1546–47 (discussing swing votes in "pro-defendant" cases during the Supreme Court's 2003–2004 Terms).

[200] Justice Kennedy has spoken out against mandatory minimum sentences. Anthony M. Kennedy, speech at the American Bar Association annual meeting (Aug 3, 2003) (transcript available at http://www.supremecourt.gov/publicinfo/speeches/viewspeeches.aspx?Filename =sp_08-09-03.html). See also Kennedy, 94 Georgetown L J at 1552 (cited in note 199) (discussing ABA speech). Joseph Kennedy has included Justice Kennedy among the Justices he believes have "a low regard for both the politics and policies of crime," citing the Justice's comments in *Roper* about "the general popularity of anti-crime legislation" and "the particular trend in recent years toward cracking down on juvenile crime." Id at 1551.

all other juvenile nonhomicide offenders sentenced to life without parole.

C. THE COURT'S APPLICATION OF THE CATEGORICAL TEST TO GRAHAM'S CASE

After the Court decided to import the categorical test for capital cases into the noncapital context, it applied the two steps of the test and determined that the punishment of life without parole was categorically unconstitutional as applied to the class of non-homicide offenders under the age of eighteen.[201] First, at Step 1, the Court determined that there were "objective indicia of [a] national consensus"[202] against sentencing that particular class of offenders to life without parole. By itself, the state of legislation did not provide evidence of the national consensus the Court was seeking to prove, since the formal statute law of thirty-seven states and the federal government authorized the imposition of life-with-out-parole sentences on juvenile nonhomicide offenders.[203] The Court therefore focused instead on "actual sentencing practices."[204] With that focus, the Court was able to find evidence of a national consensus because the imposition of a sentence of life imprisonment without parole on juvenile nonhomicide offenders was "most infrequent" in practice.[205] In reaching its desired result at the first step of the test, however, the Court did concede that the challenged sentencing practice was both more common than other practices the Court had found to violate the Eighth Amendment[206] and was allowed by more states than were those other practices.[207]

Step 2 of the categorical analysis enabled the Court to reach a result in favor of Graham and the class to which he belonged. At the second step, the Court exercised its own "independent judg-

[201] *Graham*, 130 S Ct at 2023–30.

[202] Id at 2023.

[203] Id.

[204] Id.

[205] Id. The Court supplemented the data provided by the parties and amici with its own independent research to show that "there are 129 juvenile nonhomicide offenders serving life without parole sentences," and that "only 11 jurisdictions nationwide in fact impose" such sentences on the relevant class, while 28 jurisdictions do not. Id at 2024.

[206] Id at 2024–25, citing *Enmund*, 458 US at 794.

[207] *Graham*, 130 S Ct at 2025 (analogizing to *Thompson*).

ment"[208] to evaluate "the culpability of the offenders at issue in light of their crimes [Factor 1] and characteristics [Factor 2], along with the severity of the punishment in question [Factor 3]," and "also [to] consider whether the challenged sentencing practice serves legitimate penological goals."[209] The Court determined that Factor 1 favored Graham because "defendants who do not kill, intend to kill, or foresee that life will be taken are categorically less deserving of the most serious forms of punishment than are murderers."[210] Similarly, Factor 2 favored Graham based on *Roper*'s conclusion that "juveniles have lessened culpability."[211] Factor 3 also favored Graham in the Court's analysis, because life without parole is such a severe sentence, "alter[ing] the offender's life by a forfeiture that is irrevocable," and "an especially harsh punishment for a juvenile."[212] At the second step, the Court also concluded that "none of the goals of penal sanctions that have been recognized as legitimate—retribution, deterrence, incapacitation, and rehabilitation—provides an adequate justification" for sentencing juvenile nonhomicide offenders to life without parole.[213]

After conducting the two-step analysis, the Court engaged in what it termed its "longstanding practice [of] noting the global consensus against the sentencing practice in question" and found that "the United States is the only Nation that imposes life without parole sentences on juvenile nonhomicide offenders."[214] Although this finding was "not dispositive as to the meaning of the Eighth

---

[208] Id at 2022.

[209] Id at 2026.

[210] Id at 2027.

[211] Id at 2026.

[212] Id at 2027–28.

[213] Id at 2028. See also id at 2028–30. The Court analogized the case to *Roper* to hold that retribution did not support life-without-parole sentences for offenders like Graham. Specifically, the Court reasoned: If retribution could not justify sentencing a juvenile offender to death, the most severe penalty available for people who commit homicides, it also could not justify sentencing a juvenile offender to life without parole, the most severe penalty available for people who commit nonhomicide crimes. Id at 2028. Deterrence likewise could not justify sentencing a juvenile to that punishment because the "diminished moral responsibility" of juveniles necessarily compromises the deterrent effect of punishment. Id at 2028–29. The Court likewise held that the incapacitation justification was insufficient for juveniles because it is impossible to say definitively that a specific juvenile offender will prove to be incorrigible. Id at 2029. Finally, the Court held that life without parole "forswears altogether the rehabilitative ideal" and ignores "a juvenile nonhomicide offender's capacity for change and limited moral culpability." Id at 2030.

[214] Id at 2033.

Amendment,"[215] it nevertheless supported the Court's conclusion that the punishment of life imprisonment for juvenile nonhomicide offenders was cruel and unusual.[216]

III. Some Predictions on the Future Direction of Cruel and Unusual Punishment Jurisprudence

Although the Court has opined that "[t]he case-by-case approach to sentencing must . . . be confined by some boundaries," the precise location of those boundaries remains unclear.[217] *Graham* enables us to make a few predictions and provides some lessons for future defendants seeking to establish that their respective sentences are cruel and unusual in violation of the Eighth Amendment.

Graham, and the Court's Eighth Amendment jurisprudence in general, demonstrate that defendants have a far greater chance of success if they can persuade the Court to apply the categorical framework rather than the balancing test. Given the Court's suggestion that the distinguishing feature of Graham's challenge was simply that he requested categorical treatment, while previous defendants challenging noncapital sentences had not, a defendant is most likely to be successful if he can begin his challenge by presenting himself as a member of a cognizable class.[218] He must argue that he should be treated as part of a class based either on Factor 1 (the nature of his crime) or Factor 2 (a diminished culpability based on specific characteristics). Specifically, the class must be defined either (1) by the fact that its members have committed a crime that is comparatively less serious, such as crimes that do not result in death, or (2) by diminished offender culpability, such that the members of the class are deemed to be categorically less culpable than others, regardless of the nature of their crimes. Theoretically, a defendant will have the best chance of receiving categorical treatment if he can show, as Graham did, that he and the members of his class are both categorically less culpable than others and have committed comparatively less serious crimes. That defendant can further bolster his request for

---

[215] Id at 2017.

[216] Id at 2034.

[217] Id at 2031–32.

[218] Id at 2022–23.

categorical treatment by showing that some or all of the reasons the Court articulated for abandoning the traditional case-by-case balancing test in *Graham* also apply to the class of defendants to which he belongs. Of course, this approach will not work for every definable class of offender or offense. The question is how far the Court would actually go in implementing this paradigm.

After *Graham*, members of the following classes of defendants will surely ask the Court to grant them categorical treatment and to deem their punishments unconstitutional: (1) juvenile offenders under life-without-parole sentences imposed for homicides, (2) mentally retarded defendants sentenced to life without parole, and (3) adult defendants sentenced to life without parole for committing nonhomicides.

Juvenile defendants who are sentenced to life without parole for committing homicides may well benefit from *Graham*. Significantly, the vast majority of juveniles who receive life-without-parole sentences in this country are given that punishment for crimes resulting in death; defendants like Graham, who receive life-without-parole sentences for nonhomicides, are fairly rare.[219] Again, the first question is whether this class of offenders will be able to convince the Court to consider granting them categorical treatment. Juveniles who commit nonhomicides have "a twice diminished moral culpability,"[220] because the nature of their crime (Factor 1) and their age (Factor 2) both contribute to diminished culpability, while juveniles who commit homicides have only a once-diminished culpability based on their age. Juveniles who kill might nevertheless merit categorical treatment, especially because all three of the "dilemma[s] of juvenile sentencing" that led the *Graham* Court to hold that "the case-by-case approach . . . must be confined by some boundaries"[221] apply equally to them. In addition, the strength of the Court's concern that sentencing judges may give excessive weight to the nature of the offense (Factor 1), and insufficient attention to the personal qualities of the offender (Factor 2), probably carries the greatest force when the offense is homicide.

If the Court uses a categorical analysis, it might well deem life

---

[219] Id at 2023.

[220] Id at 2027.

[221] Id at 2031–32.

without parole an unconstitutional punishment for the class of juveniles who kill. In his concurring opinion, the Chief Justice noted "the Court's apparent recognition that it is perfectly legitimate for a juvenile to receive a sentence of life without parole for committing murder."[222] Presumably he was referring to the fact that the Court's ruling specifically addresses the constitutionality of this penalty with respect to juveniles who commit nonhomicide crimes. The majority did not respond directly to the Chief Justice's assertion. However, there is no indication in the majority opinion that the Court specifically intended to limit its holding in the future to juveniles who had committed nonhomicide crimes, or that it specifically intended to exclude juveniles who commit homicides from benefiting from a possible future extension of its ruling. The closest the Court comes is its observation that "incapacitation may be a legitimate penological goal sufficient to justify life-without-parole in other contexts."[223] This observation is a far cry from stating that the penological aim of incapacitation would justify the imposition of a life-without-parole sentence on any juvenile who committed a homicide, let alone from demonstrating the constitutional validity of such sentences for the entire class of offender. Any fair reading of the majority opinion would suggest that the matter remains open.

Application of the categorical test gives rise to a strong argument that life-without-parole sentences for juveniles who commit homicides also violate the Eighth Amendment. First, application of the Step 1 analysis shows that there are objective indicia of a national consensus against sentencing juveniles who commit homicides to life without parole. The Court in *Graham* was interested in the "law in action" rather than the "law on the books": *Graham* holds that the crucial measure of national consensus is whether "an examination of actual sentencing practices in jurisdictions where the sentence in question is permitted by statute discloses a consensus against its use."[224] Although a survey of state legislative enactments shows that only six states categorically prohibit the practice,[225] a far different story is told by the frequency with which

[222] Id at 2041 (Roberts, CJ, concurring).

[223] Id at 2029.

[224] Id at 2023.

[225] The states that prohibit juvenile offenders convicted of homicides from receiving life without parole are Alaska, Colorado, Kansas, Kentucky, Montana, and Texas. See Alaska

the sentence is actually imposed.[226] Given that the *Graham* Court found a national consensus against imposing life without parole on juvenile nonhomicide offenders despite the fact that thirty-seven states authorize the sentence through legislation,[227] probably

Stat § 12.55.015(g) (2008); Colo Rev Stat Ann § 1-1.3-401(4)(b) (2009); Kan Stat Ann § 21-4622 (West 2007); Ky Rev Stat Ann § 640.040 (West 2008); Mont Code Ann § 46-18-222(1) (2009); Tex Penal Code Ann § 12.31 (West Supp 2009). See also *Shepherd v Commonwealth*, 251 SW3d 309, 320–21 (Ky 2008).

[226] Forty-four states and the federal government permit the imposition of life-without-parole sentences on juvenile offenders convicted of homicides. The states that allow juvenile offenders convicted of homicides to receive life without parole are Alabama, Arizona, Arkansas, California, Connecticut, Delaware, Florida, Georgia, Hawaii, Idaho, Illinois, Indiana, Iowa, Louisiana, Maine, Maryland, Massachusetts, Michigan, Minnesota, Mississippi, Missouri, Nebraska, Nevada, New Hampshire, New Jersey, New Mexico, New York, North Carolina, North Dakota, Ohio, Oklahoma, Oregon, Pennsylvania, Rhode Island, South Carolina, South Dakota, Tennessee, Utah, Vermont, Virginia, Washington, West Virginia, Wisconsin, and Wyoming. See Ala Code Ann § 12-15-203 (Supp 2009); § 13A-6-2(c) (2005); Ariz Rev Stat Ann §§ 13-501, 13-1105 (West 2010); Ark Code Ann § 9-27-318(b) (2009); § 5-4-501(c) (Supp 2009); Cal Penal Code § 190 (West 1999); § 1170.17 (West 2004); Conn Gen Stat § 53a-35a (2009); Del Code Ann, Title 10, § 1010 (Supp 2008); id, Title 11, § 4209 (2003); Fla Stat §§ 782.04, 985.557 (2007); Georgia Code Ann § 15-11-30.2 (2008); § 16-5-1(d) (2007); Hawaii Rev Stat § 571-22(d) (2006); § 706-656(1) (2008 Supp Pamphlet); Idaho Code § 18-4004 (Lexis 2005); §§ 19-2513, 20-509 (Lexis Supp 2009); Ill Rev Stat, ch 705, §§ 405/5-805 (West 2008); id, ch 720, § 5/9-1(b-5) (West 2008); id, ch 730, § 5/3-3-3(d) (West 2008); Ind Code § 31-30-3-6(1); § 35-50-2-3(b)(2) (West 2004); Iowa Code §§ 232.45(6), 707.2, 902.1 (2009); La Child Code Ann, Arts 305, 857(A) (West Supp 2010); La Rev Stat Ann § 14:44 (West 2007); Me Rev Stat Ann, Tit 15, § 3101(4) (Supp 2009); id, Title 17-a, § 1251 (2006); Md Cts & Jud Proc Code Ann §§ 3-8A-03(d)(1), 3-8A-06(a)(2) (Lexis 2006); Md Crim Law Code Ann § 2-201(b)(1)(ii) (Lexis Supp 2009); Mass Gen Laws, ch 119, § 74; id, ch 265, § 2 (2008); Mich Comp Laws Ann § 712A.4 (West 2002); § 750.316(1) (West Supp 2009); §§ 769.1, 791.234(6)(a) (West 2000); Minn Stat §§ 260B.125(1), 609.106, 609.185 (2008); Miss Code Ann § 43-21-157 (2009); § 97-3-21 (2007); Mo Rev Stat §§ 211.071, 565.020 (2000); Neb Rev Stat §§ 28-105, 28-303, 43-247, 43-276 (2008); Nev Rev Stat §§ 62B.330, 200.030 (2009); NH Rev Stat Ann § 169-B:24; § 628:1 (Equity 2007); § 630:1-a (Supp 2009); NJ Stat Ann § 2A:4A-26 (West Supp 2009); § 2C:11-3(b)(2) (West Supp 2009); NM Stat Ann § 31-18-14 (Supp 2009); § 31-18-15.2(A) (Westlaw 2010); NY Penal Law §§ 30.00, 60.06 (West 2009); § 70.00 (West 2008); NC Gen Stat Ann §§ 7B-2200, 14-17 (Lexis 2009); ND Cent Code Ann § 12.1-04-01 (Lexis 1997); § 12.1-16-01 (Lexis Supp 2009); § 12.1-32-01 (Lexis 1997); Ohio Rev Code Ann § 2152.10 (Lexis 2007); §§ 2903.01, 2929.02 (Lexis 2006); § 2971.03 (2010 Lexis Supp); Okla Stat, Title 10A, §§ 2-5-204, 2-5-205, 2-5-206 (West Supp 2009); id, Title 21, § 701.9 (West Supp 2007); Ore Rev Code Ann §§ 137.707, 163.105(1)(a) (2009); 42 Pa Cons Stat § 6355(a) (Purdon 2000); 18 id, § 1102(a) (2008); 61 id, § 6137(a) (2009); RI Gen Laws §§ 14-1-7, 14-1-7.1, 11-23-2 (Lexis 2002); SC Code Ann § 63-19-1210 (Supp 2008); § 16-3-20 (Westlaw 2009); SD Cod Laws § 26-11-3.1 (Supp 2009); § 26-11-4 (2004); §§ 22-3-1, 22-16-12 (2006); § 24-15-4 (2004); Tenn Code Ann §§ 37-1-134, 39-13-204 (Westlaw 2010); Utah Code Ann §§ 78A-6-602, 78A-6-703, 76-3-207.7 (Lexis 2008); Vt Stat Ann, Title 33, § 5204 (Cum Supp 2009); id, Title 13, § 2303 (Equity 2009); Va Code Ann §§ 16.1-269.1, 18.2-10, 53.1-151(B1) (2009); Wash Rev Code § 13.40.110 (2009 Supp); §§ 9A.04.050, 9.32.040, 9.94A.570 (2008); W Va Code § 49-5-10 (Lexis 2009); §§ 61-2-2, 61-11-18(b) (Lexis 2005); Wis Stat §§ 938.18, 938.183 (2007–08); §§ 939.50(3)(a), 973.014 (Westlaw 2005); Wyo Stat Ann §§ 6-2-101(c), 14-6-203 (2009); 18 USC § 1111 (2006 ed and Supp II); § 5032 (2006 ed). See also DC Code § 16-2307 (Supp 2009); § 22-2104 (Supp 2007).

[227] *Graham*, 130 S Ct at 2025–26.

the fact that an additional seven states authorize that penalty for juvenile homicide offenders would not preclude the Court from finding a national consensus against imposing that sentence on juveniles who kill.

Graham also emphasizes the importance, in measuring the relative rarity of life-without-parole sentences, of examining "the base number" of the relevant type of offense to assess "the opportunities for [the sentence's] imposition," and of then comparing that base number to the number of individuals actually serving the sentence.[228] In the past twenty-five years, juvenile offenders committed 42,000 homicides.[229] As of 2010, there were 2,445 juveniles serving life-without-parole sentences for homicides.[230] As in *Graham*, this comparison suggests that life-without-parole sentences for juveniles convicted of homicide crimes are uncommon. The *Graham* Court also took into account both the number of jurisdictions that actually impose the particular sentence on the particular class of offender and the number of offenders actually serving that sentence in each jurisdiction. Of the forty-four states which authorize life-without-parole sentences for juvenile homicide offenders, twenty-eight jurisdictions (twenty-seven states and the District of Columbia) have ten or fewer persons sentenced for homicides committed as juveniles serving that sentence,[231] while only seven states have one hundred or more persons who are serving such terms imposed for crimes committed as juveniles.[232]

---

[228] Id at 2025.

[229] According to one source, between 1980 and 2006, juvenile offenders committed 42,023 homicides. Charles Puzzanchera and Wei Kang, *Easy Access to the FBI's Supplementary Homicide Reports: 1980–2006* (National Center for Juvenile Justice 2008), online at http://ojjdp.ncjrs.gov/ojstatbb/ezashr. It is important to look at the total number of defendants convicted over an extended period of time because, as in *Graham*, the statistics regarding the number of juveniles currently serving life without parole for homicides "likely reflect nearly all juvenile []homicide offenders who have received a life without parole sentence stretching back many years." *Graham*, 130 S Ct at 2024.

[230] There are 2,574 juveniles serving life without parole for any offense. National Conference of State Legislatures, *Juvenile Life Without Parole* (*JLWOP*) 16 (2010), online at http://www.ncsl.org/documents/cj/jlwopchart.pdf. Of these, there are 129 juveniles serving life without parole for nonhomicide offenses. *Graham*, 130 S Ct at 2024.

[231] Those states are Alaska, Connecticut, Delaware, Georgia, Hawaii, Idaho, Indiana, Kansas, Kentucky, Maine, Minnesota, Montana, New Hampshire, New Jersey, New Mexico, New York, North Dakota, Ohio, Oregon, Rhode Island, South Dakota, Tennessee, Texas, Utah, Vermont, West Virginia, and Wyoming. National Conference of State Legislatures, *Juvenile Life Without Parole* (*JLWOP*) at 16 (cited in note 230).

[232] Those states are California, Florida, Illinois, Louisiana, Michigan, Missouri, and Pennsylvania. Id at 16. Notably, "the differences in the state rates of life without parole for youth do not correlate directly to differences in rates of violent crime by youth."

Taken together, the available data suggest that life-without-parole sentences for juvenile homicide offenders are rare, even if that sentence is less rare than for juvenile *non*homicide offenders.

The Court, in exercising its independent judgment at Step 2 of the categorical test and analyzing the three factors, might well determine that life without parole is a cruel and unusual punishment for juveniles who commit homicides. Both *Graham* and *Roper* establish that juveniles are generally less culpable than fully capable adults (Factor 2); *Graham* also establishes that "[l]ife without parole is an especially harsh punishment for a juvenile" (Factor 3).[233] Even Factor 1, the nature of the crime, does not automatically weigh against the defendant simply because the crime is homicide. Not all criminal homicides will be equally worthy of condemnation from a moral point of view. Moreover, not all homicides will be more morally blameworthy than all nonhomicides. The Chief Justice suggested that there is little difference, in terms of culpability, between the juvenile who kills his victim and the juvenile who simply leaves his victim for dead.[234] By the same token, the juvenile whose victim happens to die may not be sufficiently more culpable than the juvenile who leaves his victim for dead to warrant a life-without-parole sentence for the former if it is prohibited for the latter.

As part of Step 2, the Court would next examine the penological justifications for sentencing juvenile homicide offenders to life without parole, and might well conclude that none of the purposes of punishment supported such a sentence. After all, the *Graham* Court rejected the sufficiency of three of the four penological justifications for reasons that relate only to the culpability of juveniles and not to the nature of their crimes. Because those reasons relate only to the culpability of juveniles, they apply with equal force to juveniles who commit homicides. Specifically, the *Graham* Court rejected the incapacitation justification because (1) "the characteristics of juveniles make [any judgment that an individual juvenile is incorrigible] questionable,"[235] and (2) "[a] life without parole sentence improperly denies the juvenile offender a chance

---

Human Rights Watch/Amnesty International, *The Rest of Their Lives: Life Without Parole for Child Offenders in the United States* 36 (2005), online at http://www.amnestyusa.org/us/clwop/report.pdf.

[233] *Graham*, 130 S Ct at 2028.

[234] Id at 2042 (Roberts, CJ, concurring).

[235] Id at 2029.

to demonstrate growth and maturity."[236] The Court likewise focused on offender culpability in its deterrence and rehabilitation analyses. The Court found that deterrence does not justify the penalty because juveniles "are less likely to take a possible punishment into consideration when making decisions" and because they possess "diminished moral responsibility."[237] According to the Court, a juvenile offender's "capacity for change and limited moral culpability"[238] also make life without parole inconsistent with rehabilitation. These rationales likewise apply to juveniles who commit homicides. Thus, only retribution could possibly provide a legitimate penological justification for sentencing juvenile homicide offenders to life without parole. But that line of analysis is foreclosed as well. The Court held in *Roper* and reiterated in *Graham* that "the case for retribution is not as strong with a minor as with an adult,"[239] and thus emphasized that retribution, like the other penological justifications, "must be directly related to personal culpability."[240] The *Graham* Court's emphasis on offender culpability rather than on the nature of the crime suggests that the Court might well conclude at Step 2 that the purposes of punishment also render the punishment of life without parole disproportionate for juveniles who commit homicides.

After analyzing the two steps of the categorical test, the Court would likely conclude that there is also an international consensus against sentencing juveniles who commit homicides to life without parole. The two measures the Court has identified as providing "objective indicia of . . . consensus"[241]—legislation and actual sentencing practices—both lead to that conclusion. Apart from the United States, only ten countries authorize the imposition of a life-without-parole sentence on juveniles "under any circumstances."[242] Moreover, only Israel "ever impose[s] the punishment in practice," and only seven Israeli prisoners are currently serving

---

[236] Id.

[237] Id at 2028–29.

[238] Id at 2030.

[239] Id at 2028, citing *Roper v Simmons*, 543 US at 551, 571 (2005).

[240] *Graham*, 130 S Ct at 2028, quoting *Tison v Arizona*, 481 US 137, 149 (1987).

[241] *Graham*, 130 S Ct at 2023.

[242] Id at 2033.

the equivalent of life-without-parole sentences for juvenile crimes.[243]

The Court's holding in *Graham* all but ensures that another category of offenders, mentally retarded defendants who commit nonhomicides, will be given categorical treatment. As with youthful offenders like Graham, mentally retarded defendants whose crimes do not result in death fit into both the first category of defendants meriting class treatment (because they have committed a comparatively less serious crime) and the second category (because the Court in *Atkins* deemed them categorically less culpable than defendants who are not mentally retarded).[244] In addition, one of the three concerns that led the *Graham* Court to reject the case-by-case balancing test was derived directly from *Atkins*: both juveniles and the mentally retarded have less ability to assist their counsel.[245] Moreover, to the degree that the *Graham* Court refused to apply the balancing test out of a concern that judges could easily use the seriousness of the offense (Factor 1) to trump the culpability of the offender (Factor 2) in any given case, that concern is just as salient in the context of mentally retarded offenders sentenced for heinous crimes.

If the Court were to apply the categorical test to mentally retarded defendants who commit nonhomicides and receive life-without-parole sentences, it would have to determine using objective measures if there is a national consensus against the practice (Step 1), and exercise its own independent judgment (Step 2). With regard to Step 1, the data about legislation and actual sentencing practices in this area are unclear. At Step 2, however, *Graham* and *Atkins* together dictate that the Court would have little choice but to side with the defendants. At this step of the test, the Court considers the three factors, all of which favor this class of defendants. Factors 1 and 2 are discussed in the previous paragraph. Factor 3 (the harshness of the penalty) weighs in favor of mentally retarded defendants because, as with juveniles, life without parole is the most severe penalty they can face. At Step 2 of the analysis, the Court would also decide whether imposing life-without-parole sentences on mentally retarded offenders "serves legitimate pe-

---

[243] Id.

[244] *Atkins*, 536 US at 318 ("Their deficiencies . . . diminish their personal culpability.").

[245] *Graham*, 130 S Ct at 2032, quoting *Atkins*, 536 US at 320.

nological goals."[246] The Court already held in *Atkins* that the mentally retarded offender's lesser culpability means that sentencing him to death does not serve the goals of retribution and deterrence.[247] Just as the lesser culpability of juveniles diminishes the probability that they will actually be deterred by a given punishment, "the same cognitive and behavioral impairments that make [mentally retarded] defendants less morally culpable . . . also make it less likely that they can process the information of the possibility" of a given penalty and "control their conduct based upon that information."[248] This analysis applies equally whether the punishment at issue is death or life without parole.

The final class of defendants who might benefit from *Graham* consists of adults sentenced to life without parole for committing nonhomicide crimes. It is extremely unlikely that this class of offenders would be able to convince the Court to grant them categorical treatment. Offenders in this group have only a once-diminished culpability based on the nature of their crimes (Factor 1) and are thus "categorically less deserving of the most serious forms of punishment than are murderers."[249] They do not partake of any individual characteristics (such as youth or mental retardation) that would give them a "twice diminished moral culpability."[250] Moreover, it is a considerable stretch to consider this group of offenders as a discrete "class." This group of offenders is the subject of all of the Court's prior jurisprudence in the noncapital context; granting them categorical treatment would essentially mean abandoning the case-by-case balancing test. Nothing in *Graham* (or any other precedent) suggests that the Court would be inclined to take that step.

A defendant sentenced to life without parole for a nonhomicide might do best to take a different tack and hold the Court to the promise made in the Chief Justice's concurrence, namely, that the traditional balancing test has teeth and provides a viable vehicle for defendants to win Eighth Amendment challenges. In approaching the threshold analysis portion of the traditional test, a defendant could argue that Factors 1 and 3 favor him to the same

---

[246] *Graham*, 130 S Ct at 2026.

[247] *Atkins*, 536 US at 318–20.

[248] Id at 319.

[249] *Graham*, 130 S Ct at 2027.

[250] Id.

degree that they weighed in Graham's favor under Chief Justice Roberts's analysis: His crime is less serious than murder, and life without parole is the harshest penalty he can face for that crime.[251] He could then use the Chief Justice's robust interpretation of the characteristics of the offender (Factor 2) to highlight particular facts that diminish his "personal culpability."[252] Because the concurrence deems a defendant's "mental state and motive in committing the crime"[253] to be relevant to Factor 2, the defendant could show a diminished personal culpability by presenting evidence that he suffered from psychological or psychiatric disorders that related to his commission of the crime, or by focusing on his motive for committing the crime. The defendant could also use a minimal criminal history or a difficult upbringing to establish diminished culpability.[254]

While the Chief Justice's opinion gives these adult defendants a potentially more effective way of arguing that their sentences violate the Eighth Amendment, it is unlikely that those new arguments will lead to defense victories. In the final analysis, because the balancing test allows Factor 1 to trump Factor 2, a court can deny any challenge under the Cruel and Unusual Punishments Clause by determining that the defendant's crime is sufficiently heinous to outweigh any diminished personal culpability and to justify the most severe sentence available. Just as this aspect of the balancing test surely was the pivotal reason the Court rejected that test in the juvenile context, it will continue to preclude the possibility of relief for adult defendants sentenced to life without parole for committing the same crime.

IV. CONCLUSION

Justice Stevens, in a brief, elegantly crafted concurrence, responded directly to Justice Thomas's charge that the majority opinion was unfaithful to the Court's own case law. Given the central role played by "evolving standards of decency" in the Court's Eighth Amendment jurisprudence, Justice Stevens did not find it surprising that the dissenting opinions in certain Eighth

---

[251] Id at 2039–40 (Roberts, CJ, concurring).

[252] Id.

[253] Id at 2037.

[254] Id at 2040.

Amendment cases decided in 1980, 1991, and 2003 should "more accurately describe the law today than does Justice Thomas's rigid interpretation of the Amendment."[255]

Justice Stevens's brief opinion is a spirited defense of the Whiggish view of the Eighth Amendment that guides our jurisprudence. But there is another, more profound truth expressed in Justice Stevens's concurrence. Justice Stevens specifically notes that, "Society changes. Knowledge accumulates. We learn, sometimes, from our mistakes."[256] Whatever one might think of the "evolving standards of decency" paradigm, the fact is that Justice Stevens is right about change and growth. Circumstances do change; knowledge does grow; and sometimes we do learn from our mistakes, both individually and as a society. Of course, new problems develop, become more acute, mutate, and fester. If we are lucky, our knowledge grows faster than our problems, but that is far from certain. What we do know is that the approach we take to our problems must change as circumstances change and knowledge accumulates. What seemed yesterday to be an effective response to the problem of enforcing particular constitutional values will be proved inadequate today; we must look for new ways to give traction to those values today.

For example, in the years following the Court's decision in *Swain v Alabama*,[257] as one after another black criminal defendant was tried and convicted by all-white juries, despite the statistical improbability that all-white juries could be constituted from the populations from which they were drawn absent invidious discrimination, it became clear that the test articulated in *Swain* was simply ineffectual. It became clear that a new approach was needed to honor effectively the nation's commitments to racial equality and the rule of law. Thus, in *Batson v Kentucky*,[258] the Court acknowledged that the *Swain* test was unworkable and struck off in a new direction.[259] Similarly, the Court recognized in *Graham* that the rule that it had previously applied in noncapital cases was not effective in making sure that only juveniles who met a certain threshold culpability requirement would be sentenced to life with-

---

[255] Id at 2036 (Stevens, J, concurring).

[256] Id.

[257] 380 US 202 (1965).

[258] 476 US 79 (1986).

[259] Id at 92–93.

out parole in noncapital cases. Thus, the *Graham* Court also struck off in a different direction.

But the cases are not exactly similar. Whereas the Court in *Batson* acknowledged that its prior test had not worked in practice, and candidly announced the new direction it was taking, the Court in *Graham* declined to acknowledge the imperfections of its existing approach or the fact that it was heading in a new direction. In *Graham*, the Court simply pretended that it had a range of tools at its disposal, and that it was choosing to work with one of those already-available tools rather than another. While the Court's decision in *Graham* was necessary and desirable from the viewpoint of effective enforcement of the Eighth Amendment, the reasons the Court gave for its departure from precedent simply were not true. The holding in *Graham* was not the result, as the majority implied, of "business as usual." The holding in *Graham*, while undoubtedly correct, marked a significant break with past practice.

It might seem that this is a slight objection. It might even seem churlish to object to a result that we believe to be plainly correct as a matter of constitutional policy, simply because the Court did not want to acknowledge that it was doing something new and adventurous. That might seem particularly to be the case where, as here, the change not only provided a better solution to the problem at hand—fair treatment for juveniles convicted of non-capital offenses—but also opened new possibilities for other groups of defendants who might also suffer excessive punishment because of their particular characteristics. But there is more to the objection than that. Judge McCree suggested that the judicial mind requires reasons to decide anything with "spiritual quiet."[260] One might go a step further and suggest that the assignment and statement of reasons by judges is not simply a matter internal to the "spiritual quiet" of judges, but an essential condition for the legitimacy of adjudication in a democratic society. Indeed, it is essential to our system of judicial review that judges not just give reasons for their decisions, but that the reasons they give be the true reasons for their decisions. Otherwise, it is not just the "judicial mind" but the "democratic mind" that will lack the "spiritual

---

[260] Wade H. McCree, Jr., *Bureaucratic Justice*, 129 U Pa L Rev 777, 787 (1981), quoting *United States Asphalt Refining Co. v Trinidad Lake Petroleum Co.*, 222 F 1006, 1008 (SDNY 1915).

quiet" upon which the legitimacy of judicial review in a democracy depends. A mature and nonpolemical view of the Constitution recognizes that the text of the Constitution has not—and cannot—settle everything.[261] Much remains to be settled; some will be settled in the fullness of time; and some may never be settled. That means that judges necessarily have choices to make, and, at the end of the day, it is how those choices are made, and how they are explained, that matters.

H. Jefferson Powell, with his customary sensitivity to the nuance that characterizes constitutional adjudication in a democratic society, recently put the matter well:

> Because of the inescapability of judgment in the interpretation and application of the Constitution, candor is essential if the justices, or whoever is purporting to speak in the voice of the Constitution, are to ask the rest of us to take them seriously when they cannot claim their judgments are beyond dispute. Only if you and I understand the true grounds of a decision can we assent to its correctness or (and this is the point of the greatest moment) to its validity as the outcome of our system even though we think it wrong in substance.[262]

In other words, Justice Thomas was wrong on the merits, but he had a good point to make. The Court never did tell us why death was no longer different.

---

[261] Herbert Storing, *What the Anti-Federalists Were For: The Political Thought of the Opponents of the Constitution* 3 (Chicago, 1981).

[262] H. Jefferson Powell, *Constitutional Conscience* 90 (Chicago, 2008).

GEOFFREY R. STONE

UNDERSTANDING SUPREME COURT CONFIRMATIONS

My teacher and colleague Philip B. Kurland believed deeply in reasoned discourse. He founded *The Supreme Court Review* fifty years ago in no small part as a forum to promote such discourse—even on the most contentious issues of the day. I have little doubt that, if Phil were here today, he would be utterly appalled at the present state of the Supreme Court confirmation process.

Conventional wisdom says that the confirmation process for Supreme Court Justices is now terribly broken. The prevailing assumption is that the process has become so polarized and so politicized that nominees feel they must mask their views from members of the Senate in a way that makes informed consideration impossible. As one commentator has observed, many "Americans would like to think the manner in which people become justices on the Supreme Court is governed by merit and objectivity," but "recent events suggest something very different."[1] Supreme Court nominations, it is said, "have become public pitched battles in-

Geoffrey R. Stone is Edward H. Levi Distinguished Service Professor, The University of Chicago.

AUTHOR'S NOTE: I would like to thank Rachel Barkow, Rosalind Dixon, Lee Epstein, Dan Farber, Barry Friedman, Michael Gerhardt, Aziz Huq, William Landes, Richard Pildes, Richard Posner, Lori Ringhand, Louis M. Seidman, and Kenji Yoshino for their very helpful comments on earlier versions of this article; Kristin MacDonald and Jake Tracer for their terrific research assistance; and the University of Chicago Law School's Leonard Sorkin Law Faculty Fund for its generous support of this research.

[1] Richard Davis, *Electing Justice: Fixing the Supreme Court Nomination Process* 4 (Oxford, 2005).

© 2011 by The University of Chicago. All rights reserved.
978-0-226-36326-4/2011/2010-0009$10.00

volving partisans, ideological groups, single-issue groups, and the press."[2] The common refrain is that "if only we could get back to the way we did things in the past, the process would be so much better."

Of course, Phil was always skeptical of conventional wisdom, and in fact the reality is quite complicated. In this article, I explore a broad range of factors, including ethics, ideology, competence, polarization, media, and politics, that have shaped the modern Supreme Court confirmation process. Although the story is not a simple one, the confirmation process has, in recent years, evolved in a way that should leave all of us as distressed as Phil would be.

I. The Likelihood of Confirmation

To begin, let us consider the rate of confirmation. From 1790 to the present, presidents have made a total of 153 Supreme Court nominations.[3] Of these 153 nominees, 117, or 76 percent, were confirmed by the Senate. Of those who were not confirmed, twelve were rejected by the full Senate, thirteen were not voted on by the Senate before the end of the session, and eleven were withdrawn by the president before the Senate could act. Most of the withdrawn and no-action nominations occurred before the Civil War. A majority of the nominees for whom the Senate took no action were renominated in the following session. John Harlan is a recent example of a no-action nominee who was renominated and confirmed; Harriet Miers is a recent example of a withdrawn nominee.

In the first half of our nation's existence, from 1790 to 1900, the Senate confirmed 69 percent of all nominees; in the second 110 years, from 1900 to 2010, the Senate confirmed 86 percent. Thus,

[2] Id. See also Sarah A. Binder and Forest Maltzman, *Advice and Dissent: The Struggle to Shape the Federal Judiciary* 1 (Brookings, 2009); Stephen Choi and Mitu Gulati, *A Tournament of Judges?* 92 Cal L Rev 299, 301 (2004); Stephen L. Carter, *The Confirmation Mess: Cleaning Up the Federal Appointments Process* 6 (Basic, 1994); Mark Silverstein, *Judicious Choices: The New Politics of Supreme Court Confirmations* 6 (Norton, 1994); Elena Kagan, *Confirmation Messes, Old and New*, 62 U Chi L Rev 919 (1995); Michael Stokes Paulsen, *Straightening Out the Confirmation Mess*, 105 Yale L J 549 (1995); Gary J. Simson, *Mired in the Confirmation Mess*, 143 U Pa L Rev 1035 (1995); Michael J. Gerhardt, *The Confirmation Mystery*, 83 Georgetown L J 395 (1994).

[3] This excludes seven individuals who declined nomination. All data about nominations and confirmations in this article are derived from *Supreme Court Nominations, Present–1789*, online at http://www.senate.gov/pagelayout/reference/nominations/Nominations.htm.

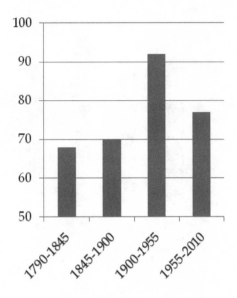

Figure 1. Percent of nominees confirmed

the rate of confirmation has increased decidedly over time. But as revealed in Figure 1, if we divide American history into four fifty-five-year periods, a more interesting pattern emerges. We see that from 1790 to 1845, thirty of forty-four, or 68 percent, of all nominees were confirmed; from 1845 to 1900, twenty-eight of forty, or 70 percent, were confirmed; from 1900 to 1955, thirty-five of thirty-eight, or 92 percent, were confirmed; and from 1955 to 2010, twenty-four of thirty-one, or 77 percent, were confirmed.

Surprisingly, the unusual period is not the most recent, but the period from 1900 to 1955. The current era only *seems* out of the ordinary because of the dramatic change from the immediately preceding period. What was going on between 1900 and 1955? The answer seems clear: At the time of every Supreme Court nomination between 1900 and 1955, the president and the majority of the Senate were from the *same* political party. Predictably, the likelihood that a nomination will fail is much greater when the president faces a Senate controlled by the opposition party.

What if we exclude nominations that were withdrawn, and examine only those nominations that came to a full Senate vote? The same pattern appears. The Senate has voted on 129 Supreme Court nominees. Of these, 117, or 91 percent, were confirmed, and twelve,

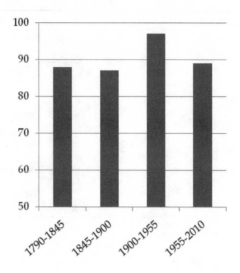

Figure 2. Percent of nominees voted on by the full Senate who were confirmed

or 9 percent, were rejected. Has the situation changed over time? From 1790 to 1900, the Senate voted on sixty-five nominees and confirmed fifty-seven, or 88 percent. From 1900 to 2010, the Senate voted on sixty-three nominees and confirmed fifty-nine, or 94 percent. Thus, it would appear that the Senate was, if anything, slightly *less* deferential to the president between 1790 and 1900 than between 1900 and 2010.

Again, however, as Figure 2 reveals, the outlier is the period from 1900 to 1955. From 1790 to 1845, the Senate confirmed thirty of the thirty-four nominees who came to a full Senate vote, or 88 percent; from 1845 to 1900, the Senate confirmed twenty-eight of thirty-two, or 87 percent; from 1900 to 1955, the Senate confirmed thirty-five of thirty-six, or 97 percent; and from 1955 to 2010, the Senate confirmed twenty-four of twenty-seven, or 89 percent.[4] Again, the explanation seems to be that no president between 1900 and 1955 sent a Supreme Court nomination to a Senate controlled by the opposition.

Indeed, all three nominees denied confirmation by the full Senate between 1955 and 2010 were nominated by a president whose party

---

[4] I do not include the 1968 nomination of Abe Fortas to serve as Chief Justice in this calculation, because his nomination was withdrawn before there was a final Senate vote.

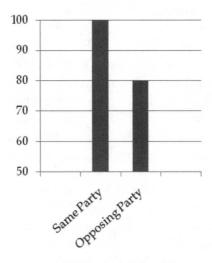

Figure 3. Percent of nominees confirmed, control of Senate (1955–2010)

did not control the Senate, and five of the six nominees denied confirmation in the last 150 years faced the same situation.[5]

Moreover, as shown in Figure 3, between 1955 and 2010, every nominee proposed by a president whose party controlled the Senate was confirmed (thirteen of thirteen), whereas only 80 percent of those nominated by a president whose party did *not* control the Senate were confirmed (twelve of fifteen).

All three nominees rejected by the full Senate between 1955 and 2010 were nominated by a Republican president facing a Democratic Senate. At first blush, this might seem to suggest that Democrats were more obstructionist than Republicans. Not so. In that era, Democratic presidents nominated eight Supreme Court Justices who were voted on by the full Senate. Each was confirmed by a Democratically-controlled Senate. During that same time, Republican presidents nominated nineteen Justices, sixteen of whom were confirmed. In four of those instances, the Republicans controlled

---

[5] The only nominee since 1870 who was denied confirmation in a vote of the full Senate when the Senate majority was of the same political party as the president was John J. Parker, who was nominated by Herbert Hoover in 1930. He was defeated by a vote of thirty-nine to forty-one, largely because of his controversial views on labor and racial issues. For a history of Parker and race, see Glenda Elizabeth Gilmore, "False Friends and Avowed Enemies: Southern African Americans and Party Allegiances in the 1920s," in Jane Dailey, Glenda Elizabeth Gilmore, and Bryant Simon, eds, *Jumpin' Jim Crow: Southern Politics from Civil War to Civil Rights* 219 (Princeton, 2000).

the Senate, and those nominees were all confirmed. In the other fifteen cases, a Democratically-controlled Senate confirmed twelve of fifteen, or 80 percent, of the Republican nominees. The key point is that the Republicans have not refused to confirm the nominee of a Democratic president in the past fifty-five years, not because they are more deferential, but because they have not had an opportunity to do so. We will never know whether a Republican-controlled Senate between 1955 and 2010 would have confirmed 100 percent, 80 percent, or 60 percent of Democratic nominees. But if we count Lyndon Johnson's 1968 nomination of Abe Fortas to succeed Chief Justice Earl Warren, which was blocked by a Republican filibuster and therefore never came to a full Senate vote, then we can say that Republicans blocked one out of five Democratic nominees, equaling the Democrats' record of defeating 20 percent of Republican nominees when the Democrats were in the majority.[6]

II. Ethics, Competence, and Ideology

When is it appropriate for a senator to vote against a Supreme Court nominee? Senators usually give one of three reasons for voting "nay." They may say that the nominee is not ethical, that he is not qualified, or that he has an "unacceptable" judicial philosophy. These factors were at play in the three most recent instances in which the Senate denied confirmation.

In 1969, Richard Nixon nominated Judge Clement Haynsworth to replace Abe Fortas after Fortas had resigned from the Court. The year before, a coalition of conservative Republicans and southern Democrats had blocked Lyndon Johnson's effort to elevate Fortas to succeed Chief Justice Earl Warren by launching the first-ever filibuster of a Supreme Court nominee.[7] This eventually led Johnson to withdraw the nomination. Fortas's critics maintained that he had had questionable financial dealings, though the coalition also had an incentive to block Johnson's effort to push Fortas's nomination (and the accompanying nomination of Homer Thornberry to replace Fortas) through the Senate less than five months before

---

[6] On the Fortas nomination, see Laura Kalman, *Abe Fortas: A Biography* 327–56 (Yale, 1992).

[7] See Lee Epstein and Jeffrey A. Segal, *Advice and Consent: The Politics of Judicial Appointments* 24 (Oxford, 2005).

the 1968 presidential election, which the Republicans fully expected to win.[8]

With the defeat of Fortas fresh in their minds,[9] the Democrats, who still controlled the Senate after the 1968 election, contested Nixon's nomination of Haynsworth. Nixon chose Haynsworth, a southerner, as part of his "Southern strategy," which was designed to bring traditionally southern Democrats into the Republican Party. A coalition of thirty-eight Democrats and seventeen liberal Republicans joined forces to defeat Haynsworth. Many senators expressed concerns about Haynsworth's views on race. Clifford Case, a New Jersey Republican, observed that "Judge Haynsworth has shown a persistent reluctance to accept . . . the Supreme Court's unanimous holdings in the *Brown* case."[10] Such concerns might not have defeated Haynsworth, however, had it not been for allegations that he, like Fortas, had engaged in improper financial dealings. The final tally was forty-five to fifty-five, with nineteen southern Democrats joining twenty-six conservative Republicans in a losing cause.[11]

The second defeated nomination between 1955 and 2010 posed the competence issue. In 1970, Nixon nominated Judge G. Harrold Carswell in place of Haynsworth. Carswell was far more troubling on race issues than Haynsworth. Not only had Carswell been involved with a racially segregated country club, but in 1948 he had declared, "I yield to no man . . . in the firm, vigorous belief in the principles of white supremacy, and I shall always be so governed."[12] Moreover, unlike Haynsworth, Carswell was a notably undistinguished jurist. Among the twenty-eight Supreme Court nominees voted on by the full Senate between 1955 and 2010, he was without

---

[8] See Henry J. Abraham, *Justices, Presidents, and Senators: A History of U.S. Supreme Court Appointments from Washington to Bush II* 227–28 (Rowman & Littlefield, 5th ed 2008).

[9] See Davis, *Electing Justice* at 40 (cited in note 1); Abraham, *Justices, Presidents, and Senators* at 10 (cited in note 8).

[10] *Consideration of the Nomination of Clement F. Haynsworth*, 91st Cong, 1st Sess 35130 (1969) (statement of Senator Case).

[11] See Abraham, *Justices, Presidents, and Senators* at 10–11 (cited in note 8). See also Trevor Parry-Giles, *The Character of Justice: Rhetoric, Law, and Politics in the Supreme Court Confirmation Process* 88–102 (Michigan State, 2006); Epstein and Segal, *Advice and Consent* at 95 (cited in note 7).

[12] Quoted in Richard Harris, *Decision* 15–16 (E. P. Dutton, 1971). See also Parry-Giles, *Character of Justice* at 103–04 (cited in note 11).

question the least qualified.[13] Yale Law School Dean Louis Pollak
went even further, telling the Senate Judiciary Committee that Carswell "presents more slender credentials than any nominee for the
Supreme Court put forth in this century."[14] It was about Carswell
that Republican Senator Roman Hruska famously remarked in a
radio interview, "Even if he were mediocre, there are a lot of mediocre judges and people and lawyers. They are entitled to a little
representation, aren't they, and a little chance? We can't have all
Brandeises and Cardozos, and Frankfurters, and stuff like that
there."[15]

Carswell's lack of distinction, combined with the charges of racism, led to his defeat by a vote of forty-five to fifty-one. As in
Haynsworth's case, liberal Republicans (thirteen) joined Democrats
(thirty-eight) in opposition, whereas southern Democrats (seventeen) joined conservative Republicans (twenty-eight) in support of
the nomination.

As suggested by the Carswell defeat, senators do take a nominee's
qualifications seriously. According to studies done by Lee Epstein
and Jeffrey Segal,[16] reflected in Figure 4, in the period 1955 to 2000
eight nominees were perceived as "very qualified" (Brennan, Whittaker, Stewart, Fortas [1965], Powell, O'Connor, Scalia, and Ginsburg). They were confirmed with an average of 97 percent of the
vote. By contrast, the six nominees who were perceived as "least
qualified" (White, Carswell, Haynsworth, Rehnquist [1986],
Thomas, and Breyer) received only 61 percent of the vote. Those

---

[13] See Abraham, *Justices, Presidents, and Senators* at 35 (cited in note 8); Epstein and
Segal, *Advice and Consent* at 104 (cited in note 7); Lee Epstein, William M. Landes, and
Richard A. Posner, *Are Judges Realists? An Empirical Study* ch 3 (Harvard, 2011); Lee
Epstein, Jeffrey A. Segal, Harold J. Spaeth, and Thomas G. Walker, *Supreme Court Com-
pendium* Table 4-17 (Congressional Quarterly, 4th ed 2007).

[14] *Hearings on the Nomination of Judge Carswell Before the Senate Committee on the Judiciary*,
91st Cong, 2d Sess 2860 (1970) (testimony of Louis H. Pollack, Yale Law School).

[15] Quoted in Harris, *Decision* at 110 (cited in note 12). Carswell's critics frequently
quoted the statement on the Senate floor. See, for example, *Hearings on the Nomination of
Judge Carswell*, 91st Cong, 2d Sess 8806 (1970) (statement of Senator Thomas Eagleton
of Missouri).

[16] See Epstein and Segal, *Advice and Consent* at 104–05 (cited in note 7). It is important
to emphasize that these rankings are not meant to reflect an objective assessment of the
actual qualifications of the nominees. Rather, they represent an evaluation of the *perceived*
qualifications of the nominees at the time they were nominated. To make this evaluation,
Epstein and Segal analyzed the content of contemporaneous newspaper editorials. Of
course, such an evaluation is subject to the risk of selection bias, but Epstein and Segal
take this into account and their data are the best available on the issue of perceived
qualifications.

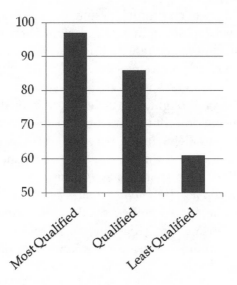

Figure 4. Percent of votes to confirm, perception of qualifications (1955–2000)

perceived as "qualified" (Harlan, Marshall, Burger, Blackmun, Rehnquist [1971], Stevens, Bork, Kennedy, and Souter) received 86 percent of the vote.

The third instance since 1955 in which the Senate rejected a nomination focused on judicial philosophy. In 1987, Ronald Reagan nominated Judge Robert Bork to succeed Lewis Powell. An accomplished scholar and jurist, Bork's extremely conservative and "originalist" views led to his rejection by the Democratically-controlled Senate. The fundamental objection of Bork's critics was that his jurisprudence was outside the "mainstream" of responsible legal thought. Bork's nomination was defeated by a largely partisan vote of forty-two to fifty-eight (fifty-two of fifty-six Democrats voted against confirmation; forty of forty-six Republicans voted for confirmation).

Certainly, it is appropriate for senators to vote against a nominee who fails to meet reasonable ethical or competence standards. But is it appropriate for them to vote "nay" merely because they do not share the nominee's judicial philosophy? In most instances, senators have put ideological differences aside. For example, between 1955 and 2010, Republican nominees Harry Blackmun, John Paul Stevens, Anthony Kennedy, Sandra Day O'Connor, and Antonin Scalia were all unanimously confirmed, despite clear liberal disagreement with their judicial philosophies. Similarly, Democratic nominees Ruth Bader Ginsburg and Stephen Breyer were confirmed with only modest Republican opposition.

Of course, if a nominee's views are truly outside the "mainstream" of responsible legal thought, it may be quite reasonable for senators to oppose confirmation. But what is the "mainstream"? To keep the concept from being defined in a purely partisan or narrowly ideological manner, I suggest that a nominee's views should be considered outside the "mainstream" *only if most liberals and most conservatives would both view the nominee that way*. It would be difficult, but not impossible, for a nominee to fail this test. An example might be a nominee who does not believe in judicial review or who believes that the incorporation doctrine or *Brown v Board of Education*[17] should be overruled.

It is unlikely, of course, that presidents would put forth such nominees and, indeed, few, if any, Supreme Court nominees have been outside the mainstream, measured by this definition. But that does not discredit the standard. It means only that presidents generally have had the good sense not to nominate such individuals. Bork's opponents tried to paint him in that light, but his views were in fact within the realm of responsible legal thought.[18] The real objection was that he would be a *very* conservative Justice whose confirmation in place of the then swing Justice, Lewis F. Powell, would have significantly shifted the ideological balance on the Court. That is a very different objection.

---

[17] 347 US 483 (1954).

[18] The problem in Bork's case was that his judicial philosophy, as he explained it in his writings and at the hearings, seemed inconsistent with the Supreme Court's precedents on a range of important issues, including the right of privacy, the constitutionality of gender discrimination, and the requirement of one person/one vote. These doctrines were fundamental elements of the Court's constitutional jurisprudence, and there seemed little doubt that Bork's own judicial philosophy of originalism would not have led him to the same conclusions as the Court on those issues. But there were dissenting views within the Court on those questions, and I do not think those dissents could fairly be said to be outside the mainstream of responsible legal thought, as I have defined that term. If it was clear that Bork intended to overrule those decisions, his position would surely have been more extreme. Interestingly, when President Reagan sought nominees for Rehnquist's associate Justice seat, he considered both Scalia and Bork. Lawyers in Reagan's Justice Department wrote a memo comparing the two and found Scalia to be slightly more conservative than Bork. See Jan Crawford Greenburg, *Supreme Conflict: The Inside Story of the Struggle for Control of the United States Supreme Court* 42–43 (Penguin, 2007).

III. Does Ideology Matter?

The Senate's consideration of Judge Bork's judicial philosophy was hardly unique in American history. In many instances, senators have objected to nominees on similar grounds. In 1795, the Senate rejected George Washington's nomination of John Rutledge because of his controversial views about the Jay Treaty.[19] In 1811, the Senate rejected James Madison's nomination of Alexander Wolcott because of Wolcott's often outspoken partisanship and vigorous enforcement of the embargo and nonintercourse acts when he was U.S. Collector of Customs.[20] When Andrew Jackson nominated Roger Taney in 1835, there was a serious debate about his views,[21] and James Polk's nomination of George Woodward was defeated in part because of his strongly nativist beliefs.[22] More recently, when Woodrow Wilson nominated Louis Brandeis, conservative senators vigorously opposed his confirmation because of Brandeis's progressive legal views (as well as his religion),[23] and Herbert Hoover's 1930 nomination of John J. Parker went down to defeat because of organized opposition to Parker's strongly conservative ideas about the rights of labor, the liberty of contract, and race.[24]

---

[19] See Davis, *Electing Justice* at 37–38 (cited in note 1); James Haw, *John and Edward Rutledge of South Carolina* 248 (Georgia, 1997).

[20] See Abraham, *Justices, Presidents, and Senators* at 71 (cited in note 8).

[21] See id at 80.

[22] See id at 32.

[23] See Melvin I. Urofsky, *Louis D. Brandeis: A Life* 437–42 (Pantheon, 2009); Abraham, *Justices, Presidents, and Senators* at 143 (cited in note 8); Philippa Strum, *Louis D. Brandeis: Justice for the People* 293–98 (Schocken, 1984); Thomas Karfunkel and Thomas W. Ryley, *The Jewish Seat: Anti-Semitism and the Appointment of Jews to the Supreme Court* 37–58 (Exposition, 1978). See generally, Parry-Giles, *Character of Justice* at 14–66 (cited in note 11).

[24] While running for governor of North Carolina in 1920, for example, Parker declared in a campaign speech that the "participation of the Negro in politics is a source of evil and danger to both races." Quoted in *Nomination of Judge John J. Parker*, 71st Cong, 2d Sess 7001 (1930). See also *Sharp Protests Hit Parker as Justice*, NY Times A3 (Mar 30, 1930). In Parker's defense, Senator Lee Overman, a Democrat from North Carolina, pleaded that "a man ought not be held responsible for what he said in a political speech." *Nomination of Judge John J. Parker*, 71st Cong, 2d Sess 7810 (1930) (statement of Senator Overman). See Christine L. Nemacheck, *Strategic Selection: Presidential Nomination of Supreme Court Justices from Herbert Hoover through George W. Bush* 46–47 (Virginia, 2007); Parry-Giles, *Character of Justice* at 60 (cited in note 11); Davis, *Electing Justice* at 26 (cited in note 1). See generally Roy M. Mersky and J. Myron Jacobstein, eds, *9 The Supreme Court of the United States: Hearings and Reports on Successful and Unsuccessful Nominations of Supreme Court Justices by the Senate Judiciary Committee, 1916–1975* 1–83 (William S. Hein, 1977) (reprinting in full the transcript of the Hearing Before the Subcommittee of the Committee on the Judiciary for Parker's nomination).

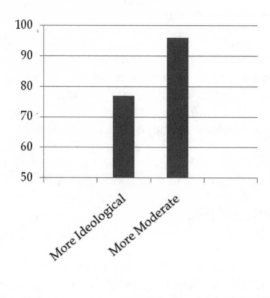

Figure 5. Percent of votes to confirm, perception of nominee's ideology (1955–2010)

Historically, then, a nominee's views have often played an important role in the confirmation process. Moreover, even when a confirmation is not particularly fractious, senators tend to vote with at least one eye on ideology. Epstein and Segal have ranked nominees in terms of the perceived intensity of their views at the time they were nominated.[25] As Figure 5 shows, those nominees perceived as having strongly ideological views (such as Brennan, Marshall, Carswell, Burger, Rehnquist [both in 1971 and 1986], Bork, Scalia, Thomas, Ginsburg, Roberts, and Alito) received, on average, 77 percent affirmative votes, whereas those nominees who were perceived as having moderate views (such as White, Stevens, O'Connor, Kennedy, Souter, and Breyer) received 96 percent affirmative votes.

Another measure of this effect is revealed in the differences in voting by party. In the twenty confirmation votes between 1969 and 2010, senators cast 76 percent of their votes in favor of confirmation. As Figure 6 shows, however, there are sharp partisan

[25] See Epstein and Segal, *Advice and Consent* at 110–11 (cited in note 7); Epstein, Landes, and Posner, *Are Judges Realists?* at Table 3-2 (cited in note 13). As noted in note 16, these data reflect the *perceived* ideology of the nominees at the time they were nominated, and are based on an analysis of contemporaneous newspaper editorials. Though necessarily imperfect, they are the best data available.

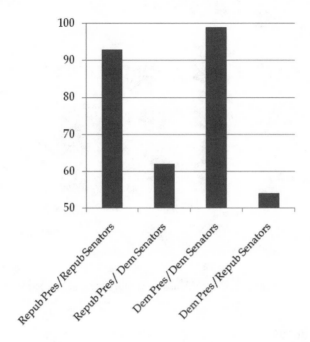

Figure 6. Percent of votes of confirm, party of president and party of senator (1969–2010)

differences. In voting on the sixteen nominations made by Republican presidents, Republican senators voted favorably 93 percent of the time, whereas Democratic senators voted favorably only 62 percent of the time. In voting on the four Democratic nominees in this era, Democratic senators voted favorably 99 percent of the time, whereas Republican senators voted favorably only 54 percent of the time.

Similarly, leaving aside party affiliation, senators are more likely to vote for nominees with whom they are ideologically aligned than for those from whom they are ideologically distant. Figure 7 reveals that when senators are closely aligned with a nominee ideologically, they vote to confirm 98 percent of the time; when they are in the same general ballpark as a nominee, they vote to confirm 82 percent of the time; and when they are ideologically distant from a nominee, they vote to confirm only 57 percent of the time.[26]

---

[26] See Epstein and Segal, *Advice and Consent* at 110–11 (cited in note 7). See also Epstein, Landes, and Posner, *Are Judges Realists?* at Table 3-2 (cited in note 13); Lee Epstein, Jeffrey A. Segal, and Chad Westerland, *The Increasing Importance of Ideology in the Nomination and Confirmation of Supreme Court Justices*, 56 Drake L Rev 609, 631 (2008).

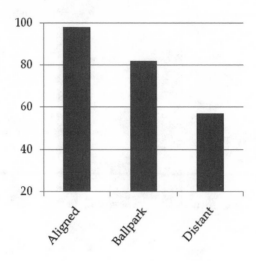

Figure 7. Percent of votes of confirm, ideological alignment (1950–2000)

We can thus say with some confidence, and without much surprise, that senators take ideology, as well as qualifications and ethics,
into account.

IV. DEFERENCE AND ITS LIMITS: HOTLY-CONTESTED
NOMINATIONS

After 220 years of history and 129 confirmation votes, there
is still no consensus about whether the Senate should consider the
substantive views of nominees.[27] One might argue that the Senate
should take into account only whether a nominee is ethical, qualified, and holds views that are within the mainstream of responsible
legal thought (as I have defined the term). On this view, the Senate
should defer to the president on matters of ideology and judicial
philosophy, except in the rare instance in which the president nominates an individual whose views are truly off the charts.

---

[27] Compare David A. Strauss and Cass R. Sunstein, *The Senate, the Constitution, and the
Confirmation Process*, 101 Yale L J 1491, 1493–94 (1992) (senators should vote on the basis
of agreement or disagreement with nominees' views), with John McGinnis, *The President,
the Senate, the Constitution, and the Confirmation Process: A Reply to Professors Strauss and
Sunstein*, 71 Tex L Rev 633, 635 (1993) (senators should not vote on that basis). See also
Henry Paul Monaghan, *The Confirmation Process: Law or Politics?* 101 Harv L Rev 1201,
1203 (1988). For a brief history of views of the Appointments Clause, see Epstein and
Segal, *Advice and Consent* at 18–20 (cited in note 7).

For the most part, the Senate takes this approach to the confirmation of cabinet members. In the entire history of the United States, the Senate has denied confirmation to only nine of more than 500 Cabinet nominees. Such a high level of deference makes sense in that context. Cabinet members directly serve the president who nominates them and their term of service does not extend beyond the president's tenure.[28]

Judicial nominations, of course, are different. Federal judges, including Supreme Court Justices, do not serve the president, they do not serve at his pleasure, and they do not serve only as long as he remains in office. Unlike Cabinet members, Justices have life tenure. Moreover, the judiciary is not a part of the executive branch but is an independent branch of government. It answers neither to the president nor to the Congress. The very sensible reasons for the Senate to give broad deference to the president's Cabinet nominations are absent in the context of Supreme Court nominations.

Moreover, a high degree of deference to the president in the realm of Supreme Court nominations is not mandated by the constitutional design. Following the lead of most state constitutions in the late eighteenth century, the Framers of the United States Constitution initially gave Congress complete control over judicial appointments.[29] The decision to assign the power to nominate judges to the president, a last-minute change at the Constitutional Convention, was intended to facilitate the process of selection (multimember bodies are not very efficient when it comes to identifying and selecting individuals for specific positions) and to ensure *dual* responsibility for the appointment of members of the third branch.[30]

Viewed in this light, it would seem quite reasonable for the Senate to exercise considerable independence in evaluating the judicial philosophies of Supreme Court nominees.[31] Indeed, senators might

---

[28] The Senate's traditional deference in confirming Cabinet members may not always be sound. It can sometimes lead it to confirm nominees it knows to be unqualified. See Carter, *Confirmation Mess* at 165–66 (cited in note 2).

[29] See Binder and Maltzman, *Advice and Dissent* at 19 (cited in note 2).

[30] See id at 23–24. For an interesting perspective, see Mary L. Clark, *Introducing a Parliamentary Confirmation Process for New Supreme Court Justices: Its Pros and Cons, and Lessons Learned from the U.S. Experience*, Public Law 464–81(July 2010).

[31] See Epstein and Segal, *Advice and Consent* at 8 (cited in note 7); Matthew D. Marcotte, Note, *Advice and Consent: A Historical Argument for Substantive Senatorial Involvement in Judicial Nominations*, 5 NYU J Leg & Pub Pol 519 (2002); Strauss and Sunstein, 101 Yale L J at 1491–1502 (cited in note 27); Christopher L. Eisgruber, *The Next Justice: Repairing the Supreme Court Appointments Process* 11–13 (Princeton, 2007).

sensibly treat Supreme Court nominations in the same way they consider legislation proposed by the president, or in the same way the president considers legislation proposed by the Senate. On this view, senators should be free to support or oppose a president's nominee based on what they independently judge to be the best interests of the nation, including whether they agree or disagree with the nominee's judicial philosophy.

Historically, though, the Senate has taken a more moderate stance. As we have seen, senators usually defer to the president in terms of judicial philosophy, even when they disagree. Indeed, even members of the opposition party vote to confirm 64 percent of the time. This generally deferential approach has significant benefits. It reduces potential fractiousness within the Senate, minimizes the risk of confirmation stalemate, reduces the risk of politicizing the judiciary, and (at least in theory) more or less averages out over time. Thus, although there is no principled or "originalist" rationale for this approach, it seems a sensible, pragmatic compromise that appears to have worked reasonably well over time.[32]

A. HOTLY-CONTESTED NOMINATIONS

Although deference has generally been the norm, it clearly has its limits, especially where the opposition party is concerned. Members of the opposition party historically have cast 64 percent of their votes to confirm, but this means they have cast 36 percent of their votes *against* confirmation. When is this most likely to happen, and why?

Consider what we might call "hotly-contested" nominations— those that generate forty or more negative votes (or, historically, 40 percent negative votes). Between 1790 and 2010, twenty-one nominations, or 16 percent, of the 129 nominations voted on by the full Senate were hotly contested. Of these twenty-one, nine were confirmed by close votes and twelve were not confirmed.[33]

---

[32] An alternative explanation is that presidents defer to the Senate. That is, presidents generally are careful to choose nominees whom the Senate is likely to confirm. Thus, when nominees are rejected or confirmed by close and contentious votes, the explanation may be that the president either miscalculated or, for one reason or another, decided not to respect the preferences of even a generally cooperative Senate. But it is probably impossible to identify—much less get reliable data on—potential Supreme Court nominees whom the president did not choose because he thought they would not be confirmed.

[33] The twenty-one were Samuel Alito (confirmed 2006); Clarence Thomas (confirmed 1991); Robert Bork (rejected 1987); G. Harrold Carswell (rejected 1970); Clement Hayns-

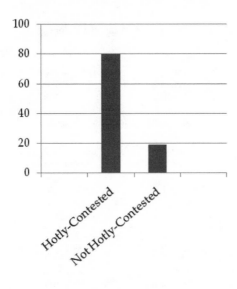

Figure 8. Percent of negative votes, senators of opposing party (1969–2010)

Why do some nominations, but not others, generate such opposition?

Between 1955 and 2010, twenty-eight nominations came to a full Senate vote. Of these, five, or 18 percent, were hotly contested: Clement Haynsworth (45–55), G. Harold Carswell (45–51), Robert Bork (42–58), Clarence Thomas (52–48), and Samuel Alito (58–42). These five nominations generated the closest votes and the sharpest conflicts. Why?

Not surprisingly, senators of the opposition party are especially likely to vote against hotly-contested nominees. Although members of the opposition party cast, on average, 36 percent of their votes against confirmation, they do not cast those votes randomly or uniformly. Rather, they vote negatively primarily in hotly-contested nominations. Indeed, as revealed in Figure 8, they vote negatively 80 percent of the time in hotly-contested nominations,

worth (rejected 1969); John Parker (rejected 1930); Wheeler Peckham (rejected 1894); William Hornblower (rejected 1894); Lucias Lamar (confirmed 1888); Stanley Matthews (confirmed 1881); Ebenezer Hoar (rejected 1870); Jeremiah Black (rejected 1861); Nathan Clifford (confirmed 1858); George Woodward (rejected 1846); Reuben Walworth (withdrawn 1844); John Spencer (rejected 1844); William Smith (declined nomination 1837); Roger Taney (postponed 1835); John Crittenden (postponed 1829); Alexander Wolcott (rejected 1811); and John Rutledge (rejected 1795). See *Supreme Court Nominations, Present–1789* (cited in note 3).

Table 1

Perceived Intensity of Ideology
(1955–2010)

Scalia	1.000
Brennan	1.000
Marshall	1.000
Fortas	1.000
Rehnquist (1986)	.990
Rehnquist (1971)	.990
Carswell	.920
Bork	.810
Alito	.800
Burger	.770
Blackmun	.770
Roberts	.760
Harlan	.750
Haynsworth	.680
Thomas	.680
Powell	.670
Sotomayor	.560
Stewart	.500
Goldberg	.500
Stevens	.500
Kagan	.460
Ginsburg	.360
Souter	.350
Kennedy	.270
O'Connor	.170
Breyer	.050
White	.000
Whittaker	.000

but only 19 percent of the time in all other nominations.

The question, then, is what makes some nominations, but not others, hotly contested? The most obvious explanation would be that hotly-contested nominations involve the most strongly ideological nominees. Such nominees would logically trigger the most fervent opposition. But when it comes to understanding Supreme Court confirmations, nothing is obvious.

Table 1 presents a ranking of all nominees voted on by the full Senate between 1955 and 2010 in terms of the perceived intensity of the nominees' ideology at the time they were nominated. In Table 1, 1.000 represents the most highly ideological and .000 represents the most moderate.[34]

---

[34] See Epstein et al, *Supreme Court Compendium* at Table 4-17 (cited in note 13); Epstein,

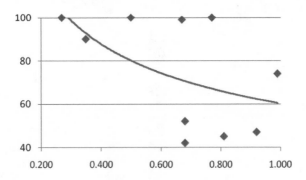

Figure 9. Percent votes to confirm, perceived intensity of ideology, opposing party in control of Senate (1968–2010).

Does intensity of ideology matter? Figure 9 shows the relationship between the perceived intensity of a nominee's ideology and the percentage of positive votes for nominees considered by a Senate *controlled by the opposition party*. Figure 9 therefore covers the confirmation votes on Haynsworth, Carswell, Burger, Blackmun, Powell, Rehnquist (1971), Stevens, Bork, Kennedy, Thomas, and Souter.

As Figure 10 reveals, a similar effect is evident when we compare the average perceived intensity of ideology of the five nominees who triggered hotly-contested confirmation battles (.778) with the average perceived intensity of the other twenty-three nominees in this era (.585). Thus, there appears to be some relationship between the perceived intensity of a nominee's ideology and the probability that the nomination will be hotly contested.

But there is a puzzle here. Although all five nominees who generated hotly-contested confirmation battles were among the

Landes, and Posner, *Are Judges Realists?* at ch 3 (cited in note 13). For Kagan and Sotomayor, see http://www.stonybrook.edu/polsci/jsegal/qualtable.pdf. A ranking of .000 would signify a perfectly moderate nominee. This is not a measure of liberal or conservative, but merely the distance from perfect moderation. This is derived by determining the absolute distance between these nominees and .500 (given their Epstein and Segal rankings) and then doubling the number to put it back onto a scale of .000 to 1.000. Thus, Stevens, for example, had a rating of .750, which means he was exactly halfway between nonideological and very conservative. The difference between .750 and perfectly neutral is .750 − .500 = .250 × 2 = .500. Ginsburg's rating was .320, which is moderately liberal (between .000 and .500). To calculate her perceived intensity: .500 − .320 = .180 × 2 = .360. The method of measuring a nominee's perceived ideology was first developed in Jeffrey A. Segal and Albert D. Cover, *Ideological Values and the Votes of U.S. Supreme Court Justices*, 83 Am Pol Sci Rev 557 (1989).

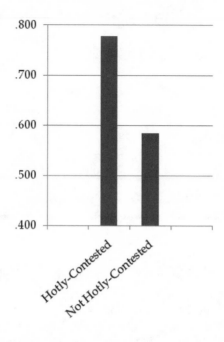

Figure 10. Perceived intensity of nominee's ideology (1955–2010)

fifteen most ideological nominees, ten other nominees who were in the same range of perceived ideological intensity did *not* trigger such battles (Harlan, Brennan, Fortas, Marshall, Burger, Blackmun, Rehnquist [1971], Rehnquist [1986], Scalia, and Roberts). What, if anything, explains this?

B. CHANGE NOMINEES

One possible explanation might be that there is greater opposition to those nominees whose confirmation would significantly alter the voting balance on the Court. We can label such nominees "change nominees." All five of the nominees whose confirmations were hotly contested between 1955 and 2010 were perceived as change nominees.

Richard Nixon nominated Clement Haynsworth and then G. Harrold Carswell to replace the very liberal Abe Fortas. With four conservatives (Warren Burger, Potter Stewart, Byron White, and John Harlan) already on the Court, the confirmation of Haynsworth or Carswell in place of Fortas would have marked a dramatic shift in the ideological balance on the Court.[35] It was therefore predictable that a coalition of liberal Democrats and liberal Republicans would push back hard against those nominees.

Similarly, Robert Bork, defeated by a vote of forty-two to fifty-eight, was nominated by Ronald Reagan to replace Lewis F. Powell, the swing Justice at the time.[36] No one doubted that Bork's confirmation would have moved the Court significantly to the right. When George H. W. Bush nominated Clarence Thomas to replace the Court's then most liberal Justice, Thurgood Marshall, Senate liberals predictably launched a campaign to defeat the nomination. Although they failed, the fifty-two to forty-eight vote was one of the narrowest confirmation margins in American history.

Finally, George W. Bush nominated Samuel Alito to succeed the then swing Justice, Sandra Day O'Connor.[37] In the fifth-closest vote since 1930, the Senate confirmed Alito by a sharply divided vote of fifty-eight to forty-two. It is noteworthy that only two months earlier the Senate had confirmed John Roberts to succeed Chief Justice William Rehnquist by a vote of seventy-eight to twenty-two. Although Roberts and Alito were both regarded as quite conservative, the significant difference in the votes was likely due to the fact that Alito's confirmation threatened significantly to alter the ideological balance on the Court, whereas Roberts's nomination did not.[38]

Thus, to understand the depth of opposition to each of these five nominees, it is helpful to recognize that not only were they perceived as highly ideological, but their nominations were seen as threatening significantly to alter the preexisting balance on the Court.[39]

What, though, of the other ten nominees who were also thought to be highly ideological—Brennan, Marshall, Burger, Scalia,

---

[35] Indeed, this would have moved the swing Justice from Hugo Black to Potter Stewart. Black was quite liberal, with a voting record of .300, whereas Stewart was a moderate conservative, with a voting record of .529. See text at note 40 and Table 2.

[36] Powell was the swing Justice in his last three years on the Court. See Epstein et al, *Supreme Court Compendium* at Table 6-2 (cited in note 13).

[37] O'Connor was the swing Justice from 1999 until she left the Court. See Epstein et al, *Supreme Court Compendium* at Table 6-2 (cited in note 13).

[38] See Greenburg, *Supreme Conflict* at 307 (cited in note 18).

[39] A similar effect is evident in lower federal court nominations. Nominations of judges to courts of appeals "with a balanced bench are less likely to be confirmed." Binder and Matlzman, *Advice and Dissent* at 84 (cited in note 2).

Table 2
Perceived Ideological Change (1955–2010)

Nominee	Perceived Ideology	Justice Replaced	Voting Record	Ideological Change
Carswell	.960	Fortas	.195	.765
Brennan	.000	Minton	.717	.717
Thomas	.840	Marshall	.133	.707
Blackmun	.885	Fortas	.195	.690
Marshall	.000	Clark	.668	.668
Haynsworth	.840	Fortas	.195	.645
Burger	.885	Warren	.263	.622
Stevens	.750	Douglas	.139	.611
Powell	.835	Black	.300	.535
Souter	.675	Brennan	.184	.491
Harlan	.125	Jackson	.612	.487
Stewart	.250	Burton	.673	.423
Rehnquist (1971)	.995	Harlan	.649	.346
Alito	.900	O'Connor	.588	.312
Ginsburg	.320	White	.606	.286
Goldberg	.250	Frankfurter	.516	.266
Breyer	.525	Blackmun	.289	.236
Bork	.905	Powell	.700	.205
Rehnquist (1986)	.995	Burger	.790	.205
White	.500	Whittaker	.696	.196
Whittaker	.500	Reed	.631	.131
Sotomayor	.220	Souter	.340	.120
Fortas	.000	Goldberg	.110	.110
Scalia	1.000	Rehnquist	.891	.109
Kennedy	.635	Powell	.700	.065
O'Connor	.585	Stewart	.529	.056
Kagan	.270	Stevens	.296	.026
Roberts	.880	Rehnquist	.891	.011

Rehnquist (1986), Rehnquist (1971), Blackmun, Harlan, Roberts, and Fortas? Table 2 presents a measure of the extent of perceived ideological change posed by each nominee from John M. Harlan to Elena Kagan. Note that in this table, the higher the number, the more conservative the nominee or Justice.[40]

---

[40] These data compare the perceived ideology of the nominee with the ideological performance of the departing Justice in civil rights and civil liberties cases. The higher the number, the more conservative; the lower the number, the more liberal. These figures are derived from Epstein, Landes, and Posner, *Are Judges Realists?* at Table 3-2 (cited in note 13), and from Epstein et al, *Supreme Court Compendium* at Table 4-17 (cited in note 13). I used the adjusted civil liberties (Adj. Civ. Lib.) column in Epstein, Landes, and Posner, which includes civil rights, criminal procedure, due process, First Amendment, and privacy issues, because it best reflects the issues of concern to this article. Several of the departing Justices changed ideologically during the course of their tenures. Blackmun and O'Connor, for example, became notably more liberal, while White became more

What can we learn from this table?[41] First, there is a correlation

conservative. See Epstein, Landes, and Posner, *Are Judges Realists?* at ch 3 (cited in note 13). Thus, Blackmun voted against civil liberties claims 50.3 percent of the time in his career, but only 28.9 percent of the time in his last five terms. O'Connor voted against civil liberties claims 70.9 percent of the time in her career, but only 58.8 percent of the time in her last five terms. This is derived from Epstein et al, *Supreme Court Compendium* at Table 6-5 (cited in note 13). Thus, if Blackmun's rating when he left the Court was .289 rather than .503 (which was his lifetime rating), then the shift of Breyer for Blackmun was .525 − .289 or .236, rather than .022. Similarly, O'Connor's rating for her last five years would be .588 rather than .709, which means the shift of Alito (.900) for O'Connor (.588) was .312 rather than .191. To calculate these data, I used Table 6-5 in Epstein et al, *Supreme Court Compendium* (cited in note 13), and subtracted the economics cases from the civil liberties column, which equates to the Adj. Civ. Lib. column in Epstein, Landes, and Posner, *Are Judges Realists?* at Table 3-2 (cited in note 13).

[41] It is worth noting that three of these nominees actually moved the Court in the "wrong" direction. That is, Breyer, although appointed by a Democratic president, was perceived to make the Court more conservative, whereas Kennedy and Roberts, although appointed by Republican presidents, were perceived to make the Court less conservative. Does the perceived ideology of the nominees predict their later behavior on the Court? The table below compares the perceived ideology of nominees at the time of confirmation with their actual record on the bench (1955–2010):

From Expectation to Reality (1955–2010)		
Nominee	Expected Ideology	Voting Record	Deviance from Expectation
Ginsburg	.320	.285	.035
Thomas	.840	.884	.044
Kennedy	.635	.695	.060
Alito	.900	.808	.092
Burger	.885	.790	.095
Rehnquist	.995	.891	.104
White	.500	.606	.106
O'Connor	.585	.709	.124
Roberts	.880	.752	.128
Marshall	.000	.133	.133
Powell	.835	.700	.135
Goldberg	.250	.110	.140
Breyer	.525	.349	.176
Brennan	.000	.184	.184
Scalia	1.000	.813	.187
Fortas	.000	.195	.195
Whittaker	.500	.696	.196
Stewart	.250	.529	.279
Souter	.675	.340	.335
Blackmun	.885	.503	.382
Stevens	.750	.296	.454
Harlan	.125	.649	.524

For seventeen of the twenty-two (I count Rehnquist only once in this table) confirmed nominees, their actual voting records on the Court were reasonably close to their expected

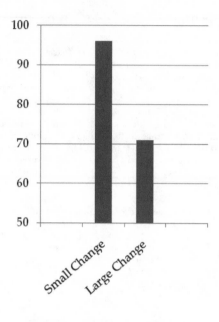

Figure 11. Percent of votes to confirm, expected change in Court (1955–2010)

between the magnitude of the predicted change on the Court and the voting behavior of senators. On average, nominees who are likely significantly to alter the balance on the Court get fewer votes to confirm than nominees who are unlikely significantly to alter the balance on the Court. As illustrated in Figure 11, the six nominees expected to bring about the least ideological change (Roberts, O'Connor, Kennedy, Scalia, Fortas, and Whittaker) received 96 percent of the votes cast, whereas the six nominees expected to have the most significant ideological impact (Brennan, Thomas, Carswell, Blackmun, Marshall, and Haynsworth) received only 71 percent of the votes cast.

Second, as Figure 12 shows, there appears to be some relationship between expected ideological change and the percentage of

ideology at the time of nomination. Of the remaining five, three were thought to be conservative, but ultimately voted liberal (Souter, Blackmun, and Stevens), and two were thought to be liberal, but ultimately voted conservative (Stewart and Harlan). Sotomayor and Kagan are excluded from this table because they have not yet voted in enough cases. See Epstein, Landes, and Posner, *Are Judges Realists?* at Table 3-2 (cited in note 13); Epstein et al, *Supreme Court Compendium* at Table 4-17 (cited in note 13).

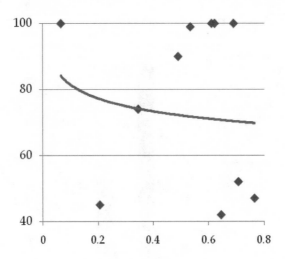

Figure 12. Percent of votes to confirm, predicted change in Court, opposing party in control of Senate (1968–2010).

votes to confirm when a nomination is made to *a Senate controlled by the opposition party*.[42]

Third, as Figure 13 shows, the average ideological change associated with the five hotly-contested nominees between 1955 and 2010 was .527, whereas the average ideological change associated with the other twenty-three nominees was only .326. Thus, the perception of significant ideological change, like the intensity of ideology, correlates with hotly-contested nominations.

Finally, Figure 14 sheds light on why five of the fifteen most ideological nominees triggered hotly-contested battles, whereas the other ten did not. The average ideological change posed by the five hotly-contested nominees was .527, whereas the average ideological change posed by the other ten highly ideological nominees was only .436. This suggests that even among the most ideological nominees, senators are more likely to vote to confirm those who are not expected to have a substantial ideological impact on the Court. Most importantly, as reflected in Table 2, the nominations of Rehnquist for Burger, Scalia for Rehnquist, Fortas for Goldberg, and Roberts for Rehnquist posed virtually no risk of

---

[42] The nominees examined in Figure 12 are Thomas, Souter, Kennedy, Bork, Stevens, Rehnquist, Powell, Blackmun, Carswell, Haynsworth, and Burger.

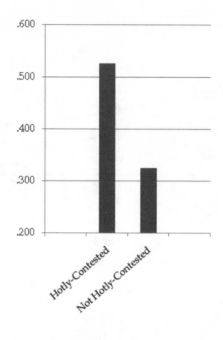

Figure 13. Average expected change in Court (1955–2010)

altering the balance on the Court, and none was hotly contested, despite the perceived intensity of the nominee's ideology.[43]

C. PARTY CONTROL

As we have seen, the intensity of a nominee's ideology and the expected impact of a nominee's confirmation on the ideological makeup of the Court both seem to influence the likelihood that a nomination will be hotly contested. But those factors still leave a lot in doubt. Another contributing factor is whether the president and Senate are of the same political party. This is hardly surprising. In Figure 3, we saw that the Senate is much more likely to confirm the nominee of a president whose party controls the Senate. Indeed, in the period 1955 to 2010, the Senate confirmed 100 percent of the individuals nominated by a president whose party controlled the Senate, but only 80 percent of nominees when the

---

[43] For additional analysis of the impact of what I call "change nominations" on the confirmation process, see L. J. Zigerell, *Senator Opposition to Supreme Court Nominations: Reference Dependence on the Departing Justice*, 35 Leg Stud Q 393 (2010).

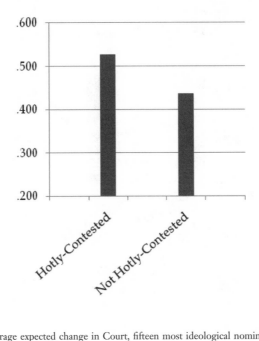

Figure 14. Average expected change in Court, fifteen most ideological nominees (1955–2010)

presidency and the Senate were in different hands. How does this play out in the realm of hotly-contested nominations?

From 1955 to 2010, twenty-eight nominees were voted on by the full Senate. Thirteen of those nominations were made by a president whose party controlled the Senate;[44] fifteen were made by a president whose party did not control the Senate.[45] In that period, there were five hotly-contested nominations. It is noteworthy that four of the five (Thomas, Bork, Carswell, and Haynsworth) occurred in the context of divided government, whereas only one (Alito) took place during a unified government.

Thus, as with failed nominations, hotly-contested nominations are much more likely to occur when the president's party does not control the Senate. Indeed, as Figure 15 reveals, from 1955 to 2010, 27 percent of nominations in the divided-government situation were hotly contested, whereas in the unified-government

---

[44] These nominees are Kagan, Sotomayor, Alito, Roberts, Breyer, Ginsburg, Scalia, Rehnquist (1986), O'Connor, Marshall, Fortas, Goldberg, and White.

[45] These nominees are Thomas, Souter, Kennedy, Bork, Stevens, Rehnquist (1971), Powell, Blackmun, Carswell, Haynsworth, Burger, Stewart, Whittaker, Brennan, and Harlan.

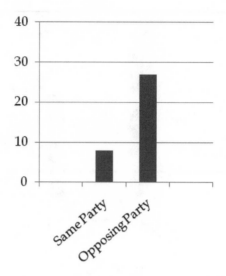

Figure 15. Percent of hotly-contested nominees, control of Senate (1955–2010)

situation only 8 percent were hotly contested. This helps explain why some highly ideological nominees who are expected to have a significant impact on the Court, such as Thurgood Marshall, are readily confirmed, whereas others, like Clarence Thomas, are hotly contested.

One might wonder, by the way, whether presidents select more moderate nominees when they face a Senate controlled by the opposition party. This surely seems sensible. Surprisingly, this has not been the case. From 1955 to 2010, the average perceived ideology of nominees put forth by a president whose party controlled the Senate was .552, whereas the average perceived ideology of nominees put forth by a president whose party did not control the Senate was .612.[46] So much for presidential deference to the preferences of the Senate.[47]

---

[46] In calculating this figure, I treated Brennan and Harlan as if they were ideologically neutral, rather than using their actual ideological ratings (1.000 and .750, respectively). I did this because they were perceived as very liberal, even though they were appointed by a Republican president (Eisenhower). If I had included them at their actual ratings, this figure would have been .643. But for purpose of this inquiry, the neutral rating seems more sensible.

[47] To add one more wrinkle, it is noteworthy that if we exclude the five hotly-contested nominees, we find that the nominees of presidents whose party controls the Senate have an average perceived ideology of .532 and the nominees of presidents whose party does

Table 3

Perceived Qualifications of
Nominees (1955–2010)

Brennan	1.000
Fortas	1.000
Ginsburg	1.000
O'Connor	1.000
Powell	1.000
Scalia	1.000
Stewart	1.000
Whittaker	1.000
Blackmun	.970
Roberts	.970
Burger	.960
Stevens	.960
Goldberg	.915
Kennedy	.890
Rehnquist (1971)	.885
Marshall	.835
Alito	.810
Sotomayor	.810
Bork	.790
Souter	.765
Harlan	.750
Kagan	.730
Breyer	.545
White	.500
Thomas	.415
Rehnquist (1986)	.400
Haynsworth	.335
Carswell	.111

D. QUALIFICATIONS

We already have seen in Figure 4 that senators pay attention to a nominee's perceived qualifications. Does that affect whether a nomination is hotly contested? Not surprisingly, it does. Table 3 sets forth the perceived qualifications of all nominees between 1955 and 2010.[48]

not control the Senate have an average perceived ideology of .449. Thus, it would appear that presidents do tend to nominate more moderate individuals when they are not in the driver's seat—except when they lose their heads and nominate individuals whose ideology pushes the envelope too far. For a fuller consideration of this issue, see David A. Yalof, *Pursuit of Justices: Presidential Politics and the Selection of Supreme Court Nominees* (Chicago, 1999); Byron J. Moraski and Charles R. Shipan, *The Politics of Supreme Court Nominations: A Theory of Institutional Constraints and Choices*, 43 Am J Polit Sci 1069 (1999).

[48] See Epstein et al, *Supreme Court Compendium* at Table 4-17 (cited in note 13). As noted in note 16, these rankings reflect the *perceived* qualifications of nominees at the time of nomination, and are the result of an analysis of cotemporaneous newspaper editorials.

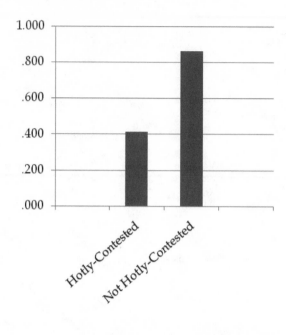

Figure 16. Perceived qualifications of nominees (1955–2010)

As Figure 16 reveals, there is a substantial correlation between perceived qualifications and hotly-contested nominees. Hotly-contested nominees have an average perceived qualifications rating of .413, whereas the twenty-three other nominees have an average perceived qualifications rating of .863.[49]

Moreover, there is a similar gap within the group of highly ideological nominees. Those within this group who triggered hotly-contested confirmation battles had an average perceived qualifications rating of .413, whereas the ten highly ideological nominees who did not generate such opposition had an average perceived qualifications rating of .878. Indeed, eight of the ten highly ideological nominees who did not generate 40 or more negative votes ranked higher in terms of perceived qualifications than *any* of the hotly-contested nominees (Brennan, Fortas, Marshall, Burger, Blackmun, Rehnquist [1971], Scalia, and Roberts).

As Figure 17 shows, perceived qualifications have a significant impact on the confirmation process when the Senate is in the hands

---

[49] The median qualifications rating of the hotly-contested nominees is .415, as compared to the median qualifications rating of the other twenty-three nominees of .960.

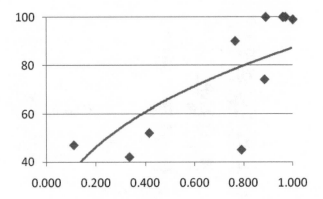

Figure 17. Percent votes to confirm, perceived qualifications, opposing party in control of Senate (1968–2010).

of the opposition party. As a nominee's perceived qualifications increase, the percentage of affirmative votes increases, even when government is divided.

Finally, Figure 18 shows the interaction of perceived qualifications and ideological alignment with senators.[50]

E. OBSERVATIONS

In a full-Senate vote, the nominee of a president whose party controls the Senate will almost always be confirmed, absent a very serious issue of competence, ethics, or extreme views. Indeed, such a nominee has been rejected only once in the last 120 years (John Parker in 1930).[51]

Similarly, the nominee of a president whose party controls the Senate is extremely unlikely to trigger a hotly-contested confir-

---

[50] Epstein and Segal, *Advice and Consent* at 114 (cited in note 7).

[51] The last time this happened was in 1930, when a Republican Senate rejected President Herbert Hoover's nomination of John Parker. Going back to 1790, roughly 90 percent of nominees were confirmed when the president's party held a Senate majority, whereas only 60 percent were confirmed when it did not. See Jeffrey A. Segal and Harold J. Spaeth, *If a Supreme Court Vacancy Occurs, Will the Senate Confirm a Reagan Nominee?* 69 Judicature 186–88 (1986). Even Bork would probably have been confirmed had the Republicans not lost control of the Senate in 1986. See Abraham, *Justices, Presidents, and Senators* at 282 (cited in note 8).

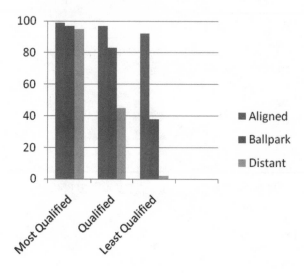

Figure 18. Interaction of perceived qualifications and ideological alignment with senators, percent of positive votes.

mation battle. This has happened only twice in the last 140 years (John Parker in 1930 and Samuel Alito in 2006).[52]

The nominee of a president whose party does *not* control the Senate is much more likely to trigger a hotly-contested confirmation. Between 1955 and 2010, four of the fifteen nominees in this situation generated forty or more negative votes (Haynsworth, Carswell, Bork, and Thomas). This represents 27 percent of these nominees.[53]

Assuming a nominee does not have a serious ethical issue, three factors seem to determine whether a nomination to a Senate controlled by the opposition party will be hotly contested: (1) whether the nominee is perceived as highly ideological, (2) whether the confirmation of the nominee is thought significantly to alter the

[52] The last time this happened before Parker was in 1870 when the Senate denied confirmation to Ebenezer Hoar by a vote of twenty-four to thirty-three. Hoar had been nominated by a Republican president (Ulysses Grant) whose party held a sixty-one to eleven margin in the Senate. In 1881, the Senate confirmed Stanley Matthews by a vote of twenty-four to twenty-three. Matthews was nominated by a Republican president (James Garfield) at a time when the Senate was divided thirty-seven to thirty-seven to two.

[53] The fifteen were Harlan, Brennan, Whittaker, Stewart, Burger, Haynsworth, Carswell, Blackmun, Powell, Rehnquist for Harlan, Stevens, Bork, Kennedy, Souter, and Thomas.

ideological balance on the Court, and (3) whether the nominee is perceived to be highly qualified.[54]

How do these three factors play out in practice? Fifteen nominees voted on by the full Senate between 1955 and 2010 were nominated by a president whose party did not control the Senate: Harlan, Brennan, Whittaker, Stewart, Haynsworth, Carswell, Burger, Blackmun, Powell, Rehnquist (1971), Stevens, Bork, Kennedy, Thomas, and Souter. Even in these circumstances, nominees perceived as ideologically moderate were easily confirmed. If we treat as "moderate" any nominee with an intensity of ideology rating of .500 or lower on Table 1, that would explain why Stewart and Souter were not hotly contested.

Similarly, even strongly ideological nominees have consistently been confirmed in this situation if they were not expected to have a significant impact on the ideological balance of the Court. If we treat as "unlikely to have a significant impact" those nominees with an expected impact of under .200 on Table 2, that would explain why Harlan[55] and Kennedy were not hotly contested.

Finally, even highly ideological nominees who are expected to have a significant impact on the Court have consistently been confirmed in this situation if they were perceived as highly qualified. If we treat as "highly qualified" those nominees with perceived qualifications ratings over .850 on Table 3, that would explain why Brennan, Burger, Blackmun, Powell, and Rehnquist (1971) were not hotly contested.

What this means is that, even when the Senate is in the hands of the opposition party, nominees have been easily confirmed if they are (1) moderate, or (2) unlikely to have a significant impact on the ideological balance of the Court, or (3) highly qualified. Indeed, Haynsworth, Carswell, Bork, and Thomas were the only nominees considered by a Senate controlled by the opposition party between 1955 and 2010 who lacked all three characteristics, and all of their nominations were hotly contested.

---

[54] Other factors are the timing of the nomination, the president's management of the confirmation process, and the president's popularity. See Segal and Cover, 83 Am Pol Sci Rev (cited in note 34); John Anthony Maltese, *The Selling of Supreme Court Nominees* 4–5 (Johns Hopkins, 1995). On the timing of the confirmation, see note 56.

[55] Harlan actually had an expected change of .487, but this was in a *liberal* direction. Given the fact that he was appointed by a Republican president facing a Democratic Congress, this is best understood as an ideological change of −.487, which is obviously much less than .200.

I do not mean to suggest, of course, that it is quite that simple. Obviously, evaluations about ideology, predicted change in the Court, and qualifications are highly subjective and imprecise. Moreover, other factors, such as timing (that is, whether the nomination is made in the final year of a president's term), presidential unpopularity, and presidential mismanagement of the process, can sabotage an otherwise credible nomination.[56] As a general rule, however, these three considerations have shaped the confirmation process when the Senate is controlled by the opposition party.[57]

---

[56] I need to say a word about Abe Fortas. In 1968, Lyndon Johnson nominated Fortas to succeed Chief Justice Earl Warren. The nomination never came to a vote, because forty-three senators (twenty-four Republicans joined by nineteen southern Democrats) initiated a filibuster, which was sustained by a vote of forty-one to forty-three. Although it is generally agreed that, but for the filibuster, Fortas would have been confirmed, this was certainly a hotly-contested nomination. Basically, this was similar to the Alito nomination, in that the president and the Senate were of the same party, and in both instances there were enough negative votes for the nomination to qualify as hotly contested, but not enough to defeat the nomination in a full vote of the Senate. The only difference is that in Alito's case the opponents did not filibuster, whereas in Fortas's case they did. That still leaves the question: Why did the Fortas nomination generate such opposition? With a perceived intensity of ideology of .690, Fortas was not seen as a moderate nominee. Moreover, his qualifications rating of .635 did not rank him as highly qualified. His perceived ideology (.155), however, was similar to Warren's (.263), so Fortas's nomination did not threaten significantly to change the balance on the Court. Moreover, a Court with Fortas and Thornberry would likely have been more *conservative* than a Court with Warren and Fortas. In such circumstances, and especially in light of the fact that the Senate was in the same hands as the presidency, his nomination "should" not have been hotly contested. The explanation turns on two other factors: ethics and timing. First, senators who opposed Fortas raised a serious ethical issue—particularly, that he had allegedly accepted a series of inappropriate speaking fees. Second, Johnson nominated Fortas to succeed Warren on June 26, 1968, less than six months before the next presidential election. Predictably, senators who had reservations about Fortas, whether for ethical or ideological reasons, were not inclined to defer to the president in such circumstances. Indeed, in all of American history, presidents have made only eight Supreme Court nominations within six months of a presidential election. This represents only 5.5 percent of all Supreme Court nominations. Moreover, only two of these nominees have been confirmed—none in almost a century. If we compare this 25 percent confirmation rate to the 79 percent confirmation rate for all other Supreme Court nominees, it is understandable why no president has tried this since 1968. Indeed, it is highly likely that Fortas would easily have been confirmed as Chief Justice, had Johnson nominated him a year earlier. See John Massaro, *Supremely Political: The Role of Ideology and Presidential Management in Unsuccessful Supreme Court Nominations* 24–31 (SUNY Press, 1990). See also Davis, *Electing Justice* at 71 (cited in note 1); Abraham, *Justices, Presidents, and Senators* at 227–28 (cited in note 8); Segal and Spaeth, 69 Judicature at 188–89 (cited in note 51). On presidential mismanagement of the confirmation process, see Massaro, *Supremely Political* at 140–49, 174–83 (cited above in this note). Massaro contends that the Fortas, Haynsworth, Carswell, and Bork failures were all due in significant part to presidential mismanagement.

[57] These same considerations are relevant when the president's party controls the Senate. By far the two weakest nominees in that situation between 1955 and 2010 in terms of these three criteria were Rehnquist (1986) and Alito, and they received thirty-three and forty-two negative votes, respectively—more than any other nominee in this situation. Rehnquist's expected intensity of ideology was .990, his predicted change in the Court

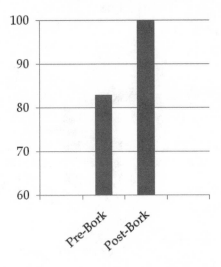

Figure 19. Percent nominees confirmed (1964–2010)

V. Borking the Confirmation Process

At the time of the Bork nomination, many commentators suggested that the harsh nature of that conflict would forever change the nomination and confirmation of Supreme Court Justices. Bork himself predicted that the aggressive questioning to which he had been subjected would limit future nominees to those who had written little and whose views were uncontroversial. Whether this has proved true is, again, more complicated than conventional wisdom suggests.

To evaluate the effects of the Bork nomination, it is useful to consider nominations between 1964 and 2010 (twenty-three years before and after the Bork nomination). One obvious question is whether the Bork nomination affected the likelihood that nominees would be confirmed. One common expectation at the time was that confirmation would become more difficult.

As revealed by Figure 19, in the twenty-three years leading up to the Bork nomination, the Senate voted on twelve nominees and confirmed ten (all but Haynsworth and Carswell). In the twenty-three years after the Bork nomination, the Senate voted on nine

---

was .205, and his perceived qualifications rating was .400. Alito's expected intensity of ideology was .800, his predicated change in the Court was .312, and his perceived qualifications rating was .810.

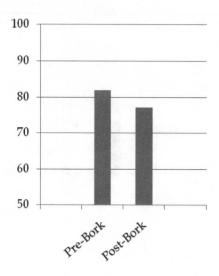

Figure 20. Percent of votes to confirm (1964–2010)

nominees and confirmed all nine. What this suggests is that the
Bork nomination had no negative impact on the probability of
confirmation.

This does not mean, however, that the process was easy. As
shown in Figure 20, in the pre-Bork era, senators cast 82 percent
of their votes to confirm, whereas post-Bork they cast 77 percent
of their votes to confirm.[58] On this measure, the Bork nomination
may have had some effect, but it is hardly substantial.

On the other hand, there was clearly a change in partisan voting.
As Figure 21 reveals, in the pre-Bork era senators voted to confirm
individuals nominated by a president of their own party 92 percent
of the time, whereas in the post-Bork era they voted to confirm
such nominees 99 percent of the time. Similarly, as Figure 22
shows, in the pre-Bork era senators voted 66 percent of the time
to confirm individuals nominated by a president of the opposition
party, whereas in the post-Bork years this figure declined to 55
percent. Thus, senators clearly became more partisan in their voting post-Bork. Indeed, in the pre-Bork years senators were 26
percent more likely to vote for a nominee of their own party than

[58] I do not include the 1965 confirmation of Abe Fortas as Associate Justice in this
calculation, because Fortas was confirmed by a voice vote.

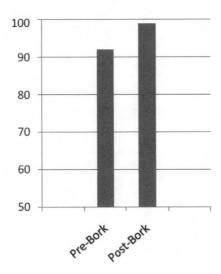

Figure 21. Percent of votes to confirm nominees of same party (1964–2010)

a nominee of the opposition party, whereas in the post-Bork years they were 44 percent more likely to vote that way.[59]

Before we read too much into this, however, it is important to note that this shift in partisan voting may be explained, at least in part, by a completely unrelated change in the demographics of the political parties. As illustrated by the Haynsworth, Carswell, and Fortas (1968) votes, the Republican and Democratic parties during much of the pre-Bork era were not neatly defined by ideology. There were many conservative (mostly southern) Democrats and many liberal Republicans. As this changed in the 1960s, '70s, and '80s, and as the parties realigned along more ideological lines, it came to pass that almost every liberal senator was a Democrat and almost every conservative senator was a Republican.[60] With this shift, it was inevitable—for reasons having nothing to do with the confirmation process—that voting behavior would conform more closely to party affiliation.[61]

---

[59] See Charles R. Shipan, *Partisanship, Ideology, and Senate Voting on Supreme Court Nominees*, 5 J Empirical Leg Stud 55 (2008).

[60] See Richard H. Pildes, *Why the Center Does Not Hold: The Causes of Hyperpolarized Democracy in America*, 98 Cal L Rev 273, 277 (2011).

[61] Perhaps the clearest example of this phenomenon in the pre-Bork years was Lyndon Johnson's 1967 nomination of Thurgood Marshall, which was confirmed by a vote of sixty-

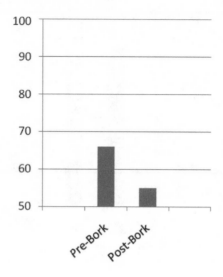

Figure 22. Percent of votes to confirm nominees of opposing party (1964–2010)

As Figure 23 shows, another measure of the possible effect of the Bork nomination is the average margin of victory of those nominees who were, in fact, confirmed. In the ten pre-Bork confirmations, the average margin of victory was seventy-six votes, whereas in the nine post-Bork confirmations the average margin had shrunk to only fifty-four votes. This suggests a significant shift in the willingness of senators to defer, even when their opposition would not affect the outcome.

Another way of evaluating the possible impact of the Bork nomination is to focus on those nominations that generated appreciable disagreement. Earlier, I highlighted what I termed "hotly-contested" nominations—those that produced forty or more negative votes. It is also instructive, however, to consider those nominations which generated twenty or more negative votes. We can call these "contested" nominations.

Between 1964 and 2010, the Senate voted on twenty-two nominations. In the pre-Bork era, the Senate voted on twelve nominations, four of which were contested (Haynsworth, Carswell, Rehnquist [1971], Rehnquist [1986]). In the post-Bork era, the Senate voted on nine nominations, five of which were contested

nine to eleven, with ten southern Democrats voting against the nominee of a Democratic president.

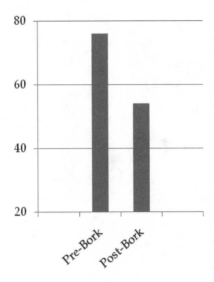

Figure 23. Average margin in successful nominations (1964–2010)

(Thomas, Roberts, Alito, Sotomayor, and Kagan). As Figure 24 shows, there was thus a substantial (33 percent to 56 percent) post-Bork increase in the percentage of contested nominations. This, too, suggests increasing contentiousness.

As already noted, Robert Bork predicted that in the wake of his failed confirmation presidents would select nominees whose views were less controversial. The evidence seems to support this prediction. As Figure 25 shows, ten of the twelve pre-Bork nominees were perceived as having strongly ideological views (above .600 in Table 1)—Marshall, Fortas, Burger, Haynsworth, Carswell, Blackmun, Powell, Rehnquist (1971), Rehnquist (1986), and Scalia; whereas only three of the nine post-Bork nominees were thought to have such views—Thomas, Roberts, and Alito. This shift, from 83 percent to 33 percent, is consistent with Bork's prediction that presidents would be more reluctant to risk appointing highly ideological nominees. What are we to make of all this?

VI. Confirmation in the New Millennium

The Bork nomination seems to have had an uneven, but significant impact on the nomination and confirmation process. A

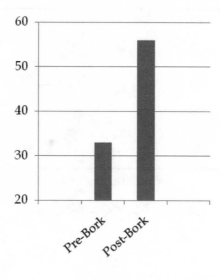

Figure 24. Percent of contested nominations (1964–2010)

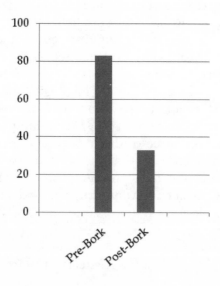

Figure 25. Percent of nominees with strongly ideological views (1964–2010)

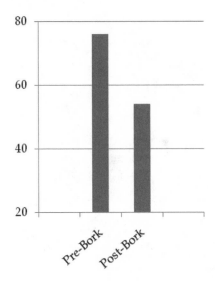

Figure 23. Average margin in successful nominations (1964–2010)

(Thomas, Roberts, Alito, Sotomayor, and Kagan). As Figure 24 shows, there was thus a substantial (33 percent to 56 percent) post-Bork increase in the percentage of contested nominations. This, too, suggests increasing contentiousness.

As already noted, Robert Bork predicted that in the wake of his failed confirmation presidents would select nominees whose views were less controversial. The evidence seems to support this prediction. As Figure 25 shows, ten of the twelve pre-Bork nominees were perceived as having strongly ideological views (above .600 in Table 1)—Marshall, Fortas, Burger, Haynsworth, Carswell, Blackmun, Powell, Rehnquist (1971), Rehnquist (1986), and Scalia; whereas only three of the nine post-Bork nominees were thought to have such views—Thomas, Roberts, and Alito. This shift, from 83 percent to 33 percent, is consistent with Bork's prediction that presidents would be more reluctant to risk appointing highly ideological nominees. What are we to make of all this?

VI. CONFIRMATION IN THE NEW MILLENNIUM

The Bork nomination seems to have had an uneven, but significant impact on the nomination and confirmation process. A

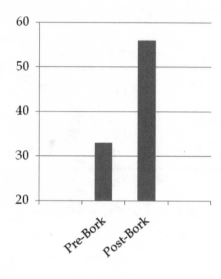

Figure 24. Percent of contested nominations (1964–2010)

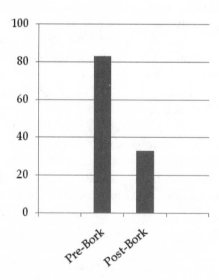

Figure 25. Percent of nominees with strongly ideological views (1964–2010)

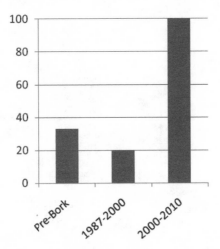

Figure 26. Percent contested nominations (1964–2010)

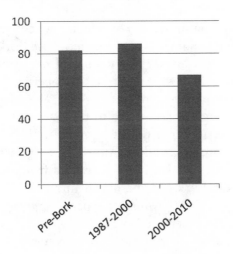

Figure 27. Percent of positive votes (1964–2010)

closer look, however, reveals a more complicated story. As we have seen, the post-Bork period saw a sharp increase in the percentage of contested nominations (from 33 percent to 56 percent). But if we divide the post-Bork era into two distinct periods, we discover some interesting differences. As Figure 26 shows, from 1987 to 2000 (the first post-Bork period), the Senate voted on and con-

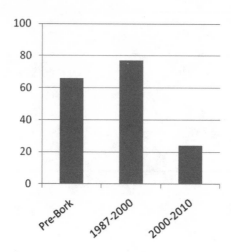

Figure 28. Percent of opposing party positive votes (1964–2010)

firmed five nominations, one of which was contested (Thomas: fifty-two to forty-eight). In the second post-Bork period (from 2000 to 2010), the Senate voted on and confirmed four nominations, *all* of which were contested (Roberts: seventy-eight to twenty-two; Alito: fifty-eight to forty-two; Sotomayor: sixty-eight to thirty-one; Kagan: sixty-three to thirty-seven).

Even more intriguing is the voting pattern. Figure 27 tracks the percentage of votes to confirm. Although, as we saw in Figure 20, the percentage of positive votes decreased from 82 percent to 77 percent after the Bork nomination, it turns out that this decrease was entirely post-2000, when the percentage of positive votes dropped to only 67 percent.

Figure 28 takes this a step further by comparing the percentage of *opposition party* positive votes. In the five nominations between 1987 and 2000, members of the opposition party (Democrats for Kennedy, Souter, and Thomas; Republicans for Ginsburg and Breyer) cast 73 percent of their votes to confirm. In the four nominations between 2000 and 2010, members of the opposition party (Democrats for Alito and Roberts; Republicans for Sotomayor and Kagan) cast only 26 percent of their votes to confirm. (Democrats cast 33 percent of their votes in favor of Roberts and Alito; Republicans cast 19 percent of their votes in favor of So-

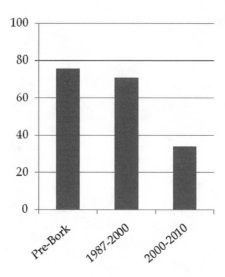

Figure 29. Average margin in successful nominations (1964–2010)

tomayor and Kagan). It is striking that the change occurs, not post-Bork, but post-2000.

This same effect is evident in the average margin of victory data. As we saw in Figure 23, the average margin of victory declined from seventy-six to fifty-four after the Bork nomination. But as Figure 29 shows, almost all of this drop-off was post-2000.

To refine our inquiry, let us exclude the "hotly-contested" nominations (those generating forty or more negative votes). There were two such nominations pre-Bork (Haynsworth and Carswell for Fortas) and two post-Bork (Thomas for Marshall and Alito for O'Connor). The intensity of the opposition in these cases makes sense, because (among other reasons) all four of these nominees threatened significantly to alter the balance within the Court. If we put these four cases aside, we are left with an even starker picture.

In the years between 1964 and 2010, five contested nominations generated between twenty and forty negative votes (Rehnquist for Harlan, Rehnquist for Burger, Roberts for Rehnquist, Sotomayor for Souter, and Kagan for Stevens). What makes these nominations especially interesting is that all of these nominees were perceived as qualified, none was accused of unethical behavior, and none threatened significantly to change the balance on the Court.

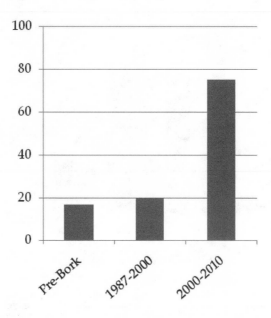

Figure 30. Percent contested nominations (20–40 negative votes) (1964–2010)

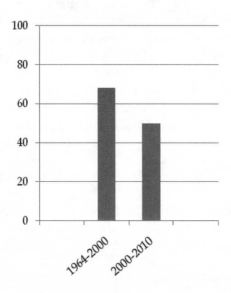

Figure 31. Percent of nominees with strongly ideological views (1964–2010)

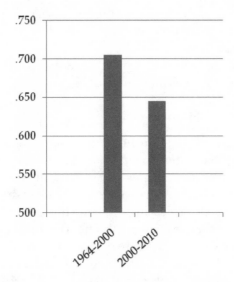

Figure 32. Average perceived ideological intensity of nominees (1964–2010)

Nonetheless, in each instance between twenty and forty senators opposed confirmation. The only plausible explanation is ideological disagreement.[62] As Figure 30 shows, these contested nominations were not evenly distributed over time.

One possible explanation for these data, of course, is that presidents between 2000 and 2010 put forward more ideologically controversial nominees than in the period 1964 to 2000. Not so. As Figure 31 shows, the sharp increase in negative voting between 2000 and 2010 occurred even though presidents in that era nominated a lower percentage of individuals with strongly ideological views[63] than in the period 1964 to 2000. Sixty-eight percent of nominees between 1964 and 2000 were strongly ideological, whereas only 50 percent were strongly ideological between 2000 and 2010. Similarly, as Figure 32 shows, nominees between 1964 and 2000 were, on average, more ideological (.705) than nominees between 2000 and 2010 (.645). Thus, the much greater level of contentiousness in the Senate between 2000 and 2010 cannot be

---

[62] As we have seen, there are other possible reasons for opposition—for example, the nomination is made in the waning days of a president's term—but no such reasons were present in these cases. On the issue of timing, see note 56.

[63] As before, I define "strongly ideological" as above .600 on Table 1.

explained on the ground that nominees in that period were more ideological than their predecessors. Indeed, if anything, the opposite is the case.

Before we try to make sense of this, we should consider changes in the confirmation hearings themselves.

VII. Borking the Hearings?

Conventional wisdom holds that the substance of confirmation hearings has deteriorated dramatically since the Bork nomination, because nominees now refuse to address serious legal issues with the Senate. Christopher Eisgruber has argued, for example, that the Bork hearings "changed the way later nominees would approach their hearings."[64] The assumption is that nominees historically were much more open in their testimony, enabling the Senate to arrive at a more nuanced understanding of their views. As then-professor Elena Kagan wrote in 1995, post-Bork hearings have become "a vapid and hollow charade, in which repetition of platitudes has replaced discussion of viewpoints and personal anecdotes have supplanted legal analysis."[65] Kagan's description of confirmation hearings may be accurate, but the perceived change is more illusory than real.

Our current practice of hearing the testimony of Supreme Court nominees is of recent vintage. The Senate did not even have public hearings on Supreme Court nominations until 1916, when the furor over Woodrow Wilson's nomination of Louis Brandeis led to the first public hearing. Moreover, of the first 102 Supreme Court nominees on whom the Senate voted, only one testified before the Senate—Harlan Fiske Stone in 1925. Stone himself requested the opportunity to appear before the Senate Judiciary Committee to respond to charges against him, which he successfully rebutted. In 1939, Felix Frankfurter was the first Justice ever "invited" by the Committee on the Judiciary, probably to answer questions about his defense of Sacco and Vanzetti in the 1920s and his support of the nascent American Civil Liberties Union. Frankfurter initially took the position that his record spoke for itself and refused to answer any questions, but in the end he did

---

[64] Eisgruber, *Next Justice* at 152 (cited in note 31).

[65] Kagan, 62 U Chi L Rev at 941 (cited in note 2). See generally David A. Yalof, *Confirmation Obfuscation: Supreme Court Confirmation Politics in a Conservative Era*, 44 Stud L, Polit & Society 141 (Emerald, 2008).

agree to take questions. He was thereafter confirmed by a voice vote.[66]

It was not until 1955 that the Senate established the current practice of inviting nominees to testify as a matter of course. When Dwight Eisenhower nominated John Marshall Harlan to succeed Robert Jackson six months after the Court's landmark decision in *Brown v Board of Education*,[67] southern senators attacked Harlan as "ultra-liberal," hostile to the South, and committed to changing the Constitution by "judicial fiat."[68] Not surprisingly, they demanded Harlan's testimony. Only twenty-eight nominees who have been voted on by the full Senate have testified in the way we now expect. For 165 years, this was not the norm. Thus, when we complain about the asserted lack of candor of nominees in their testimony it is important to keep in mind that there was no questioning at all of Supreme Court nominees until relatively recently.

Was the interrogation of nominees before 1987 more edifying than in the years since Bork? A review of a random sample of confirmation hearings between 1955 and 1987 suggests that those earlier hearings were no more illuminating than more recent ones. Indeed, just two questions into his 1955 testimony, Harlan evaded a question on civil rights.[69] Two years later, William Brennan followed suit, declining at the very outset of his hearing to answer a question on communism.[70] Similar responses can be found "within the first few pages of nearly every transcript from the 1950s onward."[71] To illustrate this custom, let us consider brief but representative excerpts from five pre-Bork hearings.

---

[66] See Lori A. Ringhand, *Aliens on the Bench: Lessons in Identity, Race and Politics from the First "Modern" Supreme Court Confirmation Hearing to Today*, 2010 Mich St L Rev (forthcoming); Abraham, *Justices, Presidents, and Senators* at 154, 174 (cited in note 8); *Nomination of Felix Frankfurter to Be Associate Justice of the Supreme Court of the United States: Hearings Before the S Comm on the Judiciary*, 76th Cong 13–14. See generally Felix Frankfurter, *The Case of Sacco and Vanzetti: A Critical Analysis for Lawyers and Laymen* (Little, Brown, 1927).

[67] 347 US 483 (1954).

[68] See Abraham, *Justices, Presidents, and Senators* at 206 (cited in note 8).

[69] *Hearings on the Nomination of John Marshall Harlan to Be Associate Justice of the Supreme Court of the United States Before the Committee on the Judiciary*, 84th Cong, 1st Sess 137–38 (1955) (testimony of John Marshall Harlan).

[70] *Hearings on the Nomination of William Joseph Brennan to Be Associate Justice of the Supreme Court of the United States Before the Committee on the Judiciary*, 85th Cong, 1st Sess 17–18 (1955) (testimony of William Joseph Brennan).

[71] Dion Farganis and Justin Wedeking, *No Hints, No Forecasts, No Previews: Analyzing*

A. JOHN MARSHALL HARLAN: "IT WOULD BE INAPPROPRIATE FOR ME
. . . TO EXPRESS MY VIEWS"

Harlan's hearings established the precedent for all that have
followed. One issue in his hearings focused on his brief membership in the Atlantic Union Committee, an organization dedi-
cated to promoting mutual security among nations of the Atlantic
community. This was controversial in some quarters because of
concerns that international treaties and organizations might undermine the sovereignty of the states and of the United States:

> **Sen. Eastland (D-MS):** Now, I would like to have you tell us, please,
> sir, . . . whether a treaty can cut across the Bill of Rights, whether it
> can override the Constitution. . . .
> **Harlan:** I will try to answer that question as fully and directly as I
> can, Senator Eastland, bearing in mind . . . the position that I am in
> as a nominee to the Supreme Court of the United States, for . . . it
> would be inappropriate for me . . . to express my views on issues that
> may come before me. . . . But in those limitations I will give an answer
> to your question, sir.
> **Sen. Eastland:** All right, sir.
> **Harlan:** First of all, as to the scope of the treaty-making power which
> has had a long history, [you have raised] questions which [have] been
> before the Supreme Court, which are likely to come again before the
> Supreme Court in one fashion or another, and as to that I must ask
> your indulgence in saying that I would not in my position be entitled
> to comment on that. . . . And although I strongly believe that in this
> dangerous period of the world's history that this country must ally itself
> with those who believe in the principles of freedom in resisting com-
> munist aggression, I believe as a citizen, and I think it is proper for
> me to say [that] my approach to any such question is that whatever
> arrangements that must be made in that area, must be done in accor-
> dance and under the Constitution and laws of the United States. That,
> I think, is as . . . fully as I can reasonably go with due regard to my
> position. . . .[72]

B. POTTER STEWART: "I HAVE NEVER GIVEN IT ANY THOUGHT"

In 1959, the Senate considered President Dwight Eisenhower's
nomination of Judge Potter Stewart. The "hot button" issue at
the time was *Brown v Board of Education*, and the southern senators

---

Supreme Court Nominee Evasiveness, 1955–2009 *10 (2010) (unpublished manuscript, June
22, 2010), online at http://papers.ssrn.com/sol3/papers.cfm?abstract_id=1628813.

[72] *Harlan Confirmation Hearings* at 137–38 (cited in note 69).

on the Judiciary Committee grilled the nominee about racial segregation and the Equal Protection Clause:

> **Sen. Eastland (D-MS):** Do you think the Supreme Court has the
> power to amend the Constitution of the United States?
> **Stewart:** Certainly not to amend it. No. . . .
> **Sen. Eastland:** Before May 1954, the Supreme Court in a number
> of cases held that the [separate-but-equal] doctrine met the test of the
> 14th Amendment. That was changed . . . in *Brown v. Board of Education.*
> Was that an amendment of the Constitution?
> **Stewart:** No, sir. I don't think it was. . . .
> **Sen. Eastland:** You don't think the courts should be bound by prec-
> edent that is a century old?
> **Stewart:** I think, certainly, the courts ought to give a very great deal
> of weight to all precedents, regardless of their age.
> **Sen. Eastland:** Isn't it true that the Constitution has the same mean-
> ing today that it had when it was adopted? . . .
> **Stewart:** The genius of the framers of that document, I think, is
> apparent when we realize that the words that they used at the end of
> the 18th Century are still alive and are still applicable . . . to a changing
> and growing society. . . .
> **Sen. Johnston (D-LA):** Do you consider yourself what is termed a
> "creative judge" or do you consider yourself a judge that follows prec-
> edent?
> **Stewart:** Well, certainly, if I can find precedents I think are appli-
> cable, I am happy; that makes the job that much easier. . . . But I don't
> really consider myself a "creative" or "non-creative judge." . . . Maybe
> I am considered creative or not creative. I don't know. I have never
> given it any thought. . . .
> **Sen. McClellan (D-AK):** [D]o you agree with the view, the reason-
> ing and logic applied . . . and the philosophy expressed by the Supreme
> Court in arriving at its decision in the case of *Brown v. Board of Education*
> on May 7, 1954?
> **Stewart:** That question I think I could not answer with an unqualified
> "yes" or "no." . . . I never read any opinion of any court that I thought
> was perfect. . . .
> **Sen. McClellan:** . . . I want to know so I am able to perform my
> duty best, my responsibility here with respect to your confirmation.
> . . . I wholly disagree with that decision. . . . But to perform my duty
> here I have a right to know . . . what is the judgment and view of the
> applicant who seeks to serve on that court. . . .
> **Stewart:** Senator McClellan, the way that question is phrased I can-
> not conscientiously give you a simple "yes" or simple "no" answer.
> **Sen. McClellan:** Give me an unsimple one with qualifications.
> **Stewart:** . . . There are now pending in the court several, many,
> cases in which the reasoning of [*Brown*] is relied upon by at least one
> of the parties. . . . If I give a simple "yes" or "no" answer . . . it would
> not only disqualify my participation in pending cases and heaven only

knows how many future cases, but it seems to me it would involve a serious problem of simple judicial ethics. It would or might be construed in a case as prejudice on my part, one way or the other, about cases that are before the court. . . .[73]

C. ABE FORTAS: "I HOPE TO GAIN MUCH MORE WISDOM"

In 1965, the Senate held hearings on President Lyndon Johnson's nomination of Abe Fortas to replace Arthur Goldberg. The hearings took place a year before the Supreme Court's 1966 decision in *Miranda v Arizona*,[74] and the issue of police interrogation was very much on the minds of some senators. Senator John McClellan questioned Fortas about the issue. Fortas, like Harlan and Stewart, responded in a manner that anticipated the answers of more recent nominees:

> **Fortas**: It is a question that has not yet been settled by the courts. . . . I know that nominees for the Supreme Court here in the past have expressed great diffidence in speaking about matters that may possibly come before the Court, and I appreciate that, and I do not want to breach that rule, but I may say that I think it is appropriate for me to repeat what I have said in the past . . . which is that I believe that an adequate opportunity in the hands of the police to interrogate persons who are accused of crime . . . is absolutely essential to law enforcement. At the same time I recognize that there comes a point at which such persons should be brought before a judicial officer, . . . and the great difficulty, the great problem, which I confess I would not be able to suggest a solution to, the great problem is where to draw that line, . . . and it is a problem of the utmost difficulty and . . . I hope to gain much more wisdom and hear many more opinions of lawyers and judges and police officers before arriving at a conclusion. I am far from it right now.[75]

D. LEWIS POWELL: "IT WOULD BE UNWISE FOR ME TO ANSWER THAT QUESTION"

In 1971, President Richard Nixon nominated Lewis Powell to

---

[73] *Hearings on the Nomination of Potter Stewart to Be Associate Justice of the Supreme Court of the United States Before the Committee on the Judiciary*, 86th Cong, 1st Sess 14–17, 26, 36–37, 40, 62–64 (19585) (testimony of Potter Stewart).

[74] 384 US 436 (1966).

[75] *Hearings on the Nomination of Abe Fortas to Be Associate Justice of the Supreme Court of the United States Before the Committee on the Judiciary*, 89th Cong, 1st Sess 42 (1965) (testimony of Abe Fortas).

succeed Hugo Black. The most salient issue at the time was whether the Court would overrule recent Warren Court decisions, especially in the realm of criminal procedure:

> **Sen. Tunney (D-CA):** Mr. Powell, when President Nixon announced your nomination, he indicated that . . . you would be a strict constructionist and a judicial conservative. What do those terms mean to you?
>
> **Powell:** . . . As a lawyer, it rarely occurs to me to think, in fact, it has never occurred to me until recently to think of judicial philosophy. . . . I would think that one's philosophy, whether it be with respect to social or economic problems or political problems, whether he is conservative, liberal, or moderate, to use the current terminology, does not necessarily relate to his concept of the role of the Court as a judicial institution. . . .
>
> **Sen. Hart (D-MI):** . . . The President who nominates you says that he believes that the Warren court . . . had moved in the directions which he would like to see reversed; that he has selected men whose philosophy indicates to him that they would share that feeling about the Warren court and would, to the extent they would be able as Members of the Court, reverse the trend. As one who has felt that the Warren court was good medicine for this country, I find myself sort of presented with a miserable dilemma. . . . How would you counsel me on this: if, indeed, I thought the Warren court made sense and that you were nominated, in order to reverse that, shouldn't I vote against you?
>
> **Powell:** . . . As a lawyer, I never had any trouble with the Warren Court. . . . I have disagreed with a good many decisions of various courts, . . . but respect for that tribunal and its role in our system has been one of the guiding lights in my professional career. . . .
>
> **Sen. Mathias (D-MD):** As a member of the President's Commission on Law Enforcement and Administration of Justice, you joined with several others in the minority statement which criticized the approach taken by the Supreme Court in the *Miranda* and *Escobedo*[76] cases, and . . . I am wondering if . . . you think these cases should be overruled?
>
> **Powell:** I would think perhaps, Senator Mathias, it would be unwise for me to answer that question directly. I will certainly say that as of the time the supplemental statement was written for the Crime Commission Report that I thought the minority opinions were the sounder opinions. . . . Now, I have not made any recent thorough study. I am aware that there are some analyses that have been made that [indicate] that some of the fears that I had with respect to on-the-scene interrogation, for example, have not materialized in fact, but I personally have not seen the data. . . .
>
> **Sen. Bayh (D-IN):** . . . Could you give us your thoughts relative to . . . the right of privacy? . . .

---

[76] *Escobedo v Illinois*, 378 US 478 (1964).

Powell: I have not read [*Griswold*⁷⁷] recently. I remember, of course,
. . . there was no specific provision of the Constitution that spelled out
a right of privacy; the right was inferred from a collection of other
rights. I suppose the correct posture for me to take at this moment is
that I would certainly view any such case with an open mind and attempt
to reach a decision based on the facts and the law and the Constitution.
. . .⁷⁸

E. ANTONIN SCALIA: "[I]T IS NOT A SLIPPERY SLOPE; IT IS A
PRECIPICE"

In 1986, President Ronald Reagan nominated Judge Antonin
Scalia to replace Justice William Rehnquist, whom Reagan had
nominated to succeed Chief Justice Warren Burger. This was the
last confirmation hearing of the pre-Bork era:

Sen. Thurmond (R-SC): Judge Scalia, the Supreme Court's decision
in *Marbury* v. *Madison*⁷⁹ is viewed as the basis of the Supreme Court's
authority to interpret the Constitution and issue decisions which are
binding on both the executive and legislative branches. Do you agree
that *Marbury* requires the President and the Congress to always adhere
to the Court's interpretation of the Constitution?
Scalia: Well, *Marbury* is of course one of the great pillars of American
law. . . . But I do not think I should answer questions regarding any
specific Supreme Court opinion, even one as fundamental as *Marbury*
v. *Madison*. . . .
Sen. Thurmond: Judge Scalia, 20 years have passed since the *Miranda* v. *Arizona* decision which defined the parameters of police conduct
when interrogating suspects in custody. . . . [W]hat is your general view
concerning the warning this decision requires? . . .
Scalia: As to [what] I think of those warnings, I am happy to answer
it as a policy matter, assuming the question is not . . . what do I think
as to the extent to which those warnings . . . are required by the
Constitution. . . .
Sen. Kennedy: . . . Judge Scalia, if you were confirmed, do you
expect to overrule *Roe* v. *Wade*?⁸⁰
Scalia: Excuse me?
Sen. Kennedy: Do you expect to overrule the *Roe* v. *Wade* . . . decision
if you are confirmed?

---

⁷⁷ *Griswold v Connecticut*, 381 US 479 (1965).

⁷⁸ *Hearings on the Nominations of William Rehnquist and Lewis F. Powell to Be Associate
Justices of the Supreme Court of the United States Before the Committee on the Judiciary*, 92nd
Cong, 1st Sess 205–06, 219, 231–32, 257–58 (1971) (testimony of Lewis F. Powell).

⁷⁹ 5 US (1 Cranch) 137 (1803).

⁸⁰ 410 US 113 (1973).

Scalia: Senator, I do not think it would be proper for me to answer that question.

Sen. Thurmond: I agree with you. I do not think it is proper to ask any question that he has to act on or may have to act on.

Scalia: I mean, if I can say why. Let us assume that I have people arguing before me to do it or not to do it. I think it is quite a thing to be arguing to somebody who you know has made a representation in the course of his confirmation hearings, and that is, by way of condition to his being confirmed, that he will do this or do that. I think I would be in a very bad position to adjudicate the case without being accused of having a less than impartial view of the matter.

Sen. Kennedy: . . . I am interested in what precedence you put on that decision being on the lawbooks. . . . What is it going to take to overrule an existing Supreme Court decision?

Scalia: As you know, Senator, they are sometimes overruled.

Sen. Kennedy: I am interested in your view.

Scalia: My view is that they are sometimes overruled. . . .

Sen. Kennedy: But what weight do you give them?

Scalia: I will not say that I will never overrule prior Supreme Court precedent.

Sen. Kennedy: Well, what weight do you give the precedents of the Supreme Court? Are they given any weight? Are they given some weight? Are they given a lot of weight? Or does it depend on your view?

Scalia: It does not depend on my view. It depends on the nature of the precedent, the nature of the issue. . . .

Sen. Mathias: One area of law that has produced shifting majorities, and some very sharp dissent, is affirmative action. . . . Do you think it is a fair observation that the Court's affirmative action decisions represent a fair measure of consensus . . . that an affirmative action program that benefits persons other than the identified victims of discrimination is permissible under the Constitution?

Scalia: Senator, I really do not think I should give my view. You are talking about an area in which it is a sure thing that there . . . is doubtless going to be a lot more litigation in that field. And I do not think here that I should commit myself to a point of view. . . .

Sen. Biden (D-DE): . . . Everything may come before the Court. There is nothing in American public life that may not come before the Court; nothing. Therefore, if you applied that across the board, you would not be able to speak to anything. . . .

Sen. Biden: Do you believe that there is such a thing as a constitutional right to privacy, not delineating whether, for example, the right to terminate a pregnancy relates to the right to privacy or the right to engage in homosexual activities in your home is a right to privacy, or the right to use contraceptives in your home is a right—but, in a philosophic sense, is there such a thing as a constitutionally protected right to privacy?

Scalia: I don't think I could answer that, Senator, without violating the line I've tried to hold. . . .

Sen. Spector (R-PA): The question I have for you is how does a Senator make a judgment on what a Supreme Court nominee is going to do if we do not get really categorical answers to fundamental questions like that? . . .

Scalia: I think at least in the present circumstances, as I see my responsibilities anyway, my problem with answering the easy question, Senator, is that what is an easy question for you may be a hard question for somebody else. . . . [I]t is not a slippery slope; it is a precipice.[81]

F. "'TIS BETTER TO BE SILENT AND BE THOUGHT A FOOL . . .'"

What seems evident is that the reluctance of nominees to answer questions about their views is nothing new. The custom has always been for nominees to bob and weave to avoid discussing past decisions, possible future cases, their own writings and judicial decisions, and their overall judicial philosophy. This is not to say, however, that nothing has changed.

A recent study by Dion Farganis and Justin Wedeking confirms that, contrary to popular belief, recent nominees are not "drastically more evasive than their predecessors,"[82] but it also concludes that they are *somewhat* less candid. Figures 33 and 34 show (*a*) that there was only a modest change in the willingness of nominees to respond forthrightly to questions about civil rights and civil liberties post-Bork, (*b*) that there was a significant decline in candor immediately after the Bork nomination, and (*c*) that the post-2000 level of candor dipped appreciably below the pre-Bork level.[83]

Figure 34 reveals that Bork and then Kennedy took the level of forthrightness to a new high—from which it then gradually declined over the next two decades to a point somewhat below

---

[81] *Hearings on the Nomination of Judge Antonin Scalia to Be Associate Justice of the Supreme Court of the United States Before the Committee on the Judiciary,* 99th Cong, 2d Sess 33–35, 37, 45, 48, 85, 102 (1986) (testimony of Antonin Scalia).

[82] Farganis and Wedeking, *No Hints* at 2 (cited in note 71). See Dion Farganis and Justin Wedeking, *Kagan's Candor: Updated Findings from the Recent Supreme Court Confirmation Hearings* (unpublished manuscript, July 6, 2010) online at http://papers.ssrn.com/ /sol3/papers.cfm?abstract_id=1635240.

[83] The least forthcoming nominees were Haynsworth, Sotomayor, Roberts, Ginsburg, Burger, Scalia, and Alito. The most forthcoming were Kennedy, Bork, Rehnquist (1986), Stevens, and Souter. These data were derived from Farganis and Wedeking, *No Hints* at 41, 45 (Figures 4 and 8) (cited in note 71); Farganis and Wedeking, *Kagan's Candor* at 8 (Figure 3) (cited in note 82).

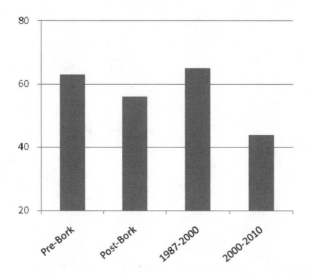

Figure 33. Percent very forthcoming answers to questions about civil rights and civil liberties (1970–2000).

the pre-Bork level. As the trend line shows, the overall trend has been modestly in the direction of less candor over the course of the past forty years. It was Bork who—for reasons of integrity, arrogance, or some combination of the two—departed dramatically from the customary practice. In the end, this did not serve him well, although there are those who believe it served the nation.[84] Ironically, had Bork been as reticent as Scalia, he too might have been confirmed (unlike Scalia, though, Bork's nomination was considered by a Senate controlled by the opposition party).[85]

In any event, after the furor over Bork had passed, subsequent nominees reverted to the safety of the traditional approach. Bork's candor therefore marked, not a critical turning point in the nature of the confirmation process, but an aberration that largely reinforced what prior nominees already knew: that, as Lincoln is said to have said, "'Tis better to be silent and be thought a fool, than to speak and remove all doubt."

[84] See Eisgruber, *The Next Justice* at 154 (cited in note 31). It may be that Bork felt he had no choice but to engage the senators in substantive debate because he had such an extensive "paper trail."

[85] See Lori A. Ringhand, *"I'm Sorry, I Can't Answer That": Positive Scholarship and the Supreme Court Confirmation Process*, 10 U Pa J Const L 331, 351–52 (2008).

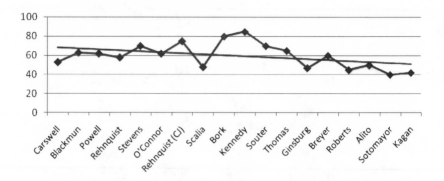

Figure 34. Percent of very forthcoming answers to questions about civil rights and civil liberties (1970–2010).

But that still leaves the question: Does it matter that nominees continue to be relatively closed-mouthed about their views and, indeed, may have become even more so over time? On the one hand, the reluctance of nominees to speak forthrightly is not necessarily a bad thing. As nominees and senators have both freely acknowledged in the hearings, there are sound reasons why nominees should not say too much about their views.

The integrity of the judicial process depends on the ability of Justices to decide cases free of prejudice or bias. If a Justice has announced under oath that she thinks that a particular decision was right or wrong, or that a particular hypothetical should be resolved one way or the other, or even that she has a specific judicial philosophy, she might later feel under considerable pressure to act in conformity with those statements when she has to decide real cases. Otherwise, she opens herself up to accusations that she lied under oath to win confirmation. There is, in other words, good reason for reticence.[86]

Moreover, the reticence of nominees does not leave senators completely in the dark. After all, for the first 165 years of our history, nominees did not testify at all. And as we saw in Figure 2, almost exactly the same percentage of nominees was denied

---

[86] There is, however, a difference between reticence and disingenuousness. Recall, for example, John Roberts's testimony about "call[ing] balls and strikes." *Hearings on the Nomination of John G. Roberts to Be Chief Justice of the Supreme Court of the United States Before the Committee on the Judiciary*, 109th Cong, 1st Sess 56 (2005) (testimony of John G. Roberts).

confirmation between 1790 and 1900 (12 percent) as between 1955 and 2010 (11 percent).[87] As in the past, a senator who wants to understand how a nominee is likely to vote on a particular issue is free to review the nominee's past writings, decisions, and actions, and to elicit the testimony of witnesses who have dealt professionally (or otherwise) with the nominee.

Although it might seem artificial to obtain such information by indirection, rather than directly from the nominee, in fact we do this sort of thing all the time in the legal system. We frequently exclude useful "evidence" because we want to serve other ends, even though this makes fact-finding more difficult. For example, a witness cannot be compelled to incriminate himself, an attorney cannot reveal statements made to her by a client, a doctor cannot disclose information provided by a patient, evidence seized in an unlawful search may not be used by the government, and so on. The practice of not requiring nominees to discuss particular issues, cases, or judicial philosophies is similar.

Of course, this privilege—it might be helpful to think of this as a "nominee privilege"—can be abused. Suppose, for example, a nominee refuses to answer *any* questions. Would senators be justified in refusing to vote for confirmation in such circumstances? Certainly, this is within the prerogative of members of the Senate, who have the authority to withhold their "consent" for pretty much any reason. Thus, the nominee "privilege" is not legally enforceable, but is merely a customary practice that senators can redefine or withdraw at will. Indeed, some senators have, on occasion, explained their opposition to particular nominees on the ground that they had not carried the burden of demonstrating to the senator's satisfaction that they had an "acceptable" judicial philosophy. This give-and-take between senators and nominees seems both inevitable and proper. Nominees understand that they take a risk if they speak too freely *and* if they stand too mute. It is a game of "chicken" that seems so far to have worked reasonably well.

Should senators demand more than they are now getting from nominees? Are they effectively being compelled to vote in igno-

---

[87] I omitted the period between 1900 and 1955 because throughout that period the president's party also controlled the Senate. If we include that period, the comparison still holds. From 1790 to 1955, 9 percent of nominees were denied confirmation; from 1955 to 2010, the same was true for 11 percent of nominees.

rance? Several factors have combined to create the impression that senators are now less well informed about nominees than in the past. First, as we have seen, recent nominees have tended to be somewhat less forthcoming in their responses. Although this may prove to be just a temporary blip,[88] I rather doubt it. My guess is that the politics of the confirmation process have changed sufficiently in recent decades that nominees are unlikely to become significantly more forthcoming in the future—unless, of course, enough senators begin to withhold their votes in order to force the issue.

Second, it is said that since the Bork nomination presidents have been more inclined to put forward "stealth" nominees, about whom relatively little is known. In considering such nominees, senators cannot as easily inform themselves from other sources. The combination of stealth nominees and a greater reticence in answering questions obviously makes it more difficult for senators. The concept of "stealth" nominee is difficult to define, but it is at least plausible that such nominees have become more common.

Among the twelve nominees voted on by the full Senate in the twenty-three pre-Bork years, ten had views that were reasonably well known—Fortas, Marshall, Burger, Haynsworth, Carswell, Blackmun, Rehnquist (1971), Stevens, Rehnquist (1986), and Scalia. Two—Powell and O'Connor—had views that were less well defined. Among the nine nominees voted on by the full Senate since 1987, six had views that were reasonably well known—Kennedy, Thomas, Ginsburg, Breyer, Roberts, and Alito; whereas three—Souter, Sotomayor, and Kagan—arguably fit the description of "stealth" nominees. Thus, although this is a very rough and highly impressionistic characterization, it is at least possible that there has been a shift (from 17 percent to 33 percent) toward nominees whose views are less well known. As Figure 35 shows, to the extent there has been such a change, it seems to have been most evident post-2000, although the numbers are obviously very small.[89]

Third, even apart from these changes, the *perception* of change has been greatly magnified. Studies show that senators now tend to ask "tougher questions more often" than they did in the past,

---

[88] See Farganis and Wedeking, *No Hints* at 31 (cited in note 71).

[89] The only nominee whose views were not well known between 1987 and 2000 was Souter. After 2000, Sotomayor and Kagan both fit into this category.

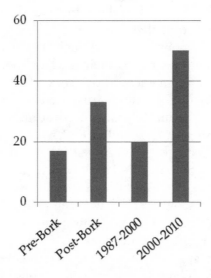

Figure 35. Percent of "stealth" nominees (1964–2010)

thus calling forth a larger number of evasive answers. As a consequence, observers "perceive nominees to be less forthcoming."[90] Moreover, the sheer number of questions asked of nominees has increased dramatically. In the 1950s, nominees typically were asked fewer than 100 questions. More recently, that number has swelled to 700.[91]

The likely explanation for this interrogative excess is no doubt publicity. Because Supreme Court confirmations now attract enormous media attention, they increasingly afford senators "an attractive opportunity" to perform for their constituents. The result is that nominees now repeatedly confront the same "tough" questions from a succession of senators, and unresponsive answers therefore must be repeated over and over again.[92] Indeed, some senators ask such questions, knowing full well what the response will be, precisely for the purpose of eliciting evasive answers.[93] And, of course, the endless dissemination of these answers on news

---

[90] Farganis and Wedeking, *No Hints* at 28 (cited in note 71). See also Davis, *Electing Justice* at 70 (cited in note 1).

[91] See Farganis and Wedeking, *No Hints* at 38 (Fig 1) (cited in note 71).

[92] Id at 4, 31.

[93] Davis, *Electing Justice* at 34 (cited in note 1).

programs, cable talk shows, and the Internet deepens still further the public's perception that nominees are being stubbornly and unreasonably unresponsive, even though they may be responding in exactly the same manner as their predecessors.[94]

What are the consequences of this state of affairs? Christopher Eisgruber argues that senators, frustrated by their inability "to engage nominees about substantive constitutional issues," have tended instead to fish "for evidence of wrongdoing." "Scandal," he asserts, has become "an argument about judicial philosophy conducted by other means."[95] Certainly, there are examples of such behavior,[96] but for the most part efforts to tar a nominee as "a rogue, a fool, or a scoundrel"[97] have been relatively few. Certainly, senators should refrain from unwarranted personal attacks, whether or not a nominee declines to answer their questions. If senators do not approve of a nominee's judicial philosophy or unwillingness to discuss it, the proper response is to vote "nay," rather than to demonize the nominee without a reasonable basis.

This still leaves the question: When *should* a senator oppose a nominee because of concerns about ideology? I will come back to that question later, but first we should try to figure out what caused the dramatic change in the nomination and confirmation process after 2000.

VIII. If It Wasn't Bork, What Was It?

As we saw in Part VI, by any number of measures post-2000 nominations generated dramatically more opposition than pre-2000 nominations. Indeed, comparing the eighteen nominations between 1964 and 2000 with the four nominations between 2000 and 2010, there was a huge increase in the percentage of contested nominations (30 percent to 100 percent), a significant decrease in the percentage of positive votes (80 percent to 67 percent), a dramatic decrease in the percentage of positive votes by members of the opposition party (69 percent to 26 percent), and a sharp decrease in the average margin of victory for those

---

[94] See Farganis and Wedeking, *No Hints* at 32 (cited in note 71).

[95] Eisgruber, *The Next Justice* at 4, 149 (cited in note 31).

[96] The effort to discover what movies Robert Bork rented and some of the accusations in the Thomas hearings might arguably be examples of such conduct.

[97] Eisgruber, *The Next Justice* at 149 (cited in note 31).

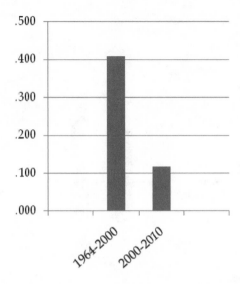

Figure 36. Average expected change in the Court (1964–2010)

nominees who were confirmed (seventy-six to thirty-eight). These changes did not begin post-Bork, but post-2000. Thus, despite conventional wisdom to the contrary, the Bork nomination was *not* a "game changer." What, then, was?

As we saw in Figures 31 and 32, the most logical hypothesis to explain this post-2000 phenomenon—that the post-2000 nominees were more ideological than their predecessors—is plainly wrong. The substantial increase in opposition to post-2000 nominees cannot be explained by the relative intensity of the nominees' ideology.

Nor, it turns out, can it be explained by expected changes in the ideological balance on the Court. As revealed in Table 2, 56 percent of nominees (ten of eighteen) between 1964 and 2000 posed a significant expected ideological change in the Court (.300 or higher), whereas only 25 percent of the post-2000 nominees (one of four) posed such an expected ideological change.[98] Moreover, as shown in Figure 36, the average expected ideological

---

[98] Among the 1964–2000 nominees, Thomas, Carswell, Blackmun, Marshall, Haynsworth, Burger, Stevens, Powell, Souter, and Rehnquist (1971) were change nominees. Among the post-2000 nominees, only Alito was a change nominee by this definition. It should also be noted that Alito's expected ideological change (.312) was lower than *all* ten other nominees on this list.

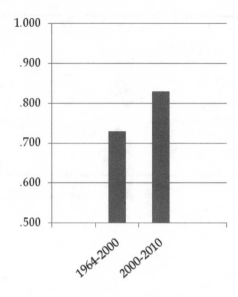

Figure 37. Average qualifications of nominees (1964–2010)

change in the Court posed by nominees between 1964 and 2000 was .409, whereas the average expected change for nominees between 2000 and 2010 was only .117.

Another logical explanation might be that nominees between 2000 and 2010 were less well qualified than prior nominees. Were that so, it is only natural that there would be stronger objections to confirmation. But as Figure 37 reveals, the opposite is the case. The average qualifications rating shown in Table 3 of nominees between 1964 and 2000 was .770, whereas the average rating for nominees between 2000 and 2010 was .830.

Thus, neither ideology, nor expected impact on the Court, nor relative qualifications can explain the dramatic shift in voting behavior post-2000. What, then, explains this phenomenon?

A. HICCUPS, RETICENCE, STEALTH, AND CONTROVERSY

One possibility is that this is merely a statistical hiccup. After all, we are talking here about only four post-2000 nominations, as compared to eighteen pre-2000 nominations. Perhaps ten or twenty years from now we will look back on these four nominations as nothing more than a hiccup. My own guess, though, is that this will not be the case. There has been no analogous series of inexplicably divisive nominations for more than a century.[99] It seems unlikely that we will revert to the old "normal" any time soon.

But if that is true, we still need an explanation. It is possible that the increasing reluctance of nominees to answer queries about their views forthrightly, combined with the increasing tendency of presidents to put forward "stealth" nominees, has driven senators to vote negatively because of their inability to determine the "real" views of nominees. Certainly, the fact that senators have become more persistent in pursuing these questions must add to their frustration when their queries are met with clichés about "call[ing] balls and strikes."[100] Moreover, Figures 33 and 35 both suggest that these issues have gotten worse since 2000. Thus, it seems reasonable to surmise that the perception of increasing reticence of nominees, combined with the perception of the increasing tendency of presidents to appoint nominees with relatively thin records, might explain the significant post-2000 increase in negative votes.

But it is not entirely clear either that nominees have been less forthright or that there have been more stealth nominees in recent years. In any event, frustration with the inability to know very much about nominees would not be particularly troubling to senators if they thought the Court was not doing anything very important or controversial. Thus, some prominent commentators—notably Judge Bork himself—have suggested, as another factor that might help explain the increasing divisiveness in the confirmation process, the growing perception of the Court itself as a "political" institution.

---

[99] Between 1887 and 1894 there were four contested nominations (Lucius Lamar, Melville Fuller, William Hornblower, and Wheeler Peckham). But in that seven-year period four other nominees were easily confirmed (David Brewer, Henry Brown, George Shiras, and Howell Jackson). Similarly, from 1835 to 1846 there was a series of contested nominations, resulting in a number of rejections, postponements, and withdrawals (Roger Taney, William Smith, John Spencer, Reuben Walworth, Edward King, John Read, and George Woodward). Again, though, during that period four other nominees were easily confirmed (Philip Barbour, John McKinley, Peter Daniel, and Samuel Nelson). Finally, the Fortas (1968), Haynsworth, and Carswell nominations were, of course, all contested. But in those instances there were ready explanations for the opposition, including timing (Fortas), ethical concerns (Fortas and Haynsworth), and competence (Carswell). None of those issues was relevant in the post-2000 confirmations.

[100] *Hearings on the Nomination of John G. Roberts to Be Chief Justice of the Supreme Court of the United States Before the Committee on the Judiciary*, 109th Cong, 1st Sess 56 (2005) (testimony of John G. Roberts).

In the 160 years before *Brown v Board of Education*,[101] the Supreme Court addressed a range of hot-button political issues. This was true, for example, in *McCulloch v Maryland*,[102] *Dred Scott v Sanford*,[103] the *Slaughter-House Cases*,[104] *Lochner v New York*,[105] and *West Virginia State Board of Education v Barnette*.[106] Many decisions during Franklin Roosevelt's first term made the Court a focal point of political controversy. But those who say that the confirmation process has been politicized because the Court is perceived as more political can certainly point to the many politically divisive issues the Court has confronted since 1954: racial segregation,[107] obscenity,[108] the free speech rights of Communists,[109] reapportionment,[110] school prayer,[111] the exclusionary rule,[112] contraception,[113] police interrogation,[114] miscegenation,[115] capital punishment,[116] abortion,[117] affirmative action,[118] flag burning,[119] the right to die,[120] *Bush v Gore*,[121] the rights of gays and lesbians,[122] the rights of terrorism suspects,[123] the rights of gun owners,[124] and the rights of corporations in the realm of campaign speech.[125] Perhaps mem-

[101] 347 US 483 (1954).

[102] 17 US 316 (1819) (national bank).

[103] 60 US (19 How) 393 (1857) (slavery).

[104] 83 US 36 (1873) (Reconstruction).

[105] 198 US 45 (1905) (liberty of contract).

[106] 319 US 624 (1943) (pledge of allegiance).

[107] See *Brown v Board of Education*, 347 US 483 (1954).

[108] See *Roth v United States*, 354 US 476 (1957).

[109] See *Scales v United States*, 367 US 203 (1961).

[110] See *Baker v Carr*, 369 US 186 (1962).

[111] See *Engel v Vitale*, 370 US 421 (1962).

[112] See *Mapp v Ohio*, 367 US 643 (1961).

[113] See *Griswold v Connecticut*, 381 US 479 (1965).

[114] See *Miranda v Arizona*, 384 US 436 (1966).

[115] See *Loving v Virginia*, 388 US 1 (1967).

[116] See *Furman v Georgia*, 408 US 238 (1972).

[117] See *Roe v Wade*, 410 US 113 (1973).

[118] See *Regents of the University of California v Bakke*, 438 US 265 (1978).

[119] See *Texas v Johnson*, 491 US 397 (1989).

[120] See *Cruzan v Director, Missouri Dept of Health*, 497 US 261 (1990).

[121] See *Bush v Gore*, 531 US 98 (2000).

[122] See *Lawrence v Texas*, 539 US 558 (2003).

[123] See *Hamdan v Rumsfeld*, 548 US 557 (2006).

[124] See *District of Columbia v Heller*, 554 US 570 (2008).

[125] See *Citizens United v Federal Elections Commission*, 130 S Ct 876 (2010).

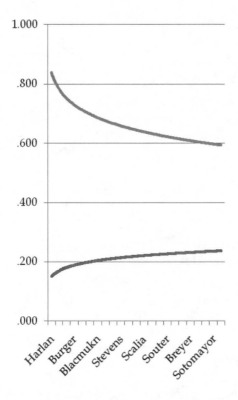

Figure 38. Intensity of ideology of nominees and percent of negative votes (1955–2010)

bers of the Senate have become less willing to defer to presidential selections of Supreme Court Justices because the Court's decisions have become increasingly controversial.[126]

To test this hypothesis, we can compare the ideological intensity of nominees over time with the percent of negative votes between 1955 and 2010 to get a sense of whether the Senate has become more oppositional. Figure 38 seems to bear out this hypothesis. As the two trend lines reveal, even as nominees tended on average

---

[126] Indeed, Robert Bork made precisely this point in attempting to explain what had happened to him. See Lee Epstein, René Lindstädt, Jeffrey A. Segal, and Chad Westerland, *The Changing Dynamics of Senate Voting on Supreme Court Nominees*, 68 J Polit 296, 297 (2006). See also Carter, *Confirmation Mess* at 77 (cited in note 2); Binder and Maltzman, *Advice and Dissent* at 56 (cited in note 2); Martin Shapiro, *Comment*, in Pietro S. Nivola and David W. Brady, eds, 2 *Red and Blue Nation? Consequences and Correction of America's Polarized Parties* 134–41 (Brookings, 2008). Jan Crawford Greenburg has suggested that Roberts and Alito may attempt "to recede from some of the divisive cultural debates." Greenburg, *Supreme Conflict* at 315 (cited in note 18). That remains to be seen.

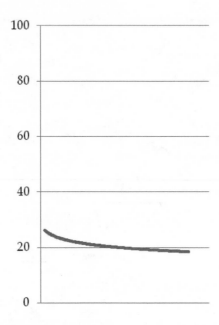

Figure 39. Percent votes against nominees (1955–2000)

to be more moderate (the top line) senators became more negative (the bottom line). This suggests that senators may have come to believe that the stakes in Supreme Court nominations have increased, and the fact that the Court was gradually taking on ever more controversial issues would surely contribute to that belief.[127]

Note that Figure 38 seems to suggest that senatorial opposition increased throughout the period from 1955 to 2010. This would tend to confirm the proposition that, as the Court increasingly attempted to resolve more controversial issues, senators became decreasingly deferential to the president. On closer examination, however, this proposition becomes less clear. Figure 39 omits the four post-2000 nominees. Thus, it charts Senate opposition to nominees only from 1955 to 2000.

The trend line in Figure 39 shows that from 1955 to 2000 the number of negative votes actually trended slightly *downward*, more

---

[127] Figures 38 and 39 do not include Brennan, Whittaker, White, Goldberg, or Fortas, because they were all confirmed by voice votes. For reasons of layout, the bottom axis lists the names only of every other nominee, but all nominees (other than the five) are included in the data.

or less tracking the slightly downward trend in Figure 38 for the ideological intensity of nominees. This suggests that senators were not more oppositional between 1955 and 2000, despite the Court's increasingly controversial docket. Moreover, Figure 39 reveals that it was the Senate's response to the post-2000 nominations that kicked the slope of the trend line upward in Figure 38. Thus, although it is logical that the Court's greater involvement in controversial issues would generate greater negativity in the Senate, this does not seem to have happened—at least not until after 2000. We therefore still need to figure out what, if anything, happened post-2000 to bring about such a dramatic change.

B. 1994–2005

Up until now, I have focused on pre- and post-2000 nominations, rather than on pre- and post-Bork nominations, because the real change seems to have occurred post-2000. But a more precise analysis might focus on pre- and post-1994. This is so because there were no nominations to the Supreme Court between 1994 (Breyer) and 2005 (Roberts). The right question, then, might not be what happened post-Bork or post-2000, but what happened between 1994 and 2005 that might explain the sharp change in the process that first became evident in 2005.

This was the longest period in American history without a Supreme Court nomination. Thus, there was ample time for changes to have occurred. But what were those changes? Several factors seem to have affected the confirmation process between 1994 and 2005.

First, from 1968 to 1993, there were twelve consecutive Republican appointments to the Court. During this quarter of a century, the Court was transformed. According to research by Lee Epstein, William Landes, and Richard Posner, as of 1968 (at the tail end of the Warren Court) the average voting record of the five most liberal Justices (Marshall, Douglas, Brennan, Fortas, and Warren) in civil liberties cases was .185. (This is on a scale in which .000 is the most liberal and 1.000 is the most conservative.) The swing Justice was Earl Warren, whose voting record was .263.[128] It was a very liberal Court.

By 1993, after twelve consecutive Republican appointments, the

---

[128] See Epstein, Landes, and Posner, *Are Judges Realists?* at Table 3-2 (cited in note 13).

Court had changed radically. The average voting record of the five most conservative Justices (Thomas, Rehnquist, Scalia, O'Connor, and Kennedy) was .798, and the swing Justice, Anthony Kennedy, had a voting record of .695.[129] Thus, the Court majority was roughly as conservative in 1993 as it had been liberal in 1968. Even more striking, by 1993 the "liberals" on the Court were almost as conservative as the "conservatives" on the Court in 1968.[130] So dramatic a change in the Court's ideology—and its decisions—would naturally heighten the attentiveness of senators to potential changes in the membership of the Court. And this is especially so in light of the Court's continuing involvement in highly controversial issues.[131]

Second, the Court's most controversial decision between 1994 and 2005, *Bush v Gore*,[132] undoubtedly highlighted the ideological inclinations of the Justices in both the public and political consciousness. In that decision, there was a bitter divide between the more conservative and more liberal Justices, with dramatic consequences for the nation, at a moment when Americans were paying close attention to the Court. The five Justices in the majority (Rehnquist, Scalia, Thomas, O'Connor, and Kennedy) had an average voting record of .695, whereas the four dissenters (Stevens, Souter, Ginsburg, and Breyer) had an average voting record of .312, and every Justice in the majority had a substantially more conservative voting record than every Justice in dissent.[133] The role of ideology could not have been more clear, and it was missed by neither the public nor their elected representatives.[134]

---

[129] See id.

[130] The four conservatives in 1968 (Harlan, White, Stewart, and Black) had an average voting record of .521, whereas the four liberals in 1993 (Stevens, Souter, Blackmun, and White) had an average voting record of .436. See Epstein, Landes, and Posner, *Are Judges Realists?* at Table 3-2 (cited in note 13).

[131] See Binder and Maltzman, *Advice and Dissent* at 102 (cited in note 2).

[132] 531 US 98 (2000).

[133] See Epstein, Landes, and Posner, *Are Judges Realists?* at Table 3-2 (cited in note 13).

[134] See Davis, *Electing Justice* at 22, 81–83 (cited in note 1). See also William G. Ross, *The Supreme Court Appointment Process: A Search for a Synthesis*, 57 Albany L Rev 993, 1020–21 (1994); Mark Silverstein, *Judicious Choices: The New Politics of Supreme Court Confirmations* 71–72 (W. W. Norton, 1994). Not surprisingly, the Court's decision in *Bush v Gore* had a strongly negative impact on the view of Democrats about the Court. Before *Bush v Gore*, 78 percent of Democrats were positive about the Court. Several years later, only 51 percent of Democrats were positive about the Court. See the Pew Research Center for the People and the Press, *Supreme Court's Image Declines as Nomination Battle Looms* (June 15, 2005), online at http://people-press.org/report/247/supreme-courts-image -declines-as-nomination-battle-looms.

Third, the notion of the confirmation process as a largely non-public event was shattered by the advent of televised hearings, round-the-clock cable coverage, and the Internet. Of course, the press has always covered the most controversial nominees, such as Alexander Wolcott in 1811, Louis Brandeis in 1916, and Hugo Black in 1937.[135] But apart from such rare exceptions, the public was largely unaware of—and uninterested in—the details of nomination and confirmation.[136] The process therefore had little political salience.

Today, however, the news media cover Supreme Court nominees as they do presidential candidates, and senators, presidents, and nominees are all acutely aware that television cameras "are beaming their faces and words to millions of Americans."[137] Today, even before the president identifies a nominee, "commentators and pundits scramble to suggest questions for the senators to ask," cable channels prepare to "provide gavel-to-gavel coverage," and people eagerly await the opportunity to watch the hearings "to see whether the nominee survives." As Christopher Eisgruber has observed, the hearings now take on the aura of "a high-stakes reality show."[138]

Supreme Court confirmation hearings were not televised until 1981, when Sandra Day O'Connor's hearings were first broadcast on public television. Several years later, during the Bork and Thomas hearings, public interest reached a fever pitch. According to one survey, 86 percent of Americans watched at least part of the Thomas hearings.[139] Today, the hearings can be seen on numerous cable and broadcast channels, as well as via the Internet. By the time the Senate votes, Americans have been bombarded with countless news and talk shows, newspaper and magazine articles, and e-mails and blog posts concerning the nomination.

---

[135] For discussions of the press coverage surrounding the Wolcott, Brandeis, and Black nominations, see Davis, *Electing Justice* at 24–27 (cited in note 1); Epstein and Segal, *Advice and Consent* at 93 (cited in note 7); Mersky and Jacobstein, 9 *Hearings and Reports* at 13–17 (cited in note 24); Thomas Karfunkel and Thomas W. Ryley, *The Jewish Seat: Anti-Semitism and the Appointment of Jews to the Supreme Court* 37–58 (Exposition, 1978); Parry-Giles, *Character of Justice* at 2 (cited in note 11); William E. Leuchtenberg, *The Supreme Court Reborn* 186 (Oxford, 1995).

[136] See Parry-Giles, *Character of Justice* at 2 (cited in note 11).

[137] Davis, *Electing Justice* at 29, 16 (cited in note 1).

[138] Eisgruber, *The Next Justice* at 151–52 (cited in note 31).

[139] CBS/New York Times survey (Oct 13, 1991), cited in Davis, *Electing Justice* at 96 (cited in note 1).

By 2005, 47 percent of all Americans regarded the identity of the next Supreme Court Justice as "very important to them personally,"[140] and 61 percent of both conservative Republicans and liberal Democrats held this view.[141] And those who regarded the identity of the next Supreme Court nominee as very important to them were more willing than ever to make their views known to members of the Senate.[142]

Fourth, the politicization of the confirmation process has been made even more dramatic by the increasingly aggressive involvement of interest groups. Such groups have long played a role in the process. As long ago as 1881, "groups opposing monopolistic railroad practices sought to block the appointment of Justice Stanley Matthews," because they feared he would vote to strike down laws regulating railroads.[143] In 1930, labor and civil rights groups flooded senators with telegrams urging them to vote against President Hoover's nominee, Judge John Parker.[144] And during the Bork nomination, many interest groups "ran ads in newspapers, sent mailings to their members," and more generally sought to undermine the nominee.[145] A record seventeen groups testified against Bork, while opposing groups made parallel efforts in his defense. There was, on both sides, a vigorous campaign "to influence senators and, crucially, their constituents."[146]

As reflected in Figure 40, there has been a dramatic increase in interest group participation in the confirmation process. An average of 1.6 interest groups participated by sending witnesses to testify in the hearings for the nine nominees between 1952 and 1967, the average rose to 8.8 for the nine nominees between 1968

---

[140] The Pew Research Center for the People and the Press, *Plurality Favors Centrist Nominee* (July 19, 2005), online at http://people-press.org/reports/pdf/250.pdf.

[141] See Pew Research Center, *Supreme Court's Image Declines* (cited in note 134).

[142] See Epstein and Segal, *Advice and Consent* at 94 (cited in note 7).

[143] Id.

[144] Id at 94–95. See Kenneth W. Goings, *The NAACP Comes of Age: The Defeat of Judge John J. Parker* 24 (Indiana, 1990); Maltese, *Selling of Supreme Court Nominees* at 59–61 (cited in note 54); Parry-Giles, *Character of Justice* at 60 (cited in note 11); Nemacheck, *Strategic Selection* at 47 (cited in note 24).

[145] Epstein and Segal, *Advice and Consent* at 95 (cited in note 7).

[146] Id. See Gregory A. Caldeira and John R. Wright, *Lobbying for Justice: Organized Interests, Supreme Court Nominations, and the United States Senate*, 42 Am J Polit Sci 499 (1998); Davis, *Electing Justice* at 24–27 (cited in note 1); Ronald D. Rotunda, *The Confirmation Process for Supreme Court Justices in the Modern Era*, 37 Emory L J 559, 586 (1988); Parry-Giles, *Character of Justice* at 116, 123 (cited in note 11); Nemacheck, *Strategic Selection* at 46–47 (cited in note 24).

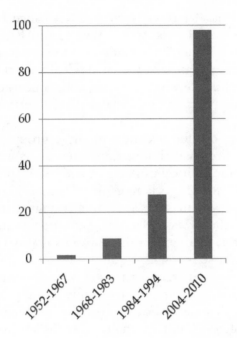

Figure 40. Number of interest groups participating in hearings (1952–2010)

and 1983, and it rose again to 27.6 for the eight nominees between 1984 and 1994. Today, "interest group mobilization and pressure has become a permanent fixture of our political landscape."[147] Indeed, the average number of interest groups skyrocketed to almost one hundred for the four nominees between 2004 and 2010.

Not only do these groups attempt directly to persuade senators to their point of view, but they often carry out aggressive public relations campaigns to gather support by portraying nominees "as either harmful or helpful to the political goals of their members," which may involve such diverse issues as abortion, affirmative action, law enforcement, capital punishment, gun control, terrorism, state's rights, women's equality, immigration, and the rights of

---

[147] Gregory A. Caldeira, *Commentary on Senate Confirmation of Supreme Court Justices: The Roles of Organized and Unorganized Interests*, 77 Ky L J 531, 538 (1989). See also Nemacheck, *Strategic Selection* at 46–52 (cited in note 24); Greenburg, *Supreme Conflict* at 301 (cited in note 18). The data in Figure 40 were derived from Epstein and Segal, *Advice and Consent* at 96 (cited in note 7); Epstein et al, *Supreme Court Compendium* at Table 4-17 (cited in note 13). The data for Roberts, Alito, Sotomayor, and Kagan are from Lee Epstein et al, *The U.S. Supreme Court Justice Database* (2010), online at http://Epstein.law.northwestern.edu/research/justicesdata.html.

gays and lesbians.[148] Groups such as the Alliance for Justice, the National Abortion Rights Action League (NARAL), People for the American Way, and the National Organization for Women (NOW) on the left, and the Christian Coalition, the Institute for Justice, the Family Research Council, and Concerned Women for America on the right, are now major players in the confirmation process.

Senators pay careful attention to these groups, because they communicate directly with their constituents, generate substantial contributions for political campaigns, and can help make or break a bid for reelection. Especially in an online world in which these organizations reach massive audiences instantly, interest groups can have a significant, even decisive, impact on a candidate's prospects. A senator who ignores these groups does so at his peril.[149] Senators, of course, know this quite well.

Fifth, the more general polarization of the political process has had a substantial impact on the confirmation process. Richard Pildes reports that the political parties are now "internally more unified and coherent, and externally more distant from each other, than anytime over the last 100 years." Indeed, "in 1970, moderates constituted 41 percent of the Senate; today, they are 5 percent." The center "has all but disappeared."[150] In the confirmation process, this has significantly magnified the effects of the other four factors.

The impact of these five factors seems clear. With a heightened public awareness of the central role the Supreme Court plays in resolving fundamental and often highly controversial conflicts in

---

[148] Davis, *Electing Justice* at 83 (cited in note 1).

[149] See Epstein and Segal, *Advice and Consent* at 87, 101 (cited in note 7); Davis, *Electing Justice* at 7 (cited in note 1).

[150] Pildes, 98 Cal L Rev at 277 (cited in note 60). On the generally more polarized political process, see Barry Friedman, *The Will of the People: How Public Opinion Has Influenced the Supreme Court and Shaped the Meaning of the Constitution* 351–52 (Farrar, Straus, and Giroux, 2009); Alan Abramowitz, *The Disappearing Center* 139–58 (Yale, 2010); David R. Stras, *Understanding the New Politics of Judicial Appointments*, 86 Tex L Rev 1033 (2008); William A. Galston, *Political Polarization and the U.S. Judiciary*, 77 UMKC L Rev 307, 323 (2008); Nolan McCarty, Keith T. Poole, and Howard Rosenthal, *Polarized America: The Dance of Ideology and Unequal Riches* 15–71 (MIT, 2006); Barbara Sinclair, *Party Wars: Polarization and the Politics of National Policy Making* 3–36 (Oklahoma, 2006); Theodore B. Olson, *The Senate Confirmation Process: Advice and Consent, or Search and Destroy?* 18 (National Legal Center, 2006); Jeffrey M. Stonecash, Mark D. Brewer, and Mack D. Mariani, *Diverging Parties: Social Change, Realignment, and Party Polarization* 18 (Westview, 2003); Sean Theriault, *Party Polarization in the U.S. Congress*, 12 Party Polit 483, 484 (2006); Binder and Maltzman, *Advice and Dissent* at 101–03 (cited in note 2).

American society, a greater public appreciation of the political/ideological nature of the Court's decision-making process, effective mechanisms—such as cable news programs, radio talk shows, the Internet, and energetic interest groups—to bring public and political pressure to bear on senators, and a political environment that is increasingly polarized for reasons unrelated to the confirmation process, the traditional understanding that senators ordinarily should err on the side of deference to reasonable presidential nominations has fallen by the wayside.[151] The consequence is a highly politicized and polarized confirmation process, unlike anything we have seen in more than a century, if ever.

The magnitude of these changes is evident in the two most recent confirmations—Sotomayor (2009) and Kagan (2010). Each of these nominees shared five essential characteristics: neither was appointed in the last year of a president's term; neither had any ethical problems; both were qualified (both had qualifications ratings well above .500 on Table 3); both were ideologically moderate (both had intensity of ideology ratings below .700 on Table 1); and neither nomination threatened any significant change in the ideological balance on the Court (both had ideological change ratings well below .500 on Table 2).

In such circumstances, rather straightforward confirmations should have followed. Indeed, between 1955 and 2010, a total of twelve nominees shared these five characteristics. All were, of course, confirmed. The ten who were confirmed before 1995 (Whittaker, Stewart, White, Goldberg, Stevens, O'Connor, Kennedy, Souter, Ginsburg, and Breyer) were confirmed with an average of only four negative votes. Moreover, four of the ten were easily confirmed even though the opposition party controlled the Senate, and even members of the opposition party in these ten cases cast 92 percent of their votes *for* confirmation. This reflects the traditional senatorial approach to moderate and reasonable presidential nominations.

Sotomayor and Kagan, however, were greeted with an average of thirty-four negative votes. The difference between the average of four negative votes for the ten pre-1995 nominees and the average of thirty-four negative votes for the two most recent nom-

---

[151] On the traditional understanding, see Joel B. Grossman and Stephen L. Wasby, *The Senate and Supreme Court Nominations: Some Reflections*, 21 Duke L J 557, 560 (1972); Massaro, *Supremely Political* at 8 (cited in note 56).

inees is a good measure of the magnitude of the politicization and polarization of the confirmation process since 1994. Even more striking is the fact that members of the opposition party cast 83 percent of their votes *against* Sotomayor and Kagan. The shift from 92 percent positive to 83 percent negative—when the twelve nominees and the circumstances of their nominations were so similar—is nothing short of remarkable.[152]

IX. The Future of Supreme Court Confirmations

It is, of course, foolhardy to predict the future. So, rather than be foolhardy, I will *assume* (rather than predict) that the forces I've identified will continue to affect the nomination and confirmation process in more or less predictable ways. What, though, does that mean?

A. THE NEW NORMAL

As we have seen, historically the nominees of a president whose party controls the Senate are almost always confirmed, absent a very serious issue of competence, ethics, or truly extreme views. In fact, no such nominee has been denied confirmation in a full-Senate vote in more than eighty years, and this has happened only once in the past 140 years. In the current environment, even if the percentage of opposition-party senators who vote negatively were to increase from 83 percent to 100 percent, they still would not have sufficient votes to defeat confirmation (assuming that the members of the president's party all support confirmation).[153]

Even so, there is the question whether opposition-party senators act appropriately if they vote "nay" even when the nominee is qualified, ethical, moderate, and unlikely to alter the balance on the Court. The answer is "yes." There is nothing in the Constitution or in our constitutional history to suggest that senators are obliged to support a Supreme Court nominee if the nominee's judicial philosophy is not to their liking.[154]

---

[152] Moreover, similar changes occurred with respect to the confirmation of lower court nominees, although those changes happened more gradually because there was not an eleven-year hiatus in lower court appointments. Confirmation rates for Court of Appeals nominees, for example, have declined from 100 percent in 1955 to approximately 70 percent in 1987 to under 50 percent in 2007. See Binder and Maltzman, *Advice and Dissent* at 1, 3, 79–80 (cited in note 2).

[153] I am putting the filibuster aside for the moment, but will return to it in Part IX.C.

[154] See Strauss and Sunstein, 101 Yale L J at 1494–1502 (cited in note 27).

As Trevor Parry-Giles has observed, virtually every serious "account of both the 'advice and consent' provisions of the Constitution and the Supreme Court nominations of the eighteenth and nineteenth centuries reveals a highly political process" in which senators independently consider and vote on nominees in light of their views. This apparently began to change near the turn of the twentieth century, when "a rhetoric took hold that divorced law from politics" and advanced the view that "judicial confirmations should be apolitical." This view, which was "rooted in a commitment to legal formalism," was useful both to presidents, who were quite happy to stifle Senate "interference in the nomination process," and to jurists, who were delighted to affirm the "mythology" of the apolitical judiciary.[155] Moreover, this custom was largely costless to senators in this era, because between 1897 and 1955 the president's party controlled the Senate for every Supreme Court nomination, and senators of the opposition party almost never paid a political price for deferring to the president.

In a sense, senators came to see the confirmation process more or less the way academics see the tenure process. Disagreement with a candidate's ideology is not a legitimate basis for opposition. But nothing in the Constitution mandates this conception of the confirmation process. To the contrary, as David Strauss and Cass Sunstein concluded in 1992, "constitutional text, history, and structure strongly suggest that the Senate is entitled to assume a far more substantial role than it has in the recent past."[156]

Assuming that recent confirmations indicate a significant turn back toward a more independent-minded Senate, is this a good or a bad development? Insofar as we assume a Senate controlled by the president's party, it probably makes little difference in terms of outcomes. The minority party is still, after all, the minority party.

On the other hand, presidents generally want their nominees to be easily confirmed, preferably by acclamation, and the recent change in Senate practice might lead presidents to select more moderate nominees in order to preserve their political capital.[157]

---

[155] Parry-Giles, *Character of Justice* at 154–55 (cited in note 11).

[156] Strauss and Sunstein, 101 Yale L J at 1502 (cited in note 27).

[157] See Moraski and Shipan, 43 Am J Polit Sci at 1069, 1071 (cited in note 47); Parry-Giles, *Character of Justice* at 141–42 (cited in note 11); Nemacheck, *Strategic Selection* at 131 (cited in note 24).

President Obama's nominations of Sonia Sotomayor and Elena Kagan can perhaps be understood in this light. Unlike President Bush II, who nominated two strongly ideological nominees when his party controlled the Senate (Roberts and Alito had an average ideological intensity of .780), Obama nominated two moderately ideological nominees (Sotomayor and Kagan had an average intensity of ideology of only .510). It is certainly plausible that Obama eschewed more liberal possibilities in order to avoid a bitter confirmation battle, even if he ultimately would have won. In the "old days," such caution would not have been necessary.[158]

What about nominees who are strongly ideological? Between 1955 and 2000, senators cast an average of only five votes against the eight nominees who were regarded as both strongly ideological (above .600 on Table 1) and well qualified (above .800 on Table 3).[159] How does that compare to the post-2000 era? Roberts and Alito were both strongly ideological (.760 and .800, respectively) and well qualified (.970 and .810). Under the old "normal," one would have expected roughly five votes against each of them. In fact, however, there was an average of thirty-two votes against them (twenty-two against Roberts, forty-two against Alito). Once again, we see the impact of the new "normal."[160]

It is interesting to compare the votes against Roberts and Alito with the votes against Sotomayor and Kagan. All received many more negative votes than one would have expected pre-2000, but what is especially striking is the difference in the degree of opposition they encountered. Roberts and Alito were much more strongly ideological (average .780) than Sotomayor and Kagan

---

[158] It is also possible that Obama chose relatively moderate nominees because he believed the nation has changed and that only such nominees would now be acceptable, not only to the Republicans in the Senate, but to the American people. Many if not most Americans today seem to think the ideal Justice is one who "strictly construes the Constitution," does "what the Framers intended," "applies rather than makes up the Constitution," and just "calls balls and strikes." Although Republican presidents have been able to sell conservative activists in this way, neither Clinton nor Obama was willing either to sell liberal activists in this way or (preferably) to explain to the American people why this understanding of the Court is nonsense. See Geoffrey R. Stone, *The Roberts Court, Stare Decisis, and the Future of Constitutional Law*, 82 Tulane L Rev 1533 (2008).

[159] This includes Brennan, Marshall, Fortas, Burger, Blackmun, Powell, Rehnquist (1971), and Scalia.

[160] The partisan nature of the votes was unmistakable. Fifty percent of Democrats voted against Roberts and 91 percent voted against Alito. The difference between Roberts and Alito in this regard is no doubt due to the fact that Roberts was replacing Rehnquist, with virtually no change in the ideological balance on the Court, whereas Alito was replacing O'Connor, creating a quite significant change in the balance on the Court.

(average .510),[161] and only Alito threatened a substantial change in the makeup of the Court. Thus, even in the world of the new normal, one would have expected a much higher percentage of negative votes against Roberts and Alito than against Sotomayor and Kagan. In fact, though, there was an average of thirty-four negative votes against Sotomayor and Kagan and thirty-two against Roberts and Alito. Why?

One possibility is differences in the relative qualifications of the nominees. The perceived qualifications of Roberts and Alito averaged .890, whereas the perceived qualifications of Sotomayor and Kagan averaged .770. It is encouraging, I suppose, to think that the difference in perceived qualifications offset the more ideological nature of the Republican nominees.

But there is another possibility. It just may be that Republicans are more aggressive in opposing Democratic nominees than Democrats are in opposing Republican nominees. It is difficult to test this hypothesis, but an indirect measure may be illuminating. Recent Democratic presidents have unquestionably been more moderate in selecting their nominees than recent Republican presidents. If we consider, for example, the eight nominations between 1990 and 2010, the average ideological intensity of the Republican nominees (Souter, Thomas, Roberts, and Alito) is .648, whereas the average ideological intensity of the Democratic nominees (Ginsburg, Breyer, Sotomayor, and Kagan) is .375. This suggests that Republicans have been much more aggressive than Democrats in pursuing their ideological agenda for the Supreme Court.[162]

B. WHAT'S WRONG WITH MODERATION?

The implications of the new normal are potentially much greater when the *opposition* party controls the Senate. As shown in Figure 3, from 1955 to 2010 the Senate confirmed 80 percent of all nominees (twelve of fifteen) when the opposition party controlled the Senate. (All of those nominations were pre-1993.) What

---

[161] See Table 1.

[162] Indeed, in the realm of civil rights and civil liberties, the eight most conservative Justices to serve on the Supreme Court since 1937 were appointed by Republican presidents between 1968 and 2010 (Thomas, Rehnquist, Scalia, Roberts, Alito, Burger, O'Connor, and Powell). On the other hand, none of the eight most liberal Justices to serve on the Court between 1937 and 2010 were appointed between 1968 and 2010. See Epstein, Landes, and Posner, *Are Judges Realists?* at Table 3-2 (cited in note 13).

would be the outcome if this were to happen in the near future? Suppose, for example, a Democratic president has an opportunity in 2014 to replace a retiring Justice Ginsburg with a nominee similar to Sotomayor or Kagan? Would she be confirmed if the Republicans control the Senate?

Historically, the answer is "yes." Far more ideological nominees, such as Burger, Blackmun, and Powell (with an average ideological intensity of .737), have easily been confirmed in such circumstances. Indeed, in those cases, 98 percent of Democratic senators voted "aye," even though Republican presidents put forth the nominees. But, as we have seen, times have changed. Suppose that, as in the Sotomayor and Kagan nominations, 83 percent of opposition senators were to vote "nay"? In that case, the Republicans would still need at least a sixty to forty majority in the Senate to deny confirmation.

But that, of course, assumes that the trends we have seen in the past decade do not accelerate in the future. By 2014, perhaps 90 percent of opposition-party senators will vote "nay," in which case even a fifty-five to forty-five majority would be sufficient to deny confirmation. Indeed, in this situation the members of the opposition party could hold out until the president puts forth a nominee who embraces *their* judicial philosophy. This could, of course, lead to serious gridlock. Indeed, this is more or less what is happening now with respect to lower federal court nominations, where the confirmation rate has dropped below 50 percent for the first time in American history and scores of federal judgeships remain vacant.[163]

We can thus see the advantages of a system in which senators err on the side of deference to the president if the nominee is ethical, qualified, and has reasonably moderate views. Such a system enables the process to function relatively smoothly and more or less averages out over time. In such circumstances, there are strong practical reasons for deference.[164]

At the same time, though, there are powerful short-term political reasons for senators not to defer. Most obviously, when members of the opposition party block a nominee, they are likely to get an ideologically "better" nominee instead. That was clearly

---

[163] See note 179. See also http://judicialnominations.org/.

[164] See Eisgruber, *The Next Justice* at 11–13, 151 (cited in note 31).

the case, for example, when the Republicans blocked Johnson's effort to elevate Fortas to succeed Warren, and wound up with Burger, and when the Democrats defeated Bork, and wound up with Kennedy. In these situations, members of the opposing party "traded up" by being aggressive. From their perspective, this was a winning strategy.

As a practical political matter, then, a potential consequence of abandoning the traditional presumption of deference, even when the opposition party controls the Senate, is that this would enable the opposition party either to block all nominations or, more modestly, to force the president to choose nominees who suit them. Anticipating this, presidents will likely try to alleviate the risk by naming ever more moderate nominees.[165]

So, one might ask, what is wrong with moderation? Why not have a Court of nine Souters, O'Connors, and Breyers? Such a Court would surely be reasonable. Without meaning to imply anything critical of Souter, O'Connor, or Breyer, I am confident that, in the long run, such a Court would be relatively toothless. It would muddle along making fine distinctions and hedging its bets. It would be a very passive Court. Some may think this is good, even great. I am not one of them. I believe the Supreme Court must (in appropriate cases)[166] play an active role in interpreting and applying the Constitution, and that to fulfill its responsibilities under the Constitution the Court must have at least some Justices who pose the hardest questions and push the boundaries of the law.

What, I wonder, would current constitutional law look like if

---

[165] It is possible, in theory, that a more independent and less deferential Senate would produce a more deliberative process, in which presidents would actually seek "advice" and opposition party senators would work collaboratively with presidents to identify the best possible nominees. Indeed, this is what David Strauss and Cass Sunstein suggested might happen if the Senate was to become more assertive. But in the twenty years that have passed since they put forth that proposition, American politics generally and the confirmation process in particular have become so polarized and politicized that the consequence of a more independent Senate is, as we have already seen, much more likely to be greater conflict than greater collaboration. See Strauss and Sunstein, 101 Yale L J at 1514–17 (cited in note 27).

[166] In my view, "appropriate cases" are those in which the exercise of judicial review is most important to the preservation of a fair and effective system of democratic self-governance. This refers especially to two situations: (1) where the government disadvantages a group that has historically been disadvantaged and lacks meaningful political power, and (2) where a transitory majority uses the levers of power to perpetuate its authority. For the Court not to act in such cases is tantamount to abdicating its fundamental constitutional responsibility. See Stone, 82 Tulane L Rev at 1553–57 (cited in note 158).

Justices like Black and Scalia, Douglas and Rehnquist, Brennan and Roberts, Marshall and Thomas, and Warren and Burger had never served on the Court? I rather doubt we would have seen many of our most important decisions, including perhaps *Roe v Wade*,[167] *Miranda v Arizona*,[168] *Citizens United v FEC*,[169] *Engel v Vitale*,[170] *Baker v Carr*,[171] *Loving v Virginia*,[172] *Heller v District of Columbia*,[173] *Lawrence v Texas*,[174] and *Brown v Board of Education*.[175]

I do not agree with all of those decisions, and I doubt anyone does. But that is not the point. If the Supreme Court is to fulfill its role in our complex constitutional system, it must have among its members Justices who think boldly as well as carefully. It is in the clash of strongly-held opposing ideas that the Court is best able to engage the often complex and vexing issues that are central to its mission. Moreover, as David Strauss and Cass Sunstein have observed, "throughout American history, dissenting opinions have helped Congress and the President—and even future generations—formulate their responses to the Court."[176] A system in which presidents are relentlessly driven to nominate only the most moderate Justices will not serve the best interests of either the Court or the nation.[177]

C. THE GORILLA IN THE ROOM

But it could be worse. Until 1968, senators never attempted to invoke the filibuster to block a judicial nominee at any level. In that year, however, a coalition of conservative Republicans and southern Democrats effectively used the filibuster to prevent the nomination of Abe Fortas as Chief Justice from coming to a vote. Although a majority of senators participating in the cloture vote

---

[167] 410 US 113 (1973).

[168] 384 US 436 (1966).

[169] 130 S Ct 876 (2010).

[170] 370 US 421 (1962).

[171] 369 US 186 (1962).

[172] 388 US 1 (1967).

[173] 554 US 570 (2008).

[174] 539 US 558 (2003).

[175] 347 US 483 (1954).

[176] Strauss and Sunstein, 101 Yale L J at 1511 (cited in note 27).

[177] See Jim Newton, *Justice for All: Earl Warren and the Nation He Made* 519 (Riverhead, 2006).

supported cloture (the vote was forty-five to forty-three), this was far short of the two-thirds then needed to invoke cloture (the rule has since been amended to enable sixty senators to invoke cloture). Beginning in the 1980s, senators for the first time began to use the filibuster against lower federal court nominees. The first such nominee to be filibustered was Stephen Breyer, when President Carter nominated him in 1980 to serve on the United States Court of Appeals for the First Circuit.[178] (Breyer, of course, was ultimately confirmed.) The use of the filibuster against lower court nominees has increased steadily ever since. Four judicial nominees were filibustered in the 1980s, four in the 1990s, and twenty-nine between 2000 and 2010.[179] Although the vast majority of these nominees eventually were confirmed, some were not.[180]

Senators from both political parties have energetically employed and self-righteously attacked the legitimacy of judicial filibusters, depending on the politics of the moment.[181] Although the constitutionality of judicial filibusters has been questioned,[182] the threat of the filibuster continues to hang over the Supreme Court nomination process. Indeed, although Fortas was the only Supreme Court nominee ever successfully filibustered, cloture had to be invoked to end filibusters against Rehnquist (1971), Rehnquist (1986), and Alito. In each of those instances, members of the opposition party supported cloture. In 2005, for example, seventeen Democrats joined fifty-five Republicans in invoking cloture to end the filibuster against Alito (the vote on cloture was seventy-

---

[178] Richard S. Beth and Betsy Palmer, *Cloture Attempts on Nominations* *6 (Congressional Research Service report, Mar 30, 2009), online at http://www.fas.org/sgp/crs/misc/RL32878.pdf. The number of cloture attempts is not identical to the number of filibusters, but it is a useful proxy.

[179] See id; *Senate Action on Cloture Motions for the 110th and 111th Congresses*, online at http://www.senate.gove/pagelayout/reference/cloture_motions/clotureCounts.htm.

[180] For example, like Fortas in 1968, three Bush II court of appeals nominees in 2003 and 2004, Miguel Estrada, William Gerry Meyers III, and Henry W. Saad, did not survive the filibuster. See Beth and Palmer, *Cloture Attempts* at 7 (cited in note 178). Senators from both parties have also invoked a variety of other procedural rules to delay and defeat lower federal court nominees. See Epstein and Segal, *Advice and Consent* at 24–25 (cited in note 7); Binder and Maltzman, *Advice and Dissent* at 55, 98–101 (cited in note 2); Nemacheck, *Strategic Selection* at 28–29 (cited in note 24).

[181] See John Cornyn, *Our Broken Judicial Confirmation Process and the Need for Filibuster Reform*, 27 Harv J L & Pub Pol 181, 206–11 (2003).

[182] See Michael J. Gerhardt, *The Federal Appointments Process: A Constitutional and Historical Analysis* 297 (Duke, 2000); Todd B. Tatelman, *Constitutionality of a Senate Filibuster of a Judicial Nomination* (Congressional Research Service report, June 14, 2005), online at www.fas.org/sgp/crs/misc/RL32102.pdf.

two to twenty-five). Note, though, that even though Republicans held a large majority in the Senate (fifty-five to forty-five), they could not have prevented the Democrats from killing the nomination, had they chosen to do so.

Whether this remnant of bipartisanship will continue is anyone's guess. The very possibility of a filibuster, however, is likely to lead presidents to nominate ever more moderate nominees—even when the president's party controls the Senate. Indeed, this threat probably contributed to President Obama's decision to play it safe by selecting Sotomayor and Kagan, rather than more traditionally "liberal" nominees, even though he held an otherwise decisive fifty-nine to forty-one margin in the Senate.

If senators in the minority ultimately resort to the filibuster to block even nominees who are qualified, ethical, within the "mainstream" of responsible legal thought (as I have defined the term), and unlikely significantly to shift the balance on the Court, then as a practical matter any group of forty-one senators will henceforth have the power to control who, if anyone, sits on the Supreme Court.

Unlike filibusters of legislation, which have long been a part of the checks and balances of our system, filibusters of judicial nominees, and especially of Supreme Court nominees, have not traditionally been part of our history. There is no persuasive reason to change that tradition. To the contrary, there is general agreement that the nomination and confirmation process worked reasonably well before it recently became so polarized and politicized. The changes that have undermined the workings of that process were not the product of thoughtful planning. Rather, they were the result of rampant politicization. The aggressive use of the filibuster is in many ways the "logical," but deeply troubling, extension of that trend.

Whether senators can resist the temptation to let this gorilla loose is a matter of fundamental importance to the future of Supreme Court confirmations. In the current climate, once the filibuster is unleashed to derail a nominee who is ethical, qualified, and in the "mainstream" of responsible legal thought, any semblance of constructive governance in this realm will be lost.[183]

---

[183] Of course, even as I have defined it, the "mainstream of responsible legal thought" is not necessarily "right." It may be that there are important voices and perspectives that are clearly outside of the mainstream at any particular time. Thus, my point is not that

This is not to say that the filibuster can never legitimately be used. It can properly be employed whenever there is clear and compelling evidence that a nominee is unqualified, unethical, or outside the "mainstream" (as I have defined the term). But it cannot properly be used, without grievously undermining the process, merely because the minority disagrees with the views of a nominee.[184]

There remains one complication. In theory, the primary justification for the filibuster is to protect minority interests. Suppose one political party controls both the presidency and the Senate for an extended period of time, and that party's presidents appoint a succession of strongly-ideological Justices who come to dominate the Court. Is there a point at which members of the minority party can legitimately say "enough!"? Is there a point at which they can appropriately use the filibuster in order to prevent the Court from being completely overtaken by one strongly held point of view?

There have been four periods between 1860 and 2010 in which presidents from a single party have made ten or more successive appointments to the Court. From 1861 to 1885, Republican presidents made sixteen consecutive appointments. During that twenty-four-year period, the Republicans controlled the Senate 92 percent of the time and held, on average, 75 percent of the seats. Between 1897 and 1912, Republican presidents made ten consecutive appointments. During this era, the Republicans controlled the Senate 100 percent of the time and, on average, held 63 percent of the seats in the Senate. In the third period, between 1937 and 1953, Democratic presidents made eighteen successive appointments. Democrats controlled the Senate 88 percent of the time and held, on average, 62 percent of the seats in the Senate. In each of these periods, there were plenty of reasons for the minority party to be frustrated, but not much opportunity to do anything about it. Given the overwhelming dominance of the majority party in the Senate during most of these years, even the filibuster might not have been of much help to the minority. In any event, it was a nonissue in those years, because no one thought it legitimate to filibuster judicial nominations until 1968.

---

nominees outside the mainstream are necessarily unqualified, but that it is reasonable for senators to be at least skeptical about such nominees.

[184] One might argue, however, that because legislation can be amended, whereas judicial appointments are permanent, a supermajority requirement is more sensible for judicial appointments than for legislation.

In the fourth period, from 1969 to 1993, Republican presidents made eleven consecutive appointments to the Court. As evident from Tables 1 and 2, all of these appointees were conservative, and seven were strongly conservative.[185] As a result, the average voting record of the Justices moved from .333 in 1968 to .637 by 1993, where .000 is the most liberal and 1.000 is the most conservative. Even more significant, the swing Justice shifted over the course of this period from .263 (Warren) to .695 (Kennedy), suggesting that the ideological transition within the Court was quite dramatic.[186]

What is striking is that all this happened during an era when *Democrats* controlled the Senate 75 percent of the time and held, on average, 55 percent of the seats in the Senate. In such unusual circumstances, a filibuster might well have been appropriate. But, of course, because the Democrats had a majority in the Senate for most of this era, a filibuster was not even necessary. Faced with this sort of situation, it would seem quite appropriate for the opposition party to take a more independent stance in the Senate. What is remarkable is that, for the most part, the Democrats in this era adhered to the tradition of senatorial deference, even though they had the votes to do otherwise, and even though the Republicans had first introduced the judicial filibuster against Fortas in 1968.[187]

X. Conclusion

It would be hard to make the case that the confirmation process is "better" today than it was in the past—pretty much any time in the past. It is not difficult to imagine a much better process.[188] Here are ten steps in the right direction:

---

[185] The strongly conservative nominees were Scalia, Rehnquist (1986), Rehnquist (1971), Burger, Blackmun, Thomas, and Powell. The moderately conservative nominees were Stevens, Souter, Kennedy, and O'Connor. I characterize as strongly conservative any appointee with a rating of .600 or higher on Table 1.

[186] These data are derived from Epstein, Landes, and Posner, *Are Judges Realists?* at Table 3-2 (cited in note 13).

[187] The Democrats confirmed eleven of fourteen Republican nominees, rejecting only Haynsworth, Carswell, and Bork. The first two, though, were at the very outset of this period. For the argument that the Democrats should not have deferred in this situation, see Strauss and Sunstein, 101 Yale L J at 1520 (cited in note 27).

[188] Many commentators have offered suggestions for improving the process. See Davis, *Electing Justice* at 35, 165, 172–73 (cited in note 1); Bruce A. Ackerman, *Transformative Appointments*, 101 Harv L Rev 1164 (1988); Michael J. Gerhardt, *Divided Justice: A Com-*

1. Presidents should nominate individuals who are ethical, qualified, and have views within the mainstream of responsible legal thought (as I have defined the term).[189]

2. In so doing, they should seek the advice of leading senators of both parties, but having sought that advice they should nominate the person who they think best serves the interests of the nation.

3. Presidents should not resort to "stealth" nominees for the purpose of preventing senators from understanding the views of their nominees.

4. Senators should inform themselves about nominees without relying too heavily on the hearings to enlighten them. We did not even have hearings until 1955. They are not indispensable.

5. Nominees should understand that they bear the burden of persuading senators that they are qualified, ethical, and hold views within the mainstream of responsible legal thought (as I have defined the term).[190]

6. If a nominee fails to meet this burden, it is appropriate for senators to vote "nay."

7. Nominees should answer questions candidly, but should not do so if the answer would in any way impair their ability to fulfill

mentary on the Nomination and Confirmation of Justice Thomas, 60 Geo Wash L Rev 969 (1992); Strauss and Sunstein, 101 Yale L J at 1518–20 (cited in note 27); Gary J. Simson, *Thomas's Supreme Unfitness—A Letter to the Senate on Advise and Consent*, 78 Cornell L Rev 619 (1993); Abraham, *Justices, Presidents, and Senators* at 327–28 (cited in note 8); Farganis and Wedeking, *No Hints* at 8–10 (cited in note 71); Gregory A. Caldeira, *Commentary on Senate Confirmation of Supreme Court Justices: The Roles of Organized and Unorganized Interests*, 77 Ky L J 531 (1989); Jeff Yates and William Gillespie, *Supreme Court Power Play: Assessing the Appropriate Role of the Senate in the Confirmation Process*, 58 Wash & Lee L Rev 1053 (2001); Robert F. Nagel, *Advice, Consent, and Influence*, 84 Nw U L Rev 858, 863 (1990); John O. McGinnis and Michael B. Rappaport, *Supermajority Rules and the Judicial Confirmation Process*, 26 Cardozo L Rev 543, 576 (2010); Stephen Choi and Mitu Gulati, *A Tournament of Judges?* 92 Cal L Rev 299 (2004); Lori A. Ringhand and Paul M. Collins, Jr., *May It Please the Senate: An Empirical Analysis of the Senate Judiciary Committee Hearings on Supreme Court Nominees, 1939–2009* *2–*5 (University of Georgia School of Law Research Paper No 10-12, July 2010, online at http://papers.ssrn.com/sol3/papers.cfm?abstract_id=1630403; Robert Post and Reva Siegel, *Questioning Justice: Law and Politics in Judicial Confirmation Hearings*, 115 Yale L J Pocket Part 38–44 (2006); Lori A. Ringhand, *In Defense of Ideology: A Principled Approach to the Supreme Court Confirmation Process*, 18 Wm & Mary Bill Rts J 131 (2009); Epstein et al, 68 J Polit at 296 (cited in note 125); Carter, *Confirmation Mess* at 187–206 (cited in note 2). But see Laurence H. Tribe, *God Save This Honorable Court: How the Choice of Supreme Court Justices Shapes Our History* 91–92 (Random House, 1985) (challenging the "myth" of a broken process).

[189] Of course, there may be circumstances in which a president might reasonably nominate an individual whose views are out of the mainstream. The mainstream, after all, may sometimes be out of whack.

[190] But see note 189.

their judicial responsibilities, including the need to preserve their independence and integrity on the bench. If a nominee reasonably and in good faith declines to answer questions for that reason, senators should not hold their reticence against them.

8. It is appropriate for senators to vote "nay" if they are not persuaded that a nominee's judicial philosophy is in the best interests of the nation. But in order to avoid undue fractiousness and confirmation paralysis, senators generally should defer to the president's judgment if the nominee holds relatively moderate views.

9. Senators should treat the confirmation hearings with respect. They should see them as having two primary functions: to evaluate the nominee and to educate the public. Indeed, the educational function may be paramount. Senators therefore should not treat the hearings as an opportunity to create a spectacle in which to wage political war. To control the grandstanding and mindless repetition, the nominee's testimony should be limited to one session and the questioning should be undertaken primarily by professional counsel, rather than by the senators themselves.

10. The filibuster is an appropriate means of protecting minority interests in those circumstances in which one political party has made a series of highly ideological appointments that have substantially altered the balance on the Court. There is, of course, no magic number for determining when this is appropriate, but three such appointments in succession might be a reasonable place to begin.

It is important to reestablish a sensible confirmation process. No one is happy with the current state of affairs, and with good reason. It is chaotic, divisive, arbitrary, dishonest, insulting, polarizing, and damaging to the public's confidence in both the Senate and the judiciary. I am reasonably certain that most thoughtful people, including presidents, senators, and nominees, would, in principle, embrace most or all of these suggestions, if short-term political advantage could be put to one side. What keeps them from embracing these suggestions is not good judgment or sound public policy, but the pursuit of short-term political self-interest.

Our government is, of course, a government of politics, even in the confirmation process. But raw politics must sometimes be tempered with at least *some* respect for the institutions, values, and aspirations of our system of self-governance. We have lost our way, and it is not at all clear we can find our way back.